SPOT GLOBE 2000

Edited by
STEEN B. BÖCHER and HENRIK B. HOFFMEYER

Geographical section:	Steen B. Böcher, Ph.D., Professor
Historical section:	Henrik B. Hoffmeyer, M.A.
Calculator of latitude and longitude:	Leif Tang Lassen, Teacher
Illustrator:	Arne Gaarn Bak, Illustrator and Cartographer

SPOT GLOBE 2000 – Special Features

Is it really possible? Can we find fresh ideas about globes? Is one globe not like another? Not always. New ideas keep cropping up, and SPOT GLOBE 2000 has completely new possibilities, offering scope for innumerable ways of use.

One of the problems of globes has been that only a limited number of place names could be printed in such a small area. SPOT GLOBE 2000 has solved that problem, and it is now possible to locate a great many more geographical names. Any place on earth can be pinpointed if the latitude and longitude are known. Given these two facts, it is possible to adjust the two scales to the required latitude and longitude. A pinpoint of light indicates where the place lies.

What if the latitude and longitude are not known? How do we overcome this difficulty? The obvious solution seems to be to provide a book in which these figures have been computed. In this way anybody can locate all the places in the index.

The day has passed when a globe was an exceptional possession, owned only by noblemen and a few scientists. By now many of us have realized that a globe provides the most accurate picture of the world where distances and directions are concerned. This point has been enlarged upon in the section on Air Traffic (p.60). The exact length of aircraft routes can be measured and, given the speed of the plane, the flying time can be calculated with the help of the time dial.

A globe is essential in the modern world, where air flight has made travel to all parts of the world possible and daily news is received from all points through television, radio, and newspapers. Like the atlas, the globe has become part of the inventory of the modern home. It is not surprising that the sale of globes has increased tenfold in some places in the past ten years.

It happens that almost daily we hear of an event in a place that is unfamiliar to us and we do not even know its position. First, we can look for it in the index of this book. If it is not there, very likely another place in the locality has been mentioned that can be found in the index. Should the distance between two places be given in miles, we only need to remember that 1° of latitude is 68.3 miles ($=110$ km).

There are many other things we want to locate besides international events. This book offers numerous other subjects that may be of interest. Let us stress that the table of contents shows only a limited selection to whet the appetite for further studies. For that reason, the book contains some blank pages on which additional information on localities can be noted. Perhaps in the future encyclopedias and dictionaries will give the latitude and longitude of place names.

We have a feeling that when you first begin to work with SPOT GLOBE 2000 and the accompanying book, you will discover a new game. The entire family can sit around the globe together and find out where the various places are located. There is no need to limit yourself to the subjects in the book. Hobbies such as travel, ham radio, and stamp collecting will lead to other investigations of the globe.

It must be mentioned that the size of the pinpoint of light (3 mm/0.039″ in diameter) results in some inaccuracy in localization. However, together with an atlas that has large-scale maps, you can first locate the place on the globe and then use the atlas to get a more accurate position. A globe is not used for its exactitude but to help locate one place in relation to others. Only a globe can give such an accurate picture.

Now try to find the location of Europe's longest bridge, 56.0° N and 16° E. It is 8.07 miles long.

The idea for SPOT GLOBE 2000 was developed at 55.5° N 12.5° E. It lies in the country of _____.

We hope that you have many pleasant hours with your globe.

Steen B. Böcher

Contents

INFORMATION

Locating places with the globe 7
The time dial 9
Adjustment of the scales 10
Replacing the bulb 11

QUIZ 12

THE EARTH

Physical Features of the Earth
The seas 14
Sea floor and sea trenches 16
Capes and peninsulas 18
Islands 20
Deserts 22
Lakes and glaciers 24
Rivers 26
Mountains and passes 28
Earthquakes 30
Meteors and meteorites 32

Climate, Plant and Animal Worlds
Climate and climate records 34
Plant and animal worlds, cultivated
plants, and domestic animals 36

Continents, Countries, and Towns
Continents and countries 38
The biggest cities of the world 40

World Resources
Sources of energy 42
Iron ore 44
Precious metals 46
Other metals 48
Other minerals 50

Industry and Traffic
Industrial zones 52
Oil refineries and atomic energy plants 54
Shipping 56
Tunnels, bridges, and dams 58
Air traffic 60

ARCHEOLOGY AND HISTORY

Prehistoric man 62
Ancient History
Mesopotamia, Egypt, Greece, and
the Roman Empire 64

The Middle Ages
Famous towns and fortresses, etc. 68
Famous buildings outside Europe 70

Modern History
Voyages of discovery and historic
battlefields 72
National parks and game preserves 74
Events that shook the world 76

INDEX 79

BIOGRAPHY OF DISCOVERERS 163

Contents

HISTORY OF THE GLOBE 171
Why a globe? 174

HOW TO USE YOUR GLOBE 175
Determination of location on the earth 175
Shortest distance between any two points on the earth 176
Time 176
Time dial 177
The international date line 178
Shape and size of the earth 178
The earth and the solar system 178
The rotation of the earth 179
The earth's revolution around the sun 182
The astronomical year 182
The seasons; astronomical zones 184
Jet streams 185
Oceans 186
Vegetation 187

WEATHER AND WEATHER INSTRUMENTS . . 188
The barometer 188
Atmospheric pressure 188
Weather rules 189
How to set a barometer 189
Barometrical rules 190
Atmospheric humidity; the hygrometer 190
The thermometer 191

Locating Places with the Globe

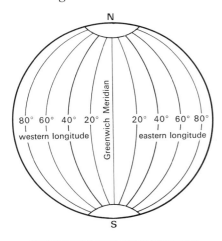

To find the position of a place on earth, you must use two groups of imaginary lines. First, lines of longitude, or meridians, which are half-circles connecting the North and South poles; second, lines of latitude, which are circles that lie parallel to the equator. The equator itself is a parallel. Lines of latitude and lines of longitude intersect at practically right angles.

A complete circle is divided into 360° (1° = 1 degree). Longitude is divided in the following way: the meridian that runs through the observatory at Greenwich, England, has been chosen as the prime meridian (0°), and from here one calculates 180° to the east and 180° to the west (altogether 360°). The location of a place is described by giving its longitude as calculated from the prime meridian together with information as to whether it lies to the east or west of the prime meridian. This has been abbreviated to E or W.

SPOT GLOBE 2000 has two horizontal scales, the upper one for time and the lower one for longitude. The prime meridian is marked as 0° on the lower scale. From 0°, this scale is subdivided into 15°, 30°, 45°, etc., to 180° both to east and west.

A register of names in this book gives latitude and longitude. To find the longitude of a place, turn the lower scale to the figure of its longitude, keeping in mind whether it lies to the east or west of the prime meridian.

Locating Places with the Globe

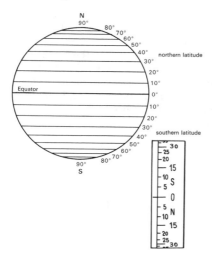

that to the south as the southern latitudes, (abbreviated as N and S).

The latitude of a place indicates its location in relation to the equator. N or S will show whether it lies to the north or south of the equator.

SPOT GLOBE 2000 has a vertical scale for degrees of latitude starting with 0°, which represents the equator, and a graduated scale above and below for north and south.

The second figure given beside a place in the index indicates the longitude, which is located by moving the lower horizontal scale (see preceding page). The first figure in the index gives the latitude. The vertical scale is adjusted to this figure. When both scales are adjusted to the latitude and longitude of a place, a pinpoint of light will indicate its position on the globe.

Normally a globe can give only a limited number of names. But SPOT GLOBE 2000 can locate more than 20,000 names with the help of the index and the two scales.

In addition, you can adjust the pinpoint of light to a place, such as New

York, and read on the scales what the corresponding latitude and longitude are.

The lines of latitude are calculated from the equator, which is called 0°. From here 90° are calculated to the north and 90° to the south, altogether 180°.

The area north of the equator is described as the northern latitudes and

The Time Dial

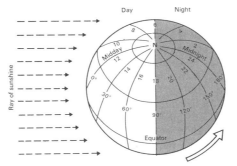

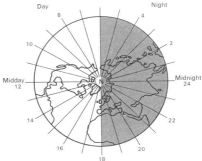

The sun rises in the east and sets in the west because the earth rotates on its axis from west to east. It is this rotation that gives us *day and night*.

Meridian means the "noon line," and the earth is divided into 360° of longitude. It takes 24 hours for the earth to make a complete rotation; so one hour represents 15°. (360° ÷ 24 = 15° per hour), or 1° of longitude is equal to four minutes (60 minutes ÷ 15 = 4 minutes per degree).

When the sun is highest in the sky, it is noon, and all points that lie on the same meridian have noon at the same time. For practical purposes the world is divided into time zones that have the same hour. Each zone is 15° wide and covers 7½° on either side of 0°, 15°, 30°, etc.

SPOT GLOBE 2000 is provided with a *time dial showing hours*. The time dial is placed above the lower horizontal scale for longitude, since a time shift of one hour is the same as 15° of longitude. If, for example, the longitudinal scale is placed on 25° E (Helsinki) and the time dial at 1400, it will be possible to read the time for all the other longitudes in relation to Helsinki at 1400.

If you fix the pinpoint of light on London (51° N, 0.5° W) by means of the two scales of latitude and longitude and adjust the time dial to 1000, you can find the corresponding time in New York (42° N, 75° W) by moving the pinpoint of light there. The time dial will show the corresponding New York time. The difference in time is calculated by simple subtraction.

SPOT GLOBE 2000 also provides a *day* and *night scale* placed at the North Pole.

That scale has hours on it and one half gives day and the other half, night. Adjust the day-and-night scale to 1000 on London's longitude (0.5° W), and the day-and-night scale will show whether it is day or night elsewhere in relation to 1000 in London.

Adjustment of the Scales

1. SPOT GLOBE 2000 has been adjusted at the factory.
2. The map on the globe is provided with a network of latitude and longitude.
3. The adjustment can be controlled by installing both the latitude and longitude scales on 0°.
4. The pinpoint of light will show on the equator (0° lat.) and the prime meridian (0° long.).
5. Apart from damage, there is only one reason to readjust the longitudinal scale: and that is after a change of light bulb if the globe has been improperly reset at 180°.
6. Adjustment will be easier if
   a. The pinpoint of light is put on the equator (0° lat.).
   b. The globe is turned so that the light shows 0° longitude (prime meridian).
   c. The globe is held firmly in this position.
   d. The scale for longitude, which is tight, is twisted to its 0° position so that 0° on the scale is next to the indicator.
   e. The scale for longitude is now adjusted to the globe's network.

Replacing the Bulb

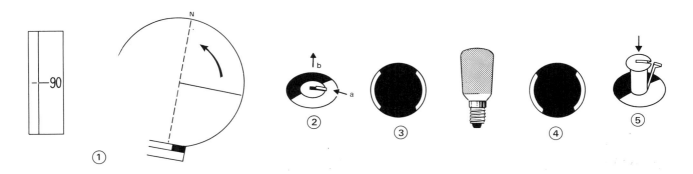

1. Adjust the vertical scale wheel for latitude to 90°N so that the pinpoint of light would indicate the North Pole if lit. This will bring the swivel arm of the lens system, which is connected to the pinpoint of light, into an upright position so that it can pass through the hole at the South Pole.
2. Push the pawl at the North Pole toward the center of the globe, withdraw the plastic tube and remove the day-and-night scale.
3. The loosened shell of the globe should now be twisted until it is free from the main chassis so that it can be lifted past the cord, bulb socket, dimmer, and lens arm.
4. After changing the bulb, replace the shell of the globe over the internal mechanism. The two indentations at the South Pole on the shell are now placed over the two projections on the revolving piece of the main support. Avoid twisting the globe 180°.
5. Place the plastic tube through the day-and-night scale and the hole at the North Pole. Push the tube gently into locking position.

With SPOT GLOBE 2000 and this book, the entire family can make their own course of programmed instruction with every member providing questions and answers. Here are some ideas for a quiz, but many more can be made using SPOT GLOBE 2000 and the accompanying book as a source for questions and answers. Here is *education and entertainment for all.*

1. **Which lies farthest north – Madrid or New York?**

   Adjust the pinpoint of light to Madrid and then turn the globe so that the light lies on the longitude that goes through New York. Read off.

2. **What are the degrees of latitude and longitude for the most southerly points of Australia, Africa, and South America?**

   Adjust the light to these points and read the scales.

3. **When it is 1200 in Hamburg, what is the time in Tokyo?**

   Adjust the light to Hamburg and the time dial to 1200. Then adjust the light to Tokyo and read off the time dial.

4. **How deep is the Philippine Trench, and where does it lie?**

   See "Sea Floor and Sea Trenches" p.17.

5. **Where is Christmas Island?**

   See "Islands" p.20.

6. **What is the name of the biggest lake in Africa? In which country does it lie?**

   See "Lakes" p.25.

7. **In which country is the world's highest waterfall?**

   See "Rivers" p.27.

8. **Which place has the most hours of sunshine in the year?**

   See "Climate Records" p.35.

9. **Which gold mine has the highest production?**

   See "Precious Metals" p.47.

10. **What is the Golden Gate? Position?**

    See "Tunnels, Bridges, and Dams" p.59.

11. **Which airport serves more travelers – London or Paris?**

    See "Air Traffic" p.61.

12. **What is Altamira? Where does it lie?**

    See "Prehistoric Man" p.63.

13. **Where is the Petrified Forest?**

    See "National Parks and Game Preserves" p.75.

14. **Where is the Kruger National Park?**

    See "National Parks and Game Preserves" p.75.

15. **Where and when did the airship *Hindenburg* burn?**

    See "Events that Shook the World" p.77.

16. **What is Canossa? Where does it lie?**

    See "The Middle Ages" p.69.

17. **Which country's capital lies 64.10° N and 21.55° W?**

    Use the vertical scale and the lower horizontal scale.

18. **When it is 0800 in San Francisco, is it morning or evening in London? In Karachi, Pakistan?**

    Use time dial and day-and-night scale.

19. **Where is Mauna Kea?**

    See "Mountains and Passes" p.29.

20. **The highest pass in the world is Cumbre, or Uspallata (3,760 m/ 12,340 feet). Give its position in latitude and longitude.**

    See "Mountains and Passes" p.29.

The Seas

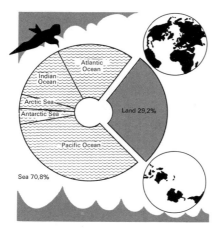

Atlantic Ocean

Indian Ocean

Arctic Sea

Antarctic Sea

Land 29,2%

Pacific Ocean

Sea 70,8%

The greatest part of the earth's surface, 70.8 percent, is covered with water.

This area is divided principally into three oceans: the Pacific Ocean, the Atlantic Ocean, and the Indian Ocean. In addition, there is a series of border seas, separated from the oceans by island chains, and inland seas, such as the Mediterranean Sea, that are almost completely surrounded by land. There is some doubt about which category the Arctic Sea belongs to, as it is very big and opens into both the Pacific and Atlantic oceans. It can be considered as an inland sea of the Atlantic Ocean or made a special case and called the Arctic Ocean. The sea around Antarctica is divided among the three great oceans.

Connections between the various seas are called straits, or sounds. Many of these are the busiest shipping areas such as the English Channel, the Strait of Gibraltar, the Strait of Malacca, etc. Indentations of water into the land are called gulfs (large) or fjords (small), but some of the gulfs are so large that it would be more correct to call them inland seas (e.g., Gulf of Mexico), or border seas (e.g., Hudson Bay or Gulf of California). On the other hand, there are some small seas that should be called straits (e.g., Kattegat and Marmara Sea).

As we all know, sea water is salty, but it is not equally salty in all parts of the world. The salt content of the oceans is generally about 3 percent. But in seas like the Red Sea, where evaporation is great and the inflow of river water low, the salinity can rise to about 4 percent. In contrast, the salinity of the Baltic in some areas is very low, only 1 percent.

Some examples of the various types of seas are given on the opposite page. Since many of the seas are very big, the latitude and longitude are located at about the middle of each sea.

Some Seas, Straits, etc.

Ocean	Latitude	Longitude
PACIFIC OCEAN *(with subsidiary seas):* 179.7 million km² (68.36 million sq. miles) surface.		
BORDER SEAS		
Sea of Okhotsk	55° N	150° E
Sea of Japan	40° N	135° E
INLAND SEAS		
Gulf of California	27° N	112° W
East China Sea	36° N	123° E
STRAITS		
Sunda Strait	6° S	105° E
Strait of Malacca	3° N	101° E
Bering Strait	66° N	170° E

Ocean	Latitude	Longitude
ATLANTIC OCEAN *(with subsidiary seas):* 106.5 million km² (41.11 million sq. miles) surface.		
BORDER SEAS		
North Sea	56° N	6° E
Gulf of Mexico	25° N	90° W
INLAND SEAS		
Baltic Sea	57° N	18° E
Mediterranean Sea	37° N	20° E
Hudson Bay	58° N	85° W
STRAITS		
English Channel with Irish Sea	50° N	0°
Kattegat	57° N	11° E
Strait of Gibraltar	36° N	6° W
INDIAN OCEAN *(with subsidiary seas):* 74.9 million km² (28.91 million sq. miles) surface.		
INLAND SEA		
Red Sea	20° N	38° E
STRAITS		
Bab-el-Mandeb	13° N	53° E
Strait of Malacca	3° N	101° E

Sea Floor and Sea Trenches

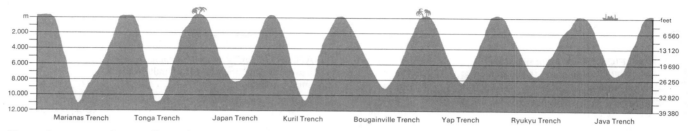

Marianas Trench	Tonga Trench	Japan Trench	Kuril Trench	Bougainville Trench	Yap Trench	Ryukyu Trench	Java Trench

From the coasts, the sea floor drops evenly down to a depth of about 660 feet. From there it descends more steeply down to the ocean floor, which on the average is about 13,126 to 19,690 feet below sea level. These descending slopes are called continental shelves. As the name suggests, they are linked to the continents. The seas that cover the area above the shelf where the depth is less than 660 feet are called transgressive seas. Politically, the U.S.A. and other countries consider this shelf to be part of the adjoining land. This distinction is made because of future oil drilling, etc. For the same reason, the North Sea has been divided among the countries that border on it.

Movements of the earth's crust have caused the ocean floor to sink into trenches in some places. This is most common near land masses. It is here that the oceans' greatest depths have been measured with the aid of echo sounders. Such movements of the earth's crust have also caused the rise of volcanoes on the ocean floor and special types of underwater mountain ranges. The Mid-Atlantic Ridge is the best example of an underwater mountain range with volcanoes. In fact, Iceland lies on the Mid-Atlantic Ridge, where it has emerged above the surface of the ocean. Other islands on the Mid-Atlantic Ridge have also been formed in this way.

Earlier, it was believed that the ocean floor was fairly even, but systematic research with echo sounders on the ocean floor has proved that this is far from true. Countless underwater ridges, mostly discovered in this century, show that the oceans are divided into a series of basins.

On the facing page is a list of the best known deep-sea trenches in the various ocean beds. Keep in mind that the figures are adjusted from time to time when new measurements are presented.

The Deepest Sea Trenches

Ocean	Depth in m/feet	Latitude	Longitude
PACIFIC OCEAN			
Marianas Trench	11,022/36,174	13° N	143° E
Tonga Trench	10,822/35,715	20° S	172° W
Tonga-Kermadec Trench	10,047/32,974	15–35° S	175° W
Kuril-Kamchatka Trench	10,542/34,599	45° N	150° E
Philippine Trench	10,540/34,592	9° N	127° E
Bougainville Trench	9,140/29,997	7° S	155° E
Yap Trench	8,597/28,215	10° N	138° E
Japan Trench	8,142/26,722	34° N	142° E
Aleutian Trench	7,822/25,672	52° N	170° E–148° W
Atacama Trench	7,820/25,665	24° S	72° W
Ryukyu Trench	7,507/24,638	26° N	128° E

Ocean	Depth in m/feet	Latitude	Longitude
ATLANTIC OCEAN			
Puerto Rico Trench	9,219/30,257	19° N	67° W
South Sandwich Trench	8,264/27,122	57° S	26° W
Cayman Trench	7,680/25,206	19° N	80° W
Romanche Trench	7,370/24,188	0°	17° W
INDIAN OCEAN			
Java Trench	7,455/24,467	10° S	100–120° E

Capes and Peninsulas

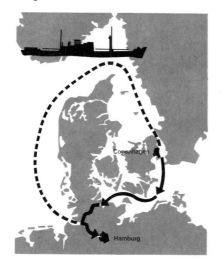

Coastal formations – such as islands, bays, capes, and peninsulas – have always been important to seafarers. This can be seen even on the early maps of the Pacific islands made by the Polynesians. The wooden maps from Greenland show capes and indentations. Ancient seafarers such as the Phoenicians and Greeks probably made similar ones, and we know that the early sea explorers placed great importance on the capes they passed. This is shown by the names they were given: Cornwall's west point, Land's End; Eire's west point, Cape Clear; Spain's west point, Cabo Finisterre (Land's End); Greenland's south point, Kap Farvel (Cape Farewell); and the Cape of Good Hope, which was thought to be the southernmost point of South Africa.

In many parts of the sea, the peninsulas extend far out, making it necessary for the boats to circumnavigate a large area. For example, to go by sea from Hamburg to Copenhagen before the Kiel Canal was built, it was necessary to sail around Skagen. To go by sea from New York to New Orleans one has to sail around the peninsula of Florida. To reach Rangoon from Bangkok by sea, ships must sail far south of the Malacca Peninsula and Singapore. At suitable places along such routes important harbors have developed.

Capes

Cape	Country	Latitude	Longitude
Nordkapp	Norway	71° N	26° E
Land's End	England	50° N	6° W
Cape Clear	Eire	51° N	9° W
Cabo Finisterre	Spain	43° N	9° W
Cabo da Roca	Portugal	39° N	10° W
Capo de Maroqui	Spain	36° N	6° W
Capo Passero	Italy	37° N	15° E
Mys Tjukotskij (East Cape)	U.S.S.R.	66° N	171° W
Cape Comorin	India	8° N	77° E
Dondra Head	Sri Lanka	6° N	82° E
Cap Blanc	Tunisia	37° N	10° E

Cape	Country	Latitude	Longitude
Cap Vert	Senegal	15° N	17° W
Cape Aghulas	South Africa	35° S	20° E
Cape York	Australia	11° S	142° E
South East Cape	Australia	42° S	146° E
North Cape	New Zealand	34° S	146° E
South West Cape	New Zealand	47° S	168° E
Kap Morris Jesup	Greenland	83° N	35° W
Kap Farvel	Greenland	59° N	44° W
Cape Prince of Wales	U.S.A.	66° N	168° W
Cape Hatteras	U.S.A.	35° N	76° W
Key West	U.S.A.	25° N	82° W
Cape Horn	Chile	57° S	67° W

Islands

We learn in school that an island is a piece of land surrounded by water. It can lie in a lake or river or in the sea. Some islands are so big that it is only on a map or globe that they can be conceived of as islands. Greenland is the biggest island. Australia is bigger still,

but it has been classified as a continent, the smallest in the world.

Most islands are connected with the continents because they lie on the continental shelf. (See p.16.) But there are more small islands in the middle of oceans, and these are generally of volcanic origin. At least the base is nearly always a volcano, and in warm seas coral reefs have grown over the bases. Coral formations can also be formed in shallow water near the coast.

Generally, coral islands lie together in a group called an archipelago (but not all archipelagoes are coral). Volcanic islands, on the other hand, tend to be completely isolated.

Many small, rocky islands were eroded by the Ice Age glaciers; if they

lie together, they are called skerries. We find some of these off the coast of Finland. It is certain that many Danish islands have been caused by glaciers, but they were not eroded and consist almost entirely of glacial deposits with the tips sticking out of the sea. These are called moraine archipelagoes.

The facing page lists the world's largest islands and their given area and also lists some of the smallest well-known islands.

The Earth's Largest Islands

Island	Area in km²	/ sq. miles	Latitude	Longitude
Greenland	2,175,000	839,550	59–83° N	11–73° W
New Guinea	785,000	303,010	5° S	143° E
Borneo	735,000	283,710	1° N	103° E
Madagascar	590,000	227,740	20° S	47° E
Baffin Island	570,000	220,020	67° N	70° W
Sumatra	450,000	173,700	0°	102° E
Great Britain	230,000	88,780	53° N	2° W
Honshu (Japan)	225,000	86,850	36° N	138° E
Celebes	180,000	69,480	2° S	120° E
New Zealand (*South Island*)	150,500	58,093	44° S	172° E
New Zealand (*North Island*)	115,000	44,390	38° S	177° E
Newfoundland	110,000	42,460	49° N	57° W

Island	Area in km²	/ sq. miles	Latitude	Longitude
Luzon	105,000	40,520	16° N	121° E
Iceland	103,000	29,758	64° N	170° W
Mindanao	95,000	36,670	8° N	125° E
Ireland	84,000	32,424	53° N	8° W
Haiti	77,000	29,722	18° N	72° W
Sakhalin	75,000	28,950	51° N	143° E
Tierra del Fuego	72,000	27,792	54° S	67° W
Tasmania	68,000	26,248	43° S	147° E
Sri Lanka	66,000	25,476	8° N	81° E
Svalbard (Western Spitzbergen)	40,000	15,440	79° N	18° E
Sicily	25,000	9,650	37° N	14° E
Sardinia	24,000	9,264	40° N	9° E

Some Well-Known Smaller Islands:

Island			Latitude	Longitude
Galapagos Islands			0°	90° W
Easter Island			27° S	110° W
Christmas Island			2° N	157° W
St. Helena			16° S	6° W
Gough Island			40° S	10° W

Deserts

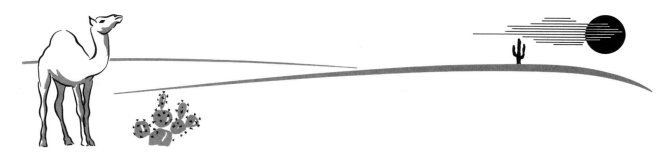

The most important causes of deserts are drought or cold. Cold deserts are found in polar regions like the whole of Antarctica, but many of the high mountains are cold deserts too.

Most of the great desert areas of the world are caused by lack of rain. This does not mean that it never rains but that there can be many years between showers of rain. In making a map of the world's deserts, it is apparent that they are generally found in areas where cold air moves toward warmer regions. Consequently this cold air can hold more moisture without condensation. The winds can blow toward the equator. These are called trade winds. Or the winds can blow from the cold seas onto the warm west side of continents. Finally, it may be that during its passage over mountain ranges or large areas of land the air has released so much condensation that there is nothing left. When an area gets less rainfall because it lies in the lee of a mountain range, in relation to the prevailing wind, it is said that it lies in the rain shadow.

Some important deserts and oases are named on the facing page. Oases are desert areas in which there is some water (wells, rivers, etc.) and plant life.

Deserts

Desert	Area in 1,000 km² / 1,000 sq.	miles	Latitude	Longitude
SAHARA				
Libyan Desert	2,000	772	15–30° N	18–35° E
Nubian Desert	400	154	27° N	25° E
OASES in Sahara				
Cufra	–	–	24° N	23° E
Siwah	–	–	29° N	25° E
ARABIAN DESERTS				
Rub al Khali	132	51	18° N	50° E
An Nefud	–	–	28° N	42° E

Desert	Area in 1,000 km² / 1,000 sq.	miles	Latitude	Longitude
AUSTRALIAN DESERTS				
Great Sandy Desert	394	150	20° S	125° E
Great Victoria Desert	657	250	28° S	130° E
Simpson Desert	145	56	25° S	137° E
Gibson Desert	–	–	24° S	125° E
Gobi	2,000	760	43° N	105° E
Kalahari	800	304	23.5° S	23° E
Takla Makan	500	190	40° N	77° E
Karakum	280	106	40° N	60° E
Thar	120	46	27° N	72° E
Atacama	368	140	23° S	70° W

Lakes and Glaciers

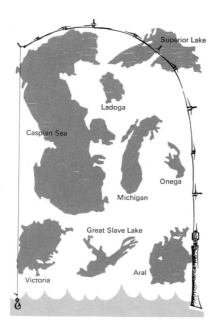

When a river flows through an area that is lower than the river's level, the area will be filled with water before the river can flow on. Many lakes must have been formed in this way, but hollows that lie below the ground-water level will also generally be filled with water.

The lake water will become salty if the evaporation from the lake is greater than the inflow, because incoming water always holds a little salt in solution. Eventually the quantity of salt will become so great that saturation is reached and salt is precipitated. Most of the world's sources of salt have been created in this way either recently or during earlier geologic periods.

If snow falls in areas where it is so cold that the snow cannot melt, it will eventually accumulate and form an ice cap. Because ice under pressure becomes plastic, the ice will under its own weight push outward and downward in the form of glaciers. The biggest coherent masses of ice are in Antarctica and Greenland.

The list on the opposite page gives the names of some of the biggest glaciers and some of the world's greatest lakes. The lakes marked with S are salt lakes.

The Largest Lakes

Lake	Area in 1,000 km²	/ 1,000 sq. miles	Latitude	Longitude
EUROPE				
Lake Ladoga	18	7	62° N	32° E
Lake Onega	10	4	63° N	36° E
AFRICA				
Lake Victoria	68	26	2° S	33° E
Lake Tanganyika	34	13	7° S	30° E
Lake Malawi	31	12	13° S	35° E
NORTH AMERICA				
Lake Superior	82	32	48° N	88° W
Lake Huron	60	23	45° N	83° W
Lake Michigan	58	22	43° N	87° W
Great Bear Lake	30	12	66° N	120° W
Great Slave Lake	29	11	62° N	115° W
Lake Erie	26	10	42° N	82° W
Lake Winnipeg	24	9	53° N	98° W
U.S.S.R.				
Caspian Sea (S)	371	143	42° N	51° E
Aral Sea (S)	67	26	45° N	60° E
Lake Baykal	32	12	54° N	107° E

Some of the Largest Glaciers

Glacier	Country	Area in km²	/ sq. miles	Latitude	Longitude
Vatnajökull	Iceland	8,800	3,397	64° N	17° W
Malaspina	U.S.A.	1,990	768	61° N	141° W
Nabesna	U.S.A.	1,350	521	62° N	147° W
Fedchenko	U.S.S.R.	1,150	444	38° N	74° E
Siachen	Mongolia	1,183	450	35° N	77° E
Aletsch	Switzerland	115	44	46° N	8° E

Rivers

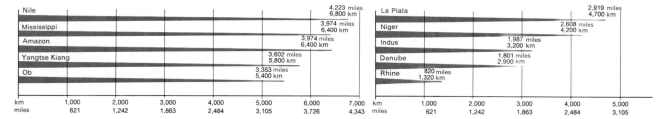

| km | | 1,000 | 2,000 | 3,000 | 4,000 | 5,000 | 6,000 | 7,000 | km | | 1,000 | 2,000 | 3,000 | 4,000 | 5,000 |
| miles | | 621 | 1,242 | 1,863 | 2,484 | 3,105 | 3,726 | 4,343 | miles | | 621 | 1,242 | 1,863 | 2,484 | 3,105 |

Nile — 4,223 miles / 6,800 km
Mississippi — 3,974 miles / 6,400 km
Amazon — 3,974 miles / 6,400 km
Yangtse Kiang — 3,602 miles / 5,800 km
Ob — 3,353 miles / 5,400 km

La Plata — 2,919 miles / 4,700 km
Niger — 2,608 miles / 4,200 km
Indus — 1,987 miles / 3,200 km
Danube — 1,801 miles / 2,900 km
Rhine — 820 miles / 1,320 km

Geographically, the word *river* indicates any water course during its flow from its source to its mouth. The latter may be in a salt lake or in the sea. Some even end in sand, but these are generally dry riverbeds, or wadis, that do not contain water all the time.

The river's source can be a spring or rain fissure that has eroded down to the subsurface water table, or it can be formed by melted water that comes from a glacier.

Some rivers erode their surrounding area (basin) and carry away the material mostly as silt. This material is deposited either in the lakes or in the sea. Such sediment deposited at the river mouth forms a delta, which stretches farther out into the sea unless it is removed by tidal or other currents or the coastline is sinking. If the coastline sinks, a funnel-shaped estuary is formed.

Some riverbeds are so hard in places that they cannot be eroded. Here waterfalls are formed, but these gradually become worn down and eventually disappear. Low waterfalls are often called cataracts.

Main rivers are those that have the biggest volume of water, but some tributaries can be longer than their main river. The Nile is considered to be the world's longest river, unless tributaries are included. In that case the Mississippi-Missouri is the longest.

The Greatest Rivers

River	Length in km	miles	Basin Area in 1,000 km²	1,000 sq. miles	Latitude	Longitude
Nile (with Kagera)	6,800	4,223	2,900	1,119	32° N	31° E
Mississippi (with Missouri)	6,400	3,974	3,250	1,255	29° N	89° W
Amazon	6,400	3,974	7,200	2,779	0°	50° W
Yangtse Kiang	5,800	3,602	1,800	695	32° N	122° E
Ob	5,400	3,353	3,000	1,158	83° N	74° E
Hwang Ho	4,900	3,043	750	290	38° N	118° E
La Plata (with Parana)	4,700	2,919	3,100	1,197	34° S	58° W
Mekong	4,500	2,795	800	309	10° N	107° E
Lena	4,400	2,732	2,500	965	74° N	126° E
Amur	4,400	2,732	1,850	714	54° N	142° E
Congo	4,300	2,670	3,700	1,428	6° S	13° E
Niger	4,200	2,608	2,100	811	4° N	6° E
Yenisey (with Angara)	4,100	2,546	2,600	1,004	83° N	80° E
Yukon	3,700	2,298	850	328	63° N	165° W
Volga	3,700	2,298	1,400	540	46° N	48° E
Mackenzie	3,500	2,174	2,100	811	69° N	135° W
St. Lawrence	3,400	2,111	1,250	489	47° N	72° W
Indus	3,200	1,987	1,000	386	24° N	68° E
Danube	2,900	1,801	820	317	45° N	30° E
Ganges	2,700	1,677	1,100	425	22° N	90° E
Zambesi	2,700	1,677	1,330	513	18° S	36° E
Rhine	1,320	820	250	97	52° N	4° E

					Latitude	Longitude
The highest waterfall in the world: Angel Falls (Venezuela)					6° N	62° W
The waterfall with the biggest volume of water: Stanley Falls (Zaire)					0°	25° E

Mountains and Passes

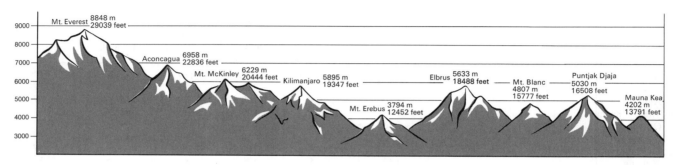

The area of the earth's surface that lies more than 660 feet (201 meters) above sea level is called highland. If such an area has an uneven surface, it is termed a mountainous area; high-lying, flat areas are called plateaus.

Mountains are of various origins and periods. The may have been caused by volcanism or by movements of the earth's crust that caused fold-mountains and fault-block mountains. The youngest fold-mountains, mostly from the Tertiary period, are the Alpine Folds and include the world's highest mountains and longest mountain ranges. The highest are the Himalayas, and the longest range is the cordilleras in North and South America. These foldings were often accompanied by volcanism, and some of the mountains in the chain may have been of volcanic origin. The older fold-mountains have become more or less completely eroded, but with later faults along lines of fracture they can be uplifted into fault-block mountains again.

Mountain ranges present obstacles to communication. But even in olden times, people, especially the Romans, were able to find places where there were gaps between the peaks. These were called passes, and at these places it was easier to cross the mountains. The best passes are those that can be used year round, such as the Brenner Pass.

The names of some of the highest mountains in various parts of the world appear on the next page. The letter V after the name indicates an active or extinct volcano. The names of some passes are given too.

The World's Highest Mountains

Mountain	Height in m*	feet*	Latitude	Longitude
EUROPE				
Mount Blanc	4,807	15,777	45° N	6° E
Etna (V)	3,340	10,962	37° N	15° E
U.S.S.R.				
Peak of Communism	7,495	24,599	38° N	72° E
Elbrus	5,633	18,488	43° N	42° E
AFRICA				
Kilimanjaro (V)	5,895	19,347	2° S	36° E
Mount Kenya (V)	5,200	17,066	0°	37° E
ASIA				
Mount Everest	8,848	29,039	28° N	86° E
Fuji (V)	3,776	12,393	35° N	138° E
NORTH AMERICA				
Mount McKinley	6,229	20,444	63° N	151° W
Citlaltepetl (V)	5,700	18,707	19° N	97° W
SOUTH AMERICA				
Aconcagua (V)	6,958	22,836	32° S	70° W
Huascaran (V)	6,768	22,213	9° S	77° W
AUSTRALIA and NEW ZEALAND				
Mount Cook	3,764	12,353	43° S	170° E
Mount Kosciusko	2,230	7,319	36° S	148° E
ANTARCTICA				
Mount Erebus (V)	3,794	12,452	77° S	167° E

* All indications of height are approximate only.

Mountain	Height in m*	feet*	Latitude	Longitude
OCEANIA				
Puntjak Djaja	5,030	16,508	3° S	137° E
Mauna Kea (V)	4,202	13,791	19° S	155° W

Passes

Mountain Range	Pass	Height in m*	feet*	Latitude	Longitude
Alps	Mount Cenis	2,083	6,836	45° N	7° E
Alps	Gt. St. Bernhard	2,469	8,103	46° N	7° E
Alps	St. Gotthard	2,091	6,863	46.5° N	8.5° E
Alps	Brenner	1,372	4,503	47° N	11.5° E
Pyrenees	Roncevalles	1,053	3,456	43° N	1° W
Trans-Sylvanian Alps	Turno Rozu	352	1,155	46° N	24° E
Balkans	Shipka	1,370	4,496	43° N	26° E
Sulajman Range	Khyber	1,070	3,512	34° N	71° E
Andes	Cumbre Uspallata	3,760	12,340	32° S	69° W

Earthquakes

The displacements, horizontal and vertical, that occur in the earth's crust (see p.28) do not take place only slowly and imperceptibly. Along the faults and folds of mountain ranges tensions may occur that can be released very suddenly, causing a tectonic earthquake. From the center of the earthquake, waves are spread that are transmitted through the earth's core as well as its crust. This is registered as a shock and is strongest just above the center of the earthquake, in the epicenter, and fades with distance from it. The strongest earthquakes can be registered all over the world at seismatic stations with seismographs. From the resulting graphs of the earthquake it is possible to establish how far from the station the earthquake occurred. The center of the earthquake can be fixed with graphs from several stations. Most earthquakes occur in the area around the Alpine Folds. This shows that the earth's surface is by no means quiescent, and folding and faulting occur all the time.

Fortunately, few earthquakes cause catastrophes, but thousands of people

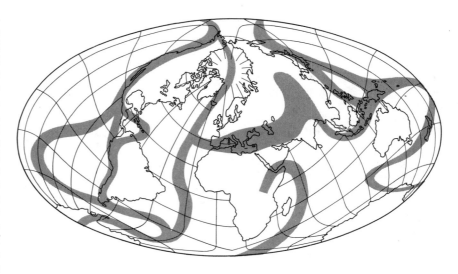

have lost their lives in some. Few areas are totally free from earthquakes, but in many cases these are very weak and may be caused by the sinking of the subsoil's bed.

The beds of the seas can be affected by earthquakes. These make great movements of water, seismatic sea waves – tsunamis – that can cause great damage when they reach the shore.

Earthquake Disasters

Locality	Year	Number of Deaths	Latitude	Longitude
Japan	1730	137,000	36° N	140° E
Lisbon	1755	32,000	39° N	10° W
Calabria (Italy)	1783	50,000	39° N	16° E
San Francisco	1906	1,000	35° N	122° W
Messina (Italy)	1908	75,000	35° N	16° E
Avezzano (Italy)	1915	30,000	42° N	13° E
Kansu (China)*	1920	180,000	36° N	104° E
Kwanto-Ebene (Japan)	1923	145,000	36° N	140° E
Kansu (China)	1932	70,000	36° N	104° E
Quetta (Pakistan)	1935	50,000	30° N	66° E
Erzingan (Turkey)	1939	45,000	39° N	39° E
Agadir (Morocco)	1960	12,000	31° N	10° W
East Turkey**	1966	3,000	39° N	43° E
East Iran**	1968	10,000	28° N	60° E
Peru**	1970	50,000	12° S	77° W
Tientsin-Tangshan (China)	1976	250,000	39° N	118° E
Mexico City (Mexico)	1985	10,000	19° N	99° W

* The earthquake released great landslides, and these caused many casualties.

** Localization not certain.

Meteors and Meteorites

Meteors are pieces of stone or metal that enter the earth's atmosphere at enormous speeds. Friction with the earth's atmosphere causes fire, and we can see a meteor's light. Meteors are commonly called shooting or falling stars.

The majority of meteors burn out before they reach the earth's surface. Others reach it and explode on impact. A meteor that reaches the earth is called a meteorite.

It is calculated that about 200 million visible meteors enter the atmosphere of the earth every day and that these increase the earth's weight by about 1,000 tons daily. Meteors belong to the solar system and occur in swarms. They are common at certain periods of the year at intervals that coincide with the occurrence of comets. It is thought that meteors are the remains of comets.

The majority of the known meteorites seem to be composed of iron and nickel. Their surfaces show signs that they have been glowing on their descent toward earth. Stone meteorites are of very varied substances, but these seem to be volcanic in character.

The facing page lists the best-known meteorites, together with a list of craters on the earth's surface that are believed to have been caused by meteorites.

It is worth noting that many of the craters found on the moon are definitely meteorite craters. Since the moon has no atmosphere, the meteorites cannot burn away; so all reach the surface of the moon.

Meteorites

Meteorite	Approx. Tonnage	Latitude	Longitude
The greatest recorded meteorite was found near Hoba in the neighborhood of Grootfontein (South West Africa).	60 t.	19° S	18° E
"The Tent"	30.4 t.		
"The Woman" Cape York	3.0 t.	76° N	67° W
"The Dog" (Greenland)	0.4 t.		
"Savic"	3.4 t.		
"Agpallilik" (near Thule)	20 t.	77° N	69° W
Found near Mexico	27 t.	26° N	108° W
Tanzania (East Africa)	26 t.	5° S	35° E
Oregon (U.S.A.)	14 t.	43° N	120° W
Mexico	14 t.	29° N	106° W
Chihuahua (Mexico)	11 t.	29° N	106° W
Cranbourne (Australia)	3.5 t.	25° S	130° E
Magura (Czechoslovakia)	1.5 t	49° N	17° E

Meteorite Scars and Craters

	Latitude	Longitude
Vanavara near Podkamenuaya, or Stony Tunguska (Siberia)	62° N	90° E
Sikhota, Alin	46° N	136° E
Deep Bay, Saskatchewan (Canada)	55° N	105° W
Nastapoga Island, Hudson Bay (Canada)	57° N	77° W
Coon Butte, or Barringer Crater, Winslow, Arizona (U.S.A.)	35° N	111° W

Climate and Climate Records

The climate of a place is generally described by its temperature, wind forces, and rainfall. Temperatures are the most important factors, but in reality the average temperature of a place does not give a true picture.

For example, the average temperature for Cambridge, England, for June is given as 58.5°F. Yet the average monthly extremes for June over a period of years range from 38°F to 82°F.

The temperature of a place is influenced by the sun's rays; that is, by the number of hours of sunshine and the height of the sun. Strangely enough, the warmest places on earth do not lie on the equator, where the sky is generally very cloudy. The hottest places are to be found in the desert areas on both sides of the equator, where there is little cloud ceiling.

The winds are caused by differences in air pressure as air masses move from places with high air pressure to those with lower air pressure. Because of the rotation of the earth, the wind is deflected to the right in the Northern Hemisphere and to the left in the Southern Hemisphere. The greater the difference in air pressure, the stronger the wind. The greatest wind forces are reached in typhoons and hurricanes.

Rain occurs when an air mass holding a certain amount of vapor is chilled so that the vapor condenses to form drops of water that fall as rain.

Climate Records

Temperature

Highest in the shade	58 °C/ 136 °F	Al Aziziyah (Libya) 32° N lat. 13° E long.
Highest yearly average	31.1 °C/ 88 °F	Lugh Ganana (East Africa) 4° N lat. 43° E long.
Lowest temperature	−88.3 °C/ −127 °F	Wostok (Antarctica) 82° S lat. 105° E long.
Lowest yearly average temperature	−17.5 °C/ 0 °F	Wostok (Antarctica) 82° S lat. 105° E long.

Air Pressure

Highest	1,079 mb	Barnaul (Mid-Siberia) 53° N lat. 84° E long.
Lowest	877 mb	near Guam (Oceania) 13° N lat. 145° E long.

Wind Force on Earth's Surface

Highest 372 km/231 miles per hour	Mt. Washington (U.S.A.) 44° N lat. 71° W long.
Most windy place with wind force over 300 km/186 miles per hour	George V Coast (Antarctica) 70° S lat. 150° E long.

Rainfall

Greatest per minute	2.12 cm/ 0.1″	Unionville (U.S.A.) 40° N lat. 115° W long.
Greatest per day	173 cm/ 65″	Reunion (Indian Ocean) 22° S lat. 56° E long.
Greatest per year	3,246 cm/ 1,278″	Cherrapunji (Assam) 28° N lat. 92° E long.
Greatest yearly average	1,200 cm/ 472″	Cherrapunji (Assam) 28° N lat. 92° E long.
Greatest number of rainy days per year	348	Bahia Felix (Chile) 45° S lat. 74° W long.
Lowest rainfall	0 cm	Atacama Desert (Chile) 24° S lat. 69° W long.
Greatest snowfall in one day	193 cm/ 76″	Silver Lake (U.S.A.) 43° N lat. 121° W long.
Greatest snowfall per year	2,541 cm/ 1,001″	Mt. Rainier (U.S.A.) 47° N lat. 121° W long.

Sunshine

Maximum 4,300 hours per year	Libyan Desert 27° N lat. 25° E long.
Minimum 6 minutes in one month	London December 1890 51.5° N lat. 0°

Plant and Animal Worlds, Cultivated Plants, and Domestic Animals

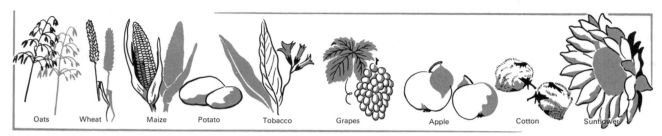

Oats Wheat Maize Potato Tobacco Grapes Apple Cotton Sunflower

Pinpointing the location of plants and animals on a globe is nearly impossible, because few species of plants and animals are associated with one single place. They do have special areas where they grow but these are not constant. Natural spreading and growth of plants and animals is becoming limited, because human beings are encroaching. In fact, some species are already lost and others have nearly been wiped out, and soon it will be possible only to say where they were last seen.

On the other hand, some plants and animals, especially cultivated plants and domestic animals, have been widely spread by man, and this happened even in prehistoric times. For many years we believed that maize was indigenous to the Americas, but it has been proved that it originated in East Asia.

Zoologists, botanists, geneticists, and geographers have been trying for years to find out where the various plants and animals of the world originated. This is difficult because the cultivated forms often look very different from the original species. It is of great importance to find the sources of the wild forms because they are of use in cross-fertilization.

Probable Place of Origin of Cultivated Plants and Domestic Animals

	Place of Origin	Latitude	Longitude
Cultivated Plants			
Wheat	Iraq	35° N	45° E
Barley	Near East	35° N	40° E
Rye	Near East	40° N	40° E
Oats	Armenia	40° N	45° E
Millet	China	35° N	115° E
Maize	Assam	28° N	95° E
Rice	Thailand	15° N	105° E
Potatoes	Peru	10° S	78° W
Sugarcane	Bangladesh	24° N	90° E
Sugar beet	Baltic Coast	54° N	12° E
Coffee	Ethiopia	5° N	40° E
Cocoa	Brazil	0°	70° W
Tea	Assam	26° N	93° E
Tobacco	Bolivia	12° S	65° W
Grapes	Armenia	42° N	42° E
Dates	Arabia	30° N	40° E
Figs	Arabia	15° N	45° E
Apple	Central Europe	52° N	12° E
Citrus fruits	Burma	23° N	97° E
(e.g., Lemon)	South China	23° N	115° E

	Place of Origin	Latitude	Longitude
Olive	Turkey	37° N	37° E
Sesame	Ethiopia	10° N	40° E
Sunflower	North America	35° N	95° W
Oil palm	West Africa	5° N	15° E
Coconut palm	Colombia	10° N	75° W
Groundnut	Brazil	15° S	45° W
Flax	Near East	40° N	45° E
Cotton	Sudan	10° N	30° E
Sisal	Mexico	20° N	90° W
Jute	Bangladesh	24° N	90° E
Domestic Animals			
Horse	Caucasus	45° N	45° E
Sheep	Afghanistan	33° N	65° E
Goat	Near East	40° N	40° E
Cattle	Near East	40° N	40° E
Donkey	North Africa	20° N	35° E
Llama	South America	12° S	72° W
Chicken	Malaysia	4° N	103° E

Continents and Countries

It is quite possible that many million years ago all the land masses were concentrated in the same area. They became split by strong internal movements of the earth. A look at a map of the world shows you that it seems likely that North and South America were connected with Europe at one time.

The great land masses are called continents, but there is no consensus as to where the divisions should be made. It would be more natural to say Eurasia instead of Europe and Asia. This would overcome the difficulty of the fact that the U.S.S.R. lies in both continents. But Europe is likely to continue its status as a continent, even though it should be called a subcontinent like India.

There are seven continents: Asia, Africa, and Europe, which constitute the Old World; North and South America, which make up the New World; and Australia and Antarctica, which might be called the Newest World. Statistically, it has been most expedient to talk of Europe without the U.S.S.R., and Asia without the U.S.S.R., and to give figures for the U.S.S.R. alone. Discussion about Australia seems to indicate that it should be included in the area of the Pacific Ocean and called Oceania.

The continents are politically divided into countries. Most of these are independent or constituent states, examples of the latter being the U.S.A., Brazil, Yugoslavia, and West Germany. There are some colonies that have not yet gained their independence.

The biggest countries in terms of area are the U.S.S.R., Canada, China, the U.S.A., Brazil, Australia, and India. Other countries are so small that it is difficult to find them on the map. The following list shows some of these.

Small States

Continent	Area in 1,000 km² / 1,000 sq.	miles	Latitude	Longitude
EUROPE				
Albania	29	11.2	42° N	20° E
Andorra	0.4	0.19	43° N	2° E
Liechtenstein	0.16	0.06	47° N	9° E
Luxembourg	2.6	1.00	49° N	7° E
Malta	0.3	0.116	36° N	14° E
Monaco	0.0015	0.00058	43° N	7° E
San Marino	0.06	0.0232	43° N	13° E
Vatican City	0.0004	0.0002	42° N	12° E
ASIA				
Bahrain	0.6	0.232	26° N	51° E
Cyprus	9.3	3.59	35° N	33° E
Israel	21	8.1	32° N	35° E
Kuwait	16	6.2	29° N	57° E
Lebanon	10	3.86	33° N	36° E
Maldive Islands	0.3	0.116	6° N	73° E
Qatar	24	8.5	25° N	52° E
Singapore	0.6	0.232	2° N	104° E

Continent	Area in 1,000 km² / 1,000 sq.	miles	Latitude	Longitude
AFRICA				
Burundi	28	10.8	4° S	30° E
Equatorial Guinea	28	10.8	2° N	10° E
Gambia	11	4.2	13° N	15° W
Lesotho	30	11.58	29° S	28° E
Mauritius	2	0.77	20° S	57° E
Rwanda	26	10.04	3° S	30° E
Swaziland	17	6.56	27° S	32° E
AMERICA				
Barbados	0.4	0.154	13° N	60° W
El Salvador	21	8.11	14° N	88° W
Haiti	27	10.4	14° N	73° W
Jamaica	11	4.25	18° N	77° W
Trinidad and Tobago	5.1	1.97	11° N	62° W
AUSTRALIA and OCEANIA				
Fiji	18	6.95	17° S	179° E
Nauru	0.02	0.0077	0°	166° E
Tonga	0.7	0.27	21° S	175° E
Western Samoa	2.8	1.98	14° S	172° E

The Biggest Cities of the World

Tokyo   New York   Shanghai   Paris   Buenos Aires   Mexico City   London   Moscow   Calcutta   Chicago   Bombay   Berlin

Due to the rapid expansion of industry since the 19th century, most towns in the industrialized countries of the world have grown quickly too. For example, in Germany the urbanized population is more than 80 percent (1816: 25 percent; 1900: 55 percent). In the U.S.S.R. about 60 percent of the people live in towns, whereas in 1900 only 12 percent lived there. This urban explosion has spread to the lesser developed countries, and they too have many big cities, that is, towns with more than 100,000 inhabitants. The reason for all this urbanization is that land dwellers have moved to the big cities, where there are greater employment possibilities and social opportunities.

This urbanization has led to the founding of single towns and also to groups of towns (conurbation). Well-known examples of this development are the Ruhr area of Germany, the Midlands of England, and Randstad Holland (the area around Amsterdam, The Hague, and Rotterdam). Many towns are surrounded by planned suburbs where the population often grows more rapidly than the actual town area. Consequently it is not always easy to calculate the actual population of a big town, and often the population of the suburbs is included. In the tables on the next page the initials "i.s." have been printed after certain population figures. This indicates "including suburbs."

There are more than 175 cities with over a million people. Most of the cities are in the U.S.S.R., the U.S.A., China, India, Japan, Germany, and Great Britain.

The Biggest Cities of the World

City	Country	Inhabitants in Millions i.s. = including suburbs	Latitude	Longitude	City	Country	Inhabitants in Millions i.s. = including suburbs	Latitude	Longitude
New York	U.S.A.	16.1 i.s.	40° N	74° W	Delhi	India	5.7 i.s.	28° N	77° E
Mexico City	Mexico	14.7 i.s.	19° N	99° W	Philadelphia	U.S.A.	5.5 i.s.	44° N	75° W
Tokyo	Japan	11.6 i.s.	35° N	139° E	Rio de Janeiro	Brazil	5.0	23° S	43° W
Los Angeles	U.S.A.	11.4 i.s.	34° N	118° W	Cairo	Egypt	5.0	30° N	31° E
Shanghai	China	10.8 i.s.	31° N	121° E	Detroit	U.S.A.	4.6 i.s.	42° N	83° W
Buenos Aires	Argentina	9.9 i.s.	34° N	58° W	Leningrad	U.S.S.R.	4.5 i.s.	60° N	30° E
Calcutta	India	9.1 i.s.	22° N	88° E	Tientsin	China	4.2	39° N	117° E
Paris	France	8.6 i.s.	48° N	2° E	Berlin (West and East)	Germany	3.0	52.5° N	13.5° E
Bombay	India	8.2	19° N	72° E					
Moscow	U.S.S.R.	8.0 i.s.	55° N	37° E					
Chicago	U.S.A.	7.8 i.s.	41° N	87° W					
Beijing (Peking)	China	7.5	40° N	116° E					
London	Great Britain	6.2	51° N	0°					

* Underlined cities are capitals.

Sources of Energy

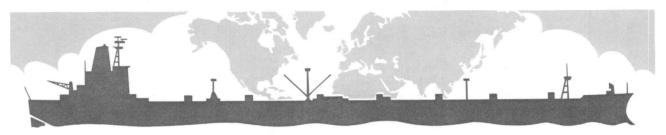

By *sources of energy* we mean the raw materials that can be developed for heat, industry, transport, etc., but we do not refer to the sources of nourishment that give energy to man and animal.

In earlier times hauling was done by man and beast, and heat was produced by wood and peat. Quite early, people learned to utilize water power and, later, wind forces. These became inadequate when the Industrial Revolution started in about 1800. Soon the problem of sufficient energy was solved by the invention of steam engines fueled by coal. In about 1900, gasoline- and oil-powered machines were introduced. Earlier, water wheels were used to provide pow-er, but by the end of the 19th century water was used to make hydraulic power-er. The introduction of alternating current at the beginning of 1900 meant that power from hydroelectric plants could be carried great distances to industrialized areas. It was not long before steam turbines and internal combustion engines contributed power to the increasing net of hydroelectric power lines. Power plants could now be built at places where raw materials for energy were found and at points to which these materials could be easily transported, for example, harbors. Later came the development of utilizing atomic energy for the production of electric power.

The countries that possess such raw materials have great advantages today because they can use them for their own industries or export the raw materials to other countries that have an insufficient supply. The demand for these materials grows greater all the time.

Location of Sources of Energy

Coal	Country	Latitude	Longitude
Yorkshire	Great Britain	55° N	1° W
Durham	Great Britain	54° N	1° W
Ruhr	West Germany	51° N	7° E
Slask	Poland	51° N	19° E
Donezbasin	U.S.S.R.	48° N	35° E
Kusnezbasin	U.S.S.R.	55° N	90° E
Karaganda	U.S.S.R.	60° N	75° E
West Virginia	U.S.A.	38° N	82° W
Pennsylvania	U.S.A.	41° N	77° W
Illinois	U.S.A.	40° N	88° W
Ranchi	India	22° N	86° E
Fuschun	China	41° N	123° E
Newcastle	Australia	38° S	152° E

Uranium	Country	Latitude	Longitude
Johannesburg	South Africa	27° S	28° E
Katanga	Zaire	8° S	25° E
Irkutsk	U.S.S.R.	53° N	104° E
Fergana	U.S.S.R.	41° N	71° E
Uranium City	Canada	59° N	109° W
Beaver Lodge	Canada	63° N	115° W
Port Radium	Canada	66° N	118° W
Shiprock	U.S.A.	37° N	109° W
Rum Jungle	Australia	13° S	131° W
Jachymov	Czechoslovakia	50° N	13° E

Oil	Country	Latitude	Longitude
Baku	U.S.S.R.	41° N	50° E
New Baku	U.S.S.R.	64° N	78° E
Kirkuk	Iraq	36° N	45° E
Kuwait		29° N	48° E
West Iran		31° N	50° E
Ghawar	Saudi Arabia	25° N	50° E
Palembang	Indonesia	3° S	105° E
Maracaibo	Venezuela	10° N	72° W
Oficina	Venezuela	8° N	66° W
Trinidad		10° N	62° W
Gulf Field	U.S.A.	24–31° N	87–97° W
Mid Continent Field	U.S.A.	33–35° N	97° W
Pembina	Canada	34° N	118° W
Hassi-Messaud	Algeria	31° N	6° E
Zelten	Libya	28° N	19° E

Iron Ore

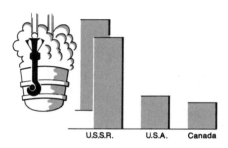

U.S.S.R. U.S.A. Canada

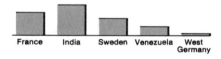

France India Sweden Venezuela West Germany

engine.

Places where both coal and iron were found in the earth became obvious areas for the establishment of heavy industry.

Iron ore is of varying quality, the best containing over 60 percent iron and the poorest having less than 20 percent. The latter, usually brown iron ore, could not be used economically in earlier times, but recently cheap methods that help to enrich the iron content have been found, and this has made it an economical proposition now.

Most iron is converted into steel, and steelworks are placed near ironworks to save transport. For the production of the many varieties of steel, many other metals are used with iron. These enhance the quality of the steel (for example, make it rustless). Manganese, chromium, and nickel are some of the metals used to make steel alloys.

The table on page 45 gives the figures for the production of iron ore in various countries for 1983; to simplify comparison, all figures quoted give the amount of iron extracted.

Iron is one of the most abundant elements of the earth's crust and the most important ore in industrial use. In ancient times iron was smelted over charcoal, and mass production first began with the introduction of blast furnaces where coke was used for the conversion of iron. The invention of blast furnaces was as important as that of the steam

Country	Iron Ore (in 1,000 tons)	Area or Location	Latitude	Longitude
U.S.S.R.	245,000	Krivoi Rog	45° N	34° E
		Magnitogorsk	53° N	59° E
U.S.A.	43,000	Mesabi Range	47° N	94° W
		Wisconsin	44° N	90° W
Australia	61,000	Hamersley Range	16° S	127° E
		Middleback Range	34° S	137° E
Canada	34,000	Schefferville	55° N	67° W
		Labrador City	62° N	68° W
Brazil	61,000	Minas Gerais	19° S	46° W
China	44,000	Anschan	41° N	123° E
Sweden	23,200	Kiruna	68° N	20° E
		Gällivare	60° N	14° E
India	40,000	Bihar/Orissa	25° N	85° E
France	31,000	Lorraine	49° N	6° E
Liberia	20,600	Bomi Hills	5° N	10° W
Venezuela	11,700	Cerro Bolivar	6° N	63° W
West Germany	1,304	Salzgitter	52° N	10° E

Precious Metals

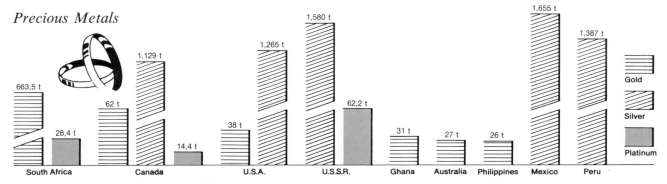

Under the heading "precious metals" we refer to platinum, gold, and silver. They are called precious because they do not combine with the oxygen of the air and are almost chemically inactive. From earliest times these qualities led to the use of gold and silver for personal ornaments, jewelry, etc., and later for coins and measures of value. Until recent years most countries had gold standards of currency, a few had silver standards, and during currency crises there is still a great demand for gold.

Gold and silver have been used in the production of jewelry because both are quite ductile and therefore malleable. In many cases the ductile quality of these two metals has been hardened by alloying them with other harder metals, such as copper. In contrast, platinum is very hard and is used for the setting of valuable jewelry. It has many technical uses in alloy form, as it is resistant to corrosion.

Most platinum and gold and some silver are found in pure form and less frequently as ore with other metals. Extraction of platinum and gold can be made partly by washing out. Grains of gold can be separated from grains of sand because gold is heavier.

The most important countries for the production of gold, silver, and platinum are shown in the table on page 47.

	Country	Annual Production in Tons	Location of Mine	Latitude	Longitude
Gold	South Africa	663.5	Witwatersrand	27° S	27° E
			Oldendalsrus	29° S	28° E
	Canada	62	Porcupine	48° N	80° W
			Val d'Or	48° N	78° W
			Yellowknife	62° N	114° W
	U.S.A.	38	Fairbanks	65° N	147° W
			Yuba	39° N	121° W
	Ghana	31	Obuasi	6° N	1° W
			Prestea	5° N	2° W
	Australia	27	Victoria	37° S	144° E
			Kalgoorlie	32° S	122° E
	Philippines	26	North Luzon	17° N	122° E
	Japan	3	Mombetsu	44° N	143° E
	Colombia	6.3	Frontino	2° N	77° W
	Mexico	6.3	San Dimas	24° N	106° W
Silver	Canada	1,129	Sudbury	47° N	81° W
			Kootenay	49° N	117° W
	U.S.A.	1,265	Butte	46° N	112° W
	Mexico	1,655	Chihuahua	29° N	106° W
	Peru	1,387	Cerro de Pasco	10° S	77° W
	U.S.S.R.	1,580	Sadon	43° N	44° E
Platinum	U.S.S.R.	62.2	Norilsk	69° N	88° E
	South Africa	28.4	Rustenburg	26° S	27° E
	Canada	14.4	Sudbury	46° N	81° W

Other Metals

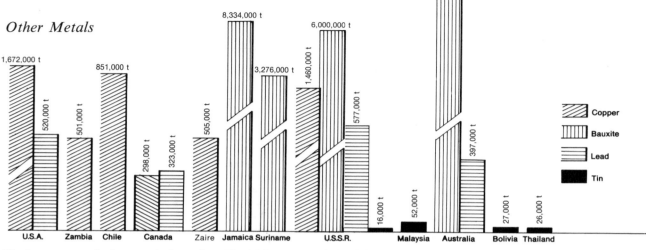

1,672,000 t — U.S.A. (Copper)
520,000 t — U.S.A. (Lead)
501,000 t — Zambia
851,000 t — Chile
298,000 t — Canada (Lead)
323,000 t — Canada (Lead)
505,000 t — Zaire
8,334,000 t — Jamaica
3,276,000 t — Suriname
1,460,000 t — U.S.S.R. (Bauxite)
6,000,000 t — U.S.S.R. (Bauxite)
577,000 t — U.S.S.R. (Lead)
16,000 t — Malaysia (Tin)
52,000 t — Malaysia (Tin)
23,621,000 t — Australia (Bauxite)
397,000 t — Australia (Lead)
27,000 t — Bolivia (Tin)
26,000 t — Thailand (Tin)

Legend:
- Copper
- Bauxite
- Lead
- Tin

The importance of other metals depends on their industrial applications and whether or not they can be used economically.

Copper is a good conducting agent for heat and electricity and is frequently made into wires, cables, and tubes. Copper alloys such as bronze and brass are used extensively in our daily life.

Aluminum is important because of its lightness. Its alloy with iron makes aluminum steel, which is both hard and light and therefore ideal for aircraft.

The main source of aluminum is bauxite, a claylike mineral that is often red in color. A great deal of electricity is needed for the extraction of aluminum, and most aluminum works are situated near hydraulic power plants.

Lead is heavy and soft. Earlier, it was used for water pipes because of its resistance to corrosion. Today it serves as a covering for all types of cables and as protection against radioactive rays and X-rays. Thick layers of lead surround reactors of atomic energy plants, and

X-ray machines are protected with lead plate.

As zinc does not rust, it is utilized in the galvanizing of iron.

Other metals – especially manganese, chrome, and nickel and even the rarer vanadium, titanium, wolfram, and molybdenum – are used primarily as alloys. Chrome, nickel, and tin function as coating metals in the automobile and canning industries.

	Country	Annual Production in 1,000 Tons	Location	Latitude	Longitude
Copper	U.S.A.	1,672	Bingham	40° N	112° W
			Morenci	33° N	110° W
			Butte	46° N	112° W
	U.S.S.R.	1,460	Dzhezkazgan	48° N	68° E
	Chile	851	Chuquieamata	22° S	64° W
			El Teniente	36° S	72° W
			Potrerillos	27° S	71° W
	Canada	298	Sudbury	46° N	81° W
			Flin Flon	55° N	102° W
	Zambia	501	Copper Belt	13° N	27° W
	Zaire	505	Katanga	10° S	27° E
Bauxite	Jamaica	8,334		18° N	77° W
	Australia	23,621	Weipa	35° S	148° E
	Surinam	3,276		4° N	56° W
	U.S.S.R.	6,000	Krasnoturinsk	60° N	68° E
			Pawlodar	56° N	63° E
	Guyana	1,545	Mackenzie	7° N	58° W
Lead	U.S.A.	520	Southeast Missouri	37° N	90° W
	U.S.S.R.	577	Leninogorsk	51° N	84° E
	Australia	397	Mt. Isa	21° S	139° E
			Broken Hill	32° S	141° E
	Canada	323	Kootenay	49° N	117° W
Tin	Malaysia	52	Kintatal	4° N	103° E
	Bolivia	27	Potosi	20° S	66° W
	U.S.S.R.	16	Borsja	50° N	127° E
	China	16	Nanning	23° N	108° E
	Thailand	26	Pilok	17° N	103° E
	Indonesia	34	Bangka	3° S	107° E

Other Minerals

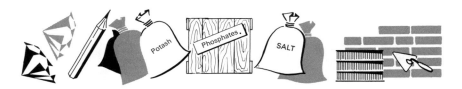

Some minerals are common all over the world rather than in only a few localities; others are rarer. Among the latter are two forms of crystallized pure carbon: diamonds and graphite. These have widely different qualities. Diamonds are the hardest material known, whereas graphite is soft and greasy. Diamonds are used as abrasives in industry. In addition, they are much valued as precious stones because of their quality of reflecting light when they are cut properly. Graphite is used in lubrication, as a moderator in atomic piles, and in making lead pencils.

One of the more common minerals is mica, which is used as insulating material in electrical equipment. Another is asbestos, which cannot burn and is used for protection against high temperatures. Workers in blast furnaces wear asbestos clothing.

A large group of minerals are used in the fertilizer industry. These are potassic salt (potash), chilean nitrate, phosphates, and chalk. The last-named is used a great deal in the building industry, in the form of cement.

In addition, sulfur and ordinary kitchen salt must be included because they are used in the chemical industry. Kitchen salt is also of importance in the human diet.

	Country	Area or Location	Latitude	Longitude
Diamonds	South Africa	Kimberley	29° S	25° E
		Premier	27° S	29° E
	Namibia (South West Africa)	Lüderitz	27° S	15° E
		Rosh Pinah	28° S	17° E
	Zaire	Tsikapa	9° S	21° E
		Mbuji-Mayi	7° S	23° E
	U.S.S.R.	Mir	55° N	31° E
		Udachnaja	64° N	102° E
		Yakutia	63° N	134° E
Potash	Germany	Lengede near Hanover	52° N	10° E
		Bernburg/Saale	52° N	12° E
	France	Bollwiller in Alsace	45° N	6° E
	U.S.S.R.	Solikamsk	56° N	56° E
	Canada	Esterhazy	51° N	102° W
	U.S.A.	Carlsbad	32° N	104° W
Phosphates	Morocco	Khouribga	33° N	7° W
		Youssoufia	32° N	9° W
	U.S.S.R.	Kirovsk	68° N	34° E
		Chulok-Tau	45° N	67° E
	U.S.A.	Mulberry	27° N	82° W
Common salt	Poland	Wieliczka	50° N	20° E
	Austria	Salzkammergut	47° N	13° E
	Israel	Dead Sea	32° N	36° E

Industrial Zones

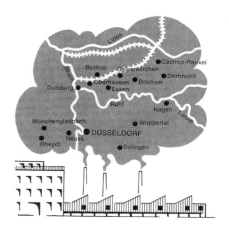

There is every reason to call our times the industrial age. Since the middle of the 19th century, industry has become more dominant, and in many countries more people are employed in industry than in any other form of labor. Now we are entering a new phase in which services of different kinds have begun to take over the employment lead. But it must be emphasized that this is possible only because mass production has made consumer goods of every sort available to all.

At the beginning of the industrial period, there was a tendency to group industries together. This was influenced by the location of raw materials, especially coal and iron, and by the availability of labor. Many industries remain where they started, but new ones have developed, especially in areas where there is a good market for industrial products.

Many industries are dependent on each other; thus proximity becomes an advantage because it reduces transportation costs. This collaboration between the different industries has been studied scientifically, and the results have influenced the placement of new factories, grouping them together in larger units.

Industrial Location	Town	Latitude	Longitude
Midlands	Birmingham	52° N	2° W
(U.K.)	Coventry	52° N	1° W
Lancashire	Manchester	53° N	3° W
(U.K.)	Preston	53° N	2° W
Yorkshire	Sheffield	55° N	1° W
(U.K.)	Leeds	54° N	1° W
Ruhr	Dortmund	52° N	7° E
(West Germany)	Bochum	51° N	7° E
	Gelsenkirchen	51° N	7° E
	Essen	51° N	7° E
	Oberhausen	51° N	7° E
	Duisburg	51° N	7° E
Randstad	Rotterdam	52° N	5° E
(The Netherlands)	Amsterdam	52° N	5° E
	The Hague	52° N	4° E
	Utrecht	52° N	5° E

Industrial Location	Town	Latitude	Longitude
Upper Silesia	Katowice	50° N	19° E
(Slask)	Zabrze	50° N	19° E
(Poland)	Gliwice	50° N	19° E
Donetsk Basin	Donetsk	48° N	38° E
(U.S.S.R.)	Makeyevka	48° N	35° E
	Gorlovka	48° N	33° E
	Voroshilovgrad	50° N	36° E
Industrial belt	Detroit	43° N	83° W
around Lake Erie	Toledo	42° N	84° W
(U.S.A.)	Cleveland	42° N	82° W
	Pittsburgh	41° N	80° W

Oil Refineries and Atomic Energy Plants

Oil has become an important world product in the past few decades. At first, oil refineries were built in areas where oil was found. But these areas had little practical use for the products, whereas in other areas the chemical industry was developing many new products from crude oil. Transportation of oil became more efficient with the building of pipelines and supertankers. It is more practical to transport the crude oil than the many finished oil products; so refineries were built outside the oil-producing areas. Such refineries are economic assets, and even small countries have refineries now.

Another modern industrial phenomenon is the atomic energy plant. Developments in this field have made it economical to build such plants in countries that use a great deal of electricity. Atomic plants are very expensive to build, but use of atomic energy leads to a saving of other raw materials originally used in the production of energy.

Oil Refineries

Location	Country	Latitude	Longitude
Grangemouth	Great Britain	56° N	3° W
Liverpool	Great Britain	53° N	3° W
Fawley	Great Britain	51° N	10° W
Thames estuary	Great Britain	51° N	10° E
Europoort	The Netherlands	52° N	40° E
Antwerp	Belgium	51° N	4° E
Ruhr	West Germany	52° N	5° E
Hamburg	West Germany	54° N	10° E
Karlsruhe	West Germany	49° N	8° E
Ingolstadt	West Germany	49° N	11° E
Le Havre	France	49° N	0°
Marseilles	France	43° N	5° E
Genoa	Italy	44° N	9° E
Augusta	Italy	37° N	15° E
Abadan	Iran	31° N	48° E

Location	Country	Latitude	Longitude
Kuwait		29° N	48° E
Tokyo	Japan	36° N	140° E
Philadelphia	U.S.A.	40° N	75° W
Chicago	U.S.A.	42° N	88° W
Houston	U.S.A.	30° N	95° W
Los Angeles	U.S.A.	33° N	110° W
San Francisco	U.S.A.	38° N	123° W
Tampico	Mexico	22° N	95° W
Trinidad		11° N	61° W
Curaçao	Dutch West Indies	12° N	69° W
Amuay	Venezuela	12° N	70° W
El Cardon	Venezuela	12° N	71° W
Baku	U.S.S.R.	41° N	50° E
Ufa	U.S.S.R.	55° N	56° E
Kuybyschew	U.S.S.R.	54° N	50° E

Atomic Energy Plants

Location	Country	Latitude	Longitude
Berkeley	Great Britain	52° N	2° W
Calder Hall	Great Britain	54° N	3° W
Hinkley Point	Great Britain	51° N	4° W
Chinon	France	47° N	0°
Marcoule	France	44° N	5° E
Kahl/Main	West Germany	50° N	8° E
Stadersand/Elbe	West Germany	54° N	9° E

Location	Country	Latitude	Longitude
Rheinsberg	East Germany	53° N	13° E
Rheinfelden	Switzerland	48° N	8° E
Voronezh	U.S.S.R.	55° N	40° E
Tokai Mura	Japan	58° N	33° E
Sioux Falls	U.S.A.	43° N	96° W
Browns Ferry	U.S.A.	40° N	76° W
Sequoyah site	U.S.A.	35° N	121° W

56

Shipping

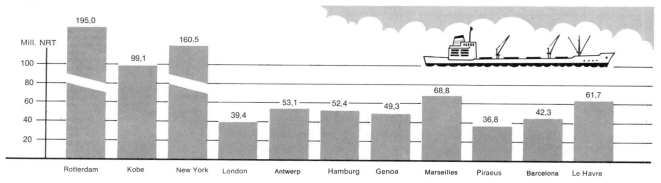

The cheapest form of transport is by boat. It is not as quick as other forms of transport, but this is not important for heavy and nonperishable goods.

At the beginning of the industrial age, it was important to transport coal, iron, and industrial goods as cheaply as possible. Horses and wagons were not practical, since the roads were badly made at that time. Consequently water transport was used, and wherever possible canals were built for this purpose. Some of these have importance today, but many remain only as tourist attractions. Inland canals that have remained impor-

tant are able to take big boats. The network in the U.S.S.R. that links Moscow to the Baltic, White, Black, and Caspian seas is one example.

Deep-draft ship canals that can take oceangoing vessels are of greatest value. Many of these have been cut through isthmuses, and long sailing distances have been reduced (Panama, Suez, and Kiel canals). Others have been cut into the land (Manchester Ship Canal, St. Lawrence Seaway, etc.).

For shipping, it has always been important that harbors be sheltered, so that ships do not have to ride at anchor

at the open roadsteads. Generally, harbors have been developed where they could supply a large industrial hinterland. It is easy to understand why Rotterdam with Europort has become the biggest harbor in the world.

Canals

	Latitude	Longitude
Suez Canal	31° N	33° E
Volga-Don Canal	48° N	44° E
Kiel Canal	54° N	9° E
Houston Canal	29° N	95° W
Alphonse XIII Canal (to Seville)	37° N	6° E
Panama Canal	9° N	80° W
Manchester Canal	53° N	2° W
Welland Canal (by Niagara Falls)	43° N	79° W

The Most Important Ports

Turnover in mill. t. net. per year (1976)		Latitude	Longitude
Rotterdam	195.0	52° N	4° E
Kobe	99.1	69° N	135° E
New York	160.5	41° N	74° W
Yokohama	181.2	35° N	139° E
Singapore	111.4	1° N	104° E
Nagoya	57.8	35° N	137° E
Osaka	84.2	35° N	135° E
London	39.4	51° N	0°
Antwerp	53.1	51° N	4° E
New Orleans	36.9	30° N	90° W
Marseilles	68.8	43° N	5° E
Hamburg	52.4	53° N	6° E
Los Angeles	59.4	33° N	118° W
Aden	9.9	13° N	45° E
San Francisco	29.4	38° N	123° W
Le Havre	61.7	49° N	0°
Genoa	43.9	44° N	9° E
Boston	14.5	42° N	71° W
Bremen	39.4	53° N	9° E
Santos	18.8	24° S	46° W
Piraeus	36.8	38° N	24° E
Southhampton	33.0	51° N	1° W
Curaçao	24.0	12° N	69° W
Barcelona	42.3	41° N	2° E
Houston	41.9	30° N	95° W
Aruba	23.1	12° N	70° W
Montreal	33.6	46° N	73° W
Copenhagen	14.4	55° N	12° E

Tunnels, Bridges, and Dams

Golden Gate

the most important uses of the lake, which can also be used for fishing. If a sluice canal is built to circumnavigate the fall, the lake can be used for water transport. These lakes give the landscape a new scenic beauty, and such areas are used for recreation. A great many such lakes have been made in the U.S.A.

Mountains and water have always been obstacles to any form of road transport. The first way of crossing mountains was by using the passes on the lowest parts of mountains. (See p.28.) Later tunnels were built.

Large stretches of water offered difficulties, for they could only be crossed by boat or ferry. Bridges can be built over fjords, straits, and big rivers where the amount of traffic justifies this expense. Tunnels can be built underwater, and these are of greatest value where there is much shipping in the area.

New features in the landscape of today are artificially built lakes. First, a barrage (artificial dam) is constructed at a suitable point on the river. The water rises behind this barrage to form a big lake. The great artificial fall of water at the barrage itself is used to make electricity. Artificial irrigation is one of

		Location		Latitude	Longitude
Tunnels Through Mountains	Simplon	Switzerland–Italy		46° N	8° E
	Apennines	Bologna–Florence		44° N	11° E
	St. Gotthard	Switzerland		47° N	9° E
Tunnels Under Water	Seikan	Tsugaru Strait (Japan)		41° N	141° E
	Kammon	Shimoseki (Japan)		34° N	131° E
	Mersey	Liverpool–Birkenhead (England)		53° N	3° W
Bridges	Öland Bridge	Sweden		56° N	16° E
	Verrazano-Narrows	New York		41° N	74° W
	Golden Gate	San Francisco		38° N	123° W
	George Washington	Hudson River		42° N	74° W
	Salazar Bridge	Lisbon		39° N	9° W
	Forth Bridge	Firth of Forth (Scotland)		56° N	4° W
	Severn	England		52° N	3° W
		Country	*River*		
Dams	Igurskaya	U.S.S.R.	Iguri	55° N	33° E
	Nurek	U.S.S.R.	Vakhsh	38° N	69° E
	Vaioul	Italy	Piave	46° N	13° E
	Mauvoisin	Switzerland	Rhônequelle	46° N	8° E
Some Big Artificial Lakes	Kariba	Zimbabwe		17° S	28° E
	Bratsk	U.S.S.R.		58° N	101° E
	Aswan	Egypt		24° N	33° E
	Akosombo	Ghana		6° N	0°

Air Traffic

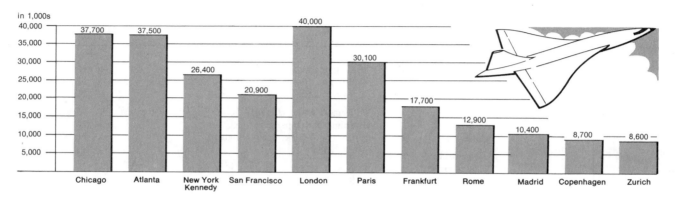

in 1,000s

Chicago	37,700
Atlanta	37,500
New York Kennedy	26,400
San Francisco	20,900
London	40,000
Paris	30,100
Frankfurt	17,700
Rome	12,900
Madrid	10,400
Copenhagen	8,700
Zurich	8,600

Today we say that the world has become smaller, and this is true. First, telecommunications have made it possible for us to contact each other over great distances in a matter of seconds. Second, almost as soon as news is made in any part of the world, it is reported to us through radio and television.

Last, and most important, we have reduced the size of the world by the speed with which we can get from one place to another by air. Travel that once took days and months now takes only a few hours. It is not surprising that the number of transatlantic ship passengers has fallen greatly. In 1954, 63 percent of the travelers came to Europe by boat but by 1967 only 9 percent did. This is not only due to the speed of modern planes but also to the fact that planes take more direct routes from airport to airport.

It is difficult to find the distance of this circular arc between two airports on a map, but on a globe it is easy. Take a piece of string and hold it tightly on the globe between the two airports. The string will lie in an arc, and the length of string between the two airports will give the distance. This can be calculated in kilometers, as each degree of latitude is 110 km ($=69.3$ miles).

Airports

	Passengers (in millions) 1982	Latitude	Longitude
U.S.A.			
Chicago	37.7	42° N	88° W
Atlanta	37.5	34° N	84° W
Los Angeles	32.3	33° N	118° W
New York (Kennedy)	26.4	40° N	74° W
Dallas	24.7	32° N	96° W
San Francisco	20.9	38° N	123° W
Miami	19.3	26° N	80° W
New York (La Guardia)	18.5	41° N	74° W
Boston	15.8	42° N	71° W
Honolulu	15.5	21° N	157° W

	Passengers (in millions) 1982	Latitude	Longitude
Europe			
London	40.0	51° N	0°
Paris	30.1	49° N	2° E
Frankfurt	17.7	50° N	9° E
Rome	12.9	42° N	12° E
Madrid	10.4	40° N	4° W
Amsterdam	9.9	52° N	5° E
Palma	8.7	39° N	3° E
Copenhagen	8.7	55° N	11° E
Zurich	8.6	47° N	9° E
Düsseldorf	7.3	51° N	6° E

Prehistoric Man

We do not know how long man has existed on earth. But there are signs that the first creature we can describe as man – because he used tools – lived about two million years ago. In this connection it is worth remembering that the first written evidence about man is only 5,000 years old and was found in Mesopotamia, now Iraq.

Judging by present-day standards, these early inhabitants were more like apes than people. This type of creature has been named *Australopithecus* (Southern Ape), as the most important discovery of this extinct group was made in Africa.

From about 500,000 B.C. there is evidence of a more human group, *Pithecanthropus*, first found in Java. Later came *Sinanthropus* (the Peking man), which is a probable variant of *Homo erectus*. The Heidelberg man, of which only the lower jaw was found, comes from a later period.

From about 60,000 B.C. the Neanderthal man seems to have dominated. This is known from many discoveries of his remains in Europe and North Africa.

Finally, from about 25,000 B.C. came the Cro-Magnon race, which resembled present-day man to a much greater degree. We know much more about them because in the last Ice Age some of them left traces in the caves where they lived in Spain and France. In cave paintings and statues, they have portrayed the animals that they hunted. Among these were the mammoth, bison, reindeer, wild horse, rhinoceros, and bear.

Excavations of Extinct Human Races

Race	Place of Discovery	Latitude	Longitude
Australopithecus	Olduvai	3° S	35° E
Pithecanthropus erectus	Java	3° S	107° E
Sinanthropus (Peking man)	near Peking	40° N	115° E
Heidelberg man	near Heidelberg	49° N	9° E
Neanderthal man	Neanderthal	51° N	7° E
Cro-Magnon	Les Eyzier	45° N	1° E

Caves with Paintings

Place	Country	Latitude	Longitude
Altamira	Spain	43° N	4° W
Lascaux	France	45° N	1° E
Font de Gaume	France	45° N	1° E
Pech Merle	France	44° N	2° E

Famous Sculptures, etc.

Place	Country	Latitude	Longitude
Venus of Willendorf	Austria	48° N	15° E
La Venus de Laussel	France	45° N	1° E
Stonehenge	England	51° N	2° W

Mesopotamia, Egypt, Greece, and the Roman Empire

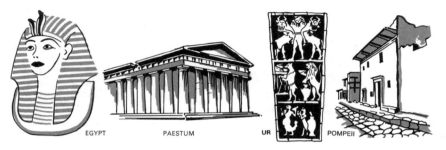

EGYPT   PAESTUM   UR   POMPEII

Mesopotamia and Egypt

Most historical remains of ancient times are to be found in the areas where civilization reached its greatest heights. This happened where artificial irrigation was used. The big artificial-irrigation areas were developed on the banks of rivers. Through ingenious canal networks the water was led into flat river valleys and used for agriculture. As the river brought fertile sediment along with it, there was no necessity to use additional fertilizer. Thus two needs for plant growth were satisfied, and high temperatures were provided by nature itself.

The conditions for establishing and maintaining an artificial-irrigation system demanded a highly organized community that could keep the rules about when and how much water should be given to each place. Many of these communities grew up in the Middle East, in the area called the Fertile Crescent, which stretches from the Euphrates and Tigris valleys to Egypt. The rulers of these kingdoms have left impressive monuments in the form of graves, pyramids, fortresses, and towns.

Jericho is thought to be the oldest of these urbanized communities. In about 7000 B.C. it was a village that gradually developed into a town, economically based on the artificial-irrigation farming of the Jordan Valley. Almost as old is Ur, Abraham's town, which lay in the land of the Sumerians. In 3000 B.C. it consisted of small, clay-lined huts flanking small streets. The town was surrounded by a wall. Dominating the town was a great temple, the ziggurat. This must have been an impressive sight with its base of 60 by 45 meters (197 by 148 feet) and height of 21 meters (69 feet). We can still see some of the wealth that was collected by the kings of the town, as 16 royal graves with valuable burial deposits have been found. Lagash was another of the Sumerian city-states.

In about 2000 B.C. the dominant rule of the Sumerians collapsed in Mesopotamia, and the Amonites became the leaders. Their most important town was Babylon, which like Ur, had a temple as focal point. This was the Marduk Temple. In about 1600 B.C. a new group of people, the Hittites, conquered Babylon. The greatest part of their kingdom

lay in Asia Minor, and from there they conquered both Syria and Lebanon, including Aleppo. The Assyrians lived on the upper reaches of the Tigris River, where Assur was the capital. Later Nineveh became the capital. By the end of 2000 B.C. the Assyrians had conquered Babylon, Syria, Palestine, and even Egypt at one point.

In Egypt there are traces of civilization from 5000 B.C., but the first real towns were developed just before 3000 B.C. The first capital of the whole country was Thebes. Later Memphis became the capital. The era from Egypt's beginnings – about 3000 B.C. – to the time when Alexander the Great conquered the land in 332 B.C. is divided into about 30 dynasties, of which there were three main periods: the Old Kingdom (about 3000–2280 B.C.), the Middle Kingdom (2050–1778 B.C.), and the New Kingdom (about 1567–1085 B.C.). Interspersed between these were periods of decline and disruption. Much of our knowledge of these old kingdoms comes from the inscriptions on clay tablets written in Egyptian script, hiero-

glyphics. In A.D. 1799, at Rosetta on the Nile delta, a find was made of a stone with three texts: one in Greek, one in hieroglyphics, and one in demotic, a later Egyptian script. A suspicion that all three sets of writing might have the same text led to the deciphering of hieroglyphics, which paved the way to a greater knowledge of ancient history.

The most beautiful monuments from these kingdoms are the pyramids, many of which are at Giza. The biggest of these is the Cheops Pyramid from about 2650 B.C.: circumference 233 meters (765 feet) and original height 146 meters (400 feet). In the period of the New Kingdom, the capital was moved from Thebes to Tel el Amarna for 20 years. Many important finds from this period have been discovered, including paintings, portraits, and cuneiform writing. The temple at Abu Simbel was also from the New Kingdom period. It was built about 1250 B.C. by the great pharaoh Ramses II.

Greece

In ancient times the greatest cultural

development in Europe took place in Greece. It started with the arrival of the Dorians in about 1100 B.C. and culminated in 5–3 B.C. Because of the many mountains that divide the country, a series of city-states developed, and these at various periods had contact and cooperation with each other. Countless relics have been preserved, and consequently only a few of the well-known ones can be listed here.

The towns of Mycenae and Troy are from the period before the Doric migration. There was a group of fortified towns on the Argos Plain, and each was ruled by a king. The best known of these are Mycenae and Tiryns, both of which were surrounded by great battlements. Some of these towns still remain. According to Homer, the king of Mycenae was a kind of overlord who could call the land to war, as Agamemnon did when hostilities against Troy broke out. This is described in the *Iliad*.

The foundation of the Golden Age of Greece was laid between 750 and 500 B.C. City-states such as Athens and Sparta developed on their own lines.

Their power and influence over the other city-states was considerable. A wave of emigration started from Athens to the coastal regions of the western Mediterranean.

Closeness in cultural interests was maintained in many ways, such as the joint athletic meeting at Olympia. Gatherings of religious importance were held too. One religious center was Delphi, where there was an Apollo cult with an oracle that interpreted the gods' prophecies.

Political agreement within Greece was strengthened when the war with the Persians took place in 499–450 B.C., and an attack from the east was successfully repelled by the Greeks. Among the famous battlefields was Marathon, about 42 km (26 miles) from Athens.

The Roman Empire

The Roman Empire became Greece's successor as a cultural influence in Europe. It was greatly influenced by the earlier Greek period. Originally, the empire consisted only of Rome and the surrounding countryside. Gradually, it developed so that at the beginning of the Christian Era it covered the whole of the Mediterranean coastal area, all of present-day western and southern Europe, the Black Sea area, Asia Minor, and all of the Italian peninsula. The Roman Empire expanded again in the first hundred years A.D. and reached its greatest power during Emperor Trajan's reign (A.D. 98–117). At that time the empire included England, all areas south of the Rhine and the Danube, plus parts of Dacia, Egypt, and Mauritania.

The Roman harbor, Ostia, was situated on the coast of Italy near Rome, and here many important relics have been found in recent years. Pompeii has been an invaluable source of knowledge about the Roman way of life at that time. The town was completely buried when Vesuvius erupted in A.D. 79. From the Greek colonization period, we have Paestum, where a great many temples from the fifth century B.C. have been preserved. Taranto, too, was one of the important Greek colonies. In a similar way, Syracuse on Sicily was a source of Greek culture. In the third and second centuries B.C. Glanum in southern France was developed as a Greek town and was later occupied and expanded by the Romans. It was destroyed in A.D. 300 but is now partially excavated.

Carthage, which lay on the north coast of Africa, was Rome's greatest enemy in the third and second centuries B.C. The town was founded by the Phoenicians, who were great traders and controlled all the shipping routes on the Mediterranean at that time. After the Punic Wars Carthage was totally destroyed by the Romans in 146 B.C.

Mesopotamia and Egypt

	Latitude	Longitude		Latitude	Longitude
Aleppo	36° N	37° E	Abu Simbel	22° N	32° E
Assur	36° N	43° E	El Faijum	29° N	31° E
Babylon	33° N	45° E	Giza	30° N	31° E
Jericho	32° N	35° E	Memphis	30° N	31° E
Nineveh	36° N	43° E	Rosetta	31° N	30° E
Telloh	31° N	47° E	Tel el Amarna	28° N	31° E
Ur	31° N	46° E	Thebes	26° N	33° E

Greece   *Roman Empire*

	Latitude	Longitude		Latitude	Longitude
Athens	38° N	24° E	Carthage	37° N	10° E
Delphi	38° N	23° E	Glanum	44° N	5° E
Marathon	38° N	26° E	Ostia	42° N	12° E
Mycenae	38° N	23° E	Paestum	40° N	15° E
Pergamon	37° N	27° E	Pompeii	41° N	15° E
Sparta	37° N	22° E	Syracuse	37° N	15° E
Troy	40° N	26° E	Taranto	41° N	17° E

Famous Towns and Fortresses, etc.

Carcassonne

Strasbourg

and power was concentrated in these two groups, and there are only a few relics to help us depict the life of the European peasant at this time. On the other hand, despite centuries of war and destruction, there are buildings of all sizes to show us how the aristocracy and clergy lived. The nobles built fortresses, castles, and walled towns such as York and Aigues Mortes. The clerics built churches, great and small, and monasteries in all parts of the Western world. The clerics were important not only as spiritual influences but also for their many innovations of practical value. Many monasteries were the leading agricultural influence of the area, and the monks were experts on such matters as drainage and plowing, types of plants, and all the technical developments of agriculture.

The monasteries were organized into religious orders. At first the majority of the cloisters lay in the country, but later in the Middle Ages, monasteries became part of the towns too. This gave their field of work a greater significance in social and educational areas.

In the Middle Ages Europe was a peasant society ruled by two powerful groups: one consisting of emperors, kings, and noblemen, and the other being the Catholic church. All the wealth

Places of the Middle Ages

		Latitude	Longitude
Towns	Aachen	51° N	6° E
	Avignon	44° N	5° E
	Bamberg	50° N	11° E
	Bruges	51° N	3° E
	Canterbury	51° N	1° E
	Hastings	52° N	1° E
	Hildesheim	52° N	10° E
	Pavia	45° N	9° E
	Salzburg	48° N	13° E
	Strasbourg	49° N	8° E
	Toulouse	44° N	1° E
	Trier	50° N	7° E
	York	54° N	1° W
Fortresses	Aigues Mortes	44° N	4° E
	Carcassonne	43° N	2° E
	Tower (London)	51° N	0°

		Latitude	Longitude
Churches	Le Puy	45° N	4° E
	Lincoln	53° N	1° W
	Lund	56° N	13° E
	Rouen	49° N	1° E
	Santiago	43° N	9° W
	Wells	51° N	3° W
Monasteries	Canossa	44° N	10° E
	Citeaux	47° N	5° E
	Cluny	46° N	5° E
	Grande Chartreuse	45° N	6° E
	Hirsau	49° N	9° E
	Ravenna	44° N	12° E

Famous Buildings Outside Europe

There are many buildings from earlier cultural periods throughout the world. Even today some of these, such as Mecca and Medina, have a great influence on cultural life.

In the ancient Asian empires many magnificent edifices were built – temples, castles, monuments, etc. Many of these were of an impressive size. The architecture of these buildings still influences the buildings of newer times. Our list includes both older and newer buildings so as to give an impression of the importance of building traditions. In some cases only the name of the town is given, e.g., Nanking, as the town has a great many characteristic buildings. In addition, from China we have included the Great Wall, a structure whose dimensions have never been surpassed.

A small group of towns from both Mexico and Peru are listed. As in Asia, many of these old buildings have had a considerable cultural influence, and in spite of the erosion of time, there are many impressive remains. In some cases there are only traces of town ruins. In others, like Cuzco, people are living in

these old buildings, although it must be added that these are people of an entirely different culture.

One of the modern cities of South America must be mentioned. This is Brasília, the new capital of Brazil, which is well known as an example of modern architecture and town planning.

Famous Buildings in Other Parts of the World

		Latitude	Longitude
Asia	Agra (Taj Mahal)	27° N	78° E
	Ajanta (Grotto)	20° N	76° E
	Angkor Wat	13° N	104° E
	Ayutthaya	14° N	101° E
	Great Wall of China	39° N	110° E
	Jaipur (Hawa Mahal)	21° N	86° E
	Kyoto (the Nijo Castle)	35° N	136° E
	Mecca	22° N	40° E
	Medina	25° N	40° E
	Nanking	32° N	119° E
	Peking	40° N	116° E
	Rangoon (the Golden Pagoda)	17° N	96° E

		Latitude	Longitude
America	Brasília	16° S	48° W
	Cuzco	14° S	72° W
	Easter Island	28° S	144° W
	Oaxaca (Monte Albán)	17° N	97° W
	San Juan Teotihuacán (Mexico)	20° N	99° W
	Uxmal	20° N	90° W

Voyages of Discovery and Historic Battlefields

From a European point of view, one of the greatest steps forward was made when voyages of discovery really became profitable about A.D. 1500. This gave an extended knowledge of the world and increased the wealth of the countries that sponsored the expeditions and merchant ships. Spain (e.g., Columbus) and Portugal pioneered such expeditions, followed by the Netherlands, England, and France. Some localities that became known through voyages of discovery are listed on the opposite page. Many places have retained their original names, but others have been named after the European who first arrived there.

The first voyages from Europe, apart from those of the Vikings who sailed to Greenland and North America, were down the coast of Africa. Areas like the Gold Coast were known to Europeans long before that terrible chapter of slave trade. This started in about 1600, and from West Africa alone, during the 16th to 19th centuries, more than 15 million slaves were shipped to the American continent. The original reason for the voyages was to find the passage to India. Vasco da Gama, a Portuguese, succeeded in doing this in 1497–98 after sailing around the Cape of Good Hope.

The European advance in America was made via the West Indies. To the north, Virginia became a favorite gateway for emigrants into the hinterland. The French founded a colony at Quebec, Canada.

The Spanish colonization of South America reached its peak after Pizarro, in 1531, conquered the Incas and their capital of Cuzco and thus gained countless riches in gold, found in the Inca empire.

One of the Europeans who gave his name to a strait was Magellan, who made a most daring voyage. In 1519 he sailed with five ships from Spain down the coast of South America around the cape into the Pacific Ocean and reached the Philippines. In 1522 he was killed there in a fight with the natives. A year later his successor sailed home around Africa with one ship carrying 18 of the original crewmen. This was the first circumnavigation of the world.

Discoveries

	Latitude	Longitude
Bahia	12° N	42° W
Bantam	7° S	106° E
Bering Strait	66° N	170° W
Cuzco	14° S	72° W
Gold Coast	4° N	2° W
Malabar Coast	11° N	75° E
Quebec	47° N	71° W
Strait of Magellan	53° S	75° W
Tanjore	11° N	49° E
Torres Strait	10° S	143° E
Virginia	51° N	76° W
West Indies	17° N	63° W

Historic Battlefields

	Latitude	Longitude
Austerlitz	49° N	17° E
El Alamein	21° N	29° E
Gettysburg	40° N	77° W
Golan Heights	33° N	36° E
Hiroshima	35° N	133° E
Narva	59° N	28° E
Normandy	49° N	0°
Pearl Harbor	21° N	158° W
Poltava	50° N	35° E
Stalingrad	49° N	44° E
Tilsit	55° N	22° E
Trafalgar	36° N	6° W
Verdun	49° N	5° E
Versailles	49° N	2° E
Waterloo	51° N	4° E

History of Europe

Europe's history of the last 300 years has been dominated by the avarice of the different nations for colonies, and this with other factors often led to wars. The longest and most cruel of these were the Thirty Years' War (1618–1648), the Napoleonic Wars (1792–1815), World War I (1914–1918), and finally World War II (1939–1945). The main actors in these wars were the European Great Powers who with changing luck defended their motherland and their colonies. Even though these wars as such did not bring any progress, many of the battlefields have become famous and are now part of history. Thus, the list contains places where Europeans have shown their clear superiority as well as places where they have displayed their worst qualities.

National Parks and Game Preserves

Today industry dominates the landscape, and many species of animals will soon be wiped out. It has become an important task not only for the industrialized countries such as the U.S.A. and those of Europe but also for the underdeveloped countries to set up preserves where nature is left unspoiled and where plants and animals may not be destroyed. Different names have been given to these areas around the world, but their purpose is the same.

The U.S.A. has been a pioneer in this type of project, passing a law creating Yellowstone National Park in 1872. This law has become a pattern for all later laws on national parks, which are grouped under a special commission, the National Park Service. In this way much important scenery has been saved as well as historical places in the U.S.A.

Preservation in Western Europe is done in the same way, but few of these areas are on the same scale as those in the U.S.A.

It is of special importance that the big mammals be preserved. This is not just for the sake of the animals but also to attract tourists and thus increase the revenue of foreign currency for many underdeveloped lands.

One of the first national parks for animals was established in South Africa: the Kruger National Park. This has been copied by many other countries, especially in East Africa, where the landscape is also being preserved and there are areas like the Murchison Falls Game Reserve in Uganda. Murchison Falls, a waterfall on the Nile, is part of this park.

National Parks and Game Preserves

	Country	Latitude	Longitude
Yellowstone National Park	U.S.A.	45° N	110° W
Grand Canyon National Park	U.S.A.	36° N	112° W
Glacier National Park	U.S.A.	49° N	114° W
Zion National Park	U.S.A.	37° N	112° W
Petrified Forest National Park	U.S.A.	35° N	110° W
Lassen Volcanic National Park	U.S.A.	40° N	121° W
Rocky Mountain National Park	U.S.A.	40° N	104° W
Lüneburger Heide	Germany	53° N	10° E
Upper Engadine	Switzerland	47° N	10° E
Peak District	England	53° N	1° W
Sarek National Park	Sweden	67° N	16° E
Kruger National Park	South Africa	24° S	32° E
Serengeti	Tanzania	3° S	35° E
Ngorongoro	Tanzania	3° S	36° E
Murchison Falls	Uganda	2° N	32° E

Events That Shook the World

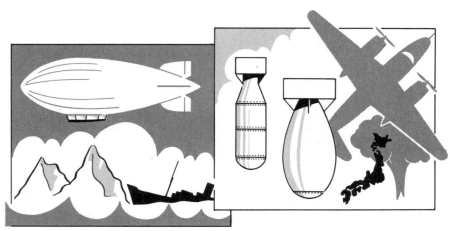

All too frequently shattering, world-shaking events come into our living rooms via newspapers, television, and radio. But where did the event take place? Probably the daily paper shows a map of the afflicted area but does not give its position in relation to the rest of the world. However, if we are given the name of an important nearby town, we can locate the area with the help of the globe.

World-shaking events have happened before, but at the time they seemed remote. On the next page we have made it easier for you to localize some of these events by giving you the respective latitudes and longitudes.

		Latitude	Longitude
1865	Murder of President Abraham Lincoln at the Ford Theatre, Washington, D.C.	39° N	77° W
1912	*Titanic,* the biggest ship of that period, sank on her maiden voyage. She hit an iceberg about 2,500 km (1,560 miles) NE of New York. About 1,500 people lost their lives.	50° N	48° W
1914	Murder of the Austrian archduke Franz Ferdinand and his wife. The assassination started World War I. It happened in the Bosnian town of Sarajevo.	44° N	18° E
1937	After several years of routine flights between Europe and the U.S.A., the airship *Hindenburg* burst into flames over Lakehurst, New Jersey.	40° N	74° W
1945	The town of Hiroshima in Japan was destroyed by the world's first atom bomb.	34° N	132° E
1961	United Nations General Secretary Dag Hammarskjöld was killed in a flying accident over Zambia.	12° S	22° E
1963	President J. F. Kennedy was assassinated in Dallas, Texas.	33° N	97° W
1972	War in Vietnam and the uprising in East Pakistan that ended with its secession as the new state of Bangladesh. Many localities have been referred to, the most important being the three capitals:		
	North Vietnam: Hanoi	21° N	105° E
	South Vietnam: Saigon – Ho Chi Minh City	11° N	106° E
	Bangladesh: Dacca	24° N	90° E
1973	In the war between Israel and Syria the decisive battles took place in the Sinai peninsula and the Golan Heights.	29° N / 33° N	34° E / 36° E
1979	Occupation of the U.S. Embassy in Teheran and seizure of hostages.	36° N	51° E
1980	Strikes in Poland, in particular at the Lenin shipyard in Danzig.	54° N	19° E

A.S.S.R. – *Autonomous Soviet Socialist Republic*
Ala. – *Alabama*
Alas. – *Alaska*
Ang. – *Angola*
Arch. – *Archipelago*
Arg. – *Argentina*
Ariz. – *Arizona*
Ark. – *Arkansas*
B. – *Baie, Bahïa, Bay, Boca, Bucht, Bugt*
B.C. – *British Columbia*
Br. – *British*
C. – *Cabo, Cap, Cape*
C. Prov. – *Cape Province*
Calif. – *California*
Chan. – *Channel*
Col. – *Colombia*
Colo. – *Colorado*
Conn. – *Connecticut*
Cord. – *Cordillera*
D.C. – *District of Columbia*
Del. – *Delaware*
Dep. – *Dependency*
Des. – *Desert*
Dist. – *District*
Dom. Rep. – *Dominican Republic*
E. – *East*
Eng. – *England*

Fd. – *Fjord*
Fed. – *Federal, Federation*
Fla. – *Florida*
Fr. – *France, French*
G. – *Golfe, Golfo, Gulf, Guba*
Ga. – *Georgia*
Gt. – *Great*
Hants. – *Hampshire*
Hd. – *Head*
Hts. – *Heights*
I.(s) – *Ile, Ilha, Insel, Isla, Island (s)*
Id. – *Idaho*
Ill. – *Illinois*
Ind. – *Indiana*
J. – *Jezero (L.)*
K. – *Kap, Kapp*
Kans. – *Kansas*
Kep. – *Kepulauan (I.)*
Kól. – *Kólpos (B.)*
Ky. – *Kentucky*
L. – *Lac, Lacul, Lago, Lagoa, Lake, Limni, Loch, Lough*
La. – *Louisiana*
Ld. – *Land*
Mad. P. – *Madhya Pradesh*
Man. – *Manitoba*
Mass. – *Massachusetts*
Md. – *Maryland*
Me. – *Maine*
Mich. – *Michigan*
Minn. – *Minnesota*

Miss. – *Mississippi*
Mo. – *Missouri*
Mont. – *Montana*
Mt.(s) – *Mont, Monte, Monti, Muntii, Montaña, Mountain (s)*
Mys. – *Mysore*
N. – *North, Northern*
N.B. – *New Brunswick*
N.C. – *North Carolina*
N.D. – *North Dakota*
N.H. – *New Hampshire*
N. Ire. – *Northern Ireland*
N.J. – *New Jersey*
N. Mex. – *New Mexico*
N.S.W. – *New South Wales*
N.Y. – *New York*
N.Z. – *New Zealand*
Nat. Park – *National Park*
Nebr. – *Nebraska*
Neth. – *Netherlands*
Nev. – *Nevada*
Newf. – *Newfoundland*
Nic. – *Nicaragua*
Nig. – *Nigeria*
O.F.S. – *Orange Free State*
Okla. – *Oklahoma*
Ont. – *Ontario*
Oreg. – *Oregon*
Os. – *Ostrov (I.)*
Oz – *Ozero (L.)*
P. – *Pass, Passo, Pasul*

P.N.G. – *Papua New Guinea*
Pa. – *Pennsylvania*
Pak. – *Pakistan*
Pass. – *Passage*
Pen. – *Peninsula*
Pk. – *Peak*
Plat. – *Plateau*
Pol. – *Poluostrov*
Port. – *Portugal, Portuguese*
Prov. – *Province, Provincial*
Pt. – *Point*
Pta. – *Ponta, Punta*
Pte. – *Pointe*
Que. – *Quebec*
Queens. – *Queensland*
R. – *Rio, River*
R.S.F.S.R. – *Russian Soviet Federal Socialist Republic*
Ra.(s) – *Range(s)*
Reg. – *Region*
Rep. – *Republic*
Res. – *Reserve, Reservoir*
S. – *South*
S. Africa – *South Africa*
S.C. – *South Carolina*
S.D. – *South Dakota*
S. Leone – *Sierra Leone*
S.S.R. – *Soviet Socialist Republic*
Sa. – *Serra, Sierra*
Sask. – *Saskatchewan*
Scot. – *Scotland*

Sd. – *Sound*
Sp. – *Spain, Spanish*
St. – *Saint*
Str. – *Strait, Stretto*
Switz. – *Switzerland*
Tanz. – *Tanzania*
Tas. – *Tasmania*
Tenn. – *Tennessee*
Terr. – *Territory*
Tex. – *Texas*
U.K. – *United Kingdom*
U.S.A. – *United States of America*
U.S.S.R. – *Union of Soviet Socialist Republics*
Ut. P. – *Uttar Pradesh*
Va. – *Virginia*
Vdkhr. – *Vodokhranilishche (Res.)*
Ven. – *Venezuela*
Vic. – *Victoria*
Vt. – *Vermont*
W. – *West*
W. Va. – *West Virginia*
Wis. – *Wisconsin*
Wyo. – *Wyoming*
Yorks. – *Yorkshire*
Yug. – *Yugoslavia*

An open square □ signifies that the name refers to an administrative division of a country while a solid square ■ follows the name of a country.

A

Aachen .... 50 47N 6 4 E
A'Ålà en Nil □ .. 8 50N 29 55 E
Aalsmeer .... 52 17N 4 43 E
Aalst .... 50 56N 4 2 E
Aalten .... 51 56N 6 35 E
Aarau .... 47 23N 8 4 E
Aare, R. .... 47 37N 8 13 E
Aarschot .... 50 59N 4 49 E
Aba .... 5 10N 7 19 E
Abā Saud .... 17 15N 43 55 E
Abadan .... 30 22N 48 20 E
Abai 25 58S 55 54W
Abakaliki .... 6 22N 8 2 E
Abakan .... 53 40N 91 10 E
Abarqu .... 31 10N 53 20 E
Abasan .... 31 19N 34 21 E
Abashiri .... 44 0N 144 15 E
Abashiri-Wan, G. . 44 0N 144 30 E
Abay .... 49 38N 72 53 E
Abaya, L. .... 6 30N 37 50 E
Abaza .... 52 39N 90 6 E
Abba Hillèl ..... 31 42N 34 38 E
Abbeville, Fr. .. 50 6N 1 49 E
Abbeville, U.S.A. . 30 0N 92 7W
Abbottabad ...... 34 10N 73 15 E
Abéché .... 13 50N 20 35 E
Ābenrå .... 55 3N 9 25 E
Abeokuta .... 7 3N 3 19 E
Aberayron 52 15N 4 16W
Aberdare 51 43N 3 27W
Aberdeen,
  Australia ..... 32 9S 150 56 E
Aberdeen, S. Africa 32 28S 24 2 E
Aberdeen, U.K. .. 57 9N 2 6W
Aberdeen, Id. ... 42 57N 112 50W
Aberdeen, Miss... 33 49N 88 13W
Aberdeen, S.D. .. 45 28N 98 29W
Aberdeen, Wash. . 46 59N 123 50W
Aberdovey 52 33N 4 3W
Aberfeldy 56 37N 3 50W
Abergavenny 51 49N 3 1W
Aberystwyth 52 25N 4 6W
Abhā .... 18 0N 42 34 E
Abidjan 5 26N 3 58W
Abilene, Kans. .. 39 0N 97 16W
Abilene, Tex. ... 32 22N 99 40W

Abingdon 51 40N 1 17W
Abkhaz A.S.S.R. .. 43 0N 41 0 E
Abkit .... 64 10N 157 10 E
Abocho .... 7 35N 6 56 E
Abohar .... 30 10N 74 10 E
Aboisso 5 30N 3 5W
Abomey .... 7 10N 2 5 E
Abong Mbang .... 4 0N 13 8 E
Abonnema 4 41N 6 49W
Aboso 5 23N 1 57W
Abou Deïa .... 11 20N 19 20 E
Aboyne 57 4N 2 48W
Abqaiq .... 26 0N 49 45 E
Abrantes 39 24N 8 7W
Abrud .... 46 19N 23 5 E
Abruzzi □ .... 42 15N 14 0 E
Absaroka Ra. 44 40N 110 0W
Abū al Khasib ... 30 25N 48 0 E
Abu Arish .... 16 53N 42 48 E
Abu Dis .... 19 12N 33 38 E
Abū Ghōsh .... 31 48N 35 6 E
Abu Hamed .... 19 32N 33 13 E
Abu Tig .... 27 4N 31 15 E
Abū Zabad .... 12 25N 29 10 E
Abū Zabī .... 24 28N 54 36 E
Abuja .... 9 16N 7 2 E
Abyad, Gebel, Reg. 17 30N 28 0 E
Abyssinia ■ =
  Ethiopia ■ .... 8 0N 40 0 E
Acajutla 13 36N 89 50W
Acámbaro 20 0N 100 40W
Acaponeta 22 30N 105 20W
Acapulco 16 51N 99 56W
Acará 1 57S 48 11W
Acatlan 18 10N 98 3W
Acayucan 17 59N 94 58W
Accra 5 35N 0 6W
Accrington 53 46N 2 22W
Aceh □ .... 4 50N 96 0 E
Achill 53 56N 9 55W
Achill, I. 53 58N 10 5W
Achinsk .... 56 20N 90 20 E
Acklins I. 22 30N 74 0W
Acme 51 33N 113 30W
Aconcagua, Mt. .. 32 39S 70 0W
Acre = Akko ..... 32 55N 35 4 E
Acre □ 9 1S 71 0W
Ad Dam .... 20 33N 44 45 E
Ad Dammam .... 26 20N 50 5 E
Ad Khālis .... 33 40N 44 55 E

Ada, Ghana ...... 5 44N 0 40 E
Ada, U.S.A. 34 50N 96 45W
Adale .... 2 58N 46 27 E
Adamaoua,
  Massif de l' ... 7 20N 12 20 E
Adamello, Mt. ... 46 10N 10 34 E
Adams, N.Y. 43 50N 76 3W
Adams, Wis. 43 59N 89 50W
Adams, Mt. 46 10N 121 28W
Adam's Bridge ... 9 15N 79 40 E
Adam's Pk. ...... 6 55N 80 45 E
Adana .... 37 0N 35 16 E
Adaut .... 8 8S 131 7 E
Adda, R. .... 45 8N 9 53 E
Addis Ababa =
  Addis Abeba ... 9 2N 38 42 E
Addis Abeba ..... 9 2N 38 42 E
Adebour .... 13 17N 11 50 E
Adelaide, Australia 34 52S 138 30 E
Adelaide, S. Afr. . 32 42S 26 20 E
Adelaide I. 67 40N 98 0W
Adelaide River .. 13 15S 131 7 E
Aden = Al 'Adan . 12 50N 45 0 E
Aden, G. of ..... 13 0N 50 0 E
Adige, R. .... 45 10N 12 20 E
Adirondack Mts. . 44 0N 74 15W
Adjohon .... 6 41N 2 32 E
Admiralty G. .... 14 20S 125 55 E
Admiralty Inlet . 48 0N 122 40W
Admiralty I. 57 50N 134 30W
Admiralty Is. ... 2 0S 147 0 E
Ado .... 6 36N 2 56 E
Ado-Ekiti .... 7 38N 5 12 E
Adoni .... 15 33N 77 18 E
Adour, R. 43 32N 1 32W
Adra 36 43N 3 3W
Adrano .... 37 40N 14 19 E
Adrar des
  Iforas, Mts. .. 19 40N 1 40 E
Adrian 41 55N 84 0W
Adriatic Sea .... 43 0N 16 0 E
Adzhar A.S.S.R. . 42 0N 42 0 E
Ægean Sea .... 37 0N 25 0 E
Æolian Is. =
  Eólie o Lípari, I. 38 30N 14 50 E
Aerhtai Shan, Mts. 48 0N 90 0 E
Afghanistan ■ ... 33 0N 65 0 E
Afgoi .... 2 7N 44 59 E
Afikpo .... 5 53N 7 54 E
Africa .... 5 0N 20 0 E

Afuá 0 15S 50 10W
Afula .... 32 37N 35 17 E
Afyon .... 38 20N 30 15 E
Agadez .... 16 58N 7 59 E
Agadir 30 28N 9 25W
Agapa .... 71 27N 89 15 E
Agartala .... 23 50N 91 23 E
Agats .... 5 34S 138 5 E
Agboville 5 55N 4 15W
Agde .... 43 19N 3 28 E
Agege .... 6 37N 3 20 E
Agen .... 44 12N 0 38 E
Agnew .... 28 1S 120 30 E
Agnibilekrou .... 7 10N 3 11 E
Agra .... 27 17N 77 58 E
Ağri Daği, Mt. .. 39 50N 44 15 E
Agrigento .... 37 19N 13 33 E
Agrinion .... 38 37N 21 27 E
Agua Clara 20 25S 52 45W
Agua Prieta 31 20N 109 32W
Aguadas 5 40N 75 38W
Aguadilla 18 27N 67 10W
Aguanish 50 14N 62 2W
Aguas Blancas ... 24 15S 69 55W
Aguascalientes .. 22 0N 102 12W
Aguascalientes □ . 22 0N 102 20W
Aguilas 37 23N 1 35W
Agulhas, K. ..... 34 52S 20 0 E
Agur .... 31 42N 34 55 E
Ahaggar, Reg. ... 23 0N 6 30 E
Ahaura .... 42 20S 171 32 E
Ahmadabad .... 23 0N 72 40 E
Ahmadnagar ...... 19 7N 74 46 E
Ahuachapán 13 54N 89 52W
Ahvāz .... 31 20N 48 40 E
Ahvenanmaa =
  Åland , I. .... 60 15N 20 0 E
Ahwar .... 13 31N 46 42 E
Aibaq .... 36 15N 68 5 E
Aichi □ .... 35 0N 137 15 E
Aigues-Mortes ... 43 35N 4 12 E
Aihun .... 49 55N 127 30 E
Aijal .... 23 40N 92 44 E
Aiken 33 44N 81 50W
Ailsa Craig, I. . 55 15N 5 7W
Aim .... 59 0N 133 55 E
Aimorés 19 30S 41 4W
Ain .... 46 5N 5 20 E
Aïn Beida .... 35 50N 7 35 E
Ain Dār .... 25 55N 49 10 E

Ainabo .... 9 0N 46 25 E
Aïr .... 18 0N 8 0 E
Airdrie 55 53N 3 57W
Aire, R. 53 44N 0 44W
Aisne, R. .... 49 26N 2 50 E
Aisne □ .... 49 42N 3 40 E
Aitush .... 39 54N 75 40 E
Aiud .... 46 19N 23 44 E
Aix-en-Provence . 43 32N 5 27 E
Aix-les-Bains ... 45 41N 5 53 E
Ajaccio .... 41 55N 8 40 E
Ajana .... 27 56S 114 35 E
Ajanta Ra. ...... 20 28N 75 50 E
Ajdābiyah .... 30 54N 20 4 E
'Ajlun .... 32 18N 35 47 E
Ajmer .... 26 28N 74 37 E
Ajo 32 18N 112 54W
Ajua 4 50N 1 55W
Akaba .... 8 10N 1 2 E
Akaroa .... 43 49S 172 59 E
Akashi .... 34 45N 135 0 E
Akershus □ ...... 60 10N 11 15 E
Aketi .... 2 38N 23 47 E
Akhelóòs, R. .... 38 36N 21 14 E
Akhisar .... 38 56N 27 48 E
Akhmîm .... 26 31N 31 47 E
Akimiski I. 52 50N 81 30W
Akita .... 39 45N 140 0 E
Akita □ .... 39 40N 140 30 E
Akjoujt 19 45N 14 15W
Akko .... 32 55N 35 4 E
Akkol .... 43 36N 70 45 E
Aklavik 68 25N 135 0W
Akola .... 20 42N 77 2 E
Akordat .... 15 30N 37 40 E
Akosombo Dam ... 6 20N 0 5 E
Akpatok I. 60 30N 68 0W
Akranes 64 19N 22 6W
Akron 41 7N 81 31W
Aksarka .... 66 31N 67 50 E
Aksehir .... 38 18N 31 30 E
Aksenovo
  Zilovskoye .... 53 20N 117 40 E
Aksu .... 41 4N 80 5 E
Aksum .... 14 5N 38 40 E
Aktogay .... 44 25N 76 44 E
Aktyubinsk ...... 50 10N 57 3 E

Aku	6 40N	7 18 E
Akure	7 15N	5 5 E
Akureyri	65 40N	18 5w
Akyab	20 15N	92 45 E
Al 'Adan	12 50N	45 0 E
Al Amārah	31 55N	47 15 E
Al 'Aqabah	29 37N	35 0 E
Al Barah	31 55N	35 12 E
Al Basrah	30 30N	47 55 E
Al Baydā	32 30N	21 40 E
Al Buraimi	24 15N	55 53 E
Al Hadithan	34 0N	41 13 E
Al Hadr	35 35N	42 44 E
Al Hasa, Reg.	25 40N	50 0 E
Al Hasakah	36 35N	40 45 E
Al Hauta	16 5N	48 20 E
Al Hawra	13 49N	47 37 E
Al Hillah, Iraq	32 30N	44 25 E
Al Hillah, Saudi Arabia	23 35N	46 50 E
Al Hilwah	23 24N	46 48 E
Al Hindiyah	32 30N	44 10 E
Al-Hoceïma	35 15N	3 58w
Al Hufūf	25 25N	49 45 E
Al Jahrah	29 25N	47 40 E
Al Jalāmid	31 20N	39 45 E
Al Jazir	18 30N	56 31N
Al Jazirah, Reg.	26 10N	21 20 E
Al Jubail	27 0N	49 50 E
Al Juwara	19 0N	57 13 E
Al Khābūrah	23 57N	57 5 E
Al Khalaf	20 30N	57 56 E
Al Khums	32 40N	14 17 E
Al Kūt	32 30N	46 0 E
Al Kuwayt	29 20N	48 0 E
Al Lādhiqiyah	35 30N	35 45 E
Al Lith	20 9N	40 15 E
Al Madīnah	24 35N	39 52 E
Al Mafraq	32 17N	36 14 E
Al Manamah	26 10N	50 30 E
Al Marj	32 25N	20 30 E
Al Masirah	20 25N	58 50 E
Al Matamma	16 43N	33 22 E
Al Mawsil	36 15N	43 5 E
Al Mazra'	31 18N	35 32 E
Al Miqdadīyah	34 0N	45 0 E
Al Mubarraz	25 30N	49 40 E
Al Muharraq	26 15N	50 40 E
Al Mukha	13 18N	43 15 E
Al Qamishli	37 10N	41 10 E
Al Qatif	26 35N	50 0 E
Al-Qatrūn	24 56N	15 3 E
Al Qunfidha	19 3N	41 4 E
Al Ubailah	21 59N	50 57 E
Al 'Ugaylah	30 12N	19 10 E
Al Wakrah	25 10N	51 40 E
Al Wari 'ah	27 50N	47 30 E
Ala Shan, Reg.	40 0N	104 0 E
Alabama, R.	31 8N	87 57w
Alabama □	31 0N	87 0w
Alagôa Grande	7 3s	35 35w
Alagôas □	9 0s	36 0w
Alagoinhas	12 0s	38 20w
Alajuela	10 2N	84 8w
Alakurtti	67 0N	30 30 E
Alameda	35 10N	106 43w
Alamogordo	32 59N	106 0w
Alamosa	37 30N	106 0w
Åland, I.	60 15N	20 0 E
Ålands hav	60 0N	19 20 E
Alapayevsk	57 52N	61 42 E
Alashanchih	38 58N	105 14 E
Alaska □	65 0N	150 0w
Alaska, G. of	58 0N	145 0w
Alaska Pen.	56 0N	160 0w
Alaska Ra.	62 50N	151 0w
Alatyr	54 45N	46 35 E
Alausi	2 0s	78 50w
Alawoona	34 45s	140 30 E
Alba	44 41N	8 1 E
Alba-Iulia	46 4N	23 35 E
Albacete	39 0N	1 50w
Albania ■	41 0N	20 0 E
Albany, Australia	35 1s	117 58 E
Albany, Ga.	31 40N	84 10w
Albany, N.Y.	42 40N	73 47w
Albany, Oreg.	44 41N	123 0w
Albany, R.	52 17N	81 31w
Albardón	31 20s	68 30w
Albarracin	40 25N	1 26w
Albarracin, Sa. de	40 30N	1 30w
Albemarle	35 27N	80 15w
Alberche, R.	39 58N	4 46w
Alberni	49 20N	124 50w
Albert	45 51N	64 38w
Albert, L.= Mobutu Sese Seko, L.	1 30N	31 0 E
Albert Lea	43 32N	93 20w
Albert Nile, R.	3 36N	32 2 E
Albert Town	18 17N	77 33w
Alberta □	54 40N	115 0w
Albertinia	34 11s	21 34 E
Alberton	38 35s	146 40 E
Albertville= Kalemie	5 55s	29 9 E
Alberz, Reshteh-Ye-Kūkhā-Ye, Mts.	36 0N	52 0 E
Albi	43 56N	2 9 E
Albina	5 37N	54 15w
Albion	42 15N	84 45w
Alboran, I.	35 57N	3 0w
Ålborg	57 2N	9 54 E
Albuquerque	35 5N	106 47w
Albury	36 3s	146 56 E
Alcalá de Henares	40 28N	3 22w
Alcalá la Real	37 27N	3 57w
Alcaniz	41 2N	0 8w
Alcántara, Brazil	2 20s	44 30w
Alcântara, Sp.	39 41N	6 57w
Alcaraz, Sa. de	38 40N	2 20w
Alcaudete	37 35N	4 5w
Alcazar de San Juan	39 24N	3 12w
Alcira	39 9N	0 30w
Alcobaça	39 32N	9 0w
Alcoy	38 43N	0 30w
Aldabra Is.	9 22s	46 28 E
Aldan, R.	63 28N	129 35 E
Aldeburgh	52 9N	1 35 E
Alderney, I.	49 42N	2 12w
Aldershot	51 15N	0 43w
Aleg	17 3N	13 55w
Alegrete	29 40s	56 0w
Aleisk	52 40N	83 0 E
Aleksandrovsk-Sakhalinskiy	50 50N	142 20 E
Aleksandrovskiy Zavod	50 40N	117 50 E
Aleksandrovskoye	60 35N	77 50 E
Alençon	48 27N	0 4 E
Alenuihaha Chan.	20 25N	156 0w
Aleppo = Halab	36 10N	37 15 E
Alert Bay	50 30N	127 35w
Alès	44 9N	4 5 E
Alessandria	44 54N	8 37 E
Ålesund	62 28N	6 12 E
Aleutian Is.	52 0N	175 0w
Alexander Arch.	57 0N	135 0w
Alexander Bay	28 36s	16 33 E
Alexander City	32 56N	85 57w
Alexander I.	69 0s	70 0w
Alexandra	45 14s	169 25 E
Alexandria=El Iskandarîya	31 0N	30 0 E
Alexandria, Canada	45 19N	74 38w
Alexandria, S. Africa	33 38s	26 28 E
Alexandria, La.	31 20N	92 30w
Alexandria, Minn.	45 50N	95 20w
Alexandria, Va.	38 47N	77 1w
Alexandria Bay	44 20N	75 52w
Alexandroúpolis	40 50N	25 24 E
Alford	53 16N	0 10 E
Alfreton	53 6N	1 22w
Alga	49 46N	57 20 E
Algarve, Reg.	37 15N	8 10w
Algeciras	36 9N	5 28w
Algemesí	39 11N	0 27w
Alger	36 42N	3 8 E
Algeria ■	35 10N	3 0 E
Alghero	40 34N	8 20 E
Algiers = Alger	36 42N	3 8 E
Algoabaai	33 50s	25 45 E
Algonquin Prov. Park	45 35N	78 35w
Alhama de Murcia	37 51N	1 25w
Alhambra	34 0N	118 10w
Aliákmon, R.	40 30N	22 36 E
Alicante	38 23N	0 30w
Alicante □	38 30N	0 37w
Alice	27 47N	98 1w
Alice Arm	55 29N	129 23w
Alice Downs	17 45s	127 56 E
Alice Springs	23 40s	135 50 E
Alicedale	33 15s	26 4 E
Aligarh	27 55N	78 10 E
Aligudarz	33 25N	49 45 E
Alingsås	57 56N	12 31 E
Alipur	29 25N	70 55 E
Alipur Duar	26 30N	89 35 E
Aliquippa	40 38N	80 18w
Aliwal Nord	30 45s	26 45 E
Aljustrel	37 55N	8 10w
Alkamari	13 27N	11 10 E
Alkmaar	52 37N	4 45 E
All American Canal	32 45N	115 0w
Allada	6 41N	2 9 E
Allahabad	25 25N	81 58 E
Allan	51 53N	106 4w
Allanridge	27 45s	26 40 E
Allard Lake	50 40N	63 10w
Allegheny Mts.	38 0N	80 0w
Allegheny, R.	40 27N	80 0w
Allende	28 20N	100 50w
Allentown	40 36N	75 30w
Alleppey	9 30N	76 28 E
Aller, R.	52 57N	9 11 E
Alliance, Nebr.	42 10N	102 50w
Alliance, Ohio	40 53N	81 7w
Allier, R.	46 58N	3 4 E
Allier □	46 25N	3 0 E
Alligator Creek	19 23s	146 58 E
Alliston	44 15N	79 55w
Alloa	56 7N	3 49w
Alma, Canada	48 35N	71 40w
Alma, U.S.A.	43 25N	84 40w
Alma Ata	43 15N	76 57 E
Almada	38 40N	9 9w
Almaden	17 22s	144 40 E
Almadén	38 49N	4 52w
Almansa	38 51N	1 5w
Almanzor, P. de	40 15N	5 18w
Almazán	41 30N	2 30w
Almeirim, Brazil	1 30s	52 0w
Almelo	52 22N	6 42 E
Almendralejo	38 41N	6 26w
Almería	36 52N	2 32w
Almirante	9 10N	82 30w
Alnwick	55 25N	1 42w
Alon	22 12N	95 5 E
Alonsa	50 50N	99 0w
Alor, I.	8 15s	124 30 E
Alor Setar	6 7N	100 22 E
Aloysius, Mt.	26 0s	128 38 E
Alpena	45 6N	83 24w
Alpes-Maritimes □	43 55N	7 10 E
Alpes-de-Haute-Provence □	44 8N	6 10 E
Alpha	23 39s	146 37 E
Alpi Carniche, Mts.	46 36N	13 0 E
Alpine	30 35N	103 35w
Alps, Mts.	47 0N	8 0 E
Alroy Downs	19 20s	136 5 E

Alsace, Reg. ...... 48 15N   7 25 E
Alsasua 42 54N   2 10W
Alston 54 48N   2 26W
Alta .... 69 55N 23 12 E
Alta Gracia ...... 31 40 S 64 30W
Alta Lake 50 10N 123 0W
Altaelv, R. ...... 69 57N 23 17 E
Altagracia 10 45N 71 30W
Altai, Mts. ...... 48 0N 90 0 E
Altai, Mts.=
  Aerhtai Shan,
  Mts. .... 48 0N 90 0 E
Altamira .... 3 0 S 52 10W
Altanbulag .... 50 19N 106 30 E
Altea 38 38N   0 2W
Alto-Alentejo,
  Reg. 38 50N   7 40W
Alto Araguaia .... 17 15 S 53 20W
Alton, U.K. 51 8N   0 59W
Alton, U.S.A. 38 55N 90 5W
Altona .... 53 32N   9 56 E
Altoona 40 32N 78 24W
Altus 34 30N 99 25W
Altyn Tagh, Mts. . 39 0N 89 0 E
Alula .... 11 50N 50 45 E
Alusi .... 7 35 S 131 40 E
Alva 36 50N 98 50W
Alvarado 18 40N 95 50W
Alvear .... 29 5 S 57 40W
Alvesta .... 56 54N 14 35 E
Alvie .... 38 15 S 143 30 E
Älvkarleby .... 60 34N 17 35 E
Alvsborgs □ ...... 58 30N 12 30 E
Älvsbyn .... 65 39N 20 59 E
Alwar .... 27 38N 76 34 E
Alyat Pristan .... 39 59N 49 28 E
Alyth 56 38N   3 15W
Am-Timan .... 11 0N 20 10 E
Amadjuak 64 0N 72 50W
Amadjuak L. 65 0N 71 0W
Amagasaki .... 34 42N 135 20 E
Amakusa-Shotō,
  Is. .... 32 15N 130 10 E
Åmål .... 59 2N 12 40 E
Amalner .... 21 5N 75 5 E
Amangeldy .... 50 10N 65 10 E
Amapá 2 5N 50 50W
Amapá □ 1 40N 52 0W
Amarante .... 6 14 S 42 50W
Amargosa .... 13 2 S 39 36W

Amarillo 35 14N 101 46W
Amaro, Mt. .... 42 5N 14 6 E
Amassama .... 5 1N   6 2 E
Amasya .... 40 40N 35 50 E
Amatikulu .... 29 3 S 31 33 E
Amatitlán 14 29N 90 38W
Amazon=
  Amazonas, R. ... 2 0 S 53 30W
Amazonas, R. ..... 2 0 S 53 30W
Amazonas □ .... 4 20 S 64 0W
Ambala .... 30 23N 76 56 E
Ambalavao .... 21 50 S 46 56 E
Ambanja .... 13 40 S 48 27 E
Ambarchik .... 69 40N 162 20 E
Ambaro, B. d' .... 13 23 S 48 38 E
Ambata-Boéni ..... 16 28 S 46 43 E
Ambato .... 1 5 S 78 42W
Ambatofinandrahana 20 33 S 46 48 E
Ambatolampy ...... 19 20 S 47 35 E
Ambatondrazaka ... 17 55 S 48 28 E
Ámbelos, Ákra .... 39 56N 23 55 E
Amberg .... 49 25N 11 52 E
Ambergris Cay 18 0N 88 0W
Amberley .... 43 9 S 172 44 E
Ambikapur .... 23 15N 83 15 E
Ambleside 54 26N   2 58W
Ambohimanga
  du Sud .... 20 52 S 47 36 E
Amboise .... 47 25N   0 59 E
Ambon .... 3 35 S 128 20 E
Ambositra .... 20 31 S 47 25 E
Ambovombé .... 25 11 S 46 5 E
Amboy 34 33N 115 51W
*Ambre, C. d' .... 12 40 S 49 10 E
Amby .... 26 30 S 148 11 E
Amderma .... 69 45N 61 30 E
Ameca 20 30N 104 0W
Ameland, I. ...... 53 27N   5 45 E
Amen .... 68 45N 180 0 E
American Falls ... 42 46N 112 56 E
American Samoa, I. 14 20 S 170 0W
Americus 32 0N 84 10W
Amersfoort, Neth . 52 9N   5 23 E
Amersfoort, S. Afr. 26 59 S 29 53 E
Amery, Australia . 31 9 S 117 5 E
Amery, Canada 56 45N 94 0W
Ames 42 0N 93 40W
Amga, R. .... 62 38N 134 32 E
Amgu .... 45 45N 137 15 E
Amherst, Burma ... 16 0N 97 40 E

Amherst, Canada .. 45 48N 64 8W
Amherstburg 42 6N 83 6W
Amiens .... 49 54N   2 16 E
Amirantes, Is. ... 6 0 S 53 0 E
Amlwch 53 24N   4 21W
'Ammān .... 32 0N 35 52 E
Ammi'ad .... 32 55N 35 32 E
Amorgós .... 36 50 25 57 E
Amos 48 35N 78 5W
Amoy=Hsiamen .... 24 25N 118 4 E
Ampanihy .... 24 40 S 44 45 E
Amper .... 9 25N   9 40 E
Amqui 48 28N 67 27W
Amroati .... 20 55N 77 45 E
Amreli .... 21 35N 71 17 E
Amritsar .... 31 35N 74 57 E
Amroha .... 28 53N 78 30 E
Amsterdam,
  Neth. .... 52 23N   4 54 E
Amsterdam, S. Afr. 26 35 S 30 45 E
Amsterdam, U.S.A. 42 58N 74 10W
Amsterdam, I. .... 37 30 S 77 30 E
Amu Darya, R. .... 43 40N 59 1 E
Amukta Pass. 52 25N 172 0W
Amundsen G. 70 30N 123 0W
Amundsen Sea .... 72 0 S 115 0W
Amur, R. .... 52 56N 141 10 E
An Najaf .... 32 3N 44 15 E
An Nasiriyah ..... 31 0N 46 15 E
An Nhon .... 13 53N 109 6 E
An Nu'ayriyah .... 27 30N 48 30 E
An Uaimh 53 39N   6 40W
Anabta .... 32 19N 35 7 E
Anaconda 46 7N 113 0W
Anacortes 48 30N 122 40W
Anadarko 35 4N 98 15W
Anadolu, Reg. .... 38 0W 39 0 E
Anadyr .... 64 35N 177 20 E
Anadyr, R. .... 64 55N 176 5 E
Anahim Lake 52 28N 125 18W
Anakapalle .... 17 42N 83 6 E
Anakie .... 23 32 S 147 45 E
Analalava .... 14 35 S 48 0 E
Anambas, Kep. .... 3 20N 106 30 E
Anambra □ .... 6 30N   7 30 E
Anan .... 33 54N 134 40 E
Anantnag .... 33 45N 75 10 E
Anápolis .... 16 15 S 48 50W
Anar .... 30 55N 55 13 E
Anatolia, Reg.=

Anadolu, Reg. ... 38 0N 39 0 E
Añatuya .... 28 20 S 62 50W
Anchorage 61 10N 149 50W
Ancohuma, Mt. .... 16 0 S 68 50W
Ancona .... 43 37N 13 30 E
Ancud .... 42 0 S 73 50W
Ancud, G. de ..... 42 0 S 73 0W
Andalsnes .... 62 35N   7 43 E
Andalusia 31 51N 86 30W
Andaman Is. ...... 12 30N 92 30 E
Andenne .... 50 30N   5 5 E
Anderson, Calif. . 40 30N 122 19W
Anderson, Ind. ... 40 5N 85 40W
Anderson, S.C. ... 34 32N 82 40W
Anderson, R. 69 43N 128 58W
Andes, Mts. ...... 20 0 S 68 0W
Andevorante ...... 18 57 S 49 6 E
Andhra Pradesh □ . 15 0N 80 0 E
Andizhan .... 41 10N 72 0 E
Andkhui .... 36 52N 65 8 E
Andorra ■ .... 42 30N   1 30 E
Andorra .... 42 31N   1 32 E
Andover 51 13N   1 29W
Andradina .... 20 54 S 51 23W
Andreanof Is. 51 0N 178 0W
Ándria .... 41 13N 16 17 E
Andriba .... 17 30 S 46 58 E
Andros, I. 24 30N 78 4W
Andros, I. .... 37 50N 24 50 E
Andros Town 24 43N 77 47W
Andújar 38 3N   4 5W
Anécho .... 6 12N   1 34 E
Anegada I. 18 45N 64 20W
Anegada Pass. 18 15N 63 45W
Aneto, Pico de ... 42 37N   0 40 E
Angamos, Pta. .... 23 1 S 70 32W
Anganki .... 47 9N 123 48 E
Angara, R. .... 58 6N 93 0 E
Angarsk .... 52 30N 104 0 E
Angaston .... 34 30 S 139 8 E
Ånge .... 62 31N 15 35 E
Angel de la
  Guarda, I. 29 30N 113 30W
Angeles .... 15 9N 120 35 E
Ängelholm .... 56 15N 12 58 E
Angels Camp 38 8N 120 30W
Ångermanälven, R. 62 48N 17 56 E
Angers .... 47 30N   0 35 E
Anglesey, I. 53 17N   4 20W
Ango .... 4 10N 26 5 E

Angoche .... 16 8 S 40 0 E
Angol .... 37 48 S 72 43W
Angola ■ .... 12 0 S 18 0 E
Angoulême .... 45 39N   0 10 E
Angoumois, Reg. .. 45 30N   0 25 E
Angren .... 41 1N 69 45 E
Anguilla, I. 8 14N 63 5W
Angurugu .... 14 0 S 136 25 E
Anhsien .... 31 30N 104 35 E
Anhwei □ .... 33 15N 116 50 E
Anie .... 7 42N   1 8 E
Anivorzno .... 18 44 S 48 58 E
Anjou, Reg. 47 20N   0 15W
Anjozorobé .... 18 22 S 47 52 E
Anju .... 39 36N 125 40 E
Anka .... 12 13N   5 58 E
Ankang .... 32 38N 109 5 E
Ankara .... 40 0N 32 54 E
Ankaramina .... 21 57 S 46 39 E
Ankazoaba .... 22 18 S 44 31 E
Ankazobé .... 18 20 S 47 10 E
Anking .... 30 31N 117 2 E
Ann Arbor 42 17N 83 45W
Anna Plains ...... 19 17 S 121 37 E
Annaba, Reg. ..... 36 50N   7 46 E
Annam, Reg.=
  Trung-Phan, Reg. 16 30N 107 30 E
Annan 54 59N   3 16W
Annan, R. 54 59N   3 16W
Annapolis 38 59N 76 30W
Annapolis Royal .. 44 44N 65 32W
Annecy .... 45 55N   6 8 E
Anning .... 24 58N 102 30 E
Anniston 33 45N 85 50W
Annobón=Pagalu . 1 35 S   3 35 E
Anoka 45 10N 93 26W
Anorotsangana ... 13 56 S 47 55 E
Anping .... 23 0N 120 6 E
Ansbach .... 49 17N 10 34 E
Anshan .... 41 3N 122 58 E
Anshun .... 26 2N 105 57 E
Ansi .... 40 21N 96 10 E
Anson, B. .... 13 20 S 130 6 E
Ansongo .... 15 25N   0 35 E
Ansonville 48 46N 80 43W
Anstruther 56 14N   2 40W
Ansuda .... 2 11 S 139 22 E
Anta .... 46 18N 125 34 E
Antakya .... 36 14N 36 10 E

* Renamed Bobraomby, T. 'i

Antalaha .... 14 57s 50 20 e
Antalya .... 36 52n 30 45 e
Antalya Körfezi ... 36 15n 31 30 e
Antananarivo .... 18 55s 47 35 e
Antarctica 90 0s 0 0
Antarctic Pen. .. 67 0s 60 0w
Antequera 37 5n 4 33w
Anthony 32 1n 106 37w
Anthony Lagoon .. 18 0s 135 30 e
Anticosti I. 49 20n 62 40w
Antigo 45 8n 89 5w
Antigonish 45 38n 61 58w
Antigua 14 34n 90 41w
Antigua, I. 17 0n 61 50w
Antilla 20 40n 75 50w
Antimony 38 7n 112 0w
Antioquia 6 40n 75 55w
Antipodes Is. .... 49 45s 178 40 e
Antofagasta 23 50s 70 30w
* Antongil, B. d' ... 15 30s 49 50 e
António Enes=
  Angoche .... 16 8s 40 0 e
Antrim 54 43n 6 13w
Antrim □ 54 55n 6 10w
Antrim, Mts. of .. 54 57n 6 10w
Antsalova .... 18 40s 44 37 e
Antsirabe .... 19 55s 47 2 e
Antsohihy .... 14 50s 47 50 e
Antung .... 40 10n 124 18 e
Antwerp=
  Antwerpen .... 51 13n 4 25 e
Antwerpen ...... 51 13n 4 25 e
Antwerpen □ .... 51 15n 4 40 e
Anupgarh .... 29 10n 73 10 e
Anuppur .... 22 58n 81 44 e
Anuradhapura .... 8 22n 80 28 e
Anvers=
  Antwerpen .... 51 13n 4 25 e
Anvik 62 40n 160 12w
Anyang .... 36 7n 114 26 e
Anyer-Lor ...... 6 6s 105 56 e
Anyi .... 28 50n 115 31 e
Anzhero
  Sudzhensk ..... 56 10n 83 40 e
Ánzio .... 41 28n 12 37 e
Aomori .... 40 45n 140 45 e
Aomori □ .... 40 45n 140 40 e
Aosta .... 45 43n 7 20 e
Aozou .... 21 49n 17 25 e
Apam 5 17n 0 44w

Apapa .... 6 25n 3 25 e
Aparri .... 18 22n 121 38 e
Apatzingán 19 0n 102 20w
Apeldoorn .... 52 13n 5 57 e
Apenam .... 8 35s 116 13 e
Apennines, Mts.=
  Appennini, Mts. . 41 0n 15 0 e
Apia 14 0s 171 55w
Apizaco 19 26n 98 9w
Apollonia=
  Marsa Susa ..... 32 52n 21 59 e
Apostle Is. 47 0n 90 30w
Apóstoles 27 55s 55 45w
Apoteri 4 2n 58 32w
Appalachian Mts. . 38 0n 80 0w
Appleby 54 35n 2 29w
Appleton 44 17n 88 25w
Approuagne 4 20n 52 0w
Apucarana 23 55s 51 33w
Aq Chah .... 37 0n 66 5 e
'Aqaba .... 29 31n 35 0 e
'Aqaba, Khalīj al .. 28 15n 33 20 e
Aqiq .... 18 14n 38 12 e
Aqraba .... 32 9n 35 20 e
Aquidauana 20 30s 55 50w
Ar Rab' al Khālī . 21 0n 51 0 e
Ar-Ramthā ...... 32 34n 36 0 e
Ar Raqqah ...... 35 56n 39 1 e
Ar Riyād .... 24 41n 46 42 e
Ar Ruska .... 23 35n 53 30 e
Arab, Bahr el, R. . 9 2n 29 28 e
Arabia, Reg. ..... 25 0n 45 0 e
Arabian Des. ..... 28 0n 32 30 e
Arabian Sea ..... 16 0n 65 0 e
Aracajú 10 55s 37 4w
Aracataca 10 38n 74 9w
Aracati 4 30s 37 44w
Araçatuba 21 10s 50 30w
Aracena 37 53n 6 58w
Araçuai 16 52s 42 4w
'Arad .... 31 17n 35 12 e
Arad .... 46 10n 21 20 e
Arafura Sea ..... 10 0s 135 0 e
Aragón, R. 42 13n 1 44w
Aragon, Reg. 41 0n 1 0w
Araguacema 8 50s 49 20w
Araguaia, R. 5 21s 48 41w
Araguari 18 38s 48 11w
Arak .... 34 0n 49 40 e

Arakan Coast ..... 19 0n 94 0 e
Arakan Yoma,
  Mts. .... 20 0n 94 30 e
Araks, R. .... 40 1n 48 28 e
Aral Sea=
  Aralskoye More . 44 30n 66 0 e
Aralsk .... 46 50n 61 20 e
Aralskoye More ... 44 30n 60 0 e
Aran, I. 55 0n 8 30w
Aran Is. 53 5n 9 42w
Aranjuez 40 1n 3 40w
Aransas P. 28 0n 97 9w
Aranyaprathet ... 13 41n 102 30 e
Arapongas 23 29s 51 28w
Araranguá 29 0s 49 30w
Araraquara 21 50s 48 0w
Ararat .... 37 16s 143 0 e
Ararat, Mt.=
  Ağri Daği, Mt. .. 39 50n 44 15 e
Arauca 7 0n 70 40w
Araxá 19 35s 46 55w
Araya, Pen. de ... 10 40n 64 0w
Arbatax .... 39 57n 9 42 e
Arbil .... 36 15n 44 5 e
Arbroath 56 34n 2 35w
Arcachon 44 40n 1 10w
Arcadia 44 13n 91 29w
Arcata 40 55n 124 4w
Archangel=
  Arkhangelsk ... 64 40n 41 0 e
Archers Post ..... 0 35n 37 35 e
Arcos de los
  Frontera 36 45n 5 49w
Arcot .... 12 53n 79 20 e
Arcoverde 8 25s 37 4w
Arctic Bay 73 2n 85 11w
Arctic Ocean 78 0n 160 0w
Arctic Red River .. 67 15n 134 0w
Arda, R. .... 41 39n 26 29 e
Ardabril .... 38 15n 48 18 e
Ardèche □ ...... 44 42n 4 16 e
Ardee 53 51n 6 32w
Ardennes, Reg. ... 49 30n 5 10 e
Ardennes □ ..... 49 35n 4 40 e
Ardestan .... 33 20n 52 25 e
Ardgour, Reg. ... 56 45n 5 25w
Ardlethan ...... 34 22s 146 53 e
Ardmore, Australia 21 39s 139 11 e
Ardmore, U.S.A. .. 34 10n 97 5w

Ardnacrusha 52 43n 8 38w
Ardnamurchan Pt. . 56 44n 6 14w
Ardrossan 55 39n 4 50w
Ards □ 54 35n 5 30w
Ards Pen. 54 30n 5 25w
Arecibo 18 29n 66 42w
Areia Branca 5 0s 37 0w
Arenal .... 39 28n 2 47 e
Arendal .... 58 28n 8 46 e
Arequipa 16 20s 71 30w
Arero .... 4 41n 38 50 e
Arévalo 41 3n 4 43w
Arezzo .... 43 28n 11 50 e
Argentia 47 18n 53 58w
Argentine Basin,
  Reg. .... 44 0s 51 0 e
Argentina ■ 35 0s 66 0w
Argentino, L. 50 10s 73 0w
Arges, R. .... 44 10n 26 45 e
Argo .... 19 28n 30 30 e
Argolikós Kól. .... 37 20n 22 52 e
Argonne, Mts. .... 49 0n 5 20 e
Árgos .... 37 40n 22 43 e
Argostólion ..... 38 12n 20 33 e
Arguello, Pt. 34 34n 120 40w
Argun, R. .... 43 22n 45 55 e
Argungu .... 12 40n 4 31 e
Argyle, L. .... 16 20s 128 40 e
Århus .... 56 8n 10 11 e
Arica, Chile 18 32s 70 20w
Arica, Col. 1 30s 75 30w
Arid, C. .... 34 1s 123 10 e
Arida .... 33 29n 135 44 e
Ariège □ .... 42 56n 1 30 e
Arima 10 38n 61 17w
Arisaig 56 50n 5 40w
Arizona 35 45s 65 25w
Arizona □ 34 20n 111 30w
Arjona 10 14n 75 22w
Arka .... 60 15n 142 0 e
Arka Tagh, Mts. .. 36 30n 90 0 e
Arkadelphia 34 5n 93 0w
Arkaig, L. 56 58n 5 10w
Arkansas, R. 33 48n 91 0w
Arkansas □ 35 0n 92 30w
Arkansas City 37 4n 97 3w
Arkhangelsk ..... 64 40n 41 0 e
Arklow 52 48n 6 10w
Arles .... 43 41n 4 40 e
Arlington, S. Afr. . 28 1s 27 53 e

Arlington, U.S.A. . 44 25n 97 4w
Arlon .... 49 42n 5 49 e
Armadale .... 32 12s 116 0 e
Armagh 54 22n 6 40w
Armagh □ 54 16n 6 35w
Armagnac, Reg. ... 43 44n 0 10 e
Armavir .... 45 2n 41 7 e
Armenia 4 35n 75 45w
Armenian S.S.R. □ 40 0n 41 10 e
Armidale .... 30 30s 151 40 e
Armstrong, B.C. .. 50 25n 119 10w
Armstrong, Ont. .. 50 20n 89 0w
Arnhem .... 51 58n 5 55 e
Arnhem, B. ...... 12 20s 136 10 e
Arnhem Land ... 13 0s 135 0 e
Arno, R. .... 43 31n 10 17 e
Arnprior 45 23n 76 25w
Arrabury .... 26 45s 141 0 e
Arrah .... 25 35n 84 32 e
Arran, I. 55 34n 5 12w
Arras .... 50 17n 2 46 e
Arrecife 28 59n 13 40w
Arrée, Mts. d' 48 26n 3 55w
Arrino .... 29 30s 115 40 e
Arrowhead 50 40n 117 55w
Arrowtown ...... 44 57s 168 50 e
Arshan .... 46 59n 120 0 e
Árta .... 39 8n 21 2 e
Artemovsk ...... 48 35n 37 55 e
Artesia 32 55n 104 25w
Arthur, Pt. ...... 22 7s 150 3 e
Artigas 30 20s 56 30w
Artois, Reg. ..... 50 20n 2 30 e
Artvin .... 41 14n 41 44 e
Aru, Kep. ...... 6 0s 134 30 e
Arua .... 3 1n 30 58 e
Aruanã 15 0s 51 10w
Aruba, I. 12 30n 70 0w
Arunachal
  Pradesh □ ..... 28 0n 95 0 e
Arusha .... 3 20s 36 40 e
Arvada 44 43n 106 6w
Arvayheer ...... 46 15n 102 48 e
Arvida 48 16n 71 14w
Arvidsjaur ...... 65 35n 19 10 e
Arvika .... 59 40n 12 36 e
Arys .... 42 26n 68 48 e
Arzamas .... 55 27n 43 55 e
Arzew 35 50n 0 23w
As Salt .... 32 2n 35 43 e

As Samawah ..... 31 15N 45 15 E
As Sulaimānīyah .. 24 8N 47 10 E
As Sulamānīyah ... 35 35N 45 29 E
As Suwaih .... 22 10N 59 33 E
As Suwayda ..... 32 40N 36 30 E
As Suwayrah .... 32 55N 45 0 E
Asaba .... 6 12N 6 38 E
Asahikawa ...... 43 45N 142 30 E
Asamankese 5 50N 0 40W
Asansol .... 23 40N 87 1 E
Asbestos 45 47N 71 58W
Asbury Park 40 15N 74 1W
Ascensión, B. de la 19 50N 87 20W
Ascension, I. 8 0s 14 15W
Aschaffenburg .... 49 58N 9 8 E
Ascoli Piceno .... 42 51N 13 34 E
Aseb .... 13 0N 42 40 E
Ash Fork 35 14N 112 32W
Ash Shāmiyah ... 31 55N 44 35 E
Ash Sharma .... 28 1N 35 18 E
Ash Shuna ..... 32 32N 35 34 E
Asha .... 35 10N 33 38 E
Ashanti □ 7 30N 2 0W
Ashburton ..... 43 53s 171 48 E
Ashburton, R. .... 37 52s 145 5 E
Ashburton Downs . 23 25s 117 4 E
Ashby-de-la-Zouch 52 45N 1 29W
Ashdod .... 31 39N 34 35 E
Ashdot Yaaqov ... 32 39N 35 35 E
Asheboro 35 43N 79 46W
Asheville 35 39N 82 30W
Ashford .... 51 8N 0 53 E
Ashikaga ...... 36 28N 139 29 E
Ashington 55 12N 1 35W
Ashkhabad ..... 38 0N 57 50 E
Ashland, Ky. 38 25N 82 40W
Ashland, Ohio ... 40 52N 82 20W
Ashland, Oreg. ... 42 10N 122 38W
Ashland, Wis. ... 46 40N 90 52W
Ashquelon ..... 31 42N 34 55 E
Ashtabula 41 52N 80 50W
Ashton 44 6N 111 30W
Ashton-under-
  Lyne 53 30N 2 8W
Asia .... 45 0N 75 0 E
Asilah 35 29N 6 0W
Asinara, G. dell' . 41 0N 8 30 E
Asinara, I. ..... 41 5N 8 15 E
Asino .... 57 0N 86 0 E
Asir, Ras .... 11 55N 51 0 E

Asir, Reg. .... 18 40N 42 30 E
Asira esh
  Shamaliya ..... 32 16N 35 16 E
Askersund ...... 58 58N 14 8 E
Asmar .... 35 10N 71 27 E
Asmera .... 15 19N 38 55 E
Aspiring, Mt. 44 23s 168 46W
Assam □ .... 25 45N 92 30 E
Asse .... 50 54N 4 6 E
Assen .... 53 0N 6 35 E
Assiniboia 49 40N 106 0W
Assiniboine, Mt. .. 50 52N 115 39W
Assiniboine, R. ... 49 53N 97 8W
Assis 22 40s 50 20W
Assisi .... 43 4N 12 36 E
Assynt, L. 58 25s 5 10W
Astara .... 38 30N 48 50 E
Asti .... 44 54N 8 11 E
Astipálaia, I. ..... 36 32N 26 22 E
Astorga 42 29N 6 8W
Astoria 46 16N 123 50W
Astrakhan ..... 46 25N 48 5 E
Asturias, Reg. ... 43 15N 6 0W
Asunción 25 21s 57 30W
Aswân .... 24 4N 32 57 E
Aswân High Dam .. 24 5N 32 54 E
Asyût .... 27 11N 31 4 E
At Ta'if ...... 21 5N 40 27 E
Atacama Des..... 24 0s 69 20W
Atacama, Pune de . 25 0s 67 30W
Atacama, Salar de . 24 0s 68 20W
Atakpamé ...... 7 31N 1 13 E
Atami .... 35 0N 139 55 E
Atar 20 30N 13 5W
Atara .... 63 10N 129 10 E
Atasu .... 48 30N 71 0 E
Atbara .... 17 42N 33 59 E
'Atbara, Nahr, R .. 17 40N 33 56 E
Atbasar .... 51 48N 68 20 E
Atchison 39 40N 95 0W
Ath .... 50 38N 3 47 E
Athabasca 54 45N 113 20W
Athabasca, L. ... 59 10N 109 30W
Athabasca, R. ... 58 40N 110 50W
Athboy 53 37N 6 55W
Athenry 53 18N 8 45W
Athens, Ala. 34 49N 86 58W
Athens, Ga. 33 56N 83 24W
Athens, Ohio 39 52N 82 64W
Athens, Tex. 32 11N 95 48W

Athens=Athínai .. 37 58N 23 46 E
Atherton ...... 17 17s 145 30 E
Athi River ...... 1 29s 36 58 E
Athiéme .... 6 37N 1 40 E
Athínai .... 37 58N 23 46 E
Athlone 53 26N 7 57W
Athol 42 36N 72 14W
Atholl, Forest of .. 56 51N 3 50W
Atholville 48 5N 67 5W
Athos, Mt. ...... 40 9N 24 22 E
Athy 53 0N 7 0W
Atka .... 60 50N 151 48 E
Atka I. 52 15N 174 30W
Atlanta 33 50N 84 24W
Atlantic 41 25N 95 0W
Atlantic City ... 39 25N 74 25W
Atlantic Ocean .. 0 0 30 0W
Atlas, Anti, Mts. .. 30 0N 8 0½
Atlas, Moyen,
  Mts. 37 0N 5 0W
Atlas Saharien,
  Mts. .... 34 10N 3 30 E
Atlin 59 31N 133 41W
Atlit .... 32 42N 34 56 E
Atmore 31 2N 87 30W
Atocha 21 0s 66 10W
Atotonilco 20 20N 98 40W
Attawapiskat ... 53 0N 82 30W
Attawapiskat L. .. 52 20N 88 0W
Attawapiskat, R. .. 52 57N 82 18W
Attil .... 32 23N 35 4 E
Attleboro 41 56N 71 18W
Attock .... 33 52N 72 20 E
Attopeu .... 14 56N 106 50 E
Attu I. .... 52 55N 173 0 E
Atura .... 2 5N 32 17 E
Atwood 39 52N 101 3W
Auasberg ...... 22 45s 17 22 E
Aube, R. .... 48 34N 3 43 E
Aube □ .... 48 15N 4 0 E
Auburn, Ala. 32 57N 85 30W
Auburn, Calif. ... 38 50N 121 10W
Auburn, Me. 44 6N 70 14W
Aubusson ...... 45 57N 2 11 E
Auch .... 43 39N 0 36 E
Auchi .... 7 6N 6 13 E
Auckland ...... 36 52s 174 46 E
Auckland Is. .... 51 0s 166 0 E
Aude, R. .... 43 13N 3 14 E
Aude □ .... 44 13N 3 15 E

Auden 50 17N 87 54W
Augathella ..... 25 48s 146 35 E
Augsburg ...... 48 22N 10 54 E
Augusta,
  Australia ...... 34 22s 115 10 E
Augusta, Italy ... 37 14N 15 12 E
Augusta, U.S.A. .. 33 29N 81 59W
Augusta 44 20N 69 46W
* Augusto Cardoso . 12 44s 34 50 E
Augustów ...... 53 51N 23 0 E
Augustus, Mt. ... 24 20s 116 50 E
Augustus Downs . 18 35s 139 55 E
Auna .... 10 9N 4 42 E
Aunis, Reg. 46 0N 0 50W
Aurangabad,
  Maharashtra .... 19 50N 75 23 E
Aurillac .... 44 55N 2 26 E
Aurora, Colo. 39 44N 104 55W
Aurora, Ill. 41 42N 88 20W
Aust-Agde □ .... 58 55N 7 40 E
Austin, Minn. ... 43 37N 92 59W
Austin, Nev. 39 30N 117 1W
Austin, Tex. 30 20N 97 45W
Australia ■ ..... 23 0s 135 0 E
Australian Alps,
  Mts. .... 36 30s 148 8 E
Australian
  Capital Terr. □ . 35 15s 149 8 E
Australian
  Dependency □ .. 73 0s 90 0 E
Austria ■ ...... 47 0N 14 0 E
Autlán 19 40N 104 30W
Autun .... 46 58N 4 17 E
Auvergne ...... 15 39s 130 1 E
Auvergne, Mts. .. 45 20N 2 45 E
Auvergne, Reg. .. 45 30N 3 20 E
Auxerre .... 47 48N 3 32 E
Avallon .... 47 30N 3 50 E
Avalon Pen. 47 0N 53 20W
Aveiro, Brazil ... 3 10s 55 5W
Aveiro, Port. 40 37N 8 38W
Avellaneda 34 50s 58 10W
Avellino .... 40 54N 14 46 E
Aversa .... 40 58N 14 11 E
Aves, Is. de 12 0N 67 40W
Avesta .... 60 9N 16 10 E
Aveyron □ ..... 44 22N 2 45 E
Aviá Terai 26 45s 60 50W
Aviemore 57 11N 3 50W
Avignon .... 43 57N 4 50 E

Ávila 40 39N 4 43W
Avilés 43 35N 5 57W
Avoca .... 37 5s 143 28 E
Avoca, R. 52 48N 6 10W
Avola, Canada ... 51 45N 119 30W
Avon, R,
  Australia ...... 31 40s 116 7 E
Avon, R., Avon .. 51 30N 2 43W
Avon, R., Dorset . 50 43N 1 46W
Avon, R.,
  Gloucester 51 59N 2 10W
Avon □ 51 30N 2 40W
Avonmouth 51 30N 2 42W
Avranches 48 40N 1 20W
Awaji-Shima, I. .. 34 30N 134 50 E
Awali .... 26 0N 50 30 E
Awash .... 9 1N 40 10 E
Awatere, R. .... 41 37s 174 10 E
Awe, L. 56 15N 5 15W
Awgu .... 6 4N 7 24 E
Awjilah .... 29 8N 21 7 E
Awka .... 6 12N 7 5 E
Axel Heiberg
  Ld. 80 0N 90 0W
Axim 4 41N 2 15W
Axminster 50 47N 3 1W
Ayabe .... 35 20N 135 20 E
Ayacucho, Arg. .. 37 5s 58 20W
Ayacucho, Peru .. 13 0s 74 0W
Ayaguz .... 48 10N 80 0 E
Ayamonte 37 12N 7 24W
Ayan .... 56 30N 138 16 E
Aykin .... 62 20N 49 56 E
Aylesbury, Canada 50 55N 105 53W
Aylesbury, U.K. .. 51 48N 0 49W
Aylmer, L. 64 0N 109 0W
Ayr, Australia ... 19 35s 147 25 E
Ayr, U.K. 55 28N 4 37W
Ayr, R. 55 29N 4 28W
Ayre, Pt. of 54 27N 4 21W
Aytos .... 42 47N 27 16 E
Ayvalik .... 39 20N 26 46 E
Az Zahiriya .... 31 25N 34 58 E
Az Zahrān ..... 26 10N 50 7 E
Az-Zarqā' ..... 32 5N 36 4 E
Az Zilfi .... 26 12N 44 52 E
Az Zubayr ..... 30 20N 47 50 E
Azamgarh ..... 26 35N 83 13 E
Āzārbāījān □ ... 37 0N 44 30 E
Azare .... 11 55N 10 10 E

Renamed Metangula

Azbine=Aïr ...... 18 0N   8 0 E
Azerbaijan
  S.S.R. □ .... 40 20N 48 0 E
Azov .... 32 2N 34 48 E
Azores, Is. 38 44N 29 0w
Azov= .... 47 3N 39 25 E
Azov Sea=
  Azovskoye More 46 0N 36 30 E
Azovskoye More .. 46 0N 36 30 E
Azovy .... 64 55N 64 35 E
Aztec 36 54N 108 0w
Azua 18 25N 70 44w
Azuaga 38 16N   5 39w
Azuero, Pen. de ... 7 40N 80 30w
Azul 36 42s 59 43w

B

Ba Don .... 17 45N 106 26 E
Baba, Koh-i-, Mts. 34 40N 67 20 E
Babahoyo 1 40s 79 30w
Babakin .... 32 11s 117 52 E
Babana .... 10 31N   5 9 E
Babati .... 4 13s 35 45 E
Babelthuap, I. .. 7 30N 134 36 E
Babinda .... 17 27s 146 0 E
Babo .... 2 30s 133 30 E
Bâbol .... 36 40N 52 50 E
Babol Sar ...... 36 45N 52 45 E
Babura .... 12 51N   8 59 E
Babuyan Chan. .. 18 58N 122 0 E
Babuyan Is. .... 19 0N 122 0 E
Babylon .... 32 40N 44 30 E
Bacabal 5 20s 56 45w
Bacan, I. ...... 1 0s 127 30 E
Bachelina ...... 57 45N 67 20 E
Back, R. 67 15N 95 15w
Bacolod .... 10 50N 123 0 E
Bad Ischl ...... 47 44 13 38 E
Badagara .... 11 35N 75 40 E
Badagri .... 6 25N   2 55 E
Badajoz 38 50N   6 59w
Badakhshan □ ... 36 30N 71 0 E
Badalona .... 41 26N   2 15 E
Badalzal .... 29 50N 65 35 E
Badanah .... 30 58N 41 30 E
Badas .... 4 20N 114 37 E

Baden .... 48 1N 16 13 E
Baden-Baden .... 48 45N   8 14 E
Baden
  Württemberg □ . 48 40N   9 0 E
Badenoch, Reg. .. 57 0N   4 0w
Badgastein ..... 47 7N 13 9 E
Badghis □ ...... 35 0N 63 0 E
Badin .... 24 38N 68 54 E
Baeza 37 57N   3 25w
Bafang .... 5 9N 10 11 E
Baffin B. 72 0N 65 0w
Baffin I. 68 0N 77 0w
Bafia .... 4 40N 11 10 E
Bafilo .... 9 22N   1 22 E
Bâft 29 15N 56 38w
Bagamoyo .... 6 28s 38 55 E
Bagdarin .... 54 26N 113 36 E
Baghdâd .... 32 20N 44 30 E
Baghin .... 30 12N 56 45 E
Baghlan .... 36 12N 69 0 E
Baghlan □ ...... 36 0N 68 30 E
Bagotville 48 22N 70 54w
Bagrash Kol, L. . 42 0N 87 0 E
Baguio .... 16 26N 120 34 E
Bahamas ■ 24 0N 74 0w
Bahawalpur ..... 29 37N 71 40 E
* Bahawalpur □ .. 29 5N 71 3 E
Bahi .... 5 58s 35 21 E
Bahia=
  Salvador 13 0s 38 30w
Bahia, Is. de la . 16 45N 86 15w
Bahia .... 12 0N 42 0 E
Bahia Blanca ... 38 35s 62 13w
Bahia de
  Caráquez 0 40s 80 27w
Bahia Laura 48 10s 66 30w
Bahia Negra 20 5s 58 5w
Bahr el Ghazâl □ 7 0N 28 0 E
Bahraich .... 27 38N 81 50 E
Bahrain ■ ...... 26 0N 50 35 E
Baia Mare ...... 47 40N 23 37 E
Baião 2 50s 49 15w
Baie Comeau 49 12N 68 10w
Baie T. Paul ... 47 28N 70 32w
Ba 'iji .... 35 0N 43 30 E
Baile Atha
  Cliath=Dublin . 53 20N   6 18w
Bainbridge 30 53N 84 34w

Baird Mts. 67 10N 160 15w
Bairnsdale ..... 37 48s 147 36 E
Baixo-Alentejo,
  Reg. 38 0N   8 40w
Baja .... 46 12N 18 59 E
Baja California
  Norte □ 30 0N 116 0w
Baja California
  Sur □ 26 0N 112 0w
Bajima, Mt. .... 29 17s 152 6 E
Bajoga .... 10 57N 11 20 E
Bajool .... 24 30s 150 35 E
Bakchar .... 57 0N 82 5 E
Baker, Calif. .. 36 16N 116 2w
Baker, Mont. ... 46 22N 104 12w
Baker I. .... 0 10N 176 35 E
Baker L. 64 0N 97 0w
Baker, Mt. 48 50N 121 49w
Baker Lake 64 20N 96 10w
Baker's Dozen Is. 57 30N 79 0w
Bakersfield 35 25N 119 0w
Bakhtiari □ .... 32 0N 49 0 E
Bakinskikh
  Komissarov .... 39 20N 49 15 E
Bakony Forest=
  Bakony Hegyseg,
  Reg. .... 47 10N 17 30 E
Bakori .... 11 34N   7 27 E
Baku .... 40 25N 49 45 E
Bal'a .... 32 20N 35 6 E
Bala, L. 52 53N   3 38w
Balabac I. ..... 8 0N 117 0 E
Balabac Str. ... 7 53N 117 5 E
Balaghat .... 21 49N 80 12 E
Balaghat Ra. ... 18 50N 76 30 E
Balaguer .... 41 50N   0 50 E
Balaklava,
  Australia ..... 34 7s 138 22 E
Balaklava,
  U.S.S.R. ...... 44 30N 33 30 E
Balakovo .... 52 4N 47 55 E
Balashov .... 51 30N 43 10 E
Balasore .... 21 35N 87 3 E
Balaton, L. .... 46 50N 17 40 E
Balboa 9 0N 79 30w
Balbriggan 53 35N   6 10w
Balcarce 38 0s 58 10w
Balclutha ...... 46 15s 169 45 E
Bald, Hd. ...... 35 6s 118 1 E
Baldy Pk. 33 55N 109 35w

Baleares, Is. ...... 39 30N   3 0 E
Balearic Is.=
  Baleares, Is. .... 39 30N   3 0 E
Balfe's Creek .. 20 12s 145 55 E
Balfour .... 26 38s 28 35 E
Bali .... 5 54N 10 0 E
Bali, I. .... 8 20s 115 0 E
Balikesir ...... 39 35s 27 58 E
Balikpapan ..... 1 0s 116 55 E
Balintang Chan. . 19 50N 122 0 E
Balipara .... 26 50N 92 45 E
Baliza 16 0s 52 20w
Balkan Pen. .... 42 0N 22 0 E
Balkans, Mts. .. 42 45N 25 0 E
Balkh .... 36 30N 67 0 E
Balkhash .... 46 50N 74 50 E
Balkhash, Oz. .. 46 0N 74 50 E
Ballachulish ... 56 40N   5 10w
Balladonia ..... 32 27s 123 51 E
Ballarat .... 37 33s 143 50 E
Ballard, L. .... 29 20s 120 10 E
Ballater 57 2N   3 2w
Ballidu .... 30 35s 116 45 E
Ballina,
  Australia ..... 28 50s 153 31 E
Ballina, Mayo .. 54 7N   9 10w
Ballina, Tipperary 52 49N   8 27w
Ballinasloe 53 20N   8 12w
Ballinger 31 45N 99 58w
Ballinrobe 53 36N   9 13w
Ballycastle 55 12N   6 15w
Ballymena 54 53N   6 18w
Ballymena □ 54 53N   6 18w
Ballymoney 55 5N   6 30w
Ballymoney □ ... 55 5N   6 30w
Ballyshannon ... 54 30N   8 10w
Balmaceda 46 0s 71 50w
Balmoral 57 3N   3 13w
Balovale .... 13 30s 23 15 E
Balrampur ...... 27 30N 82 20 E
Balranald ...... 34 38s 143 33 E
Balsas, R. 17 55N 102 10w
Balta .... 48 2N 29 45 E
Baltic Sea ..... 56 0N 20 0 E
Baltimore, Eire 51 29N   9 22w
Baltimore, U.S.A. 39 18N 76 37w
Baluchistan, Reg. 27 0N 62 0 E
Bam .... 29 7N 58 14 E
Bama .... 11 33N 13 33 E
Bamako 12 34N   7 55w

Bambari .... 5 40N 20 35 E
Bambaroo .... 18 50s 146 10 E
Bamberg .... 49 54N 10 53 E
Bamenda .... 5 57N 10 11 E
Bamian .... 35 0N 67 0 E
Bampur .... 27 15N 60 21 E
Ban Kantang .... 7 25N 99 35 E
Banadar Daryay
  Oman □ .... 25 30N 56 0 E
Banalia .... 1 32N 25 5 E
Banamba 13 29N   7 22w
Banana .... 24 32s 150 12 E
Bananal, I. de .. 11 30s 50 30w
Banaras = Varanasi 25 22N 83 8 E
Bânâs, Ras ..... 23 57N 35 50 E
Banat, Reg. .... 45 30N 21 30 E
Banbridge 54 26N   6 16w
Banbridge □ 54 21N   6 16w
Banbury 52 4N   1 21w
Banchory 57 3N   2 30w
Bancroft 45 3N 77 51w
Band-e Charak .. 26 45N 54 20 E
Band-e Nakhîlu . 26 58N 53 30 E
Banda .... 25 30N 80 26 E
Banda Aceh ..... 5 35N 95 20 E
Banda Banda, Mt. 31 10s 152 28 E
Banda Sea ...... 6 0s 130 0 E
Bandar=
  Machilipatnam . 16 12N 81 12 E
Bandar Abbas ... 27 15N 56 15 E
Bandar Maharani . 2 3N 102 34 E
Bandar Seri
  Begawan .... 4 52N 115 0 E
* Bandar-e Bushetir 28 55N 50 55 E
Bandar-e Lengeh . 26 35N 54 58 E
Bandar-e Ma'shur 30 35N 49 10 E
* Bandar-e-Pahlavi 37 30N 49 30 E
Bandar-e Rig ... 29 30N 50 45 E
‡ Bandar-e Shâh . 37 0N 54 10 E
† Bandar-e Shahpur 30 30N 49 5 E
Bandawe .... 11 58s 34 5 E
Bandeira, Pico da 20 26s 41 47w
Bandera 28 55s 62 20w
Bandiagara 14 12N   3 29w
Bandirma .... 40 20N 28 0 E
Bandon 51 44N   8 45w
Bandon, R. 51 40N   8 35w
Bandundu 3 15s 1722¼
Bandung .... 6 36s 107 48 E
Banes 20 58N 75 43w

* Renamed Bandar Anzalī
† Renamed Bandar Khomeynī
‡ Renamed Bandar-e Torkeman

Banff, Canada 51 20N 115 40w
Banff, U.K. 57 40N   2 32w
Banff Nat. Park ... 51 38N 116 22w
Bang Saphan ..... 11 14N   99 28 E
Bangala Dam 21   7s 31 25 E
Bangalore .... 12 59N   77 40 E
Bangassou .... 4 55N   23 55 E
Banghazi .... 32 11N   20   3 E
Bangil .... 7 36s 112 50 E
Bangka, I., Selatan 3 30s 105 30 E
Bangka, I., Utara .. 1 50N 12s   5 E
Bangkalan 7   2s 112 46 E
Bangkok=Krung
    Thep .... 13 45N 100 31 E
Bangladesh ■ 24   0N   90   0 E
Bangor, Gwynedd . 53 13N   4   9w
Bangor, N. Down . 54 40N   5 40w
Bangor, Me. 44 48N   68 42w
Bangued .... 17 40N 120 37 E
Bangui .... 4 23N   18 35 E
Bangweulu, L. 11   0s 30   0 E
Bani 18 16N   70 22w
Bani Na'im ...... 31 31N   35 10 E
Banïnah 32   0N   20 12 E
Banja Luka ...... 44 49N   17 26 E
Banjar .... 7 24s 108 30 E
Banjarmasin ..... 3 20s 114 35 E
Banjarnegara ..... 7 24s 109 42 E
Banjul 13 28N   16 40w
Banka Banka .... 18 50s 134   0 E
Bankipore .... 25 35N   85 10 E
Banks I. 73 30N 120   0w
Banks, Pen. ..... 43 45s 173 15 E
Bankura .... 23 11N   87 18 E
Bann, R. 55   2N   6 35w
Banning 48 44N   91 56w
Bannu 33   0N   70 18s
Bannockburn 56   5N   3 55w
Banská Bystrica ... 48 46N   19 14 E
Banswara .... 23 32N   74 24 E
Banten 6   5s 106   8 E
Bantry 51 40N   9 28w
Bantry, B. 51 35N   9 50w
Bantul .... 7 55s 110 19 E
Bapatla .... 15 55N   80 30 E
Baqa el Gharbiya . 32 25N   35   2 E
Bar 42   8N   19   8 E
Barabai .... 2 32s 115 34 E
Barabinsk .... 55 20N   78 20 E
Baraboo 43 28N   89 46w

Baracoa 20 20N   74 30w
Barahona 18 13N   71   7w
Barail Ra. .... 25 15N   93 20 E
Barak ■ .... 38 20N 140   0 E
Barakhola 25   0N   92 45 E
Baramula .... 34 15N   74 20 E
Baran 25   9N   76 40 E
Baranof 57   0N 135 10w
Baranof I. 57   0N 135 10w
Baranovichi ...... 53 10N   26   0 E
Barat□, Java 7   0s 107   0 E
Barat□,
    Kalimantan 0   0s 111   0 E
Barat□, Sumatera .. 0   0s 101   0 E
Barat Daja,
    Kep. .... 7 30s 128   0 E
Barbacena 21 15s   43 56w
Barbacoas 1 45N   78   0w
Barbados ■ 13   0N   59 30w
Barberton,
    S. Africa ..... 25 42s   31   2 E
Barberton, U.S.A. . 41   0N   81 40w
Barbuda, I. 17 30N   61 40w
Barcaldine ...... 22 33s 145 13 E
Barce=Al Marj ... 32 25N   20 40 E
Barcelona, Sp. ... 41 21N   2 10 E
Barcelona, Ven. ... 10 10N   64 40w
Barcelos 1   0s 63   0w
Bardaï .... 21 25N   17   0 E
Bardera 2 20N   42   0s
Bardiyah .... 31 45N   25   0 E
Bardsey I. 52 46N   4 47w
Bareilly .... 28 22N   79 27 E
Barents Sea 73   0N   39   0 E
Barfleur, Pte. de . 49 42N   1 17w
Bargal .... 11 25N   51   0 E
Bargara .... 24 50s 152 25 E
Barguzin .... 53 37N 109 37 E
Bari 41   6N   16 52 E
Bari Doab, Reg. .. 30 20N   73   0 E
Bari Sadri .... 24 25N   74 29 E
Barinas 8 36N   70 15w
Baring, C. 70   0N 116 30w
Bâris .... 24 42N   30 31 E
Barisal .... 22 30N   90 20 E
Barisan,
    Bukit, Mts. .... 3 30s 102 15 E
Barito, R. 4   0s 114 50 E
Barkah .... 24 30N   58   0 E
Barkha 31   0N   81 45 E

Barkly East ...... 30 58s   27 33 E
Barkly Tableland .. 19 50s 138 40 E
Barkly West ..... 28 38s   24 11 E
Bar-le-Duc ...... 48 47N   5 10 E
Barlee, L. .... 29 15s 119 30 E
Barletta .... 41 20N   16 17 E
Barmedman 34   9s 147 21 E
Barmer .... 25 45N   71 20 E
Barmera .... 34 15s 140 28 E
Barmouth 52 44N   4   3w
Barnard Castle ... 54 33N   1 55w
Barnaul .... 53 20N   83 40 E
Barnesville 33   6N   84   9w
Barnet 51 37N   0 15w
Barneveld 52   7N   5 36 E
Barnsley 53 33N   1 29w
Barnstaple 51   5N   4   3w
Baroda=
    Vadodara .... 22 20N   73 10 E
Barpeta .... 26 20N   91 10 E
Barqa 27   0N   20   0 E
Barquisimeto 9 58N   69 13w
Barra 11   5s 43 10w
Barra, I. 57   0N   7 30w
Barra de Corda ... 5 30s 45 10w
Barra do Piraí ... 22 30s   43 50w
Barraba .... 30 21s 150 35 E
Barranca 10 45s   77 50w
Barrancabermeja . 7   0N   73 50w
Barrancas 8 55N   62   5w
Barrancos 38 10N   6 58w
Barranqueras 27 30s   59   0w
Barranquilla 11   0N   74 50w
Barras 1 45s 73 13w
Barraute 47 30N   76 50w
Barre 44 15N   73 30w
Barreiras 12   8s 45 0w
Barreirinhas 2 30s 42 50w
Barreiro 38 40N   9   6w
Barreiros 8 49s   35 12w
Barretos 20 30s   48 35w
Barrhead 54 10N 114 30w
Barrie 44 25N   79 45w
Barrow, U.K. 54   8N   3 15w
Barrow, U.S.A. .. 71 16N 156 50w
Barrow, I. ...... 20 45s 115 20 E
Barrow, R. 52 46N   7   0w
Barrow Creek ... 21 30s 133 55 E
Barry 51 23N   3 19w
Barry's Bay 45 30N   77 40w

Barsaloi .... 1 20N   36 52 E
Barsi .... 18 10N   75 50 E
Barstow 34 58N 117   2w
Bartica 6 25N   58 40w
Bartlesville 36 50N   95 58w
Barton Siding ... 30 31s 132 39 E
Barton-upon-
    Humber 53 41N   0 27w
Bartow 27 53N   81 49w
Baruun Urt ..... 46 46N 113 15 E
Bas Rhin □ ..... 48 40N   7 30 E
Basel .... 47 35N   7 35 E
Bashkir
    A.S.S.R. □ 54   0N   57   0 E
Basilan, I. .... 6 35N 122   0 E
Basilan City=
    Lamitan ...... 6 37N 122   0 E
Basilan Str. ...... 13 10s 122   0 E
Basildon .... 51 34N   0 29 E
Basilicata □ ..... 40 30N   16   0 E
Basim 20   4N   77   4 E
Basingstoke 51 15N   1   5w
Baskatong Res. .. 46 46N   75 50w
Basle=Basel ..... 47 35N   7 35 E
Basoka .... 1 16N   23 40 E
Basque □ 42 50N   2 45w
Basra=Al Basrah . 30 30N   47 55 E
Bass Rock 56   5N   2 40w
Bass, Str. .... 39 15s 146 30 E
Bassano del
    Grappa ...... 45 45N   11 45 E
Bassari 9   9N   0 57 E
Bassas da
    India, I. 22   0s 39   0 E
Basse Terre 16   0N   61 40w
Bassein, Burma .. 16 45N   94 30 E
Basseterre 17 17N   62 43w
Bassett 42 37N   99 30w
Bassigny, Reg. .. 48   0N   5 10 E
Bastak .... 27 15N   54 25 E
Basti .... 26 52N   82 55 E
Bastia .... 42 40N   9 30 E
Bastogne 50   1N   5 43 E
Basutoland=
    Lesotho ■ ... 29 40s   28   0 E
Bat Yam 32   2N   34 44 E
Bata .... 1 57N   9 50 E
Bataan, Pen. .... 14 38N 120 30 E
Batabanó, G. de . 22 30N   82 30w
Batagoy .... 67 38N 134 38 E

Batalha 39 40N   8 50w
Batamay .... 63 30N 129 15 E
Batan Is. .... 20 25N 121 59 E
Batang .... 6 55s 109 40 E
Batangas .... 13 35N 121 10 E
Bataszék .... 46 12N   18 44 E
Batavia 43   0N   78 10w
Batchelor 13   4s 131   1 E
Batesville 35 48N   91 40w
Bath, U.K. 51 22N   2 22w
Bath, N.Y. 42 20N   77 17w
Bathgate 55 54N   3 38w
Bathurst=Banjul . 13 28N   16 40w
Bathurst,
    Australia ..... 33 25s 149 31 E
Bathurst, Canada . 47 37N   65 43w
Bathurst, C. 70 30N 128 30w
Bathurst, I.,
    Australia ..... 11 30s 130 10 E
Bathurst I., Canada 76 30N 130 10w
Bathurst Inlet ... 67 15N 108 30w
Bathurst Mines .. 47 30N   65 47w
Batinah, Reg. ... 24   0N   57   0 E
Batna .... 35 34N   6 15 E
Baton Rouge 30 30N   91   5w
Batouri .... 4 30N   14 25 E
Battambang 13   7N 103 12 E
Batticaloa .... 7 43N   81 45 E
Battir .... 31 44N   35   8 E
Battle .... 50 55N   0 30 E
Battle, R. 52 45N 108 15w
Battle Creek 42 20N   85 10w
Battle Harbour .. 52 13N   55 42w
Battle Mountain . 40 45N 117   0w
Battleford 52 45N 108 15w
Batu, Kep. ...... 0 30s 98 25 E
Batu Pahat= Bandar
    Penggaram .... 1 50N 102 56 E
Batumi .... 41 30N   41 30 E
Baturadja .... 4 11s 104 15 E
Baturité 4 28s 38 45w
Baubau .... 5 25s 123 50 E
Bauchi .... 10 22N   9 48 E
Bauchi □ .... 10 25N   10   0 E
Bauhinia Downs . 24 35s 149 18 E
Bauru 22 10s 49   0w
Baus 18 22s 5247½
Bautzen 51 11N   14 25w
Bavaria□=
    Bayern □ 49   7N   11 30 E

Bawdwin	23 5N	97 50 E
Bawean, I.	5 46S	112 35 E
Bawku	11 3N	0 19W
Bawlake	19 11N	97 21 E
Bay City, Mich.	43 35N	83 51W
Bay City, Tex.	28 59N	95 55W
Bay Shore	40 44N	73 15W
Bay View	3925N	176 50 E
Bayamón	18 24N	66 10W
Bayan	47 20N	107 55 E
Bayan Kara Shan, Mts.	34 0N	98 0 E
Bayan-Uul	49 6N	112 12 E
Bayanaul	50 45N	75 45 E
Bayantsogt	47 58N	105 1 E
Bayern □	49 7N	11 30 E
Bayeux	49 17N	0 42W
Baykal, Oz.	53 0N	108 0 E
Baykal, L.= Baykal, Oz.	53 0N	108 0 S
Baykir	61 50N	95 50 E
Baykonur	47 48N	65 50 E
Baynes Mts.	22 40S	12 50 E
Bayonne	43 30N	1 28 E
Bayreuth	49 56N	11 35 E
Bayrūt	33 53N	35 31 E
Bayt Aula	31 37N	35 2 E
Bayt Jālā	31 43N	35 11 E
Bayt Lahm	31 43N	35 12 E
Bayt Sāhūr	31 42N	35 13 E
Baytin	31 56N	35 14 E
Baytown	29 42N	94 57W
Baza	37 30N	2 47W
Bazaruto, I. do	21 40S	35 28 E
Beach	46 57N	104 0W
Beachy Hd.	50 44N	0 16 E
Beacon	30 20S	117 55 E
Beacon, U.S.A.	41 32N	73 58W
Beagle	55 0S	68 30W
Bealey	43 2S	171 36 E
Beardmore	49 36N	87 59W
Beardstown	40 0N	90 25W
Béarn, Reg	43 28N	0 36W
Beatrice	40 20N	96 40W
Beauceville	46 13N	70 46W
Beaudesert	27 59S	153 0 E
Beaufort, Malaysia	5 30N	115 40 E
Beaufort, Australia	37 25S	143 25 E
Beaufort, U.S.A.	34 45N	76 40W
Beaufort Sea	70 30N	146 0W
Beaufort West	32 18S	22 36 E
Beauharnois	45 20N	73 20W
Beaujolais, Reg.	46 0N	4 25 E
Beauly	57 29N	4 27W
Beaumaris	53 16N	4 7W
Beaumont	30 5N	94 8W
Beaune	47 2N	4 50 E
Beausejour	50 5N	96 35 E
Beauvais	49 25N	2 8 E
Beauval	55 9N	107 35W
Beaver, U.S.A.	66 40N	147 50W
Beaver Dam	43 28N	88 50W
Beaver Falls	40 44N	80 20W
Beawar	26 3N	74 18 E
Beccles	52 27N	1 33 E
Béchar	31 38N	2 18 E
Bechuanaland ■= Botswana ■	23 0S	24 0 E
Bechuanaland, Reg.= Betsjoeanaland, Reg.	26 30S	22 30 E
Beckley	37 50N	81 8W
Bedford, Canada	45 10N	73 0W
Bedford, S. Africa	32 40S	26 10 E
Bedford, U.K.	52 8N	0 29W
Bedford, Ohio	41 23N	81 32W
Bedford, Ind.	38 50N	86 30W
Bedford □	52 4N	0 28W
Bednesti	53 50N	123 10W
Bedourie	24 30S	139 30 E
Beenleigh	27 43S	153 10 E
Be'er Sheva	31 15N	34 48 E
Be'erotayim	32 19N	34 59 E
Beeston	52 55N	1 11W
Beeville	28 27N	97 44W
Bega	36 41S	149 51 E
Begoro	6 23N	0 23W
Behbehan	30 30N	50 15 E
Behshahr	36 45N	53 35 E
Beilen	52 52N	6 27 E
Beira	19 50S	34 52 E
Beira-Alta, Reg.	41 0N	7 20W
Beira-Baixa, Reg.	40 0N	7 30W
Beira Litoral, Reg.	40 0N	8 30W
Beirut=Bayrut	33 53N	35 31 E
Beit Hanun	31 32N	34 32 E
Beit'Ur et Tahta	31 54N	35 5 E
Beitbridge	22 12S	30 0 E
Beituniya	31 54N	35 10 E
Beja, Port.	38 2N	7 53W
Beja, Tunisia	36 10N	9 0 E
Béjaïa	36 42N	5 2 E
Békéscsaba	46 40N	21 10 E
Bekily	24 13S	45 19 E
Bekwai	6 25N	1 37W
Bela, India	25 50N	82 0 E
Bela, Pak.	26 12N	66 20 E
Bela Vista	17 0S	49 0W
Belawan	3 33N	98 32 E
Belaya Tserkov	49 45N	30 10 E
Belcher Is.	56 20N	79 20W
Belebey	54 72N	54 7 E
Belém	1 20S	48 30W
Belén	27 40S	67 5W
Belen	34 40N	106 50W
Belet Uen	4 30N	45 5 E
Belfast, S. Afr.	25 42S	30 2 E
Belfast, U.K.	54 35N	5 56W
Belfast, U.S.A.	44 30N	69 0W
Belfast, L.	54 40N	5 50W
Belfast □	54 35N	5 56W
Belfort	47 38N	6 50 E
Belfort, Terr. de □	47 38N	6 52 E
Belgaum	15 55N	74 35 E
Belgium ■	51 30N	5 0 E
Belgooly	51 44N	8 30W
Belgorod	50 35N	36 35 E
Belgorod-Dnestrovskiy	46 11N	30 23 E
Belgrade= Beograd	44 50N	20 37 E
Belitung, Pulau, I.	3 10S	107 50 E
Belize ■	17 0N	88 30W
Belize City	17 25N	88 0W
Bell Ville	32 40S	62 40W
Bella Coola	52 25N	126 40W
Bella Vista	28 33S	59 0W
Bellaire	40 1N	80 46W
Bellary	15 10N	76 56 E
Bellata	29 53S	149 46 E
Belle I.	47 20N	3 10W
Belle I., Str. of	51 30N	56 30W
Belle Fourche	44 43N	103 52W
Belle Glade	26 43N	80 38W
Bellefontaine	40 20N	83 45 E
Belleville, Canada	44 15N	77 37W
Belleville, U.S.A.	38 30N	90 0W
Bellevue	46 35N	84 10W
Bellin	60 0N	70 0W
Bellingen	30 25S	152 50 E
Bellingham	48 45N	122 27W
Bellingshausen Sea	66 0S	80 0W
Bellinzona	46 11N	9 1 E
Bellows Falls	43 10N	72 30W
Belluno	46 8N	12 6 E
Bélmez	38 17N	5 17W
Belmont	33 4S	151 42 E
Belmonte, Brazil	16 0S	39 0W
Belmopan	17 18N	88 30W
Belmullet	54 13N	9 58W
Belo Horizonte	19 55S	43 56W
Belogorsk	51 0N	128 20 E
Beloit	42 35N	89 0W
Belomorsk	64 35N	34 30 E
Beloretsk	53 58N	58 24 E
Belo-sur-Tsiribihina	19 40S	44 30 E
Belovo	54 30N	86 0 E
Beloye, Oz.	60 10N	37 35 E
Beloye More	66 0N	38 0 E
Belozersk	60 0N	37 30 E
Belsty	47 48N	28 0 E
Beltana	30 48S	138 25 E
Belterra	2 45S	55 0W
Belton	31 4N	97 30W
Belturbet	54 6N	7 28W
Belvidere	42 15N	88 55W
Belyy Os.	73 30N	71 0 E
Belyy Yar	58 26N	84 30 E
Bemidji	47 30N	94 50W
Ben Cruachan, Mt.	56 26N	5 8W
Ben Gardane	33 11N	11 11 E
Ben Hope, Mt.	58 24N	4 36W
Ben Lawers, Mt.	56 33N	4 13W
Ben Lomond, Mt., Australia	30 1S	151 43 E
Ben Lomond, Mt., U.K.	56 12N	4 39W
Ben Macdhui, Mt.	57 4N	3 40W
Ben More, Mt.	56 26N	6 2W
Ben More Assynt, Mt.	58 7N	4 51W
Ben Nevis, Mt.	56 48N	5 0W
Ben Wyvis, Mt.	57 40N	4 35W
Bena	11 20N	5 50 E
Bena Dibele	4 4S	22 50 E
Benalla	36 30S	146 0 E
Benares=Varanasi	25 22N	83 8 E
Benbecula, I.	57 26N	7 20W
Benbonyathe Hill	30 25S	139 11 E
Bencubbin	30 48S	117 52 E
Bend	44 2N	121 15W
Bendel □	6 0N	5 40 E
Bender Beila	9 30N	50 48 E
Bendering	32 23S	118 18 E
Bendery	46 50N	29 50 E
Bendigo	36 40S	144 15 E
Bene Beraq	32 5N	34 50 E
Benenitra	23 27S	45 5 E
Benevento	41 7N	14 45 E
Bengal, B. of	15 0N	90 0 E
Benghazi= Banghazi	32 11N	20 3 E
Bengkalis	1 30N	102 10 E
Bengkulu	3 50S	102 12 E
Bengkulu □	3 50S	102 10 E
Bengough	49 25N	105 10W
Benguela	12 37S	13 25 E
Beni	32 11S	148 43 E
Beni Mazar	28 32N	30 44 E
Beni Mellal	32 21N	6 21W
Benī Suēf	29 5N	31 6 E
Benidorm	38 33N	0 9W
Benin ■	8 0N	2 0 E
Benin, B. of	5 0N	3 0 E
Benin City	6 20N	5 31 E
Benjamin Constant	4 40S	70 15W
Benlidi	24 35S	144 50 E
Bennettsville	34 38N	79 39W
Bennington	42 52N	73 12W
Benoni	26 11S	28 18 E
Benson	31 59N	110 19W
Benteng	6 10S	120 30 E
Benton, Ark.	34 30N	92 35W
Benton, Ill.	38 0N	88 55W
Benton Harbor	42 10N	86 28W
Benue, R.	7 47N	6 45 E
Benue □	7 20N	8 20 E
Beograd	44 50N	20 37 E
Beppu	33 15N	131 30 E
Ber Dagan	32 1N	34 49 E
Berati	40 43N	19 59 E
Berber	18 0N	34 0 E

Berbera .... 10 30N 45 2 E
Berbérati .... 4 15N 15 40 E
Berdicher .... 49 57N 28 30 E
Berdsk .... 54 47N 83 2 E
Berdyansk .... 46 45N 36 50 E
Bereda .... 11 45N 51 0 E
Berekum 7 29N 2 34W
Berens River 52 25N 97 0W
Berevo .... 19 44S 44 58 E
Berezniki .... 59 24N 56 46 E
Berezovo .... 64 0N 65 0 E
Bérgamo .... 45 42N 9 40 E
Bergen, Neth. .... 52 40N 4 42 E
Bergen, Norway ... 60 23N 5 27 E
Bergen-op-Zoom . 51 30N 4 18 E
Bergerac .... 44 51N 0 30 E
Bergum .... 53 13N 5 59 E
Berhampore ..... 24 2N 88 27 E
Berhampur ...... 19 15N 84 54 E
Bering Sea 59 0N 175 0W
Bering Str. 66 0N 170 0W
Beringen .... 51 3N 5 14 E
Beringovskiy .... 63 3N 179 19 E
Berja 36 50N 2 56W
Berkeley 38 0N 122 20W
Berkner I. 79 30S 50 0W
Berkshire □ 51 30N 1 20W
Berlin, Germany .. 52 32N 13 24 E
Berlin, U.S.A. 44 29N 7 36W
Bermejo, R. 26 51S 58 23W
Bermuda, I. 32 45N 65 0W
Bern .... 46 57N 7 28 E
Bernalilo 35 17N 106 37W
Bernardo de
  Irigoyen 26 15S 53 40W
Bernburg .... 51 48N 11 44 E
Bernier, I. ...... 24 50S 113 12 E
Bernina, Piz .... 46 20N 9 54 E
Beroun .... 49 57N 14 5 E
Berowra .... 33 35S 151 12 E
Berrechid 33 18N 7 36W
Berri .... 34 14S 140 35 E
Berrigan .... 35 38S 145 49 E
Berry, Reg. ..... 47 0N 2 0 E
Bertoua .... 4 30N 13 45 E
Berwick 41 4N 76 17W
Berwick-upon-
  Tweed 55 47N 2 0W
Berwyn Mts. 52 54N 3 26W
Besalampy ...... 16 43S 44 29 E

Besançon .... 47 9N 6 0 E
Beskids, Mts.=
  Vychodné
  Beskydy ...... 49 30N 22 0 E
Bessemer 46 27N 90 0W
Bessin, Reg. 49 21N 1 0W
Bet Ha 'Emeq ... 32 58N 35 8 E
Bet Ha Shitta ... 32 31N 35 27 E
Bet Ha'tmeq .... 32 58N 35 8 E
Bet Oren .... 32 43N 34 59 E
Bet Qeshet ..... 32 41N 35 21 E
Be't She'an .... 32 30N 35 30 E
Bet Shemesh .... 31 45N 35 0 E
Bet Yosef ...... 32 34N 35 33 E
Betafo .... 19 50S 46 51 E
Bétaré-Oya ..... 5 40N 14 5 E
Bethal .... 26 27S 29 28 E
Bethanien ...... 26 31S 17 8 E
Bethany=
  Eizariya ...... 31 47N 35 15 E
Bethlehem,
  Jordan=
  Bayt Lahm .... 31 43N 35 12 E
Bethlehem,
  S. Africa ...... 28 14S 28 18 E
Bethlehem, U.S.A. 40 39N 75 24W
Bethulie .... 30 30S 25 29 E
Betioky .... 23 48S 44 20 E
Betoota .... 25 40S 140 42 E
Betroka .... 23 16S 46 6 E
Betsjoeanaland,
  Reg. .... 26 30S 22 30 B
Bettiah .... 26 48N 84 33 E
Betul .... 21 48N 77 59 E
Betung .... 2 0S 103 10 E
Beulah, Australia . 35 58S 142 29 E
Beulah, Canada .. 50 16N 101 2W
Beverley,
  Australia ...... 32 9S 116 56 E
Beverley, U.K. ... 53 52N 0 26W
Beverly 53 36N 113 21W
Beverly Hills 34 4N 118 29W
Beverwijk ...... 52 28N 4 38 E
Beyla 8 30N 8 38W
Bexhill .... 50 51N 0 29 E
Beyneu .... 45 10N 55 3 E
Beypazari ...... 40 10N 31 48 E
Beyşehir Gölü, L. . 37 40N 31 45 E
Bezet .... 33 4N 35 8 E
Bezhitsa .... 53 19N 34 17 E

Béziers .... 43 20N 3 12 E
Bhachau 23 10N 70 15W
Bhadgaon .... 27 42N 85 27 E
Bhadrakh .... 21 10N 86 30 E
Bhagalpur ...... 25 10N 87 0 E
Bhamo .... 24 15N 97 15 E
Bhandara .... 21 5N 79 42 E
Bhanrer Ra. ..... 23 40N 79 45 E
Bharatpur ...... 27 15N 77 30 E
Bharuch .... 21 47N 73 0 E
Bhatinda .... 30 15N 74 57 E
Bhatpara .... 22 50N 88 25 E
Bhavnagar ...... 21 45N 72 10 E
Bhilwara .... 25 25N 74 38 E
Bhima, R. ...... 17 20N 76 30 E
Bhimavaram ..... 16 30N 81 30 E
Bhind .... 26 30N 78 46 E
Bhiwandi .... 19 15N 73 0 E
Bhiwani .... 28 50N 76 9 E
Bhopal .... 23 20N 77 53 E
Bhubaneswar ... 20 15N 85 50 E
Bhusaval .... 21 1N 75 56 E
Bhutan ■ .... 27 25N 89 50 E
Biafra, B. of=
  Bonny, B. of .. 4 0N 8 0 E
Biała Podlaska ... 52 4N 23 6 E
Białystok .... 53 10N 23 10 E
Biarritz 43 29N 1 33W
Biberach .... 48 5N 9 49 E
Bibiani 6 30N 2 8W
Bic 48 20N 68 41W
Bida .... 9 3N 5 58 E
Bicester 51 53N 1 9W
Bidar .... 17 55N 77 35 E
Biddeford .... 43 30N 70 28 E
Bideford 51 1N 4 13W
* Bié .... 12 22S 16 55 E
Bié Plat. .... 12 0S 16 0 E
Bieber 41 4N 121 6W
Biel .... 47 8N 7 14 E
Bielé Karpaty,
  Mts. .... 49 5N 18 0 E
Bielefeld .... 52 2N 8 31 E
Biella .... 45 33N 8 3 E
Bielsko-Biała .... 49 50N 19 8 E
Biên Hoa .... 10 57N 106 49 E
Big Beaver House . 52 59N 89 50W
Big Bend Nat.
  Park 29 15N 103 15W
Big Delta 64 15N 145 0W

Big Rapids 43 42N 85 27W
Big River 53 50N 107 0W
Big Salmon 61 50N 136 0W
Big Spring 32 10N 101 25W
Big Stone Gap ... 36 52N 82 45W
Big Trout L. 53 40N 90 0W
Biggar, Canada .. 52 10N 108 0W
Biggar, U.K. 55 38N 3 31W
Bigge, I. .... 14 35S 125 10 E
Biggenden ...... 25 31S 152 4 E
Bighorn Mts. 44 30N 107 20W
Bigorre, Reg. .... 43 5N 0 2 E
Bigtimber 45 33N 110 0W
Bihác .... 44 49N 15 57 E
Bihar .... 25 5N 85 40 E
Bihar □ .... 25 0N 86 0 E
Biharamulo ..... 2 25S 31 25 E
Bijagos,
  Arquipélago dos 11 15N 16 10W
Bijapur .... 16 50N 75 55 E
Bijnor .... 29 27N 78 11 E
Bikaner .... 28 2N 73 18 E
Bikin .... 46 50N 134 20 E
Bilara .... 26 14N 73 53 E
Bilaspur .... 22 2N 82 15 E
Bilbao 43 16N 2 56W
Bilecik .... 40 5N 30 5 E
Bilibino .... 68 3N 166 20 E
Bilir .... 65 40N 131 20 E
Billabong ...... 27 25S 115 49 E
Billiluna ...... 19 37S 127 41 E
Billingham 54 36N 1 18W
Billings 45 43N 108 29W
Bilma .... 18 50N 13 30 E
Biloela .... 24 34S 150 31 E
Biloxi 30 30N 89 0W
Biltine .... 14 40N 20 50 E
Bilyana .... 18 5S 145 50 E
Bima .... 8 22S 118 49 E
Bina-Etawah ... 24 13N 78 14 E
Binalbagan ..... 10 12N 122 50 E
Binatang ...... 2 10N 111 40 E
Binbee .... 20 19S 147 56 E
Binche .... 50 26N 4 10 E
Bindi Bindi .... 30 37S 116 22 E
Bindura .... 17 18S 31 18 E
Bingara, N.S.W. . 29 40S 150 40 E
Bingara, Queens. . 25 0S 149 10 E
Bingham Canyon . 40 31N 112 10W
Binghamton 42 9N 75 54W

Binh Son .... 15 20N 104 40 E
Binjai .... 3 50N 98 30 E
Binyamina ...... 32 32N 34 56 E
Binzerte .... 37 15N 9 50 E
Bir Atrun .... 18 15N 26 40 E
Bir Nabala ...... 31 52N 35 12 E
Bîr Shalatein .... 23 5N 35 25 E
Bir Zeit .... 31 59N 35 11 E
Birch Hills 53 10N 105 10W
Birchip .... 35 52S 143 0 E
Bird, I. .... 22 20S 155 20 E
Birdsville .... 25 51S 139 20 E
Birdum .... 15 50S 133 0 E
Bireuen .... 5 14N 96 39 E
Bırjand .... 32 57N 59 10 E
Birkenhead 53 24N 3 1W
Bîrlad .... 46 15N 27 38 E
Birmingham, U.K. . 52 30N 1 55W
Birmingham,
  U.S.A. 33 31N 86 50W
Birni Ngaouré ... 13 5N 2 51 E
Birni Nkonni .... 13 55N 5 15 E
Birnin Gwari .... 11 0N 6 45 E
Birnin-Kebbi .... 12 32N 4 12 E
Birnin Kuku .... 11 30N 9 29 E
Birobidzhan .... 48 50N 132 50 E
Birr 53 7N 7 55W
Birtle 50 30N 101 5W
Bisbee 31 30N 110 0W
Biscay, B. of ... 45 0N 2 0W
Bishop 37 20N 118 26W
Bishop Auckland . 54 40N 1 40W
Bishop's Falls .. 49 2N 55 24W
Bishop's
  Stortford ..... 51 52N 0 11 E
Biskra .... 34 50N 5 23 E
Bismarck 46 49N 100 49W
Bismark Arch. .. 3 30S 148 30 E
Bispfors .... 63 2N 16 40 E
Bissau 11 45N 15 45W
Bissett 51 18N 95 43W
Bistrita .... 47 9N 24 35 E
Bistrita, R. .... 46 30N 26 57 E
Bitola .... 41 5N 21 21 E
Bitterfontein ... 31 0S 18 32 E
Bitterroot Ra. .. 46 0N 114 20W
Bittou 11 17N 0 18W
Biu .... 10 40N 12 3 E
Biwa-Ko, L. .... 35 15N 135 45 E
Biysk .... 52 40N 85 0 E

* Renamed Kuito

Bizen .... 34 44N 134 9 E
Bizerte=Binzerte .. 37 15N 9 50 E
Bjelovar .... 45 56N 16 49 E
Black Forest=
  Schwarzwald .... 48 0N 8 0 E
Black Hills, Mts ... 44 0N 103 50w
Black Mts........ 51 52N 3 50w
Black Sea .... 43 30N 35 0 E
Black Volta, R. ... 8 41N 1 33w
Blackall .... 24 26 s 145 27 E
Blackbull .... 18 0 s 141 7 E
Blackfoot 43 13N 112 12w
Blackheath ...... 33 39 s 150 17 E
Blackpool 53 48N 3 3w
Blacks Harbour ... 45 3N 66 49w
Blackville 47 5N 65 58w
Blackwater ...... 23 35 s 149 0 E
Blackwater, R.,
  Cork 51 51N 7 50w
Blackwater, R.,
  Dungannon 54 31N 6 34w
Blackwater, R.,
  Meath 53 39N 6 43w
Blackwell 36 55N 97 20w
Blaenau
  Ffestiniog ... 53 0N 3 57w
Blagodarnoye .... 45 7N 43 37 E
Blagoveshchensk .. 50 20N 127 30 E
Blaine Lake 52 51N 106 52w
Blair Atholl,
  Australia ..... 22 42 s 147 31 E
Blair Atholl, U.K. .. 56 46N 3 50w
Blairgowrie 56 36N 3 20w
Blairmore 49 40N 114 25w
Blanc, C.=
  Ras Nouadhibou 37 15N 9 56 E
Blanc, Mt. .... 45 50N 6 52 E
Blanca, B. 39 10s 61 30w
Blanca Pk. 37 35N 105 29w
Blanco .... 33 57s 22 24 E
Blandford 50 52N 2 10w
Blanding 37 35N 109 30w
Blantyre .... 15 45s 35 0 E
Blarney 51 57N 8 35w
Blåvands Huk .... 55 33N 8 5 E
Blaydon 54 56N 1 47w
Blayney .... 33 32 s 149 14 E
Bleiburg .... 46 35N 14 49 E
Blekinge □ .... 56 15N 15 15 E

Blenheim .... 41 38 s 174 5 E
Bletchley 51 59N 0 54w
Blida .... 36 30N 2 49 E
Blind River 46 15N 83 0w
Blitar .... 8 5 s 112 11 E
Blitta .... 8 23N 1 6 E
Block I. 41 13N 71 35w
Bloemfontein .... 29 6s 26 14 E
Bloemhof .... 27 38 s 25 32 E
Blois .... 47 35N 1 20 E
Bloomington, Ill. .. 40 25N 89 0w
Bloomington, Ind. . 39 10N 86 30w
Bloomsburg 41 0N 76 30w
Blue Island 41 40N 87 41w
Blue Mud, B. .... 13 30 s 136 0 E
Blue Mts. 45 15N 119 0w
Blue Nile, R.=
  Nîl el Azraq, R. .. 10 30N 35 0 E
Blue Ridge, Mts ... 36 30N 80 15w
Bluefield 37 18N 81 14w
Bluefields 12 0N 83 50w
Bluff, Australia ... 23 40 s 149 0 E
Bluff, N.Z. ...... 46 36 s 168 21 E
Bluff Knoll, Mt. ... 34 23 s 118 20 E
Bluffton 40 43N 85 9w
Blumenau .... 27 0 s 49 0w
Blyth 55 8N 1 32w
Blythe 33 40N 114 33w
Blytheville 35 56N 89 55w
Bo 7 55N 11 50w
Boa Vista 2 48N 60 30w
Boaco 12 29N 85 35w
Boali .... 4 48N 18 7 E
Bobadilla 36 58N 5 10w
Bobbili .... 18 35N 83 30 E
Bobcaygeon 44 33N 78 35w
Bobo-Dioulasso ... 11 8N 4 13w
Bobruysk .... 53 10N 29 15 E
Bocaiuva 17 7s 43 49w
Bocas del Toro ... 9 15N 82 20w
Bocholt .... 51 50N 6 35 E
Bochum .... 51 28N 7 12 E
Boda .... 4 19N 17 26 E
Bodaybo .... 57 50N 114 0 E
Boddington ..... 32 50 s 116 30 E
Boden .... 65 50N 21 42 E
Bodensee, L. .... 47 35N 9 25 E
Bodhan .... 18 40N 77 55 E
Bodinga .... 12 58N 5 10 E
Bodmin 50 28N 4 44w

Bodmin Moor, Reg. 50 33N 4 36w
Bodø .... 67 17N 14 27 E
Bodrog, R. ...... 48 15N 21 35 E
Bogalusa 30 50N 89 55w
Bogan Gate ..... 33 6s 147 44 E
Bogantungan .... 23 41 s 147 17 E
Bogenfels ...... 27 25 s 15 25 E
Boggabri .... 30 45 s 150 0 E
Bognor Regis ... 50 47N 0 40w
Bogor .... 6 36 s 106 48 E
Bogorodskoye ... 52 22N 140 30 E
Bogota 4 34N 74 0w
Bogotal .... 56 15N 89 50 E
Bogra .... 24 26N 89 22 E
Boguchany ...... 58 40N 97 30 E
Bohemia □ ...... 49 50N 14 0 E
Bohemian Forest=
  Böhmerwald .... 14 30N 12 40 E
Böhmerwald, Mts.. 49 30N 12 40 E
Bohol, I. .... 9 58N 124 20 E
Bohotleh .... 8 20N 46 25 E
Boi .... 9 34N 9 27 E
Boiestown 46 27N 66 26w
Boise 43 43N 116 9w
Boissevain 49 15N 100 0w
Bojonegoro ..... 7 9s 111 52 E
Boju .... 7 22N 7 55 E
Boké 10 56N 14 17w
Bokkos .... 9 19N 9 1 E
Bokna, Fd. ...... 59 12N 5 30 E
Bokote .... 0 12s 21 8 E
Bokpyin .... 11 18N 98 42 E
Bol, Kuh-e ...... 30 40N 52 45 E
Bolama 11 30N 15 30w
Bolan Pass ..... 29 50N 67 20 E
Bolangir .... 20 42N 83 20 E
Bolbec .... 49 30N 0 30 E
Bolgatanga 10 44N 0 53w
Bolívar, Arg. 36 2s 60 53w
Bolívar, Col. 2 0N 77 0w
Bolivia ■ 17 6s 64 0w
Bolivian Plat. ... 19 0s 69 0w
Bollnäs .... 61 20N 16 28 E
Bologna .... 44 30N 11 20 E
Bologoye .... 57 55N 34 0 E
Bolsena, L. di ... 42 35N 11 55 E
Bolshevik, Os. ... 78 30N 102 0 E
Bolshoi Kavkaz .. 42 50N 44 0 E
Bolshoy Atlym .. 62 25N 66 50 E
Bolshoy Shantar,Os. 55 0N 137 42 E

Bolton 53 35N 2 26w
Bolzano .... 46 30N 11 20 E
Bom Despacho .. 19 46 s 45 15w
Bom Jesus da Lapa 13 15s 43 30w
Boma .... 5 50 s 13 4 E
Bomaderry ..... 34 52 s 150 37 E
Bomadi .... 5 9N 6 0 E
Bombala .... 36 56 s 149 15 E
Bombay .... 18 55N 72 50 E
Bomboma ...... 2 25N 18 55 E
Bomda .... 29 59N 96 25 E
Bon, C. .... 37 1N 11 2 E
Bonaire, I........ 12 10N 68 15w
Bonaparte Arch. .. 15 0 s 124 30 E
Bonaventure 48 5N 63 32w
Bonavista 48 40N 53 5w
Bonavista B. 48 58N 53 25w
Bondoukoro 9 51N 4 25w
Bondoukou 8 2N 2 47w
Bondowoso ..... 7 56 s 113 49 E
Bone, Teluk, G... 4 10 s 120 50 E
Bo'ness 56 0N 3 38w
Bongor .... 10 35N 15 20 E
Bonham 33 30N 96 10w
Bonifacio ...... 41 24N 9 10 E
Bonifacio,
  Bouches de ... 41 23N 9 10 E
Bonn .... 50 43N 7 6 E
Bonners Ferry .. 48 38N 116 21w
Bonnie Rock ... 30 29 s 118 22 E
Bonny, R. ...... 4 20N 7 10 E
Bonny, B. of .... 4 0N 8 0 E
Bonnyville 54 20N 110 45w
Bontang .... 0 10N 117 30 E
Bonthain ...... 5 34 s 119 56 E
Boom .... 51 6N 4 20 E
Boonah .... 28 0 s 152 35 E
Boone 42 5N 93 46w
Boonville, Ind. .. 38 3N 87 13w
Boonville, Mo. .. 38 57N 92 45w
Boonville, N.Y. .. 43 31N 75 20w
Boothia, G. of ... 70 0N 90 0w
Boothia Pen. ... 70 30N 95 0w
Bootle 53 28N 3 1w
Boué .... 0 5N 11 55 E
Bopeechee ..... 29 35 s 137 30 E
Borås .... 57 42N 13 1 E
Borba 4 12s 59 34w
Bordeaux 44 50N 0 36w
Borden, Australia . 34 3s 118 12 E

Borden, Canada ... 46 18N 63 47w
Borders □ 55 30N 3 0w
Bordertown ...... 36 14 s 140 58 E
Borger, Neth. .... 52 54N 7 33 E
Borger, U.S.A. ... 35 40N 101 20w
Borgholm .... 56 54N 16 48 E
Borisoglebsk .... 51 27N 42 5 E
Borisov .... 54 17N 28 28 E
Borja .... 4 20 s 77 40w
Borkou .... 18 15N 18 50 E
Borlänge .... 60 28N 14 33 E
Borneo, I. ...... 1 0N 115 0 E
Bornholm, I. .... 55 8N 14 55 E
Borno □ .... 12 0N 12 0 E
Bornu Yassu .... 12 14N 12 25 E
Borogontsy ..... 62 42N 131 8 E
Boromo 11 45N 2 58w
Borovichi ...... 58 25N 33 55 E
Borroloola ...... 16 4 s 136 17 E
Borsod-Abaúj-
  Zemplén □ .... 48 20N 21 0 E
Borujerd .... 33 55N 48 50 E
Borzya .... 50 24N 116 31 E
Bosa .... 40 17N 8 32 E
Bosanska
  Gradiška ..... 45 9N 17 15 E
Bosaso .... 11 13N 49 8 E
Boscastle 50 42N 4 42w
Boshof .... 28 31 s 25 13 E
Bosna, R. ...... 45 4N 18 29 E
Bosna i
  Hercegovina □ .. 44 0N 18 0 E
Bosporus, Str.=
  Karadeniz
  Boğazi .... 41 10N 29 5 E
Bossangoa ..... 6 35N 17 30 E
Bossier City 32 28N 93 38w
Bosso .... 13 30N 13 15 E
Boston, U.K. 52 59N 0 2w
Boston, U.S.A. .. 42 20N 71 0w
Botany B. ...... 34 2 s 151 6 E
Bothaville ...... 27 23 s 26 34 E
Bothnia, G. ..... 63 0N 21 0 E
Bothwell 42 37N 81 54w
Botletle, R. ..... 20 10 s 24 10 E
Botoşani .... 47 42N 26 41 E
Botswana ■ .... 23 0 s 24 0 E
Botucatu ...... 22 55 s 48 30w
Botwood 49 6N 55 23w
Bou Saâda ..... 35 11N 4 9 E

Bouaké 7 40N 5 2w
Bouar .... 6 0N 15 40 E
Bouârfa .... 32 32N 1 58 E
Bouches-du-Rhône 43 37N 5 2 E
Bougainville, C. . 13 57 s 126 4 E
Bougouni 11 30N 7 20w
Boukombé .... 10 11N 1 6 E
Boulder 40 3N 105 10w
Boulder City 36 0N 114 58w
Boulia .... 22 52 s 139 51 E
Boulogne-sur-Mer . 50 42N 1 36 E
Boulsa 12 39N 0 34w
Bouna 9 10N 3 0N
Bountiful 40 57N 111 58w
Bourbonnais, Reg. 46 28N 3 0 E
Bourem 17 0N 0 24w
Bourg en Bresse . 46 13N 5 12 E
Bourges .... 47 5N 2 22 E
Bourgogne, Reg. . 47 0N 4 30 E
Bourke .... 30 8 s 145 55 E
Bourlamaque 48 5N 77 56w
Bournemouth 50 43N 1 53w
Bouvet, I. ...... 55 0 s 3 30 E
Bow Island 49 50N 111 23w
Bowelling ..... 33 25 s 116 30 E
Bowen .... 20 0 s 148 16 E
Bowie 32 15N 109 30w
Bowland Forest .. 54 0N 2 30w
Bowling Green, Ky. 37 0N 86 25w
Bowling Green,
  Ohio 41 22N 83 40w
Bowling Green, C. 19 19 s 147 25 E
Bowman 46 12N 103 21w
Bowmanville 43 55N 78 40w
Bowmore 55 45N 6 18w
Bowness 50 55N 114 25w
Bowser ...... 36 19 s 146 23 E
Bowsman 52 15N 101 12w
Boxtel .... 51 36N 5 9 E
Boyle 53 58N 8 19w
Boyne, R. 53 40N 6 34w
Boyoma, Chutes . 0 12N 25 25 E
Boyup Brook ... 33 47 s 116 40 E
Bozeman 45 40N 111 0w
Bozoum .... 6 25N 16 35 E
Brabant □ .... 49 15N 5 20 E
Brac, I. .... 43 20N 16 40 E
Bracebridge 45 5N 79 20w
Bräcke .... 62 42N 15 32 E
Brad .... 46 10N 22 50 E

Bradenton 27 25N 82 35w
Bradford, U.K. .. 53 47N 1 45w
Bradford, U.S.A. .. 41 58N 78 41w
Bradore Bay 51 27N 57 18w
Brady 31 8N 99 25w
Braemar 57 2N 3 20w
Braga 41 35N 8 32w
Bragança, Brazil .. 1 0 s 47 2w
Bragança, Port. .. 41 48N 6 50w
Brahmanbaria ... 23 50N 91 15 E
Brahmani, R. ... 21 0N 85 15 E
Brahmaputra, R. . 26 30N 93 30 E
Braich-y-Pwll, Pt. . 52 47N 4 46w
Brăila ...... 45 19N 27 59 E
Brainerd 46 20N 94 10w
Braintree ...... 51 53N 0 34 E
Brak, R. .... 29 35 s 22 55 E
Bralorne 50 50N 123 15w
Brampton 43 42N 79 46w
Branco, R. 1 30N 61 15w
Brandenburg ... 52 24N 12 33 E
Brandon 49 50N 100 0w
Brandvlei ..... 30 25 s 20 30 E
Braniewo ...... 54 25N 19 50 E
Brańsk .... 52 45N 22 51 E
Brantford 43 15N 80 15w
Branxholme ... 37 52 s 141 49 E
Brasília ...... 15 55 s 47 40w
Brasilia Legal .. 3 45 s 55 40w
Braşov .... 45 7N 25 39 E
Brasschaat ... 51 19N 4 27 E
Bratislava .... 48 10N 17 7 E
Bratsk .... 56 10N 101 3 E
Brattleboro ... 42 53N 72 37w
Braunschweig . 52 17N 10 28 E
Braunton 51 6N 4 9w
Brava .... 1 20N 44 8 E
Brawley 32 58N 115 30w
Bray 53 12N 6 6w
Bray, Reg. ..... 49 40N 1 40 E
Brazil ■ .... 10 0 s 50 0w
Brazil 39 30N 87 8w
Brazilian
  Highlands, Mts. . 18 0 s 46 30w
Brazol, R. 30 30N 96 20w
Brazzaville ... 4 9 s 15 12 E
Breadalbane .. 23 48 s 139 33 E
Breadalbane, Reg. . 56 30N 4 15w
Bream, B. .... 35 56 s 174 35 E
Bream Head ... 35 51 s 174 36 E

Brebes .... 6 52 s 109 3 E
Brechin 56 44N 2 40w
Breckenridge ... 32 48N 98 55w
Breckland, Reg. . 52 30N 0 40 E
Brecon 51 57N 3 23w
Brecon Beacons,
  Mts. 51 53N 3 27w
Breda .... 51 35N 4 45 E
Bredasdorp ... 34 33 s 20 2 E
Bredbo ..... 35 58 s 149 10 E
Bregenz ...... 47 30N 9 45 E
Breidafjördur .. 65 20N 23 0w
Brejo .... 3 41 s 42 50w
Bremen ...... 53 4N 8 47 E
Bremerhaven .. 53 34N 8 35 E
Bremerton 47 30N 122 48w
Brenham 30 5N 96 27w
Brenner P. .... 47 0N 11 30 E
Brent, Canada .. 46 0N 78 30w
Brent, U.K. ... 51 33N 0 18w
Brentwood ... 51 37N 0 19w
Bréscia ...... 45 33N 10 13 E
Breslau = Wrocław . 51 5N 17 5 E
Bressanone ... 46 43N 11 40 E
Bressay, I. 60 10N 1 5w
Bresse, Reg. .. 46 20N 5 10 E
Brest, Fr. 48 24N 4 31w
Brest, U.S.S.R. .. 52 10N 23 40 E
Bretagne, Reg. . 48 0N 3 0w
Bretçu .... 46 7N 26 18 E
Brett, C. ..... 35 10 s 174 20 E
Breves .... 1 38 s 50 25w
Brewarrina ... 30 0 s 146 51 E
Brewer 44 43N 68 50w
Brewton 31 9N 87 2w
Breyten ..... 26 16 s 30 0 E
Bria .... 6 30N 21 58 E
Briançon .... 44 54N 6 39 E
*Brickaville .... 18 49 s 49 4 E
Bridgend 51 30N 3 35w
Bridgeport ... 41 12N 73 12w
Bridgeton 39 29N 75 10w
Bridgetown,
  Australia ...... 33 58 s 116 7 E
Bridgetown,
  Barbados 13 0N 59 30w
Bridgewater, Can. . 44 55N 65 12w
Bridgwater,
  Australia ...... 36 36 s 143 59 E
Bridgwater, Can. . 44 25N 64 31w

Bridgnorth 52 33N 2 25w
Bridgwater 51 7N 3 0w
Bridlington 54 4N 0 10w
Bridport 50 43N 2 45w
Brie, Reg. .... 48 35N 3 10 E
Brig .... 46 18N 7 59 E
Brigg 53 33N 0 30w
Brigham City ... 41 30N 112 1w
Brighton,
  Australia ...... 35 1 s 138 30 E
Brighton,
  Canada 44 3N 77 44w
Brighton, U.K. .. 50 50N 0 9w
Brindisi .... 40 39N 17 55 E
Brisbane .... 27 25 s 152 54 E
Bristol, U.K. .. 51 26N 2 35w
Bristol, U.S.A. .. 41 44N 72 37w
Bristol B. 58 0N 159 0w
Bristol Chan. .. 51 18N 3 30w
Bristow 35 5N 96 28w
British Antarctic
  Terr. ...... 66 0 s 45 0w
British
  Columbia □ ... 55 0N 125 15w
British
  Honduras ■ =
  Belize ■ 17 0N 88 30w
British Is. 55 0N 4 0w
Brits ...... 25 37 s 27 48 E
Britstown ... 30 37 s 23 30 E
Britt 45 46N 80 35w
Brittany, Reg. =
  Bretagne, Reg. . 48 0N 3 0w
Britton 45 50N 97 47w
Brixton ...... 23 32 s 144 52 E
Brno .... 49 10N 16 35 E
Broad Arrow ... 30 23 s 121 15 E
Broad Law, Mt. . 55 30N 3 22w
Broadford .... 37 14 s 145 4 E
Broads, The ... 52 30N 1 15 E
Brock 51 27N 108 42w
Brocken, Mt. .. 51 48N 10 40 E
Brockton 42 8N 71 2w
Brockville ... 44 37N 75 38w
Brod .... 41 35N 21 17 E
Brodeur Pen. .. 72 0N 88 0w
Brodick 55 34N 5 9w
Broken Bow .. 41 25N 99 35w
Broken Hill .. 31 58 s 141 29 E
Bromley .... 51 20N 0 5 E

Brönderslev ..... 57 17N 9 55 E
Brong-Ahafo □ ... 7 50N 2 0w
Bronkhorstspruit .. 25 46 s 28 45 E
Bronte Pk. .... 42 8 s 146 30 E
Brookfield 39 50N 92 50w
Brookhaven ... 31 40N 90 25w
Brookings 44 19N 96 48w
Brooks Ra. ... 68 40N 147 0w
Brookton .... 32 22N 116 57 E
Brookville ... 41 10N 79 6w
Broom, L. .... 57 55N 5 15 E
Broome ..... 18 0 s 122 15w
Broomehill ... 33 40 s 117 36 E
Brora 58 0N 3 50w
Brosna, R. 53 8N 8 0w
Broughton I. .. 67 35N 63 50w
Broughty Ferry . 56 29N 2 50w
Brown Willy, Mt. . 50 35N 4 34w
Brownfield ... 33 10N 102 15w
Browning 48 35N 113 10w
Brownlee 50 43N 105 59N
Brownsville ... 25 54N 97 30w
Brownwood ... 31 45N 99 0w
Bruce, Mt. ... 22 31 s 118 6 E
Bruce Mines .. 46 20N 83 45w
Bruce Rock .. 31 51 s 118 2 E
Bruck ...... 47 24N 15 16 E
Brue, R. 51 10N 2 50w
Brugge ..... 51 13N 3 13 E
Brule 53 15N 117 38w
Brumado .... 14 13 s 41 40w
Brunei ...... 4 52N 115 0 E
Brunette Downs . 18 38 s 135 57 E
Brünn = Brno .. 49 10N 16 35 E
Brunner .... 42 27 s 171 20 E
Bruno 52 20N 105 30w
Brunssum ... 50 57N 5 59 E
Brunswick, Ga. . 31 10N 81 30w
Brunswick, Me. . 43 53N 69 50w
Brunswick, Pen. . 53 30 s 71 30w
Brunswick Junction 33 15 s 115 50 E
Brusque ..... 27 5 s 49 0w
Brussel .... 50 51N 4 21 E
Bruthen ..... 37 43 s 147 48 E
Bruxelles =
  Brussel ...... 50 51N 4 21 E
Bryan, Ohio ... 41 30N 84 30w
Bryan, Tex. ... 30 40N 96 27w
Bryansk .... 53 13N 34 25 E
Bryne ...... 58 45N 5 36 E

* Renamed Vohibinany

Brzeg .... 50 52N 17 30 E
Bucak .... 37 28N 30 36 E
Bucaramanga 7 0N 73 0w
Buchan, Reg. 57 32N 2 8w
Buchan Ness, Pt. .. 57 29N 1 48w
Buchanan, Canada 51 40N 102 45w
Buchanan, Liberia . 5 57N 10 2w
Buchans 49 0N 57 2w
Bucharest =
  Bucureşti .... 44 27N 26 10 E
Buckeye 33 28N 112 40w
Buckhannon 39 2N 80 10w
Buckíe 57 40N 2 58w
Buckingham,
  U.S.A. 45 37N 75 24w
Buckinghamshire □ 51 50N 0 55w
Buctouche 46 30N 64 45w
Bucureşti .... 44 27N 26 10 E
Bucyrus 40 48N 83 0w
Budalin .... 22 20N 95 10 E
Budapest .... 47 29N 19 5 E
Budaun .... 28 5N 79 10 E
Bude 50 49N 4 33w
Buea .... 4 10N 9 9 E
Buenaventura 29 15s 69 40w
Buenos Aires 34 30s 58 20w
Buenos Aires, L. .. 46 35s 72 30w
Buffalo, Canada .. 50 49N 110 42w
Buffalo, U.S.A. .. 42 55N 78 50w
Buffalo Narrows .. 55 52N 108 28w
Bug, R. .... 51 20N 23 40 E
Buga 4 0N 77 0w
Bugondo .... 1 33N 33 10 E
Bugulma .... 54 38N 52 40 E
Buguma .... 4 42N 6 55 E
Bugun Shara, Mts. . 48 30N 102 0 E
Buturuslan ...... 53 39N 52 26 E
Bui .... 58 23N 41 27 E
Builth Wells 52 10N 3 26w
Bujumbura .... 3 16s 29 18 E
Bukachacha ...... 52 55N 116 50 E
Bukavu .... 2 20s 28 52 E
Bukene .... 4 15s 32 48 E
Bukhara .... 39 50N 64 10 E
Bukit Mertajam .. 5 22N 100 28 E
Bukittinggi ..... 0 20s 100 20 E
Bukoba .... 1 20s 31 49 E
Bukombe .... 3 31s 32 3 E
Bukuru .... 9 42N 8 48 E

Bulak .... 45 2N 82 5 E
Bulawayo .... 20 7s 28 32 E
Bulgaria ■ ...... 42 35N 25 30 E
Bulhar .... 10 25N 44 30 E
Bullabulling .... 31 0s 120 55 E
Bullara .... 22 30s 114 2 E
Bullaring .... 32 28s 117 40 E
Bullock Creek ... 17 40s 144 30 E
Bulls .... 40 10s 175 24 E
Bulo Burti ...... 3 50N 45 33 E
Bulsar .... 20 40N 72 58 E
Bultfontein ..... 28 18s 26 10 E
Bulun .... 70 37N 127 30 E
Bulundshahr ..... 28 30N 77 45 E
Bumba .... 2 13N 22 30 E
Bumbum .... 14 0N 8 10 E
Bumhpa Bum, Mt. . 26 40N 97 20 E
Bunbury .... 33 20s 115 35 E
Buncrana 55 8N 7 28w
Bundaberg .... 24 54s 152 22 E
Bundi .... 25 30N 75 35 E
Bundooma .... 24 54s 134 16 E
Bunia .... 1 35N 30 20 E
Bununu Dass ..... 10 6N 9 25 E
Bununu Kasa ..... 9 51N 9 32 E
Bunza .... 12 8N 4 0 E
Bura .... 1 6s 39 57 E
Bura Hills ...... 3 25s 38 20 E
Burdwan .... 23 16N 87 54 E
Bure, R. .... 52 38N 1 38 E
Burgas .... 42 33N 27 29 E
Burgenland □ .... 47 20N 16 20 E
Burgeo 47 36N 57 34w
Burgersdorp ..... 31 0s 26 20 E
Burgos 42 21N 3 41w
Burgsvik .... 57 3N 18 19 E
Burias, I. ...... 13 5N 122 55 E
Burica, Pta 8 3N 82 51w
Burin .... 32 11N 35 15 E
Buriram .... 15 0N 103 0 E
Burketown .... 17 45s 139 33 E
Burks Falls 45 37N 79 10w
Burley 42 37N 113 55w
Burlington,
  Canada 43 25N 79 45w
Burlington, Colo. . 39 21N 102 18w
Burlington, Iowa . 40 50N 91 5w
Burlington, Kans. . 38 15N 95 47w
Burlington, N.C. .. 36 7N 79 27w
Burlington, N.J. ... 40 5N 74 50w

Burlington, Vt. 44 27N 73 14w
Burlington, Wash. . 48 29N 122 19w
Burlyu-Tyube .... 46 30N 79 10 E
Burma ■ .... 21 0N 96 30 E
Burngup .... 33 0s 118 35 E
Burnie .... 41 4s 145 56 E
Burnley 53 47N 2 15w
Burns 43 40N 119 4w
Burns Lake 54 20N 125 45w
Burntwood, L. ... 55 35N 99 40w
Burqa .... 32 18N 35 11 E
Burra .... 33 40s 138 55 E
Burrendong Res. . 32 45s 149 10 E
Burruyacú 26 30s 64 45w
Burry Port 51 41N 4 17w
Bursa .... 40 15N 29 5 E
Burton-on-Trent . 52 48N 1 39w
Buru, I. .... 3 30s 126 3 E
Burundi ■ .... 3 15s 30 0 E
Burung .... 0 21N 108 25 E
Burutu .... 5 20N 5 29 E
Bury 53 36N 2 19w
Bury St. Edmunds . 52 15N 0 42 E
Buryat A.S.S.R. □ . 53 0N 110 0 E
Busembatia ...... 0 45N 33 32 E
Bushenyi .... 0 32s 30 11 E
Busia .... 0 25N 34 6 E
Buskerud □ ...... 60 20N 9 0 E
Busselton .... 33 42s 115 15 E
Bussum .... 52 16N 5 10 E
Busto Arsizio ... 45 38N 8 50 E
Busu-Djanoa ..... 1 50N 21 5 E
Busuanga, I. .... 12 10N 120 0 E
Buta .... 2 50N 24 53 E
Butare .... 2 31s 29 52 E
Bute, I. 55 48N 5 2w
Butembo .... 0 9N 29 18 E
Butere .... 0 14N 34 51 E
Butiaba .... 1 50N 31 20 E
Butler 40 52N 79 52w
Butt of Lewis,
  Pt. 58 30N 6 20w
Butte, Mont. 46 0N 112 31w
Butte, Neb. 42 56N 98 54w
Butterworth ..... 5 24N 100 23 E
Butuan .... 8 52N 125 36 E
Butung, I. ...... 5 0s 122 45 E
Buturlinovka .... 50 50N 40 35 E
Buxton, S. Afr. .. 27 38s 24 42 E
Buxton, U.K. 53 16N 1 54w

Buyaga .... 59 50N 127 0 E
Buyr Nuur, L. ... 47 50N 117 35 E
Buzău .... 45 10N 26 50 E
Buzău, R. .... 45 10N 27 20 E
Buzen .... 33 35N 131 5 E
Buzuluk .... 52 48N 52 12 E
Buzzards Bay 41 45N 70 38w
Bydgoszcz .... 53 10N 18 0 E
Byelorussian
  S.S.R. □ ...... 53 30N 27 0 E
Bylas 33 11N 110 9w
Bylot I. 73 0N 78 0w
Byrd Ld. 79 30s 125 0w
Byrock .... 30 40s 146 27 E
Byron Bay .... 28 30s 153 30 E
Byske .... 64 59N 21 17 E
Byrranga, Gory .. 75 0N 100 0 E
Bytom .... 50 25N 19 0 E
Byumba .... 1 35s 30 4 E

C

Cabana 8 25s 78 5w
Cabanatuan ...... 15 30N 121 5 E
Cabedelo 7 0s 34 50w
Cabimas 10 30N 71 25w
Cabinda .... 5 40s 12 11 E
Cabinet Mts. 48 8N 115 46w
Cabo Blanco 47 56s 65 47w
Cabo Frio 22 51s 42 3w
Cabonga Res. 47 35N 76 40w
Caboolture ...... 27 5s 152 47 E
Cabora Bassa
  Dam .... 15 30s 32 40 E
Caborca 30 40N 112 10w
Cabot Str. 47 15N 59 40w
Cabri 50 35N 108 25w
Cabriel, R. 39 14N 1 3w
Cabruta 7 50N 66 10w
Čačak .... 43 54N 20 20 E
Cáceres 39 26N 6 23w
Cache Bay 46 26N 80 0w
Cache Lake 49 55N 74 35w
Cachinal 24 59s 69 35w
Cachoeira 12 30s 39 0w
Cachoeiro de

Itapemirim 20 51s 41 7w
Cachoeira do Sul . 30 3s 52 53w
Caconda .... 13 48s 15 8 E
Cadillac, Canada . 49 45N 108 0w
Cadillac, U.S.A. .. 44 16N 85 25w
Cadiz, Philippines . 11 30N 123 15 E
Cádiz, Sp. 36 30N 6 20w
Cádiz, G. de 36 35N 6 20w
Cadomin 52 59N 117 28½
Cadoux .... 30 47s 117 8 E
Caen 49 10N 0 22w
Caernarfon 53 8N 4 17w
Caernarfon B. ... 53 4N 4 40w
Caerphilly 51 34N 3 13w
Caesarea=Qesari . 32 30N 34 53 E
Caetité 13 50s 42 50w
Cagayan de Oro .. 8 30N 124 40 E
Cágliari .... 39 15N 9 6 E
Cágliari, G. di .. 39 8N 9 10 E
Caguas 18 14N 66 4w
Caher 52 23N 7 56w
Cahirciveen 51 57N 10 13w
Cahore Pt. 52 34N 6 11w
Cahors .... 44 27N 1 27 E
Caibarién 22 30N 79 30w
Caicara 7 50N 66 10w
Caicó 6 20s 37 0w
Caicos Is. 21 40N 71 40w
Cairn Gorm, Mt. .. 57 7N 3 40w
Cairngorm Mts. .. 57 6N 3 42w
Cairns .... 16 55s 145 51 E
Cairo, Egypt=
  El Qâhira ..... 30 1N 31 14 E
Cairo, Ga. 30 52N 84 12w
Cairo, Mo. 37 0N 89 10w
Cajamarca 7 5s 78 28w
Cajazeiras 7 0s 38 30w
Cala Millor ..... 39 34N 3 18 E
Calabar .... 4 57N 8 20 E
Calaboza 9 0N 67 20w
Calabria □ ...... 39 4N 16 30 E
Calafate 50 25s 72 25w
Calahorra 42 18N 1 59w
Calais .... 50 57N 1 56 E
Calama 22 30s 68 55w
Calamar 10 15N 74 55w
Calamian Group,
  Is. .... 11 50N 119 55 E
Calamocha 40 50N 1 17w
Călăraşi .... 44 14N 27 23 E

Calatayud 41 20N   1 40w
Calauag .... 13 55N 122 15 E
Calcutta .... 22 36N 88 24 E
Calder R. 53 44N   1 21w
Caldera .... 27 5 s 70 55w
Caldwell 43 45N 116 42w
Caledon .... 34 14 s 19 26 E
Caledon, R. ...... 30 31 s 26 5 E
Calella .... 41 37N   2 40 E
Calf of Man, I. .. 54 4N   4 48w
Calgary 51 0N 114 10w
Cali 3 25N 76 35w
Calicut .... 11 15N 75 43 E
Caliente 37 43N 114 34w
California 37 25N 120 0w
California, G. de . 27 0N 111 0w
California,
   Baja, Reg. ... 30 0N 115 0w
Calingasta .... 31 15 s 69 30w
Calipatria 33 8N 115 30w
Calitzdorp .... 33 30 s 21 41 E
Callan 52 33N   7 25w
Callao .... 12 0 s 77 0w
Callide .... 24 23 s 150 33 E
Calliope .... 24 0 s 151 16 E
Calo .... 31 37 s 27 33 E
Caloundra .... 26 45 s 153 10 E
Calatagirone ..... 37 13N 14 30 E
Caltanissetta .... 37 30N 14 3 E
Calvados □ 49 5N   0 15w
Calvi .... 42 34N   8 45 E
Calvinia .... 31 28 s 19 45 E
Cam, R. .... 52 21N   0 15 E
Camagüey 21 20N 78 0w
Camarones .... 44 50 s 66 0w
Cambay .... 22 23N 72 33 E
Cambay, G. of .... 20 45N 72 30 E
Cambodia ■ .... 12 15N 105 0 E
Camborne 50 13N   5 18w
Cambrai .... 50 11N   3 14 E
Cambrian Mts. 52 10N   3 52w
Cambridge, Canada 43 23N 80 19w
Cambridge, N.Z. .. 37 54 s 175 29 E
Cambridge, U.K. .. 52 13N   0 8 E
Cambridge, Mass. . 42 20N 71 8w
Cambridge, Ohio .. 40 1N 81 22w
Cambridge □ ...... 52 21N   0 5 E
Cambridge B. 69 10N 105 0w
Cambridge, G. .... 14 45 s 128 0 E
Camden, Australia 34 5 s 150 38 E

Camden, Ala. 31 59N 87 15w
Camden, Ark. 33 30N 92 50w
Camden, S.C. 34 17N 80 34w
Cameron 30 53N 97 0w
Cameroon ■ .... 3 30N 12 30 E
Cameroun, Mt. ... 4 45N   8 55 E
Cametá .... 2 0 s 49 30w
Caminha 41 50N   8 50w
Camira Creek ..... 29 15 s 153 10 E
Camocim .... 2 55 s 40 50w
Camooweal .... 19 56 s 138 7 E
Camopi 3 45N 52 50w
Campania □ .... 40 50N 14 45 E
Campana, I. ...... 48 20 s 75 10w
Campbell I. ...... 52 30 s 169 0 E
Campbell River .. 50 1N 125 15w
Campbell Town .. 41 52 s 147 30 E
Campbelltown,
   Australia ...... 34 5 s 150 48 E
Campbellton, N.B. 47 57N 66 43w
Campbellton, Alta. 53 32N 113 15w
Campbeltown 55 25N   5 36w
Campeche 19 50N 90 32w
Campeche □ 19 50N 90 32w
Campeche, B. de .. 19 30N 93 0w
Camperdown .... 38 4 s 143 12 E
Campino Grande .. 7 5 s 35 47w
Campinas .... 22 50 s 47 0w
Campo Formoso .. 10 30 s 40 20w
Campo Gallo ...... 26 35 s 62 50w
Campo Grande .... 20 25 s 54 40w
Campo Maior,
   Brazil .... 4 50 s 42 12w
Campalegre 2 48N 75 20w
Campobasso .... 41 34N 14 40 E
Campos .... 21 50 s 41 20w
Campos Belos ..... 13 10 s 46 45w
Camrose 53 0N 112 50w
Can Tho .... 10 2N 105 46 E
Canada ■ 60 0N 100 0w
Cañada de
   Gómez .... 32 55 s 61 30w
Canadian, R. 35 27N 95 3w
Canal Zone 9 10N 79 48w
Cananea 31 0N 110 20w
Canarreos, Arch.
   de los 21 35N 81 40w
Canary Is.=
   Canarias, Is. .. 29 30N 17 0w

Canaveral, C. 28 28N 80 31w
Canavieiras ...... 15 45 s 39 0w
Canberra .... 35 15 s 149 8 E
Candia=Iráklion .. 35 20N 25 12 E
Candle 65 55N 161 56w
Canelones .... 34 32 s 56 10w
Cañete .... 37 50 s 73 10w
Cangamba .... 13 40 s 19 54w
Cangas de Narcea . 43 10N   6 32w
Canguaretama .... 6 20 s 35 5w
Canguçu .... 31 22 s 52 43w
Canipaan .... 8 33N 117 15 E
Canmore 51 7N 115 18w
Cann River .... 37 35 s 149 6 E
Canna, I. 57 3N   6 33w
Cannakale .... 40 5N 27 20 E
Cannakale Boǧazi=
   Dardenelles, Str. 40 10N 27 20 E
Cannanore .... 11 53N 75 27 E
Cannes .... 43 32N   7 0 E
Cannock 52 42N   2 2w
Canon City 39 30N 105 20w
Canora 51 40N 102 30w
Canso 45 20N 61 0w
Cantabrian Mts.=
   Cantábrica, Cord. 43 0N   5 10w
   Cantábrica, Cord. . 43 0N   5 10w
Cantal □ .... 45 4N   2 45 E
Canterbury □ ..... 43 45 s 171 19 E
Canterbury,
   Australia .... 33 55 s 151 7 E
   U.K. .... 51 17N   1 5 E
Canterbury Bight . 44 16 s 171 55 E
Canterbury Plain . 43 55 s 171 22 E
Canton, China=
   Kwangchow ..... 23 10N 133 10 E
Canton, Mo. 40 10N 91 33w
Canton, N.Y. 44 32N 75 3w
Canton, Ohio 40 47N 81 22w
Canton I. 36 12N 98 40w
Canutillo 31 55N 106 36w
Canyon 44 43N 110 36w
Canyonlands
   Nat. Park 38 25N 109 30w
Cap Breton, I. ... 46 0N 61 0w
Cap Chat 49 6N 66 40w
Cap Haïtien 19 40N 72 20w
Cape Barren I. ... 40 25 s 184 15 E
Cape Coast 5 5N   1 15w
Cape Dorset 64 30N 77 0w

Cape Dyer 66 30N 61 0w
Cape Girardeau ... 37 20N 89 30w
Cape Province □ .. 32 0 s 23 0 E
Cape Town .... 33 55 s 18 22 E
Cape Verde Is. ... 17 10N 25 20w
Cape York Pen... 13 30 s 142 30 E
Capela .... 10 15 s 37 0w
Capella .... 23 2 s 148 1 E
Capraia, I. ...... 43 2N   9 50 E
Capreol 46 40N 80 50w
Caprera, I. ...... 41 12N   9 28 E
Capri, I. .... 40 34N 14 15 E
Caprivi Strip, Reg. 18 0 s 23 0 E
Caquetá, R. ...... 3 8 s 64 46w
Caracal .... 44 8N 24 22 E
Caracas 10 30N 66 50w
Caracol .... 9 15 s 64 20w
Caragabal .... 33 54 s 147 50 E
Carangola .... 20 50 s 42 5w
Carani .... 30 57 s 116 28 E
Caransebeş .... 45 28N 22 18 E
Caratasca, L. 15 30N 83 40w
Caratinga .... 19 50 s 42 10w
Caraúbas .... 5 50 s 37 33w
Caravaca 38 8N   1 52w
Caravelas .... 17 50 s 39 20w
Carballo 43 13N   8 41w
Carberry 49 50N 99 25w
Carbonara, C. .... 39 8N   9 30 E
Carbondale, Colo. 39 30N 107 10w
Carbondale, Ill. . 37 45N 89 10w
Carbondale, Pa. .. 41 37N 75 30w
Carbonear 47 42N 53 13w
Carcassonne ...... 43 13N   2 20 E
Carcross 60 20N 134 40w
Cardabia .... 23 2 s 113 55 E
Cardamon Hills ... 9 30N 77 15 E
Cárdenas, Cuba .. 23 0N 81 30w
Cárdenas, Mexico . 22 0N 99 41w
Cardiff 51 28N   3 11w
Cardigan 52 6N   4 41w
Cardigan Bay 52 30N   4 30w
Cardross 49 50N 105 40w
Cardston 49 0N 113 20w
Cardwell .... 18 14 s 146 2 E
Carei .... 47 40N 22 29 E
Carey, L. .... 29 0 s 122 15 E
Cargados
   Garajos,Is. ..... 17 0 s 59 0 E

Caribbean Sea 15 0N 75 0w
Cariboo Mts. 53 0N 121 0w
Carinhanha .... 14 15 s 44 0w
Carinthia□=
   Kärnten .... 46 52N 13 30 E
Caripito 10 2N 63 0w
Carleton Place ... 45 8N 76 11w
Carletonville .... 26 23 s 27 22 E
Carlin 40 50N 116 5w
Carlingford L. ... 54 0N   6 5w
Carlinville 39 20N 89 55w
Carlisle, U.K. ... 54 54N   2 55w
Carlisle, U.S.A. . 40 12N 77 10w
Carlow 52 50N   6 58w
Carlow □ 52 43N   6 50w
Carlsbad 32 20N 104 7w
Carlsruhe=
   Karlsruhe ...... 49 3N   8 23 E
Carmacks 62 0N 136 0w
Carman 49 30N 98 0w
Carmarthen 51 52N   4 20w
Carmel, Mt. ...... 32 45N 35 3 E
Carmelo .... 34 0 s 58 10w
Carmen, Col. 9 43N 75 6w
Carmen de
   Patagones ...... 40 50 s 63 0w
Carmila .... 21 53 s 149 5 E
Carmona .... 37 28 s   5 42w
Carnac 47 13N   3 10w
Carnarvon,
   Australia .... 24 51 s 113 42 E
Carnarvon,
   S. Africa .... 30 56 s 22 8 E
Carnatic, Reg. .. 12 0N 79 0 E
Carndonagh 55 15N   7 16w
Carnegie, L. ..... 26 5 s 122 30 E
Carnsore Pt. 52 10N   6 20w
Carolina, Brazil . 7 10 s 47 30w
Carolina, S. Afr. . 26 5 s 30 6 E
Caroline Is. ..... 8 0N 150 0 E
Caron 50 30N 105 50w
Carpathians, Mts. . 46 20N 26 0 E
Carpatii
   Meridionali, Mts. 45 30N 25 0 E
Carpentaria, G. of. 14 0 s 139 0 E
Carpentaria Downs 18 44 s 144 20 E
Carrara .... 44 5N 10 7 E
Carrick-on-
   Shannon 53 57N   8 7w
Carrick-on-Suir .. 52 22N   7 30w

Carrickfergus 54 43N 5 50w
Carrickfergus □ 54 43N 5 50w
Carrickmacross 54 0N 6 43w
Carrieton .... 32 27s 138 27 E
Carrizal Bajo 28 5s 71 20w
Carrizozo 33 40N 105 57w
Carroll 42 2N 94 55w
Carrollton 33 36N 85 5w
Carrot River 53 50N 101 17w
Carson City 39 12N 119 52w
Carson Sink 39 50N 118 40w
Carstairs 55 42N 3 41w
Cartagena, Col. ... 10 25N 75 33w
Cartagena, Sp. ... 37 38N 0 59w
Cartago, Col. 4 45N 75 55w
Cartago, Costa Rica 9 50N 84 0w
Cartersville 34 11N 84 48w
Carterton .... 41 2s 175 31 E
Carthage, Mo. 37 10N 94 20w
Carthage, N.Y. ... 43 59N 75 37w
Cartwright 53 41N 56 58w
Caruaru 8 15s 35 55w
Carúpano 10 45N 63 15w
Caruthersville ... 36 10N 89 40w
Casa Grande 32 53N 111 51w
Casa Nova 9 10s 41 5w
Casablanca 33 43N 7 24w
Casale
  Monferrato ..... 45 8N 8 28 E
Casas Grandes 30 22N 108 0w
Cascade Ra. 44 0N 122 10w
Caserta .... 41 5N 14 20 E
Cashel 52 31N 7 53w
Casilda 33 10s 61 10w
Casino .... 28 52s 153 3 E
Casiquiare, R. ... 2 1N 67 7w
Caspe 41 14N 0 1w
Casper 42 52N 106 27w
Caspian Sea ...... 42 30N 51 0 E
Cassel=Kassel .... 51 19N 9 32 E
Cassiar Mts. 39 30N 130 30w
Cassinga .... 15 5s 16 23 E
Castellammare del
  Golfo .... 38 2N 12 53 E
Castellammare di
  Stábia .... 40 47N 14 29 E
Castellón de la
  Plana 39 58N 0 3w
Castelo Branco ... 39 50N 7 31w
Castelvetrano .... 37 40N 12 46 E

Casterton .... 37 30s 141 30 E
Castilla la Nueva,
  Reg. 39 45N 3 20w
Castilla la
  Vieja, Reg. 41 55N 4 0w
Castle Douglas ... 54 57N 3 57w
Castle Harbour ... 32 17N 64 44w
Castle Rock 46 20N 122 58w
Castlebar 53 52N 9 17w
Castleblayney 54 7N 6 44w
Castleford 53 43N 1 21w
Castlegar 49 20N 117 40w
Castlemaine ...... 37 2s 144 12 E
Castlereagh 53 47N 8 30w
Castlereagh □ 53 47N 8 30w
Castletown 54 4N 4 40w
Castletown
  Bearhaven 51 39N 9 54w
Castlevale .... 24 30s 146 48 E
Castor 52 15N 111 50w
Castres .... 43 37N 2 13 E
Castries 14 0N 60 50w
Castro, Brazil ... 24 45s 50 0w
Castro, Chile 42 30s 73 50w
Castro Alves 12 46s 39 33w
Castro del Rio ... 37 41N 4 29w
Cat I. 24 30N 75 30w
Catalão 18 5s 47 52w
Catalina 25 13s 69 43w
Cataluña, Reg. ... 41 40N 1 15 E
Catamarca 28 30s 65 50w
Catánia .... 37 31N 15 4 E
Catanzaro .... 38 54N 16 38 E
Catarman .... 12 28N 124 1 E
Cathcart .... 32 18s 27 10 E
Catine, Reg. 46 30N 0 15w
Cato, I. .... 23 15s 155 32 E
Catoche, C. 21 40N 87 0w
Catriló 36 23s 63 24w
Catrimani 0 27N 61 41w
Catskill 42 14N 73 52w
Catskill Mts. 42 15N 74 15w
Caucasus Mts.=
  Bolshoi Kavkaz . 42 50N 44 0 E
Caucia 3 40s 38 55w
Cauquenes 36 0s 72 30w
Causapscal 48 19N 67 12w
Cauvery, R. ...... 11 10N 79 51 E
Caux, Reg. .... 49 38N 0 35 E
Cavan □ 53 58N 7 10w

Cavan 54 0N 7 22w
Cavendish .... 37 31s 142 2 E
Caviana, I. 0 15N 50 0w
Cavite .... 14 20N 120 55 E
Caxias 5 0s 43 27w
Caxias do Sul 29 10s 51 10w
Caxito .... 8 30s 13 30 E
Cayambe 0 3N 78 22w
Cayenne 5 0N 52 18w
Cayman Is. 19 40N 79 50w
* Cayo 17 10N 89 0w
Cazombo .... 12 0s 22 48 E
Ceanannas Mor 53 42N 6 53w
Ceara □ 5 0s 40 0w
Ceará=Fortaleza .. 3 35s 38 35w
Cebollar 29 10s 66 35w
Cebu .... 10 30N 124 0 E
Cebu, I. .... 10 23N 123 58 E
Cedar City 37 41N 113 3w
Cedar Creek Res. . 32 15N 96 0w
Cedar Falls 42 39N 92 29w
Cedar L. 53 30N 100 30w
Cedar Rapids 42 0N 91 38w
Cedartown 34 1N 85 15w
Cedarvale 55 1N 128 22w
Cedarville 41 37N 120 13w
Cedro 6 34s 39 3w
Cedros, I. de 28 10N 115 20w
Ceduna .... 32 7s 133 46 E
Cefalù .... 38 3N 14 1 E
Cegléd .... 47 11N 19 47 E
Celaya 20 31N 100 37w
Celbridge 53 20N 6 33w
Celebes, I.=
  Sulawesi, I. ... 2 0s 120 0 E
Celebes Sea ...... 3 0N 123 0 E
Celje .... 46 16N 15 18 E
Celle .... 52 37N 10 4 E
Centerville 31 15N 95 56w
Central 32 46N 108 9w
Central □, Ghana . 5 40N 1 20w
Central □, U.K. .. 56 12N 4 25w
Central Africa ■ . 7 0N 20 0 E
Central Makan Ra. 26 30N 64 15 E
Central Russian
  Uplands .... 54 0N 36 0 E
Central Siberian
  Plat. .... 65 0N 105 0 E
Centralia, Ill. .. 38 32N 89 5w
Centralia, Wash. . 46 46N 122 59w

Cephalonia, I.=
  Kefallinía, I. .. 38 28N 20 30 E
Ceram, I.=
  Seram, I. ...... 3 10s 129 0 E
Ceres, Arg. 29 55s 61 55w
Ceres, S. Africa . 33 21s 19 18 E
Cerignola .... 41 17N 15 53 E
Çerkeş .... 40 40N 32 58 E
Cernavodă .... 44 22N 28 3 E
Cerralvo, I. ..... 24 20N 109 45 E
Cerritos 22 20N 100 20w
Cervera .... 41 40N 1 16 E
Cesena .... 44 9N 12 14 E
České Budějovice . 48 55N 14 25 E
Ceskomoravská
  Vrchovina ...... 49 20N 15 30 E
Český Těšín ...... 49 45N 18 39 E
Cessnock .... 33 0s 151 15 E
Cetinje .... 42 23N 18 59 E
Ceuta 35 52N 5 26w
Cevennes, Mts. ... 44 10N 3 50 E
Ceyhan .... 37 4N 35 47 E
Ceylon=
  Sri Lanka ■ .... 7 30N 80 50 E
Chablais, Reg. ... 46 20N 6 45 E
Chachran .... 28 55N 70 28 E
Chaco Austral, Reg. 27 30s 61 40w
Chaco Boreal, Reg. 22 30s 60 10w
Chaco Central, Reg. 24 0s 61 0w
Chad ■ .... 12 30N 17 15 E
Chad, L. 13 30N 14 30w
Chadron 42 50N 103 0w
Chafe .... 11 56N 6 55 E
Chagai Hills ..... 29 30N 63 0 E
Chagos Arch. ..... 6 0s 72 0 E
Chah Bahar .... 25 20N 60 40 E
Chake Chake ...... 5 15s 39 45 E
* Chakhansur □ ... 30 25N 62 0 E
Chakradharpur .... 22 45N 85 40 E
Chakwal .... 32 50N 72 45 E
Chaling .... 26 55N 113 30 E
Chalisgaon .... 20 30N 75 10 E
Challapata 19 0s 66 50w
Chalon-sur-Saône . 46 48N 4 50 E
Châlons-sur-
  Marne .... 48 58N 4 20 E
Chaman .... 30 55N 66 22 E
Chamba, India .... 32 35N 76 10 E
Chamba, Tanz. .... 11 35s 36 58 E

Chambersburg 39 53N 77 41w
Chambéry .... 45 34N 5 55 E
Chambeshi .... 10 58s 31 5 E
Chambord 48 25N 72 6w
Chamdo .... 31 21N 97 2 E
Chamical 30 22s 66 19w
Chamonix .... 45 55N 6 51 E
Champagne, Reg. . 49 0N 4 40 E
Champaign 40 8N 88 14w
Champlain, L. ... 44 30N 73 20w
Champotón 19 20N 90 50w
Chañaral 26 15s 70 50w
Chanchiang=
  Chankiang ..... 21 7N 110 21 E
Chanda .... 19 57N 79 25 E
Chandalar 67 30N 148 30w
Chandeleur Sd. .. 29 58N 88 40w
Chandigarh ...... 30 44N 76 47 E
Chandler, Canada . 48 18N 64 46w
Chandler, U.S.A. . 33 20N 111 56w
Chandpur .... 23 8N 78 19 E
Changane, R. .... 24 45s 33 37 E
Changchih .... 36 7N 113 0 E
Changchow,
  Fukien .... 24 32N 117 44 E
Changchow,
  Kiangsu .... 31 45N 120 0 E
Changchow,
  Shantung ...... 36 55N 118 3 E
Changchun .... 43 58N 125 9 E
Changhua .... 24 2N 120 30 E
Changkiakow ..... 40 52N 114 45 E
Changkiang ...... 21 7N 110 21 E
Changli .... 39 40N 119 19 E
Changpai .... 41 26N 128 0 E
Changpai
  Shan, Mts. .... 42 0N 128 0 E
Changping, Fukien 25 30N 117 33 E
Changping, Peiping 40 15N 116 15 E
Changsha .... 28 5N 113 1 E
Changtai .... 24 34N 117 50 E
Changteh .... 29 12N 111 43 E
Changting .... 25 46N 116 30 E
Changwu .... 42 21N 122 45 E
Changyeh .... 39 0N 100 59 E
Channaptna ...... 12 40N 77 15 E
Channel Is. 49 30N 2 40w
Chantada 42 37N 7 46w

* Renamed San Ignacio   * Renamed Nīmrūz

Chanthaburi ...... 12 38N 102 12 E
Chanute 37 45N 95 25W
Chanyi .... 25 56N 104 1 E
Chao Phraya, R. .. 13 32N 100 36 E
Chaoan .... 23 45N 117 11 E
Chaochow .... 23 45N 116 32 E
Chaohwa .... 32 16N 105 41 E
Chaotung .... 27 30N 103 40 E
Chaoyang .... 41 46N 120 16 E
Chapata, L. 20 10N 103 20W
Chapayevo .... 50 25N 51 10 E
Chapayevsk ...... 53 0N 49 40 E
Chapel Hill 35 53N 79 3W
Chapleau 47 45N 83 30W
Chapra .... 25 48N 84 50 E
Charadai 27 40s 59 55W
Charagua 19 45s 63 10W
Charambira, Pta. .. 4 20N 77 30W
Charaña 17 30s 69 35W
Charchan .... 38 4N 85 16 E
Charchan, R. ..... 39 0N 86 0 E
Chard, U.K. 50 52N 2 59W
Chard, U.S.A. 55 55N 111 10W
Chardara .... 41 16N 67 59 E
Chardzhou .... 39 0N 63 20 E
Charente □ 45 50N 0 36W
Charente-
  Maritime □ 45 50N 0 35W
Chari, R. .... 12 58N 14 31 E
Charikar .... 35 0N 69 10 E
Charkhlikh .... 39 16N 88 17 E
Charleroi .... 50 24N 4 27 E
Charles, C. 37 10N 75 52W
Charles City 43 2N 92 41W
Charleston, Mass. . 34 2N 90 3W
Charleston, S.C. .. 32 47N 79 56W
Charleston, W.Va. . 38 24N 81 36W
Charlestown, Nevis 17 8N 62 37W
Charlestown, S. Afr. 27 30s 29 55 E
Charleville,
  Australia .... 26 24s 146 15 E
Charleville, Eire=
  Rath Luire 52 21N 8 40W
Charleville ...... 26 24s 146 15 E
Charleville-
  Mézières ..... 49 44N 4 40 E
Charlotte 35 16N 80 46W
Charlotte Amalie . 18 22N 64 56W
Charlottenburg ... 52 31N 13 16 E
Charlottesville ... 38 1N 78 30W

Charlottetown 46 19N 63 3W
Charlton .... 36 16s 143 24 E
Charlton 40 59N 93 20W
Charlton I. 52 0N 79 20W
Charny 46 43N 71 15W
Charolles .... 46 27N 4 16 E
Charters Towers .. 20 5s 146 13 E
Chartres .... 48 29N 1 30 E
Chascomús 35 30s 58 0W
Chatanika 65 7N 147 31W
Château Salins ... 48 49N 6 30 E
Châteaubriant 47 43N 1 23W
Châteauroux ..... 46 50N 1 40 E
Châtellerault ..... 46 50N 0 30 E
Chatham, U.K. ... 51 22N 0 32 E
Chatham, N.B. ... 47 2N 65 28W
Chatham, Ont. ... 42 23N 82 15W
Chatham, Alas. ... 57 30N 135 0W
Chatham Is. 44 0s 176 40W
Chatham Str. 57 0N 134 40W
Chatrapur .... 19 21N 85 0 E
Chattahoochee 30 43N 84 51W
Chattanooga 35 2N 85 17W
Chaumont .... 48 7N 5 8 E
Chaves, Brazil 0 15s 49 55W
Chaves, Port. 41 45N 7 32W
Cheb .... 50 9N 12 20 E
Cheboksary ...... 56 8N 47 30 E
Cheboygan 45 38N 84 29W
Chefoo=Yentai ... 37 30N 121 21 E
Chegdomyn ...... 51 7N 132 52 E
Chehallis 46 44N 122 59W
Cheju .... 33 28N 126 30 E
Cheju Do, I. ..... 33 29N 126 34 E
Chekiang □ ...... 29 30N 120 0 E
Chelforó 39 0s 66 40W
Chelkar .... 47 40N 59 32 E
Chelkar Tengiz
  Solonchak .... 48 0N 62 30 E
Chelm .... 51 8N 23 30 E
Chelmno .... 53 20N 18 30 E
Chelmsford ...... 51 44N 0 29 E
Chelmza .... 53 10N 18 39 E
Chelsea .... 38 5s 145 8 E
Cheltenham 51 55N 2 5W
Chelyabinsk ..... 55 10N 61 35 E
Chemainus 48 54N 123 41W
Chemba .... 17 11s 34 53 E
Chemikovsk 54 58N 56 0W
Chemnitz=

Karl Marx Stadt . 50 50N 12 55 E
Chemult 43 14N 121 54W
Chenab, R. ...... 29 23N 71 2 E
Chengchou=
  Chengchow .... 34 47N 113 46 E
Chengchow ...... 34 47N 113 46 E
Chengkiang ...... 24 58N 102 59 E
Chengteh .... 41 0N 117 55 E
Chengting .... 38 8N 114 37 E
Chengtu .... 30 45N 104 0 E
Chengyang ...... 36 20N 120 16 E
Chenhsien .... 25 45N 112 37 E
Chenning .... 25 57N 105 51 E
Chentung .... 46 2N 123 1 E
Chenyuan .... 27 0N 108 20 E
Chepo 9 10N 79 6W
Chepstow 51 39N 2 41W
Chequamegon B. . 46 40N 90 30W
Cher, R. .... 47 21N 0 29 E
Cher □ .... 47 10N 2 30 E
Cherbourg 49 39N 1 40W
Cherchell .... 36 35N 21 63 E
Cherdyn .... 60 20N 56 20 E
Cheremkhovo .... 53 32N 102 40 E
Cherepanovo .... 54 15N 83 30 E
Cherepovets ..... 59 5N 37 55 E
Cherkassy .... 49 30N 32 0 E
Chernigov .... 51 28N 31 20 E
Chernovtsy ...... 48 0N 26 0 E
Chernoye .... 70 30N 89 10 E
Cherokee 42 40N 95 30W
Cheropovets ..... 59 5N 37 55 E
Cherquenco 38 35s 72 0W
Cherrapunji ...... 25 17N 91 47 E
Cherskogo
  Khrebet .... 65 0N 143 0 E
Cherwell, R. 51 44N 1 15W
Chesapeake B. ... 38 0N 76 12W
Cheshire □ 53 14N 2 30W
Chester, U.K. 53 12N 2 53W
Chester, Pa. 39 54N 75 20W
Chester, S.C. 34 44N 81 13W
Chesterfield 53 14N 1 26W
Chesterfield Inlet . 63 30N 91 0W
Chesterfield Is. ... 19 52s 158 15 E
Chetumal 18 30N 88 20W
Chetumal, B. de .. 18 40N 88 10W
Cheviot, The, Mt. . 55 28N 2 8W
Cheviot Hills 55 20N 2 30W
Chew Bahir, L. ... 4 40N 30 50 E

Chewelah 48 25N 117 56W
Cheyenne 41 9N 104 49W
Cheyenne, R. 44 40N 101 15W
Chhindwara ..... 22 2N 78 59 E
Chi, R. .... 15 13N 104 45 E
Chiai .... 23 29N 120 25 E
Chianje .... 15 35s 13 40 E
Chiapas □ 17 0N 92 45W
Chiávari .... 44 20N 9 20 E
Chiavenna ...... 46 18N 9 23 E
Chiba .... 35 30N 140 7 E
Chiba □ .... 35 30N 140 20 E
Chibemba .... 15 48s 14 8 E
Chibougamau ... 49 56N 74 24W
Chibuk .... 10 52N 12 50 E
Chicago 41 45N 87 40W
Chicago Heights . 41 29N 87 37W
Chichagof I. 58 0N 136 0W
Chichester 50 50N 0 47W
Chichén Itzá 20 40N 88 34W
Chichibu .... 36 5N 139 10 E
Chichirin .... 50 35N 123 45 E
Chickasha 35 0N 98 0W
Chiclana de la
  Frontera 36 26N 6 9W
Chiclayo 6 42s 79 50W
Chico 39 45N 121 54W
Chico, R. 43 50s 66 25W
Chicopee 42 6N 72 37W
Chicoutimi 48 28N 71 5W
Chidley, C. 60 30N 64 15W
Chiengi .... 8 38s 29 10 E
Chiengmai ...... 18 55N 98 55 E
Chieti .... 42 22N 14 10 E
Chiguana 21 0s 67 50W
Chihfeng .... 42 10N 118 56 E
Chihing .... 25 2N 113 45 E
Chihkiang .... 27 21N 109 45 E
Chihli, G. of=
  Po Hai, G. .... 38 30N 119 0 E
Chihsien .... 35 29N 114 1 E
Chihuahua 28 40N 106 3W
Chihuahua □ 28 40N 106 3W
Chiili .... 44 10N 66 55 E
Chilas .... 35 25N 74 5 E
Childers .... 25 15s 152 17 E
Childress 34 30N 100 50W
Chile ■ 35 0s 71 15W
Chilecito 29 0s 67 40W
Chilete 7 10s 78 50W

Chililabombwe .... 12 18s 27 43 E
Chilin=Kirin .... 43 58N 126 31 E
Chilka L. .... 19 40N 85 25 E
Chillán 36 40s 72 10W
Chillicothe, Mo. ... 39 45N 93 30W
Chillicothe, Ohio. . 39 53N 82 58W
Chilliwack 49 10N 122 0W
Chiloé, I. de 42 50s 73 45W
Chilpancingo 17 30N 99 40W
Chiltern .... 36 10s 146 36 E
Chiltern Hills ... 51 44N 0 42W
Chilumba .... 10 28N 34 12 E
Chilung .... 25 3N 121 45 E
Chilwa, L. ...... 15 15s 35 40 E
Chimai .... 34 0N 101 39 E
Chimala .... 8 55s 34 4 E
Chimborazo, Mt. .. 1 20s 78 55W
Chimbote 9 0s 78 35W
Chimkent .... 42 40N 69 25 E
Chin □ .... 22 0N 93 0 E
China ■ .... 35 0N 100 0 E
Chinan=Tsinan ... 34 50N 105 40 E
Chinandega 12 30N 87 0W
Chincha Alta 13 20s 76 0W
Chinchilla ...... 26 45s 150 38 E
Chinchow .... 41 10N 121 2 E
Chinde .... 18 45s 36 30 E
Chindwin, R. .... 21 26N 95 15 E
Chingola .... 12 31s 27 53 E
Chingole .... 13 4s 34 17 E
Ch'ingtao=
  Tsingtao ..... 36 0N 120 25 E
Chinhae .... 35 9N 128 58 E
Chiniot .... 31 45N 73 0 E
Chinju .... 35 12N 128 2 E
Chinkiang ...... 32 2N 119 28 E
Chino Valley 34 54N 112 28W
Chinon .... 47 10N 0 15 E
Chinook, Canada . 51 28N 110 59W
Chinook, U.S.A. .. 48 35N 109 19W
Chintheche ..... 11 50s 34 5 E
Chinwangtao .... 40 0N 119 31 E
Chióggia .... 45 13N 12 15 E
Chios, I.=
  Khíos, I. ..... 38 20N 26 0 E
Chip Lake 53 35N 115 35W
Chipata .... 13 38s 33 28 E
* Chipinga .... 20 13s 32 36 E
Chippenham 51 27N 2 7W

* Renamed Chipinge

Chippewa, R. 44 25N 92 10W
Chippewa Falls.... 44 56N 91 24W
Chiquimula 14 51N 89 37W
Chiquinquira 5 37N 73 50W
Chirala ..... 15 50N 80 20 E
Chirchik ..... 81 58N 69 15 E
Chirikof I. 55 50N 155 35W
Chiriquí, G. de ... 8 0N 82 10W
Chiriquí, L. de ... 9 10N 82 0W
Chiriquí, Mt.... 8 55N 82 35W
Chiromo ..... 16 30S 35 7 E
Chisamba ..... 14 55S 28 20 E
Chita ..... 52 0N 113 25 E
Chitembo ..... 13 30S 16 50 E
Chitorgarh ..... 24 52N 74 43 E
Chitré 7 59N 80 27W
Chittagong ..... 22 19N 91 55 E
Chittagong □ ..... 24 5N 91 25 E
Chittoor ..... 13 15N 79 5 E
Chiusi ..... 43 1N. 11 58 E
Chivasso ..... 45 10N 7 52 E
Chivilcoy 35 0S 60 0W
Chiwanda ..... 11 22S 34 54 E
Chobe Nat. Park .. 18 25S 24 15 E
Choele Choel 39 11S 65 40W
Choinice ..... 53 42N 17 40 E
Cholet 47 4N 0 52W
Choluteca 13 20N 87 14W
Choma ..... 16 48S 26 59 E
Chomutov ..... 50 28N 13 23 E
Chon Buri ..... 13 21N 101 1 E
Chonan ..... 36 56N 127 3 E
Chone 0 40S 80 0W
Chongjin ..... 41 51N 129 58 E
Chŏngju, N. Korea 39 41N 125 13 E
Chŏngju, S. Korea 36 39N 127 27 E
Chŏnju ..... 35 50N 127 4 E
Chonos, Arch.
de los 45 0S 75 0W
Chorley 53 39N 2 39W
Chorzow ..... 50 18N 19 0 E
Chos-Malal 37 20S 70 15W
Chóshi ..... 35 45N 140 45 E
Choszczno ..... 53 7N 15 25 E
Choteau 47 50N 112 10W
Chotila ..... 22 25N 71 11 E
Choybalsan ..... 48 3N 114 28 E
Christchurch, N.Z. 43 33S 172 47W
Christchurch, U.K. 50 44N 1 47W
Christiana ..... 27 52S 25 8 E

Christmas Creek .. 18 29S 125 23 E
Christmas I.
Indian Oc. ..... 10 0S 105 40 E
† Christmas I.
Pacific Oc. 1 58N 157 27W
Chu ..... 43 36N 73 42 E
Chu Kiang, R. .. 24 50N 113 37 E
Chuanchow ..... 24 57N 118 31 E
Chuanhsien ..... 25 50N 111 12 E
Chūbu □ ..... 36 45N 137 0 E
Chubut, R. 43 20S 65 5W
Chucheng ..... 36 0N 119 16 E
Chuchow ..... 27 56N 113 3 E
Chudskoye, Oz. .. 58 13N 27 30 E
Chugiak 61 25N 149 30W
Chūgoku □ ..... 35 0N 133 0 E
Chūgoku-Sanchi,
Mts. ..... 35 0N 133 0 E
Chuhsien ..... 30 51N 107 1 E
Chuka ..... 0 23S 37 38 E
Chukai ..... 4 13N 103 25 E
Chukotskiy Khrebet 68 0N 175 0 E
Chukotskoye More 68 0N 175 0 E
Chula Vista 33 44N 117 8W
Chumatien ..... 33 0N 114 4 E
Chumbicha 29 0S 66 10W
Chumikan ..... 54 40N 135 10 E
Chumphon ..... 10 35N 99 14 E
Chunchŏn ..... 37 58N 127 44 E
Ch'ungch'ing=
Chungking ..... 29 30N 106 30 E
Chunghsien ..... 30 17N 108 4 E
Chungking ..... 29 30N 106 30 E
Chungtien ..... 28 0N 99 30 E
Chungwei ..... 37 35N 105 10 E
Chunya ..... 8 30S 33 27 E
Chur ..... 46 52N 9 32 E
Churchill 58 45N 94 5W
Churchill, R.,
Man. 58 47N 94 12W
Churchill, R.,
Newf. 58 47N 60 10W
Churchill Pk. 58 10N 125 10W
Churu ..... 28 20N 75 0 E
Chusan, I. ..... 30 0N 122 20 E
Chuvash
A.S.S.R. □ ..... 55 30N 48 0 E
Chuvovoy ..... 58 15N 57 40 E
Cianjur ..... 6 81S 107 7 E
Cibatu ..... 7 8S 107 59 E

Cicero 41 48N 87 48W
Ciechanów □ ..... 53 0N 20 0 E
Ciego de Avila ... 21 50N 78 50W
Ciénaga 11 0N 74 10W
Cienfuegos 22 10N 80 30W
Cieszyn ..... 49 45N 18 35 E
Cieza 38 17N 1 23W
Cilacap ..... 7 43S 109 0 E
Cimarron, R. 36 10N 96 17W
Cimahi ..... 6 53S 107 33 E
Cîmpina ..... 45 10N 25 45 E
Cîmpulung ..... 45 17N 25 3 E
Cinca, R. ..... 41 26N 0 21 E
Cincinnati 39 10N 84 26W
Cinto, Mt. ..... 42 24N 8 54 E
Circle 47 26N 105 35W
Circleville, Ohio .. 39 35N 82 57W
Circleville, Utah .. 38 12N 112 24W
Cirebon ..... 6 45S 108 32 E
Cirencester 51 43N 1 59W
Cisco 32 25N 99 0W
Citlaltepetl, Mt. .. 19 0N 97 20W
Citrusdal ..... 32 35S 19 0 E
Ciudad Acuña ... 29 20N 101 10W
Ciudad Bolívar .. 8 5N 63 30W
Ciudad Camargo .. 27 41N 105 10W
Ciudad de Valles .. 22 0N 98 30W
Ciudad del
Carmen 18 20N 97 50W
Ciudad Guayana .. 8 20N 62 35W
Ciudad Guzmán .. 19 40N 103 30W
Ciudad Juárez ... 31 40N 106 28W
Ciudad Madero .. 22 19N 97 50W
Ciudad Mante ... 22 50N 99 0W
Ciudad Obregón .. 27 28N 109 59W
Ciudad Piar 7 27N 63 19W
Ciudad Real 38 59N 3 55W
Ciudad Rodrigo .. 40 35N 6 32W
Ciudad Victoria .. 23 41N 99 9W
Civitanova
Marche ..... 43 18N 13 41 E
Civitavécchia ..... 42 6N 11 46 E
Çivril ..... 38 20N 29 55 E
Clackline ..... 31 40S 116 32 E
Clacton ..... 51 47N 1 10 E
Clanwilliam ..... 32 11S 18 52 E
Clara 53 20N 7 38W
Clare ..... 33 20S 143 50 E
Clare □ 52 52N 8 55W
Clare, R. 53 20N 9 3W

Claremont 43 23N 72 20W
Claremore 36 20N 95 20W
Claremorris 53 45N 9 0W
Clarence, I. 54 0S 72 0W
Clarence, Str. ..... 12 0S 131 0 E
Clarence, R. ..... 42 10S 173 56 E
Clarendon 34 41N 91 20W
Clarenville 48 10N 54 1W
Claresholm 50 0N 113 45W
Clarinda 40 45N 95 0W
Clark Fork, R. .. 48 9N 116 15W
Clarkdale 34 53N 112 3W
Clarke City 50 12N 66 38W
Clarkes Harbour .. 43 25N 65 38W
Clarksburg 39 18N 80 21W
Clarksdale 34 12N 90 33W
Clarkston 46 28N 117 2W
Clarksville 36 32N 87 20W
Clayton 44 14N 76 5W
Clear, I. 51 26N 9 30W
Clearfield 41 0N 78 27W
Clearwater,
Canada 51 38N 120 2W
Clearwater, U.S.A. 27 58N 82 45W
* Clearwater L. 56 10N 75 0W
Cleburne 32 18N 97 25W
Clee Hills 55 25N 2 35W
Cleethorpes 53 33N 0 2W
Clermont,
Australia ..... 22 46S 147 38 E
Clermont-Ferrand . 45 46N 3 4 E
Clevedon 51 27N 2 51W
Cleveland,
Australia ..... 27 31S 153 3 E
Cleveland, Miss. .. 33 34N 90 43W
Cleveland, Ohio .. 41 28N 81 43W
Cleveland, Tenn. .. 35 9N 84 52W
Cleveland, Tex. .. 30 18N 95 0W
Cleveland □ 54 30N 1 12W
Cleveland, Mt. .. 48 56N 113 51W
Cleveleys 53 53N 3 3W
Clew B. 53 54N 9 50W
Clifden, Ire. 53 30N 10 2W
Clifden, N.Z. ..... 46 1S 167 42 E
Clifton 33 8N 109 23W
Clifton Forge 37 49N 79 51W
Clingmans Dome,
Mt. 35 35N 83 30W
Clinton, B.C. 51 0N 121 40W
Clinton, Ont. 43 38N 81 33W

Clinton, N.Z. ..... 46 12S 169 23 E
Clinton, Ark. 35 37N 92 30W
Clinton, Ill. 40 8N 89 0W
Clinton, Iowa ... 41 50N 90 18W
Clinton, Mass. ... 42 26N 71 40W
Clinton, Mo. 38 20N 93 40W
Clinton, N.C. ... 35 5N 78 15W
Clinton Colden L. . 64 0N 107 0W
Clipperton I. 10 18N 109 13W
Clocolan ..... 28 55S 27 34 E
Clonakilty 51 37N 8 53W
Cloncurry ..... 20 40S 140 28 E
Clones 54 10N 7 13W
Clonmel 52 22N 7 42W
Cloquet 46 40N 92 30W
Clovis, Calif. 36 54N 119 45W
Clovis, N.Mex ... 34 20N 103 10W
Cluj ..... 46 47N 23 38 E
Clutha, R. ..... 46 20S 169 49 E
Clwyd □ 53 0N 3 15W
Clwyd, R. 53 20N 3 30W
Clyde, Canada ... 70 30N 68 30W
Clyde, N.Z. ..... 45 12S 169 20 E
Clyde, R. 55 56N 4 29W
Clyde, Firth of .. 55 42N 5 0W
Clydebank 55 54N 4 25W
Coachella 33 44N 116 13W
Coachman's Cove . 50 6N 56 20W
Coahuila □ 27 0N 112 30W
Coaldale,
Canada 49 45N 112 35W
Coalinga 36 10N 120 21W
Coalville 52 43N 1 21W
Coast Mts. 52 0N 126 0W
Coast Ra. 40 0N 124 0W
Coastal Plains
Basin ..... 30 10S 115 30 E
Coatbridge 55 52N 4 2W
Coatepeque 14 46N 91 55W
Coaticook 45 10N 71 46W
Coats I. 62 30N 82 0W
Coatzacoalcos ... 18 7N 94 35W
Coazapá 26 0S 56 35W
Cobalt 47 25N 79 42W
Coban 15 30N 90 21W
Cobar ..... 31 27S 145 48 E
Cobh 51 50N 8 18W
Cobham ..... 30 10S 142 0 E
Cobourg 44 0N 78 20W
Coburg ..... 50 15N 10 58 E

† Renamed Kiritimati

* French nameform
Eau Claire, L. à l'

Cocanada=
  Kakinada...... 16 55N 82 20 E
Cochabamba.... 17 15s 66 20w
Cochin-China,
  Reg.=Nam-
  Phan, Reg.... 10 30N 106 0 E
Cochrane, Alta. .. 51 20N 114 30w
Cochrane, Ont. ... 49 0N 81 0w
Cochrane, L...... 47 10s 72 0w
Cockburn,
  Australia...... 32 5s 141 2 E
Cockburn,
  Canada...... 54 30s 72 0w
Coco, R. 15 0N 83 8w
Cocos Is. .... 12 12s 96 54 E
Cod, C. 42 8N 70 10w
Codajás........ 3 40s 62 0w
Codó 4 30s 43 55w
Codrington 17 43N 61 49w
Cody 44 35N 109 0w
Coen .... 13 52s 143 12 E
Coeur d'Alene ... 47 45N 116 51w
Coffeyville 37 0N 95 40w
Coffs Harbour ... 30 16s 153 5 E
Cognac.......... 45 41N 0 20w
Cohoes.......... 42 47N 73 42w
Cohuna .... 35 45s 144 15 E
Coiba, I. 7 30N 81 40w
Coig, R. 51 0s 69 10w
Coihaique 45 35s 72 8w
Coimbatore ...... 11 2N 76 59 E
Coimbra 40 15N 8 27w
Coín 36 40N 4 48w
Cojimies 0 20N 80 0w
Cojutepeque 13 41N 88 54w
Colac .... 38 10s 143 30 E
Colby 39 27N 101 2w
Colchester ...... 51 54N 0 55 E
Cold Lake 54 27N 110 10w
Coldstream 55 39N 2 14w
Coldwell 48 45N 86 30w
Colebrook 44 54N 71 29w
Coleman 31 52N 99 30w
Colenso .... 28 44s 29 50 E
Coleraine,
  Australia ...... 37 36s 141 40 E
Coleraine, U.K. ... 55 8N 6 40w
Coleraine □ 55 8N 6 40w
Colesburg .... 30 45s 25 5 E
Colhué Huapí, L. . 45 30s 69 0w

Coligny .... 26 17s 26 18 E
Colima 19 10N 103 50w
Colima □ 19 10N 103 40w
Colinas 6 0s 44 10w
Colinton .... 35 50s 149 10 E
Coll, I. 56 40N 6 35w
College Park 33 42N 84 27w
Collie .... 33 25s 116 30 E
Collier, B. .... 16 0s 124 0 E
Collingwood,
  Australia ...... 22 20s 142 31 E
Collingwood,
  Canada 44 30N 80 20w
Collingwood, N.Z.. 40 42s 172 40 E
Collinsville ...... 20 30s 147 56 E
Collooney 54 11N 8 28w
Colmar .... 48 5N 7 20 E
Colne 53 51N 2 11w
Colo, R. .... 33 20s 150 40 E
Cologne=Köln ... 50 56N 9 58 E
Colombia ■ 3 45N 73 0w
Colombia 3 24N 79 49w
Colombo .... 6 56N 79 58 E
Colón 9 20N 80 0w
Colonia del
  Sacramento..... 34 25s 57 50w
Colonia 25 de
  Mayo 38 0s 67 32w
Colonsay, I. 56 4N 6 12w
Colorado □ 37 40N 106 0w
Colorado, R., Arg. 39 50s 62 8w
Colorado, R.
  Mex.-U.S.A... 31 45N 114 40w
Colorado, R.,
  U.S.A. 28 36N 95 58w
Colorado Aqueduct 34 0N 115 20w
Colorado City ... 32 25N 100 50w
Colorado Plat. ... 36 40N 110 30w
Colorado Springs . 38 55N 104 50w
Columbia, La. ... 32 7N 92 5w
Columbia, Mo. ... 38 58N 92 20w
Columbia, S.C.... 34 0N 81 0w
Columbia, Tenn. .. 35 40N 87 0w
Columbia,
  District of □ ... 38 55N 77 0w
Columbia, Mt. ... 52 20N 117 30w
Columbia, R. 45 49N 120 0w
Columbia Falls ... 48 25N 114 16w
Columbia Heights . 45 5N 93 10w

Columbia Plat. ... 47 30N 118 30w
Columbus, Ga. ... 32 30N 84 58w
Columbus, Ind. .. 39 14N 85 55w
Columbus, Miss. .. 33 30N 88 26w
Columbus, N.D... 48 52N 102 48w
Columbus, Ohio.. 39 57N 83 1w
Colville, C. ...... 36 29s 175 21 E
Colville, R. 70 25N 150 30w
Colwyn Bay 53 17N 3 44w
Comácchio ...... 44 41N 12 10 E
Comallo 41 0s 70 5w
Comet .... 23 36s 148 38 E
Comilla .... 23 22N 91 18 E
Comino, I. ...... 36 0N 14 22 E
Comitán 16 18N 92 9w
Committee B. 68 0N 87 0w
Commerce 33 15N 95 50w
Como .... 45 48N 9 5 E
Como, L. di ..... 46 5N 9 17 E
Comodoro
  Rivadavia 45 50s 67 40w
Comorin, C. ..... 8 3N 77 40 E
Comoro Is. ...... 12 10s 44 15 E
Comox 49 42N 125 0w
Compiègne ...... 49 24N 2 50 E
Conakry......... 9 29N 13 49w
Conard Junction .. 41 48s 143 70 E
Concarneau 47 52N 3 56w
Conceição do
  Araguaia 8 0s 49 2w
Conceiçao do
  Barra 18 50s 39 50w
Concepción, Chile . 36 50s 73 0w
Concepción,
  Paraguay 23 30s 57 20w
Concepción, Canal. 50 50s 75 0w
Concepción, Pt. .. 34 30N 120 34w
Concepción del Oro 24 40N 101 30w
Concepción del
  Uruguay 32 35s 58 20w
Concord, N.C. ... 35 28N 80 35w
Concord, N.H. ... 43 5N 71 30w
Concordia, Arg. .. 31 20s 58 2w
Concordia, U.S.A.. 39 35N 97 40w
Condamine ...... 26 55s 150 3 E
Condobolin ...... 33 4s 147 6 E
Congleton 53 10N 2 12w
Congo ■ .... 1 0s 16 0 E
Congo (Kinshasa)■
  =Zaïre ■ ...... 3 0s 22 0 E

Congo, R.=
  Zaïre, R. ...... 6 4s 12 24 E
Congo Basin ..... 1 0s 23 0 E
Congress 34 11N 112 56w
Coniston 46 32N 80 51w
Conjeeveram=
  Kanchipuram .. 12 52N 79 45 E
Conjuboy .... 18 35s 144 45 E
Connacht □ 53 23N 8 40w
Conneaut 41 55N 80 32w
Connecticut □ ... 41 40N 72 40w
Connecticut, R. .. 41 17N 72 21w
Connemara 53 29N 9 45w
Connersville 39 40N 85 10w
Conquest 53 35N 107 0w
Conroe 30 15N 95 28w
Conselheiro 20 40s 43 8w
Consett 54 51N 1 49w
Consort 52 1N 110 46w
Constance, L.=
  Bodensee ..... 47 35N 9 25 E
Constanţa ...... 44 14N 28 38 E
Constantine ..... 36 25N 6 42 E
Constitución 35 20s 72 30w
Conway, Ark. ... 35 5N 92 30w
Conway, N.H. ... 43 58N 71 8w
Conway, S.C. ... 33 49N 79 2w
Conwy 53 17N 3 50w
Conwy R. 53 17N 3 50w
Cooch Behar .... 26 22s 89 29 E
Cook .... 30 42s 130 48 E
Cook, B. 55 10s 70 0w
Cook Inlet....... 59 0N 151 0w
Cook Is. 22 0s 157 0w
Cook, Mt. .... 43 36s 170 9 E
Cook, Str. .... 41 15s 174 29 E
Cookeville 36 12N 85 30w
Cookhouse ...... 32 44s 25 47 E
Cooktown .... 15 30s 145 16 E
Cookstown □ 54 40N 6 43w
Coolabah .... 31 0s 146 15 E
Coolangatta ..... 28 11s 153 29 E
Coolgardie ...... 30 55s 121 8 E
Coolidge 33 1N 111 35w
Coolidge Dam ... 33 10N 110 30w
Cooma .... 36 12s 149 8 E
Coonabarabran .. 31 14s 149 18 E
Coonamble ...... 30 56s 148 27 E
Coonana .... 31 0s 123 0 E
Coongoola ...... 27 43s 145 47 E

Cooper. 39 57N 75 7w
Cooper
  Creek, R., L. ... 28 0s 139 0 E
Coorong, The .... 35 50s 139 20 E
Coorow .... 29 50s 115 59 E
Cooroy .... 26 22s 152 54 E
Coos Bay 43 26N 124 7w
Cootamundra .... 34 36s 148 1 E
Cootehill 54 5N 7 5w
Copenhagen=
  København .... 55 41N 12 34 E
Copiapó .... 27 15s 70 20 E
Copper Center ... 62 10N 145 25w
Copper Cliff 46 30N 81 4w
Copper Mountain . 49 20N 120 30w
Coppermine 68 0N 116 0w
Coquet, R. 55 22N 1 37w
Coquilhatville=
  Mbandaka ..... 0 1N 18 18 E
Coquimbo 30 0s 71 20w
Corabia .... 43 48N 24 30 E
Coracora 15 5s 73 45w
Coral Harbour ... 64 0N 83 0w
Coral Rapids 50 20N 81 40w
Coral Sea .... 15 0s 150 0 E
Corbin 37 0N 84 3w
Corby 52 29N 0 41w
Corcoran 36 6N 119 35w
Corcubión 42 56N 9 12w
Cordele 31 55N 83 49w
Córdoba, Arg. ... 31 20s 64 10w
Córdoba, Mexico . 20 26N 103 20w
Córdoba, Sp. 37 50N 4 50w
Córdoba, Sa. de .. 31 10s 64 25w
Cordon .... 16 42N 121 32 E
Cordova 60 36N 145 45w
Corfield .... 21 40s 143 21 E
Corfu, I.=
  Kérkira, I. ..... 39 38N 19 50 E
Corigliano ...... 39 36N 16 31 E
Corinth 34 54N 88 30w
Corinto, Nic. 12 30N 87 10w
Corinto,
  Brazil 18 20s 44 30w
Cork 51 54N 8 30w
Cork □ 51 54N 8 30w
Çorlu .... 41 11N 27 49 E
Cormorant 54 5N 100 45w
Corn Is. 12 0N 83 0w

Corner Brook 49 0N 58 0w
Corning, Calif. 39 56N 122 9w
Corning, N.Y. 42 10N 77 3w
Cornwall 45 5N 74 45w
Cornwall □ 50 26N   4 40w
Coro 11 30N 69 45w
Coroatá 4 20s 44 0w
Corocoro 17 15s 69 19w
Coromandel ...... 36 45s 175 31 E
Coromandel Coast
   Reg. .... 12 30N 81 0 E
Corona 33 49N 117 36w
Coronado 32 45N 117 9w
Coronado, B. de . 9 0N 83 40w
Coronation G. 68 0N 114 0w
Coronel 37 0s 73 10w
Coronel Dorrego . 38 40s 61 10w
Coronel Pringles . 38 0s 61 30w
Coronel Suárez .. 37 30s 62 0w
Corpus Christi 27 50N 97 28w
Correntes, C. das . 24 11s 35 34 E
Corrèze □ .... 45 20N   1 50 E
Corrib, L. 53 25N   9 10w
Corrientes 27 30s 58 45w
Corrientes, C.,
   Cuba 21 43N 84 30N
Corrientes, C.,
   Col. 5 30N 77 34w
Corrigin .... 32 18s 117 45 E
Corry 41 55N 79 39w
Corse, C. .... 43 1N   9 25 E
Corse, I. .... 42 0N   9 0 E
Corse du Sud □ ... 41 40N   9 0 E
Corsica, I. =
   Corse, I. ...... 42 0N   9 0 E
Corsicana 32 5N 96 30w
Cortez 37 24N 108 35w
Cortland 42 35N 76 11w
Cortona .... 43 16N 12 0 E
Çorum .... 40 30N 35 5 E
Corumbá 19 0s 57 30w
Corunna =
   La Coruña 43 20N   8 25w
Corvallis 44 36N 123 15w
Cosamalopan 18 23N 95 50w
Cosenza .... 39 17N 16 14 E
Coshocton 40 17N 81 51w
Costa, Cord. de la . 30 0s 71 0w
Costa Blanca, Reg. 38 25N   0 10w
Costa Brava, Reg. . 41 30N   3 0 E

Costa del Sol, Reg. 36 30N   4 30w
Costa Dorada, Reg. 40 45N   1 15 E
Costa Rica ■ 10 0N 84 0w
Cotabato .... 7 8N-124 13 E
Côte d'Or □ ..... 47 30N   4 50 E
Côte d'Or, Reg. ... 47 10N   4 50 E
Cotentin, Reg. 49 30N   1 30w
Côtes-du-Nord □ . 48 28N   2 50w
Cotonou .... 6 20N   2 25 E
Cotopaxi, Mt. 0 30s 78 30w
Cotswold Hills ... 51 42N   2 10w
Cottage Grove ... 43 48N 123 2w
Cottbus .... 51 44N 14 20 E
Cottonwood 34 48N 112 1w
Coulee City 47 44N 119 12w
Council, Alas. 64 55N 163 45w
Council, Id. 44 45N 116 30w
Council Bluffs 41 20N 95 50w
Courtenay 49 45N 125 0w
Coventry 52 25N   1 32w
Covilhã 40 17N   7 31w
Covington, Ga. ... 33 36N 83 50w
Covington, Ky. ... 39 5N 84 30w
Cowan 52 5N 100 45w
Cowan, L. .... 31 45s 121 45 E
Cowangie .... 35 12s 141 26 E
Cowansville 45 14N 72 46w
Cowdenbeath 56 7N   3 20w
Cowell .... 33 38s 136 40 E
Cowes 50 45N   1 18w
Cowra .... 33 49s 148 42 E
Coxim 18 30s 54 55w
Cox's Bazar ..... 21 25N 92 3 E
Cozumel, I. de ... 20 30N 86 40w
Cracow =
   Kraków .... 50 4N 19 57 E
Cradock .... 32 8s 25 36 E
Craig 40 32N 107 44w
Craigavon □ 54 27N   6 26w
Craiova .... 44 21N 23 48 E
* Crampel .... 7 8N 19 8 E
Cranberry Portage . 54 36N 101 22w
Cranbrook,
   Tas. .... 42 0s 148 5 E
Cranbrook,
   W. Australia ... 34 20s 117 35 E
Cranbrook
   Canada 49 30N 115 55w
Crateús 5 10s 40 50w
Crato, Brazil 7 10s 39 25w

Crawfordsville 40 2N 86 51w
Crawley 51 7N   0 10w
Crécy .... 48 50N   2 53 E
Cree L. 57 30N 107 0w
Cremona .... 45 8N 10 2 E
Cres, I. .... 44 58N 14 25 E
Crescent City 41 45N 124 12w
Cressman 47 40N 72 55w
Creston, Canada . 49 10N 116 40w
Creston, U.S.A. ... 41 0N 94 20w
Crestview 30 45N 86 35w
Crete, I. .... 35 10N 25 0 E
Creus, C. .... 42 20N   3 19 E
Creuse □ .... 46 0N   2 0 E
Creuse, R. ...... 47 0N   0 34 E
Crewe 53 6N   2 28w
Criciúma 28 40s 49 23w
Crieff 56 22N   3 50w
Crimea =
   Krymskaya, Reg. 45 0N 34 0 E
Crinan 56 4N   5 30w
Cristóbal 9 10N 80 0w
Crişul Alb, R. .... 46 42N 21 17 E
Crişul Negru, R. .. 46 42N 21 16 E
Crna, R. .... 41 35N 21 59 E
Crna Gora □ .... 42 40N 19 20 E
Crna Gora, Mts. .. 42 20N 19 20 E
Crockett 31 20N 95 30w
Croker, I. .... 11 12s 132 32 E
Cromarty 57 40N   4 2w
Cromer .... 52 56N   1 18 E
Cromwell .... 45 3s 169 14 E
Cronulla .... 34 3s 151 8 E
Crooked I. 22 50N 74 10w
Crookston 47 50N 96 40w
Cross Fell, Mt. ... 54 44N   2 29w
Cross River □ .... 6 20N   8 20 E
Crosshaven 51 48N   8 19w
Crotone .... 39 5N 17 6 E
Crow Agency 45 40N 107 30w
Crow Hd. 51 34N 10 9w
Crowley 30 15N 92 20w
Crowsnest P. 49 40N 114 40w
Croydon,
   Australia ..... 18 15s 142 14 E
Croydon, U.K. ... 51 18N   0 5w
Crozet Is. .... 46 27s 52 0 E
Cruz Alta 28 40s 53 32w
Cruz del Eje 30 45s 64 50w
Cruzeiro 22 50s 45 0w

Cruzeiro do Sul .. 7 35s 72 35w
Crystal Brook .... 33 21s 138 13 E
Crystal City 38 15N 90 23w
Csongrád .... 46 43N 20 12 E
Cuamba .... 14 45s 36 22 E
Cuando, R. ...... 14 0s 19 30 E
Cuba ■ 22 0N 79 0w
Cuballing .... 32 50s 117 15 E
Cubango, R. ..... 18 50s 22 25 E
Cucui 1 10N 66 50w
Cúcuta 7 54N 72 31w
Cuddalore .... 11 46N 79 45 E
Cuddapah .... 14 30N 78 47 E
Cue .... 27 20s 117 55 E
Cuenca, Ecuador . 2 50s 79 9w
Cuenca, Sa. de .. 39 55N   1 50w
Cuernavaca 18 50N 99 20w
Cuero 29 5N 97 17w
Cuevas de
   Almanzora 37 18N   1 58w
Cuiabá 15 30s 56 0w
Cuillin Hills 57 14N   6 15w
Cuito, R. .... 18 1s 20 48 E
Cuitzeo, L. 19 55N 101 5w
Culcairn .... 35 41s 147 3 E
Culebra, Sa. de la . 41 55N   6 20w
Culiacán 24 50N 107 40w
Cullen 57 45N   2 50w
Cullen, Pt. ...... 11 50s 141 47 E
Cullera 39 9N   0 17w
Culloden Moor ... 57 29N   4 7w
Culverden .... 42 47s 172 49 E
Cumaná 10 30N 64 5w
Cumberland,
   Canada, ... 49 40N 125 0w
Cumberland,
   U.S.A. 39 40N 78 43w
Cumberland Pen. . 67 0N 65 0w
Cumberland Plat. . 36 0N 84 30w
Cumberland Sd. .. 65 30N 66 0w
Cumbria □ 54 44N   2 55w
Cumbrian, Mts. .. 54 30N   3 0w
Cumbum .... 15 40N 79 10 E
Cunderdin ...... 31 37s 117 15 E
Cunene, R. ...... 17 20s 11 50 E
Cúneo .... 44 23N   7 32 E
Cunnamulla ..... 28 4s 145 41 E
Cupar, Canada .. 51 0N 104 10w
Cupar, U.K. 56 20N   3 0w
Cupica, G. de ... 6 25N 77 30w

Curaçao 12 10N 69 0w
Curiapo 8 33N 61 5w
Curicó 34 55s 71 20w
Curitiba 25 20s 49 10w
Currais Novos ... 6 13s 36 30w
Curralinho 1 35s 49 30w
Currawilla ...... 25 10s 141 20 E
Currie 40 16N 114 45w
Curtis, I. .... 23 40s 151 15 E
Curuçá 0 35s 47 50w
Cururupu 1 50s 44 50w
Curuzú Cuatiá ... 29 50s 58 5w
Curvelo 18 45s 44 27w
Curya .... 35 53s 142 54 E
Cushing 31 43N 94 50w
Custer 43 45N 103 38w
Cut Bank 48 40N 112 15w
Cuttack .... 20 25N 85 57 E
Cuvier, C. ...... 23 14s 113 22 E
Cuxhaven .... 53 52N   8 42 E
Cuyahoga Falls .. 41 8N 81 30w
Cuzco, Mt. 20 0s 66 50w
Cuzco 13 32s 72 0w
Cyclades, Is. =
   Kikládhes, Is. .. 37 20N 24 30 E
Cygnet .... 43 8s 147 1 E
Cyprus ■ .... 35 0N 33 0 E
Cyrenaica = Barqa
   Reg. .... 27 0N 20 0 E
Cyrene = Shahhat . 32 39N 21 18 E
Czechoslovakia ■ . 49 0N 17 0 E
Częstochowa ..... 50 49N 19 7 E

D

Da, R. .... 16 0N 107 0 E
Da Lat .... 12 3N 108 32 E
Da Nang .... 16 10N 108 7 E
Dabai .... 11 25N   5 15 E
Dabakala 8 15N   4 20w
Dąbie .... 53 27N 14 45 E
Dabola 10 50N 11 5w
* Dacca .... 23 43N 90 26 E
Dacca □ .... 24 0N 90 0 E
Dadanawa 3 0N 59 30w
Dadiya .... 9 35N 11 24 E
Dadu .... 26 45N 67 45 E

* Renamed Kaga Bandoro

* Renamed Dhākā

Dagesta
A.S.S.R. □ ..... 42 30N 47 0 E
Dagupan .... 16 3N 120 33 E
Dahomey ■=
  Benin ■ .... 8 0N 2 0 E
Daingean 53 18N 7 15w
Dairen=Talien .. 39 0N 121 31 E
Dairût .... 27 34N 30 43 E
Dairy Creek .... 25 12s 115 48 E
Daisetsu-Zan, Mt. . 43 30N 142 57 E
Dajarra .... 21 42s 139 30 E
Dakar 14 34N 17 29w
Dakhla 23 50N 15 53w
Dakhovskaya .... 44 13N 40 13 E
Dakingari ...... 11 37N 4 1 E
Dalai Nor, L. ... 49 0N 117 50 E
Dalälven, R. .... 60 38N 17 27 E
Dalandzadgad ... 43 35N 104 30 E
Dalarö .... 59 8N 18 24 E
Dalbandin ...... 28 53N 64 25 E
Dalbeattie 54 56N 3 49w
Dalby .... 27 11s 151 16 E
Dalhart 36 4N 102 31w
Dalhousie 48 0N 66 26w
Daliyat el Karmel . 32 41N 35 3 E
Dalkeith 55 54N 3 4w
Dallas 32 47N 96 48w
Dalma, I. ...... 24 30N 52 20 E
Dalmacija, Reg. .. 43 0N 17 0 E
Dalmatia, Reg.=
  Dalmacija, Reg. . 43 0N 17 0 E
Dalmellington 55 20N 4 25w
Dalnerechensk ... 45 50N 133 40 E
Daloa 6 53N 6 27w
Dalton, Canada .. 60 10N 137 0w
Dalton, Neb. 41 27N 103 0w
Daly, R. .... 13 20s 130 19 E
Daly Waters .... 16 15s 133 22 E
Daman .... 20 25N 72 57 E
Daman, Dadra &
  Nagar Haveli □ . 20 25N 72 58 E
Damanhûr .... 31 2N 30 28 E
Damaraland, Reg. .. 22 33s 17 6 E
Damascus=
  Dimashq ...... 33 30N 36 18 E
Damataru .... 11 45N 11 55 E
Damävand .... 35 45N 52 10 E
Damävand,
  Qolleh-ye, Mt. .. 35 56N 52 8 E
Dâmboviţa, R. ... 44 40N 26 0 E

Dâmäghan .... 36 10N 54 17 E
Damietta=
  Dumyât .... 31 24N 31 48 E
Damiya .... 32 6N 35 34 E
Damoh .... 23 50N 79 28 E
Dampier .... 20 39s 116 45 E
Dampier, Selat ... 0 40s 130 40 E
Dan .... 33 13N 35 39 E
Dan Dume .... 11 28N 7 8 E
Dan Gulbi ...... 11 40N 6 15 E
Dan Yashi ...... 12 0N 8 5 E
Danané 7 16N 8 9w
Danbury 41 23N 73 29w
Dandenong ...... 37 52s 145 12 E
Dangora .... 11 25N 8 7 E
Daniel's Harbour . 50 13N 57 35w
Danilov .... 58 16N 40 13 E
Danja .... 11 29N 7 30 E
Dankama .... 13 20N 7 44 E
Dankhar Gompa .. 32 9N 78 10 E
Dannemora ...... 60 11N 16 49 E
Dannevirke ..... 40 12s 176 8 E
Dannhauser ..... 28 0s 30 3 E
Dansville 42 32N 77 41w
Danube,
  R. (Donau)
  =Dunárea, R. .. 45 20N 29 40 E
Danville, Ill. ... 40 10N 87 45w
Danville, Ky. ... 37 40N 84 45w
Danville, Va. ... 36 40N 79 20w
Danzig=
  Gdánsk .... 54 22N 18 40 E
Dapango .... 10 52N 0 12 E
Dapto .... 34 30s 150 47 E
Dar'a .... 32 37N 36 6 E
Dar-es-Salaam ... 6 50s 39 12 E
Dârâb .... 28 50N 54 30 E
Darazo .... 11 1N 10 24 E
Darband .... 34 30N 72 50 E
Darbhanga ...... 26 15N 86 3 E
D'Arcy 50 35N 122 30w
Dardanelles=
  Cannakale
  Boğazi, Str. .... 40 0N 26 20 E
Dârfûr □ .... 15 35N 25 0 E
Dârfûr, Reg. .... 12 35N 25 0 E
Dargai .... 34 25N 71 45 E
Dargan Ata ..... 40 40N 62 20 E
Dargaville ..... 35 57s 173 52 E
Darhan .... 49 27N 105 57 E

Darién, G. del 9 0N 77 0w
Darmstadt .... 49 51N 8 40 E
Darnall .... 29 23s 31 18 E
Darnley, B. 69 30N 124 30w
Darr .... 24 34s 144 52 E
Dart, R. 50 34N 3 56w
Dartmoor .... 37 56s 141 19 E
Dartmoor, Reg. .. 50 36N 4 0w
Dartmouth,
  Australia .... 23 30s 144 40 E
Dartmouth
  Canada 44 40N 63 30w
Dartmouth, U.K. .. 50 21N 3 35w
Darjeeling ...... 27 3N 88 18 E
Dark Cove 49 54s 54 5w
Darkan .... 33 19s 116 37 E
Darling, R. ..... 34 4s 141 54 E
Darling Downs ... 27 30s 150 30 E
Darling Ra. ..... 32 0s 116 30 E
Darlington 54 33N 1 33w
Darłowo .... 54 26N 16 23 E
Darvaza .... 40 12N 58 24 E
Darwin .... 12 20s 130 50 E
Darwin River .... 12 49s 130 58 E
* Daryächeh-ye
  Reza'iyeh, L. ... 37 30N 45 30 E
Das .... 35 5N 75 4 E
Dashen, Ras, Mt. .. 13 10N 38 26 E
Dashinchilen .... 47 50N 103 60 E
Dasht, R. .... 25 10N 61 40 E
Dasht-e Kavir,
  Des. .... 34 30N 55 0 E
Dasht-e Lút,
  Des. .... 31 30N 58 0 E
Datia .... 25 39N 78 27 E
Daugavpils ..... 55 53N 26 32 E
Daulat Yar ..... 34 33N 65 46 E
Dauphin 51 15N 100 5w
Dauphiné, Reg. .. 45 15N 5 25 E
Daura .... 13 2N 8 21 E
Davangere ...... 14 25N 75 50 E
Davao .... 7 0N 125 40 E
Davao G. .... 6 30N 125 48 E
Davenport,
  Iowa 41 30N 90 40w
Davenport,
  Wash. 47 40N 118 5w
Daventry 52 16N 1 10w
David 8 30N 82 30w
Davis, Alas. 51 52N 176 39w

Davis, Calif. 38 39N 121 45w
Davis Inlet 55 50N 60 45w
Davis Str. 68 0N 58 0w
Davos .... 46 48N 9 50 E
Dawson 64 4N 139 25w
Dawson Creek ... 55 46N 120 14w
Dawson, I. 53 50s 70 50w
Dayr al-Ghusūn .. 32 21N 35 5 E
Dayr az Zawr ... 35 20N 40 9 E
Dayral Balah .... 31 25N 34 21 E
Dayton, Ohio ... 39 45N 84 10w
Dayton, Wash. ... 46 20N 118 0w
Daytona Beach .. 29 14N 81 0w
D'Entrecasteaux,
  Pt. .... 34 50s 116 0 E
De Aar .... 30 39s 24 0 E
De Grey .... 20 30s 120 0 E
De Grey, R. ..... 20 12s 119 11 E
De Kalb 41 55N 88 45w
De Land 29 1N 81 19w
De Ridder 30 48N 93 15w
De Soto= 38 8N 90 34w
Dead Sea=
  Miyet, Bahr el .. 31 30N 35 30 E
Deadwood 44 25N 103 43w
Deakin .... 30 46s 129 0 E
Deal .... 51 13N 1 25 E
Dean, Forest of .. 51 50N 2 35w
Deán Funes 30 20s 64 20w
Dease Arm, B. ... 66 45N 120 0w
Dease Lake 58 40N 130 5w
Death Valley 36 0N 116 40w
Death Valley
  Nat. Mon. 36 30N 117 0w
Death Valley
  Junction 36 15N 116 30w
Deba Habe ...... 10 14N 11 20 E
Debre Markos ... 10 20N 37 40 E
Debre Tabor .... 11 50N 38 5 E
Debrecen .... 47 33N 21 42 E
Decatur, Ala. ... 34 35N 87 0w
Decatur, Ga. 33 47N 84 17w
Decatur, Ill. ... 39 50N 89 0w
Decatur, Ind. ... 40 52N 85 28w
Deccan, Reg. .... 18 0N 77 0 E
Decorah 43 20N 91 50w
Dédougou 12 30N 3 35w
Dee, R., Scot. ... 57 4N 3 7w
Dee, R., Wales ... 53 15N 3 7w
Deep Well ...... 24 25s 134 5 E

Deepwater ...... 29 25s 151 51 E
Deer Lake 49 11N 57 27w
Deer Lodge 46 25N 112 40w
Deesa .... 24 18N 72 10 E
Defiance 41 20N 84 20w
Deganya .... 32 43N 35 34 E
Degeh Bur ...... 8 14N 43 35 E
Degema .... 4 50N 6 48 E
Deggendorf ..... 48 49N 12 59 E
Deh Bîd .... 30 39N 53 11 E
Dehra Dun ...... 30 20N 78 4 E
Deir Dibwan .... 31 55N 35 15 E
Dej .... 47 10N 23 52 E
Del Norte 37 47N 106 27w
Del Rio 29 15N 100 50w
Delagoa B. ..... 25 50s 32 45 E
Delano 35 48N 119 13w
Delareyville .... 26 41s 25 26 E
Delaware 40 20N 83 0w
Delaware □ 39 0N 75 40w
Delaware, R. 41 50N 75 15w
Delft .... 52 1N 4 22 E
Delfzijl .... 53 20N 6 55 E
Delgado, C. .... 10 45s 40 40 E
Delgo .... 20 6N 30 40 E
Delhi .... 28 38N 77 17 E
Delicias 28 10N 105 30w
Delmiro Gonveia .. 9 24s 38 6w
Delong, Os. .... 76 30N 153 0 E
Deloraine ...... 41 30s 146 40 E
Delphos 40 51N 84 17w
Delray Beach ... 26 27N 80 4w
Delta 38 44N 108 5w
Delungra .... 29 40s 150 45 E
Demanda, Sa. de .. 42 15N 3 0w
Deming 48 49N 122 13w
Demmit 55 26N 119 54w
Demopolis 32 31N 87 50w
Dempo, Mt. ..... 4 2s 103 9 E
Den Helder ..... 52 54N 4 45 E
Denau .... 38 16N 67 54 E
Denbigh 53 11N 3 25w
Dendang .... 3 5s 107 54 E
Dendermonde ... 51 2N 4 7 E
Denge .... 12 52N 5 21 E
Dengi .... 9 25N 9 55 E
Denham .... 25 55s 113 32 E
Denholm 52 40N 108 0w
Denia .... 38 49N 0 8 E
Deniliquin ..... 35 32s 144 58 E

Denison	33 45N	96 33W
Denizli	37 46N	29 6 E
Denmark	34 57S	117 21 E
Denmark ■	56 0N	10 0 E
Denmark Str.	67 0N	25 0W
Denpasar	8 39S	115 13 E
Denton	33 13N	97 8W
Denver	39 43N	105 1W
Deoghar	24 30N	86 59 E
Deolali	19 56N	73 50 E
Deosai Mts.	35 10N	75 20 E
Depot Springs	27 55S	120 3 E
Deputatskiy	69 18N	139 54 E
Dera Ghazi Khan	30 3N	70 38 E
Dera Ismail Khan	31 50N	70 50 E
† Dera Ismail Khan □	31 50N	70 54 E
Derbent	42 3N	48 18 E
Derby, Australia	17 18S	123 38 E
Derby, U.K.	52 55N	1 29W
Derby □	52 55N	1 29W
Derg, L.	53 0N	8 20W
* Derna	32 40N	22 35 E
Derrinallum	37 57S	143 13 E
Derriwong	33 6S	147 21 E
Derry=		
Londonderry	55 0N	7 20W
Derryveagh Mts.	55 0N	8 40W
Derudub	17 31N	36 7 E
Derwent R.		
Cumbria	54 42N	3 22W
Derwent, R.		
Derby	53 26N	1 44W
Derwent, R.		
Yorks	54 13N	0 35W
Derwentwater, L.	53 34N	3 9W
Des Moines	41 35N	93 37W
Des Moines, R.	41 15N	93 0W
Deseado, R.	40 0S	69 0W
Desert Center	33 45N	115 27W
Desna, R.	52 0N	33 15 E
Desolación, I.	53 0S	74 10W
Dessau	51 50N	12 14 E
Detmold	51 56N	8 52 E
Detroit	42 20N	83 3W
Detroit Lakes	46 49N	95 57W
Deurne, Belgium	51 13N	4 28 E
Deurne, Neth.	51 28N	5 47 E
Deutsche, B.	54 30N	7 30 E
Deux-Sèvres □	46 30N	0 20W
Deva	45 53N	22 55 E
Deventer	52 15N	6 10 E
Deveron, R.	57 22N	3 0W
Devils Lake	48 7N	98 59W
Devizes	51 22N	1 59W
Devon □	53 22N	113 44W
Devon □	50 45N	3 50W
Devon I.	75 0N	87 0W
Devonport,		
Australia	41 11S	146 21 E
Devonport, N.Z.	36 49S	174 48 E
Devonport, U.K.	50 22N	4 10W
Dewas	22 57N	76 4 E
Dewsbury	53 42N	1 37W
Deyhūk	33 17N	57 30 E
Deyyer	27 50N	51 55 E
Dezfūl	32 23N	48 24 E
† Dezh Shāhpūr	35 31N	46 10 E
Dhahaban	21 58N	39 3 E
Dhahran=		
Az Zahrān	26 10N	50 7 E
Dhamar	14 46N	44 23 E
Dhamtari	20 42N	81 33 E
Dhanbad	23 47N	86 26 E
Dhar	22 36N	75 18 E
Dharmapuri	12 8N	78 10 E
Dharwar	15 28N	75 1 E
Dhaulagiri, Mt.	28 42N	83 31 E
Dhenkanal	20 45N	85 35 E
Dhidhimotikhon	41 21N	26 30 E
Dhodhekánisos, Is.	36 35N	27 10 E
Dholpur	26 42N	77 54 E
Dhrol	22 34N	70 25 E
Dhubri	26 1N	89 59 E
Dhula	15 5N	48 5 E
Dhulia	20 54N	74 47 E
Diamante	32 5S	60 35W
Diamantina	18 5S	43 40W
Diamantina, R.	26 45S	139 10 E
Diamantino	14 25S	56 27W
Diamond Harbour	22 11N	88 14 E
Diapangou	12 5N	0 10 E
Dibaya Lubue	4 12S	19 54 E
Dibba	25 45N	56 16 E
Dibi	4 12N	41 58 E
Dibrugarh	27 29N	94 55 E
Dickinson	46 53N	102 47W
Didsbury	51 40N	114 8W
Diefenbaker L.	51 0N	106 55W
Diego Garcia, I.	7 20S	72 25 E
Diego Ramirez,		
Is.	56 30S	68 44W
* Diégo-Suarez	12 16S	49 17 E
* Diégo-Suarez □	14 0S	49 0 E
Dieppe	49 56N	1 5 E
Differdange	49 32N	5 32 E
Digby	44 41N	65 50W
Dighinala	23 15N	92 5 E
Digne	44 6N	6 14 E
Dihang, R.	27 30N	96 30 E
Dijlah, Nahr	30 0N	47 50 E
Dijon	47 19N	5 1 E
Dikson	73 30N	80 35 E
Dikwa	12 2N	13 56 E
Dili	8 33S	125 35 E
Dillon, Mont.	45 13N	112 38W
Dillon, S.C.	34 25N	79 22W
Dimashq	33 30N	36 18 E
Dimbokro	6 39N	4 42W
Dimboola	36 27S	142 2 E
Dimitrovgrad,		
Bulgaria	42 3N	25 36 E
Dimitrovgrad,		
U.S.S.R.	54 25N	49 33 E
Dinagat, I.	10 10N	125 35 E
Dinajpur	35 38N	88 38 E
Dinan	48 27N	2 2W
Dinant	50 16N	4 55 E
Dinar	38 4N	30 10 E
Dinar, Kuh-e,		
Mt.	30 48N	51 40 E
Dinara Planina,		
Mts.	43 50N	16 35 E
Dinard	48 38N	2 4W
Dinaric Alps,		
Mts.	43 50N	16 35W
Dindigul	10 21N	77 58 E
Dingle	52 8N	10 15W
Dingle, B.	52 5N	10 15W
Dingo	23 39S	149 20 E
Dinguiraye	11 18N	10 43W
Dingwall	57 35N	4 29W
Dinosaur Nat.		
Mon.	40 32N	108 58W
Dinuba	36 32N	119 23W
Diourbel	14 40N	16 15W
Dipolog	8 36N	123 20 E
Dire Dawa	9 37N	41 52 E
Diriamba	11 53N	86 15W
Dirico	17 50S	20 42 E
Dirk Hartog, I.	25 48S	113 0 E
Dirranbandi	28 35S	148 14 E
Disappointment.C.	46 18N	124 3W
Disappointment, L.	23 30S	122 50 E
Discovery	63 0N	115 0W
Discovery, B.	38 12S	141 7 E
Disina	11 35N	9 50 E
Disko, I.	69 50N	53 30W
Diss	52 23N	1 6 E
Disteghil Sar, Mt.	36 22N	75 12 E
Districto Federal □	15 45S	47 45W
Distrito		
Federal □	19 15N	99 10W
Diu	20 43N	70 69 E
Divnoye	45 55N	43 27 E
Dixon	41 50N	89 29W
Dixon Entrance	54 25N	132 30W
Diyarbakir	37 55N	40 14 E
Djajapura=		
Jayapura	2 28S	140 38 E
Djakarta=		
Jakarta	6 9S	106 49 E
Djambala	2 33S	14 45 E
Djangeru	2 20S	116 29 E
Djawa, I.=		
Java, I.	7 0S	110 0 E
Djelfa	34 30N	3 20 E
Djema	6 3N	25 19 E
Djerba, I. de	33 56N	11 0 E
Djerid, Chott el,		
Reg.	35 50N	8 30 E
Djibouti	11 36N	43 9 E
Djibouti ■	11 30N	42 15 E
Djidjelli	36 52N	5 50 E
Djirlagne	11 44N	108 15 E
Djolu	0 37N	22 21 E
Djougou	9 42N	1 40 E
Djourab, Erg du	16 40N	18 50 E
Djugu	1 55N	30 30 E
Djúpivogur	64 40N	14 10W
Dnepr, R.	46 30N	32 18 E
Dneprodzerzhinsk	48 30N	34 37 E
Dnepropetrovsk	48 30N	35 0 E
Dnestr, R.	46 18N	30 17 E
Dnieper, R.=		
Dnepr, R.	46 30N	32 18 E
Dniester, R.=		
Dnestr, R.	46 18N	30 17 E
Doba	8 39N	16 51 E
Doberai, Jazirah	1 25S	133 0 E
Doblas	37 5S	64 0W
Dobo	5 46S	134 13 E
Dobruja, Reg.	44 30N	28 30 E
Dodecanese Is.=		
Dhodhekánisos,		
Is.	36 35N	27 10 E
Dodge City	37 45N	100 1W
Dodoma	6 11S	35 45 E
Dodsland	51 48N	108 49W
Doetinchem	51 58N	6 17 E
Dog Creek	51 35N	122 18W
Dogondoutchi	13 38N	4 2 E
Doha	25 15N	51 36 E
Dohad	22 50N	74 15 E
Dohazari	22 10N	92 5 E
Dolbeau	48 53N	72 14W
Dôle	47 6N	5 30 E
Dolgellau	52 44N	3 53W
† Dolisie	4 12S	12 41 E
Dolo, Somali Rep.	4 13N	42 8 E
Dolomiti, Mts.	46 25N	11 50 E
Dolores, Arg.	36 19S	57 40W
Dolores, Uruguay	33 33S	58 13W
Dolphin, C.	51 15S	58 58W
Dolphin &		
Union Str.	69 5N	114 45W
Doma	8 25N	8 18 E
Dombarovskiy	50 46N	59 39 E
Dombås	62 5N	9 8 E
Dombes, Reg.	46 0N	5 3 E
Dominica, I.	15 30N	61 20W
Dominica Pass	15 10N	61 20W
Dominican Rep. ■	19 0N	70 40W
Domodossola	46 7N	8 17 E
Don, R., Eng.	53 39N	0 59W
Don, R., Scot.	57 10N	2 4W
Don, R., U.S.S.R.	47 4N	39 18 E
Donaghadee	54 39N	5 33W
Donalda	52 35N	112 34W
Donau, R.=		
Dunárea, R.	45 20N	29 40 E
Donauwörth	48 43N	10 46 E
Doncaster	53 32N	1 7W
Dondra Hd.	5 55N	80 35 E
Donegal	54 39N	8 7W
Donegal □	54 50N	8 0W
Donegal, B.	54 30N	8 35W
Donetsk	48 0N	37 48 E
Dong Hoi	17 18N	106 36 E
Dongara	29 15S	114 56 E
Dongola	19 9N	30 22 E

† Now part of
North West Frontier

* Darnah

† Renamed Marīvān

* Renamed Antsiranana

* Jijel

† Renamed Loubomo

Donnacona 46 40N 71 47w
Donnelly's Crossing 35 43 s 173 33 E
Donnybrook ...... 33 35 s 115 48 E
Donor's Hills ..... 18 42 s 140 33 E
Doodlakine .... 31 35 s 117 28 E
Doon, R. 55 26N 4 38w
Dor .... 32 37N 34 55 E
Dora Báltea, R. .. 45 11N 8 5 E
Dorchester 50 43N 2 26w
Dorchester, C. ... 65 29N 77 30w
Dordogne □ ...... 45 10N 0 45 E
Dordogne, R. 45 2N 0 35w
Dordrecht, Neth. .. 51 49N 107 45w
Dordrecht, S. Afr. . 31 20 s 27 3 E
Dore, Mt. .... 45 32N 2 50 E
Dore Lake 54 56N 107 45w
Dori 14 3N 0 2w
Dorion 45 23N 74 3w
Dornie 57 17N 5 30w
Dornoch 57 52N 4 2w
Dornoch Firth 57 52N 4 2w
Döröö Nuur, L. ... 47 40N 93 30 E
Dorre, I. .... 25 9 s 113 7 E
Dorrigo .... 30 21 s 152 43 E
Dorset □ 50 47N 2 20w
Dortmund .... 51 31N 7 28 E
Dos Bahias, C. ... 44 55 s 65 32w
Doshi .... 35 37N 68 41 E
Dosso .... 13 3N 3 12 E
Dot 50 12N 121 25w
Dothan 31 13N 85 24w
Douai .... 50 22N 3 4 E
Douala .... 4 3N 9 42 E
Douarnenez 48 6N 4 20w
Doubs □ .... 47 10N 6 25 E
Doubtless, B. .... 34 55 s 173 27 E
Doucet 48 15N 76 35w
Douentza 14 58N 2 48w
Douglas, S. Afr. .. 29 4 s 23 46 E
Douglas, U.K. 54 9N 4 29w
Douglas, Ariz. ... 31 21N 109 33w
Douglas, Ga. 31 31N 82 51w
Douglas, Wyo. 42 45N 105 24w
Dounreay 58 40N 3 28w
Dourada, Sa. ..... 13 10 s 48 45w
Douro, R. 41 8N 8 40w
Douro
  Litoral, Reg. ... 41 5N 8 20w
Dove, R. 54 20N 0 55w
Dover, Australia .. 43 19 s 147 1 E

Dover, U.K. ...... 51 8N 1 19 E
Dover, Del. 39 10N 75 32w
Dover, N.H. 43 12N 70 56w
Dover, Ohio 40 32N 81 30w
Dover, Str. of ... 51 0N 1 30 E
Dovey, R. 52 32N 4 0w
Dovrefjell, Mts. .. 62 6N 9 25 E
Dowagiac 41 59N 86 6w
Dowlàtābad ...... 28 18N 56 40 E
Down □ 54 24N 5 55w
Downham Market . 52 36N 0 23 E
Downpatrick 54 20N 5 43w
Draguignan ...... 43 32N 6 28 E
Drake Pass....... 58 0s 70 0w
Drakensberg, Mts. . 27 0s 30 0 E
Dráma .... 41 9N 24 8 E
Drammen .... 59 44N 10 15 E
Drava, R. .... 45 33N 18 55 E
Drayton Valley ... 53 13N 114 59w
Drenthe □ .... 52 45N 6 30 E
Dresden .... 51 3N 13 44 E
Dreux .... 48 44N 1 22 E
Driffield 54 0N 0 27w
Drina, R. .... 44 53N 19 21 E
Drini, R. .... 41 17N 20 2 E
Drøbak .... 59 39N 10 48 E
Drogheda 53 43N 6 21w
Drogobych ...... 49 20N 23 30 E
Droitwich 52 16N 2 9w
Drôme □ .... 44 35N 5 10 E
Dromedary, C. .... 36 17 s 150 10 E
Dronfield .... 53 19 s 1 27w
Dronning Maud
  Ld. .... 75 0s 10 0 E
Drouin .... 38 8 s 145 57 E
Drumheller 51 28N 112 42w
Drummondville .. 45 53N 72 30w
Druzhina .... 68 11N 14 51 9 E
Dryden 49 47N 92 50w
Drysdale, R. ..... 13 59 s 126 51 E
Dschang .... 5 27N 10 4 E
Du Bois 41 7N 78 46w
Du Quoin 38 0N 89 10w
Duaringa .... 23 42 s 149 42 E
Dubā .... 27 10N 35 40 E
Dubawnt L. 63 0N 102 0w
Dubayy .... 25 18N 55 18 E
Dubbo .... 32 15 s 148 36 E
Dublin, Eire 53 20N 6 15w
Dublin, U.S.A. 32 32N 82 54w

Dublin □ 53 20N 6 15w
Dubois 44 10N 112 14w
Dubovka .... 49 5N 44 50 E
Dubreka 9 48N 13 31w
Dubrovnik .... 42 38N 18 7 E
Dubrovskoye .... 47 28N 42 40 E
Dubuque 42 30N 90 41w
Duchesne 40 10N 110 24w
Duchess .... 21 22 s 139 52 E
Ducie I. .... 24 47 s 124 50w
Duck Lake 52 47N 106 13w
Duck Mt. Prov.
  Park 51 36N 100 55w
Dudinka .... 69 25N 86 15 E
Dudley 52 30N 2 5w
Duero, R. 41 37N 4 25w
Dufftown 57 26N 3 9w
Dugi Otok, I. ..... 44 0N 15 0 E
Duisburg .... 51 27N 6 42 E
Duiwelskloof .... 23 42 s 30 10 E
Dukhan .... 25 25N 50 50 E
Duku .... 10 43N 10 43 E
Dulce, G. 8 40N 83 20w
Dullstroom ...... 25 24 s 30 7 E
Dululu .... 23 48 s 150 15 E
Duluth 46 48N 92 10w
Dum Duma ...... 27 40N 95 40 E
Dumai .... 1 35N 101 20 E
Dumas 35 50N 101 58w
Dumbarton 55 58N 4 35w
Dumbleyung ..... 33 17 s 117 42 E
Dumfries 55 4N 3 37w
Dumfries-
  Galloway □ 55 12N 3 30w
Dumosa .... 35 52 s 143 6 E
Dumyāt .... 31 25N 31 48 E
Dun Leary=
  Dun Laoghaire .. 53 17N 6 9w
Dunaföldvár ..... 46 50N 18 57 E
Dunárea, R. ..... 45 20N 29 40 E
Dunaújváros ..... 47 0N 18 57 E
Dunback .... 42 23 s 170 36 E
Dunbar 56 0N 2 32w
Dunblane, Canada . 51 11N 106 52w
Dunblane, U.K. ... 56 10N 3 58w
Duncan, Canada .. 48 45N 123 40w
Duncan, U.S.A. ... 34 25N 98 0w
Duncan Town 22 20N 75 80w
Dundalk, U.K. 53 55N 6 45w

Dundas 43 17N 79 59w
Dundas, L. .... 32 35 s 121 50 E
Dundas, Str. ..... 11 15 s 131 35 E
Dundee,
  S. Africa ...... 28 11 s 30 15 E
Dundee, U.K. 56 29N 3 0w
Dundrum 54 17N 5 50w
Dundrum, B. 54 12N 5 40w
Dunedin .... 45 50 s 170 33 E
Dunfermline 56 5N 3 28w
Dungannon 54 30N 6 47w
Dungannon □ 54 30N 6 47w
Dungarvan 52 6N 7 40w
Dungeness, Pt. ... 50 54N 0 59 E
Dungu .... 3 42N 28 32 E
Dunkeld, Australia 37 40 s 142 22 E
Dunkeld, U.K. ... 56 34N 3 36w
Dunkerque ...... 51 2N 2 20 E
Dunkery Beacon . 51 15N 3 37w
Dunkirk 42 30N 79 18w
Dunkwa, Ghana .. 6 0N 1 47w
Dunkwa, Ghana .. 5 30N 1 0w
Dunmara .... 16 42 s 133 25 E
Dunmore 41 27N 75 38w
Dunmore Hd. 53 37N 8 44w
Dunn 35 18N 78 36w
Dunnet Hd. 58 38N 3 22w
Dunoon 55 57N 4 56w
Duns 55 47N 2 20w
Dunsmuir 41 0N 122 10w
Dunstable 51 53N 0 31w
D'Urville, I. ..... 40 50 s 173 55 E
Dūrā .... 31 30N 35 2 E
Durack, R. .... 15 33 s 127 52 E
Durance, R. ...... 43 55N 4 44 E
Durango, Mexico .. 24 3N 104 39w
Durango, Sp. 43 13N 2 40w
Durango, U.S.A. .. 37 10N 107 50w
Durango □ 25 0N 105 0w
Duranillin .... 33 30 s 116 45 E
Durant 34 0N 96 25w
Durazno .... 33 25 s 56 38w
Durban .... 29 49 s 31 1 E
Durg .... 21 15N 81 22 E
Durham, Canada .. 44 10N 80 48w
Durham, U.K. 54 47N 1 34w
Durham, U.S.A. .. 36 0N 78 55w
Durham □ 54 42N 1 45w

Durrësi .... 41 19N 19 28 E
Dushak .... 37 20N 60 10 E
Dushanbe .... 38 40N 68 50 E
Dusky, Sd. ...... 45 47 s 166 29 E
Düsseldorf ...... 51 15N 6 46 E
Dutch Harbor ... 53 54N 166 35w
Duzce .... 40 50N 31 10 E
Drinskaya Guba .. 65 0N 39 45 E
Dwarka .... 22 18N 69 8 E
Dwellingup ...... 32 38 s 115 58 E
Dyersburg 36 2N 89 20w
Dyfed □ 52 0N 4 30w
Dzerzhinsk ...... 56 15N 43 15 E
Dzhalal Abad .... 41 0N 73 0 E
Dzhalinda .... 53 50N 124 0 E
Dzhambul .... 43 10N 71 0 E
Dzhankoi .... 45 40N 34 30 E
Dzhardzhan ..... 68 43N 124 2 E
Dzhelinde .... 70 0N 114 20 E
Dzhezkazgan .... 47 10N 67 40 E
Dzhizak .... 40 20N 68 0 E
Dzhugdzur
  Khrebet, Ra.... 57 30N 138 0 E
Dzungaria, Reg.... 44 10N 88 0 E
Dzungarian Gate=
  Dzungarskiye
  Vorota .... 45 25N 82 25 E
Dzungarskiye
  Vorota .... 45 25N 82 25 E
Dzuunbulag ..... 46 58N 115 30 E
Dzuunmod ...... 47 45N 106 58 E

E

Eagle 64 44N 141 29w
Eagle Pass 28 45N 100 35w
Eaglehawk ...... 36 43 s 144 16 E
Ealing 51 30N 0 19w
Earlimart 35 57N 119 14w
Earn, L. 56 23N 4 14w
Earnslaw, Mt. ... 44 32 s 168 27 E
Easley 34 52N 82 35w
East, C. .... 37 42 s 178 35 E
East Angus 45 30N 71 40w
East Bengal, Reg. . 23 0N 90 0 E
East C. 65 50N 168 0w
East Chicago 41 40N 87 30w

East China Sea .... 30 0N 126 0 E
East Cleveland 41 32N 81 35W
East Falkland 51 30s 58 30W
East Germany ■ .. 52 0N 12 30 E
East Grand
  Forks 47 55N 97 5W
East Indies, Is. ... 0 0 120 0 E
East Kilbride 55 48N   4 12W
East Lansing 42 44N 84 37W
East Liverpool ... 40 39N 80 35W
East London ..... 33 0s 27 55 E
East Main 52 20N 78 30W
East Orange 40 45N 74 15W
East Pine 55 48N 120 5W
East Point 33 40N 84 28W
East Retford 53 19N   0 55W
East St. Lovis ... 38 36N 90 10W
East Siberian
  Sea .... 73 0N 160 0 E
East Sussex □ .... 50 55N   0 20 E
Eastbourne, N.Z. .. 41 19s 174 55 E
Eastbourne, U.K. . 50 46N   0 18 E
Eastend 49 32N 108 50W
Easter Is. 27 0s 109 0W
Eastern Ghats, Mts. 15 0N 80 0 E
Eastern □, Ghana . 6 20N   1 0W
* Eastern
  Malaysia □ ..... 3 0N 112 30 E
Eastleigh 50 58N   1 21W
Eastmain, R. 52 20N 78 30W
Easton 40 41N 75 15W
Eastport 44 57N 67 0W
Eastview 45 27N 75 40W
Eatonia 51 20N 109 25W
Eau Claire 44 46N 91 30W
Ebbw Vale 51 47N   3 12W
Ebden .... 36 10s 147 1 E
Ebeltoft .... 56 12N 10 41 E
Eberswalde ...... 52 49N 13 50 E
Eboli .... 40 39N 15 2 E
Ebro, R. .... 40 43N   0 54 E
Echuca .... 36 3s 144 46 E
Ecija 37 30N   5 10W
Ecuador ■ 2 0s 78 0W
Ed Dâmer .... 17 27N 34 0 E
Ed Debba .... 18 0N 30 51 E
Ed Dueim .... 10 10N 28 20 E
Edah .... 28 16s 117 10 E
Edam .... 52 31N   5 3 E
Eday, I. 59 11N   2 47W

Eddystone Rock .. 50 11N   4 16W
Ede, Neth. .... 52 4N   5 40 E
Ede, Nigeria ..... 7 45N   4 29 E
Edea .... 3 51N 10 9 E
Eden, R. 54 57N   3 1W
Edenburg .... 29 43s 25 58 E
Edenderry 53 21N   7 3W
Edenville .... 27 37s 27 34 E
Eder, R. .... 51 13N   9 27 E
Edge Hill 52 7N   1 28W
Edgeley 46 27N 98 41W
Edgemont 43 15N 103 53W
Edhessa .... 40 48N 22 5 E
Edievale .... 45 49s 169 22 E
Edinburg 26 22N 98 10W
Edinburgh 55 57N   3 12W
Edirne .... 41 40N 26 45 E
Edith River ...... 14 12s 132 2 E
Edmond 35 37N 97 30W
Edmonton,
  Australia ...... 17 2s 145 45 E
Edmonton, Canada 53 30N 113 30W
Edmundston 47 23N 68 20W
Edremit .... 39 40N 27 0 E
Edson 53 40N 116 28W
Edward, L.=Idi
  Amin Dada, L. .. 0 25s 29 40 E
Edwards Plat. 30 30N 101 5W
Eekloo .... 51 11N   3 33 E
Eersterus .... 25 45s 28 20 E
Effingham 39 8N 88 30W
Égadi, Is. .... 37 55N 12 10 E
Eganville 45 32N 77 5W
Eger .... 47 53N 20 27 E
Egersund=
  Eigersund ..... 58 2N   6 1 E
Eginbah .... 20 53s 119 47 E
Egmont, Mt. ..... 39 17s 174 5 E
Egume .... 7 30N   7 14 E
Egvekinot 66 19N 179 10W
Egypt ■ .... 28 0N 31 0 E
Eha Amufu ...... 6 30N   7 40 E
Ehime □ .... 33 30N 132 40 E
Eidsvold .... 25 25s 151 12 E
Eidsvoll .... 60 19N 11 14 E
Eifel, Mts. ...... 50 10N   6 45 E
Eiffel Flats ...... 18 20s 30 9 E
Eigersund .... 58 2N   6 1 E
Eigg, I. 56 54N   6 10W
Eighty Mile

Beach .... 19 30s 120 40 E
Eil, L. .... 56 50N   5 15 E
Eildon, L. .... 37 10s 146 0 E
Einasleigh .... 18 32s 144 5 E
Eindhoven .... 51 26N   5 30 E
Eire ■=
  Irish Rep. ■ ... 53 0N   8 0W
Eisenerz .... 47 32N 15 54 E
Eizariya .... 31 47N 35 15 E
Ejura .... 7 25N   1 25 E
Ekenäs .... 59 58N 23 26 E
Eket 4 38N   7 56W
Eketahuna .... 40 38s 175 43 E
Ekibastuz .... 51 40N 75 22 E
Ekimchan 53 0N 133 0W
El Aaiun 27 0N 12 0W
El Alamein ...... 30 48N 28 58 E
El Aricha 34 13N   1 16W
El Arîha .... 31 52N 35 27 E
El Arish .... 17 49s 146 1 E
El'Arîsh .... 31 8N 33 50 E
* El Asnam .... 36 10N   1 20 E
El Bawiti .... 28 25N 28 45 E
El Bayadh .... 33 40N   1 1 E
El Cajon 32 49N 117 0W
El Campo 29 10N 96 20W
El Centro 32 50N 115 40W
El Cuy 39 55s 68 25W
El Dere .... 3 50N 47 8 E
El Diviso 1 22N 78 14W
El Djouf .... 20 0N 11 30 E
El Dorado, Ark. .. 33 10N 92 40W
El Dorado, Kans. . 37 55N 96 56W
El Dorado,
  Venezuela 6 55N 61 30W
El Escorial 40 35N   4 7W
El Faiyûm .... 29 19N 30 50 E
El Fâsher .... 13 33N 25 26 E
El Ferrol 43 29N   3 14W
El Geneina .... 13 27N 22 45 E
El Geteina .... 14 50N 32 27 E
El Gezira .... 14 0N 33 0 E
El Gîza .... 30 0N 31 10 E
El Goléa .... 30 30N   2 50 E
El Harrach .... 36 45N   3 5 E
El Iskandarîya .... 31 0N 30 0 E
El Istwa'ya □ .... 5 0N 32 0 E
El Jadida 33 16N   9 31W
El Jebelein ...... 12 30N 32 45 E
El Kef .... 36 12N   8 47 E

El Khandaq ...... 18 30N 30 30 E
El Khârga .... 25 30N 30 33 E
El Khartûm ...... 15 31N 32 35 E
El Khartum
  Bahrî .... 15 40N 32 31 E
El Mafâza .... 13 38N 34 30 E
El Mahalla el
  Kubra .... 31 0N 31 0 E
El Mansura ...... 31 0N 31 19 E
El Minyâ .... 28 7N 30 33 E
El Niybo .... 4 32N 39 59 E
El Obeid .... 13 8N 30 18 E
El Oro 3 30s 79 50W
El Oued .... 33 20N   6 58 E
El Paso 31 50N 106 30W
El Progreso 15 26N 87 51W
El Qâhira .... 30 1N 31 14 E
El Qantara ...... 30 51N 32 20 E
El Qasr .... 25 44N 28 42 E
El Qubba .... 11 10N 27 5 E
El Reno 35 30N 98 0W
El Suweis .... 29 58N 32 31 E
El Tigre 8 55N 64 15W
El Tocuyo 9 47N 69 48W
El Turbio 51 30s 72 40W
El Uqsur .... 25 41N 32 38 E
El Vigia 8 38N 71 39W
El Wâhat el-
  Dakhla .... 26 0N 27 50 E
El Wâhât el
  Khârga .... 24 0N 23 0 E
El Wak .... 2 49N 40 56 E
Elaine .... 37 44s 144 2 E
Elat .... 5 40s 133 5 E
Elazig .... 38 37N 39 22 E
Elba, I. .... 42 48N 10 15 E
Elbasani .... 41 9N 20 9 E
Elbe, R. .... 53 50N   9 0 E
Elbert, Mt. 39 12N 106 36W
Elberton 34 7N 82 51W
Elbeuf .... 49 17N   1 2 E
Elblag .... 54 10N 19 25 E
Elbrus, Mt. ...... 43 30N 42 30 E
Elburz Mts.=
  Alberz, Reshteh-
  Ye-Kakha-Ye .. 36 0N 52 0 E
Elche de la
  Sierra 38 27N   2 3W
Eldama .... 0 3N 35 43 E
Elde, R. .... 53 17N 12 40 E

Eldorado 59 35N 108 30W
Eldoret .... 0 30N 35 25 E
Elefantes, R. ..... 24 10s 32 40 E
Elele .... 5 5N   6 50 E
Elephant Butte
  Res. 33 45N 107 30W
Eleuthera I. 25 0N 76 20W
Elgin, U.K. 57 39N   3 20W
Elgin, Ill. 42 0N 88 20W
Elgin, Ore. 45 37N 118 0W
Elgin, Tex. 30 21N 97 22W
Elgon, Mt. .... 1 10N 34 30 E
Eliase .... 8 10s 130 55 E
Elisabethville=
  Lubumbashi .... 11 32s 27 38 E
Elista .... 46 16N 44 14 E
Elizabeth,
  Australia ...... 34 45s 138 39 E
Elizabeth, U.S.A. . 40 37N 74 12W
Elizabeth City 36 18N 76 16W
Elizabethton 36 20N 82 13W
Elizabethtown 37 40N 85 54W
Elk City 35 25N 99 25W
Elk Lake 47 40N 80 25W
Elk Point 54 10N 110 55W
Elkhart 41 42N 85 55W
Elkhorn 50 0N 101 11W
Elkhovo .... 42 10N 26 40 E
Elkins 38 53N 79 53W
Elko, Canada 49 20N 115 10W
Elko, U.S.A. 40 40N 115 50W
Ellen Mt. 38 4N 110 56W
Ellendale,
  Australia ...... 17 56s 124 48 E
Ellendale, U.S.A. . 46 3N 98 30W
Ellensburg 47 0N 120 30W
Ellesmere I. 79 30N 80 0W
Ellesmere Port ... 53 17N   2 55W
Ellice Is=
  Tuvalu ■ .... 8 0s 176 0 E
Elliot .... 31 22s 27 48 E
Elliot Lake 46 35N 82 35W
Elliott .... 41 5s 145 38 E
Elliston .... 33 39s 134 55 E
Ellon 57 21N   2 5W
Ellore=Eluru ..... 16 48N 81 8 E
Ellsworth 38 47N 98 15W
Ellsworth Ld. 75 30s 80 0W
Ellwood City 40 52N 80 19W
Elma .... 47 0N 123 30 E

Elmali .... 36 44N 29 56 E
Elmenteita ...... 0 32s 36 14 E
Elmhurst 41 52N 87 58w
Elmina 5 5N 1 21w
Elmira 42 8N 76 49w
Elmore .... 36 30s 144 37 E
Elrose 51 20N 108 0w
Elsinore 33 40N 117 15w
Eltham .... 39 26s 174 19 E
Eluru .... 16 48N 81 8 E
Elvas 38 50N 7 17w
Elverum .... 60 55N 11 34 E
Elwood 40 20N 85 50w
Ely, U.K. .... 52 24N 0 16 E
Ely, U.S.A. 47 54N 91 52w
* Elyashiv .... 32 23N 34 55 E
Elyria 41 22N 82 8w
Emba .... 48 50N 58 8 E
Embarcación 23 10s 64 0w
Embu .... 0 32s 37 38 E
Emden .... 53 22N 7 12 E
Emerald .... 23 30s 148 11 E
Emerson 49 0N 97 10w
Emilia Romagna □ 44 33N 10 40 E
Emmen .... 52 48N 6 57 E
Emmett 24 45s 144 30w
Empalme 28 1N 110 49w
Empangeni ...... 28 50s 31 52 E
Empédrado 28 0s 58 46w
Emporia, Kans. ... 38 25N 96 16w
Emporia, Va. 36 41N 77 32w
Emporium 41 30N 78 17w
Ems. R. .... 51 9N 9 26 E
'En Kerem ...... 31 47N 35 6 E
En Nahud ...... 12 45N 28 25 E
'En Yahav ...... 30 37N 35 11 E
Ena .... 35 25s 137 25 E
Encarnación 27 15s 56 0w
Encarnación de
  Diaz 21 30N 102 20w
Enchi 5 53N 2 48w
Encontrados 9 3N 72 14w
Ende .:....... 8 45s 121 30 E
Endeavour, Str. ... 10 45s 142 0 E
Enderby 50 35N 119 10w
Enderby, I. ...... 20 35s 116 30 E
Enderby Ld. ..... 66 0s 53 0 E
Endicott 42 6N 76 2w
Enfield 51 38N 0 4w
Engaño, C.,

Dom. Rep. 18 30N 68 20w
Engaño, C.,
  Philippines .... 18 35N 122 23 E
Engcobo .... 31 39s 28 1 E
Engels .... 51 28N 46 6 E
Enggano .... 5 20s 102 40 E
England ■ 53 0N 2 0w
Englee 50 45N 56 5w
Englehart 47 49N 79 52w
Englewood, Colo. . 39 39N 104 59w
English, R. 50 12N 95 0w
English Bazar .... 24 58N 88 21 E
English Chan. 50 0N 2 30w
Enid 36 26N 97 52w
Enkeldoorn ...... 19 2s 30 52 E
Enkhuizen .... 52 42N 5 17 E
Enna .... 37 34N 14 15 E
Ennedi .... 17 15N 22 0 E
Ennis, Eire 52 51N 8 59w
Ennis, U.S.A. 32 15N 96 40w
Enniscorthy 52 30N 6 35w
Enniskillen 54 20N 7 40w
Ennistymon 52 56N 9 18w
Enontekio .... 68 23N 23 38 E
Enschede .... 52 13N 6 53 E
Entebbe .... 0 4N 32 28 E
Enterprise 45 25N 117 17w
† Entre Rios .... 14 57s 37 20 E
Entre Rios, Reg. .. 30 0s 58 30w
Enugu .... 6 30N 7 30 E
Enugu Ezike ..... 7 0N 7 29 E
Eólie o
  Lípari, I. ...... 38 30N 14 50 E
Epe, Neth. ...... 52 21N 5 59 E
Epe, Nigeria ..... 6 36N 3 59 E
Épernay .... 49 3N 3 56 E
Ephraim 39 30N 111 37w
Épinal .... 48 19N 6 27 E
Epping .... 51 42N 0 8 E
Equatorial
  Guinea ■ ..... 2 0N 8 0 E
Er Rahad .... 12 45N 30 32 E
Er Rif 35 1N 4 1w
Er Roseires ...... 11 55N 34 30 E
Eradu .... 28 40s 115 2 E
Ercha .... 69 45N 147 20 E
Erdene .... 44 30N 111 0 E
Erdenedalay ..... 46 3N 105 1 E
Erechim 27 35s 52 15w
Eregli .... 41 15N 31 30 E

Erfurt .... 50 58N 11 2 E
Ergani .... 38 26N 39 49 E
Ergeni
  Vozvyshennost .. 47 0N 44 0 E
Erhlien .... 43 42N 112 2 E
Eriboll, I. 58 28N 4 41w
Erie 42 10N 80 7w
Erie, L. 42 30N 82 0w
Erigavo .... 10 35N 47 35 E
Eriksdale 50 52N 98 5w
Erimanthos, Mt... 37 57N 21 50 E
Erith 53 25N 116 46w
Eritrea □ ...... 14 0N 41 0 E
Erlangen .... 49 35N 11 0 E
Erldunda .... 25 14s 133 12 E
Ermelo, Neth. .... 52 35N 5 35 E
Ermelo, S. Afr. ... 26 31s 29 59 E
Ernakulam .... 9 59N 76 19 E
Erne, L. 54 14N 7 30w
Erne, R. 54 30N 8 16w
Erode .... 11 24N 77 45 E
Erramala Hills ... 15 30N 78 15 E
Eruwa .... 7 33N 3 26 E
Erzgebirge Mts. ... 50 25N 13 0 E
Erzurum .... 39 57N 41 15 E
Es Sider .... 30 50N 18 21 E
Esbjerg .... 55 29N 8 29 E
Escanaba 45 44N 87 5w
Esch .... 49 32N 6 0 E
Escondido 33 9N 117 4w
Escuintla 14 20N 90 48w
Esfahan .... 32 40N 51 38 E
Esfahan □ ...... 33 0N 53 0 E
Esh Shimâliya □ .. 20 0N 31 0 E
Eshowe .... 28 50s 31 30 E
Eshta'ol .... 31 47N 35 0 E
Esk, R., Eng. 54 29N 0 37w
Esk, R., Scot. 54 58N 3 2w
Eskilstuna .... 59 22N 16 32 E
Eskimo Point 61 10N 94 15w
Eskisehir .... 39 50N 30 35 E
Esla, R. 41 29N 6 4w
Esmeraldas 1 0N 79 40w
Espanola 46 15N 81 46w
Espe .... 44 0N 74 5 E
Esperance .... 33 51s 121 53 E
Esperance, B. .... 33 48s 121 55 E
Esperanza 31 29s 61 3w
Espichel, C. 38 22N 9 16w
Espinal 4 9N 74 53w

Espinhaço, Sa. do . 17 30s 43 30w
Espírito Santo,
  B. del 19 15N 79 40w
Espírito Santo □ .. 19 30s 40 30w
Esquel 42 40s 71 20w
Essaouira 31 32N 9 42w
Essen, Belgium ... 51 28N 4 28 E
Essen,
  W. Germany ... 51 28N 6 59 E
Essex □ .... 51 48N 0 30 E
Esslingen .... 48 43N 9 19 E
Essonne □ ...... 48 30N 2 20 E
Estados,
  I. de los 54 40s 64 30w
Estância, Brazil ... 11 15s 37 30w
Estancia, U.S.A. .. 34 50N 106 1w
Estcourt .... 28 58s 29 53 E
Estelí 13 9N 86 22w
Esterhazy 50 37N 102 5w
Estevan 49 10N 103 0w
Estheville 43 25N 94 50w
Estonian S.S.R. □ . 48 30N 25 30 E
Estoril 38 42N 9 23w
Estrêla, Sa. da 40 10N 7 45w
Estremadura, Reg. 39 0N 9 0w
Estrondo, Sa. de .. 7 20s 48 0w
Esztergom .... 47 47N 18 44 E
Etawah .... 26 48N 79 6 E
Ethel Creek ...... 22 55s 120 11 E
Ethelbert 51 32N 100 25w
Ethiopia ■ ..... 8 0N 40 0 E
Ethiopian
  Highlands, Mts. . 10 0N 37 0 E
Etive, L. 56 30N 5 12w
Etna, Mt. .... 37 45N 15 0 E
Etoshapan .... 18 40s 16 30 E
Ettrick, R. 55 31N 2 55w
Etzatlán 20 48N 104 5w
Euclid 41 32N 81 31w
Eucumbene, L. ... 36 2s 148 40 E
Eufaula 31 55N 85 11w
Eugene 44 0N 123 8w
Eunice 30 35N 92 28w
Eupen .... 50 37N 6 3 E
Euphrates, R.=
  Furat, Nahr al . 33 30N 43 0 E
Eure □ .... 49 6N 1 0 E
Eureka, Calif. 40 50N 124 0w
Eureka, Nev. 39 32N 116 2w
Eureka, Utah 40 0N 112 0w

Eure-et-Loir □ .... 48 22N 1 30 E
Euroa .... 36 44s 145 35 E
Europa, Île ...... 22 20s 40 22 E
Europa, Picos de . 43 10N 5 0w
Europa, Pta. de .. 36 3N 5 21w
Europe .... 50 0N 20 0 E
Europoort .... 51 57N 4 10 E
Evans Head ...... 29 7s 153 27 E
Evanston, Ill. 42 0N 87 40w
Evanston, Wyo. ... 41 10N 111 0w
Evansville 38 0N 87 35w
Eveleth 47 35N 92 40w
Even Yehuda ..... 32 16N 34 53 E
Everest, Mt. ..... 28 5N 86 58 E
Everett 48 0N 122 10w
Everglades
  Nat. Park 25 50N 80 40w
Evesham 52 6N 1 57w
Evora 38 33N 7 57w
Évreux .... 49 0N 1 8 E
Evron .... 32 59N 35 6 E
Evvoia □ ...... 38 40N 23 40 E
Ewe, L. 57 49N 5 38w
Excelsior Springs . 39 20N 94 10w
Exe, R. 50 37N 3 25w
Exeter 50 43N 3 31w
Exmoor, Reg. 51 10N 3 55w
Exmouth,
  Australia ...... 22 6s 114 0 E
Exmouth, U.K. ... 50 37N 3 24w
Exmouth, G. ..... 22 15s 114 15 E
Extremadura, Reg. 39 30N 6 5w
Exuma Sd. 24 30N 76 20w
Eyasi, L. .... 3 30s 35 0 E
Eye Pen. .... 58 20N 0 51 E
Eyemouth 55 53N 2 5w
Eyre, L. .... 28 30s 136 45 E
Eyre, Pen. ...... 33 30s 137 17 E

F

Fabens 31 30N 106 8w
Fabriano .... 43 20N 12 52 E
Facatativa 4 49N 74 22w
Fada N'Gourma ... 12 10N 0 30 E
Faenza .... 44 17N 11 53 E
Fafa .... 15 22N 0 48 E

* Renamed Chivhu
† Renamed Malema

Fagam .... 11 1N 10 1 E
Fagaraş .... 45 48N 24 58 E
Fagernes ...... 61 0N 9 16 E
Fagersta .... 61 1N 15 46 E
Fagnano, L. 54 30s 68 0w
Fahraj .... 29 0N 59 0 E
Fahsien .... 21 19N 110 33 E
Fahud .... 22 18N 56 28 E
Fair Haven 43 36N 76 16w
Fairbank 31 44N 110 12w
Fairbanks 64 59N 147 40w
Fairbury 40 5N 97 5w
Fairfield,
  Australia ...... 37 45s 175 17 E
Fairfield, Ala. ... 33 30N 87 0w
Fairfield, Calif. .. 38 14N 122 1w
Fairfield, Ill. 38 20N 88 20w
Fairfield, Iowa .. 41 0N 91 58w
Fairfield, Tex..... 31 40N 96 0w
Fairlie .... 44 5s 170 49 E
Fairmont, Minn... 43 37N 94 30w
Fairmont, W. Va. . 39 29N 80 10w
Fairport 43 8N 77 29w
Fairview,
  Australia ...... 15 31s 144 17 E
Fairview, Canada .. 56 5N 118 25w
Fairweather, Mt. .. 58 55N 137 45w
Faizabad,
  Afghanistan .... 37 7N 70 33 E
Faizabad, India .. 26 45N 82 10 E
Fajardo 18 20N 65 39w
Fakenham .... 52 50N 0 51 E
Fakfak .... 3 0s 132 15 E
Faku .... 42 31N 123 26 E
Falaise 48 54N 0 12w
Falam .... 23 0N 93 45 E
Falcone, C. ..... 41 0N 8 10 E
Falfurrias .... 27 8N 98 8 E
Falkenberg ...... 56 54N 12 30 E
Falkirk 56 0N 3 47w
Falkland, Sd. 52 0s 60 0w
Falkland Is. □ 51 30s 59 0w
Falkland Is.
  Dependencies □ . 57 0s 40 0w
Falköping ...... 58 12N 13 33 E
Fall River 41 45N 71 5w
Fallon 39 31N 118 51w
Falls City 40 0N 95 40w
Falmouth, Jamaica 18 30N 77 40w
Falmouth, U.K. .. 50 9N 5 5w

Falso, C. 17 45N 71 40w
Falster, I......... 54 48N 11 58 E
Falsterbo .... 55 23N 12 50 E
Falun .... 60 37N 15 37 E
Famagusta ...... 35 8N 33 55 E
Fandriana .... 20 14s 47 21 E
Fangcheng .... 31 2N 118 13 E
Fanning I. 3 51N 159 22w
Fano .... 43 50N 13 0 E
Fanshaw 57 11N 133 30w
Faradje .... 3 50N 29 45 E
Farafangana ..... 22 49s 47 50 E
Faranah 10 2N 10 45w
Farar .... 32 30N 62 17 E
Farar □ .... 32 25N 62 10 E
Farasān, Jazā'ir, I. . 16 45N 41 55 E
Faratsiho .... 19 24s 46 57 E
Fareham 50 52N 1 11w
Farewell, C.,
  Greenland=
  Farvel, K. 66 0N 44 0w
Farewell, C., N.Z. . 40 29s 172 43 E
Fargo 47 0N 97 0w
Faribault 44 15N 93 19w
Faridpur .... 23 36N 89 53 E
Farina .... 30 3s 138 15 E
Farmington,N. Mex. 36 45N 108 28w
Farmington, Utah . 41 0N 111 58w
Farnborough 51 17N 0 46w
Farne Is. 55 38N 1 37w
Faro, Brazil...... 2 0s 56 45w
Faro, Port. 37 2N 7 55w
Faroe Is. 62 0N 7 0w
Farquhar, C. ..... 23 38s 113 36 E
Farrāshband ..... 28 57N 52 5 E
Farrell 41 13N 80 29w
Farrell Flat ..... 33 48s 138 48 E
Fars □ .... 29 30N 55 0 E
Farsund .... 58 5N 6 55 E
Faru .... 12 48N 6 12 E
Farvel, K. 60 0N 44 0w
Faryab □ .... 36 0N 65 0 E
Fastnet Rock 51 22N 9 27w
Fatehgarh .... 27 25N 79 35 E
Fatehpur,
  Rajasthan ..... 28 0N 75 4 E
Fatehpur, Ut.P. .. 27 8N 81 7 E
Fatshan .... 23 0N 113 4 E
Faulkton 45 4N 99 8w
Faure, I. .... 25 52s 113 50 E

Fauresmith ...... 29 44s 25 17 E
Fauske .... 67 17N 15 25 E
Favara .... 37 19N 13 39 E
Favignana, I...... 37 56N 12 18 E
Faxaflói, B. 64 29N 23 0w
Fayetteville, Ark.. 36 0N 94 5w
Fayetteville, N.C.. 35 0N 78 58w
Fazilka .... 30 27N 74 2 E
F'Dérik .... 22 40N 12 45 E
Feale, R. 52 26N 9 28w
Fear, C. 33 45N 78 0w
Featherston ..... 41 6s 175 20 E
Fécamp .... 49 45N 0 22 E
Fehmarn, I. ..... 54 26N 11 10 E
Fehmarn Bælt .... 54 35N 11 20 E
Feilding .... 40 13s 175 35 E
Feira de
  Santana 12 15s 38 57w
Feldkirch .... 47 15N 9 37 E
Felipe
  Carillo Puerto ... 19 38N 88 3w
Felixstowe 51 58N 1 22w
Femund, L. ..... 62 5N 11 55 E
Fen Ho, R. ..... 35 36N 110 42 E
* Fénérive .... 17 22s 49 25 E
Fencheng .... 28 2N 115 46 E
Fengcheng,
  Heilungkiang ... 45 41N 128 54 E
Fengcheng,
  Liaoning ...... 40 28N 124 4 E
Fenghsien .... 33 56N 106 41 E
Fengkieh .... 31 0N 109 33 E
Fengtai .... 39 57N 116 21 E
Fengyuan .... 24 10N 120 45 E
Fenoarivo ...... 18 26s 46 34 E
Fens, Reg. ...... 52 45N 0 2 E
Fenyang .... 37 19N 111 46 E
Feodosiya ...... 45 2N 35 28 E
Fergana .... 40 23N 71 46 E
Fergus 43 43N 80 24w
Fergus Falls 46 25N 96 0w
Ferland 50 19N 88 27w
Fermanagh □ 54 21N 7 40w
Fermoy 52 4N 8 18w
Fernando de
  Noronha, Is. ... 4 0s 33 10w
† Fernando Póo, I.=
  Macias Nguema
  Biyoga .... 3 30N 8 4 E
Fernie 49 30N 115 5w

Fernlees .... 23 51s 148 7 E
Ferozepore ...... 30 55N 74 40 E
Ferrara .... 44 50N 11 36 E
Fès 34 0N 5 0½
Fetlar, I. 60 36N 0 52w
Fezzan .... 27 0N 15 0 E
Fianarantsoa ..... 21 26s 47 5 E
Fianarantsoa □ .... 21 30s 47 0 E
Fichtelgebirge, Mts. 50 10N 12 0 E
Ficksburg ...... 28 51s 27 53 E
Fiditi .... 7 45N 3 53 E
Fier, Portile de ... 44 42N 22 30 E
Fife □ 56 13N 3 2w
Figeac .... 44 37N 2 2 E
Figtree .... 20 22s 28 20 E
Figueira da
  Foz 40 7N 8 54w
Figueras .... 42 18N 2 58 E
Figuig 32 5N 1 11w
Fihaonana ...... 18 36s 47 12 E
Fiji ■ .... 17 20s 179 0 E
Filey 54 13N 0 18w
Filiatrá .... 37 9N 21 35 E
Filingué .... 14 21N 3 19 E
Filipstad ...... 59 43N 14 9 E
Fillmore 34 23N 118 58w
Findhorn 57 30N 3 45w
Findlay 41 0N 83 41w
Finisterre □ 48 20N 4 20w
Finisterre, C. 42 50N 9 19w
Finke .... 25 34s 134 35 E
Finland ■ ...... 70 0N 27 0 E
Finland, G. of 60 0N 26 0¼
Finley .... 35 38s 145 35 E
Finnegan 51 7N 112 5w
Finnigan, Mt. ... 15 49s 145 17 E
Finniss, C. ..... 33 38s 134 51 E
Finnmark □ ..... 69 30N 25 0 E
Firenze .... 43 47N 11 15 E
Firozabad ...... 27 10N 78 25 E
Fīrūzābād ...... 28 52s 52 35 E
Fīrūzkūh ...... 35 50N 52 40 E
Fisher .... 30 30s 131 0 E
Fishguard 51 59N 4 59w
Fitchburg 42 35N 71 47w
Fitz Roy 47 10s 67 0w
Fitzgerald 31 45N 83 10w
Fitzroy, R., Queens. 23 32s 150 52 E
Fitzroy, R.,
  W. Australia .... 17 31s 138 35 E

Fitzroy Crossing ... 18 9s 125 38 E
Fizi .... 4 17s 28 55 E
Flagstaff 35 10N 111 40w
Flåm .... 60 52N 7 14 E
Flamborough Hd. . 54 8N 0 4w
Flaming Gorge L. . 41 15N 109 30w
Flanders=
  Flandres,
  Plaines des ..... 51 10N 3 15 E
Flandre
  Occidentale □ .. 51 0N 3 0 E
Flandre
  Orientale □ ..... 51 0N 4 0 E
Flandres, Plaines
  des .... 51 10N 3 15 E
Flannan Is. 58 9N 7 52w
Flathead L. 47 50N 114 0w
Flattery, C.,
  Australia ...... 14 58s 145 21 E
Flattery, C.,
  U.S.A. 48 21N 124 31w
Fleetwood ...... 53 55N 3 .1w
Flekkefjord ..... 58 18N 6 39 E
Flensburg ...... 54 46N 9 28 E
Fletton 52 34N 0 13w
Flin Flon 54 46N 101 53w
Flinders, B. ..... 34 19s 114 9 E
Flinders, I. ..... 40 0s 148 0 E
Flinders, Ras. ... 31 30s 138 30 E
Flint, U.K. 53 15N 3 7w
Flint, U.S.A. 43 0N 83 40w
Flint I. 11 26s 151 48w
Flodden 55 37N 2 8w
Flora 38 40N 88 30w
Florence, Italy=
  Firenze .... 43 47N 11 15 E
Florence, Ala. 34 50N 87 50w
Florence, Ariz. ... 33 0N 111 25w
Florence, Oreg. ... 44 0N 124 3w
Florence, S.C. 34 5N 79 50w
Florencia 1 36N 75 36w
Flores, I. 16 50N 89 40w
Flores Sea ..... 6 30s 124 0 E
Floriano 6 50s 43 0w
Florianópolis ... 27 30s 48 30w
Florida 34 7s 56 10w
Florida □ 28 30N 82 0w
Florida Str. 25 0N 80 0w
Flórina .... 40 48N 21 26 E

* Renamed Fenoarivo Atsinanana
† Renamed Bioko

Florø . . . . 61 35N   5 1 E
Flushing=
  Vlissingen . . . . . 51 26N   3 34 E
Fly, R. . . . . 7 50 S 141 20 E
Foam Lake 51 40N 103 15W
Focşani . . . . 45 41N 27 15 E
Fóggia . . . . 41 28N 15 31 E
Foggo . . . . 11 21N   9 57 E
Fogo 49 43S 54 17W
Foix, Reg. 43   0N   1 30 E
Foleyet 48 15N 82 25W
Foligno . . . . 42 58N 12 40 E
Folkestone . . . . . . 51 5N   1 11 E
Fond du Lac,
  Canada 59 20N 107 10W
Fond-du-Lac,
  U.S.A. 43 46N 88 26W
Fondi . . . . 41 21N 13 25 E
Fonsagrada 43 8N   7 4W
Fonseca, G. de 13 10N 87 40W
Fontainebleau . . . . 48 24N   2 40 E
Fonte Boa 2 25S 66 0W
Fontem . . . . 5 32N   9 52 E
Fontenay-le-
  Comte 46 28N   0 48W
Foochow . . . . 26 5N 119 18 E
Forbes . . . . 33 22S 148 0 E
Forest Lawn 51 4N 114 0W
Forestburg 52 35N 112 1W
Forestville 48 48N 69 20W
Forez, Mts. du . . . 45 40N   3 50 E
Forfar 56 40N   2 53W
Forlí . . . . 44 14N 12 2 E
Formby Pt. 53 33N   3 7W
Formentera, I. . . . 38 40N   1 30 E
Formiga 20 27S 45 25W
Formosa, Arg. . . . 26 15S 58 10W
Formosa, Brazil . . 15 32S 47 20W
Formosa=
  Taiwan ■ 24   0N 121 0 E
Formosa, Sa. 12   0S 55 0W
Formosa Str. . . . . 24 40N 124 0 E
Forres 57 37N   3 38W
Forrest . . . . 38 22S 143 40 E
Forrest City 35 1N 90 47W
Forsayth . . . . 18 33S 143 34 E
Forst . . . . 51 43N 15 37 E
Forsyth 46 14N 106 37W
Fort Albany 52 15N 81 35W
Fort-Archambault

=Sarh . . . . 9 5N 18 23 E
Fort Assinboine . . 54 20N 114 45W
Fort Augustus . . . 57 9N   4 40W
Fort Beaufort . . . 32 46S 26 40 E
Fort Benton 47 50N 110 40W
Fort Bragg 39 28N 123 50W
Fort Bridger 41 22N 110 20W
Fort Chimo 58 9N 68 12W
Fort Chipewyan . . 58 46N 111 9W
Fort Collins 40 30N 105 4W
Fort Coulonge . . . 45 50N 76 45W
* Fort-Dauphin . . . 25 2S 47 0 E
Fort Dodge 42 29N 94 10W
Fort Frances 48 35N 93 25W
Fort Franklin 65 30N 123 45W
Fort Good Hope . . 66 14N 128 40W
Fort Graham 56 38N 124 35W
Fort Hancock 31 19N 105 56W
Fort Hope 51 30N 88 10W
Fort Kent 47 12N 68 30W
Fort-Lamy=
  Ndjamena . . . . . 12 4N 15 8 E
Fort Laramie 42 15W 104 30W
Fort Lauderdale . . 26 10N 80 5W
Fort Liard 60 20N 123 30W
Fort Mackay 57 12N 111 41W
Fort McKenzie . . . 56 50N 69 0W
Fort Macleod 49 45N 113 30W
Fort MacMahon . . 29 51N   1 45 E
Fort Madison 40 39N 91 20W
Fort Mirabel . . . . 29 31N   2 55 E
Fort Morgan 40 10N 103 50W
Fort Munro . . . . . 30 0N 69 55 E
Fort Myers 26 30N 82 0W
Fort Nelson 58 50N 122 30W
Fort Norman 64 57N 125 30W
Fort Payne 34 25N 85 44W
Fort Peck 47 1N 105 30W
Fort Peck Res. . . . 47 40N 107 0W
Fort Pierce 27 29N 80 19W
Fort Portal . . . . . . 0 40N 30 20 E
Fort Providence . . 61 20N 117 30W
Fort Qu'Appelle . . 50 45N 103 50W
Fort Resolution . . 61 10N 114 40W
Fort-Rousset . . . . 0 29S 15 55 E
Fort Rupert 51 30N 78 40W
Fort St. James . . . 54 30N 124 10W

Fort St. John 56 15N 120 50W
Fort Sandeman . . 31 20N 69 25 E
Fort Saskatchewan 53 40N 113 15W
Fort Scott 38 0N 94 40W
Fort Selkirk 62 43N 137 22W
Fort Severn 56 0N 87 40W
Fort Simpson 61 45N 121 30W
Fort Shevchenko . 44 30N 50 10 E
Fort Smith 35 25N 94 25W
Fort Stockton . . . 30 48N 103 2W
Fort Sumner 34 24N 104 18W
Fort Valley 32 33N 83 52W
Fort Vermilion . . . 58 30N 115 57W
* Fort Victoria . . . 20 8S 30 55 E
Fort Wayne 41 5N 85 10W
Fort William,
  Canada=
  Thunder Bay . . . 48 20N 89 10W
Fort William, U.K. 56 48N   5 8W
Fort Worth 32 45N 97 25W
Fort Yukon 66 35N 145 12W
Fortaleza 3 35S 38 35W
Fort-de-France . . 14 36N 61 5W
Fortescue, R. . . . . 21 20S 116 5 E
Forth, Firth of . . . 56 5N   2 55W
Fortrose 57 35N   4 10W
Fortuna 48 38N 124 8W
Forty Mile 64 20N 140 30W
Fostoria 41 8N 83 25W
Fougères 48 21N   1 14W
Foula, I. 60 10N   2 5W
Foulness, I. . . . . . 51 26N   0 55 E
Fouman . . . . 5 45N 10 50 E
Fourcroy, C. . . . . 11 45S 130 2 E
Fouriesburg . . . . . 28 38S 28 14 E
Fouta Djalon, Mts. 11 20N 12 10W
Foveaux, Str. . . . . 46 42S 168 10 E
Fowey 50 20N   4 39W
Fowlers, B. . . . . . 31 59S 132 34 E
Fowning . . . . 33 30N 119 40 E
Fox Valley 50 30N 109 25W
Foxe Basin 68 30N 77 0W
Foxe Chan. 66 0N 80 0W
Foxe Pen. 65 0N 76 0W
Foxton . . . . 40 29S 175 18 E
Foyle, L. 55 6N   7 18W
Foynes 52 37N   9 6W
Foz do Iguaçu . . . 25 30S 54 30W
Franca 20 25S 47 30W
Francavilla

Fontana . . . . 40 32N 17 35 E
France ■ . . . . 47 0N   3 0 E
Franceville . . . . . . 1 38S 13 35 E
Franche Comté,
  Reg. . . . . 46 30N   5 50 E
Francis Harbour . . 52 34N 55 44W
Francistown . . . . . 21 11S 27 32 E
François 47 34N 56 44W
Franconia . . . . . . 50 0N   9 0 E
Frankfort, S. Afr. . 27 16S 28 30 E
Frankfort, Ind. . . . 40 20N 86 33W
Frankfort, Ky. . . . 38 12N 85 44W
Frankfurt am Main 50 7N   8 40 E
Frankfurt an der
  Oder . . . . 52 50N 14 31 E
Fränkische Alb. . . 49 20N 11 0 E
Franklin, Nebr. . . 40 9N 98 55W
Franklin, N.H. . . . 43 28N 71 39W
Franklin, Pa. 41 22N 79 45W
Franklin, Tenn. . . 35 54N 86 53W
Franklin, W. Va. . 38 38N 79 21W
* Franklin, Reg. . . 71 0N 99 0W
Franklin D.
  Roosevelt L. . . . 48 30N 118 16W
Franklin Mts. . . . 66 0N 125 0W
Franklin Str. 72 0N 96 0W
Frankston . . . . . . 38 8S 145 8 E
Frantsa Iosifa,
  Zemlya, Is. . . . . 76 0N 62 0 E
Franz 48 25N 85 0W
Fraser, I. . . . . 25 15S 153 10 E
Fraser, R. 49 9N 123 12W
Fraser Lake 54 0N 124 50W
Fraserburg . . . . . 31 55S 21 30 E
Fraserburgh . . . . . 47 41N   2 0½ E
Fray Bentos 33 10S 58 15W
Frazier Downs . . . 18 48S 121 42 E
Fredericia . . . . . . 55 34N   9 45 E
Frederick, Md. . . . 39 25N 77 23W
Frederick, Okla. . . 34 22N 99 0W
Fredericksburg . . . 38 16N 77 29W
Fredericton 45 57N 66 40W
Frederikshavn . . . 57 28N 10 31 E
Fredonia 42 26N 79 20W
Fredrikstad . . . . . 59 13N 10 57 E
Freeport, Bahamas 26 30N 78 35W
Freeport, Ill. 42 18N 89 40W
Freeport, N.Y. . . . 40 39N 73 35W
Freeport, Tex. . . . 28 55N 95 22W
Freetown 8 30N 13 10W

Freiburg . . . . 48 0N   7 50 E
Freire 39 0S 72 50W
Freising . . . . 48 24N 11 27 E
Freistadt . . . . 48 30N 14 30 E
Fréjus . . . . 43 25N   6 44 E
Fremantle . . . . . . 32 1S 115 47 E
Fremont, Nebr. . . 41 30N 96 30W
Fremont, Ohio . . . 41 20N 83 5W
French, I. . . . . . . 38 20S 145 22 E
French Guiana ■ . . 4 0N 53 0W
French Terr. of the
  Afars & Issas■=
  Djibouti ■ . . . . 11 30N 42 15 E
Fresco, R. 6 39S 51 59W
Fresnillo 23 10N 103 0W
Fresno 36 47N 119 50W
Frewena . . . . 19 50S 135 50 E
Frías 28 40S 65 5W
Fribourg . . . . 46 49N   7 9 E
Friedrichshafen . . 47 39N   9 29 E
Friendly Is.=
  Tonga Is. 20 0S 173 0W
Friesian Is.=
  Waddeniladen . . 53 30N   5 30 E
Friesland □ . . . . . 53 5N   5 50 E
Frio, C. . . . . 18 0S 12 0 E
Friuli Venezia
  Giulia □ . . . . . 46 0N 13 0 E
Frobisher B. 63 0N 67 0W
Frome 51 16N   2 17W
Front Royal 38 55N 78 10W
Frontera 18 30N 92 40W
Frosinone . . . . . . 41 38N 13 20 E
Frostburg 39 43N 78 57W
Frunze . . . . 42 54N 74 36 E
Frutal 20 0S 49 0W
Frýdek Místek . . . 49 40N 18 20 E
Fuchin . . . . 47 10N 132 0 E
Fuchou=Foochow . 26 5N 119 18 E
Fuchow . . . . 27 50N 116 14 E
Fuchu . . . . 34 34N 133 14 E
Fuchun Kiang, R. . 30 10N 120 0 E
Fuente Ovejuna . . 38 15N   5 25W
Fuentes de Oñoro . 40 33N   6 52W
Fuerteventura, I. . 28 30N 14 0W
Fujaira . . . . 25 7N 56 18 E
Fuji . . . . 35 9N 138 39 E
Fuji-san, Mt. . . . 35 22N 138 44 E
Fuji-no-miya . . . . 35 20N 138 40 E
Fujisawa . . . . . . 35 22N 139 29 E

* Renamed Faradofay
† French nameform
  La Grande, R.

* Renamed Masvingo

* Renamed Kitikmeot

Fukien □	26 0N	117 30 E
Fukuchiyama	35 25N	135 9 E
Fukui	36 0N	136 10 E
Fukui □	36 0N	136 12 E
Fukuoka	33 30N	130 30 E
Fukuoka □	33 30N	131 0 E
Fukushima	37 30N	140 15 E
Fukushima □	37 30N	140 15 E
Fukuyama	34 35N	133 20 E
Fulda	50 32N	9 41 E
Fullerton	33 52N	117 58W
Fulton, Mo.	38 50N	91 55W
Fulton, N.Y.	43 20N	76 22W
Funabashi	35 45N	140 0 E
Funafuti, I.	8 30S	179 0 E
Funchal	32 45N	16 55W
Fundación	10 31N	74 11W
Fundão	40 8N	7 30W
Fundy, B. of	45 0N	66 0W
Funtua	11 31N	7 17 E
Furat, Nahr al, R.	33 30N	43 0 E
Furness	54 14N	3 8W
Fürth	49 29N	11 0 E
Fury & Hecla Str.	69 40N	81 0W
Fusagasugá	4 21N	74 22W
Fushan	37 30N	121 5 E
Fushun	42 0N	123 59 E
Fusin	42 12N	121 33 E
Futing	27 15N	120 10 E
Futsing	25 46N	119 29 E
Fuyang	30 5N	119 56 E
Fuyu	45 10N	124 50 E
Fyen, I.=Fyn, I.	55 20N	10 30 E
Fylde, R.	53 47N	2 56W
Fyn, I.	55 20N	10 30 E
Fyne, L.	56 0N	5 20W

G

Gaanda	10 10N	12 27 E
Gabès	33 53N	10 2 E
Gabès, G. de	34 0N	10 30 E
Gabon ■	0 10S	10 0 E
Gaborone	24 37S	25 57 E
Gabrovo	42 52N	25 27 E
Gach-Sarán	30 15N	50 45 E
Gada	13 38N	5 36 E

Gadag	15 30N	75 45 E
Gadarwara	22 50N	78 50 E
Gadhada	22 0N	71 35 E
Gadsden, Ala.	34 1N	86 0W
Gadsden, Ariz.	32 35N	114 47W
Gadwal	16 10N	77 50 E
Gaeta	41 12N	13 35 E
Gaffney	35 10N	81 31W
Gafsa	34 24N	8 51 E
Gagetown	45 46N	66 29W
Gagnoa	6 4N	5 55W
Gagnon	51 50N	68 5W
Gainesville, Fla.	29 38N	82 20W
Gainesville, Ga.	34 17N	83 47W
Gainesville, Tex.	33 40N	97 10W
Gainsborough	53 23N	0 46W
Gairdner, L.	32 0S	136 0 E
Gairloch, L.	57 43N	5 45W
Gajiram	12 29N	13 9 E
Galangue	13 48S	16 3 E
Galápagos, Is.	0 0	89 0W
Galashiels	55 37N	2 50W
Galaţi	45 27N	28 2 E
Galatina	40 10N	18 10 E
Galax	36 42N	80 57W
Galdhøpiggen, Mt.	61 45N	8 40 E
Galena	27 50S	114 41 E
Galesburg	40 57N	90 23W
Galich	58 23N	42 18 E
Galicia, Reg.	42 43N	8 0W
Galilee=		
Hagalil, Reg.	32 53N	35 18 E
Galilee, Sea of=		
Kinneret, Yam	32 49N	35 36 E
Gallatin	36 24N	86 27W
Galle	6 5N	80 10 E
Gállego, R.	41 39N	0 51W
Gallegos, R.	51 35S	69 0W
Gallinas, Pta.	12 28N	71 40W
Gallipoli	40 8N	18 0 E
Gallipolis	38 50N	82 10W
Gällivare	67 7N	20 32 E
Galloway, Reg.	55 0N	4 25W
Galloway, Mull of .	54 38N	4 50W
Gallup	35 30N	108 54W
Galt:=		
Cambridge	43 23N	80 19W
Galty Mts.	52 20N	8 10W
Galveston	29 15N	94 48W
Galveston B.	29 30N	94 50W

Gálvez	32 0S	61 20W
Galway	53 16N	9 4W
Galway, B.	53 10N	9 20W
Galway □	53 16N	9 3W
Gamagori	34 50N	137 14 E
Gamawa	12 10N	10 31 E
Gambaga	10 30N	0 28W
Gambia ■	13 20N	15 45W
Gambia, R.	13 28N	16 34W
Gambier, C.	11 56S	130 57 E
Gamboa	9 8N	79 42W
Gamerco	35 33N	108 56W
Gamtoos, ■.	33 58S	25 1 E
Gan Shamu'el	32 28N	34 56 E
Gan Yavne	31 48N	34 42 E
Gananoque	44 20N	76 10W
Gand=Gent	51 2N	3 37 E
Gandak, R.	25 32N	85 5 E
Gander	49 1N	54 33W
Gandi	12 55N	5 49 E
Ganga, R.	23 22N	90 32 E
Ganganagar	29 56N	73 56 E
Gangaw	22 5N	94 15 E
Ganges, R.=		
Ganga, R.	23 22N	90 32 E
Gangtok	27 20N	88 40 E
Gao	18 0N	1 0 E
Gaoua	10 20N	3 8W
Gaoual	11 45N	13 25W
Gap	44 33N	6 5 E
Garanhuns	8 50S	36 30W
Garberville	40 11N	123 50W
Garcia	25 32S	32 13 E
Gard □	44 2N	4 10 E
Garda, L. di	45 40N	10 40 E
Garden City	38 0N	100 45W
Gardez	33 31N	68 59 E
Gardiner	45 3N	110 53W
Gardner	42 35N	72 0W
Gardo	9 18N	49 20 E
Garfield	47 3N	117 8W
Gargano, Mte.	41 43N	15 40 E
Garissa	0 25S	39 40 E
Garkida	10 27N	12 36 E
Garko	11 45N	8 53 E
Garland	41 47N	112 10W
Garm	39 0N	70 20 E
Garmsar	35 20N	52 25 E
Garoe	8 35N	48 40 E
Garonne, R.	45 2N	0 36W

Garoua	9 19N	13 21 E
Garrison	46 37N	112 56W
Garrison Res.	47 30N	102 0W
Garry, L.	65 40N	100 0W
Garson	50 5N	96 50W
Gartok	31 59N	80 30 E
Garut	7 14S	107 53 E
Garvie, Mts.	45 27S	169 59 E
Gary	41 35N	87 20W
Garzón	2 10N	75 40W
Gascogne, Reg.	43 45N	0 20 E
Gascogne, G. de	44 0N	2 0W
Gascony, Reg.=		
Gascogne, Reg.	43 45N	0 20 E
Gascoyne, R.	24 52S	113 37 E
Gascoyne Junction	25 3S	115 12 E
Gashaka	7 20N	11 29 E
Gashua	12 54N	11 0 E
Gaspé	48 52N	64 30W
Gaspé, C.	48 48N	64 7W
Gaspé Pass.	49 10N	64 0W
Gaspé Pen.	48 45N	65 40W
Gaspesian Prov.		
Park	49 0N	66 45W
Gastonia	35 17N	81 10W
Gastre	42 10S	69 15W
Gata, C. de	36 41N	2 13W
Gata, Sa. de	40 20N	6 20W
Gatehouse of		
Fleet	54 53N	4 10W
Gateshead	54 57N	1 37W
Gaths	26 2S	30 32 E
Gatineau Nat.		
Park	45 30N	75 52W
Gatooma	18 21S	29 55 E
Gatun	9 16N	79 55W
Gatun L.	9 7N	79 56W
Gauhati	26 5N	91 55 E
Gaula, R.	63 21N	10 14 E
Gavater	25 10N	61 31 E
Gavle	60 41N	17 13 E
Gävleborgs □	61 20N	16 15 E
Gawilgarh Hills	21 15N	76 45 E
Gawler	34 30S	138 42 E
Gaya, India	24 47N	85 4 E
Gaya, Nigeria	11 57N	9 0 E
Gayndah	25 35S	151 39 E
Gaza	31 30N	34 28 E
Gaza □	23 0S	33 0 E
Gaza Strip	31 29N	34 25 E

Gazaoua	13 32N	7 55 E
Gaziantep	37 6N	37 23 E
Gboko	7 17N	9 4 E
Gbongan	7 28N	4 20 E
Gcuwa	32 20S	28 11 E
Gdańsk	54 22N	18 40 E
Gdańska, Zatoka	54 30N	19 15 E
Gdynia	54 35N	18 33 E
Gebeit Mine	21 3N	36 29 E
Gedaref	14 2N	35 28 E
Gedera	31 49N	34 46 E
Gedser	54 35N	11 55 E
Geelong	38 2S	144 10 E
Geelvink, Chan.	28 30S	114 10 E
Geeraadsbergen	50 45N	3 53 E
Geidam	12 57N	11 57 E
Geili	16 1N	32 37 E
Geita	2 48S	32 12 E
Gela	37 3N	14 15 E
Gelderland □	52 5N	6 10 E
Geldrop	51 25N	5 32 E
Geleen	50 57N	5 49 E
Gelibolu	40 28N	26 43 E
Gelsenkirchen	51 30N	7 5 E
Gemas	2 37N	102 36 E
Gembloux	50 34N	4 43 E
Gemena	3 20N	19 40 E
General Acha	37 20S	64 38W
General Alvear	36 0S	60 0W
General Belgrano	36 2S	58 40W
General Guido	36 40S	57 40W
General Juan		
Madariaga	37 0S	57 0W
General Paz	27 45S	57 36W
General Pico	35 45S	63 50W
General Pinedo	27 15S	61 30W
General Roca	30 0S	67 40W
General Villegas	35 0S	63 0W
Geneva, Switz.=		
Genève	46 12N	6 9 E
Geneva, U.S.A.	42 53N	77 0W
Geneva, L.=		
Léman, L.	46 26N	6 30 E
Genève	46 12N	6 9 E
Genil, R.	37 42N	5 19W
Genissiat	46 1N	5 48 E
Genk	50 58N	5 32 E
Genoa=Genova	44 24N	8 56 E
Genova	44 24N	8 56 E
Génova, G. di	44 0N	9 0 E

* French nameform
  Honguedo, Dét. d'
† Renamed Kadoma
‡ Renamed Sakakawea, Lake

Gent . . . . 51 2N 3 37 E
Geographe, B. . . . 33 30s 115 15 E
Geographe, Chan. . 24 30s 113 0 E
George . . . . 33 58s 22 29 E
George, L. 43 30N 73 30w
George R.=Port
  Nouveau-Quebec 58 30N 65 50w
George Town
  Australia . . . . 41 5s 148 55 E
George Town,
  W. Malaysia . . . . 5 25N 100 19 E
Georgetown,
  Australia . . . . . . 18 17s 143 33 E
Georgetown, Ont. . 43 40N 80 0w
Georgetown, P.E.I. 46 13N 62 24w
Georgetown,
  Gambia 13 30N 14 47w
Georgetown,
  Guyana 6 50N 58 12w
Georgetown,
  U.S.A. 33 22N 79 15w
Georgia □ 32 0N 82 0w
Georgia Str. 49 20N 124 0w
Georgian B. 45 15N 81 0w
Georgian S.S.R. □ . 41 0N 45 0 E
Georgiu-Dezh . . . 51 3N 39 20 E
Georgiyevsk . . . . . 44 12N 43 28 E
Gera . . . . 50 53N 12 5 E
Geraldton,
  Australia . . . . . . 28 48s 114 32 E
Geraldton,
  Canada 49 44N 86 59w
Gerdine, Mt. 61 32N 152 50w
Gerede . . . . 40 45N 32 10 E
Gerlogubi . . . . . . 6 53N 45 3 E
Germansen
  Landing 55 43N 124 40w
Germiston . . . . . 26 15s 28 5 E
Gero . . . . 35 48N 137 14 E
Gerona . . . . 41 58N 2 46 E
Gers □ . . . . 43 35N 0 38 E
Gevaudan, Reg. . . 44 40N 3 40 E
Geyser 47 17N 110 30w
Geysir 64 19N 20 18w
Gezer . . . . 31 52N 34 55 E
Ghaghara, R. . . . . 25 45N 84 40 E
Ghana ■ 6 0N 1 0w
Ghardaïa . . . . 32 31N 3 37 E
Ghat . . . . 24 59N 10 19 E
Ghazal, Bahr

el, R. . . . . 9 31N 30 25 E
Ghazaouet 35 8N 1 50w
Ghaziabad . . . . . . 28 42N 77 35 E
Ghazipur . . . . 25 38N 83 35 E
Ghazni . . . . 33 30N 68 17 E
Ghazni □ . . . . 33 0N 68 0 E
Ghent=Gent . . . . 51 2N 3 37 E
Ghor □ . . . . 34 0N 64 20 E
Ghost River 51 25N 83 20w
Ghudames . . . . . . 30 11N 9 29 E
Ghugus . . . . 19 55N 79 15 E
Ghulam
  Mohammed Barr. 25 30N 67 0 E
Ghurian . . . . 34 17N 61 25 E
Giant Mts.=
  Krkonose . . . . . 50 50N 16 10 E
Giant's Causeway . 55 15N 6 30w
Giarre . . . . 37 44N 15 10 E
Gibara 21 0N 76 20w
Gibeon . . . . 25 7s 17 45 E
Gibraltar ■ 36 7N 5 22w
Gibraltar, Str. of . 35 55N 5 40w
Gibson, Des. . . . . 24 0s 126 0 E
Giessen . . . . 50 34N 8 40 E
Gifu . . . . 35 30N 136 45 E
Gifu □ . . . . 36 0N 137 0 E
Giganta, Sa. de la . 25 30N 111 30w
Gigha, I. 55 42N 5 45w
Gijón 43 32N 5 42w
Gila, R. 32 43N 114 33w
Gila Bend 32 57N 112 43w
Gilan □ . . . . 37 0N 49 0 E
Gilbedi . . . . 13 40N 5 45 E
• Gilbert Is. . . . . . 1 0N 176 0 E
Gilbert Plains . . . 51 9N 100 28w
Gilbert River . . . 18 9s 142 50 E
Gilgai . . . . 31 15s 119 56 E
Gilgandra . . . . . . 31 42s 148 39 E
Gilgil . . . . 0 30s 36 20 E
Gilgit . . . . 35 50N 74 15 E
Gillam 56 20N 94 40w
Gilliat . . . . 20 40s 141 28 E
Gillingham . . . . . 51 23N 0 34 E
Gilmour 44 48N 77 37w
Gilroy 37 10N 121 37w
Gindie . . . . 23 45s 148 10 E
Gingin . . . . 31 22s 115 37 E
Ginnosar . . . . . . 32 51N 35 32 E
Giong, Teluk, B. . . 4 50N 118 20 E
Girardot 4 18N 74 48w

Girdle Ness 57 9N 2 2w
Giresun . . . . 40 45N 38 30 E
Girga . . . . 26 17N 31 55 E
Giridih . . . . 24 10N 86 21 E
Girishk . . . . 31 47N 64 24 E
Gironde, R. 45 30N 1 0w
Gironde □ 44 45N 0 30w
Girvan 55 15N 4 50w
Gisborne . . . . . . 38 39s 178 5 E
Gisenyi . . . . 1 41s 29 30 E
Gitega . . . . 3 26s 29 56 E
Giurgiu . . . . 43 52N 25 57 E
Giv'at Olga . . . . 32 28N 34 53 E
Giv'atayim . . . . . 32 4N 34 49 E
Giza=El Gîza . . . 30 0N 31 10 E
Gizhiga . . . . 62 0N 150 27 E
Gizhiginskaya
  Guba . . . . 61 0N 158 0 E
Gizycko . . . . 54 2N 21 48 E
Gjoa Haven 68 20N 96 0w
Gjøvik . . . . 60 47N 10 43 E
Glace Bay 46 11N 59 58w
Glacier B. Nat.
  Monument 58 45N 136 30w
Glacier Nat. Park . 48 40N 114 0w
Gladewater 32 30N 94 58w
Gladstone, Queens. 23 52s 151 16 E
Gladstone,
  S. Australia . . . . 33 17s 138 22 E
Gladstone, Canada 50 20N 99 0w
Glâma, R. . . . . . 59 12N 10 57 E
Glasgow, U.K. . . 55 52N 4 14w
Glasgow, U.S.A. . 37 2N 85 55w
Glastonbury 51 9N 2 42w
Glauchau . . . . . . 50 50N 12 33 E
Glazov . . . . 58 0N 52 30 E
Gleichen 50 50N 113 0w
Glen Affric 57 15N 5 0w
Glen Canyon Dam 37 0N 111 25w
Glen Canyon
  Nat. Recreation
  Area 37 30N 111 0w
Glen Coe 56 40N 5 0w
Glen Garry 57 3N 5 7w
Glen More . . . . . 57 12N 4 30 E
Glen Thompson . 37 38s 142 35 E
Glenalbyn . . . . . 36 30s 143 48 E
Glenbrook . . . . . 33 46s 150 37 E
Glencoe . . . . . . 28 11s 30 11 E
Glendale . . . . . . 17 22s 31 5 E

Glendale, Ariz. . . 33 40N 112 8w
Glendale, Calif. . . 34 7N 118 18w
Glendale, Oreg. . . 42 44N 123 29w
Glendive 47 7N 104 40w
Glenelg . . . . 34 58s 138 30 E
Glenelg, R. . . . . 38 3s 141 9 E
Glengariff 51 45N 9 33w
Glengyle . . . . . . 24 48s 139 37 E
Glenn Innes . . . . 29 44s 151 44 E
Glennies Creek . . 32 30s 151 8 E
Glenorchy . . . . . 36 55s 142 41 E
Glenore . . . . 17 50s 141 12 E
Glenormiston . . . 22 55s 138 50 E
Glenrock 42 53N 105 55w
Glenrothes 56 12N 3 11w
Glens Falls 43 20N 73 40w
Glenties 54 48N 8 18w
Glenwood, Canada 49 21N 113 24w
Glenwood, U.S.A. 45 38N 95 21w
Glenwood Springs 39 39N 107 15w
Gliwice . . . . 50 22N 18 41 E
Globe 33 25N 110 53w
Głogów . . . . 51 37N 16 5 E
Glorieuses, Is. . . 11 30s 47 20 E
Glossop 53 27N 1 56w
Gloucester,
  Australia . . . . . 32 0s 151 59 E
Gloucester, U.K. . 51 52N 2 15w
Gloucestershire □ . 51 44N 2 10w
Gloversville 43 5N 74 18w
Glückstadt . . . . . 53 46N 9 28 E
Gmünd . . . . 48 45N 15 0 E
Gmunden . . . . . 47 55N 13 48 E
Gniezno . . . . . . 52 30N 17 35 E
Gnowangerup . . . 33 58s 117 59 E
Gô Công . . . . . . 10 12N 107 0 E
Goa . . . . 15 33N 73 59 E
Goa □ . . . . 15 33N 73 59 E
Goaso 6 48N 2 30w
Goat Fell, Mt. . . 55 37N 5 11w
Goba . . . . 7 1N 39 59 E
Gobabis . . . . . . 22 16s 19 0 E
Gobi, Des. . . . . . 44 0N 111 0 E
Godavari, R. . . . . 16 37N 82 18 E
Godavari Pt. . . . 17 0N 82 20 E
Godbout 49 20N 67 38w
Goderich 43 45N 81 41w
Godhra . . . . 22 49N 73 40 E
Gods L. 54 40N 94 10w

Godthåb 64 10N 51 46w
Goei Hoop, K.die
  =Good Hope,
  C. of . . . . 34 24s 18 30 E
Goeree . . . . 51 50N 4 0 E
Goes . . . . 51 30N 3 55 E
Gogama 47 35N 81 35w
Gogango . . . . . . 23 40s 150 2 E
Gogriâl . . . . 8 30N 28 0 E
Goiânia 16 35s 49 20w
Goias □ 12 10s 48 0w
Gojo . . . . 34 21N 135 42 E
Gojra . . . . 31 10N 72 40 E
Gokteik . . . . . . 22 26N 97 0 E
Gold Coast 4 0N 1 40w
Golden, Canada . 51 20N 117 0w
Golden, U.S.A. . . 39 42N 105 30w
Golden B. . . . . . 40 45s 172 50 E
Goldfields 37 45N 117 13w
Goldsboro 35 24N 77 59w
Goldsworthy . . . . 20 21s 119 30 E
Goleniów . . . . . . 53 35N 14 50 E
Golfito 8 41N 83 5w
Golfo Aranci . . . 41 0N 9 38 E
Golspie 57 58N 3 58w
Goma . . . . 1 37s 29 10 E
Gombe . . . . 10 19N 11 2 E
Gomel . . . . 52 28N 31 0 E
Gomera, I. 28 10N 17 5w
Gómez Palacio . . 25 40N 104 40w
Gonābād . . . . . . 34 15N 58 45 E
Gonaïves 19 20N 72 50w
Gonda . . . . 27 9N 81 58 E
Gonder . . . . 12 23N 37 30 E
Gondia . . . . 21 30N 80 10 E
Gonen . . . . 33 7N 35 39 E
Gongola, R. . . . . 9 30N 12 10 E
Goniri . . . . 11 30N 12 15 E
Gonja . . . . 4 15s 38 0 E
Gonzales 29 30N 97 30w
Good Hope, C. of . 34 24s 18 30 E
Goole 53 42N 0 52w
Goolgowi . . . . . . 33 58s 154 39 E
Goomalling . . . . 31 19s 116 49 E
Goondiwindi . . . . 28 30s 150 21 E
Goor . . . . 52 13N 6 33 E
Goose Bay 53 15N 60 20w
Gop . . . . 22 5N 69 50 E
Gorakhpur . . . . . 26 47N 83 32 E
Gorda, Pta. 14 10N 83 10w

* *Renamed Kiribati*

Gordon 42 49N 102 6w
Gordon River .... 34 10s 117 15 E
Gordonia, Reg. .. 28 13 s 21 10 E
Gordonvale ...... 17 5 s 145 50 E
Gore, Australia ... 28 17 s 151 29 E
Gore, Ethiopia ... 8 12N 35 32 E
Gore, N.Z. .... 46 5 s 168 58 E
Gorey 52 41N   6 18w
Gorgona, I. 3 0N 78 10w
Goris .... 39 31N 46 23 E
Gorízia .... 45 56N 13 37 E
Gorki=Gorkiy .... 56 20N 44 0 E
Gorkiy .... 56 20N 44 0 E
Gorkovskoye
   Vdkhr .... 57 2N 43 4 E
Görlitz .... 51 10N 14 59 E
Gorlovka .... 48 25N 37 58 E
Gorna
   Oryakhovitsa ... 43 7N 25 40 E
Gorno Filinskoye . 60 5N 70 0 E
Gornyatski ...... 67 49N 64 20 E
Gorontalo .... 0 35N 123 13 E
Goronyo .... 13 29N   5 39 E
Gort 53 4N   8 50w
Goryn, R. .... 52 8N 27 17 E
Gorzów
   Wielkopolski .. 52 43N 15 15 E
Gosford .... 33 23 s 151 18 E
Goshen 41 36N 85 46w
Goslar .... 51 55N 10 23 E
Gospič .... 44 35N 15 23 E
Gosport 50 48N   1 8w
Göta kanal ...... 58 45N 14 15 E
Göteborg .... 57 43N 11 59 E
Göteborgs och
   Bohus □ ...... 58 30N 11 30 E
Gotha .... 50 56N 10 42 E
Gothenburg=
   Göteborg ..... 57 43N 11 59 E
Gotland, I. ...... 57 30N 18 30 E
Götland, Reg. .... 58 0N 14 0 E
Gōtsu .... 35 0N 132 14 E
Göttingen .... 51 31N   9 55 E
Gottwaldov ..... 49 14N 17 40 E
Gouda .... 52 1N   4 42 E
Gough, I. .... 40 10 s   9 45w
Goulburn .... 32 22 s 149 31 E
Goundam 16 25N   3 45w
Gounou-Gaya .... 9 38N 15 31 E

Governor's
   Harbour 25 10N 76 14w
Gower, Pen. 51 35N   5 10w
Goya .... 29 10 s 59 10w
Gozo, I. .... 36 0N 14 13 E
Graaff-Reinet .... 32 13 s 24 32 E
Gračac .... 44 18N 15 57 E
Gracias a
   Dios, C. 15 0N 83 20w
Grado .... 45 40N 13 20 E
Grafton, Australia . 29 35 s 152 0 E
Grafton, U.S.A. ... 48 30N 97 25w
Graham, Canada .. 49 20N 90 30w
Graham, N.C. 36 5N 79 22w
Graham, Tex. 33 7N 98 38w
Graham I. 53 40N 132 30w
Graham Ld. ..... 65 0 s 64 0w
Grahamdale 51 30N 98 34w
Grahamstown .... 33 19 s 26 31 E
Grain Coast, Reg. . 4 20N 10 0w
Grajaú .... 5 50 s 46 30w
Grampian □ 57 20N   2 45w
Grampian
   Highlands, Mts. . 56 50N   4 0w
Gran Canaria, I. .. 27 55N 15 35w
Gran Chaco, Reg. . 25 0 s 61 0w
Gran Paradiso, Mt. 49 33N   7 17 E
Gran Sasso
   d'Italia, Mts. ... 42 25N 13 30 E
Granada, Nic. 11 58N 86 0w
Granada, Sp. 37 10N   3 35w
Granard 53 47N   7 30w
Granby 45 25N 72 45w
Grand Bahama I. .. 26 40N 78 30w
Grand Bank 47 6N 55 48w
Grand Bassam 5 10N   3 49w
Grand Bourg 15 53N 61 19w
Grand Canyon ... 36 10N 112 45w
Grand Canyon
   Nat. Park 36 15N 112 20w
Grand Cayman, I. . 19 20N 81 20w
Grand Coulee Dam 48 0N 118 50w
Grand Falls 47 2N 67 46w
Grand Abaco I. ... 47 2N 67 46w
Grand Forks,
   Canada 49 0N 118 30w
Grand Forks,
   U.S.A. 48 0N 97 3w
Grand Haven 43 3N 86 13w
Grand Island 40 59N 98 25w
Grand Junction ... 39 0N 108 30w

Grand Lahou 5 10N   5 0w
Grand Marais 47 45N 90 25w
Grand' Mère 46 36N 72 40w
Grand Rapids,
   Canada 53 12N 99 19w
Grand Rapids,
   Mich. 42 57N 85 40w
Grand Rapids,
   Minn. 47 19N 93 29w
Grand St-Bernard,
   Col. du .... 45 53N   7 11 E
Grand Teton, Mt. . 43 45N 110 57w
Grande, B. ...... 50 30 s 68 20w
Grande, R. 25 57N 97 9w
Grand Baie 48 19N 70 52w
Grande-Entrée ... 47 30N 61 40w
Grande Prairie ... 55 15N 118 50w
Grande Rivière ... 48 26N 64 30w
Grangemouth 56 1N   3 43w
Grangeville 45 57N 116 4w
Granite City 38 45N 90 3w
Granity .... 41 39 s 171 51 E
Granja .... 3 17 s 40 50w
Granollers ...... 41 39N   2 18 E
Grantham 52 55N   0 39w
Grantown-on-Spey 57 19N   3 36w
Grants 35 14N 107 57w
Grants Pass 42 30N 123 22w
Grantsville 40 35N 112 32w
Granville, France .. 48 50N   1 35w
Granville, U.S.A. .. 43 24N 73 16w
Graskop .... 24 56 s 30 49w
Grass Valley 39 18N 121 0w
Grasse .... 43 38N   6 56 E
Gravelbourg 49 50N 105 35w
Gravenhurst 44 52N 79 20w
Gravesend,
   Australia ..... 29 35 s 150 20 E *
Gravesend, U.K. .. 51 25N   0 22 E
Grays .... 51 28N   0 23 E
Grayson 50 45N 102 40w
Graz .... 47 4N 15 27 E
Great Abaco I. ... 26 15N 77 10w
Great Australian
   Basin .... 24 30 s 143 0 E
Great Australian
   Bight. .... 33 30 s 130 0 E
Great Bahama
   Bank 23 15N 78 0w
Great Barrier I. ... 37 12 s 175 25 E

Great Barrier
   Reef .... 19 0 s 149 0 E
Great Basin 40 0N 116 30w
Great Bear L. 65 0N 120 0w
Great Bend 38 25N 98 55w
Great Bitter
   Lake .... 30 15N 32 40 E
Great Blasket, I. .. 52 5N 10 30w
Great Bushman
   Land .... 29 20 s 19 0 E
Great Divide, Mts. . 23 0 s 146 0 E
Great Dividing
   Range .... 25 0 s 147 0 E
Great Exuma I. ... 23 30N 75 50w
Great Falls 47 27N 111 12w
Great Fish, R. ... 33 30 s 27 8 E
Great Inagua I. ... 21 0N 73 20w
Great Indian Des. . 28 0N 72 0 E
Great L. =
   Tonlé Sap ..... 13 0N 104 0 E
Great
   Namaqualand=
   Groot
   Namaqualand .. 26 0 s 18 0 E
Great Orme's Hd. . 53 20N   3 52w
Great Ouse, R. ... 52 47N   0 22 E
Great Plains 42 0N 100 0w
Great Ruaha, R. .. 7 56 s 37 52 E
Great Salt L. 41 0N 112 30w
Great Salt Lake
   Des. 40 20N 113 50w
Great Sandy Des. . 21 0 s 124 0 E
Great Slave L. ... 61 30N 114 20w
Great Smoky Mt.
   Nat. Park 35 39N 83 30w
Great Victoria
   Des. .... 29 30 s 126 30 E
Great Whale, R. .. 55 20N 77 45 E
Great Whale
   River=Poste
   de la Baleine ... 55 20N 77 40 E
Great Whernside,
   Mt. 54 9N   1 59w
Great Yarmouth .. 52 40N   1 45 E
Greater Antilles .. 20 0N 74 0w
Greater
   Manchester □ .. 53 35N   2 15w
Greater Sunda Is. . 4 30 s 113 0 E
Gredos, Sa. de .. 40 20N   5 0w
Greece ■ ...... 40 0N 23 0 E

Greeley 40 30N 104 40w
Green Bay 44 30N 88 0w
Green B. 45 0N 87 30w
Green Island .... 45 54 s 170 27 E
Green River, Utah 39 0N 110 10w
Green River, Wyo. 41 32N 109 28w
Greencastle 39 40N 86 48w
Greeneville 31 50N 86 38w
Greenfield, Ind. .. 39 47N 85 51w
Greenfield, Mass. . 42 38N 72 38w
Greenland ■ 66 0N 45 0w
Greenock 55 57N   4 45w
Greenore 54 2N   6 8w
Greenough, R. ... 28 51 s 114 38 E
Greensboro 36 7N 79 46w
Greensburg, Ind. . 39 20N 85 30w
Greensburg, Pa. .. 40 18N 79 31w
Greenville, Liberia 5 7N   9 6w
Greenville, Mich. .. 43 12N 85 14w
Greenville, Miss. .. 33 25N 91 0w
Greenville, N.C. .. 35 37N 77 26w
Greenville, Pa. ... 41 23N 80 22w
Greenville, S.C. .. 34 54N 82 24w
Greenville, Tex. .. 33 5N 96 5w
Greenwich, U.K. .. 51 28N   0 0
Greenwood, Miss. . 33 30N 90 4w
Greenwood, S.C. . 34 13N 82 13w
Gregory Downs .. 18 35 s 138 45 E
Gregory L. .... 20 10 s 127 30 E
Greifswalder
   Bodden .... 54 12N 13 35 E
Gremikha .... 67 50N 39 40 E
Grenada 33 45N 89 50w
Grenada, I. 12 10N 61 40w
Grenfell .... 33 52 s 148 8 E
Grenen, C. ...... 57 46N 10 34 E
Grenoble .... 45 12N   5 42 E
Gresik .... 9 13 s 112 38 E
Gretna 30 0N 90 2w
Gretna Green ... 55 0N   3 3w
Grevenmacher ... 49 41N   6 26 E
Grey, R. .... 42 27 s 171 12 E
Grey Res. 48 20N 56 30w
Greybull 44 30N 108 3w
Greymouth ..... 42 29 s 171 13 E
Greytown, N.Z. .. 41 5 s 175 29 E
Greytown,
   S. Africa ...... 29 1 s 30 36 E
Gridley 39 27N 121 47w
Griekwastad ..... 28 49 s 23 15 E

* French nameform
Grande Baleine, R.

Griffin 33 15N 84 16w
Griffith . . . . 34 14s 145 46 E
Griffith Mine 50 47N 93 25w
Grimsby 53 35N 0 5w
Grimsey, I. 66 33N 18 0w
Grimshaw 56 10N 117 40w
Grimstad . . . . 58 22N 8 35 E
Grinnell 41 45N 92 50w
Griqualand East,
Reg. . . . . 30 30s 29 0 E
Griqualand West,
Reg. . . . . 28 40s 23 30 E
Gris Nez, C. . . . . . . 50 50N 1 35 E
Groblersdal . . . . . . 25 15s 29 25 E
Grodno . . . . 53 42N 23 52 E
Grodzisk
Mazowiecki . . . . . 52 7N 20 37 E
Grong . . . . 64 25N 12 8 E
Groningen . . . . 53 15N 6 35 E
Groningen □ . . . . . . 53 16N 6 40 E
Groot-Brakrivier . . 34 2 s 22 18 E
Groot Karasberge,
Mts. . . . . 27 10s 18 45 E
Groot Karoo, Reg. 32 35s 23 0 E
Groot Kei, R. . . . . . 32 41s 28 22 E
Groot
Namakwaland =
Namaland, Reg. . 26 0s 18 0 E
Groot Winterberg,
Mt. . . . . 32 45s 26 50 E
Groote Eylandt, I. . 14 0s 136 50 E
Grootfontein . . . . . 19 31s 18 6 E
Gross
Glockner, Mt. . . . 47 5N 12 40 E
Grosseto . . . . 42 45N 11 7 E
Groveton 44 34N 71 30w
Groznyy . . . . 43 20N 45 45 E
Grudziądz . . . . 53 30N 18 47 E
Gryazi . . . . 52 30N 39 58 E
Gua . . . . 22 13N 85 20 E
Guachípas 25 40s 65 30w
Guacanayabo,
G. de 20 40N 77 20w
Guadalajara,
Mexico 20 40N 103 20w
Guadalajara, Sp. . . 40 37N 3 12w
Guadalcanal . . . . . 10 0s 160 0 E
Guadalete, R. 36 35N 6 13w
Guadalquivir, R. . . . 36 47N 6 22w
Guadalupe 34 59N 120 33w

Guadalupe, Sa. de . 39 26N 5 25w
Guadalupe Pk. 31 50N 105 30w
Guadarrama,
Sa. de 41 0N 4 0w
Guadeloupe, I. 16 20N 61 40w
Guadeloupe Pass. . 16 50N 68 15w
Guadiana, R. 37 14N 7 22w
Guadix 37 18N 3 11w
Guafo, B. del 43 35s 74 0w
Guaíra 24 5s 54 10w
Guaitecas, Is. 44 0s 74 30w
Guajira, Pen.
de la 12 0N 72 0w
Gualeguay 33 10s 59 20w
Gualeguaychú 33 3s 58 31w
Guam, I. . . . . 13 27N 144 45 E
Guanabacoa 23 8N 82 18w
Guanabara □ 23 0s 43 25w
Guanacaste 10 40N 85 30w
Guanajay 22 56N 82 42w
Guanajuato 21 0N 101 20w
Guanajuato □ 20 40N 101 20w
Guanare 8 42N 69 12w
Guandacol 29 30s 68 40w
Guantánamo 20 10N 75 20w
Guaporé, R. 29 10s 51 54w
Guaqui 16 41s 68 54w
Guarapuava 25 20s 51 30w
Guarda 40 32N 7 20w
Guardafui, C.=
Asir, Ras . . . . . 11 55N 51 0 E
Guasaualito 7 15N 70 44w
Guasipati 7 28N 61 54w
Guatemala 14 38N 90 31w
Guatemala ■ 15 40N 90 30w
Guaviare, R. 4 3N 67 44w
Guaxupé 21 10s 47 5w
Guayama 17 59N 66 7w
Guayaquil 2 15s 79 52w
Guayaquil, G. de . . 3 10s 81 0w
Gubin . . . . 51 58N 14 45 E
Gubio . . . . 12 30N 12 42 E
Guchin-Us . . . . 45 28N 102 10 E
Gudbrandsdalen . . 62 0N 9 14 E
Gudivada . . . . 16 30N 81 15 E
Gudur . . . . 14 12N 79 55 E
Guecho 43 21N 2 59w
Guéckédou 8 40N 10 5w
Guelma . . . . 36 25N 7 29 E
Guelph 43 35N 80 20w

Güemes 24 50s 65 0w
Guéret . . . . 46 11N 1 51 E
Guérin Kouka . . . . 9 40N 0 40 E
Guernica 43 19N 2 40w
Guernsey, I. 49 30N 2 35w
Guerrero □ 17 30N 100 0w
Guiana Highlands,
Mts. 5 0N 60 0w
Guibes . . . . 26 41s 16 49 E
Guider . . . . 9 55N 13 59 E
Guildford 51 14N 0 34w
Guilvinec 47 48N 4 17w
Guimarães 2 9s 44 35w
Guimaras, I. . . . . . 10 35N 122 37 E
Guinea, Reg. . . . . . 9 0N 3 0 E
Guinea ■ 10 20N 10 0w
Guinea, G. of . . . . 3 0N 2 30 E
Guinea-Bissau ■ . . 12 0N 15 0w
Güines 22 50N 82 0w
Guingamp 48 34N 3 10w
Guiria 10 32N 62 11w
Guiuan . . . . 11 2N 125 44 E
Gujarat □ . . . . 23 20N 71 0 E
Gujranwala . . . . . . 32 10N 74 12 E
Gujrat . . . . 32 40N 74 2 E
Gulbarga . . . . 17 20N 76 50 E
Gulfport 30 28N 89 3w
Gull Lake 50 10N 108 55w
Gulshad . . . . 46 45N 74 25 E
Gulu . . . . 2 48N 32 17 E
Gulwe . . . . 6 30s 36 25 E
Gum Lake . . . . 32 42s 143 9 E
Guma . . . . 37 37N 78 18 E
Gumbiro . . . . 10 1s 35 20 E
Gumla . . . . 23 3N 84 32 E
Gumma . . . . 36 30N 138 20 E
Gummi . . . . 12 4N 5 9 E
Guna . . . . 24 40N 77 19 E
Gundagai . . . . 35 3s 148 6 E
Gunnedah . . . . 30 59s 150 15 E
Gunning . . . . 34 47s 149 14 E
Gunnison, Colo. . . 38 32N 106 56w
Gunnison, Utah . . 39 11N 111 48w
Guntakal . . . . 15 11N 77 27 E
Guntersville 34 18N 86 16w
Guntur . . . . 16 23N 80 30 E
Gunungsitoli . . . . . 1 15N 97 30 E
Gunworth 51 20N 108 10w
Gürchän . . . . 34 55N 49 25 E
Gurdaspur . . . . . . 32 5N 75 25 E

Gurgaon . . . . 28 33N 77 10 E
Gurley . . . . 29 45s 149 48 E
Gurupá 1 20s 51 45w
Guryev . . . . 47 5N 52 0 E
Gusau . . . . 12 18N 6 31 E
Güstrow . . . . 53 47N 12 12 E
Gutha . . . . 28 58s 115 55 E
Guthrie 35 55N 97 30w
Guyana ■ 5 0N 59 0w
Guyenne, Reg. . . . 44 30N 0 40 E
Guyra . . . . 30 15s 151 40 E
Gwa . . . . 17 30N 94 40 E
Gwadabawa . . . . . 13 20N 5 15 E
Gwādar . . . . 25 10N 62 18 E
Gwagwada . . . . . . 10 15N 7 15 E
Gwalia . . . . 28 55s 121 20 E
Gwalior . . . . 26 12N 78 10 E
Gwanda . . . . 20 55s 29 0 E
Gwandy . . . . 12 30N 4 41 E
Gwaram . . . . 11 15N 9 51 E
Gwasero . . . . 9 30N 3 30 E
Gweedore 55 4N 8 15w
† Gwelo . . . . 19 27s 29 49 E
Gwent □ 51 45N 3 0w
Gwio Kura . . . . . . 12 40N 11 2 E
Gwynedd □ 53 0N 4 0w
Gwoza . . . . 11 12N 13 40 E
Gydanskiy Pol. . . . 70 0N 78 0 E
Gympie . . . . 26 11s 152 38 E
Gyöngyös . . . . 47 48N 20 15 E
Györ . . . . 47 41N 17 40 E
Gypsumville 51 45N 98 40w
Gyula . . . . 46 38N 21 17 E

H

Ha Dong . . . . 20 58N 105 46 E
Haarlem . . . . 52 23N 4 39 E
Haast, R. . . . . 43 50s 169 2 E
Hab Nadi Chauki . . 25 0N 66 50 E
Habaswein . . . . . . 1 1N 39 29 E
Hachinohe . . . . . . 40 30N 141 29 E
Hachiōji . . . . 33 3N 139 55 E
Hackett . . . . 52 9N 112 28 E
Hadar Ramatayim . 52 8N 34 45 E
Hadd, Ras al . . . . . 22 35N 59 50 E

Haddington 55 57N 2 48w
Hadejia . . . . 12 30N 9 59 E
Hadera . . . . 32 27N 34 55 E
Hadhramawt, Reg. 15 30N 49 30 E
Hadrian's Wall . . . 55 0N 2 30 E
Haeju . . . . 38 12N 125 41 E
Haerhpin=Harbin . 45 46N 126 51 E
Hafar al Bâtin . . . . 28 25N 46 50 E
Hafizabad . . . . 32 5N 73 40 E
Haflong . . . . 25 10N 93 5 E
Hafnarfjördur 64 3N 21 55w
Hagalil, Reg. . . . . . 32 53N 35 18 E
Hagen . . . . 51 21N 7 29 E
Hagerstown 39 39N 77 46w
Hagfors . . . . 60 3N 13 45 E
Hagi, Iceland 65 28N 23 25w
Hagi, Japan . . . . . 34 30N 131 30 E
Hague, C. de la . . . 49 43N 1 57w
Hague, The=
s'Gravenhage . . 52 7N 4 17 E
Haguenau . . . . 48 49N 7 47 E
Haifa . . . . 32 46N 35 0 E
Haig . . . . 30 55s 126 10 E
Haikow . . . . 20 0N 110 20 E
Hailar . . . . 49 12N 119 37 E
Hailar, R. . . . . 49 35N 117 55 E
Hailey 43 30N 114 15w
Haileybury 47 30N 79 38w
Hailun . . . . 47 24N 127 0 E
Hailung . . . . 42 46N 125 57 E
Haimen . . . . 31 48N 121 8 E
Hainan, I. . . . . 19 0N 110 0 E
Hainaut □ . . . . 50 30N 4 0 E
Haines Junction . . 60 45N 137 30w
Haining . . . . 30 16N 120 47 E
Haiphong . . . . 20 55N 105 42 E
Haitan Tao, I. . . . . 25 30N 119 45 E
Haiti ■ 19 0N 72 30w
Haiyen . . . . 30 28N 120 57 E
Hajdúböszörmény . 47 40N 21 30 E
Hajnówka . . . . 52 45s 23 36 E
Hajr, Reg. . . . . 24 0N 56 34 E
Hakodate . . . . 41 45N 140 44 E
Hakos, Mt. . . . . . . 23 25s 16 25 E
Haku-San, Mt. . . . 36 9N 136 46 E
Hakui . . . . 36 53s 136 47 E
Hala . . . . 25 49N 68 25 E
Ḥalab . . . . 36 10N 37 15 E
Halaib . . . . 22 5s 36 30 E
Halberstadt . . . . . 51 53N 11 2 E

Halcombe .... 40 8 s 175 30 e
Halden .... 59 7 n 11 30 e
Haldia .... 22 4 n 88 4 e
Haldwani .... 29 25 n 79 30 e
Haleakala, Mt. ... 20 42 n 156 15 w
Half Assini .... 5 1 n 2 50 w
Halhul .... 31 35 n 35 7 e
Hali .... 18 40 n 41 15 e
Haliburton ...... 45 3 n 78 30 w
Halifax, Canada ... 44 38 n 63 35 w
Halifax, U.K. .... 53 43 n 1 51 w
Hall Lake .... 68 30 n 81 0 w
Hallands .... 57 0 n 12 37 e
Halle, Belgium ... 50 44 n 4 13 w
Halle, E. Germany 51 29 n 12 0 e
Hällefors .... 59 46 n 14 30 e
Hallett .... 33 25 s 138 55 e
Hallingdal ...... 60 40 n 8 45 e
Hällnäs .... 64 18 n 19 40 e
Halls Creek ..... 18 20 s 128 0 e
Halmahera, I. .... 0 40 n 128 0 e
Halmstad .... 56 37 n 12 56 e
Halq el Oued .... 36 53 n 10 10 e
Hals .... 56 59 n 10 20 e
Halvad .... 23 3 n 71 12 e
Hamä .... 35 5 n 36 40 e
Hamada .... 34 50 n 132 10 e
Hamadän .... 34 52 n 48 32 e
Hamadän □ ..... 35 0 n 48 40 e
Hamamatsu ..... 34 45 n 137 45 e
Hamar .... 60 48 n 11 7 e
Hamburg .... 53 32 n 9 59 e
Häme □ .... 61 30 n 24 30 e
Hämeenlinna .... 61 3 n 24 26 e
Hamelin Pool .... 26 22 s 114 20 e
Hameln .... 52 7 n 9 24 e
Hamersley Ra. ... 22 0 s 117 45 e
Hamhung .... 40 0 n 127 30 e
Hami .... 42 54 n 93 28 e
Hamilton,
   Australia ...... 37 37 s 142 0 e
Hamilton, Bermuda 32 15 n 64 45 w
Hamilton, Canada . 43 20 n 79 50 w
Hamilton, N.Z. ... 37 47 s 175 19 e
Hamilton, U.K. ... 55 47 n 4 2 w
Hamilton, Mont. .. 46 20 n 114 6 w
Hamilton, N.Y. ... 42 49 n 75 31 w
Hamilton, Ohio ... 39 20 n 84 35 w
Hamilton Hotel ... 22 45 s 140 40 e
Hamiota .... 50 11 n 100 38 w

Hamlet .... 34 56 n 79 40 w
Hamm .... 51 40 n 7 58 e
Hammerfest ..... 70 33 n 23 50 e
Hammond, Ind. ... 41 40 n 87 30 w
Hammond, La. .... 30 30 n 90 28 w
Hampden .... 45 18 s 170 50 e
Hampshire □ .... 51 3 n 1 20 w
Hampton .... 37 4 n 76 6 w
Hamra .... 24 2 n 38 55 e
Han Kiang, R. .... 30 32 n 114 22 e
Han Pijesak ..... 44 3 n 18 59 e
Hanau .... 50 8 n 8 56 e
Hanchung .... 33 10 n 107 2 e
Hancock .... 47 10 n 88 35 w
Handa, Japan .... 34 53 n 137 0 e
Handa, Somalia ... 10 37 n 51 2 e
Handeni .... 5 25 s 38 2 e
Hanegev, Reg. ... 30 50 n 35 0 e
Haney .... 49 12 n 122 40 w
Hanford .... 36 25 n 119 45 w
Hangchou=
Hangchow ...... 30 12 n 120 1 e
Hangchow ...... 30 12 n 120 1 e
Hangchow Wan, G. 30 30 n 121 30 e
Hangö .... 59 59 n 22 57 e
Hanh .... 51 32 n 100 35 e
Hanita .... 33 5 n 35 10 e
Hankow .... 30 32 n 114 20 e
Hanku .... 39 16 n 117 50 e
Hanmer .... 42 32 s 172 50 e
Hanna .... 51 40 n 112 0 w
Hannibal .... 39 42 n 91 22 w
Hannover .... 52 23 n 9 43 e
Hanoi .... 21 5 n 105 40 e
Hanover, Canada .. 44 9 n 81 2 w
Hanover, Germany=
Hannover ...... 52 33 n 9 43 e
Hanover, S. Afr. .. 31 4 s 24 29 e
Hanover, N.H. .... 43 43 n 72 17 w
Hanover, Pa. .... 39 46 n 76 59 w
Hanover, I. ...... 50 58 s 74 40 w
Hansi .... 29 10 n 75 57 e
Hantan .... 36 42 n 114 30 e
Hanyang .... 30 30 n 114 19 e
Haparanda ...... 65 52 n 24 8 e
Happy Valley .... 155 53 n 40 10 w
Hapur .... 28 45 n 77 45 e
Har-Ayrag ...... 45 50 n 109 30 e
Har Us Nuur, L. .. 48 0 n 92 0 e
Har Yehuda, Reg. . 31 40 n 35 0 e

Harad .... 24 15 n 49 0 e
Haradera .... 4 33 n 47 38 e
Harbin .... 45 46 n 126 51 e
Harbour Breton ... 47 29 n 55 50 w
Harbour Deep .... 50 25 n 56 30 w
Harbour Grace ... 47 40 n 53 22 w
Harburg .... 53 27 n 9 58 e
Hardanger Fd. ... 60 15 n 6 0 e
Hardap Dam ..... 24 28 s 17 48 e
Harderwijk ..... 52 21 n 5 36 e
Harding .... 30 22 s 29 55 e
Hardoi .... 27 26 n 80 15 e
Hardwar .... 29 58 n 78 16 e
Hardy, Pen. ..... 55 30 s 68 20 w
Harer .... 9 20 n 42 8 e
Hargeisa .... 9 30 n 44 2 e
Hargshamn ...... 60 12 n 18 30 e
Harlech .... 52 52 n 4 7 w
Harlem .... 48 29 n 108 39 w
Harlingen, Neth. .. 53 11 n 5 25 e
Harlingen, U.S.A. . 26 30 n 97 50 w
Harlow .... 51 47 n 0 9 e
Harlowton ...... 46 30 n 109 54 w
Harney L. ...... 43 0 n 119 0 w
Harney Basin .... 43 30 n 119 0 w
Harney Pk. ..... 43 52 n 103 33 w
Härnösand ...... 62 38 n 18 5 e
Harriman .... 36 0 n 84 35 w
Harrington
   Harbour ...... 50 31 n 59 30 w
Harris, I. .... 57 50 n 6 55 w
Harrisburg, Ill. ... 37 42 n 88 30 w
Harrisburg, Pa. ... 40 18 n 76 52 w
Harrismith ...... 28 15 s 29 8 e
Harrison, Ohio ... 36 10 n 93 4 w
Harrison B. ..... 70 25 n 151 0 w
Harrisonburg .... 38 28 n 78 52 w
Harrisonville .... 38 45 n 93 45 w
Harriston .... 43 57 n 80 53 w
Harrogate ...... 53 59 n 1 32 w
Harrow .... 51 35 n 0 15 w
Hartford .... 41 47 n 72 41 w
Hartland .... 46 20 n 67 32 w
Hartland Pt. .... 51 2 n 4 32 w
Hartlepool ..... 54 42 n 1 11 w
Hartley .... 18 10 s 30 7 e
Hartley Bay ..... 46 4 n 80 45 w
Hartmannberge ... 18 0 s 12 30 e
Hartney .... 49 30 n 100 35 w
Hartsville ...... 34 23 n 80 2 w

Harvey, Australia . 33 4 s 115 48 e
Harvey, U.S.A. ... 41 40 n 87 40 w
Harwich .... 51 56 n 1 18 e
Haryana □ ...... 29 0 n 76 10 e
Harz, Mts. ...... 51 40 n 10 40 e
Haslemere ...... 51 5 n 0 41 w
Hassan .... 13 0 n 76 5 e
Hasselt .... 50 56 n 5 21 e
Hassi Messaoud .. 31 15 n 6 35 e
Hassi R'Mel ..... 32 35 n 3 24 e
Hastings, N.Z. ... 39 39 s 176 52 e
Hastings, U.K. ... 50 51 n 0 36 e
Hastings, Mich. ... 42 40 n 85 20 e
Hastings, Neb. ... 40 34 n 98 22 w
Hatch .... 32 45 n 107 8 w
Hatgal .... 50 40 n 100 0 e
Hathras .... 27 36 n 78 6 e
Hatia .... 22 30 n 91 15 e
Hatteras, C. ..... 35 10 n 75 30 w
Hattiesburg ..... 31 20 n 89 20 w
Hatvan .... 47 40 n 19 45 e
Haugesund ...... 59 23 n 5 13 e
Haura .... 13 50 n 47 35 e
Hauraki, G. ..... 36 35 s 175 5 e
Haut-Rhin □ .... 48 0 n 7 15 e
Haute-Corse □ ... 42 30 n 9 20 e
Haute-Garonne □ . 43 28 n 1 30 e
Haute-Loire □ ... 45 5 n 3 50 e
Haute-Marne □ ... 48 10 n 5 20 e
Hauterive ...... 49 10 n 68 25 w
Haute-Saône □ ... 47 45 n 6 10 e
Haute-Savoie □ .. 46 0 n 6 20 e
Haute-Vienne □ .. 45 50 n 1 10 e
Hautes-Alpes □ .. 44 40 n 6 30 e
Hautes-Pyrénées □ 43 0 n 0 10 e
Hauts-de-Seine □ . 48 52 n 2 15 e
Havana=
   La Habana ..... 23 0 n 82 41 w
Havant .... 50 51 n 0 59 w
Havel, R. .... 52 53 n 11 58 e
Havelock .... 44 26 n 77 53 w
Havelock North .. 39 42 s 176 53 e
Haverfordwest ... 51 48 n 4 59 w
Haverhill ...... 42 50 n 71 2 w
Havering .... 51 33 n 0 20 e
Havlíckuv Brod ... 49 36 n 15 33 e
Havre St. Pierre .. 50 18 n 63 33 w
Havza .... 41 0 n 35 35 e
Hawaii □ .... 20 0 n 155 0 w

Hawaii, I. .... 20 0 n 155 0 w
Hawea, L. .... 44 28 s 169 19 e
Hawera .... 39 35 s 174 19 e
Hawick .... 55 25 n 2 48 w
Hawk Junction ... 48 5 n 84 35 w
Hawke, B. ...... 39 25 s 177 20 e
Hawker .... 31 59 s 138 22 e
Hawke's Bay □ ... 39 45 s 176 35 e
Hawke's Harbour . 53 2 n 55 50 w
Hawkesbury,
   Nova Scotia ... 45 40 n 61 10 w
Hawkesbury, Ont. . 45 35 n 74 40 w
Hawthorne ...... 38 37 n 118 47 w
Hay, Australia ... 34 30 s 144 51 e
Hay, U.K. .... 52 4 n 3 9 w
Hay River ...... 60 50 n 115 50 w
Hayden .... 40 30 n 107 22 w
Haydon .... 18 0 s 141 30 e
Hayes, Mt. ..... 63 37 n 146 43 w
Hayes, R. .... 57 3 n 92 .9 w
Hayling I. ...... 50 48 n 1 0 w
Hays .... 38 55 n 99 25 w
Haywards Heath .. 51 0 n 0 5 w
Hazarân,
   Küh-e, Mt. .... 29 35 n 57 20 e
Hazard .... 37 18 n 83 10 w
Hazaribagh ..... 23 58 n 85 26 e
Hazelton .... 55 20 n 127 42 w
Hazleton .... 40 58 n 76 0 w
Hazor .... 33 30 n 35 2 e
Hazrat Imam .... 37 15 n 68 50 e
Headlands ...... 18 15 s 32 2 e
Healdsburg ..... 38 33 n 122 51 w
Heanor .... 53 1 n 1 20 w
Heard I. .... 53 0 s 74 0 e
Hearst .... 49 40 n 83 41 w
Heart's Content .. 47 54 s 53 27 w
Heath Steele .... 48 30 n 66 20 w
Hebel .... 28 59 s 147 48 e
Hebertville ..... 47 0 n 71 30 w
Hebrides, Inner, Is. 57 20 n 6 40 w
Hebrides, Outer, Is. 57 50 n 7 25 w
Hebron, Canada .. 58 10 n 62 50 w
Hebron, Jordan .. 31 32 n 35 6 e
Hecate Str. ..... 53 10 n 130 30 w
Hedaru .... 4 30 s 37 54 e
Hede .... 62 22 n 13 43 e
Hedemora ...... 60 18 n 15 48 e
Hedmark □ ..... 61 45 n 11 0 e
Heemstede ..... 52 19 n 4 37 e

* Renamed Chegutu

Heerde.......... 52 24N 6 2 E
Heerenveen...... 52 57N 5 55 E
Heerlen.......... 50 55N 6 0 E
Heidelberg,
C. Prov........ 34 6s 20 59 E
Heidelberg, Trans.. 26 30s 28 23 E
Heidelberg,
W. Germ...... 49 23N 8 41 E
Heilbron........ 27 16s 27 59 E
Heilbronn....... 49 8N 9 13 E
Heilungkiang □ ... 47 30N 129 0 E
Heinola......... 61 13N 26 10 E
Heinsburg...... 53 50N 110 30w
Heinze Is....... 14 25N 97 45 E
Hekla, Mt...... 63 56N 19 35w
Helena, Ark..... 34 30N 90 35w
Helena, Mont... 46 40N 112 0w
Helensburgh..... 56 0N 4 44w
Helensville..... 36 41s 174 29 E
Helez.......... 31 36N 34 39 E
Heligoland, I.... 54 10N 7 51 E
Hell-Ville...... 13 25s 48 16 E
Hellendoorn..... 52 24N 6 27 E
Hellín......... 38 31N 1 40w
Helmand, Hamun . 31 0N 61 0 E
Helmand □...... 31 0N 64 0 E
Helmand, R..... 31 12N 61 34 E
Helmond....... 51 29N 5 41 E
Helmsdale...... 58 7N 3 40w
Helsingborg..... 56 3N 12 42 E
Helsingfors=
Helsinki........ 60 15N 25 3 E
Helsingør...... 56 2N 12 35 E
Helsinki....... 60 15N 25 3 E
Helston........ 50 7N 5 17w
Helvellyn, Mt.... 54 31N 3 1w
Helwân........ 29 50N 31 20 E
Hemel
Hempstead..... 51 45N 0 28w
Hempstead..... 40 42N 73 37w
Hemse......... 57 15N 18 20 E
Henares, R...... 40 24N 3 30w
Hendaye....... 43 23N 1 47w
Henderson, Ky... 37 50N 87 38w
Henderson, N.C.. 36 18N 78 23w
Henderson, Tex.. 32 5N 94 49w
Hendersonville.... 35 21N 82 28w
Hendon........ 28 5s 151 50 E
Hendrik Verwoerd
Dam.......... 30 38s 25 30 E

Hengelo......... 52 15N 6 48 E
Hengyang....... 26 57N 112 28 E
Henrietta Maria, C. 55 10N 82 30w
Henrique de
Carvalho....... 9 39s 20 24 E
Henryetta...... 35 2N 96 0w
Henty......... 35 30N 147 0 E
Henzada....... 17 38N 95 35 E
Heppner....... 45 27N 119 34w
Herat......... 34 20N 62 7 E
Herat □ .... 34 20N 62 7 E
Hérault □ ...... 43 34N 3 15 E
Herbert........ 50 30N 107 10w
Herbert Downs .. 23 0s 139 11 E
Hercegnovi..... 42 30N 18 33 E
Hercegovina □ ... 43 20N 18 0 E
Hereford, U.K.... 52 4N 2 42w
Hereford, U.S.A.. 34 50N 102 28w
Hereford and
Worcester □ ... 52 14N 1 42w
Herentals...... 51 12N 4 51 E
Herford........ 52 7N 8 40 E
Hermanus...... 34 27s 19 12 E
Hermidale...... 31 30s 146 42 E
Hermiston..... 45 50N 119 16w
Hermitage...... 43 44s 170 5 E
Hermite, I...... 55 50s 68 0w
Hermon, Mt.=
Sheikh, Jabal ash 33 20N 26 0 E
Hermosillo..... 29 10N 111 0w
Hernad R....... 47 56N 21 8 E
Herne Bay...... 51 22N 1 8 E
Herning....... 56 8N 9 0 E
Heron Bay..... 48 40N 85 25w
* Herowabad..... 37 37N 48 32 E
Herrera del
Duque........ 39 10N 5 3w
Herrin......... 37 50N 89 0w
Herstal........ 50 40N 5 38 E
Hertford....... 51 47N 0 4w
Hertford □ 51 51N 0 5w
Herzliyya...... 32 10N 34 50 E
Hessen □ ...... 50 57N 9 20 E
Hewett, C...... 70 30N 68 0w
Hexham....... 54 58N 2 7w
Heysham...... 54 5N 2 53w
Heywood...... 38 8s 141 37 E
Hibbing....... 47 30N 93 0w
Hickory....... 35 46N 81 17w
Hida Sammyaku,

Mts. .... 36 0N 137 10 E
Hidalgo □ 20 30N 99 10w
Hidalgo del Parral . 26 10N 104 50w
Hierro, I....... 27 57N 17 56w
Hifung........ 22 59N 115 17 E
Higashiōsaka.... 34 39N 135 35 E
Higginsville.... 31 42s 121 38 E
High Lava Plat. ... 3 40N 36 45 E
High Point..... 35 57N 79 58w
High Prairie..... 55 30N 116 30w
High River..... 50 30N 113 50w
High Wycombe .. 51 37N 0 45w
High Veld...... 26 30s 30 0 E
Highland □ 57 30N 4 50w
Highland Park, Ill.. 42 10N 87 50w
Highland Park,
Mich........ 42 25N 83 6w
Hijāz, Reg...... 26 0N 37 30 E
Hikari........ 33 58N 131 56 E
Hikone....... 35 15N 136 10 E
Hikurangi..... 37 54s 178 5 E
Hildersheim.... 52 9N 9 55 E
Hillegom...... 52 18N 4 35 E
Hillingdon..... 51 33N 0 29w
Hillsboro, Kan... 38 28N 97 10w
Hillsboro, Oreg... 45 31N 123 0w
Hillsboro, Tex... 32 0N 97 10w
Hillsport...... 49 27N 85 34w
Hillston...... 33 30s 145 31 E
Hilo......... 19 44N 155 5w
Hilversum..... 52 14N 5 10 E
Himachal
Pradesh □ ..... 31 30N 77 0 E
Himalaya, Mts..... 29 0N 84 0 E
Himatnagar..... 23 36N 72 58 E
Himeji........ 34 50N 134 40 E
Himi......... 36 50N 137 0 E
Hims=Homs.... 34 40N 36 45 E
Hinchinbrook, I.. 18 20s 146 15 E
Hinckley...... 52 33N 1 21w
Hindmarsh, L.... 35 50s 141 55 E
Hindubagh..... 30 56N 67 57 E
Hindukush, Mts... 36 0N 71 0 E
Hindupur..... 13 49N 77 32 E
Hines Creek.... 56 20N 118 40w
Hingan....... 25 39N 110 43 E
Hingcheng..... 40 21N 120 10 E
Hingham..... 48 40N 110 29w
Hingi........ 25 4N 105 2 E
Hingning..... 24 2N 115 55 E

Hingoli.......... 19 41N 77 15 E
Hingwa Wan, G.. . 25 0N 120 0 E
Hinnoy, I....... 68 40N 16 28 E
Hinton, Canada .. 53 26N 117 28w
Hinton, U.S.A.... 37 40N 80 51w
Hirakud Dam.... 21 32N 83 45 E
Hiratsuka...... 35 40N 139 36 E
Hirosaki........ 40 35N 140 25 E
Hiroshima...... 34 30N 132 30 E
Hiroshima □ .... 34 30N 133 0 E
Hispaniola, I..... 19 0N 71 0w
Hissar........ 29 12N 75 45 E
Hita.......... 33 42N 130 52 E
Hitachi........ 36 40N 140 35 E
Hitchin........ 51 57N 0 16w
Hitoyoshi...... 32 13N 130 45 E
Hitra, I........ 63 30N 8 45 E
Hjälmaren, L..... 59 18N 15 40 E
Hjørring...... 57 29N 9 59 E
Ho........... 6 37N 0 27 E
Hoadley....... 52 45s 114 30w
Hoai Nhon..... 14 28N 103 37 E
Hobart, Australia . 42 50s 147 21 E
Hobart, U.S.A. ... 35 0N 99 5w
Hobbs........ 32 40N 103 3w
Hoboken...... 51 11N 4 21 E
Hobro........ 56 39N 9 46 E
Hichih....... 24 43N 107 43 E
Hochwan...... 30 0N 106 15 E
Hodaka-Dake, Mt. 36 20N 137 30 E
Hodeida...... 14 50N 43 0 E
Hodgson...... 51 20N 97 40w
Hódmezóvásárhely 46 28N 20 22 E
Hodna, Chott el .. 35 30N 5 0 E
Hodonin...... 48 50N 17 0 E
Hoek van Holland . 52 0N 4 7 E
Hoëveld...... 26 30s 30 0 E
Hofei........ 31 45N 116 36 E
Hōfu......... 34 0N 130 30 E
Hoggar=
Ahaggar, Mts. .. 23 0N 6 30 E
Hohpi....... 35 59N 114 13 E
Hoima....... 1 26N 31 21 E
Hokang...... 47 36N 130 28 E
Hokien...... 38 30N 116 2 E
Hokitika..... 42 42s 171 0 E
Hokkaidō □ .... 43 30N 143 0 E
Hokkaidō, I..... 43 30N 143 0 E
Hokow...... 22 39N 103 57 E
Holan Shan.... 38 40N 105 50 E

Holbrook,
Australia .... 35 42s 147 18 E
Holbrook, U.S.A. . 35 0N 110 0w
Holdenville..... 35 5N 96 25w
Holderness, Pen... 53 45N 0 5w
Holguín....... 20 50N 76 20w
Hollams Bird I... 24 40s 14 30 E
Holland■=
Netherlands ■ .. 52 0N 5 30 E
Holland 42 47N 86 0w
Hollandia=
Jayapura .... 2 28N 140 38 E
Hollywood, Calif. . 34 0N 118 10w
Hollywood, Fla... 26 0N 80 9w
Holman Island ... 70 43N 117 43w
Holmsund ..... 63 41N 20 20 E
Holon .... 32 2N 34 47 E
Holstebro ..... 56 22N 8 33 E
Holy Cross 62 12s 159 47w
Holy, I., Eng. ... 55 42N 1 48w
Holy, I., Wales .. 53 17N 4 37w
Holyhead 53 18N 4 38w
Holyoke 42 14N 72 37w
Homalin ..... 24 55N 95 0 E
Hombori ..... 15 20N 1 38 E
Home Hill .... 19 43s 147 25 E
Homedale 43 42N 116 59w
Homer 59 40N 151 35w
Homestead ... 20 20s 145 40 E
Homs .... 34 40N 36 45 E
Honan □ .... 33 50N 113 15 E
Honda 5 12N 74 45w
Hohoe ..... 7 8N 0 32 E
Hondeklipbaai .. 30 19s 17 17 E
Hondo, R. 19 26N 99 13w
Hondo 14 40N 86 30w
Honduras ■ ... 14 40N 86 30w
Honduras, G. de . 16 50N 87 0w
Hønefoss .... 60 10N 10 12 E
Honfleur .... 49 25N 0 10 E
Hongha, R. .... 22 0N 104 0 E
Hong Kong ■ .. 22 11N 114 14 E
Honiton 50 48N 3 11w
Honolulu 21 19N 157 52w
Honshū, I. .... 36 0N 138 0 E
Hood, Pt. .... 34 23s 119 34 E
Hoogeveen ... 52 44N 6 30 E
Hoogezand ... 53 11N 6 45 E
Hooghly, R. ... 21 56N 88 4 E
Hook Hd. 52 8N 6 57w
Hoonah 58 15N 135 30w

Hoopeston 40 30N 87 40w
Hoorn . . . . 52 38N   5 4 E
Hoover Dam . . . 36 0N 114 45w
Hope, Canada . . . . 49 25N 121 25 E
Hope, U.S.A. 33 40N 93 30w
Hope, Pt. 68 20N 166 40w
Hope Town 26 30N 76 30w
Hopefield . . . . 33 3s 18 22 E
Hopei □ . . . . 39 25N 116 45 E
Hopetown . . . . 29 34s 24 3 E
Hopetoun, Vic. . . . 35 48s 142 25 E
Hopetoun,
   W. Australia . . 33 54s 120 6 E
Hopkinsville 36 52N 87 26w
Hoppo . . . . 21 32N 109 6 E
Hoquiam 47 0N 123 55w
Hordaland □ . . . . . 60 25N   6 45 E
Hormoz . . . . 27 35N 55 0 E
Hormoz, Jazireh-ye . 27 4N 56 28 E
Hormoz, Küh-e . . . 27 40N 55 30 E
Hormuz, Str. of . . . 26 30N 56 30 E
Horn . . . . 48 39N 15 40 E
Horn, C.=
   Hornos, C. de . . 55 50s 67 30w
Horncastle 53 13N   0 8w
Hornell 42 23N 77 41w
Hornepayne 49 14N 84 48w
Hornsby . . . . 33 42s 151 2 E
Hornsea 53 55N   0 10w
Horqueta 23 15s 56 55w
Horsens . . . . 55 52N   9 51 E
Horsham,
   Australia . . . . 36 44s 142 13 E
Horsham, U.K. . . . 51 4N   0 20w
Horten . . . . 59 25N 10 32 E
Hoshangabad . . . . 22 45N 77 44 E
Hoshiarpur . . . . . . 31 30N 75 58 E
Hospet . . . . 15 15N 76 20 E
Hospitalet de
   Llobregat . . . . . 41 21N   2 6 E
Hoste, I. 55 0s 69 0w
Hot Springs, Alas. . 64 55N 150 10w
Hot Springs, Ark. . . 34 30N 93 0w
Hot Springs, S.D. . 43 25N 103 30w
Hotien . . . . 37 6N 79 59 E
Hoting . . . . 64 8N 16 15 E
Houghton-le-
   Spring 54 51N   1 28w
Houhora . . . . 34 49s 173 9 E

Houlton 46 5N 68 0w
Houma 29 35N 90 50w
Hourne, L. 57 7N   5 35w
Houston 29 50N 95 20w
Hove 50 50N   0 10w
Hövsgöl Nuur, L. . . 51 0N 100 30 E
Howard . . . . 25 16s 152 32 E
Howatharra . . . . . . 28 29s 114 33 E
Howe, C. . . . . 37 30s 150 0 E
Howick . . . . 29 28s 30 14 E
Howrah . . . . 22 37N 88 27 E
Howth Hd. . . . . . . 53 21N   6 4 E
Hoy, I. 58 50N   3 15w
Høyanger . . . . 61 25N   6 50 E
Hradec Králové . . . 50 15N 15 50 E
Hron, R. . . . . 47 49N 18 45 E
Hrvatska □ . . . . . . 45 20N 16 0 E
Hsenwi . . . . 23 22N 97 55 E
Hsiamen . . . . 24 28N 118 7 E
Hsian=Sian . . . . . 34 2N 109 0 E
Hsiao Shan . . . . . 34 0N 111 30 E
Hsinchow . . . . 19 37N 109 17 E
Hsinchu . . . . 24 55N 121 0 E
Hsuchang . . . . . . 34 2N 114 0 E
Hsüchou=Suchow . 34 10N 117 20 E
Huacho 11 10s 77 35w
Hualien . . . . 24 0N 121 30 E
Huancane 15 10s 69 50w
Huancavelica 12 50s 75 5w
Huancayo 12 5s 75 0w
Huangliu . . . . 18 30N 108 46 E
Huánuco 9 55s 76 15w
Huaraz 9 30s 77 32w
Huascarán, Mt. . . . 9 0s 77 30w
Huasco 28 24s 71 15w
Huatabampo 26 50N 109 50w
Hubli . . . . 15 22N 75 15 E
Huchow . . . . 30 57N 120 1 E
Huchuetenango . . . 15 25N 91 30w
Huddersfield 53 38N   1 49w
Hudiksvall . . . . . . 61 43N 17 10 E
Hudson 42 15N 73 46w
Hudson, R. 40 42N 74 2w
Hudson B. 60 0N 86 0w
Hudson Falls 43 18N 73 34w
Hudson Hope 56 0N 121 54w
Hudson Str. 62 0N 70 0w
Hué . . . . 16 30N 107 35 E
Huelva 37 18N   6 57w
Huesca 42 8N   0 25w

Hughenden . . . . . . 20 52s 144 10 E
Hughes, Australia . . 30 40s 129 30 E
Hughes, U.S.A. . . . 66 3N 154 16w
Huhehot . . . . 40 52N 111 36 E
Huila, Mt. 3 0N 76 0w
Huiling Shan, I. . . . 21 35N 111 57 E
Huinca Renancó . . 34 51s 64 22w
Huixtla 15 9N 92 28w
Hukawng Valley . . . 26 30N 96 30 E
Hukow . . . . 29 38N 116 25 E
Hulan . . . . 46 0N 126 44 E
Hülda . . . . 31 50N 34 51 E
Hulin . . . . 45 45N 133 0 E
Hull, Canada 45 20N 75 40w
Hull, U.K. 53 45N   0 20w
Hull, R. 53 44N   0 19w
Huma . . . . 51 44N 126 42 E
Huma, R. . . . . 51 40N 126 44 E
Humahuaca 23 10s 65 25w
Humaitá 7 35s 62 40w
Humansdorp . . . . . 34 2s 24 46 E
Humber, R. . . . . . . 53 32N   0 8 E
Humberside □ 53 45N   0 20w
Humboldt, Canada . 52 15N 105 9w
Humboldt, U.S.A. . . 35 50N 88 55w
Humboldt, R. 40 2N 118 31w
Hün . . . . 29 2N 16 0 E
Hunaflói, B. 65 50N 21 0w
Hunan □ . . . . 27 30N 111 30 E
Hunchun . . . . 42 49N 130 31 E
Hunedoara . . . . . . 45 40N 22 50 E
Hung Ho, R. . . . . . 33 0N 117 0 E
Hungary ■ . . . . . . 47 20N 19 20 E
Hunghai Wan, G. . . 20 30N 115 0 E
Hungshui Ho, R. . . 23 70N 110 30 E
Hunghu . . . . 29 49N 113 30 E
Hungkiang . . . . . . 27 0N 109 49 E
Hungnam . . . . 39 59N 127 40 E
Hungtze Hu, L. . . . 33 20N 118 35 E
Hunsberge . . . . . . 27 45s 17 12 E
Hunsruck, Mts. . . . 50 0N   7 30 E
Hunstanton . . . . . 52 57N   0 30 E
Hunter, R. . . . . . . 32 50s 151 40 E
Hunterville . . . . . . 39 56s 175 35 E
Huntingdon,
   Canada 45 10N 74 10w
Huntingdon, U.K. . . 52 20N   0 11w
Huntington, Ind. . . 40 52N 85 30w
Huntington, W. Va. . 38 20N 82 30w

Huntington Beach . 34 40N 118 0w
Huntington Park . . 33 58N 118 15w
Huntly, N.Z. . . . . . 37 34s 175 11 E
Huntly, U.K. 57 27N   2 48w
Huntsville, Canada . 45 20N 79 14w
Huntsville, Ala. . . . 34 45N 86 35w
Huntsville, Tex. . . . 30 50N 95 35w
Huonville . . . . 43 0s 147 5 E
Hupei □ . . . . 31 5N 113 5 E
Huron 44 30N 98 20w
Huron, L. 45 0N 83 0w
Hurricane 37 10N 113 12w
Hurunui, R. . . . . . . 42 54s 173 18 E
Húsavík 66 3N 17 13w
Huskvarna . . . . . . 57 47N 14 15 E
Hussein Bridge . . . 31 53N 35 33 E
Hutag . . . . 49 25N 102 34 E
Hutchinson 38 3N 97 59w
Huwará . . . . 32 9N 35 15 E
Huy . . . . 50 31N   5 15 E
Hvar, I. . . . . 43 11N 16 28 E
Hvítá, R., Iceland . 63 50N 21 0w
Hvítá, R., Iceland . 64 40N 22 0w
Hwainan . . . . 32 44N 117 1 E
Hwang Ho, R. . . . . 37 32N 118 19 E
Hwangshih . . . . . . 30 27N 115 0 E
Hweian . . . . 25 2N 118 56 E
Hweitseh . . . . 26 32N 103 6 E
Hwo Shan, Mts. . . 37 0N 112 30 E
Hwohsien . . . . 36 30N 111 42 E
Hyannis 42 3N 101 45w
Hyargas Nuur, L. . . 49 0N 92 30 E
Hydaburg 55 15N 132 45w
Hyden . . . . 32 24s 118 46 E
Hyderabad, India . . 17 10N 78 29 E
Hyderabad, Pak. . . 25 23N 68 36 E
• Hyderabad □ . . . . 25 3N 68 24 E
Hyères . . . . 43 8N   6 9 E
Hyères, Îs. d' . . . . 43 0N   6 28 E
Hyndman Pk. 44 4N 114 0w
Hyōgo □ . . . . 35 15N 135 0 E
Hyrum 41 35N 111 56w
Hythe . . . . 51 4N   1 5 E
Hyvinkää . . . . 60 38N 25 0 E

I

Iakora . . . . 23 6s 46 40 E
Ialomiţa, R. . . . . . 44 42N 27 51 E
Iaşi . . . . 47 10N 27 40 E
Iaurête 0 30N 69 5w
Ibadan . . . . 7 22N   3 58 E
Ibagué 4 27N 73 14w
Ibar, R. . . . . 43 43N 20 45 E
Ibarra 0 21N 78 7w
Ibb . . . . 14 1N 44 10 E
Iberian Pen. 40 0N   5 0w
Iberville 5 19N 73 17w
Ibicuy 33 55s 59 10w
Ibiza . . . . 38 54N   1 26 E
Ibiza, I. . . . . 39 0N   1 30 E
Ibonma . . . . 3 22s 133 31 E
Ibusuki . . . . 31 16N 130 39 E
Icá 14 0s 75 30w
Içana 0 21N 67 19w
Iceland ■ 65 0N 19 0w
Icha . . . . 55 30N 156 0 E
Ichang . . . . 30 48N 111 29 E
Ichchapuram . . . . 19 10N 84 40 E
Ichihara . . . . 35 35N 140 6 E
Ichinomiya . . . . . . 35 20N 136 50 E
Ichun . . . . 47 42N 129 8 E
Idah . . . . 6 10N   6 40 E
Idaho □ 44 10N 114 0w
Idaho Falls 43 30N 112 10w
Idaho Springs . . . 39 49N 105 30w
Idd el Ghanam . . . 11 30N 24 25 E
Idehan Marzúq . . . 24 50N 13 51 E
Idfû . . . . 25 0N 32 49 E
Idi . . . . 4 55N 97 45 E
† Idi Amin Dada, L. .
Idlip . . . . 35 55N 36 38 E
Idna . . . . 31 34N 34 58 E
Idutywa . . . . 32 8s 28 18 E
Ieper . . . . 50 51N   2 53 E
Ifakara . . . . 8 10s 36 53 E
Ifanadiana . . . . . . 21 29s 47 39 E
Ife . . . . 7 30N   4 31 E
Ifon . . . . 6 58N   5 40 E
Igarapava 20 3s 47 47w
Igarapé Açu 1 4s 47 33w
Igarka . . . . 67 30N 87 20 E
Igawa . . . . 8 45s 34 23 E

Igbetti .... 8 44N 4 8 E
Igbo-Ora .... 7 10N 3 15 E
Igboho .... 8 40N 3 50 E
Igbor .... 7 30N 8 32 E
Iggesund .... 61 39N 17 10 E
Iglésias .... 39 19N 8 27 E
Igloolik Island .. 69 20N 81 30W
Ignace 49 30N 91 40W
Iguaçu, R. 25 30S 53 10W
Iguaçu Falls 25 40S 54 33W
Iguala 18 20N 99 40W
Igualada .... 41 37N 1 37 E
Iguape 24 43S 47 33W
Iguatu 6 20S 39 18W
Ihiala .... 5 40N 6 55 E
Ihosy .... 22 24S 46 8 E
Ihsien .... 41 45N 121 3 E
Iida .... 35 35N 138 0 E
Iisalmi .... 63 32N 27 10 E
Iizuka .... 33 38N 130 42 E
Ijebu-Igbo .... 6 56N 4 1 E
Ijebu-Ode .... 6 47N 3 52 E
Ijmuiden .... 52 28N 4 35 E
Ijsel, R. .... 52 30N 6 0 E
Ijsselmeer, L. ... 52 45N 5 20 E
Ikaría, I. .... 37 35N 26 10 E
Ikeda .... 34 1N 133 48 E
Ikeja .... 6 28N 3 45 E
Ikerre-Ekiti ..... 7 25N 5 19 E
Iki, I. .... 33 45N 129 42 E
Ikire .... 7 10N 4 15 E
Ikom .... 6 0N 8 42 E
Ikot Ekpene ...... 5 12N 7 40 E
Ikurun .... 7 55N 4 41 E
Ila .... 8 0N 4 51 E
Ilagan .... 17 9N 121 53 E
Ilan .... 46 14N 129 33 E
Ilanskiy .... 56 14N 96 3 E
Ilaro .... 6 53N 3 3 E
Ilbilbie .... 21 45S 149 20 E
Île de France,
  Reg. .... 49 0N 2 20 E
Ilebo .... 4 17S 20 47 E
Ilero .... 8 0N 3 20 E
Ilesha .... 8 57N 3 28 E
Ilfracombe,
  Australia ...... 23 30S 144 30 E
Ilfracombe, U.K. . 51 13N 4 8W
Ilha Grande, B. da. 23 10S 44 30W
Ilhéus 15 0S 39 10W

Iliamna L. 59 30N 155 0W
Iliamna, Mt. 60 5N 153 9W
Ilich .... 41 0N 68 10 E
Ilion 43 0N 75 3W
Iliysk=Kapchagai . 44 10N 77 20 E
Ilkeston 52 59N 1 19W
Ilkhuri Shan, Mts. 51 30N 124 0 E
Illapel 32 0S 71 10W
Ille-et-
  Vilaine □ 48 10 1 30W
Illimani, Mt. 16 30S 67 50W
Illinois, R. 38 58N 90 27W
Illinois □ 40 15N 89 30W
Illizi .... 26 31N 8 32 E
Ilmen, Oz. .... 5 15N 31 10 E
Ilo 17 40S 71 20W
Ilobu .... 7 45N 4 25 E
Iloilo .... 10 45N 122 33 E
Ilongero .... 4 45S 34 55 E
Ilora .... 7 45N 3 50 E
Ilorin .... 8 30N 4 35 E
Ilwaki .... 7 55S 126 30 E
Imabari .... 34 4N 133 0 E
Iman .... 45 50N 133 40 E
Imandra, Oz. ..... 67 45N 33 0 E
Imari .... 33 15N 129 52 E
Immingham 53 37N 0 12W
Imo □ .... 4 15N 7 30 E
Imola .... 44 20N 11 42 E
Imperatriz 5 30S 47 29W
Impéria .... 43 52N 8 0 E
Imperial,
  Canada 51 21N 105 28W
Imperial, U.S.A. . 32 52N 115 34W
Imperial Dam 32 50N 114 30W
Impfondo .... 1 40N 18 0 E
Imphal .... 24 15N 94 0 E
Imwas .... 31 51N 34 59 E
In Salah .... 27 10N 2 32 E
Inangahua
  Junction .... 41 52S 171 59 E
Inari .... 68 54N 27 5 E
Inari, L. .... 69 0N 28 0 E
Inca .... 39 43N 2 54 E
Inchon .... 37 32N 126 45 E
Indaw .... 24 15N 96 5 E
Independence,
  Kans. 37 10N 95 50W
Independence, Mo. 39 3N 94 25W
Independence,
  Oreg. 44 53N 123 6W
India ■ .... 23 0N 77 30 E
Indian Cabin 59 50N 117 12W
Indian Head 50 30N 103 35W
Indian Ocean ..... 5 0S 75 0 E
Indiana 40 38N 79 9W
Indiana □ 40 0N 86 0W
Indianapolis 39 42N 86 10W
Indianola 41 20N 93 38W
Indiga .... 67 50N 48 50 E
Indonesia ■ ...... 5 0S 115 0 E
Indore .... 22 42N 75 53 E
Indramaju .... 6 21S 108 20 E
Indravati, R. .... 18 43N 80 17 E
Indre □ .... 46 45N 1 30 E
Indre-et-Loire □ . 47 12N 0 40 E
Indus, R. .... 24 20N 67 47 E
Inebolu .... 41 55N 33 40 E
Inegöl .... 40 5N 29 31 E
Ingersoll 43 4N 80 55W
Ingham .... 18 43S 146 10 E
Ingleborough, Mt. . 54 11N 2 23W
Inglewood, N.S.W. 28 25S 151 8 E
Inglewood, Vic. .. 36 29S 143 53 E
Inglewood, N.Z. .. 33 58N 174 14 E
Inglewood 33 58N 118 27W
Ingolstadt .... 48 45N 11 26 E
Ingulec .... 47 42N 33 4 E
Inhambane .... 23 54S 35 30 E
Inhambane □ ...... 22 30S 34 20 E
Inharrime .... 24 30S 35 0 E
Ining, Kwangsi-
  Chuang .... 25 8N 109 57 E
Ining =
  Sinkiang-Uigur . 43 57N 81 20 E
Inishmore, I. 53 8N 9 45W
Inishowen, Pen. .. 55 14N 7 15W
Inland Sea=
  Setonaikai ..... 34 10N 133 10 E
Inn, R. .... 48 35N 13 28 E
Inner Mongolian
  Autonomous
  Rep. □ .... 44 50N 117 40 E
Innisfail,
  Australia ...... 17 33S 146 5 E
Innisfail, Canada. 52 0N 114 0W
Innsbruck .... 47 16N 11 23 E
Inowrocław .... 52 50N 18 20 E
Inscription, C. .. 25 29S 112 59 E
Insein .... 16 46N 96 18 E

Inta .... 66 2N 60 8 E
Interlaken .... 46 41N 7 50 E
International Falls. 48 30N 93 25W
Intiyaco 28 50S 60 0W
Inútil, B. 53 30S 70 15W
Inuvik 68 25N 133 30W
Inveraray 56 13N 5 5W
Inverbervie 56 50N 2 17W
Invercargill ..... 46 24S 168 24 E
Inverell .... 29 48S 151 36 E
Invergordon 57 41N 4 10W
Invermere 50 51N 116 9W
Inverness, Canada. 46 15N 61 19W
Inverness, U.K. .. 57 29N 4 12W
Inverurie 57 15N 2 21W
Inverway .... 17 50S 129 38 E
Investigator, Str. 35 30S 137 0 E
Inyangani, Mt. ... 18 20S 32 20 E
Inyokern 35 37N 117 54W
Inza .... 53 55N 46 25 E
Ioánnina .... 39 42N 20 55 E
Iola 38 0N 95 20W
Iona, I. 56 20N 6 25W
Ionia 42 59N 85 7W
Ionian Is.=
  Iónioi Nísoi ... 38 40N 20 8 E
Ionian Sea .... 37 30N 17 30 E
Iónioi Nísoi, Is. . 38 40N 20 8 E
Íos, I. .... 36 41N 25 20 E
Iowa □ 42 18N 93 30W
Iowa City 41 40N 91 35W
Iowa Falls 42 30N 93 15W
Ipameri 17 44S 48 9W
Ipiales 1 0N 77 45W
Ipin .... 28 58N 104 45 E
Ipiros □ .... 39 30N 20 30 E
Ipoh .... 4 36N 101 4 E
Ipswich,
  Australia ...... 27 38S 152 37 E
Ipswich, U.K. .... 52 4N 1 9 E
Ipu 4 23S 40 44W
Iquique 20 19S 70 5W
Iquitos 3 45S 73 10W
Iracoubo .... 5 .N 53 10W
Iráklion .... 35 20N 25 12 E
Iran ■ .... 33 0N 53 0 E
Iran, Plat. of ... 32 0N 57 0 E
Iranshahr .... 27 75N 60 40 E
Irapuato 20 40N 101 40W
Iraq ■ .... 33 0N 44 0 E

Irbid .... 32 35N 35 48 E
Ireland, I., Bermuda 32 19N 64 50W
Ireland, I., Europe 53 0N 8 0W
Irele .... 7 40N 5 40 E
Iret .... 60 10N 154 5 E
Iri .... 35 59N 127 0 E
Irian Jaya □ ..... 5 0S 140 0 E
Iriba .... 15 7N 22 15 E
Iringa .... 7 48S 33 43 E
Iriri, R. 3 52S 52 37W
Irish Republic ■ . 53 0N 8 0W
Irish Sea .... 54 0N 145 12 E
Irkineyeva .... 58 30N 96 49 E
Irkutsk .... 52 10N 104 20 E
Iron Mountain 45 49N 88 4W
Ironbridge 52 38N 2 29W
Ironton 38 35N 82 40W
Ironwood 46 30N 90 10W
Iroquois Falls ... 48 40N 80 40W
Irrawaddy, R. .... 15 50N 95 6 E
Irshih .... 47 8N 119 57 E
Irtysh, R. .... 61 4N 68 52 E
Irumu .... 1 32N 29 53 E
Irún 43 20N 1 52W
Irvine 55 37N 4 40W
Irvinestown 54 28N 7 38W
Irwin, Pt. .... 35 4S 116 56 E
Irymple .... 34 14S 142 8 E
Isa .... 13 14N 6 24 E
Ísafjördur 66 5N 23 9W
Isahaya .... 32 50N 130 3 E
Isaka .... 3 56S 32 59 E
Isangi .... 0 52S 24 10 E
Isar, R. .... 48 49N 12 58 E
Íschia, I. .... 40 45N 13 51 E
Iscia Baidoa ..... 3 40N 43 0 E
Ise .... 34 29S 136 42 E
Ise-Wan, G. ...... 34 45N 136 45 E
Isère, R. .... 44 59N 4 51 E
Isère □ .... 45 10N 5 50 E
Iseyin .... 8 0N 3 58 E
Isfahan=Esfahan .. 32 40N 51 38 E
Ishan .... 24 30N 108 41 E
Ishikari-Wan ..... 43 20N 141 20 E
Ishikawa □ .... 36 30N 136 30 E
Ishim, R. .... 57 45N 71 10 E
Ishinomaki .... 38 32N 141 20 E
Ishkuman .... 36 40N 73 50 E
Ishpeming 46 30N 87 40W
Isiolo .... 0 24N 37 33 E

Isipingo Beach ..... 29 59 s 30 57 E
Isiro .... 2 53 N 27 58 E
Isisford .... 24 15 s 144 21 E
Iskenderun .... 36 32 N 36 10 E
Isla, R. .... 56 30 N   3 25 W
Islamabad .... 33 40 N 73 0 E
Island, Pt. .... 30 20 s 115 2 E
Island L. .... 53 40 N 94 30 W
Island Falls ...... 49 35 N 81 20 W
Island Pond ...... 44 50 N 71 50 W
Islands, B. of ..... 49 11 N 58 15 W
Islas Malvinas=
  Falkland Is. ..... 51 30 s 59 0 W
Islay, I. .... 55 46 N   6 10 W
Isle of Man □ ..... 54 15 N   4 30 W
Isle of Wight □ .. 36 54 N 76 43 W
Ismâ'ilîya .... 30 37 N 32 18 E
Isna .... 25 17 N 32 30 E
Isoka .... 10 4 s 32 42 E
Isparta .... 37 47 N 30 30 E
Ispica .... 36 47 N 14 53 E
Israel ■ .... 32 0 N 34 50 E
Isseka .... 28 22 s 114 35 E
Issyk Kul, L. ..... 42 30 N 77 30 E
Istanbul .... 41 0 N 29 0 E
Istra, Pen. .... 45 10 N 14 0 E
Itabira .... 19 29 s 43 23 W
Itabuna .... 1448 E 39 16 W
Itacaré .... 14 18 s 39 0 W
Itaeté .... 13 0 s 41 5 W
Itaituba ....   4 10 s 55 50 W
Itajaí .... 27 0 s 48 45 W
Italy ■ .... 42 0 N 13 0 E
Itapecuru-Mirim ..   3 20 s 44 15 W
Itaperaba .... 12 32 s 40 18 W
Itaperuna .... 21 10 s 42 0 W
Itaquatiana ......   2 58 s 58 30 W
Itaquí .... 29 0 s 56 30 W
Ithaca .... 42 25 N 76 30 W
Itháki, I. .... 38 25 N 20 40 E
Itigi ....   5 42 s 34 29 E
Ito .... 34 58 N 139 5 E
Itu, Brazil .... 23 10 s 47 15 W
Itu, Nigeria ......   5 10 N   7 58 E
Ituiutaba .... 19 0 s 49 25 W
Ituliho .... 50 40 N 121 30 E
Itumbiara .... 18 20 s 49 10 W
Ituna .... 51 10 N 103 30 W
Iturbe .... 23 0 s 65 25 W
Ivalo .... 68 38 N 27 35 E

Ivanhoe .... 32 56 s 144 20 E
Ivano-Frankovsk ː 49 0 N 24 40 E
Ivanovo .... 57 0 N 40 55 E
Iviza, I.=Ibiza, I. . 39 0 N   1 30 E
Ivohibe .... 22 29 s 46 52 E
Ivory Coast ■ ....   7 30 N   5 0 E
Ivrea .... 45 30 N   7 52 E
Ivugivik .... 62 18 N 77 50 W
Iwaki .... 37 3 N 140 55 E
Iwakuni .... 34 15 N 132 8 E
Iwata .... 34 49 N 137 59 E
Iwate □ .... 39 30 N 141 30 E
Iwo ....   7 39 N   4 9 E
Ixtepec .... 16 40 N 95 10 W
Ixtlán .... 21 5 N 104 28 W
Izamal .... 20 56 N 89 1 W
Izegem .... 50 55 N   3 12 E
Izhevsk .... 56 50 N 53 0 E
Izmir .... 38 25 N 27 8 E
Izmit .... 40 45 N 29 50 E
Izra .... 32 51 N 36 15 E
Izumi-sano .... 34 40 N 135 43 E
Izumo .... 35 20 N 132 55 E

J

Jaba .... 32 20 N 35 13 E
Jabalïya .... 31 32 N 34 27 E
Jabalpur .... 23 9 N 79 58 E
Jablah .... 35 20 N 36 0 E
Jablonec .... 50 43 N 15 10 E
Jaca .... 42 35 N   0 33 W
Jacareí .... 23 20 s 46 0 W
Jacarèzinho ...... 23 5 s 50 0 W
Jackson,
  Australia ...... 26 40 s 149 30 E
Jackson, Ky. ..... 37 35 N 83 22 W
Jackson, Mich. ... 42 18 N 84 25 W
Jackson, Minn. ... 43 35 N 95 30 W
Jackson, Tenn. ... 35 40 N 88 50 W
Jackson Bay ...... 50 32 s 125 57 W
Jacksons .... 42 46 N 171 32 E
Jacksonville, Fla. . 30 15 N 81 38 W
Jacksonville, Ill. .. 39 42 N 90 15 W
Jacksonville, Ill. .. 39 42 N 90 15 W
Jacksonville, N.C. . 34 50 N 77 29 W
Jacksonville, Tex. . 31 58 N 95 12 W

Jacksonville Beach 30 19 N 81 26 W
Jacmel .... 18 20 N 72 40 W
Jacobabad .... 28 20 N 68 29 E
Jacobina .... 11 11 s 40 30 W
Jacob's Well ..... 32 13 N 35 13 E
Jacques Cartier, Mt. 48 57 N 66 0 W
Jacques Cartier
  Pass. .... 49 50 N 62 30 W
Jaén .... 37 44 N   3 43 W
Jaffa=Tel Aviv-
  Yafo .... 32 4 N 34 48 E
Jaffna ....   9 45 N 80 2 E
Jagdalpur .... 19 3 N 82 6 E
Jagersfontein .... 29 44 s 25 27 E
Jaghbub .... 29 42 N 24 38 E
Jagraon .... 30 50 N 75 25 E
Jagtial .... 18 50 N 79 0 E
Jaguarão .... 32 30 s 53 30 W
Jaguariaíva ...... 24 10 s 49 50 W
Jaguey .... 22 35 N 81 7 W
Jagungal, Mt. .... 36 12 s 148 28 W
Jahrom .... 28 30 N 53 31 E
Jaipur .... 26 54 N 72 52 E
Jakarta ....   6 9 s 106 49 E
Jakobstad .... 63 40 N 22 43 E
Jalalabad .... 34 30 N 70 29 E
Jalapa,
  Guatemala ..... 14 45 N 89 59 W
Jalapa, Mexico ... 19 30 N 96 50 W
Jalgaon .... 21 0 N 75 42 E
Jalingo ....   8 55 N 11 25 E
Jalisco □ .... 20 0 N 104 0 W
Jalna .... 19 48 N 75 57 E
Jalor .... 25 20 N 72 41 E
Jalpaiguri .... 26 32 N 88 46 E
Jamaari .... 11 44 N   9 53 E
Jamaica ■ .... 18 10 N 77 30 W
Jamalpur,
  Bangladesh .... 24 52 N 90 2 E
Jamalpur, India .. 25 18 N 86 28 E
Jamari .... 11 2 N 11 0 E
Jambi ....   1 38 s 103 30 E
Jambi □ ....   1 30 s 103 30 E
James B. .... 53 30 N 80 30 W
James, R. .... 44 50 N 98 0 W
Jamestown,
  Australia ...... 33 10 s 138 32 E
Jamestown, S.Afr. 31 6 s 26 45 E
Jamestown, N.D. .. 47 0 N 98 30 W
Jamestown, N.Y. .. 42 5 N 79 18 W

Jamkhandi .... 16 30 N 75 15 E
Jammu .... 32 46 N 75 57 E
Jammu and
  Kashmir □ ..... 34 25 N 77 0 W
Jamnagar .... 22 30 N 70 0 E
Jamshedpur ...... 22 44 N 86 20 E
Jämtlands □ ...... 62 40 N 13 50 E
Jan Mayen, I. .... 71 0 N 11 0 W
Jand .... 33 30 N 72 0 E
Jandowae .... 26 45 s 151 7 E
Janesville .... 42 39 N 89 1 W
Jansenville .... 32 57 s 24 39 E
Januária .... 15 25 s 44 25 W
Jaora .... 23 40 N 75 10 E
Japan ■ .... 36 0 N 136 0 E
Japara ....   6 30 s 110 40 E
Japurá, R. ....   3 8 s 64 46 W
Jarales .... 34 44 N 106 51 W
Jarama, R. .... 40 2 N   3 39 W
Jaramillo .... 47 10 s 67 7 W
Jardines de la
  Reina, Is. ...... 20 50 N 78 50 W
Jargalant .... 47 2 N 115 1 E
Jarosław .... 50 2 N 22 42 E
Jarvis I. ....   0 15 s 159 55 W
Jarwa .... 27 45 N 82 30 E
Jāsk .... 25 38 N 57 45 E
Jasło .... 49 45 N 21 30 E
Jason Is. .... 51 0 s 61 0 W
Jasper, Canada ... 52 55 N 118 0 W
Jasper, U.S.A. .... 30 31 N 82 58 W
Jasper Nat.
  Park .... 52 53 N 118 3 W
Jasper Place ...... 53 33 N 113 25 W
Jászberény .... 47 30 N 19 55 E
Jataí .... 17 50 s 51 45 W
Jatibarang ....   6 28 s 108 18 E
Jatinegara ....   6 13 s 106 52 E
Jatobal ....   4 35 s 49 33 W
Jatt .... 32 24 N 35 2 E
Jaú .... 22 10 s 48 30 W
Jaunpur .... 25 46 N 82 44 E
Java ....   7 0 s 110 0 E
Java Sea ....   4 35 s 107 15 E
Java Trench ...... 10 0 s 110 0 E
Jaya, Puncak, Mt. .   4 0 s 137 20 E
Jayapura ....   2 28 s 140 38 E
Jayawijaya,
  Pegunungan ...   4 50 s 139 0 E

Jaydot .... 49 15 N 110 15 W
Jean Marie River . 62 0 N 121 0 W
Jebāl Barez,
  Küh-e .... 29 0 N 58 0 E
Jebba, Morocco .. 35 11 N   4 43 W
Jebba, Nigeria ...   9 9 N   4 48 E
Jebel, Bahr el, R. .   9 40 N 30 30 E
Jedburgh .... 55 28 N   2 33 W
Jędrzejów .... 50 35 N 20 15 E
Jefferson, Mt. .... 38 51 N 117 0 W
Jefferson City .... 36 8 N 93 30 W
Jeffersonville .... 38 20 N 85 42 W
Jega .... 12 15 N   4 23 E
Jelenia Góra ..... 50 50 N 15 45 E
Jelgava .... 56 41 N 22 49 E
Jember ....   8 11 s 113 41 E
Jemeppe .... 50 37 N   5 30 E
Jena .... 50 56 N 11 33 E
Jenkins .... 37 13 N 82 41 W
Jennings .... 30 10 N 92 45 W
Jequié .... 13 51 s 40 5 W
Jequitinhonha ... 16 30 s 41 0 W
Jerada .... 34 40 N   2 10 W
Jerantut ....   3 56 N 102 22 E
Jérémie .... 18 40 N 74 10 W
Jerez de Gacia
  Salinas .... 22 39 N 103 0 W
Jerez de la
  Frontera ...... 36 41 N   6 7 W
Jericho, Australia . 23 38 s 146 6 E
Jericho, Jordan=
  El Arīha .... 31 52 N 35 27 E
Jerilderie .... 35 20 s 145 41 E
Jerome .... 34 50 N 112 0 W
Jersey, I. .... 49 15 N   2 10 W
Jersey City ...... 40 41 N 74 8 W
Jersey Shore ..... 41 17 N 77 18 W
Jerseyville .... 39 5 N 90 20 W
Jerusalem .... 31 47 N 35 10 E
Jervis Bay .... 35 8 s 150 46 E
Jesselton=Kota
  Kinabalu ......   6 0 N 116 12 E
Jessore .... 23 10 N 89 10 E
Jeypore .... 18 50 N 82 38 E
Jhal Jhao .... 26 20 N 65 35 E
Jhang Maghiana .. 31 15 N 72 15 E
Jhansi .... 25 30 N 78 36 E
Jharsuguda ...... 21 51 N 84 1 E
Jhelum .... 33 0 N 73 45 E

Jhelum, R.	31 12N	72 8 E
Jhunjhunu	28 10N	75 20 E
Jiddah	21 29N	39 16 E
Jifna	31 58N	35 13 E
Jihchao	35 18N	119 28 E
Jihlava	49 28N	15 35 E
Jihlava, R.	48 55N	16 37 E
Jijiga	9 20N	42 50 E
Jiloca, R.	41 21N	1 39W
Jima	7 40N	36 55 E
Jiménez	27 10N	105 0W
Jinja	0 25N	33 12 E
Jinnah Barrage	32 58N	71 33 E
Jinné	51 32N	121 25 E
Jinotega	13 6N	85 59W
Jinotepe	11 50N	86 10W
Jipijapa	1 0S	80 40W
Jisr ash Shughur	35 49N	36 18 E
Jitarning	32 48S	117 57 E
Jiu, R.	43 47N	23 48 E
Joaçaba	27 5S	51 31W
João Belo	25 7S	33 32 E
João Pessoa	7 10S	34 52W
Joaquin Villa González	25 10S	64 0W
Jodhpur	26 23N	73 2 E
Joggins	45 42N	64 27W
Johannesburg	26 10S	28 8 E
John O'Groats	58 39N	3 3W
Johnson City, N.Y.	42 9N	67 0W
Johnson City, Tenn.	36 18N	82 21W
Johnson's Crossing	60 33N	133 27W
Johnstown	43 1N	74 20W
Johor Baharu	1 45N	103 47 E
Joinvile	26 15S	48 55 E
Jokkmokk	66 35N	19 50 E
Joliet	41 30N	88 0W
Joliette	46 3N	73 24W
Jolo, I.	6 0N	121 0 E
Jombang	7 32S	112 12 E
Jones, C.	54 33N	79 35W
Jonesboro	35 50N	90 45W
Jönköping	57 45N	14 10 E
Jönköpings □	57 30N	14 30 E
Joplin	37 0N	94 25W
Jordan ■	31 0N	36 0 E
Jordan, R.	31 46N	35 33 E
Jorhat	26 45N	94 20 E
Jörn	65 5N	20 12 E
Jos	9 53N	8 51 E
Jos Plat.	9 45N	8 45 E
José Batlle y Ordóñez	33 20S	55 10W
José de San Martín	44 4S	70 26W
Joseph Bonaparte, G.	14 0S	29 0 E
Jotunheimen, Mts.	61 30N	9 0 E
Jounieh	33 59N	35 30 E
Jouzjan □	22 40N	81 10W
Juan de Fuca Str.	48 15N	124 0W
Juan Fernández, Arch. de	33 50S	80 0W
Juárez	37 40S	59 43W
Juàzeiro	9 30S	40 30W
Juazeiro do Norte	7 10S	39 18W
Jûbâ	4 57N	31 35 E
Jubaila	24 55N	46 25 E
Juby, C.	28 0N	12 59W
Júcar, R.	39 40N	2 18W
Juchitán	16 27N	95 5W
Judaea=Har Yehuda, Reg.	31 35N	34 57 E
Juiz de Fora	21 43S	43 19W
Juli	16 10S	69 25W
Julia Creek	20 40S	141 55 E
Juliaca	15 25S	70 10W
Julianatop, Mt.	3 40N	56 30W
Julianehåb	60 43N	46 0W
Jullundur	31 20N	75 40 E
Jumento Cays	23 40N	75 40 E
Jumet	50 27N	4 25 E
Jumilla	38 28N	1 19W
Jumna, R.= Yamuna, R.	25 25N	81 50 E
Junagadh	21 30N	70 30 E
Junction City, Kans.	39 4N	96 55W
Junction City, Oreg.	44 20N	123 12W
Jundah	24 46S	143 2 E
Jundiaí	23 10S	47 0W
Juneau	58 26N	134 30W
Junee	34 49S	147 32 E
Junín	34 33S	60 57W
Junin de los Andes	39 45S	71 0W
Juquiá	24 19S	47 38W
Jura, I.	56 0N	5 50W
Jura, Mts.	46 45N	6 30 E
Jura □	46 47N	5 45 E
Jurado	7 7N	77 46W
Jurm	36 50N	70 45 E
Juruá, R.	2 37S	65 44W
Juruti	2 9S	56 4W
Justo Daract	33 52S	65 12W
Juticalpa	14 40N	85 50W
Jutland= Jylland, Reg.	56 25N	9 30 E
Južna Morava, R.	43 35N	21 20 E
Jyekundo	33 0N	96 50 E
Jylland, Reg.	56 25N	9 30 E
Jyväskylä	62 12N	25 47 E

K

K2, Mt.	36 0N	77 0 E
Kaap Plato	28 30S	24 0 E
Kaapstad= Cape Town	33 55S	18 22 E
Kabaena, I.	5 15S	122 0 E
Kabale	9 38N	11 37W
Kabalo	6 0S	27 0 E
Kabambare	4 41S	27 39 E
Kabarega Falls	2 15S	31 38 E
Kabarnet	0 35N	35 50 E
Kabba	7 57N	6 3 E
Kabinda	6 23S	24 38 E
Kabongo	7 22S	25 33 E
Kabra	23 25S	150 25 E
Kabul	34 28N	69 18 E
Kabul □	34 0N	68 30 E
Kabwe	14 30S	28 29 E
Kachin □	26 0N	97 0 E
Kachiry	53 10N	75 50 E
Kachung	1 48N	32 50 E
Kadan Kyun	12 30N	98 20 E
Kade	6 7N	0 56W
Kadina	34 0S	137 43 E
* Kadiyerka	48 35N	38 30 E
Kaduna	10 30N	7 21 E
Kaduna □	11 0N	7 30 E
Kaelé	10 15N	14 15 E
Kaerh	31 45N	80 22 E
Kaesŏng	37 58N	126 35 E
Kafanchan	9 40N	8 20 E
Kafulwe	9 0S	29 1 E
Kafia Kingi	9 20N	24 25 E
Kafirévs, Ákra	38 9N	24 8 E
Kafr Kanna	32 45N	35 20 E
Kafr Ra'i	32 23N	35 9 E
Kafue, R.	15 56S	28 55 E
Kafulwe	9 0S	29 1 E
Kagan	39 43N	64 33 E
Kagawa □	34 15N	134 0 E
Kagoshima	31 36N	130 40 E
Kagoshima □	30 0N	130 0 E
Kahama	4 8S	32 30 E
Kahe	3 30S	37 25 E
Kai, Kep	5 55S	132 45 E
Kaiapoi	42 24S	172 40 E
Kaifeng	34 50N	114 27 E
Kaikohe	35 25S	173 49 E
Kaikoura	42 25S	173 43 E
Kailua	21 24N	157 44W
Kainji Res.	10 1N	4 40 E
Kaipara, Harbour	36 25S	174 14 E
Kaiping	40 28N	122 10 E
Kairouan	35 45N	10 5 E
Kaiserslautern	49 30N	7 43 E
Kaitaia	35 8S	173 17 E
Kaitangata	46 17S	169 51 E
Kaiyuan	42 33N	124 4 E
Kajaani	64 17N	27 46 E
Kajiado	1 53S	36 48 E
Kakamega	0 20N	34 46 E
Kake	34 6N	132 19 E
Kakegawa	34 45N	138 1 E
Kakhovka	46 46N	34 28 E
Kakinada= Cocanada	16 50N	82 11 E
Kakogawa	34 46N	134 51 E
Kala	12 2N	14 40 E
Kalabagh	33 0N	71 28 E
Kalabahi	8 13S	124 31 E
Kalabáka	39 42N	21 39 E
Kalach	50 22N	41 0 E
Kaladan, R.	20 9N	92 57 E
Kalahari, Des.	24 0S	22 0 E
Kalakan	55 15N	116 45 E
Kalamata	37 3N	22 10 E
Kalamazoo	42 20N	85 35W
Kalamunda	32 0S	116 0 E
Kalan	39 7N	39 32 E
Kalannie	30 22S	117 5 E
Kalat	29 8N	66 31 E
Kalat-i- Ghilzai	32 15N	66 58 E
Kalemie	5 55S	29 9 E
Kalewa	22 41N	95 32 E
Kalgoorlie	30 40S	121 22 E
Kaliakra, Nos.	43 21N	28 30 E
Kalibo	11 43N	122 22 E
Kalimantan □	0 0	115 0 E
Kálimnos, I.	37 0N	27 0 E
Kalinin	56 55N	35 55 E
Kaliningrad	54 44N	20 32 E
Kalispell	48 10N	114 22 E
Kalisz	53 17N	15 55 E
Kaliua	5 5S	31 48 E
Kallia	31 46N	35 30 E
Kalmalo	13 40N	5 20 E
Kalmar	56 40N	16 20 E
Kalmar □	57 25N	16 15 E
Kalmyk A.S.S.R. □	46 5N	46 1 E
Kalmykovo	49 0N	51 35 E
Kalocsa	46 32N	19 0 E
Kalomo	17 0S	26 30 E
Kaltag	64 20N	158 44W
Kaltungo	9 48N	11 19 E
Kaluga	54 35N	36 10 E
Kalundborg	55 41N	11 5 E
Kama, R.	55 45N	52 0 E
Kamachumu	1 37S	31 37 E
Kamaishi	39 20N	142 0 E
Kamaran, I.	15 28N	42 35 E
Kamba	11 50N	3 45 E
Kambalda	31 10S	121 37 E
Kambarka	56 17N	54 12 E
Kamchatka Pol.	57 0N	160 0 E
Kamembe	2 29S	28 54 E
Kamen	53 50N	81 30 E
Kamenets Podolskiy	48 40N	26 30 E
Kamenka	65 58N	44 0 E
Kamensk Shakhtinskiy	48 23N	40 20 E
Kamensk Uralskiy	56 28N	61 54 E
Kamenskoye	62 45N	165 30 E
Kameoka	35 0N	135 35 E
Kamina	8 45S	25 0 E
Kamloops	50 40N	120 20W
Kampala	0 20N	32 30 E
Kampen	52 33N	5 53 E
Kampot	10 36N	104 10 E

* Renamed Stakhanov

Kampuchea■ =
Cambodia ■ .... 12 15N 105 0 E
Kamsack 51 35N 101 50W
Kamskoye Vdkhr. . 58 0N 56 0 E
Kamyshin .... 50 10N 45 30 E
Kan Kiang, R. ... 29 45N 116 10 E
Kanab 27 3N 112 29W
Kananga .... 5 55S 22 18 E
Kanash .... 55 48N 47 32 E
Kanazawa .... 36 30N 136 38 E
Kanchanaburi ... 14 8N 99 31 E
Kanchenjunga,
Mt. .... 27 50N 88 10 E
Kanchipuram ... 12 52N 79 45 E
Kanchow .... 25 51N 114 59 E
Kanchwan ...... 36 29N 109 24 E
Kandagach ..... 49 20N 57 15 E
Kandahar .... 31 32N 65 30 E
Kandahar □ ..... 31 0N 65 0 E
Kandalaksha ... 67 9N 32 30 E
Kandalakshskiy
Zaliv .... 66 0N 35 0 E
Kandangan ..... 2 50S 115 20 E
Kandavu, I. .... 19 0S 178 15 E
Kandi, Benin ... 11 7N 2 55 E
Kandi, India ... 23 58N 88 5 E
Kandy .... 7 42N 80 37 E
Kane 41 39N 78 53W
Kane Basin 79 0N 70 0W
Kangar .... 6 27N 100 12 E
Kangaroo, I. ... 35 45S 137 0 E
Kangāvar ...... 34 40N 48 0 E
Kangnŭng ...... 37 45N 128 54 E
Kangshan ...... 22 43N 120 14 E
Kangsu □ ...... 38 0N 101 40 E
Kangto, Mt. .... 27 50N 92 35 E
Kanin, Pol. .... 68 0N 45 0 E
Kaniva .... 36 22S 141 18 E
Kankakee 41 6N 87 50W
Kankakee, R. ... 41 23N 88 16W
Kankan 10 30N 9 15W
Kannapolis 35 32N 80 37W
Kano, Benin .... 12 2N 8 30 E
Kano □ .... 12 0N 8 30 E
Kanoya .... 31 23N 130 51 E
Kanpetlet ...... 21 10N 93 59 E
Kanpur .... 26 35N 80 20 E
Kanrach .... 25 35N 65 20 E
Kansas, R. 39 7N 94 36W
Kansas □ 38 40N 98 0W

Kansas City,
Kans. 39 0N 94 40W
Kansas City, Mo. . 39 3N 94 30W
Kansk .... 56 20N 96 37 E
Kantché .... 13 31N 8 30 E
Kantō □ .... 36 0N 120 0 E
Kantse .... 31 30N 100 29 E
Kanturk 52 10N 8 55W
Kanuma .... 36 44N 139 42 E
Kanye .... 25 0S 25 28 E
Kanyu .... 34 53N 119 9 E
Kaohsiung ..... 22 35N 120 16 E
Kaokoveld ..... 19 0S 13 0 E
Kaolack 14 5N 16 8w
Kaomi .... 36 25N 119 45 E
Kaoping .... 35 48N 112 55 E
Kaoyu Hu, L. ... 32 50N 119 25 E
Kapela, Ra. .... 45 0N 15 15 E
Kapfenberg .... 47 26N 15 18 E
Kapiri Mposha ... 13 59s 28 43 E
Kapisa □ ...... 34 45N 69 30 E
Kapps .... 22 32s 17 18 E
Kapsabet ...... 0 14N 35 5 E
Kapuas, R. .... 0 25s 109 24 E
Kapunda .... 34 20s 138 56 E
Kapuskasing ... 49 25N 82 30w
Kaputar, Mt. ... 30 15s 130 10 E
Kaputir .... 2 5N 35 28 E
Kara .... 69 10N 65 25 E
Kara Bogaz Gol,
Zaliv .... 41 0N 53 30 E
Kara Kalpak
A.S.S.R. □ .... 43 0N 59 0 E
Kara Sea ...... 75 0N 70 0 E
Karabük .... 41 12N 32 37 E
Karabutak ..... 49 59N 60 14 E
Karachi □ ..... 25 30N 67 0 E
Karad .... 17 54N 74 10 E
Karadeniz
Bogazi .... 41 10N 29 5 E
Karadeniz
Dağlari, Mts. ... 41 30N 35 0 E
Karaganda ..... 49 50N 73 0 E
Karagayly ..... 49 26N 76 0 E
Karaikkudi .... 10 0N 78 45 E
Karaj .... 35 4N 51 0 E
Karakas .... 48 20N 83 30 E
Karakorum, Mts. . 35 20N 76 0 E
Karakoram P. ... 35 33N 77 46 E
Karaköse ...... 39 44N 43 3 E

Karalon .... 57 5N 115 50 E
Karambu .... 3 53s 116 6 E
Karasburg ..... 28 0S 18 44 E
Karasino ...... 66 50N 86 50 E
Karasjok ...... 69 27N 25 30 E
Karasuk .... 53 44N 78 2 E
Karatau .... 43 10N 70 28 E
Karatau Ra. ... 44 0N 69 0 E
Karatsu .... 33 30N 130 0 E
Karawanken,
Mts. .... 46 30N 14 40 E
Karazhal ...... 48 2N 70 49 E
Karbalā .... 32 47N 44 3 E
Karcag .... 47 19N 21 1 E
Kareeberge .... 30 50s 22 0 E
Karelian
A.S.S.R. □ .... 65 30N 32 30 E
Kargasok ...... 59 3N 80 53 E
Kargat .... 55 10N 80 15 E
Kargil .... 34 32N 76 12 E
Kargopol ...... 61 30N 38 58 E
Kariba L. ...... 16 40s 28 25 E
Karikal .... 10 59N 79 50 E
Karima .... 18 30N 21 40 E
Karimata, Selat, Str. . 2 0s 108 20 E
Karimnagar .... 18 26N 79 10 E
Kariya .... 34 58N 137 1 E
Karkaralinsk ... 49 30N 75 10 E
Karkinitskiy
Zaliv .... 45 36N 32 35 E
Karkur .... 32 29N 34 57 E
Karl-Marx-Stadt . 50 50N 12 55 E
Karlovac ...... 45 31N 15 36 E
Karlovy Vary ... 50 13N 12 51 E
Karlsborg ...... 58 33N 14 33 E
Karlshamn ..... 56 10N 14 51 E
Karlskoga ..... 59 22N 14 33 E
Karlskrona .... 56 10N 15 35 E
Karlsruhe ...... 49 3N 8 23 E
Karlstad .... 59 23N 13 30 E
Karluk 57 30N 155 0w
Karnal .... 29 42N 77 2 E
Karnaphuli Res. . 22 40N 92 20 E
Karnataka □ ... 13 15N 77 0 E
Karnische Alpen,
Mts. .... 46 36N 13 0 E
Kärnten □ ..... 46 52N 13 30 E
Karonga .... 9 57s 33 55 E
Karoonda ...... 35 1s 139 59 E
Kárpathos, I. ... 35 37N 27 10 E

Karpogory ..... 63 59N 44 27 E
Kars .... 40 40N 43 5 E
Karsakpay ..... 47 55N 66 40 E
Karshi .... 38 53N 65 48 E
Kartaly .... 53 3N 60 40 E
Karumo .... 2 25s 32 50 E
Karungu .... 0 50s 34 10 E
Karur .... 10 59N 78 2 E
Karwar .... 14 44N 74 5 E
Kasai, R. ...... 3 2s 16 57 E
Kasama .... 10 16s 31 9 E
Kasangulu ..... 4 15s 15 15 E
Kasaragod ..... 12 30N 74 58 E
Kasenyi .... 1 24N 30 26 E
Kasese .... 0 13N 30 3 E
Kāshān .... 34 5N 51 30¼ E
Kashgar .... 39 46N 75 52 E
Kashing .... 30 45N 120 41 E
Kashmir □ ..... 34 0N 78 0 E
Kasimov .... 54 55N 41 20 E
Kaslo 49 55N 117 0w
Kasongo .... 4 30s 26 33 E
Kásos, I. ...... 35 20N 26 55 E
Kassala .... 15 23N 36 26 E
Kassalâ □ ..... 15 20N 36 26 E
Kassel .... 51 19N 9 32 E
Kassue .... 6 58s 139 21 E
Kastamonu .... 41 25N 33 43 E
Kasulu .... 4 37s 30 5 E
Kasur .... 31 5N 74 25 E
Kata .... 58 46N 102 40 E
Katako Kombe ... 3 25s 24 20 E
Katanga, Reg.=
Shaba, Reg. ... 8 30s 25 0 E
Katanning ..... 33 40s 117 33 E
Katha .... 24 10N 96 30 E
Katherine ..... 14 27s 132 20 E
Kathiawar, Reg. . 22 0N 71 0 E
Katiet .... 2 21s 99 14 E
Katihar .... 25 34N 87 36 E
Katima Mulilo ... 17 28s 24 13 E
Katmai Mt. 58 20N 154 59w
Katmandu ..... 27 45N 85 12 E
Katombora ..... 18 0S 25 30 E
Katcompi ...... 6 2s 26 23 E
Katoomba ...... 33 41s 150 19 E
Katowice ...... 50 17N 19 5 E
Katrine, L. .... 56 15N 4 30 E
Katrineholm ... 59 9N 16 12 E
Katsina .... 7 10N 9 20 E

Kattawaz
Urgan □ .... 32 10N 62 20 E
Kattegat, Str. ... 57 0N 11 20 E
Katwijk-aan-Zee . 52 12N 4 22 E
Kauai, I. 19 30N 155 30w
Kaukauveld .... 20 0S 20 15 E
Kaukonen ..... 67 42N 24 58 E
Kaunas .... 54 54N 23 54 E
Kaura Namoda ... 12 37N 6 33 E
Kautokeino .... 69 0N 23 4 E
Kavacha .... 60 16N 169 51 E
Kavála .... 40 57N 24 28 E
Kaw 4 30N 52 15w
Kawagoe .... 35 55N 139 29 E
Kawaguchi ..... 35 52N 138 45 E
Kawaihae 20 5N 155 50w
Kawambwa ..... 9 48s 29 3 E
Kawanoe ...... 34 1N 133 34 E
Kawasaki ...... 35 35N 138 42 E
Kawerau 45 4N 91 15w
Kawhia
Harbour ...... 38 4s 174 49 E
Kawnro .... 22 48N 99 8 E
Kawthaung ..... 10 5N 98 36 E
Kawthoolei □ ... 18 0N 97 30 E
Kaya 13 25N 1 10w
Kayah □ .... 19 15N 97 15 E
Kayambi .... 9 28s 31 59 E
Kayenta .... 36 46N 110 15 E
Kayes 14 25N 11 30w
Kayrunnera .... 30 40s 142 30 E
Kayseri .... 38 45N 35 30 E
Kayuagung .... 3 28s 104 46 E
Kazachye ...... 70 52N 135 58 E
Kazakh S.S.R. □ . 50 0N 58 0 E
Kazan .... 55 48N 49 3 E
Kazanlŭk ...... 42 38N 25 35 E
Kazbek, Mt. .... 42 30N 44 30 E
Kāzerūn .... 29 38N 51 40 E
Kazym, R. ..... 63 54N 65 50 E
Kéa, I. .... 37 30N 24 22 E
Kearney 40 45N 99 3w
Kebnekaise, Mt. . 67 48N 18 30 E
Kebri Dehar ... 6 45N 44 17w
Kebumen ...... 7 42s 109 40 E
Kecskemet .... 46 57N 19 35 E
Kedgwick 47 40N 67 20w
Kediri .... 7 51s 112 -1 E
Keeling Is.=

Cocos Is. . . . . . . 12 12 s   96 54 E
Keelung=Chilung . 25   3 N 121 45 E
Keene . . . . 42 57 N 72 17 W
Keetmanshoop . . . . 26 35 s 18   8 E
Keewatin . . . . 47 23 N 93   0 W
Keewatin, Reg. . . . 63 20 N 94 40 W
Kefallinía, I. . . . . 38 28 N 20 30 E
Kefamenanu . . . . . 9 28 s 124 38 E
Kefar Gil'adi . . . . 33 14 N 35 35 E
Kefar Sava . . . . . 32 11 N 34 54 E
Kefar Szold . . . . . 33 11 N 35 34 E
Kefar Tavor . . . . 32 42 N 35 24 E
Kefar Vitkin . . . . . 32 22 N 34 53 E
Kefar Yona . . . . . 32 20 N 34 54 E
Kefar Zetim . . . . . 32 49 N 35 27 E
Keffi . . . . 8 55 N   7 43 E
Keflavik 64   2 N 22 35 W
Keighley . . . . 53 52 N   1 54 W
Keimoes . . . . 28 41 s 21   0 E
Keita . . . . 14 46 N   5 46 E
Keith, Australia . . . 36   0 s 140 20 E
Keith, U.K. . . . . 57 33 N   2 58 W
Keith Arm, B. . . . . 65 20 N 122   0 W
Kël . . . . 69 30 N 124 10 E
Kelang 3   2 N 101 26 E
Kelibia . . . . 36 50 N 11   3 E
Kellerberrin . . . . . 31 36 s 117 38 E
Kellogg . . . . 47 30 N 116   5 W
Kells=Ceanannas
   Mor . . . . 53 42 N   6 53 W
Kelowna . . . . 49 50 N 119 25 W
Kelsey Bay . . . . 50 25 N 126   0 W
Kelso, N.Z. . . . . 45 54 s 169 15 E
Kelso, U.K. . . . . 55 36 N   2 27 W
Kelso, U.S.A. . . . 46 10 N 122 57 W
Keluang 2   3 N 103 18 E
Kelvington . . . . . 52 20 N 103 30 W
Kem 65   0 N 34 38 E
Kem, R. . . . . 64 57 N 34 41 E
Kemerovo . . . . . . 55 20 N 85 50 E
Kemi . . . . 65 47 N 24 32 E
Kemijärvi . . . . . . 66 43 N 27 22 E
Kemijoki, R. . . . . 65 47 N 24 30 E
Kemmerer . . . . . 41 52 N 110 30 W
Kempsey 31   1 s 152 50 E
Kempten . . . . . . 47 42 N 10 18 E
Kemptville 45   0 N 75 38 W
Ken, R. . . . . 54 50 N   4   4 W
Kendal, Indonesia . 6 56 s 110 14 E
Kendal, U.K. . . . . 54 19 N   2 44 W

Kendari . . . . 3 50 s 122 30 E
Kende . . . . 11 30 N   4 12 E
Kendenup . . . . . . 34 30 s 117 38 E
Kendi . . . . 60 30 N 151   0 W
Kendrapara . . . . . 20 35 N 86 30 E
Kenema . . . . 7 50 N 11 14 W
Keng Tawng . . . . 20 45 N 98 18 E
Keng Tung 21   0 N 99 30 E
Kenho . . . . 50 43 N 121 30 E
Kenitra . . . . 34 15 N   6 40 W
Kenmare . . . . . . 51 52 N   9 35 W
Kennedy, C.=
   Canaveral, C. . . . 28 28 N 80 31 W
Kennet, R. . . . . . 51 28 N   0 57 W
Kennett 36   7 N 90   0 W
Kennewick . . . . . 46 11 N 119   2 W
Kenora . . . . 49 50 N 94 35 W
Kenosha . . . . . . 42 33 N 87 48 W
Kensington . . . . . 46 25 N 63 34 W
Kent 41   8 N 81 20 W
Kent □ . . . . 51 12 N   0 40 E
Kent Pen. . . . . . 68 30 N 107   0 W
Kentau . . . . 43 32 N 68 36 E
Kenton . . . . 40 40 N 83 35 W
Kentucky, R. . . . . 38 41 N 85 11 W
Kentucky □ . . . . . 37 20 N 85   0 W
Kenya ■ . . . . . . 2 20 N 38   0 E
Kenya, Mt. . . . . . 0 10 s 37 18 E
Keokuk . . . . 40 25 N 91 30 W
Kephallinia, I.=
   Kefallinia, I. . . . 38 28 N 20 30 E
Kerala □ 11   0 N 76 15 E
Kerang . . . . 35 40 s 143 55 E
Keray . . . . 26 15 N 57 30 E
Kerch . . . . 45 20 N 36 20 E
Kerem Maharal . . . 32 39 N 34 59 E
Kerguelen, I. . . . . 48 15 s 69 10 E
Kericho . . . . 0 22 s 35 15 E
Kerinci, Mt. 2   5 s 101   0 E
Kerkenna, Is. . . . 34 48 N 11   1 E
Kerki . . . . 37 10 N 65   0 E
Kérkira . . . . 39 38 N 19 50 E
Kérkira, I. . . . . . 39 35 N 19 45 E
Kerkrade . . . . . . 50 53 N   6   4 E
Kermadec Is. 31   8 s 175 16 W
Kermān . . . . . . 30 15 N 57   1 E
Kermān □ 30   0 N 57   0 E
* Kermānshāh . . . . 34 23 N 47   0 E

* Kermānshāh □ 34   0 N 46 30 E
Kermit . . . . 31 56 N 103   3 W
Kerripi . . . . 3 55 N 31 52 E
Kerrobert 52   0 N 109 11 W
Kerrville 30   1 N 99   8 W
Kerry □ 52   7 N   9 35 W
Kerry Hd. . . . . . . 52 26 N   9 56 W
Kerulen, R. . . . . . 48 48 N 117   0 E
Kerzaz . . . . 29 29 N   1 25 W
Keski-Suomen □ . . 63   0 N 25   0 E
Kestell . . . . 28 17 s 28 42 E
Keswick . . . . 54 35 N   3   9 W
Keta . . . . 5 49 N   1   0 E
Keta Lagoon . . . . 5 50 N   1   0 E
Ketapang . . . . . . 1 55 s 131 40 E
Ketchikan . . . . . 55 25 N 131 40 W
Kete Krachi . . . . . 7 55 N   0   1 W
Ketrzyn 54   7 N 21 22 E
Kettering . . . . . . 52 24 N   0 44 W
Kettle Falls . . . . 48 41 N 118   2 W
Kewanee . . . . . . 41 18 N 90   0 W
Keweenaw B. 47   0 N 88   0 W
Keweenaw Pt. . . . 47 26 N 87 40 W
Key West . . . . . . 24 40 N 82 15 W
Keyser . . . . 39 26 N 79   0 W
Kezhma . . . . . . 59 15 N 100 57 E
Khabarovo . . . . . 69 30 N 60 30 E
Khaborovsk . . . . 48 20 N 135   0 E
Khairagarh . . . . . 21 27 N 81   2 E
Khairpur . . . . . . 27 32 N 68 49 E
Khalij-e Fars . . . . 28 20 N 51 45 E
Khalkís . . . . 38 27 N 23 42 E
Khalmer Yu . . . . 67 58 N 65   1 E
Khalturin . . . . . . 58 40 N 48 50 E
Khamas Country . . 21 45 s 26 30 E
Khamir . . . . 16 10 N 43 45 E
Khan Tengri,
   Mt. . . . . 42 25 N 80 10 E
Khān Yūnis . . . . 31 21 N 34 18 E
Khanabad . . . . . . 36 45 N 69   5 E
Khānaqin . . . . . . 34 23 N 45 25 E
Khandwa . . . . . . 21 49 N 76 22 E
Khandyga . . . . . 62 30 N 134 50 E
Khanewal . . . . . . 30 20 N 71 55 E
Khaniá . . . . 35 30 N 24   4 E
Khaníon, Kól. . . . 35 33 N 23 55 E
Khanka, Oz. 45   0 N 132 30 E
Khanty-
   Mansiysk 61   0 N 69   0 E
Khapcheranga . . . 49 40 N 112   0 E

Kharagpur . . . . . . 22 20 N 87 25 E
Kharfa 22   0 N 46 35 E
Kharkov . . . . 49 58 N 36 20 E
Kharovsk . . . . . . 59 56 N 40 13 E
Kharsaniya . . . . . 27 10 N 49 10 E
Khartoum=El
   Khartûm . . . . . 15 31 N 32 35 E
Khasab . . . . 26 14 N 56 15 E
Khāsh . . . . 28 15 N 61   5 E
Khashm el Girba . 14 59 N 35 58 E
Khashmor . . . . . 28 30 N 69 31 E
Khaskovo . . . . . 41 56 N 25 30 E
Khatanga 72   0 N 102 20 E
Khatanga, R. . . . 73 30 N 109   0 E
Khavari . . . . . . 37 20 N 46   0 E
Khed Brahma . . . 24   2 N 73   3 E
Khemis Miliana . . 36 11 N   2 14 E
Khenchela . . . . . 35 28 N   7 11 E
Khenifra . . . . . . 32 58 N   5 46 W
Kherson . . . . . . 46 35 N 32 35 E
Khetinsiring . . . . 32 54 N 92 50 E
Khilok . . . . 51 30 N 110 45 E
Khíos . . . . 38 27 N 26   9 E
Khíos, I. . . . . . . 38 20 N 26   0 E
Khiva . . . . 41 30 N 60 18 E
Khmelnitsky . . . . 49 23 N 27   0 E
Khojak P. . . . . . 30 55 N 66 30 E
Kholm . . . . 57 10 N 31 15 E
Kholmsk 35   5 N 139 48 E
Khong, R. 14   7 N 105 51 E
Khonh Hung . . . . 9 37 N 105 50 E
Khonu . . . . 66 30 N 143 25 E
Khoper, R. 52   0 N 43 20 E
Khorasan □ 34   0 N 58   0 E
Khorat=Nakhon
   Ratchasima . . . 14 59 N 102 12 E
Khorog . . . . . . 37 30 N 71 36 E
Khorramābād . . . 33 30 N 48 25 E
Khorromshahr . . . 30 29 N 48 15 E
Khouribga . . . . . 32 58 N   6 57 W
Khugiani . . . . . . 31 28 N 66 14 E
Khulna . . . . 22 45 N 89 34 E
Khulna □ . . . . . 22 45 N 89 35 E
Khushab . . . . . 32 20 N 72 20 E
Khuzestan □ 31   0 N 50   0 E
Khvor . . . . 33 45 N 55   0 E
Khvormūj . . . . . 28 40 N 51 30 E
Khvoy . . . . 38 35 N 45   0 E
Khyber P. . . . . . 34 10 N 71   8 E
Kialing

Kiang, R. 30   2 N 106 18 E
Kiama . . . . 34 40 s 150 50 E
Kiamal . . . . 34 58 s 142 18 E
Kiambu 1   8 s 36 50 E
Kiamusze . . . . . 46 45 N 130 30 E
Kian 27   1 N 114 58 E
Kiangling . . . . . 30 28 N 113 16 E
Kiangsi □ . . . . . 27 45 N 115   0 E
Kiangsu □ 33   0 N 119 50 E
Kiangyin . . . . . . 31 51 N 120   0 E
Kiaohsien . . . . . 36 20 N 120   0 E
Kibau . . . . 8 35 s 35 18 E
Kiberege . . . . . . 7 55 s 36 53 E
Kibiti . . . . 7 40 s 38 54 E
Kibombo . . . . . . 3 57 s 25 53 E
Kibwezi . . . . . . 2 27 s 37 57 E
Kichiga . . . . . . 59 50 N 163   5 E
Kicking Horse P. . 51 27 N 116 25 W
Kidderminster . . . 52 24 N   2 13 W
Kidete . . . . 6 25 s 37 17 E
Kidugallo . . . . . 6 49 s 38 15 E
Kiel . . . . 54 16 N 10   8 E
Kieler B. . . . . . 54 30 N 10 30 E
Kienko . . . . . . 31 50 N 105 30 E
Kienow 27   0 N 118 16 E
Kienshui . . . . . . 23 57 N 102 45 E
Kiensi . . . . 26 58 N 106   0 E
Kienteh . . . . . . 29 30 N 119 28 E
Kienyang . . . . . 27 30 N 118   0 E
Kiev=Kiyev . . . . 50 30 N 30 28 E
Kiffa . . . . 16 50 N 11 15 W
Kigali 1   5 s 30   4 E
Kigoma-Ujiji . . . 5 30 s 30   0 E
Kihurio . . . . . . 4 32 s 38   5 E
Kii-Suido,
   Chan. 33   0 N 134 50 E
Kijabe . . . . 0 56 s 36 33 E
Kikiang . . . . . . 28 58 N 106 44 E
Kikinda . . . . . . 45 50 N 20 30 E
Kikládhes, Is. . . . 37 20 N 24 30 E
Kikládhes □ . . . . 37 20 N 24 30 E
Kilcoy . . . . 26 59 s 152 30 E
Kildare . . . . . . 53 10 N   6 50 W
Kildare □ . . . . . 53 10 N   6 50 W
Kilembe . . . . . . 0 15 N 30   3 E
Kilgore . . . . . . 32 22 N 94 40 W
Kilifi . . . . 3 40 s 39 48 E
Kilimanjaro, Mt. . 3   7 s 37 20 E
Kilimatinde . . . . 5 55 s 34 58 E
Kilindini 4   4 s 39 40 E

* Renamed Qahremānshahr   * Renamed Qahremānshahr

Kilis .... 36 50N 37 10 E
Kilkee 52 41N 9 40w
Kilkenny 52 40N 7 17w
Kilkenny □ 52 35N 7 15w
Killala 54 13N 9 12w
Killaloe 52 48N 8 28w
Killarney, Canada . 49 10N 99 40w
Killarney, Eire ... 52 2N 9 30w
Killary Harbour .. 53 38N 9 52w
Killiecrankie,
   P. of 56 44N 3 46w
Killin 56 27N 4 20w
Killybegs 54 38N 8 26w
Kilmany .... 38 8s 146 55 E
Kilmarnock 55 36N 4 30w
Kilmore .... 37 25s 144 53 E
Kilosa .... 6 48s 37 0 E
Kilrush 52 39N 9 30w
Kilwa Kisiwani ... 8 58s 39 32 E
Kilwa Kivinje .... 8 45s 39 25 E
Kimba .... 33 8s 136 23 E
Kimball 41 17N 103 20w
Kimberley, Canada 49 40N 116 10w
Kimberley,
   S. Africa ..... 28 43s 24 46 E
Kimberley Downs . 17 24s 124 22 E
Kimberly 42 33N 114 25w
Kimchaek .... 40 41N 129 12 E
Kimchon .... 36 11N 128 4 E
Kimry .... 56 55N 37 15 E
Kinabalu, Mt. ... 6 0N 116 0 E
Kincaid 49 40N 107 0w
Kincardine 44 10N 81 40w
Kindersley 51 30N 109 10w
Kindia 10 0N 12 52w
Kindu .... 2 55s 25 50 E
Kineshma .... 57 30N 42 5 E
King, I. .... 39 50s 144 0 E
King, Mt. .... 25 10s 147 31 E
King Edward, R. .. 14 14s 126 35 E
King George B. .. 51 30s 60 30w
King George Is. .. 53 40N 80 30w
King Leopold,
   Ras. .... 17 20s 124 20 E
King Sd. .... 16 50s 123 20 E
King William I. ... 69 0N 98 0w
King William's
   Town .... 32 51s 27 22 E
Kingaroy .... 26 32s 151 51 E
Kingku .... 23 49N 100 30 E

Kingman 35 12N 114 2w
Kingoonya .... 30 54N 135 18 E
Kingpeng .... 43 30N 117 25 E
Kings Canyon
   Nat. Park 37 0N 118 45w
Kings Lynn ...... 52 45N 0 25 E
Kingsbridge 50 14N 3 46w
Kingscourt 53 55N 6 48w
Kingston, Canada . 44 20N 76 30w
Kingston, Jamaica . 18 0N 76 50w
Kingston, N.Z. ... 45 20s 168 43 E
Kingston, N.Y. ... 41 55N 74 0w
Kingston, Pa. 41 19N 75 58w
Kingston South
   East .... 36 52s 139 51 E
Kingstown 13 10N 61 10w
Kingsville,
   Canada 42 3N 82 45w
Kingsville, U.S.A. . 27 30N 97 53w
Kingtai .... 37 4N 103 59 E
Kingtehchen ..... 29 8N 117 21 E
Kingtzekwan ..... 33 25N 111 10 E
Kingussie 47 5N 4 2w
Kinhsien .... 36 6N 107 49 E
Kinhwa .... 29 5N 119 32 E
Kinistino 52 59N 105 0w
Kinkala .... 4 18s 14 49 E
Kinki □ .... 33 30N 136 0 E
Kinleith .... 38 20s 175 56 E
Kinloch .... 44 51s 168 20 E
Kinmen, I. ...... 24 25N 118 24 E
Kinneret .... 32 44N 35 34 E
Kinneret,
   Yam, L. ...... 32 49N 35 36 E
Kinross 56 13N 3 25w
Kinsale 51 42N 8 31w
Kinsale, Old Hd. . 51 37N 8 32w
Kinsha, R. ...... 32 30N 98 0 E
Kinshasa .... 4 20s 15 15 E
Kinsiang .... 35 4N 116 25 E
Kinston 35 18N 77 35w
Kintiku .... 6 0s 35 20 E
Kintyre, Pen. 55 30N 5 35w
Kinyangiri ...... 4 35s 34 37 E
Kioga, L. .... 1 35N 33 0 E
Kioshan .... 32 50N 114 0 E
Kiparissía ...... 37 15N 21 40 E
Kól. .... 37 25N 21 25 E
Kipawa Reserve

Prov. Park 47 0N 78 30w
Kipembawe ...... 7 38s 33 23 E
Kipengere Ra. .... 9 12s 34 15 E
Kipili .... 7 28s 30 32 E
Kipini .... 2 30s 40 32 E
Kirensk .... 57 50N 107 55 E
Kirgiz S.S.R. □ .. 42 0N 75 0 E
Kirikkale .... 39 51N 33 32 E
Kirillov .... 59 51N 38 14 E
Kirin .... 43 58N 126 31 E
Kirin □ .... 43 45N 125 20 E
Kirkcaldy 56 7N 3 10w
Kirkcudbright 54 50N 4 3w
Kirkee .... 18 34N 73 56 E
Kirkenes .... 69 40N 30 5 E
Kirkintilloch 55 57N 4 10w
Kirkland Lake 48 15N 80 0w
Kirksville 40 8N 92 35w
Kirkük .... 35 30N 44 21 E
Kirkwall 58 59N 2 59w
Kirkwood .... 33 22s 25 15 E
Kirov .... 58 35N 49 40 E
Kirovabad .... 40 45N 46 10 E
Kirovograd ...... 48 35N 32 20 E
Kirovsk .... 67 48N 33 50 E
Kirovskiy .... 45 51N 48 11 E
Kirriemuir 56 41N 3 0w
Kirsanov .... 52 35N 42 40 E
Kirthar Ra. ..... 27 0N 67 0 E
Kiruna .... 67 50N 20 20 E
Kirup .... 33 40s 115 50 E
Kiryū .... 36 25N 139 20 E
Kisaki .... 7 27s 37 40 E
Kisangani .... 0 35N 25 15 E
Kisaran .... 2 47N 99 29 E
Kisaratzu .... 35 25s 139 59 E
Kiselevsk .... 54 5N 86 6 E
Kisengwa .... 6 0s 25 50 E
Kiserawe .... 6 53s 39 0 E
Kishanda .... 1 42s 31 34 E
Kishanganj ...... 26 3N 88 14 E
Kishangarh ...... 27 50N 70 30 E
Kishi .... 9 1N 3 45 E
Kishinev .... 47 0N 28 50 E
Kishiwada .... 34 28N 135 22 E
Kishon .... 32 33N 35 12 E
Kishtwar .... 33 20N 75 48 E
Kisi .... 45 21N 131 0 E
Kisii .... 0 40s 34 45 E

Kisiju .... 7 23s 39 19 E
Kiska I. .... 52 0N 177 30 E
Kiskörös .... 46 37N 19 20 E
Kiskunfélegyháza . 46 42N 19 53 E
Kiskunhalas ..... 46 28N 19 37 E
Kislovodsk ...... 43 50N 42 45 E
Kiso-Gawa, R. ... 35 2N 136 45 E
Kisoro .... 1 17s 29 48 E
Kissidougou 9 5N 10 0w
Kistna, R.=
   Krishna, R. ... 15 43N 80 55 E
Kisumu .... 0 3s 34 45 E
Kitai .... 44 0N 89 27 E
Kitaibaraki ...... 36 50N 140 45 E
Kitakyūshū ...... 33 50N 130 50 E
Kitale .... 1 0N 35 12 E
Kitangari .... 10 40s 39 20 E
Kitchener,
   Australia ...... 30 55s 124 8 E
Kitchener,
   Canada 43 30N 80 30w
Kitega .... 3 30s 29 58 E
Kitgum .... 3 17N 32 52 E
Kitimat 53 55N 129 0w
Kitoma .... 1 5N 30 55 E
Kitsuki .... 33 35N 131 37 E
Kittanning 40 49N 79 30w
Kitui .... 1 17s 38 0 E
Kitwe .... 12 54s 28 7 E
Kityang .... 23 30N 116 29 E
Kiukiang .... 29 37N 116 2 E
Kiuling Shan,
   Mts. .... 28 40N 115 0 E
Kiungchow ...... 19 57N 110 17 E
Kiungchow-
   Haihsia, Str. .. 20 40N 110 0 E
Kivu, L. .... 1 48s 29 0 E
Kiyang .... 26 36N 111 42 E
Kiyev .... 50 30N 30 28 E
Kiyevskoye, Vdkhr. 51 0N 30 0 E
Kizel .... 59 3s 57 40 E
Kizlyar .... 43 51N 46 40 E
Kizyl-Arvat ..... 38 58N 56 15 E
Kizyl Kiva ...... 40 20N 72 35 E
Kladno .... 50 10N 14 7 E
Klagenfurt ...... 46 38N 14 20 E
Klaipeda .... 55 43N 21 10 E

Klamath Falls 42 20N 121 50w
Klarälven, R. .... 59 23N 13 32 E
Klaten .... 7 43s 110 36 E
Klatovy .... 49 23N 13 18 E
Klawak 55 35N 133 0w
Klawer .... 31 44s 18 36 E
Kleena Kleene ... 52 0N 124 50w
Klein Karoo ..... 33 45s 21 30 E
Klerksdorp ...... 26 51s 26 38 E
Klipplaat .... 33 0s 24 22 E
Kłodzko .... 50 28N 16 38 E
Klondike 64 0N 139 40w
Klouto .... 6 57N 0 44 E
Kluane, L. 61 25N 138 50w
Knaresborough .. 54 1N 1 29w
Knighton 52 21N 3 2w
Knokke .... 51 20N 3 17 E
Knoxville, Iowa .. 41 20N 93 5w
Knoxville, Tenn. . 35 58N 83 57w
Knysna .... 34 2s 23 2 E
Koartac 61 5N 69 36w
Koba .... 6 37s 134 37 E
Kobarid .... 46 15N 13 30 E
Kobe .... 34 45N 135 10 E
København ...... 55 41N 12 34 E
Koblenz .... 50 21N 7 36 E
Kočani .... 41 55N 22 25 E
Kočevje .... 45 39N 14 50 E
Kōchi .... 33 30N 133 35 E
Kōchi □ .... 33 40N 133 30 E
Kodiak 57 48N 152 23w
Kodiak I. .... 57 30N 152 45 E
Kodok .... 9 53N 32 7 E
Koffiefontein .... 29 22s 24 58 E
Koforidua 6 3N 0 17w
Kōfu .... 35 40N 138 30 E
Kogin Baba ..... 7 55N 11 35 E
Kohat .... 33 40N 71 29 E
Kohima .... 25 35N 94 10 E
Kojonup 33 48s 117 10w
Kokand .... 40 30N 70 57 E
Kokanee Glacier
   Prov. Park 49 47N 117 10w
Kokchetav ...... 53 20N 69 10 E
Kokhav Mikha'el . 31 37N 34 40 E
Kokiu .... 23 22N 103 6 E
Kokkola .... 63 50N 23 8 E
Koko .... 11 28N 4 29 E
Koko Nor, L. .... 37 0N 100 0 E
Kokomo 40 30N 86 6w

Koksoak, R. 58 30N 68 10W
Kokstad .... 30 32S 29 29 E
Kokuora ...... 61 30N 145 0 E
Kola .... 68 45N 33 8 E
Kolan .... 38 43N 111 32 E
Kolar .... 13 12N 78 15 E
Kolar Gold
  Fields ...... 12 58N 78 16 E
Kolarovgrad ...... 43 27N 26 42 E
Kolayat .... 27 51N 72 59 E
Kolding ...... 55 30N 9 29 E
Kolepom, I. ...... 8 0S 138 30 E
Kolguyev ...... 69 20N 48 30 E
Kolhapur .... 16 43N 74 15 E
Kolín .... 50 2N 15 9 E
Köln .... 50 56N 9 58 E
Koło .... 52 14N 18 40 E
Kołobrzeg ...... 54 10N 15 35 E
Kołomna ...... 55 8N 38 45 E
Kolomyja ...... 48 31N 25 2 E
Kolosib ...... 24 15N 92 45 E
Kolpashevo ...... 58 20N 83 5 E
Kolskiy Pol. .... 67 30N 38 0 E
Kolskiy Zaliv .... 69 23N 34 0 E
Kolwezi ...... 10 40S 25 25 E
Kolyma, R. .... 64 40N 153 0 E
Komandorskiye Is. 55 0N 167 0 E
Kómárno ...... 47 49N 18 5 E
Komatipoort .... 25 25S 31 57 E
Komatsu ...... 36 25N 136 30 E
Komenda 5 4N 1 28W
Komga .... 32 37S 27 56 E
Komi A.S.S.R. .. 64 0N 55 0 E
Komoro ...... 36 19N 138 26 E
Komotiri ...... 41 9N 25 26 E
Kompong Bang ... 12 24N 104 40 E
Kompong Cham ... 11 54N 105 30 E
Kompong Som ... 10 38N 103 30 E
Komsberge ...... 32 40S 20 45 E
Komsomolets, Os... 80 30N 95 0 E
Komsomolsk .... 50 30N 137 0 E
Kondakovo ...... 69 20N 151 30 E
Kondinin .... 32 34S 118 8 E
Kondoa .... 4 0S 36 0 E
Konduga ...... 11 35N 13 26 E
Koudougou 12 10N 2 20W
Kondratyevo .... 57 30N 98 30 E
Kong, Koh .... 11 20N 103 0 E
Kongju ...... 36 30N 127 0 E
Konglu ...... 27 13N 97 57 E

Kongmoon .... 22 35N 113 1 E
Kongolo .... 5 22S 27 0 E
Kongsberg ...... 59 39N 9 39 E
Königsberg=
  Kaliningrad..... 54 42N 20 32 E
Kongsvinger ..... 60 12N 12 2 E
Kongwa .... 6 11S 36 26 E
Kønig Haakon
  VII Sea .... 66 0S 35 0 E
Konin .... 52 12N 18 15 E
Konjic .... 43 42N 17 58 E
Konongo 6 40N 1 15W
Konosha .... 61 0N 40 5 E
Konotop .... 51 12N 33 7 E
Końskie .... 51 15N 20 23 E
Konstanz......... 47 39N 9 10 E
Kontagora ...... 10 23N 5 27 E
Konya .... 37 52N 32 35 E
Konza .... 1 45S 37 0 E
Kookynie ...... 29 17S 121 22 E
Kooline ...... 22 57S 116 20 E
Koolyanobbing .. 30 48S 119 46 E
Koonibba ...... 31 58S 133 27 E
Koorda .... 30 48S 117 35 E
Kootenay Nat.
  Park 51 0N 116 0W
Koo-wee-rup .... 38 13S 145 28 E
Kopaonik
  Planina, Mts. .. 43 10N 21 0 E
Kopervik ...... 59 17N 5 17 E
Kopeysk ...... 55 7N 61 37 E
Köping .... 59 31N 16 3 E
Kopparberg .... 59 53N 14 59 E
Kopparbergs □.. 61 20N 14 15 E
Korça .... 40 37N 20 50 E
Korčula, I....... 42 57N 17 0 E
Kordestān □ .... 36 0N 47 0 E
Kordofân □ .... 13 0N 29 0 E
Korea B. .... 39 0N 124 0 E
Korhogo .... 9 29N 5 28 E
Korinthiakós
  Kól. .... 38 16N 22 30 E
Kórinthos ...... 37 26N 22 55 E
Kōriyama ...... 37 24N 140 23 E
Korla .... 41 45N 86 4 E
Koro 14 1N 2 58W
Koro Sea 17 30S 179 45W
Korogwe ...... 5 5S 38 25 E
Koroit .... 38 18S 142 24 E
Körös, R. ...... 46 30N 142 42 E

Korsakov .... 46 30N 142 42 E
Korsør .... 55 20N 11 9 E
Kortrijk .... 50 50N 3 17 E
Korumburra ... 38 26S 145 50 E
Koryakskiy
  Khrebet, Mts.... 61 0N 171 0 E
Kos, I. .... 36 50N 27 15 E
Kościan .... 52 5N 16 40 E
Kosciusko 33 3N 89 34W
Kosciusko I. 56 0N 133 40W
Kosciusko, Mt. .. 36 27S 148 16 E
Košice .... 48 42N 21 15 E
Koslan .... 63 28N 48 52 E
Kosovska-
  Mitrovica ...... 42 54N 20 52 E
Koster .... 25 52S 26 54 E
Kôstî .... 13 8N 32 43 E
Kostroma ...... 57 50N 41 58 E
Kostrzyn ...... 52 24N 17 14 E
Koszalin ...... 54 12N 16 8 E
Kota .... 25 14N 75 49 E
Kota Baharu .... 6 7N 102 14 E
Kota Kinabalu .. 6 0N 116 12 E
Kota Tinggi ...... 1 44N 103 53 E
Kotabaru ...... 3 20S 116 20 E
Kotabumi ...... 4 49S 104 46 E
Kotawaringin ... 2 28S 111 27 E
Kotelnich ...... 58 20N 48 10 E
Kotka .... 60 28N 26 55 E
Kotlas .... 61 15N 47 0 E
Kotlik 63 2N 163 33W
Kotor .... 42 25N 18 47 E
Kottagudem ... 17 30N 80 40 E
Kottayam ...... 9 35N 76 33 E
Kotturu ...... 14 45N 76 13 E
Kotzebue 66 53N 162 39W
Koudougou 12 10N 2 20W
Kougaberge ..... 33 40S 23 55 E
Koula-Moutou ... 1 15S 12 25 E
Koumala ...... 21 38S 149 15 E
Kounradskiy ... 47 20N 75 0 E
Kourou 5 9N 52 39W
Kouroussa 10 45N 9 45W
Kouvé .... 6 30N 1 30 E
Kovdor .... 67 34N 30 22 E
Kovel .... 51 10N 25 0 E
Kovrov .... 56 25N 41 25 E
Kowloon ...... 22 20N 114 15 E
Koyiu .... 23 2N 112 28 E
Koyukuk, R. 64 56N 157 30W

Kozáni □ .... 40 20N 21 45 E
Kozhikode=
  Calicut .... 11 15N 75 43 E
Kozhva .... 65 10N 57 0 E
Kpandu .... 7 2N 0 18 E
Kpessi .... 7 50N 1 25 E
Kra, Isthmus of=
  Kra, Kho Khot.. 10 15N 99 30 E
Kra, Kho Khot .. 10 15N 99 30 E
Kracków .... 50 4N 19 57 E
Kragerø .... 58 56N 9 30 E
Kragujevac ...... 44 2N 20 56 E
Krakatau, I.=
  Rakatau, P...... 6 10S 105 20 E
Kraksaan ...... 7 43S 113 23 E
Kraljevo .... 43 44N 20 41 E
Kramatorsk ..... 48 50N 37 30 E
Kramfors ...... 62 55N 17 48 E
Kras, Reg ...... 45 30N 14 0 E
Krasavino ...... 60 58N 46 26 E
Kraskino ...... 42 45N 130 58 E
Krasnik ...... 50 55N 22 5 E
Krasnodar ...... 45 5N 38 50 E
Krasnokamsk ..... 58 0N 56 0 E
Krasnoselkupsk .. 65 20N 82 10 E
Krasnoturinsk ... 59 39N 60 1 E
Krasnoufimsk ... 56 57N 57 37 E
Krasnouralsk .... 58 0N 60 0 E
Krasnovodsk .... 40 0N 52 52 E
Krasnovishersk ... 60 23N 56 59 E
Krasnoyarsk .... 56 8N 93 0 E
Krasnyy Yar .... 46 43N 48 23 E
Kratie .... 12 32N 106 10 E
Krefeld .... 51 20N 6 22 E
Kremenchug .... 49 5N 33 25 E
Kremenchugskoye,
  Vdkhr. .... 49 20N 32 30 E
Kremnica......... 48 45N 18 50 E
Krishna, R. .... 15 43N 80 55 E
Krishnanagar ... 23 24N 88 33 E
Kristiansand .... 58 5N 7 50 E
Kristianstad .... 56 5N 14 7 E
Kristianstads □.. 56 0N 14 0 E
Kristiansund ... 63 10N 7 45 E
Kristinehamn ... 59 18N 14 13 E
Kristinestad ... 62 18N 21 25 E
Kriti, I. .... 35 15N 25 0 E
Kriti □ .... 35 15N 25 0 E
Krivoy Rog ...... 47 51N 33 20 E
Krk, I. .... 45 5N 14 56 E

Krkonose, Mts. .. 50 50N 16 10 E
Krokodil, R. ...... 25 26S 32 0 E
Kronobergs □.... 56 45N 14 30 E
Kronshtadt ...... 60 5N 29 35 E
Kroonstad ...... 27 43S 27 19 E
Kropotkin ...... 58 50N 115 10 E
Krosno .... 49 35N 21 56 E
Krotoszyn ...... 51 42N 17 23 E
Krugersdorp ... 26 5S 27 46 E
Kruisfontein .... 34 0S 24 43 E
Krung Thep ...... 13 45N 100 35 E
Kruševac ...... 43 35N 21 28 E
Krymskaya ...... 44 57N 37 50 E
Ksar El
  Boukhari ...... 35 5N 2 52 E
Ksar-el-Kebir ... 35 0N 6 0W
Kuala Dungun ... 2 46N 105 47 E
Kuala Kerai .... 5 32N 102 12 E
Kuala Kubu
  Baharu .... 3 35N 101 38 E
Kuala Lipis ...... 4 22N 102 5 E
Kuala Lumpur .. 3 9N 101 41 E
Kuala Selangor .. 3 20N 101 15 E
Kuala Trengganu . 5 20N 103 8 E
Kualakapuas ... 2 55S 114 20 E
Kualakurun ...... 1 10S 113 50 E
Kualapembuang .. 3 14S 112 38 E
Kualasimpang ... 4 16N 98 4 E
Kuantan ...... 3 49N 103 20 E
Kuba .... 41 21N 48 22 E
Kubak .... 27 10N 63 10 E
Kuban, R. ...... 45 20N 37 30 E
Kubokawa ...... 33 12N 133 8 E
Kucha .... 41 50N 82 30 E
Kuching .... 1 33N 110 25 E
Kuchinotsu ...... 32 36N 130 11 E
Kuda .... 23 10N 71 18 E
Kudat .... 7 0N 116 42 E
Kudus .... 6 48N 110 51 E
Kueiyang=
  Kweiyang ...... 25 30N 106 35 E
Kufra, El
  Wâhât et ...... 24 17N 23 15 E
Kufstein ...... 47 35N 12 11 E
Kûhpâyeh ...... 32 44N 52 20 E
Kukawa .... 12 58N 13 27 E
Kukerin .... 33 13S 118 0 E
Kulgera ...... 25 50S 133 18 E
Kulin .... 32 40S 118 2 E

Kulja . . . . 30 35s 117 31 E
Kulsary . . . . 46 59N 54 1 E
Kululu . . . . 9 28N 33 1 E
Kulunda . . . . 52 45N 79 15 E
Kulyab . . . . 37 55N 69 50 E
Kum Darya, R. . . . 41 0N 89 0 E
Kum Tekei . . . . 43 10N 79 30 E
Kumaganum . . . . . 13 8N 10 38 E
Kumai . . . . 2 52s 111 45 E
Kumamoto . . . . . . 32 45s 130 45 E
Kumamoto □ . . . . . 32 30N 130 40 E
Kumara . . . . 42 37s 171 12 E
Kumari . . . . 32 45s 121 30 E
Kumasi . . . . 6 41N 1 38 E
Kumba . . . . 4 36N 9 24 E
Kumbarilla . . . . . . 27 15s 150 55 E
Kumbo . . . . 6 15N 10 36 E
Kumagaya . . . . . . 36 9N 139 22 E
Kumertau . . . . 52 46N 55 47 E
Kumi . . . . 1 30N 33 58 E
Kumla . . . . 59 8N 15 10 E
Kumo . . . . 10 1N 11 12 E
Kumon Bum, Mts. . 26 0N 97 15 E
Kunar □ . . . . 35 15N 71 0 E
Kundip . . . . 33 42s 120 10 E
Kunduz . . . . 36 50N 68 50 E
Kunduz □ . . . . 36 50N 68 50 E
Kunene, R. . . . . . . 17 20s 11 50 E
Kungchuling . . . . . 43 31N 124 58 E
Kungho . . . . 36 28N 100 45 E
Kungrad . . . . 43 6N 58 54 E
Kungram . . . . 25 45N 89 35 E
Kungsbacka . . . . . 57 30N 12 7 E
Kunhsien . . . . 32 30N 111 17 E
Kuningan . . . . 6 59s 108 29 E
Kunlong . . . . 23 20N 98 50 E
Kunlun Shan, Mts. 36 0N 82 0 E
Kunming . . . . 25 11N 102 37 E
Kunsan . . . . 35 59N 126 35 E
Kununurra . . . . . . 15 40s 128 39 E
Kunwarara . . . . . . 22 25s 150 7 E
Kuopio . . . . 62 53N 27 35 E
Kuopio □ . . . . 63 25N 27 10 E
Kupa, R. . . . . 45 28N 16 24 E
Kupang . . . . 10 19s 123 39 E
Kupreanof I. 56 50N 133 30w
Kura, R. . . . . 39 24N 49 24 E
Kurashiki . . . . 34 40N 133 50 E
Kurayoshi . . . . 35 26N 133 50 E
Kure . . . . 34 14N 132 32 E

Kurgaldzhino . . . . 50 35N 70 20 E
Kurgan . . . . 55 30N 65 0 E
Kurilskiye Os. . . . 45 0N 150 0 E
Kurino . . . . 31 57N 130 43 E
Kurnool . . . . 15 45N 78 0 E
Kurow . . . . 44 4s 170 29 E
Kurri Kurri . . . . . 32 50s 151 28 E
Kursk . . . . 51 42N 36 11 E
Kurume . . . . 33 15N 130 30 E
Kurunegala . . . . . . 7 30N 80 18 E
Kurya . . . . 61 15N 108 10 E
Kushan . . . . 39 58N 123 30 E
Kushikino . . . . . . 31 44N 130 16 E
Kushima . . . . 31 29N 131 14 E
Kushimoto . . . . . . 33 28N 135 47 E
Kushiro . . . . 43 0N 144 30 E
Kushk . . . . 34 55N 62 30 E
Kushka . . . . 35 20N 62 18 E
Kushtia . . . . 23 55N 89 5 E
Kuskokwim, R. . . . 60 17N 162 27w
Kuskokwim B. . . . 59 45N 162 25w
Kustanai . . . . 53 20N 63 45 E
Kut, Ko . . . . 11 40N 102 35 E
Kutahya . . . . 39 25N 29 59 E
Kutaisi . . . . 42 19N 42 40 E
Kutaraja=Banda
Aceh . . . . 5 35N 95 20 E
Kutch, G. of . . . . 22 50N 69 15 E
Kutch, Rann of,
Reg. 24 0N 70 0N
Kutno . . . . 52 15N 19 23 E
Kuttabul . . . . 21 5s 148 48 E
Kutum . . . . 14 20N 24 10 E
Kuwait ■ . . . . 29 30N 47 30 E
Kuwana . . . . 35 0N 136 43 E
Kuyang . . . . 41 8N 110 1 E
Kuybyshev,
Kuyb. Obl. . . . . 53 12N 50 9 E
Kuybyshev,
Tatar A.S.S.R. . . 54 57N 49 5 E
Kuybyshev,
Novosibirsk
Obl. . . . . 55 27N 78 19 E
Kuybyshevskoye
Vdkhr. . . . . 55 2N 49 30 E
Kuyumba . . . . 61 10N 97 10 E
Kuyto, Oz. . . . . . 64 40N 31 0 E
Kuznetsk . . . . 53 12N 46 40 E
Kuzomen . . . . 66 22N 36 50 E
Kvarner, G. . . . . . 44 50N 14 10 E

Kvarneric . . . . 44 43N 14 37 E
Kwabhaca . . . . . . 30 51s 29 0 E
Kwakoegron 5 25N 55 25w
Kwale . . . . 4 15s 39 31 E
Kwando, R. . . . . . 16 48s 22 45 E
Kwangan . . . . 30 35N 106 40 E
Kwangchou=
Kwangchow . . . 23 10N 113 10 E
Kwangchow . . . . 23 10N 113 10 E
Kwangchow
Wan, G. . . . . . . 21 0N 111 0 E
Kwangju . . . . 35 10N 126 45 E
Kwangnan . . . . . . 24 10N 105 0 E
Kwangsi-Chuang
Aut.Dist. □ . . . . 23 30N 108 55 E
Kwangtseh . . . . . . 27 30N 117 25 E
Kwangtung □ . . . . 23 35N 114 0 E
Kwangyuan . . . . . 32 30N 105 49 E
Kwanhsien . . . . . . 30 59N 103 40 E
Kwantung . . . . . . 25 12N 101 37 E
Kwara □ . . . . 8 30N 5 0 E
Kwatisore . . . . . . 3 7s 139 59 E
Kwei Kiang, R. . . 23 30N 110 30 E
Kweichih . . . . 30 40N 117 30 E
Kweichow=
Fengkieh . . . . . . 31 0N 109 33 E
Kweichow □ . . . . . 26 40N 107 0 E
Kweihsien . . . . . . 22 59N 109 44 E
Kweiki . . . . 28 10N 117 8 E
Kweilin . . . . 25 16N 110 15 E
Kweiping . . . . 23 12N 110 0 E
Kweiting . . . . 26 0N 113 35 E
Kweiyang . . . . . . 25 30N 106 35 E
Kwidzyń . . . . 54 5N 18 58 E
Kwiguk Island . . . 62 45N 164 28w
Kwinana . . . . 32 15s 115 47 E
Kwo Ho, R. . . . . . 33 20N 116 50 E
Kwoka, Mt. . . . . . 0 31s 132 27 E
Kwolla . . . . 8 55N 9 18 E
Kyakhta . . . . 50 30N 106 25 E
Kyancutta . . . . . . 33 8s 135 34 E
Kyaukpadaung . . . 20 52N 95 8 E
Kyaukpyu . . . . . . 19 28N 93 30 E
Kyaukse . . . . 21 36N 96 10 E
Kyenjojo . . . . 0 40N 30 37 E
Kyle Dam . . . . . . 20 14s 31 0 E
Kyoga, L. . . . . . . 1 35N 33 0 E
Kyogle . . . . 28 40s 153 0 E
Kyongju . . . . 35 59N 129 26 E

Kyonpyaw . . . . . . 17 12N 95 10 E
Kyōto . . . . 35 0N 135 45 E
Kyōto □ . . . . 35 15N 135 30 E
Kyrínia . . . . 35 20N 33 19 E
Kystatyam . . . . . . 67 15N 123 0 E
Kytal Ktakh . . . . 65 30N 123 40 E
Kyunhla . . . . 23 25N 95 15 E
Kyūshū, I. . . . . . . 32 30N 131 0 E
Kyūshū □ . . . . . . 32 30N 131 0 E
Kyustendil . . . . . . 42 25N 22 41 E
Kyusyur . . . . 70 30N 127 0 E
Kyzyl . . . . 51 50N 94 30 E
Kyzyl Orda . . . . . 44 50N 65 10 E

L

La Alcarria, Reg. . . 40 31N 2 45w
La Asunción 11 2N 63 53w
La Banda 27 45s 64 10w
La Barca 20 20N 102 40w
La Blanquilla, I. . . 11 51N 64 37w
La Boca . . . . 9 0N 79 30 E
La Calera 32 50s 71 10w
La Carlota 33 30s 63 20w
La Carolina 38 17N 3 38w
La Ceiba,
Honduras 15 40N 86 50w
La Ceiba, Ven. . . . 9 35N 64 10w
La Chaux-de-Fonds 47 7N 6 50 E
La Cocha 27 50s 65 40w
La Coruña 43 20N 8 25w
La Crosse 43 48N 91 13w
La Dorada 5 30N 74 40w
La Estrada 42 43N 8 27w
La Fayette 40 22N 86 52w
La Folette 36 23N 84 9w
La Grande 45 15N 118 0w
La Grange 33 4N 85 0w
La Guaira 10 36N 66 56w
La Habana 23 0N 82 41w
La Mabana 23 8N 82 22w
La Junta 38 0N 103 30w
La Linea de la
Concepción . . . 36 15N 5 23w
La Loche 56 29N 109 27w
La Louvière . . . . . 50 27N 4 10 E
La Malbaie 47 40N 70 10w

La Mancha, Reg. . . 39 10N 2 54w
La Martre, L. 63 0N 118 0w
La Mesa 32 48N 117 0w
La Orchila, I. . . . 12 30N 67 0w
La Oroya 11 32s 75 54w
La Palma 37 21N 6 38w
La Palma 8 15N 78 0w
La Palma, I. 28 40N 17 52w
La Paragua 6 50N 63 20w
La Paz, Arg. 30 50s 59 45w
La Paz, Bolivia . . . 16 20s 68 10w
La Paz, Mexico . . . 24 10N 110 20w
La Pedrera 1 18s 69 43w
La Perouse, Str. . . 45 40N 142 0 E
La Piedad 20 20N 102 1w
La Pine 40 53N 80 45w
La Plata 35 0s 57 55w
La Porte 41 40N 86 40w
La Reine 48 50N 79 30w
La Rioja 29 20s 67 0w
La Rioja, Reg. . . . 42 20N 2 20w
La Robla 42 50N 5 41w
La Roche-sur-
Yon 46 40N 1 25w
La Rochelle 46 10N 1 9w
La Roda 39 13N 2 15w
La Romana 18 27N 68 57w
La Salle 41 20N 89 5w
La Sarre 48 45N 79 15w
La Serena 29 55s 71 10w
La Spézia . . . . . . 44 8N 9 50 E
La Tagua 0 3N 74 40w
La Tortuga, I. . . . 10 56N 65 20w
La Tuque 47 30N 72 50w
La Unión,
Chile 40 10s 73 0w
La Union,
Salvador 13 20N 87 50w
La Urbana 7 8N 66 56w
La Vega 19 20N 70 30w
La Vela 11 30N 69 30w
La Verendrye
Prov. Park 47 15N 77 0w
La Victoria 10 14N 67 20w
Laaland=
Lolland, I. . . . . 54 45N 11 30 E
Labbézenga . . . . . 14 57N 0 42 E
Labé 11 24N 12 16w
Labis . . . . 2 22N 103 2 E
Laboulaye 34 10s 63 30w

Labrador, Reg..... 53 20N   61 0W
Labrador City..... 52 42N   67 0W
Labuha .... 0 30s 127 30 E
Labuhan .... 6 26s 105 50 E
Lac la Biche 54 45N 111 50W
Lac Seul 50 28N   92 0W
Laccadive Is. .... 10 0N 72 30 E
Lachine 45 30N 73 40W
Lachlan, R. ...... 34 21s 143 57 E
Lachute 45 39N 74 21W
Lackawanna 42 49N 78 50W
Lacombe 52 30N 113 50W
Laconia 43 32N 71 30W
Ladakh Ra. ...... 34 0N 78 0 E
Ladismith .... 33 28s 21 15 E
Lādiz .... 28 55N 61 15 E
Ladozhskoye, Oz. . 61 15N 30 30 E
Ladrone Is. ...... 17 0N 145 0 E
Lady Grey .... 30 43s 27 13 E
Ladybrand ...... 29 9s 27 29 E
Ladysmith,
    Canada 49 0N 124 0W
Ladysmith,
    S. Africa ..... 28 32s 29 46 E
Laesø, I. .... 57 15N 10 53 E
Lafayette 30 18N   92 0W
Lafia .... 8 30N   8 34 E
Lafiagi .... 8 52N   5 20 E
Laforest 47 4N 81 12W
Lågen, R. .... 61 8N 10 25 E
Laghman □ ...... 34 20N 70 0 E
Laghouat .... 33 50N   2 59 E
Lagonoy G. ...... 13 50N 123 50 E
Lagos, Nigeria .... 6 25N   3 27 E
Lagos, Port. 37 5N   8 41W
Lagos □ .... 6 25N   3 35 E
Lagos de
    Moreno 21 21N 101 55W
Lagrange .... 14 13s 125 46 E
Laguna .... 28 30s 48 50 E
Laguna Beach ... 33 31N 117 52W
Lagunas 21 0s 69 45W
Laha .... 48 9N 124 30 E
Lahad Datu ..... 5 0N 118 30 E
Lahaina 20 52s 156 41W
Lahat .... 3 45s 103 30 E
Lahn, R. .... 50 18N   7 37 E
Laholm .... 56 30N 13 2 E
* Lahore .... 31 32N 74 22 E

Lahore □ .... 31 55N 74 5 E
Lai Chau .... 22 5N 103 3 E
Laichow Wan, G. . 37 30N 119 30 E
Laidley .... 27 39s 152 20 E
Laila .... 22 10N 46 40 E
Laingsburg ...... 33 9s 20 52 E
Laipin .... 23 42N 109 16 E
Lairg 58 1N   4 24W
Lais .... 3 35s 102 0 E
Laisamis .... 1 38N 37 50 E
Laiyang .... 36 58N 120 41 E
Lajes 27 48s 50 20W
Lake Charles 31 10N 93 10W
Lake City, Fla. 30 10N 82 40W
Lake City, S.C. ... 33 51N 79 44W
Lake Grace ...... 33 7s 118 28 E
Lake Harbour 62 30N 69 50W
Lake Havasu
    City 34 25N 114 20W
Lake King .... 33 5s 119 45 E
Lake Mead Nat.
    Rec. Area 36 20N 114 30W
Lake Nash ...... 20 57s 138 0 E
Lake Superior
    Prov. Park 47 45N 85 0W
Lake Traverse ... 45 56N 78 4w
Lake Worth 26 36N 80 3w
Lakefield 44 25N 78 16w
Lakeland 28 0N 82 0w
Lakeport 39 1N 122 56w
Lakes Entrance .. 37 50s 148 0 E
Lakeview 34 12N 109 59w
Lakewood 41 28N 81 50w
Lakhimpur ...... 27 14N 94 7 E
Lakonikós Kól. ... 36 40N 22 40 E
Lakselv .... 70 2N 24 56 E
Lala Ghat .... 24 30N 92 40 E
Lalín 42 40N   8 5w
Lalin .... 45 14N 126 52 E
Lalitpur .... 24 42N 78 28 E
Lama-Kara ...... 9 30N   1 15 E
Lamaing .... 15 25N 97 53 E
Lambaréné ...... 0 20s 10 12 E
Lame .... 10 27N   9 12 E
Lamego 41 5N   7 52w
Lameroo .... 35 19s 140 33 E
Lamesa 32 45N 101 57w
Lamía .... 38 55N 22 41 E
* Lamitan .... 6 40N 122 10 E
Lammermuir Hills . 55 50N 24 0w

Lamon B. .... 14 30N 122 20 E
Lampedusa, I. .... 35 36N 12 40 E
Lampeter 52 6N   4 6w
Lampman 49 25N 102 50w
Lampung □ ...... 5 30s 105 0 E
Lamu .... 2 10s 40 55 E
Lanark 55 40N   3 48w
Lancashire □ 53 40N   2 30w
Lancaster, Canada . 45 17N 66 10w
Lancaster, U.K. ... 54 3N   2 48w
Lancaster, Calif. .. 34 47N 118 8w
Lancaster, Ky. 37 40N 84 40w
Lancaster, N.H. ... 44 29N 71 34w
Lancaster, S.C. ... 34 45N 80 47w
Lancaster Sd. 74 0N 84 0w
Lanchi .... 29 11N 119 30 E
Lanchou=
    Lanchow ...... 36 4N 103 44 E
Lanchow .... 36 4N 103 44 E
Lanciano .... 42 15N 14 22 E
Landeck .... 47 9N 10 34 E
Lander □ 42 50N 108 49w
Landes □ 43 57N   0 48w
Landes, Reg. 44 0N   1 5w
Landi Kotal ..... 34 7N 71 6 E
Land's End 50 4N   5 42w
Landshut .... 48 31N 12 10 E
Landskrona ..... 56 53N 12 50 E
Lanett 33 0N 85 15w
Langchung ...... 31 31N 105 58 E
Langeberg ...... 33 55s 21 20 E
Langfeng .... 48 4N 121 10 E
Langholm 55 9N   2 59w
Langkawi, Pulau . 6 25N 99 45 E
Langlade, I. 46 50N 56 20w
Langreo 43 13N   5 42w
Langres .... 47 52N   5 20 E
Langres, Plat.
    de .... 47 45N   5 20 E
Langsa .... 4 30N 97 57 E
Langson .... 21 52N 106 42 E
Languedoc, Reg. .. 43 58N   3 22 E
Lansdowne House . 52 5N 88 0w
L'Anse au Loup .. 51 32s 56 50w
Lansing 42 47N 84 32w
Lanzarote, I. 29 0N 13 40w
Lao Cai .... 22 30N 103 57 E
Laoag .... 18 7N 120 34 E
Laoang .... 12 32N 125 8 E
Laois □ 53 0N   7 20w

Laon .... 49 33N   3 35 E
Laos ■ .... 17 45N 105 0 E
Lapeer 43 3N 83 20w
Lappi □ .... 64 33N 25 10 E
Lappland, Reg. ... 68 7N 24 0 E
Laptev Sea ..... 76 0N 125 0 E
L'Aquila .... 42 21N 13 24 E
Lãr .... 27 40N 54 14 E
Larache 35 10N   6 5w
Laramie 41 15N 105 29w
Larder Lake 48 5N 79 40w
Laredo 27 34N 99 29w
† Largeau .... 17 58N 19 6 E
Largs 55 48N   4 51w
Lárisa .... 39 38N 22 28 E
Larkana .... 27 32N 68 2 E
Lárnax .... 35 0N 33 35 E
Larne 54 52N   5 50w
Larne □ 54 55N   5 55w
Larrimah .... 15 35s 133 12 E
Larvik .... 59 4N 10 0 E
Laryak .... 61 15N 80 0 E
Las Anod .... 8 26N 47 19 E
Las Cruces 32 25N 106 50w
Las Flores 36 0s 59 0w
Las Heras 32 51s 68 49w
Las Khoreh ..... 11 4N 48 20 E
Las Lajas 38 30s 70 25w
Las Lomitas 24 35s 60 50w
Las Palmas 28 10N 15 28w
Las Plumas 43 40s 67 15w
Las Rosas 32 30s 61 40w
Las Varillas 32 0s 62 50w
Las Vegas, Nev. ... 36 10N 115 5w
Las Vegas, N. Mex. 35 35N 105 10w
Lashburn 53 10N 109 40w
Lashio .... 22 56N 97 45 E
Lassen Pk. 40 20N 121 0w
Latacunga 0 50s 78 35w
Latakia=
    Al Ladhiqiya ... 35 30N 35 45 E
Latchford 47 20N 79 50w
Latham .... 29 44s 116 20 E
Latina .... 41 26N 12 53 E
Latouche 60 0N 147 55w
Latrobe,
    Australia ..... 41 14s 146 30 E
Latrun .... 31 50N 34 58 E
Latur .... 18 25N 76 40 E
Latvian S.S.R. □ .. 57 0N 25 0 E

Lau Is. 17 0s 178 30w
Lauchhammer .... 51 35N 13 40 E
Launceston,
    Australia .... 41 24s 147 8 E
Launceston, U.K. .. 50 38N   4 21w
Laura .... 33 10s 138 18 E
Laurel, Miss. 31 50N 89 0w
Laurel, Mont. 45 46N 108 49w
Laurencekirk 56 50N   2 30w
Laurens 34 32N 82 2w
Laurentian Plat. .. 51 30N 65 0w
Laurentides
    Prov. Park 47 50N 71 50w
Lauringburg 34 50N 79 25w
Lausanne .... 46 32N   6 38 E
Lauzon 46 48N 71 4w
Laverton .... 28 44s 122 29 E
Lavi .... 32 47N 35 25 E
Lavrentiya 65 35N 171 0w
Lawra 10 39N   2 51w
Lawrence, N.Z. ... 45 55s 169 41 E
Lawrence, U.S.A. .. 42 40N 71 9w
Lawrence 39 0N 95 10w
Lawrenceburg ... 35 12N 87 19w
Lawton 34 33N 98 25w
Lawu, Mt. ...... 7 40s 111 13 E
Layras 21 20s 45 0w
Laysan I. 25 30N 167 0w
Lazio □ .... 42 10N 12 30 E
Le Creusot ..... 46 50N   4 24 E
Le François 14 38N 60 57w
Le Havre ...... 49 30N   0 5 E
Le Maire,
    Estrecho de ... 54 50s 65 0w
Le Mans .... 48 0N   0 10 E
Le Marinel ..... 10 25s 25 17 E
Le Mars 43 0N 96 0w
Le Moule 16 20N 61 22w
Le Puy .... 45 3N   3 52 E
Le Tréport ..... 50 3N   1 20 E
Le Verdon 45 32N   1 5w
Lea, R. .... 51 30N   0 1 E
Lead 44 20N 103 40w
Leader 50 50N 109 30w
Leadhills 55 25N   3 47w
Leadville 39 17N 106 23w
Lealui .... 15 10s 23 2 E
Leamington,
    Canada 42 10N 82 30w
Leamington, U.K. . 52 18N   1 32w

* Now part of Punjab   * Renamed Isabela   † Renamed Faya-Largeau

Learmonth .... 22 40 s 114 10 E
Leask 53 5N 106 45w
Leavenworth 39 25N 95 0w
Lebanon, Ind. ... 40 3N 86 55w
Lebanon, Mo. 37 40N 92 40w
Lebanon, N.H. ... 43 38N 72 15w
Lebanon, Ore. ... 44 31N 122 57w
Lebanon, Pa. 40 20N 76 28w
Lebanon, Tenn. .. 36 15N 86 20w
Lebanon ■ .... 34 0N 36 0 E
Lebombo-berg .. 24 30s 32 0 E
Lebrija 36 53N   6 5w
Lebu 37 40s 73 47w
Lecce .... 40 20N 18 10 E
Lecco .... 45 50N   9 27 E
Łęczyca .... 52 5N 19 45 E
Ledbury 52 3N   2 25w
Ledesma 41 6N   5 59w
Leduc 53 20N 113 30w
Lee, R. 51 51N   9 2w
Leeds 53 48N   1 34w
Leek 53 7N   2 2w
Leesburg 28 47N 81 52w
Leeu-Gamka .... 32 43s 21 59 E
Leeuwarden ..... 53 15N   5 48 E
Leeuwin, C. .... 34 20s 115 9 E
Leeward Is. 16 30N 63 30w
Legazpi .... 13 10N 123 46 E
Leghorn =
  Livorno .... 43 32N 10 18 E
Legnica .... 51 12N 16 10 E
Leh .... 34 15N 77 35 E
Leicester 52 39N   1 9w
Leicester □ 52 40N   1 10w
Leichow Pantao,
  Pen. .... 20 40N 110 10 E
Leiden .... 52 9N   4 30 E
Leigh Creek ..... 30 28s 138 24 E
Leine, R. .... 48 54N 10 1 E
Leinster □ 53 0N   7 10w
Lienyünchiangshih=
  Sinhailien ...... 34 31N 119 0 E
Leipzig .... 51 20N 12 23 E
Leiria 39 46N   8 53w
Leith 55 59N   3 10w
Leith Hill 51 10N   0 23w
Leitrim 54 0N   8 5w
Leitrim □ 54 8N   8 0w
Leiyang .... 26 24N 112 51 E
Leland 33 25N 90 52w

Leleque 42 15s 71 0w
Léman, L. .... 46 26N   6 30 E
Lembeni .... 3 48s 37 33 E
Lemery .... 13 58N 120 56 E
Lemesós .... 34 42N 33 1 E
Lemnos, I.=
  Límnos, I. ..... 39 50N 25 5 E
Lemvig .... 56 33N   8 20 E
Lena .... 72 25N 126 40 E
Lena, R. .... 66 30N 126 3 E
Leninabad ...... 40 17N 69 37 E
Leninakan ...... 41 0N 42 50 E
Leningrad .... 59 55N 30 20 E
Leninogorsk .... 50 20N 83 30 E
Leninsk .... 48 40N 45 15 E
Leninsk
  Kuznetskiy .... 55 10N 86 10 E
Leninskoye ..... 47 56N 132 38 E
Lenkoran .... 39 45N 48 50 E
Lenoir 35 55N 81 36w
Lenoir City 35 40N 84 20w
Lens .... 50 26N   2 50 E
Lensk .... 60 48N 114 55 E
Lentini .... 37 18N 15 0 E
Leo 11 3N   2 2w
Leoben .... 47 22N 15 5 E
Leominster, U.K... 52 15N   2 43w
Leominster, U.S.A. 42 30N 71 44w
León, Mexico 21 7N 101 30w
León, Nic. 12 20N 86 51w
León, Sp. 42 38N   5 34w
León, Reg. 41 30N   6 0w
Léon, Mt. de 42 30N   6 18w
Leongatha .... 38 30s 145 58 E
Leonora .... 28 49s 121 19 E
Léopold II, L.=
  Mai-Ndombe, L. . 2 0s 18 0 E
Léopoldville=
  Kinshasa .... 4 20s 15 15 E
Leoville 53 39N 107 33w
Lepel .... 54 50N 28 40 E
Lepikha .... 64 45N 125 55 E
Lere .... 9 39N 14 13 E
Lérida .... 41 37N   0 39 E
Lerwick 60 10N   1 10w
Les Cayes 18 15N 73 46w
Les Sables-
  d'Olonne 46 30N   1 45w
Les Tres Marías,
  Is. 12 20N 106 30w

Lesbos, I.=
  Lésvos, I. ...... 39 0N 26 20 E
Leskovac .... 43 0N 21 58 E
Leslie .... 26 16s 28 55 E
Lesotho ■ .... 29 40s 28 0 E
Lesozarodsk ..... 45 30N 133 20 E
Lesser Antilles,
  Is. 12 30N 61 0w
Lesser Sunda
  Is. .... 7 30s 117 0 E
Lesuru .... 1 0N 35 15 E
Lésvos, I. .... 39 0N 26 20 E
Letchworth 51 58N   0 13w
Lethbridge 49 45N 112 45w
Lethem 3 20N 59 50w
Leti, Kep. ...... 8 10s 128 0 E
Letiahau, R. ..... 21 16s 24 0 E
Leticia 4 0s 70 0w
Letlhakane ...... 24 0s 24 59 E
Letpadan .... 17 45N 96 0 E
Letpan .... 19 28N 93 52 E
Letsôk-au-Kyun .. 11 37N 98 15 E
Letterkenny 54 57N   7 42w
Leuser, Mt. ..... 4 0N 96 51 E
Leuven .... 50 52   4 42 E
Levanger .... 63 45N 11 19 E
Levelland 33 38N 102 17w
Leven 56 12N   3 0w
Leven, L. 56 12N   3 2w
Leveque, C. ..... 16 20s 123 0 E
Levin .... 40 37s 175 18 E
Levis 46 48N 71 9w
Lévka, Mt. ...... 35 18N 24 3 E
Levkás, I. ...... 38 40N 20 43 E
Levkôsia .... 35 10N 33 25 E
Lewes .... 50 53N   0 2 E
Lewis, I. 58 10N   6 40w
Lewis Ra. .... 20 3s 128 50 E
Lewisporte 49 15N 55 3w
Lewiston, Id. 45 58N 117 0w
Lewiston, Me. 44 6N 70 13w
Lewistown, Mont. . 47 0N 109 25w
Lewistown, Pa. ... 40 37N 77 33w
Lexington, Ky. ... 38 6N 84 30w
Lexington, Mo. ... 39 7N 93 55w
Lexington, Neb. .. 40 48N 99 45w
Lexington, N.C. .. 35 50N 80 13w
Leyte, I. .... 11 0N 125 0 E
Lhasa .... 29 39N 91 6 E

Lhatse Dzong .... 29 10N 87 45 E
Lhokseumawe .... 5 20N 97 10 E
Li Kiang, R. ..... 18 25N 98 45 E
Liangsiang ...... 39 44N 116 8 E
Liaoning □ ...... 41 15N 122 0 E
Liaotung, Pen. ... 40 0N 122 22 E
Liaotung Wan, G. . 40 30N 121 30 E
Liaoyang .... 41 17N 123 11 E
Liaoyuan .... 42 55N 125 10 E
Liard, R. 61 52N 121 18w
Liberal 37 4N 101 0w
Liberec .... 50 47N 15 7 E
Liberia ■ 6 30N   9 30w
Liberty 41 48N 74 45w
Lîbîya, Sahrâ', Des. 27 35N 25 0 E
Libourne 44 55N   0 14w
Libreville .... 0 25N   9 26 E
Libya ■ .... 28 30N 17 30 E
Licantén 34 55s 72 0w
Licata .... 37 6N 13 55 E
Lichfield 52 40N   1 50w
Lichinga .... 13 13s 35 11 E
Lichtenburg ..... 26 8s 26 8 E
Lidköping .... 58 31N 13 14 E
Liebenwalde .... 52 51N 13 23 E
Liechtenstein ■ . . 47 8N   9 35 E
Liège .... 50 38N   5 35 E
Liège □ .... 50 32N   5 35 E
Lienz .... 46 50N 12 46 E
Liepaja .... 56 30N 21 0 E
Lier .... 51 7N   4 34 E
Liffey, R. 53 21N   6 16w
Lifford 54 50N   7 30w
Ligúria □ .... 44 30N   9 0 E
Ligurian Sea .... 43 15N   9 0 E
Lihou Reef and
  Cays .... 17 25s 151 40 E
Lihue 21 59N 152 24w
Likasi .... 10 55s 26 48 E
Likiang .... 26 50N 100 15 E
Likati .... 3 20N 24 0 E
Liling .... 27 47N 113 30 E
Lille .... 50 38N   3 3 E
Lille Bælt .... 55 30N   9 45 E
Lillehammer .... 61 8N 10 30 E
Lillesand .... 58 15N   8 23 E
Lillestrøm .... 59 58N 11 5 E
Lilliput .... 22 30s 29 55 E
Lillooet 50 42N 121 56w
Lilongwe .... 14 0s 33 48 E

Lima, Peru 12 0s 77 0w
Lima, Mont. 44 41N 112 38w
Lima, Ohio 40 42N 84 5w
Liman Katagum .. 10 5N   9 42 E
Limavady 55 0N 655½
Limavady □ 55 3N   6 58w
Limay, R. 39 0s 68 0w
Limay Mahuida .. 37 10s 66 45w
Limburg .... 50 22N   8 4 E
Limburg □ ...... 51 20N   5 55 E
Limeira 22 35s 47 28w
Limerick 52 40N   8 38w
Limerick □ 52 30N   8 50w
Limfjorden ..... 56 55N   9 0 E
Límnos, I. ...... 39 50N 25 5 E
Limoeiro do
  Norte 5 5s 38 0w
Limoera 7 52s 35 27w
Limoges .... 45 50N   1 15 E
Limón 10 0N 83 2w
Limousin, Reg. .. 46 0N   1 0 E
Limpopo, R. .... 25 15s 33 30 E
Limuru .... 1 2s 36 35 E
Linares, Chile ... 35 50s 71 40w
Linares, Mexico .. 24 50N 99 40w
Linares, Sp. 38 10N   3 40w
Lincheng .... 37 26N 114 34 E
Lincoln, Arg. 34 55N 61 30w
Lincoln, N.Z. .... 43 38s 172 30 E
Lincoln, U.K. 53 14N   0 32w
Lincoln, Ill. 40 10N 89 20w
Lincoln, Neb. 40 50N 96 42w
Lincoln Wolds ... 53 20N   0 5w
Lindi .... 9 58s 39 38 E
Lindsay, Canada . 44 22N 78 43w
Lindsay, U.S.A. .. 36 14N 119 6w
Lindley .... 27 52s 27 56 E
Linfen .... 36 5N 111 32 E
Lingayen .... 16 1N 120 14 E
Lingayen G. ..... 16 10N 120 15 E
Lingen .... 52 32N   7 21 E
Lingga, Kep. .... 0 10 E 104 30 E
Lingling .... 26 13N 111 37 E
Linglo .... 24 20N 105 25 E
Lingshui .... 18 27N 110 0 E
Linguéré 15 25N 15 5w
Linhai .... 28 51N 121 7 E
Linho .... 40 50N 107 30 E
Lini .... 35 5N 118 20 E

Linkao . . . . 19 56N 109 42 E
Linkiang . . . . 46 2N 133 56 E
Linköping . . . . . . 58 28N 15 36 E
Linkow . . . . 45 16N 130 18 E
Linlithgow . . . . . . 55 58N 3 38 E
Linnhe, L. 56 36N 5 25W
Linping . . . . 24 25N 114 32 E
Lins . . . . 21 40 S 49 44W
Linsi . . . . 43 30N 118 5 E
Linsia . . . . 35 50N 103 0 E
Lintan . . . . 34 59N 103 49 E
Linton 39 0N 87 10W
Lintsing 36 50N 115 45W
Linville . . . . 26 50 S 152 11 E
Linz . . . . 48 18N 14 18 E
Lion, G. du . . . . . . 43 0N 4 0 E
Lípari, I. . . . . . . 38 26N 14 58 E
Lipari Is. . . . . . . 38 40N 15 0 E
Lipetsk . . . . 52 45N 39 35 E
Liping . . . . 26 16N 109 8 E
Lipno . . . . 52 49N 19 15 E
Lippe, R. . . . . . . 51 39N 6 38 E
Liptrap, C. . . . . . 38 50 S 145 55 E
Lira . . . . 2 17N 32 57 E
Liria 39 37N 0 35W
Lisala . . . . 2 12N 21 38 E
Lisboa 38 42N 9 10W
Lisboa □ 39 0N 9 12W
Lisbon = Lisboa . . 39 0N 9 12W
Lisburn 54 30N 6 9W
Lisburn □ 54 30N 6 5W
Lisburne, C. 68 50N 166 0W
Lishui 28 20N 119 48W
Lisieux . . . . 49 10N 0 12 E
Lismore,
  Australia . . . . . . 28 44 S 153 21 E
Lismore, Eire 52 8N 7 58W
Listowel, Canada . . 44 4N 80 58W
Listowel, Eire 52 27N 9 30W
Litchfield 39 10N 89 40W
Lithgow . . . . 33 25 S 150 8 E
Lithuanian S.S.R. □ 55 30N 24 0 E
Litoměřice . . . . . . 50 33N 14 10 E
Little Abaco I. . . . 26 50N 77 30W
Little Barrier, I. . 36 12 S 175 8 E
Little Bushman
  Land . . . . 29 10 S 18 10 E
Little Current 45 55N 82 0W
Little Colorado, R. 36 11N 111 48W
Little Falls, Minn. . 45 58N 94 19W

Little Falls, N.Y. . . 43 3N 74 50W
Little Inagua I. . . . 21 40N 73 50W
Little Longlac 49 42N 86 58W
Little Namaqualand 29 0 S 17 10 E
Little Ouse, R. . . . 52 30N 0 22 E
Little Rann . . . . . 23 25N 71 25 E
Little River . . . . . 43 45 S 172 49 E
Little Rock 34 41N 92 10W
Littlefield 33 57N 102 17W
Littlehampton . . . 50 48N 0 32W
Liuan . . . . 31 45N 116 30 E
Liucheng . . . . . . 24 39N 109 14 E
Liuchow . . . . . . 24 10N 109 10 E
Liuwa Plain . . . . . 14 20 S 22 30 E
Livermore, Mt. . . . 30 45N 104 8W
Liverpool,
  Australia . . . . . . 33 55 S 150 52 E
Liverpool,
  Canada 44 5N 64 41W
Liverpool, U.K. . . 53 25N 3 0W
Livingston,
  Guatemala 15 50N 88 50W
Livingston, U.S.A. 45 40N 110 40W
Livingstone . . . . . 17 46 S 25 52 E
Livingstone Mts. . 9 40 S 34 20 E
Livingstonia . . . . 10 38 S 34 5 E
Livny . . . . 52 30N 37 30 E
Livorno . . . . 43 32N 10 18 E
Liwale . . . . 9 48 S 37 58 E
Lizard Pt. 49 57N 5 11W
Ljubljana . . . . . . 46 4N 14 33 E
Ljungan, R. . . . . . 62 19N 17 23 E
Ljungby . . . . 56 49N 13 55 E
Ljusdal . . . . 61 46N 16 3 E
Ljusnan, R. . . . . . 61 12N 17 8 E
Llandeilo 51 54N 4 0W
Llandovery 51 59N 3 49W
Llandrindod
  Wells 52 15N 3 23W
Llandudno 53 19N 3 51W
Llanelli 51 41N 4 11W
Llanes 43 25N 4 50W
Llangollen 52 58N 3 10W
Llanidloes 52 28N 3 31W
Llano Estacado,
  Reg. 34 0N 103 0W
Llanos, Reg. 3 25N 71 35W
Llanquihue, L. . . . 41 10 S 72 50W
Lloret de Mar . . . 41 41N 2 53 E
Lloydminster 53 20N 110 0W

Llullaillaco, Mt. . . 24 30 S 68 30W
Lobatse . . . . 25 12 S 25 40 E
Lobería . . . . 38 10 S 58 40W
Lobito . . . . 12 18 S 13 35 E
Locarno . . . . 46 10N 8 47 E
Lochaber, Reg. . . . 56 55N 5 0W
Lochalsh, Kyle of . 57 17N 5 43W
Lochboisdale 57 10N 7 20W
Lochgilphead 56 2N 5 37W
Lochmaddy 57 36N 7 10W
Lochnagar, Mt. . . . 56 57N 3 14W
Lochy, L. 56 58N 4 55W
Lock . . . . 33 34 S 135 46 E
Lockeport 43 47N 65 4W
Lockerbie 55 7N 3 21W
Lockhart 29 55N 97 40W
Lod . . . . 31 57N 34 54 E
Lodi 38 12N 121 16W
Lodja . . . . 3 30 S 23 23 E
Lodwar . . . . 3 10N 35 40 E
Łódź . . . . 51 45N 19 27 E
Lofoten, Is. . . . . . 68 10N 13 0 E
Logan, Ohio 39 35N 82 22W
Logan, Utah 41 45N 111 50W
Logan, W. Va. . . . 37 51N 81 59W
Logan, Mt. 60 40N 140 0W
Logansport 31 58N 93 58W
Logar □ . . . . 33 50N 69 0 E
Logroño 42 28N 2 32W
Loheia . . . . 15 45N 42 40 E
Loho . . . . 33 33N 114 5 E
Loimaa . . . . 60 50N 23 5 E
Loir, R. 47 33N 0 32W
Loir-et-Cher □ . . . 47 40N 1 20 E
Loire □ . . . . 45 40N 4 5 E
Loire, R. 47 16N 2 11W
Loire-Atlantique □ 47 25N 1 40W
Loiret □ . . . . 47 58N 2 10 E
Loja, Ecuador . . . 3 59 S 79 16W
Loja, Sp. 37 10N 4 10W
Lokeren . . . . 51 6N 3 59 E
Lokitaung . . . . . . 4 12N 35 48 E
Lokka, L. . . . . . . 68 0N 27 50 E
Løkken . . . . 57 22N 9 41 E
Lokoja . . . . 7 47N 6 45 E
Lokolama . . . . . . 2 35 S 19 50 E
Lokwei . . . . 19 12N 110 30 E
Lolland, L. . . . . . 54 45N 11 30 E
Lom . . . . 43 48N 23 20 E
Lomami, R. . . . . . 0 46N 24 16 E

Lombardia □ . . . . 45 35N 9 45 E
Lomblen, I. . . . . . 8 30 S 116 20 E
Lombok, I. . . . . . 8 35 S 116 20 E
Lomé . . . . 6 9N 1 20 E
Lomela . . . . 2 5 S 23 52 E
Lomela, R. . . . . . 0 14 S 20 42 E
Lomond 50 24N 112 36W
Lomond, L. 56 8N 4 38W
Lompoc 34 41N 120 32W
Łomza . . . . 53 10N 22 2 E
Loncoche . . . . . . 39 20 S 72 50W
Londiani . . . . . . 0 10 S 35 33 E
London, Canada . . 43 0N 81 15W
London, U.K. . . . 51 30N 0 5W
London □ 51 30N 0 5W
Londonderry 55 0N 7 20W
Londonderry □ . . 55 0N 7 20W
Londonderry, C. . . 13 45 S 126 55 E
Londonderry, I. . . 55 0 S 71 0W
Londrina . . . . . . 23 0 S 51 10W
Lone Pine 36 35N 118 2W
Long Beach 33 46N 118 12W
Long Eaton 52 54N 1 16W
Long I.,
  Bahamas 23 20N 75 10W
Long I.,
  Canada 44 23N 66 19W
Long I., U.S.A. . . . 40 50N 73 20W
Long Range Mts. . 48 0N 58 30W
Long Xuyen . . . . 10 19N 105 28 E
Longford 53 43N 7 50W
Longford □ 53 42N 7 45W
Longiram . . . . . . 0 5 S 115 45 E
Longmont 40 10N 105 4W
Longreach . . . . . . 23 28 S 144 14 E
Longview, Tex. . . . 32 30N 94 45W
Longview, Wash. . 46 9N 122 58W
Lons-le-Saunier . . 46 40N 5 31 E
Lønsdal . . . . 66 46N 15 26 E
Looe 50 21N 4 26W
Loomis 49 15N 108 45W
Loon Lake 54 2N 109 10W
Loongana . . . . . . 30 52 S 127 5 E
Loop Hd. 52 34N 9 55W
Lop Nor, L. . . . . . 40 30N 90 30 E
Lopez, C. . . . . . . 0 47 S 8 40 E
Lorain 41 20N 82 5W
Loralaï . . . . 30 29N 68 30 E
Lorca 37 41N 1 42W
Lord Howe I. . . . . 31 33 S 159 6 E

Lordsburg 32 15N 108 45W
Lorestan □ . . . . . 33 0N 48 30 E
Loreto, Brazil . . . . 7 5 S 45 30W
Loreto, Italy . . . . 43 26N 13 36 E
Lorient 47 45N 3 23N
Lorn, Firth of . . . . 56 20 S 5 40W
Lorne, Reg. 56 26N 5 10W
Lorraine, Reg. . . . 49 0N 6 0 E
Lorrainville 47 21N 79 23W
Lorugumu . . . . . . 2 50N 35 15 E
Los Alamos 35 57N 106 17W
Los Andes . . . . . . 32 50 S 70 40W
Los Angeles,
  Chile . . . . 37 28 S 72 23W
Los Angeles,
  U.S.A. 34 0N 118 10W
Los Angeles
  Aqueduct 35 0N 118 20W
Los Banos 37 8N 120 56W
Los Blancos . . . . . 23 45 S 62 30W
Los Hermanos,
  Is. 11 45N 64 25W
Los Lagos . . . . . . 39 51 S 72 50W
Los Mochis 25 45N 109 5W
Los Roques, Is. . . 11 50N 66 45W
Los Testigos, Is. . . 11 23N 63 6W
Los Vilos . . . . . . 32 0 S 71 30W
Loshkalakh . . . . . 62 45N 147 20 E
Losinj . . . . 44 35N 14 28 E
Lossiemouth 57 43N 3 17W
Lot . . . . 44 39N 1 40 E
Lot, R. . . . . 44 18N 0 20 E
Lot-et-
  Garonne □ . . . . . 44 22N 0 30 E
Lota . . . . 37 5 S 73 10W
Lotagipi Swamp . . 4 55N 35 0 E
Lothian □ . . . . . . 55 55 S 3 35W
Loto . . . . 28 50 S 22 28 E
Loughborough . . . 52 46N 1 11W
Loughrea 53 11N 8 33W
Louis Trichardt . . 23 0 S 25 55 E
Louisbourg 45 55N 60 0W
Louiseville 46 20N 73 0W
Louisiade Arch. . . 11 10 S 153 0 E
Louisiana □ 30 50N 92 0W
Louisville, Ky. . . . 38 15N 85 45W
Louisville, Miss. . . 33 7N 89 3W
Loulé 37 9N 8 0W
Loup City . . . . . . 41 19N 98 57 E
Lourdes 43 6N 0 3W

Lourenço
  Marques=
    Maputo .... 25 58s 32 32 E
Louth, Australia .. 30 30s 145 8 E
Louth, Eire 53 47N 6 33w
Louth, U.K. 53 23N 0 0
Louth □ 53 55N 6 30w
Love 53 29N 104 9w
Loveland 40 27N 105 4w
Lovelock 40 17N 118 25w
Lovisa .... 60 28N 26 12 E
Lowell 42 38N 71 19w
Lower Hutt ...... 41 10s 174 55 E
Lowestoft .... 52 29N 1 44 E
Łowicz .... 52 6N 19 55 E
Lowville 43 48N 75 30w
Loxton .... 34 28s 140 31 E
Loyang .... 34 41N 112 28 E
Loyung .... 24 25N 109 25 E
Lozère □ .... 44 35N 3 30 E
Lu-ta .... 39 0N 121 31 E
Lualaba, R. ...... 0 26N 25 20 E
Luanda .... 8 58s 13 9 E
Luang Prabang .. 19 45N 102 10 E
Luangwa, R. ..... 15 40N 30 25 E
Luanshya .... 13 3s 28 28 E
Luarca 43 32N 6 32w
Lubang Is. ...... 13 50N 120 12 E
Lubban .... 32 9N 35 14 E
Lubbock 33 40N 102 0w
Lübeck .... 53 52N 10 41 E
Lubefu .... 4 47s 24 27 E
Lublin .... 51 12N 22 38 E
Lubnân, Mts. .... 34 0N 36 0 E
Lubuklinggau .... 3 15s 102 55 E
Lubuksikaping ... 0 10N 100 15 E
Lubumbashi ..... 11 32s 27 28 E
Lubushi .... 10 32s 30 30 E
Lubutu .... 0 45s 26 30 E
Lucania, Mt. 60 48N 141 25w
Lucca .... 43 50N 10 30 E
Luce B. 54 45N 4 48w
Lucena, Philippines 13 56N 121 37 E
Lucena, Sp. 37 27N 4 31w
Lučenec .... 48 18N 19 42 E
Luchow .... 29 2N 105 10 E
Luckenwalde .... 52 5N 13 11 E
Lucknow .... 26 50N 81 0 E
Lüderitz .... 26 41s 15 8 E

Ludhiana .... 30 57N 75 56 E
Ludington 43 58N 86 27w
Ludlow 52 23N 2 42w
Ludvika .... 60 8N 15 14 E
Ludwigsburg .... 48 53N 9 11 E
Ludwigshafen ... 49 27N 8 27 E
Lufkin 31 25N 94 40w
Luga .... 58 40N 29 55 E
Lugano .... 46 0N 8 57 E
Lugansk=
  Voroshilovgrad.. 48 35N 39 29 E
Lugazi .... 0 32N 30 42 E
Lugh Ganana .... 3 48N 42 40 E
Lugo 43 2N 7 35w
Lugoj .... 45 42N 21 57 E
Lugovoy .... 43 0N 72 20 E
Luis Correia 3 0s 41 35w
Luján 34 45s 59 5w
Lukang .... 24 0N 120 19 E
Łuków .... 51 56N 22 23 E
Lukulu .... 14 35s 23 25 E
Luleå .... 65 35N 22 10 E
Lulonga, R. ..... 0 43N 18 23 E
Lulua, R. .... 5 2s 21 7 E
Luluabourg=
  Kananga ...... 5 55s 22 18 E
Lumberton 34 37N 78 59w
Lumbwa .... 0 12s 35 28 E
Lumsden .... 45 44s 168 27 E
Lun .... 47 55N 105 1 E
Lund .... 55 41N 13 12 E
Lundazi .... 12 20s 33 7 E
Lundy, I. 51 10N 4 41w
Lune, R. 54 2N 2 50w
Lüneburg .... 53 15N 10 23 E
Lüneburger
  Heide, Reg. ... 53 0N 10 0 E
Lunenburg 44 22N 64 18w
Lunéville .... 48 36N 6 30 E
Lunghwa .... 41 15N 117 51 E
Lungkiang ...... 47 22N 123 4 E
Lungkow .... 37 40N 120 25 E
Lungleh .... 22 55N 92 45 E
Lungsi .... 35 0N 104 35 E
Luni .... 26 0N 73 6 E
Luni, R. .... 24 40N 71 15 E
Luofu .... 0 1s 29 15 E
Luqa .... 35 35N 14 28 E
Lurgan 54 28N 6 20w
Lusaka .... 15 28s 28 16 E

Lushoto .... 4 47s 38 20 E
Lushun .... 38 48N 121 16 E
* Luso .... 11 47s 19 52 E
Lü-ta .... 39 0N 122 0 E
Luton 51 53N 0 24w
Lutong .... 4 30N 114 0 E
Lutsk .... 50 50N 25 15 E
Luwingu .... 10 15s 30 4 E
Luxembourg ..... 49 37N 6 9 E
Luxembourg ■ ... 50 0N 6 0 E
Luxembourg □ ... 49 58N 5 30 E
Luxor=El Uqsur .. 25 41N 32 38 E
Luza .... 60 39N 47 10 E
Luzern .... 47 3N 8 18 E
Luziania 16 20s 48 0w
Luzon, I. .... 16 0N 121 0 E
Lvov .... 49 40N 24 0 E
Lwanhsien ...... 39 45N 118 45 E
Lwasamaire ..... 0 53s 30 7 E
Lyakhovskiye Os. . 73 40N 141 0 E
* Lyallpur .... 31 30N 73 5 E
Lybster 58 18N 3 16w
Lyckele .... 64 38N 18 40 E
Lydda=Lod ...... 31 57N 34 54 E
Lydenburg ...... 25 10s 30 29 E
Lyell .... 41 48s 172 4 E
Lyell, Ra. ...... 41 38s 172 20 E
Lyme Regis 50 44N 2 57w
Lymington 50 46N 1 32w
Lynchburg 37 23N 79 10w
Lyndhurst, N.S.W. . 33 41N 149 2 E
Lyndhurst, Queens. 18 56s 144 30 E
Lyndonville 44 32N 72 1w
Lynn 42 28N 70 57w
Lynn Lake 56 51N 101 3w
Lynton 51 14N 3 50w
Lyon .... 45 46N 4 50 E
Lyonnais, Reg. ... 45 45N 4 15 E
Lyons=Lyon ..... 45 46N 4 50 E
Lyons, G. of=
  Lion, G. du ... 43 0N 4 0 E
Lyons, R. 25 2N 115 9w
Lysra .... 57 7N 57 47 E
Lytham
  St. Annes 53 45N 2 58w
Lyttelton .... 43 35s 172 44 E

M

Ma'ad .... 32 37N 35 36 E
Maanshan .... 31 40N 118 30 E
Maas, R. .... 51 49N 5 1 E
Maastricht ...... 50 50N 5 40 E
Mablethorpe .... 53 21N 0 14 E
Mabuki .... 2 57s 33 12 E
Macaé 20 20s 41 55w
McAllen 26 12N 98 15w
McAlester 34 57N 95 40w
Macapá 0 5N 51 10w
McArthur, R. .... 15 54s 136 40 E
Macau 5 0s 36 40w
Macau ■ .... 22 16N 113 35 E
McBride 53 20N 120 10w
McCammon 42 41N 112 11w
Macclesfield 53 16N 2 9w
McClintock 57 45N 94 15w
M'Clintock Chan. . 71 0N 103 0w
McComb 31 20N 90 30w
McCook 40 15N 100 35w
McDonald I. ..... 54 0s 73 0 E
Macdonnell, Ras. .. 23 40s 133 0 E
Macdougall, L. ... 66 20N 98 30w
Macduff 57 40N 2 30w
Mace 48 55N 80 0w
Macedonia□,
  Greece=
  Makedhonia □ . 40 39N 22 0 E
Macedonia□,
  Y.-slav.=
  Makedonija □ .. 41 53N 21 40 E
Maceió 9 40s 35 41w
Macenta 8 35N 9 20w
Macerata .... 43 19N 13 28 E
McGill 35 27N 114 50w
Macgillycuddy's
  Reeks, Mts. ... 52 2N 9 45w
Mach .... 29 50N 67 20 E
Machakos .... 1 30s 37 15 E
Machala 3 10s 79 50w
Macheŕna .... 61 20N 172 20 E
Machilipatnam ... 16 11N 81 8 E
Machiques 10 4N 72 34w
Machynlleth 52 36N 3 51w
† Macias Nguema
  Biyoga, I. ... 3 30N 8 40 E

Macintyre, R. .... 28 38s 150 47 E
Mackay, Australia . 21 36s 148 39 E
Mackay, U.S.A. .. 43 58N 113 37w
Mackay, L. ...... 22 40s 128 35 E
McKeesport 40 29N 79 50w
‡ Mackenzie, Reg. .. 63 30N 144 30w
Mackenzie 55 20N 123 5w
Mackenzie, R. ... 23 30s 150 0 E
Mackenzie, R. ... 69 15N 134 8w
Mackenzie City .. 6 0N 58 10w
Mackenzie Mts. .. 64 0N 130 0w
McKinlay .... 21 16s 141 17 E
McKinley, Mt. ... 63 10N 151 0w
McKinney 33 10N 96 40w
Mackinnon Road . 3 40s 39 0 E
Macklin 52 20N 109 56w
Macksville ...... 30 40s 152 56 E
Maclean .... 29 26s 153 16 E
Maclear .... 31 2s 28 23 E
Macleay, R. ..... 30 52s 153 1 E
McLennan 55 42N 116 50w
McLeod, L. ...... 24 9s 113 47 E
McLure 50 55N 120 20w
M'Clure Str. 74 40N 117 30w
McMinnville,
  Oreg. 45 16N 123 11w
McMinnville,
  Tenn. 35 43N 85 45w
McMurray 56 45N 111 27w
McNary 34 4N 109 53w
Macomb 40 25N 90 40w
Mâcon .... 46 19N 4 50 E
Macon 32 50N 83 37w
McPherson 38 25N 97 40w
Macquarie Is. ... 54 36s 158 55s
Macquarie, R. ... 30 7s 147 24 E
Macroom .... 51 54s 8 57 E
Madā'in Sâlih ... 26 51N 37 58 E
Madagali .... 10 56N 13 33 E
Madagascar ■ ... 20 0s 47 0 E
Madama .... 22 0N 14 0 E
Madang .... 5 0s 145 46 E
Madaoua .... 14 5N 6 27 E
Madara .... 11 45N 10 35 E
Madaripur ...... 23 2N 90 15 E
Madauk .... 17 56N 96 52 E
Madaya .... 22 20N 96 10 E
Madden L. 9 20N 79 37w
Madeira, I. 32 50N 17 0w
Madeira, R. 3 22s 58 45w

* Renamed Luena
* Renamed Faisalabad
† Renamed Bioko
‡ Renamed Fort Smith

Madera 37 0N 120 1w
Madhya Pradesh □ 21 50N 81 0 E
Madinat al
  Shaab .... 12 50N 45 0 E
Madingou .... 4 10s 13 33 E
Madison, Ind. 38 42N 85 20w
Madison, S.D. 44 0N 97 8w
Madison, Wis. 43 5N 89 25w
Madisonville 37 42N 86 30w
Madiun .... 7 38s 111 32 E
Mado Gashi ...... 0 47N 39 12 E
Madras, India .... 13 8N 80 19 E
Madras, U.S.A. ... 44 40N 121 10w
Madre, Laguna ... 25 0N 97 30w
Madre de Dios, R. 10 59s 66 8w
Madre de Dios,
  I. 50 20s 75 10w
Madre del
  Sur, Sa. 17 30N 100 0w
Madre Occidental,
  Sa. 27 0N 107 0w
Madre Oriental,
  Sa. 25 0N 100 0w
Madrid 40 25N   3 45w
Madura, I. .... 7 0N 113 20 E
Madura, Selat ... 7 30s 113 20 E
Madura Motel ... 31 55s 127 0 E
Madurai .... 9 55N 78 10 E
Madurantakam ... 12 30N 79 50 E
Mae Sot .... 16 43N 98 34 E
Maebashi .... 36 23N 139 4 E
Maesteg 51 36N   3 40w
Maestra, Sa. 20 15N 77 0w
Maestrazgo, Mts.
  de 40 30N   0 25w
Maevatanana .... 16 56s 46 49 E
Mafeking, Canada . 52 40N 101 10w
Mafeking, S.Africa 25 50s 25 38 E
Mafia I. .... 7 45s 39 50 E
Mafra, Brazil 26 7s 49 49w
Mafra, Port. 38 56N   9 20w
Mafupa .... 10 30s 29 7 E
Magadan .... 59 30N 151 0 E
Magadi .... 1 54s 36 19 E
Magallanes,
  Estrecho de, Str. 52 30s 75 0w
Magangue 9 14N 74 45w
Magdalen Is. 47 30N 61 40w
Magdalena, Arg. .. 35 4s 57 32w

Mexico 30 50N 112 0w
Magdalena, U.S.A. 34 10N 107 20w
Magdalena, I.,
  Chile 44 42s 73 10w
Magdalena, I.,
  Mexico 24 40N 112 15w
Magdeburg ...... 52 8N 11 36 E
Magdi'el .... 32 10N 34 54 E
Magee, I. 54 48N   5 44w
Magelang .... 7 29s 110 13 E
Magellan's Str.=
  Magallanes,
  Estrecho de 52 30s 75 0w
Maggiore, L. ..... 46 0N   8 35 E
Maghar .... 32 54N 35 24 E
Magherafelt 54 45N   6 36w
Magherafelt □ ... 54 45N   6 36w
Magnitogorsk .... 53 20N 59 0 E
Magnolia 33 18N 93 12w
Magog 45 18N 72 9w
Magrath 49 25N 112 50w
Maguarinho, C. .. 0 15s 48 30w
Magwe .... 20 10N 95 0 E
Mahābād .... 36 50N 45 45 E
Mahabo .... 20 23s 44 40 E
Mahaddei Uen ... 3 0N 45 32 E
Mahagi .... 2 20N 31 0 E
Mahagi Port ..... 2 3N 31 17 E
Mahalapye ...... 23 1s 26 51 E
Mahallat .... 33 55N 50 30 E
Mahanadi, R. .... 20 0N 86 25 E
Mahanoro .... 19 59s 48 48 E
Maharashtra □ ... 19 30N 75 30 E
Mahbubnagar ... 16 45N 77 59 E
Mahdia .... 35 28N 11 0 E
Mahenge .... 8 45s 36 35 E
Maheno .... 45 10s 170 50 E
Mahia Pen. ...... 39 9s 177 55 E
Mahón .... 39 50N   4 18 E
Mahone Bay 44 27N 64 23w
Mahuta .... 11 32N   4 58 E
Mai-Ndombe, L. .. 2 0s 18 0 E
Maidenhead ..... 51 31n' 0 42w
Maidstone,
  Canada 53 5N 109 20w
Maidstone, U.K. .. 51 16N   0 31 E
Maiduguri ...... 12 0N 13 20 E
Maijdi .... 22 48N 91 10 E
Maikala Ra. ..... 22 0N 81 0 E
Main, R. 54 43N   6 18w

Main, R. .... 50 0N   8 18 E
Maine □ 45 20N 69 0w
Maine, Reg. ..... 48 0N   0 0 E
Maine-et-Loire □ . 47 31N   0 30w
Maingkwan ..... 26 15N 96 45 E
Mainland, I.,
  Orkney 59 0N   3 10w
Mainland, I.,
  Shetland 60 15N   1 22w
Mainpuri .... 27 18N 79 4 E
Maintirano ...... 18 3s 44 5 E
Mainz .... 50 0N   8 17 E
Maipú 37 0s 58 0w
Maiquetía 10 36N 66 57w
Mairabari .... 26 30N 92 30 E
Maisí, C. 20 10N 74 10w
Maitland .... 32 44s 151 36 E
Maiyema .... 12 5N   4 25 E
Maizuru .... 35 25N 135 22 E
Majalengka ...... 6 55s 108 14 E
Majd el Kurum .. 32 56N 35 15 E
Majene .... 3 27s 118 57 E
Majorca, I.=
  Mallorca, I. .... 39 30N   3 0 E
Majunga .... 17 0s 47 0 E
Majunga □ ...... 16 30s 46 30 E
Makania .... 4 21s 37 49 E
Makarovo .... 57 40N 107 45 E
Makasar, Selat,
  Str. .... 1 0s 118 20 E
Makat .... 47 39N 53 19 E
Makedhona .... 40 39N 22 0 E
Makedonija □ ... 41 53N 21 40 E
Makeni 8 55N 12 5w
Makeyevka ...... 48 0N 38 0 E
Makgadikgadi Salt
  Pans .... 20 40s 25 45 E
Makhachkala .... 43 0N 47 15 E
Makindu .... 2 17s 37 49 E
Makinsk .... 52 37N 70 26 E
Makkah .... 21 30N 39 54 E
Makkovik 55 0N 59 10w
Maklakovo ...... 58 16N 92 29 E
Makó .... 46 14N 20 33 E
Makokou .... 0 40N 12 50 E
Makongolosi .... 8 23s 33 10 E
Makran Coast Ra. 25 40N   4 0 E
Maktau .... 3 25s 38 2 E
Māku .... 39 15N 44 31 E
Makurazaki ..... 31 15N 130 20 E

Makurdi .... 7 45N   8 32 E
Mal Usen, R. ..... 48 50N 49 39 E
Malabar Coast,
  Reg. .... 11 0N 75 0 E
Malacca=Melaka . 2 15N 102 15 E
Malacca, Str. of . 3 0N 101 0 E
Malad City 41 10N 112 20w
Maladetta, Mt. ... 42 40N   0 30 E
Málaga 36 43N   4 23w
Malagarasi ...... 5 5s 30 50 E
Malagasy Rep.=
  Madagascar ■ . 19 0s 46 0 E
Malaimbandy .... 20 20s 45 36 E
Malakāl .... 9 33N 31 50 E
Malakand .... 34 40N 71 55 E
Malamyzh .... 50 0N 136 50 E
Malang .... 7 59s 112 35 E
Malangali .... 8 33s 34 57 E
† Malanje .... 9 30s 16 17 E
Mälaren, L. ..... 59 30N 17 10 E
Malargüe 35 40s 69 30w
Malartic 48 9N 78 9w
Malatya .... 38 25N 38 20 E
Malawi ■ .... 13 0s 34 0 E
Malawi, L. ...... 12 30s 34 30 E
* Malaya □ .... 4 0N 102 0 E
Malayer .... 28 22N 56 38 E
Malaysia ■ ...... 5 0N 110 0 E
Malbon .... 21 5s 140 17 E
Malbork .... 54 3N 19 10 E
Malcolm .... 28 51s 121 25 E
Malden I. 4 3s 154 59w
Maldive Is. 2 0N 73 0w
Maldonado 35 0s 55 0w
Malea, Ákra .... 36 58N 23 7 E
Malegaon .... 20 30N 74 30 E
Malha .... 15 8N 26 12 E
Malhão, Sa. do .. 37 20N   8 0w
Mali 15 0N 10 0w
Malimba Mts. ... 7 30s 29 30 E
Malin Hd. 55 18N   7 16w
Malindi .... 3 12s 40 5 E
Malingping ...... 6 45s 106 2 E
Maliwun .... 10 14N 98 37 E
Mallacoota, Inlet . 34 40s 149 40 E
Mallaig 57 0N   5 50w
Mallawi .... 27 44N 30 44 E
Mallorca, I. ..... 39 30N   3 0 E
Mallow 52 8N   8 39w
Malmberget ..... 67 11N 20 40 E

Malmédy .... 50 26N   6 2 E
Malmesbury ..... 33 28s 18 41 E
Malmö .... 55 36N 12 59 E
Malmöhus □ .... 55 45N 13 30 E
Malolos .... 14 50N 21 2 E
Malone 44 50N 74 19w
Malta .... 48 20N 107·55w
Malta ■ .... 35 50N 14 30 E
Malton 54 9N   0 48w
Maluku, Js. ...... 3 0s 128 0 E
Malumfashi ..... 11 48N   7 39 E
Malvan .... 16 2N 73 30 E
Malvern, U.K. ... 52 7N   2 19w
Malvern, U.S.A. .. 34 22N 92 50w
Malvern Hills ... 52 0N   2 19w
Malvinas, Is.=
  Falkland Is. □ .. 51 30s 59 0w
Mamanguape 6 50s 35 4w
Mamasa .... 2 55s 119 20 E
Mambrui .... 3 5s 40 5 E
Mamfe .... 5 50N   9 15 E
Mammoth 32 46N 110 43w
Mamoi .... 26 0N 119 25 E
Mamoré, R. 10 23s 65 53w
Mamou 10 15N 12 0w
Mampawah ...... 0 30N 109 5 E
Man 7 30N   7 40w
Man, I. of 54 15N   4 30w
Man Na .... 23 27N 97 19 E
Mana 5 45N 53 55w
Manacapuru 3 10s 60 50w
Manacor .... 39 32N   3 12 E
Manado .... 1 40N 124 45 E
Managua 12 0N 86 20w
Managua, L. de .. 12 20N 86 30w
Manakara ...... 22 8s 48 1 E
Mananjary ...... 21 13s 48 20 E
Manantenina .... 24 17s 47 19 E
Manaos=Manaus . 3 0s 60 0w
Manapouri, L. ... 45 32s 167 32 E
Manass .... 44 0N 86 10 E
Manaung Kyun, I. 18 45N 93 40 E
Manaus 3 0s 60 0w
Manche □ 49 10N   1 20w
Manchester, U.K. . 53 30N   2 15w
Manchester, U.S.A. 42 58N 71 29w
Manchouli ...... 49 46N 117 24 E
Manchuria, Reg. . 44 0N 126 0 E
Manda .... 10 30s 34 40 E
Mandal .... 58 2N   7 25 E

* Renamed Mafikeng
² French nameform
³ Madeleine, Îs. de la

* Renamed Mahajanga

† Renamed Malanje
* Renamed Peninsular Malaysia

Mandala, Puncak,
Mt. . . . .   4 30 s 141 0 e
Mandalay . . . . 22 0 n 96 10 e
Mandalgovi . . . . . 45 40 n 106 22 e
Mandali . . . . 33 52 n 45 28 e
Mandan . . . . 46 50 n 101 0 w
Mandar, Teluk, G.   3 35 s 119 4 e
Mandasaur . . . . . . 24 4 n 75 4 e
Mandimba . . . . . . 14 22 s 35 33 e
Mandoto . . . . 19 34 s 46 17 e
Mandritsara . . . . . 15 50 s 48 49 e
Mandurah . . . . . . 32 32 s 115 43 e
Mandya . . . . 12 30 n 77 0 e
Manengouba, Mts..   5 15 n   9 15 e
Manfalût . . . . 27 20 n 30 52 e
Manfredónia, G. di 41 30 n 16 10 e
Mangalore . . . . . . 12 55 n 74 47 e
Mangaweka . . . . . 39 48 s 175 47 e
Manggar . . . .   2 50 s 108 10 e
Mangla Dam . . . . 33 32 n 73 50 e
Mangole, I. . . . . . . 1 50 s 125 55 e
Mangonui . . . . . . 35 1 s 173 32 e
Mangueira, L. . . . . 33 0 s 52 50 w
Mangyai . . . . 38 6 n 91 37 e
Mangyshlak Pol. . . 43 40 n 52 30 e
Manhattan . . . . . . 39 10 n 96 40 w
Manhuaçu . . . . . . 20 15 s 42 2 w
Manica et
Sofala □ . . . . . . 19 10 s 33 45 e
Manicaland □ . . . . 19 0 s 32 30 e
Manicoré . . . . 6 0 s 61 10 w
Manicouagan, L. . . 51 25 n 68 15 w
Manihiki, I. . . . . . 11 0 s 161 0 w
Manikpur . . . . 25 5 n 81 5 e
Manila . . . . 14 40 n 121 3 e
Manila B. . . . . 14 0 n 120 0 e
Manildra . . . . 33 11 s 148 41 e
Manilla . . . . 30 45 s 150 43 e
Manipur □ . . . . . . 24 30 n 94 0 e
Manisa . . . . 38 38 n 27 30 e
Manistee . . . . 44 15 n 86 20 w
Manistique . . . . . . 45 59 n 86 18 w
Manitoba □ . . . . . 55 30 n 97 0 w
Manitoba, L. . . . . . 50 40 n 98 30 w
Manitou Springs . . 38 52 n 104 55 w
Manitoulin I. . . . . 45 40 n 82 30 w
Manitowoc . . . . . . 44 8 n 87 40 w
Manizales . . . . 5 5 n 75 32 w
Manja . . . . 21 26 s 44 20 e
Manjakandriana . . 18 55 s 47 47 e
Manjhand . . . . 25 50 n 68 10 e
Manjil . . . . 36 46 n 49 30 e
Manjimup . . . . . . 34 15 s 116 6 e
Manjra, R. . . . . . . 18 49 n 77 52 e
Mankato, Kans. . . 39 49 n 98 11 w
Mankato, Minn. . . 44 8 n 93 59 w
Mankono . . . . 8 10 n   6 10 w
Mankulam . . . . . . 9 7 n 80 26 e
Manly . . . . 33 48 s 151 14 e
Manmad . . . . 20 18 n 74 28 e
Mannahill . . . . . . 32 26 s 139 59 e
Mannar, G. of . . . . 8 30 n 79 0 e
Mannar, I. . . . . . . 9 4 n 79 45 e
Mannheim . . . . . . 49 28 n   8 29 e
Manning . . . . 56 53 n 117 39 w
Mannum . . . . 34 57 s 139 12 e
Manokwari . . . . . . 0 54 n 134 0 e
Manombo . . . . . . 22 57 s 43 28 e
Manono . . . . 7 18 s 27 25 e
Mansa, Zambia . . . 11 13 s 28 55 e
Mansel I. . . . . 62 0 n 80 0 w
Mansfield,
Australia . . . . . . 37 0 s 146 0 e
Mansfield, U.K. . . 53 8 n   1 12 w
Mansfield, U.S.A. . 40 45 n 82 30 w
Mansura=
El Mansura . . . . 31 0 n 31 19 e
Manta . . . . 1 0 s 80 40 w
Manteca . . . . 37 50 n 121 12 w
Mantes-la-Jolie . . . 49 0 n   1 41 e
Manti . . . . 39 23 n 111 32 w
Mantiqueira, Sa.
da . . . . 22 0 s 44 0 w
Mántova . . . . 45 10 n 10 47 e
Mantua =Mantova 45 9 n 10 48 e
Manukan . . . . 8 14 n 123 3 e
Manukau . . . . 37 2 s 174 54 e
Manych-Gudilo,
Oz. . . . . 46 24 n 42 38 e
Manyoni . . . . 5 45 s 34 55 e
Manzai . . . . 32 20 n 70 15 e
Manzanares . . . . . 39 0 n   3 22 w
Manzanillo, Cuba . 20 20 n 77 10 w
Manzanillo, Mexico 19 0 n 104 20 w
Manzanillo, Pta. . . 9 30 n 79 40 w
Manzini . . . . 26 30 s 31 25 e
Mao . . . . 14 4 n 15 19 e
Maple Creek . . . . . 49 55 n 109 27 w
Maplewood . . . . . 38 33 n 90 18 w
Maputo . . . . 25 58 s 32 32 e
Maputo, B. de . . . . 26 0 s 32 50 e
Maputo □ . . . . . . 26 30 s 32 40 e
Maqnã . . . . 28 25 n 34 50 e
Maquinchao . . . . . 41 15 s 68 50 w
Mar Sa. do . . . . . . 25 30 s 49 0 w
Mar Chiquita, L. . . 30 40 s 62 50 w
Mar del Plata . . . . 38 0 s 57 30 w
Mara . . . . 1 30 s 34 32 e
Marabá . . . . 5 20 s 49 5 w
Maracaibo . . . . . . 10 40 n 71 37 w
Maracaibo, L. de . . 9 40 n 71 30 w
Maracay . . . . 10 15 n 67 36 w
Maradah . . . . 29 4 n 19 4 e
Maradi . . . . 13 35 n   8 10 e
Maragheh . . . . . . 37 30 n 46 12 e
Marajó, I. de . . . . . 1 0 s 49 30 w
Maralal . . . . 1 0 n 36 58 e
Maramba =
Livingstone . . . . 17 50 s 25 50 e
Marand . . . . 38 30 n 45 45 e
† Marandellas . . . . . 18 5 s 31 42 e
Maranguape . . . . . 3 55 s 38 50 w
Maranhão=São
Luís . . . . 2 39 s 44 15 w
Maranhão □ . . . . . 5 0 s 46 0 w
Marañón, R. . . . . . 4 50 s 75 35 w
Maraş . . . . 37 37 n 36 53 e
Marathón . . . . . . 38 11 n 23 58 e
Marathon . . . . . . 20 51 s 143 32 e
Marbat . . . . 17 0 n 54 45 e
Marble Bar . . . . . . 21 9 s 119 44 e
March . . . . 57 33 n   0 5 e
Marche □ . . . . 43 22 n 13 10 e
Marche, Reg. . . . . 46 5 n   2 10 e
Marche-en-
Famenne . . . . . . 50 14 n   5 19 e
Marchena . . . . . . 37 18 s   5 23 w
Mardan . . . . 34 12 n 72 2 e
Mardin . . . . 37 20 n 40 36 e
Maree, L. . . . . 57 40 n   5 30 w
Mareeba . . . . 16 59 s 145 28 e
Margaret Bay . . . . 51 20 n 127 20 w
Margaret River . . . 18 0 s 126 30 e
Margarita, I. de . . . 11 0 n 64 0 w
Margate, S. Afr. . . 30 50 s 30 20 e
Margate, U.K. . . . . 51 23 n   1 24 e
Margherita, Mt. . . . 0 22 n 29 51 e
Mari A.S.S.R. □ . . 56 30 n 48 0 e
Maria van
Diemen, C. . . . . 34 29 s 172 40 e
Mariakani . . . . 3 50 s 39 27 e
Mariana Is. . . . . . . 17 0 n 145 0 e
Marianao . . . . 23 8 n 82 24 w
Marianna . . . . 30 45 n 85 15 w
* Mariano Machado . 13 2 s 14 40 e
Marib . . . . 15 25 n 45 20 e
Maribor . . . . 46 36 n 15 40 e
Maricourt . . . . . . 61 36 n 71 57 w
Marie-Galante, I. . . 15 56 n 61 16 w
Mariehamn . . . . . 60 5 n 19 57 e
Mariental . . . . 24 36 s 18 0 e
Mariestad . . . . . . 58 43 n 13 50 e
Marietta, Ga. . . . . 34 0 n 84 30 w
Marietta, Ohio . . . 39 27 n 81 27 w
Marigot . . . . 15 32 n 61 18 w
Marniisk . . . . 56 10 n 87 20 e
Marília . . . . 22 0 s 50 0 w
Marin . . . . 42 23 n   8 42 w
Marinduque, I. . . . 13 25 n 122 0 e
Marinette . . . . 45 4 n 87 40 w
Maringá . . . . 23 35 s 51 50 w
Marion, Ill. . . . . . 37 45 n 88 55 w
Marion, Ind. . . . . 40 35 n 85 40 w
Marion, Iowa . . . . 42 2 n 91 36 w
Marion, Ohio . . . . 40 38 n 83 8 w
Marion, S.C. . . . . 34 11 n 79 22 w
Marion, Va. . . . . . 36 51 n 81 29 w
Maritsa . . . . 42 1 n 25 50 e
Marjan . . . . 32 5 n 68 20 e
Market Drayton . . 52 55 n   2 30 w
Market Harborough 52 29 n   0 55 w
Market Rasen . . . . 53 24 n   0 20 w
Marks . . . . 51 45 n 46 50 e
Marlborough . . . . 22 46 s 149 52 e
Marlborough
Downs . . . . 51 25 n   1 55 w
Marlin . . . . 31 25 n 96 50 w
Marmagao . . . . . . 15 25 n 73 56 e
Marmara Denizi,
Sea . . . . 40 45 n 28 15 e
Mármora . . . . 44 28 n 77 41 w
Marne □ . . . . 49 0 n   4 10 e
Marne, R. . . . . . . 48 49 n   2 24 e
Maroantsetra . . . . 15 26 s 49 44 e
Maroochydore . . . 26 35 s 153 10 w
Maroua . . . . 10 40 n 14 20 e
Marovoay . . . . . . 16 6 s 46 39 e
Marquard . . . . . . 28 40 s 27 28 e
Marquesas Is. . . . . 9 0 s 139 30 w
Marquette . . . . . . 46 30 n 87 21 w
Marra, J. . . . . 7 20 n 27 35 e
Marrakech . . . . . . 31 40 n   8 0 w
Marrakesh=
Marrakech . . . . . 31 40 n   8 0 w
Marrawah . . . . . . 40 56 s 144 41 e
Marree . . . . 29 39 s 138 1 e
Marsa Brega . . . . . 30 30 n 19 20 e
Marsa Susa . . . . . 32 52 n 21 59 e
Marsabit . . . . 2 18 n 38 0 e
Marsala . . . . 37 48 n 12 25 e
Marsden . . . . 33 47 n 147 32 e
Marseille . . . . 43 18 n   5 23 e
Marseilles=
Marseille . . . . . . 43 18 n   5 23 e
Marshall, Minn. . . 44 25 n 95 45 w
Marshall, Mo. . . . 39 8 n 93 15 w
Marshall, Tex. . . . 32 29 n 94 20 w
Marshall Is. . . . . . 9 0 n 171 0 e
Marshalltown . . . . 42 0 n 93 0 w
Marshfield . . . . . . 44 42 n 90 10 w
Martaban . . . . 16 30 n 97 35 e
Martaban, G. of . . 15 40 n 96 30 e
Martapura,
Kalimantan . . . . 3 22 s 114 56 e
Martapura,
Sumatera . . . . . . 4 19 s 104 22 e
Marte . . . . 12 23 n 13 46 e
Marthaguy Creek . 30 16 s 147 35 e
Martha's Vineyard . 41 25 n 70 35 w
Martigny . . . . 46 6 n   7 3 e
Martinique, I. . . . . 14 40 n 61 0 w
Martinique Pass. . . 15 15 n 61 0 w
Martins Ferry . . . . 40 5 n 80 46 w
Martinsburg . . . . . 39 30 n 77 57 w
Martinsville, Ind. . 39 29 n 86 23 w
Martinsville, Va. . . 36 41 n 79 52 w
Marton . . . . 40 4 s 175 23 e
Martos . . . . 37 44 n   3 58 w
Maru . . . . 12 22 n   6 22 e
Marugame . . . . . . 34 15 n 133 55 e
Marulan . . . . 34 43 s 150 3 e
Marungu Mts. . . . . 7 30 s 30 0 e
Marwar . . . . 25 43 n 73 45 e
Mary . . . . 37 40 n 61 50 e
Mary Kathleen . . . 20 35 s 139 48 e
Mary River . . . . . 70 30 n 78 0 w
Maryborough,
Queens. . . . . . . 25 31 s 152 37 e
Maryborough, Vic. 37 0 s 143 44 e

† Renamed Marondera   * Renamed Ganda

Maryland □ 39 10N 76 40w
Maryport 54 43N 3 30w
Marystown 47 10N 55 10w
Marysvale 38 25N 112 17w
Marysville 39 14N 121 40w
Maryville 35 50N 84 0w
Marzūq .... 25 53N 14 10 E
Masai Steppe .... 4 30s 36 30 E
Masaka .... 0 21s 31 45 E
Masakali .... 13 2N 12 32 E
Masamba .... 2 30s 120 15 E
Masan .... 35 11N 128 32 E
Masandam, Ras.. 26 30N 56 30 E
Masasi .... 10 45s 38 52 E
Masaya 12 0N 86 7w
Masba .... 10 35N 13 1 E
Masbate .... 12 20N 123 30 E
Masbate, I. .... 12 20N 123 30 E
Mascara .... 35 26N 0 6 E
Maseru .... 29 18s 27 30 E
Mashhad .... 36 20N 59 35 E
Mashi .... 13 0N 7 54 E
Mashkode 47 2N 84 7w
Mashonaland
  North □ .... 16 30s 30 0 E
Mashonaland
  South □ .... 18 0s 31 30 E
Masindi .... 1 40N 41 43 E
Masindi Port ..... 1 43N 32 2 E
Masisi .... 1 23s 28 49 E
Masjed Soleyman . 31 55N 49 25 E
Mask, L. 53 36N 9 24w
Masoala, C. ...... 15 59s 50 13 E
Mason City 48 0N 119 0w
Masqat .... 23 37N 58 36 E
Massa .... 44 2N 10 7 E
Massachusetts □ .. 42 25N 72 0w
Massawa=Mitsiwa . 15 35N 39 25 E
Massena 44 52N 74 55w
Masset 54 0N 132 0w
Massif Central
  Reg. .... 45 30N 2 21 E
Massillon 40 47N 81 30w
Masterton .... 40 56s 175 39 E
Mastung .... 29 50N 66 42 E
Mastura .... 23 7N 38 52 E
Masuda .... 34 40N 131 51 E
Masurian Lakes=
  Mazurski,
  Pojezierze ...... 53 50N 21 0 E

Matabeleland □ ... 20 0s 27 30 E
Mataboor .... 1 41s 138 3 E
Matachewan 47 50N 80 55w
Matad .... 47 12N 115 29 E
Matadi .... 5 52s 13 31 E
Matagalpa 13 10N 85 40w
Matagami 49 45N 77 34w
Matale .... 7 30N 80 44 E
Matamoros 18 2N 98 17w
Matane 48 50N 67 33w
Matanuska 61 38N 149 0w
Matanzas 23 0N 81 40w
Mataram .... 8 41s 116 10 E
Mataranka .... 14 55s 133 4 E
Mataró .... 41 32N 2 29 E
Matatiele .... 30 20s 28 49 E
Mataura .... 46 11s 168 51 E
Matehuala 23 40N 100 50w
Mateke Hills .... 21 48s 31 0 E
Matera .... 40 40N 16 37 E
Mathura .... 27 30N 77 48 E
Matlock 53 8N 1 32w
Matmata .... 33 30N 9 59 E
Mato Grosso □ ... 14 0s 54 0w
Matombo .... 7 3s 37 46 E
Matopo .... 20 36s 28 20 E
Matopo Hills .... 20 36s 28 20 E
Matozinhos 41 11N 8 42w
Matrah .... 23 37N 58 30 E
* Matrûh .... 31 19N 27 9 E
Matsena .... 13 5N 10 5 E
Matsu, I. .... 26 9N 119 56 E
Matsue .... 35 25N 133 10 E
Matsumoto ..... 36 15N 138 0 E
Matsusaka .... 34 34N 136 32 E
Matsuyama ...... 33 45N 132 45 E
Mattancheri ..... 9 50N 76 15 E
Mattawa 46 20N 78 45w
Matterhorn, Mt... 45 58N 7 39 E
Matthew Town ... 20 57N 73 40w
Mattoon 39 30N 88 20w
Matua .... 2 58s 110 52 E
Maturín 9 45N 63 11w
Mau Ranipur .... 25 16N 79 8 E
Maués 3 20s 57 45w
Maui, I. .... 20 45N 156 20 E
Maulamyaing .... 16 30N 97 40 E
Maumere .... 8 38s 122 13 E
Maun .... 20 0s 23 26 E
Mauna Loa, Mt... 19 50N 155 28 E

Maungmagan Is. .. 41 0s 97 48 E
Maungu .... 3 32s 38 42 E
Mauritania ■ 20 50N 10 0w
Mauritius .... 20 0s 57 0 E
Maurienne, Reg. . 45 15N 6 20 E
Mavqi'im .... 31 38N 34 32 E
Mawkmai .... 20 14N 97 50 E
Mawlaik .... 23 40N 94 26 E
Maxwelton .... 39 51s 174 49 E
May Pen 17 58N 77 15w
Maya Mts. 16 30N 89 0w
Mayaguana I. ... 21 30N 72 44w
Mayagüez 18 12N 67 9w
Mayanup .... 33 58s 116 25 E
Maydena .... 42 45s 146 39 E
Mayenne 48 20N 0 38w
Mayenne □ 48 10N 0 40w
Mayerthorpe 53 57N 115 15w
Mayfield 36 45N 88 40w
Maykop .... 44 35N 40 25 E
Maynooth, Canada 45 14N 77 56w
Maynooth, Eire .. 53 22N 6 38w
Mayo 63 38N 135 57w
Mayo □ 53 47N 9 7w
Maysville 38 43N 84 16w
Mayumba .... 3 25s 10 39 E
Mayya .... 61 44N 130 18 E
Mazabuka .... 15 52s 27 44 E
Mazagão 0 20s 51 50w
Mazama 49 43N 120 8w
Mazan Deran □ .. 36 30N 53 30 E
Mazar-i-Sharif .... 36 41N 67 0 E
Mazarredo 47 10s 66 50w
Mazarrón 37 38N 1 19w
Mazatenango 14 35N 91 30w
Mazatlán 23 10N 106 30w
Mazurski,
  Pojezierze ...... 53 50N 21 0 E
Mbabane .... 26 18s 31 6 E
M'Baiki .... 3 53N 18 1 E
Mbala .... 8 46s 31 17 E
Mbale .... 1 8N 34 12 E
Mbalmayo .... 3 33N 11 33 E
Mbamba Bay .... 11 13s 34 49 E
Mbandaka .... 0 1s 18 18 E
Mbanga .... 4 30N 9 33 E
Mbarara .... 0 35s 30 25 E
Mbeya .... 8 54s 33 29 E
Mbulamuti .... 0 57N 33 0 E

Mbulu .... 3 45s 35 30 E
Mchinja .... 9 46s 39 45 E
Mchinji .... 13 47s 32 58 E
Mdina .... 35 51N 14 25 E
Mead, L. 36 10N 114 10w
Meadow .... 26 35s 114 30 E
Meadow Lake 54 10N 108 10w
Meadow Lake
  Prov. Park 52 25N 109 0w
Meadville 41 39N 80 9w
Meaford 44 40N 80 36w
Meath □ 53 32N 6 40w
Meaux .... 48 58N 2 50 E
Mecca=Makkah .. 21 30N 39 54 E
Mechelen .... 51 2N 4 29 E
Mecklenburger, B.. 54 20N 11 40 E
Meda P.O. ..... 17 20s 123 59 E
Medan .... 3 40N 98 38 E
Medanosa, Pta. .. 48 0s 66 0w
Médéa .... 36 12N 2 50 E
Medellín 6 15N 75 35w
Médenine .... 33 21N 10 30 E
Mederdra 17 0N 15 38w
Medford 42 20N 122 52w
Mediaş .... 46 9N 24 22 E
Medicine Bow ... 41 56N 106 11w
Medinine Bow Ra. 41 10N 106 25w
Medicine Hat 50 0N 110 45w
Medina 43 15N 78 27w
Medina del Campo 41 18N 4 55w
Medina-Sidonia .. 36 28N 5 57w
Mediterranean
  Sea .... 35 0N 15 0 E
Médoc, Reg. 45 10N 0 56w
Medveditsa, R. .. 49 0N 43 58 E
Medvezhi Oshova . 71 0N 161 0 E
Medvezhyegorsk . 63 0N 34 25 E
Medway, R. ..... 51 27N 0 44 E
Meeberrie .... 26 57s 116 0 E
Meekatharra .... 26 32s 118 29 E
Meerut .... 29 1N 77 50 E
Mega .... 3 57N 38 30 E
Mégantic 45 36N 70 56w
Mégara .... 37 58N 23 22 E
Meghalaya □ .... 25 50N 91 0 E
Megiddo .... 32 36N 15 11 E
Mehadia .... 44 56N 22 23 E
Mehsana .... 23 39N 72 26 E
Meihokow .... 42 37N 125 46 E
Meihsien .... 24 20N 116 0 E

Meiktila .... 21 0N 96 0 E
Meissen .... 51 10N 13 29 E
Mejillones 23 10s 70 30w
Mekele .... 13 33N 39 30 E
Mekhtar .... 30 33N 69 20 E
Meknès 33 57N 5 33w
Meko .... 7 30N 3 0 E
Mekong, R. ..... 10 33N 105 24 E
Melaka .... 2 15N 102 15 E
Melalap .... 5 10N 116 5 E
Melbourne .... 37 40s 145 0 E
Melchor Múzquiz . 27 50N 101 40w
Melekess=
  Dimitrovgrad ... 54 25N 49 33 E
Melfort, Canada .. 52 50N 105 40w
Melfort, Rhod. ... 18 0s 31 25 E
Melilla 35 21N 2 57w
Melilot .... 31 22N 34 37 E
Melita 49 15N 101 5w
Melitopol .... 46 50N 35 22 E
Melk .... 48 13N 15 20 E
Mellerud .... 58 41N 12 28 E
Melo 32 20s 54 10w
Melrose 55 35N 2 44w
Melton Mowbray . 52 46N 0 52w
Melun .... 48 32N 2 39 E
Melville .... 32 2s 115 48 E
Melville, I.,
  Australia .... 11 30s 131 0 E
Melville, I.,
  Canada 75 30N 111 0w
Melville, L. 53 45N 59 40w
Melville Pen. 68 0N 84 0w
Memel .... 27 38s 29 36 E
Memel=Klaipeda . 55 43N 21 10 E
Memmingen ..... 47 59N 10 12 E
Memphis 35 7N 90 0w
Menai Str. 53 7N 4 20w
Ménaka .... 15 59N 2 18 E
Menasha 44 13N 88 27w
Menate .... 0 12s 112 47 E
Mencheng .... 33 27N 116 45 E
Mende .... 44 31N 3 30 E
Mendip Hills 51 17N 2 40w
Mendocino 39 26N 123 50w
Mendota 36 46N 120 24w
Mendoza 32 50s 68 52w
Mene de Mauroa . 10 45N 70 50w
Mene Grande 9 49N 70 56w
Menemen .... 38 36N 27 4 E

* Renamed Marsá Maṭruḥ

Menen .... 50 47N   3 7 E
Menfi .... 37 36N 12 57 E
Menggala .... 4 20s 105 15 E
Mengtz .... 23 20N 103 20 E
Menindee .... 32 20N 142 25 E
Menominee 45 9N 87 39w
Menomonie 44 50N 91 54w
Menor, Mar 37 40N   0 45w
Menorca, I. ...... 40 0N   4 0 E
Mentawai,
  Kep. .... 2 0s 99 0 E
Menton .... 43 50N   7 29 E
Menzel Temime ... 36 46N 11 0 E
Menzelinsk ...... 55 43N 53 8 E
Menzies .... 29 40s 120 58 E
Me'ona .... 33 1N 35 15 E
Meppel .... 52 42N   6 12 E
Merak .... 5 55s 106 1 E
Merano .... 46 40N 11 10 E
Merauke .... 8 29s 120 24 E
Merca .... 1 48N 44 50 E
Mercara .... 12 30N 75 45 E
Merced 37 25N 120 30w
Mercedes,
  Buenos Aires .. 34 40s 59 30w
Mercedes,
  Corrientes 29 10s 58 5w
Mercedes,
  San Luis 33 40s 65 30w
Mercedes,
  Uruguay 33 12s 58 0w
Merceditas 28 20s 70 35w
Mercer .... 37 16s 175 5 E
Mercy, C. 65 0N 62 30w
Mere 51 5N   2 16w
Meredith, C. 52 15s 60 40w
Mergui .... 12 30N 98 35 E
Mergui Arch.=
  Myeik Kyunzu .. 11 0N 98 0 E
Mérida, Mexico ... 20 50N 89 40w
Mérida, Sp. 38 55N   6 25w
Mérida, Ven. 8 36N 71 8w
Meriden 41 33N 72 47w
Meridian, Id. 43 41N 116 20w
Meridian, Miss. ... 32 20N 88 42w
Meriruma 1 15N 54 50w
Merksem .... 51 16N   4 25 E
Merowe .... 18 29N 31 46 E
Merredin .... 31 28s 118 18 E
Merrill 45 11N 89 41w

Merritt 50 10N 120 45w
Merroe .... 27 53s 117 50 E
Mersa Fatma ..... 14 57N 40 17 E
Mersea I. .... 51 48N   0 55 E
Merseburg ...... 51 20N 12 0 E
Mersey, R. 53 25N   3 0w
Merseyside □ 53 25w   2 55w
Mersin .... 36 51N 34 36 E
Mersing .... 2 25N 103 50 E
Merthyr Tydfil .. 51 45N   3 23w
Mértola .... 37 40N   7 40 E
Mertzon 31 17N 100 48w
Meru .... 0 3N 37 40 E
Meru, Mt. ...... 3 15s 36 46 E
Mesa 33 20N 111 56w
Meshed=Mashhad . 36 20N 59 35 E
Mesilla 32 20N 107 0w
Mesolóngion .... 38 27N 21 28 E
Mesopotamia,
  Reg.=Al
  Jazirah, Reg.... 33 30N 44 0 E
Messina, S.Africa . 22 20s 30 12 E
Messina, Str. di . 38 5N 15 35 E
Messíni .... 37 4N 22 1 E
Messiniakós Kól. .. 36 45N 22 5 E
Mesta, R. .... 40 41N 24 44 E
Meta, R. 6 12N 67 28w
Metagama 47 0N 81 55w
Metán 25 30s 65 0w
Methven .... 43 38s 171 40 E
Metlakatia 55 8N 131 35w
Metropolis 37 10N 88 47w
Metulla .... 33 17N 35 34 E
Metz .... 49 8N   6 10 E
Meulaboh .... 4 11N 96 3 E
Meureudu .... 5 19N 96 10 E
Meurthe-et-
  Moselle □ ..... 48 52N   6 0 E
Meuse □ .... 49 8N   5 25 E
Meuse, R. ...... 51 49N   5 1 E
Mexia 31 38N 96 32w
Mexiana, I. 0 0 49 30w
Mexicali 32 40N 115 30w
Mexico, Mexico .. 19 20N 99 10w
Mexico, U.S.A. .. 39 10N 91 55w
Mexico ■ 20 0N 100 0w
México □ 19 20N 99 10w
Mezen, R. ...... 66 11N 43 59 E
Mezen .... 65 50N 44 20 E
Mezökövesd ..... 47 49N 20 35 E

Mezötur .... 47 0N 20 41 E
Mhlaba Hills .... 18 30s 30 30 E
Mhow .... 22 33N 75 50 E
Miahuatlán 16 21N 96 36w
Miami 25 52N 80 15w
Miami Beach 25 49N 80 6w
Miandowāb ...... 37 0N 46 5 E
Miandrivaso .... 19 31s 45 28 E
Miāneh .... 37 30N 47 40 E
Mianwali .... 32 38N 71 28 E
Miaoli .... 24 34N 120 48 E
Miass .... 54 59N 60 6 E
Michelson, Mt. ... 69 19N 144 17w
Michigan □ 44 40N 85 40w
Michigan, L. 44 0N 87 0w
Michigan City ... 41 42N 86 56w
Michikamau L. ... 54 0N   6 0w
Michipicoten I. ... 47 55N 85 45w
Michipicoten River 47 50N 84 58w
Michoacán □ 19 0N 102 0w
Michurinsk ..... 52 58N 40 27 E
Mid Glamorgan □ . 51 40N   3 25w
Middelburg, Neth. . 51 30N   3 36 E
Middelburg,
  C. Prov. .... 31 30s 25 0 E
Middelburg, Trans. 25 49s 29 28 E
Middelveld, Reg. .. 26 30s 26 0 E
Middle Brook 48 40N 54 20w
Middlebury 44 0N 73 9w
Middlesboro 36 40N 83 40w
Middlesbrough .. 54 35N   1 14w
Middletown, Conn. 41 37N 72 40w
Middletown, N.Y. . 41 28N 74 28w
Middletown, Ohio . 39 29N 84 25w
Middleton 44 50N 65 5w
Middleton P.O. .. 22 22s 141 32 E
Midi, Canal du ... 43 45N   1 21 E
Midland,
  Australia ..... 31 54s 115 59 E
Midland, Canada .. 44 45N 79 50w
Midland, Mich. .. 43 37N 84 17w
Midland, Tex..... 32 0N 102 3w
Midlands □ ..... 19 0s 29 30 E
Midnapore ..... 22 25N 87 21 E
Midongy du Sud .. 23 35s 47 1 E
Midway Is. 28 13N 177 22w
Midwest 43 27N 106 11w
Mie □ .... 34 20N 136 20 E
Międzychod .... 52 35N 15 53 E
Międzyrzec

Podlaski .... 51 58N 22 45 E
Mienyang ...... 31 18N 104 26 E
Miercurea Ciuc .. 46 21N 25 48 E
Mieres 43 18N   5 48w
Migdal .... 32 51N 35 30 E
Migdal Ha'Emeq . 32 41N 35 14 E
Mihara .... 34 25N 133 5 E
Mikese .... 6 48s 37 55 E
Mikindani ...... 10 15s 40 2 E
Mikkeli □ ...... 61 56N 28 0 E
Mikun .... 62 20N 50 0 E
Milagro 2 0s 79 30w
Milan=Milano .. 45 28N   9 10 E
Milang .... 35 20s 138 55 E
Milano .... 45 28N   9 10 E
Milazzo .... 38 13N 15 13 E
Mildenhall ..... 52 20N   0 30 E
Mildura .... 34 13s 142 9 E
Miles .... 26 37s 150 10 E
Miles City 46 30N 105 50w
Milestone 50 0N 104 30w
Milford, Conn. ... 41 13N 73 4w
Milford, Del. ... 38 52N 75 26w
Milford, Utah ... 38 20N 113 0w
Milford Haven .. 51 43N   5 2w
Miling .... 30 30s 116 17 E
Millau .... 44 8N   3 4 E
Millertown Junction 48 49N 56 28w
Millicent .... 37 34s 140 21 E
Millinocket 45 45N 68 45w
Millom 54 13N   3 16w
Millville 39 22N 74 0w
Milne Inlet 72 30N 80 0w
Milo .... 24 28N 103 23 E
Mílos, I. .... 36 44N 24 25 E
Milton, N.Z. .... 46 7s 169 59 E
Milton, U.S.A. .. 41 0N 76 53w
Milton Keynes .. 52 3N   0 42w
Miltown Malbay .. 52 51N   9 25w
Milwaukee 43 9N 87 58w
Milwaukie 45 33N 122 39w
Minā al
  Ahmadī ...... 29 5N 48 10 E
Mina Saud ..... 28 45N 48 20 E
Mināb .... 27 10N 57 1 E
Minamata ...... 32 10N 130 30 E
Minas 34 20s 55 15w
Minas de Rio
  Tinto 37 42N   6 22w
Minas Gerais □ .. 18 50s 46 0w

Minatitlán 17 58N 94 35w
Minbu .... 20 10N 95 0 E
Minch, Little,
  Chan. 57 40N   6 50w
Minch, North,
  Chan. 58 0N   6 0w
Mindanao, I. .... 8 0N 125 0 E
Mindanao Sea ... 9 0 124 0 E
Mindanao Trench . 8 0N 128 0 E
Minden .... 52 18N   8 54 E
Minden 32 40N 93 20w
Mindoro, I. ..... 13 0N 121 0 E
Mindoro Str. .... 12 30N 120 30 E
Minehead 51 12N   3 29w
Mineral Wells ... 32 50N 98 5w
Mingan 50 20N 64 0w
Mingechaurskoye,
  Vdkhr. .... 40 56N 47 20 E
Mingela .... 19 52s 146 38 E
Mingenew ...... 29 12s 115 21 E
Minho, R. 41 52N   8 51w
Minho Reg. 41 40N   8 30w
Minhow=Foochow 26 5N 119 18 E
Minilya .... 23 55s 114 0 E
Min Kiang, R. ... 26 0N 119 30 E
Minkiang ...... 32 30N 114 10 E
Minna .... 9 37N   6 30 E
Minneapolis 44 58N 93 20w
Minnedosa 50 20N 99 50w
Minnesota □ 46 40N 94 0w
Minnipa .... 32 51s 135 9 E
Mino .... 35 32N 136 55 E
Minorca, I.=
  Menorca ...... 40 0N   4 0 E
Minot 48 10N 101 15w
Minsk .... 53 52N 27 30 E
Mińsk Mazowiecki . 52 10N 21 33 E
Minto .... 34 1s 150 51 E
Minto, L. 48 0N 84 45w
Minturn 39 45N 106 25w
Minusinsk ...... 53 50N 91 20 E
Minutang ...... 28 15N 96 30 E
Minya Konka, Mt. . 29 34N 101 53 E
Miquelon, I. 47 8N 56 24w
Miraj .... 16 50N 74 45 E
Miranda 20 10s 50 15w
Miranda de Ebro . 42 41N   2 57w
Miranda do Douro . 41 30N   6 16w
Miri .... 4 18N 114 0 E
Miriam Vale .... 24 20s 151 39 E

Mirim, L.......... 32 45 s 52 50w
Mirpur Khas ..... 25 30N 69 0 E
Mirzapur .... 25 10N 82 45 E
Mishan .... 45 31N 132 2 E
Mishawaka 41 40N 86 8w
Mishima .... 35 10N 138 52 E
Mishmar Alyalon . 31 52N 34 57 E
Mishmar Ha
  'Emeq .... 32 37N 35 7 E
Mishmar Ha Negev 31 22N 34 48 E
Mishmar Ha
  Yarden .... 33 0N 35 56 E
Miskin .... 2344⅛ 56 52 E
Miskitos, Cayos . 14 26N 82 50w
Miskolc .... 48 7N 20 50 E
Misool, I. .... 2 0 s 130 0 E
Misrātah .... 32 18N 15 3 E
Mission 26 15N 98 30w
Mission City 49 10N 122 15w
Mississippi □ 33 0N 90 0w
Mississippi, R. ... 29 0N 89 15w
Mississippi,
  Delta of the ... 29 10N 89 15w
Missoula 47 0N 114 0w
Missouri □ 38 25N 92 30w
Missouri, Plat. du
  Coteau du 46 0N 99 30w
Missouri, R. 38 50N 90 8w
Mistassini, L. 51 0N 73 40w
Mitchell,
  Australia .... 26 29 s 147 58 E
Mitchell, U.S.A. .. 43 40N 98 0w
Mitchell, Mt. 35 40N 82 20w
Mitchelstown ... 52 16N   8 18w
Mitylene, I.=
  Lésvos, I. ...... 39 0N 26 20 E
Mitilíni .... 39 6N 26 35 E
Mitla 16 55N 96 17w
Mito .... 36 20N 140 30 E
Mitsinjo .... 16 1 s 45 52 E
Mitsiwa .... 15 35N 39 25 E
Mittagong .... 34 28 s 150 29 E
Mittyack .... 35 8 s 142 36 E
Mitumba,
  Chaîne des .... 10 0 s 26 20 E
Mityana .... 0 24N 32 3 E
Miyagi □ .... 38 15N 140 45 E
Miyako .... 39 40N 141 75 E
Miyakonojo ..... 31 32N 131 5 E
Miyazaki .... 31 56N 131 30 E

Miyazaki .... 32 0N 131 30 E
Miyet, Bahr el .... 31 30N 35 30 E
Miyoshi .... 34 48N 132 32 E
Miyun .... 40 22N 116 49 E
Mizen Hd., Cork . 51 27N   9 50w
Mizen Hd.,
  Wicklow 52 52N   6 4w
Mizoram □ ...... 23 0N 92 40 E
Mizpe Ramon ... 20 36N 34 48 E
Mjanji .... 0 17N 33 59 E
Mjölby .... 58 20N 15 10 E
Mjøsa, L. .... 60 45N 11 0 E
Mkobela .... 10 57 s 38 5 E
Mkushi .... 14 20 s 29 20 E
Mkwaya .... 6 17 s 35 40 E
Mladá Boleslav .. 50 27N 14 53 E
Mława .... 53 9N 20 25 E
Mlanje, Mt. ..... 16 2 s 35 33 E
Mme .... 6 18N 10 14 E
Mo .... 66 15N 14 8 E
Moa, I. .... 8 0 s 128 0 E
Moab 38 40N 109 35w
Moama .... 36 3 s 144 45 E
Moba .... 7 3 s 29 47 E
Mobaye .... 4 25N 21 5 E
Moberly 39 25N 92 25w
Mobert 48 41N 85 40w
Mobile 30 41N 88 3w
Mobutu Sese
  Seko, L. .... 1 30N 31 0 E
Moçambique ..... 15 3 s 40 42 E
*Moçâmedes ...... 16 35 s 12 30 E
Mochudi .... 24 27 s 26 7 E
Moçimboa da Praia 11 25 s 40 20 E
Mocoa 1 15N 76 45w
Moctezuma, R.... 21 59N 98 34w
Mocuba .... 16 54 s 37 25 E
Modane .... 45 12N   6 40 E
Modderrivier .... 29 2 s 24 38 E
Módena .... 44 39N 10 55 E
Modesto 37 43N 121 0w
Módica .... 36 52N 14 45 E
Moe .... 38 12 s 146 19 E
Moengo 5 45N 54 20w
Moero, L. .... 9 0 s 28 45 E
Moffat 55 20N   3 27w
Mogadishu □ .... 2 2N 45 25 E
Mogadishu=
  Mogadiscio ... 2 2N 45 25 E
Mogador=

Essaouira 31 32N   9 42w
Mogaung .... 25 20N 97 0 E
Mogi das Cruzes . 23 45 s 46 20w
Mogi Mirim ..... 22 20 s 47 0w
Mogilev .... 53 55N 30 18 E
Mogilev
  Podolskiy ..... 48 20N 27 40 E
Mogocha .... 53 40N 119 50 E
Mogollon Mesa .. 43 40N 110 0w
Mogumber ...... 31 2 s 116 3 E
Mohács .... 45 58N 18 41 E
Moho .... 53 15N 122 27 E
Mohoro .... 8 6 s 39 8 E
Mointy .... 47 40N 73 45 E
Mojave 35 8N 118 8w
Mojave Des. 35 0N 117 30w
Mojokerto .... 7 29 s 112 25 E
Mokau .... 38 42 s 174 37 E
Mokpo .... 34 50N 126 30 E
Mokwa .... 9 18N   5 2 E
Mol .... 51 11N   5 5 E
Mold 53 10N   3 10w
Moldanan S.S.R. □ 47 0N 28 0 E
Molde .... 62 46N   7 12 E
Molepolole ...... 24 28 s 25 28 E
Molfetta .... 41 12N 16 35 E
Moline 41 30N 90 30w
Molise □ .... 41 45N 14 30 E
Mollendo .... 17 0 s 72 0w
Mölndal .... 57 40N 12 3 E
Molokai, I. 21 8N 156 0w
Molong .... 33 5 s 148 54 E
Molopo, R. ...... 28 30 s 20 13 E
Molteno .... 31 22 s 26 22 E
Molucca Sea .... 4 0 s 124 0 E
Moluccas, Is.=
  Maluku, Is. ... 1 0 s 127 0 E
Moma .... 16 47 s 39 4 E
Mombasa .... 4 2 s 39 43 E
Mombo .... 4 57 s 38 20 E
Mompos 9 14N 74 26w
Møn, I. .... 54 57N 12 15 E
Mona, Pta. 9 37N 82 36w
Mona, I. 18 5N 67 54w
Monach Is. 57 32N   7 40w
Monaco ■ ...... 43 46N   7 23 E
Monadhliath Mts. 57 10N   4 4w
Monaghan 54 15N   6 58w
Monaghan □ 54 10N   7 0w
Monahans 31 35N 102 50w

Monastir .... 35 50N 10 49 E
Monchegorsk .... 67 54N 32 58 E
Mönchengladbach . 51 12N   6 23 E
Monchique 37 19N   8 38w
Monclava 26 50N 101 30w
Moncton 46 7N 64 51w
Mondego, R. 40 9N   8 52w
Mondovi .... 44 23N   7 56 E
Monessen 40 9N 79 50w
Monet 48 10N 75 40w
Monforte de
  Lemos 42 31N   7 33w
Mong Kung ..... 21 35N 97 35 E
Mong Pan ...... 20 19N 98 22 E
Mong Pawk ..... 22 4N 99 16 E
Mong Ton ...... 20 25N 98 45 E
Mong Wa .... 21 26N 100 27 E
Mong Yai ...... 22 28N 98 3 E
Monger, L. ...... 29 25 s 117 5 E
Monghyr .... 25 23N 86 30 E
Mongo .... 12 14N 18 43 E
Mongolia ■ ..... 47 0N 103 0 E
Mongonu .... 12 40N 13 32 E
Mongu .... 15 16 s 23 12 E
Monk 47 7N 69 59w
Monkira .... 24 46 s 140 30 E
Monmouth, U.K. . 51 48N   2 43w
Monmouth, U.S.A. 40 50N 90 40w
Mono, Pta. del ... 12 0N 83 30w
Monópoli .... 40 57N 17 18 E
Monroe, La. 32 32N 92 4w
Monroe, Mich. .. 41 55N 83 26w
Monroe, N.C. 35 2N 80 37w
Monroe, Wis. 42 38N 89 40w
Monrovia, Liberia . 6 18N 10 47w
Monrovia, U.S.A. . 34 7N 118 1w
Mons .... 50 27N   3 58 E
Mont Joli 48 37N 68 10w
Mont Laurier 46 35N 75 30w
Mont St.
  Michel 48 40N   1 30w
Mont Tremblant
  Prov. Park 46 30N 74 30w
Montagu .... 33 45 s 20 8 E
Montague, I. 31 40N 144 46w
Montalbán 40 50N   0 45w
Montana □ ...... 6 0 s 73 0w
Montargis .... 48 0N   2 43 E
Montauban ...... 44 0N   1 21 E

Montauk Pt. 41 4N 71 52w
Montbéliard ..... 47 31N   6 48 E
Mont-de-
  Marsan 43 54N   0 31w
Monte Alegre ... 2 0 s 54 0w
Monte Azul ..... 15 9 s 42 53w
Monte Carlo .... 43 46N   7 23 E
Monte Caseros .. 30 10 s 57 50w
Monte Comán ... 34 40 s 68 0w
Monte Sant
  'Angelo .... 41 42N 15 59 E
Montebello 45 40N 74 55w
Montecristi ..... 1 0 s 80 40w
Montego Bay 18 30N 78 0w
Montejinnie ..... 16 40 s 131 45 E
Montélimar ..... 44 33N   4 45 E
Montemorelos .. 25 11N 99 42w
Montenegro □ =
  Crna Gora .... 42 40N 19 20 E
Monterey 36 35N 121 57w
Montería 8 46N 75 53w
Monterrey 25 40N 100 30w
Montes Claros .. 16 30 s 43 50w
Montesano 47 0N 123 39w
Montevideo ..... 34 50 s 56 11w
Montgomery, U.K. 52 34N   3 9w
Montgomery,
  U.S.A. 32 20N 86 20w
Montgomery=
  Sahiwal .... 30 45N 73 8 E
Monticello, Utah . 37 55N 109 27w
Montijo 38 52N   6 39w
Montilla 37 36N   4 40w
Montivideo 44 55N 95 40w
Montluçon ..... 46 22N   2 36 E
Montmagny ..... 46 58N 70 43 E
Montmorency ... 46 53N 71 11w
Monto .... 24 52 s 151 12 E
Montoro 38 1N   4 27w
Montpelier, Id. .. 42 15N 111 29w
Montpelier, Vt. .. 44 15N 72 38w
Montpellier ..... 43 37N   3 52 E
Montreal 45 31N 73 34w
Montreuil ...... 50 27N   1 45 E
Montreux .... 46 26N   6 55 E
Montrose, U.K. .. 56 43N   2 28w
Montrose, U.S.A. . 38 30N 107 52w
Montserrat, I. ... 16 40N 62 10w
Monywa .... 22 7N 95 11 E
Monze .... 16 17 s 27 29 E

* Renamed Namibe

Monze, C. .... 24 47N 66 37 E
Monzón .... 41 52N 0 10 E
Mooliabeenee ..... 31 20s 116 2 E
Moonbeam 49 20N 82 10w
Moonie .... 27 46s 150 20 E
Moonta .... 34 6s 137 32 E
Moora .... 30 37s 115 58 E
Mooraberree ..... 25 13s 140 54 E
Moorarie .... 25 56s 117 35 E
Moore, L. ...... 29 50s 117 35 E
Moore River .... 31 6s 115 32 E
Moorreesburg .... 33 6s 18 38 E
Moorfoot Hills .. 55 44N 3 8w
Moorhead 47 0N 97 0w
Moose, R. 43 37N 75 22w
Moose Factory .. 52 20N 80 40w
Moose Jaw 50 30N 105 30w
Moose Lake 46 27N 92 48w
Moosomin 50 9N 101 40w
Moosonee 51 25N 80 40w
Mopeia Velha ... 17 30s 35 40 E
Mopti 14 30N 4 0w
Moquegua 17 15s 70 46w
Mora, Sweden ... 61 2N 14 38 E
Moradabad ...... 28 50N 78 50 E
Moramanga ..... 18 56s 48 12 E
Morant Pt. 17 55N 76 12w
Morar, L. 56 57N 5 40w
Moratuwa ...... 6 45N 79 55 E
Morava, R. ..... 48 10N 16 59 E
Morawa .... 29 13s 116 0 E
Morawhanna 8 30N 59 40w
Moray Firth 57 50N 3 30w
Morbihan □ 47 55s 2 50w
Morden 49 15N 98 10w
Mordialloc ..... 38 1s 145 6 E
Mordovian
  A.S.S.R. □ ..... 54 20N 44 30 E
Møre og
  Romsdal □ .... 63 0N 9 0 E
Morecambe 54 5N 2 52w
Morecambe B. .. 54 7N 3 0w
Moree .... 29 28s 149 54 E
Moorhead City .. 34 46N 76 44w
Moravian Hts.=
  Ceskomoravská V. 49 20N 15 30 E
Morea□=
  Pelopónnisos .. 37 40N 22 15 E
Morelia 19 40N 101 11w
Morella .... 23 0s 143 47 E

Morelos □ 18 40N 99 10w
Morena, Sa. 38 20N 4 0w
Morenci 33 7N 109 20w
Moreton, I. ..... 27 10s 153 25 E
Morgan City 29 40N 91 15w
Morganton 35 46N 81 48w
Morgantown 39 39N 75 58w
Morgenzon ..... 26 45s 29 36 E
Moriki .... 12 52N 6 30 E
Morinville 53 49N 113 41w
Morioka .... 39 45N 141 8 E
Morlaix 48 36N 3 52w
Mornington, I.,
  Australia ... 16 30s 139 30 E
Mornington, I.,
  Chile 49 50s 75 30w
Moro G. .... 6 30N 123 0 E
Morocco ■ 32 0N 5 50w
Morogoro ...... 6 50s 37 40 E
Moroleón 20 8N 101 32w
Morombé ...... 21 45s 43 22 E
Morón 22 0N 78 30w
Mörön, R. ..... 47 14N 110 37 E
Morón de la
  Frontera 37 6N 5 28w
Morondavo .... 20 17s 44 27 E
Morotai, I. .... 2 10N 128 30 E
Moroto .... 2 28N 34 42 E
Moroto, Mt. .... 2 30N 34 43 E
Morpeth 55 11N 1 41w
Morrilton 35 10N 92 45w
Morrinhos 17 45s 49 10w
Morrinsville .. 37 40s 175 32 E
Morris 49 25N 97 30w
Morris, Mt. ... 26 9s 131 4 E
Morrisburg 44 55N 75 7w
Morristown, Tenn. 36 18N 83 20w
Morro Bay 35 27N 120 54w
Morrosquillo, G. de 9 35N 75 40w
Morshansk .... 53 28N 41 50 E
Morteros 30 50s 62 0w
Mortes, R. 11 45s 50 44w
Mortlake ..... 38 5s 142 50 E
Morundah ..... 34 57s 146 19 E
Morven .... 26 22s 147 5 E
Morvern, Reg. .. 56 38N 5 44w
Morwell ...... 38 10s 146 22 E
Moscos Is. .... 14 0N 97 45 E
Moscow 46 45N 116 59w
Moscow=Moskva . 55 45N 37 35 E

Mosel, R. .... 50 22N 7 36 E
Moselle, R. ...... 50 22N 7 36 E
Moselle □ .... 48 59N 6 33 E
Mosgiel .... 45 53s 170 21 E
Moshi .... 3 22s 37 18 E
Mosjøen .... 65 51N 13 12 E
Moskva .... 55 45N 27 35 E
Moskva, R. ...... 55 5N 38 50 E
Mosquera 2 35N 78 30w
Mosquitos,
  G. de los 9 15N 81 0w
Moss .... 59 27N 10 40 E
Moss Vale ...... 34 32s 150 25 E
Mossbank 50 0N 106 0w
Mossburn .... 45 41s 168 15 E
Mosselbaai ..... 34 11s 22 8 E
Mossendjo ...... 2 55s 12 42 E
Mossgiel .... 33 15s 144 30 E
Mossman .... 16 28s 145 23 E
Mossoró 5 10s 37 15w
Mossuril .... 14 58s 40 42 E
Most .... 50 31N 13 38 E
Mosta .... 35 53N 14 26 E
Mostaganem .... 35 54N 0 5 E
Mostar .... 43 22N 17 50 E
Mostardas 31 2s 50 51w
Mosul=Al
  Mawsil .... 36 20N 43 5 E
Motala .... 58 32N 15 1 E
Motherwell 55 48N 4 0w
Motihari ...... 26 37N 85 1 E
Motril 36 44N 3 37w
Motueka .... 41 7s 173 1 E
Mouila .... 1 50s 11 0 E
Moulins .... 46 35N 3 19¼ E
Moulmein=
  Maulamyaing .. 16 30N 97 40 E
Moultrie 31 11N 83 47w
Moundou ...... 8 40N 16 10 E
Moundsville ... 39 53N 80 43w
Mount Airy 36 31N 80 37w
Mount Barker .. 34 38s 117 40 E
Mount Carmel, Ill. 38 20N 87 48w
Mount Carmel, Pa. 40 46N 76 25w
Mount Coolon .. 21 25s 147 25 E
Mount Darwin .. 16 47s 31 38 E
Mount Douglas . 21 35s 146 50 E
Mount Eden ... 36 53s 174 46 E
Mount Edgecumbe 57 3N 135 21w
Mount Elizabeth . 16 0s 125 50 E

Mount Forest 43 59N 80 43w
Mount Gambier ... 37 50s 140 46 E
Mount Garnet .... 17 41s 145 7 E
Mount Hope .... 34 7s 135 23 E
Mount Isa ..... 20 42s 139 26 E
Mount Keith .... 27 15s 120 30 E
Mount Larcom .. 23 48s 150 59 E
Mount Lavinia .. 6 50N 79 50 E
Mount Magnet .. 28 2s 117 47 E
Mount
  Maunganui .... 37 40s 176 14 E
Mount Molloy ... 16 42s 145 20 E
Mount Morgan .. 23 40s 150 25 E
Mount Narryer .. 26 30s 115 55 E
Mount Newman .. 23 18s 119 45 E
Mount Pleasant,
  Iowa 41 0N 91 35w
Mount Pleasant,
  Mich. 43 38N 84 46w
Mount Pleasant,
  Texas 33 5N 95 0w
Mount Pleasant,
  Utah 39 40N 111 29w
Mount Rainier
  Nat. Park 46 50N 121 20w
Mt. Revelstoke
  Nat. Park 51 6N 118 0w
Mount Robson .. 52 56N 119 15w
Mount Sterling .. 38 0N 84 0w
Mount Surprise .. 18 10s 144 17 E
Mount Vernon, Ill. 38 19N 88 55w
Mount Vernon,
  N.Y. 40 57N 73 49w
Mount Vernon,
  Ohio 40 20N 82 30w
Mount
  Vernon, Wash. .. 48 27N 122 18w
Mount
  Willoughby .... 27 58s 134 8 E
Mountain Home .. 43 3N 115 52w
Mountain Park .. 52 50N 117 15w
Mountain View .. 37 26s 122 5w
Mountainair ... 34 35N 106 15w
Mountmellick .. 53 7N 7 20w
Moura, Australia . 24 35s 149 58 E
Moura, Brazil ... 1 25s 61 45w
Mourdi,
  Depression du .. 18 10N 23 0 E
Mouri 5 6N 1 14w
Mourne, Mts. 54 10N 6 0w

Mourne, R. 54 45N 7 25w
Mouscron .... 50 45N 3 12 E
Moutohora ...... 38 27s 177 32 E
Mowming .... 21 50N 110 32 E
Mowping .... 37 25N 121 34 E
Moyale .... 3 30N 39 0 E
Moyle □ 55 10N 6 15w
Moza .... 31 48N 35 8 E
Mozambique ■ .. 19 0s 35 0 E
Mozambique Chan. 20 0s 39 0 E
Mozyr .... 52 0N 29 15 E
Mpanda .... 6 23s 31 40 E
Mpika .... 11 51s 31 25 E
Mporokoso ..... 9 25s 30 5 E
Mpulungu ...... 8 51s 31 5 E
Mpwapwa ...... 6 30s 36 30 E
Msaken .... 35 49N 10 33 E
Msoro .... 13 35s 31 50 E
Mtito Andei .... 2 41s 38 12 E
Mtwara .... 10 20s 40 20 E
Muaná 1 25s 49 15w
Muang Chiang
  Rai .... 19 52N 99 50 E
Muar=Bandar
  Maharani ..... 2 3N 102 34 E
Muarabungo .... 1 40s 101 10 E
Muarakaman .... 0 2s 116 45 E
Muaratembesi .. 1 42s 103 2 E
Muaratewe ..... 0 50s 115 0 E
Mubairik ...... 23 22s 39 8 E
Mubende .... 0 33N 31 22 E
Mubi .... 10 18N 13 16 E
Muck, I. 56 50N 6 15w
Mucuri 18 0s 40 0w
Mueda .... 11 36s 39 28 E
Mufulira 12 32s 28 15w
Muhammad Qol .. 20 53s 37 9 E
Muheza .... 5 9s 38 48 E
Mühlhausen .... 51 12N 10 29 E
Muine Bheag ... 52 42N 6 59w
Mukalla .... 14 33N 49 2 E
Mukden=Shenyang 41 48N 123 27 E
Mukeiras ...... 13 59N 45 52 E
Mukinbudin ... 30 55s 118 5 E
Mukomuko ..... 2 20s 101 10 E
Mukono .... 0 28N 32 37 E
Muktsar .... 30 30N 74 30 E
Mulatas, Arch.
  de las 6 51N 78 31w
Mulchén 37 45s 72 20w

Mulde, R., ... 51 10N   12 48 E
Muleba .... 1 50 S   31 37 E
Mulgrave 45 38N   61 31w
Mulhacén, Mt. 37 4N   3 20w
Mülheim 51 26N   6 53w
Mulhouse .... 47 40N   7 20 E
Mull of Galloway,
   Pt. 54 40N   4 55w
Mull of Kintyre,
   Pt. 55 20N   5 45w
Mull, I. 56 27N   6 0w
Mullengudgery ... 31 43 S 147 29 E
Mullet, Pen. 54 10N   10 2w
Mullewa .... 28 29 S 115 30 E
Mullingar 53 31N   7 20w
Mullumbimby ..... 28 30 S 153 30 E
Multan .... 30 15N   71 30 E
Mulwala .... 35 59 S 146 0 E
Mumias .... 0 20N   34 29 E
Mun, R. .... 15 19N 105 31 E
Muna, I. .... 5 0 S 122 30 E
Munabao .... 25 45N   70 17 E
München .... 48 8N   11 33 E
Muncie 40 10N   85 20w
Münden .... 51 25N   9 42 E
Mundiwindi ...... 23 47 S 120 9 E
Mundo Novo ...... 11 50 S   40 29w
Mundrabilla ..... 31 52 S 127 51 E
Mungallala ...... 26 25 S 147 34 E
Mungana .... 17 8 S 144 27 E
Mungindi .... 28 58 S 149 1 E
Munhango .... 12 9 S   18 36 E
Munich=
   München ...... 48 8N   11 33 E
Muñoz Gamero,
   Pen. .... 52 30 S   73 5 E
Munster □ 52 20N   8 40w
Münster .... 51 58N   7 37 E
Muntadgin .... 31 48 S 118 30 E
Muntok .... 2 5 S 105 10 E
Muonio, R. ...... 67 48N   23 25 E
Mur, R. .... 46 18N   16 53 E
Murallón, Mt. ... 49 55 S   73 30w
Murangá .... 0 45 S   37 9 E
Muranisgar Mts. .. 0 30 S   35 0 E
Murashi .... 59 30N   49 0 E
Murchison,
   Australia .... 36 39 S 145 14 E
Murchison, N.Z. .. 41 49 S 172 21 E
Murchison, R. .... 26 1 S 117 6 E

Murcia 38 2N   1 10w
Murcia, Reg. 38 35N   1 50w
Mureş, R. .... 46 15N   20 13 E
Murfreesboro 35 50N   86 21w
Murgab .... 38 10N   73 59 E
Murgon .... 26 15 S 151 54 E
Muritz See ...... 53 25N   12 40 E
Murmansk .... 68 57N   33 10 E
Murom .... 55 35N   42 3 E
Muroran .... 42 25N 141 0 E
Murphysboro 37 50N   89 20w
Murray, Ky. 36 40N   88 20w
Murray, Utah 40 41N 111 58w
Murray, R. ...... 35 22 S 139 22 E
Murray Bridge .... 35 6 S 139 14 E
Murraysburg ..... 31 58 S   23 47 E
Murrayville ..... 35 16 S 141 11 E
Murree .... 33 56N   73 28 E
Murrin Murrin ... 28 50 S 121 45 E
Murrumbidgee, R. . 34 43 S 143 12 E
Murrurundi ...... 31 42 S 150 51 E
Murtoa .... 36 35 S 142 28 E
Murupara .... 38 30 S 178 40 E
Murwara .... 23 46N   80 28 E
Murwillumbah .... 28 18 S 153 27 E
Mürzzuschlag .... 47 36N   15 41 E
Musala, Mt. ..... 41 13N   23 37 E
Muscat=Masqat .. 23 37N   58 36 E
Muscatine 41 25N   91 5w
Mushao .... 2 2 S   29 20 E
Mushie .... 2 56 S   17 4 E
Mushin .... 6 32N   3 21 E
Muskegon 43 15N   86 17w
Muskegon
   Heights 43 12N   86 17w
Muskogee 35 50N   95 25w
Musmar .... 18 6N   35 40 E
Musoma .... 1 30 S   33 48 E
Musselburgh 55 57N   3 3w
Musters, L. ..... 45 20 S   69 25w
Muswellbrook .... 32 16 S 150 56 E
Mût .... 25 28N   28 58 E
Mutankiang ...... 44 35N 129 30 E
Muttaburra ...... 22 38 S 144 29 E
Mutton Bay 50 50N   59 2w
Muya .... 56 27N 115 39 E
Muzaffarabad .... 34 25N   73 30 E
Muzaffarnagar ... 29 26N   77 40 E
Muzaffarpur ..... 26 7N   85 32 E
Muzhi .... 65 25N   64 40 E

Muztagh, Mt. .... 36 30N   87 22 E
Mvadhi Ousye .... 1 13N   13 12 E
Mvomero .... 6 18 S   37 28 E
Mwanza, Tanzania . 2 30 S   32 58 E
Mwanza, Zaire ... 7 55 S   26 43 E
Mwaya .... 9 32 S   33 55 E
Mweka .... 4 50 S   21 40 E
Mweru, L. .... 9 0 S   28 45 E
Mwirasandu ...... 0 56 S   30 22 E
My Tho .... 10 29N 106 23 E
Myanaung .... 18 25N   95 10 E
Myaungmya .... 16 30N   95 0 E
Myeik Kyunzu .... 11 0N   98 0 E
Myingyan .... 21 30N   95 30 E
Myitkyina .... 25 30N   97 26 E
Mymensingh=
   Nasirabad .... 24 42N   90 30 E
Myrtle Creek 43 0N 123 0w
Myrtle Point 43 0N 124 4w
Mysore .... 12 17N   76 41 E
Mývatn, L. 65 36N   17 0w
Mzimvubu, R. .... 31 30 S   29 30 E

N

Na'an .... 31 53N   34 52 E
Naantali .... 60 27N   21 57 E
Naas 53 12N   6 40w
Nababeep .... 29 36 S   17 46 E
Nabadwip .... 23 34N   88 20 E
Nabenl .... 36 30N   10 51 E
Nabi Rubin ...... 31 56N   34 44 E
Naboomspruit .... 24 32 S   28 40 E
Nābulus .... 32 14N   35 15 E
Nachingwea ...... 10 49 S   38 49 E
Nackara .... 32 48 S 139 12 E
Nacogdoches 31 33N   95 30w
Nacozari 30 30N 109 50w
Nadiad .... 22 41N   72 56 E
Nadūshan .... 32 2N   53 35 E
Nadvoitsy .... 63 52N   34 15 E
Nadym .... 63 35N   72 42 E
Nafada .... 11 8N   11 20 E
Naga .... 13 38N 123 15 E
Nagaland □ ...... 26 0N   95 0 E
Nagano .... 36 40N 138 10 E
Nagano □ .... 36 15N 138 0 E

Nagaoka .... 32 27N 138 51 E
Nagappattinam ... 10 46N   79 51 E
Nagasaki .... 32 47N 129 50 E
Nagasaki □ ...... 3250⅛N 129 40 E
Nagato .... 36 15N 138 16 E
Nagaur .... 27 15N   73 45 E
Nagercoil .... 8 12N   77 33 E
Nagornyy .... 55 58N 124 57 E
Nagoya .... 35 10N 136 50 E
Nagpur .... 21 8N   79 10 E
Nagykanizsa ..... 46 28N   17 0 E
Nagykörös .... 47 2N   19 48 E
Naha .... 26 12N 127 40 E
Nahannai Butte ... 61 5N 123 30w
Nahariyya .... 33 1N   35 5 E
Nahavand .... 34 10N   48 30 E
Nahf .... 32 56N   35 18 E
Nahuel Huapi, L. . 41 0 S   71 32w
Naicam 52 30N 104 30w
Nain 56 34N   61 40w
Nainpur .... 22 26N   80 6 E
Nairn 57 35N   3 54w
Nairobi .... 1 17 S   36 48 E
Naivasha .... 0 40 S   36 30 E
Najafābād .... 32 40N   51 15 E
Najd, Reg. ...... 26 30N   42 0 E
Najibabad .... 29 40N   78 20 E
Nakamura .... 33 0N 133 0 E
Nakasongola ..... 1 19N   32 28 E
Nakhi Mubarak ... 24 10N   38 10 E
Nakhichevan ..... 39 14N   45 30 E
Nakhodka .... 43 10N 132 45 E
Nakhon Phanom ... 17 23N 104 43 E
Nakhon Ratchasima 14 59N 102 12 E
Nakhon Sawan .... 15 35N 100 12 E
Nakhon Si
   Thammarat .... 8 29N 100 0 E
Nakina 50 10N   86 40w
Nakskov .... 54 50N   11 8 E
Nakuru .... 0 15 S   35 5 E
Nakusp 50 20N 117 45w
Nal, R. .... 26 2N   65 19 E
Nalayh .... 47 43N 107 22 E
Nalchik .... 43 30N   43 33 E
Nalgonda .... 17 6N   79 15 E
Nallamalai Hills . 15 30N   78 50 E
Nālūt .... 31 54N   11 0 E
Nam Dinh .... 20 25N 106 5 E
Nam-Phan, Reg. .. 10 30N 106 0 E
Nam Tok .... 14 21N   99 0 E

Nam Tso, L. ..... 30 40N   90 30 E
Namaland, Reg. .. 29 43 S   19 5 E
Namangan .... 41 30N   71 30 E
Namapa .... 13 43 S   39 50 E
Namasagali ...... 1 2N   33 0 E
Namber .... 1 2 S 134 57 E
Nambour .... 26 38 S 152 49 E
Nambucca Heads .. 30 45 S 152 48 E
Namcha Barwa, Mt. 29 30N   95 10 E
Namib Des.=
   Namibwoestyn .. 22 30 S   15 0w
Namibia■=
   S.W. Africa ■ .. 22 0 S   18 0 E
Namibwoestyn .... 22 30 S   15 0w
Namlea .... 3 10 S 127 5 E
Nampa 43 40N 116 40w
Nampula .... 15 6 S   39 7 E
Namrole .... 3 46 S 126 46 E
Namsen, R. ...... 64 27N   11 28 E
Namsos .... 64 29N   11 30 E
Namtu .... 23 5N   97 28 E
Namur .... 50 27N   4 52 E
Namur □ .... 50 17N   5 0 E
Namutoni .... 18 49 S   16 55 E
Namwala .... 15 44 S   26 30 E
Namyung .... 25 15N 114 5 E
Nan .... 18 48N 100 46 E
Nan Shan, Mts. .. 38 30N   98 0 E
Nanaimo 49 10N 124 0w
Nanango .... 26 40 S 152 0 E
Nanao .... 37 0N 137 0 E
Nanchang .... 28 34N 115 48 E
Nancheng .... 27 30N 116 28 E
Nancheng=
   Hanchung ..... 33 10N 107 2 E
Nanching=
   Nanking ...... 32 10N 118 50 E
Nanchung .... 30 47N 105 59 E
Nancy .... 48 42N   6 12 E
Nanda Devi, Mt. .. 30 30N   80 30 E
Nander .... 19 10N   77 20 E
Nandi .... 17 25 S 176 50 E
Nandurbar .... 21 20N   74 15 E
Nandyal .... 15 30N   78 30 E
Nanga-Eboko ..... 4 40N   12 26 E
Nanga Parbat, Mt. 35 10N   74 35 E
Nangal Dam ...... 31 25N   76 38 E
Nangarhar .... 34 15N   70 30 E
Nankang .... 25 42N 114 35 E
Nanking .... 32 10N 118 50 E

Nankoku .... 33 39N 133 44 E
Nannine .... 26 51s 118 18 E
Nanning .... 22 51N 108 18 E
Nannup .... 33 59s 115 45 E
Nanping .... 26 45N 118 5 E
Nansei-Shotō, Is. .. 29 0N 129 0 E
Nanson .... 28 34s 114 46 E
Nantan .... 25 0N 107 35 E
Nantes 47 12N   1 33w
Nanticoke 41 12N 76 1w
Nanton 50 20N 113 50w
Nantou .... 23 57N 120 35 E
Nantucket I. 41 16N 70 3w
Nantung .... 32 0N 120 50 E
Nanuque 17 50s 40 21w
Nanyang .... 33 2N 112 35 E
Nanyuan .... 39 48N 116 23 E
Nanyuki .... 0 2N 37 4 E
Nao, C. de la ... 38 44N   0 14 E
Naoetsu .... 37 12N 138 10 E
Napa 38 18N 122 17w
Napanee 44 15N 77 0w
Napier .... 39 30s 176 56 E
Napier Broome, B. 14 0s 127 0 E
Napier Downs .... 16 20s 124 30 E
Naples=
  Nápoli .... 40 50N 14 5 E
Napo, R. 3 20s 72 40w
Napoleon 46 32N 99 49w
Nápoli .... 40 50N 14 5 E
Nara .... 34 40N 135 49 E
Nara .... 34 30N 136 0 E
Naracoorte ..... 36 50s 140 44 E
Narasapur ...... 16 26N 81 50 E
Narayanganj ..... 23 31N 90 33 E
Narayanpet ..... 16 45N 77 30 E
Narbonne .... 43 11N   3 0 E
Narembeen ...... 32 4s 118 24 E
Naretha .... 31 0s 124 50 E
Narmada, R. .... 21 35N 72 35 E
Narok .... 1 20s 33 30 E
Narrabri .... 30 19s 149 46 E
Narran, R. ..... 29 45s 147 20 E
Narrandera ..... 34 42s 146 31 E
Narrogin .... 32 58s 117 14 E
Narromine ...... 32 12s 148 12 E
Narsinghpur .... 22 54N 79 14 E
Naruto .... 35 36N 140 25 E
Narvik .... 68 28N 17 26 E
Narym .... 59 0N 81 58 E

Narymskoye ..... 49 10N 84 15 E
Naryn .... 41 30N 76 10 E
Nasarawa .... 8 32N   7 41 E
Naser, Buheiret en 23 0N 32 30 E
Nashua, Mont. ... 48 10N 106 25w
Nashua, N.H. 42 50N 71 25w
Nashville 36 12N 86 46w
Nasik .... 20 2N 73 50 E
Nasirabad,
  Bangladesh .... 26 15N 74 45 E
Nasirabad, Pak. .. 28 25N 68 25 E
Nassau 25 0N 77 30w
Nassau, B. 55 20s 68 0w
Nasser, L.=Naser,
  Buheiret en ... 23 0N 32 30 E
Nässjö .... 57 38N 14 45 E
Nastapoka Is. ... 57 0N 77 0w
Nat Kyizio ..... 14 55N 98 0 E
Natagaima 3 37N 75 6w
Natal, Brazil ... 5 47s 35 13w
Natal, Indonesia .. 0 35N 99 0 E
Natal .... 28 30s 30 30 E
Natashquan 50 14N 61 46w
Natashquan, R. .. 50 6N 61 49w
Natchez 31 35N 91 25w
Natchitoches 31 47N 93 4w
Natimuk .... 36 35s 141 59 E
Natitingou ..... 10 20N   1 26 E
National City ... 32 45N 117 7w
Natividade 11 43s 47 47w
Natron, L. ...... 2 20s 36 0 E
Natuna Besar,
  Kep. .... 4 0N 108 0 E
Natuna Selatan,
  Kep. .... 3 0N 109 55 E
Naumburg .... 51 10N 11 48 E
Naushahra ...... 33 9N 74 15 E
Nautanwa .... 27 26N 83 25 E
Navajo Res. 36 55N 107 30w
Navalcarnero 40 17N   4 5w
Navan=An Uaimh 53 39N   6 40w
Navarino, I. 55 0s 67 30w
Navarra, Reg. ... 42 40N   1 40w
Navassa, I. 18 30N 75 0w
Navoi .... 40 9N 65 22 E
Navojoa 27 0N 109 30w
Navolok .... 62 33N 39 57 E
Návpaktos ...... 38 23N 21 42 E
Navplion .... 37 33N 22 50 E
Navsari .... 20 57N 72 59 E

Nawabshah ...... 26 15N 68 25 E
Nawalgarh ...... 27 50N 75 15 E
Náxos, I. ...... 37 5N 25'30 E
Nāy Band .... 27 20N 52 40 E
Nayakhan .... 62 10N 159 0 E
Nayarit 22 0N 105 0w
Nazaré, Brazil .. 13 0s 39 0w
Nazareth, Israel .. 32 42N 35 17 E
Nazir Hat ...... 22 35N 91 55 E
Ndala .... 4 46s 33 16 E
N'Délé .... 8 25N 20 36 E
Ndendé .... 2 29s 10 46 E
Ndjamena .... 12 4N 15 8 E
Ndola .... 13 0s 28 34 E
Ndumbwe .... 10 14s 39 58 E
Ndungu .... 4 28s 38 4 E
Neagh, L. 54 35N   6 25w
Near Is. 53 0N 172 0w
Neath 51 39N   3 49w
Nebo 39 27N 90 47w
Nebraska 41 30N 100 0w
Nebraska City ... 40 40N 95 52w
Nebrodi, Monti .. 37 55N 14 35 E
Neckar, R. ..... 49 31N   8 26 E
Necochea 38 30s 58 50w
Needles 34 50N 114 35w
Neemuch .... 24 30N 74 50 E
Neenah 44 10N 88 30w
Neepawa 50 20N 99 30w
Nefta .... 33 53N   7 58 E
Neftyannyye
  Kamni .... 40 20N 50 55 E
Nefyn 52 57N   4 31w
Negaunee 46 30N 87 36w
Negoiu, Mt. .... 45 48N 24 32 E
Negombo .... 7 12N 79 50 E
Negotin .... 44 16N 22 37 E
Negra Pt. ...... 18 40N 120 50 E
Negra, Pta. 6 6s 81 10w
Negro, R., Arg. .. 41 2s 62 47w
Negro, R., Brazil . 3 10s 59 58w
Negros, I. ..... 10 0N 123 0 E
Nehbandān ...... 31 35N 60 5 E
Neikiang .... 29 35N 105 10 E
Neisse, R. ..... 52 4N 14 47 E
Neiva 2 56N 75 18w
Nekemte .... 9 4N 36 30 E
Neksø .... 55 4N 15 8 E
Nelkan .... 57 50N 136 15 E
Nellore .... 14 27N 79 59 E

Nelma .... 47 30N 139 0 E
Nelson, Canada .. 49 30N 117 20w
Nelson, N.Z. .... 41 18s 173 16 E
Nelson, U.K. 53 50N   2 14w
Nelson .... 42 11s 172 15 E
Nelson, Estrecho . 51 30s 75 0w
Nelson, R. 55 30N 96 50w
Nelson Forks ... 59 30N 124 0w
Nelspruit ...... 25 29s 30 59 E
Néma 16 40N   7 15w
Nemuro .... 43 20N 145 35 E
Nemuro-Kaikyō,
  Str. .... 43 30N 145 30 E
Nemuy .... 55 40N 135 55 E
Nenagh 52 52N   8 11w
Nenana 63 34N 149 7w
Nene, R. .... 52 48N   0 13 E
Neosho 35 59N 95 10w
Nepal .... 28 0N 84 30 E
Nepalganj ...... 28 0N 81 40 E
Nephi 39 43N 111 52w
Nerchinsk ...... 52 0N 116 39 E
Nerchinskiyzavod . 51 10N 119 30 E
Nerva 37 42N   6 30w
Nes Ziyyona 31 56N 34 48w
Nesher .... 32 45N 35 3 E
Ness, L. 57 15N   4 30w
Nesttun .... 60 19N   5 21 E
Netanya ...•.... 32 20N 34 51 E
Netherlands .. 52 0N   5 30 E
Nettilling L. ... 66 30N 71 0w
Neu Brandenburg . 53 33N 13 17 E
Neuchâtel ...... 47 0N   6 55 E
Neuchâtel, L. de . 46 53N   6 50 E
Neumünster ..... 54 4N   9 58 E
Neunkirchen .... 49 23N   7 6 E
Neuquén 38 0s 68 0w
Neustrelitz ..... 53 22N 13 4 E
Nevada 37 20N 94 40w
Nevada 39 20N 117 0w
Nevada, Sa. 37 3N   3 15w
Nevada de Sta.
  Marta, Sa. ... 10 55N 73 50w
Nevanka .... 56 45N 98 55 E
Nevers .... 47 0N   3 9 E
Nevertire ...... 31 50s 147 44 E
Nevis, I. 17 0N 62 30w
New Albany 38 20N 85 50w
New Amsterdam .. 6 15N 57 30w
New Bedford 41 40N 70 52w

New Bern 35 8N 77 3w
New Braunfels ... 29 43N 98 9w
New Brighton ... 43 29s 172 43 E
New Britain 41 41N 72 47w
New Britain, I. .. 6 0s 151 0 E
New Brunswick .. 40 30N 74 28w
New Brunswick . 46 50N 66 30w
New Bussa .... 9 55N   4 33 E
New Caledonia, I. . 21 0s 165 0 E
New Castile=
  Castilla la
  Nueva 39 45N   3 20w
New Castle, Ind. . 39 55N 85 23w
New Castle, Pa. .. 41 0N 80 20w
New Delhi ...... 28 37N 77 13 E
New Denver 50 0N 117 25w
New Forest, Reg... 50 53N   1 40w
New Glasgow 45 35s 62 36w
New Guinea, I. .. 5 0s 141 0 E
New Hampshire . 43 40N 71 40w
New Hanover .... 29 22s 30 31 E
New Haven 41 20N 72 54w
New Hebrides, I. .. 15 0s 168 0 E
New Iberia 30 2N 91 54w
New Ireland, I. .. 3 0s 151 30 E
New Jersey 39 50N 74 10w
New Kensington .. 40 36N 79 43w
New Liskeard ... 47 31N 79 41w
New London 41 23N 72 8w
New Mexico 34 30N 106 0w
New Norcia ..... 30 58s 116 13 E
New Norfolk .... 42 46s 147 2 E
New Orleans 30 0N 90 5w
New Philadelphia . 40 29N 81 25w
New Plymouth ... 39 4s 174 5 E
New Providence I. . 25 0N 77 30w
New Radnor 52 15N   3 10w
New Romney .... 50 59N   0 57 E
New South Wales . 33 0s 146 0 E
New Ulm 44 15N 94 30w
New Waterford ... 46 13N 60 4w
New Westminster . 49 10N 122 52w
New York 40 45N 74 0w
New York 42 40N 76 0w
New Zealand ... 40 0s 173 0 E
Newala .... 10 58s 39 10 E
Newark, U.K. ... 53 6N   0 48w
Newark, N.J. ... 40 41N 74 12w
Newark, N.Y. ... 43 2N 77 10w
Newberry 46 20N 85 32w

* Renamed Vanuatu

Newburgh	41 30N	74 1W
Newbury	51 24N	1 19W
Newburyport	42 48N	70 50W
Newcastle, Australia	32 52S	151 49 E
Newcastle, Canada	47 1N	65 38W
Newcastle, Eire	52 27N	9 3W
Newcastle, S.Africa	27 45S	29 58 E
Newcastle, N. Ireland	54 13N	5 54W
Newcastle, Tyne and Tees	54 59N	1 37W
Newcastle Emlyn	52 2N	4 29W
Newcastle Waters	17 30S	133 28 E
Newcastle-under-Lyme	53 2N	2 15W
Newdegate	33 17N	118 58 E
Newe Etan	32 30N	35 32 E
Newe Sha'anan	32 47N	34 59 E
Newe Zohar	31 9N	35 21 E
Newenham, C.	58 37N	162 12W
Newfoundland □	48 28N	56 0W
Newfoundland, I.	48 30N	56 0W
Newhaven	50 47N	0 4 E
Newman, Mt.	23 20S	119 34 E
Newmarket, Eire	52 13N	9 0W
Newmarket, U.K.	52 15N	0 23 E
Newnan	33 22N	84 48W
Newport, Gwent	51 35N	3 0W
Newport, I. of Wight	50 42N	1 18W
Newport, Ark.	35 38N	91 15W
Newport, Ky.	39 5N	84 23W
Newport, Oreg.	44 41N	124 2W
Newport, Rhode I.	41 13N	71 19W
Newport, Vt.	44 57N	72 17W
Newport Beach	33 40N	117 58W
Newport News	37 2N	76 54W
Newquay	50 24N	5 6W
Newry	54 10N	6 20W
Newry & Mourne □	54 10w	6 20W
Newton, Iowa	41 40N	93 3W
Newton, Kans.	38 2N	97 30W
Newton, Mass.	42 21N	71 10W
Newton, N.J.	41 3N	74 46W
Newton Abbot	50 32N	3 37W
Newton Stewart	54 57N	4 30W
Newtonmore	57 4N	4 7W
Newtown, Australia	34 30S	151 10 E
Newtown, U.K.	52 31N	3 19W
Newtownabbey □	54 40N	5 55W
Newtownards	54 37N	5 40W
Neya	58 21N	43 49 E
Neyshābūr	36 10N	58 20 E
Nezhin	51 5N	31 55 E
Ngala	12 15N	14 15 E
Ngami Depression	20 30S	22 46 E
Ngamo	19 3S	27 25 E
Nganjuk	7 32S	111 55 E
Ngaoundéré	7 15N	13 35 E
Ngapara	44 57S	170 46 E
Ngawi	7 24S	111 26 E
Ngerengere	6 47S	38 10 E
Ngomba	8 20S	32 53 E
Ngong	1 25S	36 39 E
Ngoring Nor, L.	34 50N	98 0 E
Ngorongoro Crater	3 11S	35 32 E
Ngudu	2 58S	33 25 E
Nguru	12 56N	10 29 E
Nguru Mts.	6 0S	37 30 E
Nha Trang	12 16N	109 10 E
Nhill	36 18S	141 40 E
Niagara Falls, Canada	43 7N	79 5W
Niagara Falls, U.S.A.	43 5N	79 0W
Niah	3 58S	113 46 E
Niamey	13 27N	2 6 E
Niangara	3 50N	27 50 E
Nias, I.	1 0N	97 40 E
Nicaragua ■	11 40N	85 30W
Nicastro	39 0N	16 18 E
Nice	43 42N	7 14 E
Nichinan	31 28N	131 26 E
Nicholson Ra.	27 12S	116 40 E
Nicobar Is.	9 0N	93 0 E
Nicola	50 8N	120 40W
Nicolet	46 17N	72 35W
Nicosia=Levkosia, Cyprus	35 10N	33 25 E
Nicoya, G. de	10 0N	85 0w
Nicoya, Pen. de	9 45S	85 40W
Nidd, R.	54 1N	1 12W
Nieder-Osterreich □	48 25N	15 40 E
Niedersachsen □	52 45N	9 0 E
Nienburg	52 38N	9 15 E
Nieuw Amsterdam	5 53N	55 5W
Nieuw Nickerie	6 0N	57 10W
Nièvre □	47 10N	5 40 E
Niğde	37 59N	34 42 E
Nigel	26 27S	28 25 E
Niger ■ R.	13 30N	10 0 E
Niger, R.	5 33N	6 33 E
Niger Delta	4 0N	5 30 E
Niger □	10 0N	5 30 E
Nigeria ■	8 30N	8 0 E
Nightcaps	45 57S	168 14 E
Niigata	37 58N	139 0 E
Niigata □	37 15N	138 45 E
Niihama	33 55N	133 10 E
Niihau, I.	21 55N	160 10w
Niimi	34 59N	133 28 E
Nijkerk	52 13N	5 30 E
Nijmegen	51 50N	5 52 E
Nike	6 26N	7 29 E
Nikiniki	9 40S	124 30 E
Nikki	9 58N	3 21 E
Nikolayev	46 58N	32 7 E
Nikolayevsk	50 10N	45 35 E
Nikolayevskna-Am	53 40N	140 50 E
Nikopol	47 35N	34 25 E
Nîl, Nahr en, R.	30 10N	31 6 E
Nîl el Abyad, R.	15 40N	32 30 E
Nîl el Azraq, R.	11 40N	32 30 E
Nîl el Azraq □	12 30N	34 30 E
Niland	33 16N	115 30w
Nile, R.= Nîl, Nahren, R.	30 10N	31 6 E
Niles	41 8N	80 40W
Nîmes	43 50N	4 23 E
Nimmitabel	36 29S	149 15 E
Nimneryskiy	58 0N	125 10 E
Nimule	3 32N	32 3 E
Ninety Mile Beach, The	38 30S	147 10 E
Nineveh	36 25N	43 10 E
Ningming	22 10N	107 59 E
Ningpo	29 50N	121 30 E
Ningsia Hui □	37 45N	106 0 E
Ningteh	26 45N	120 0 E
Ningwu	39 2N	112 15 E
Ninh Binh	20 15N	105 55 E
Ninove	50 51N	4 2 E
Niobrara, R.	42 45N	98 0W
Nioro	13 40N	15 50W
Niort	46 19N	0 29W
Nipawin	53 20N	104 0W
Nipawin Prov. Park	54 0N	104 40W
Nipigon	49 0N	88 17W
Nipigon, L.	49 40N	88 30W
Niquelandia	14 27S	48 27W
Nirasaki	35 42N	138 27 E
Niš	43 19N	21 58 E
Nisab	14 25N	46 29 E
Nishinomiya	34 45N	135 20 E
Niterói	22 52S	43 0W
Nith, R.	55 0N	3 5W
Nitra	48 19N	18 4 E
Nitra, R.	47 46N	18 10 E
Nivelles	50 35N	4 20 E
Nivernais, Reg.	47 0N	3 40 E
Nizamabad	18 45N	78 7 E
Nizamghat	28 20N	95 45 E
Nizhne Kolymsk	68 40N	160 55 E
Nizhne-Vartovskoye	60 56N	76 38 E
Nizhneangarsk	56 0N	109 30 E
Nizhneudinsk	55 0N	99 20 E
Nizhniy Tagil	57 45N	60 0 E
Nizip	37 1N	37 46 E
Nizké Tatry, Mts.	48 55N	20 0 E
Nizzanim	31 42N	34 37 E
Njombe	9 0S	34 35 E
Nkambe	6 35N	10 40 E
Nkawkaw	6 36N	0 49W
Nkhata Bay	11 33S	34 16 E
Nkhota Kota	12 55S	34 15 E
Nkonge	0 15S	31 10 E
Nkongsamba	4 55N	9 55 E
Noakhali=Maijdi	22 48N	91 10 E
Noatak	67 34N	162 59W
Nobeoka	32 36N	131 41 E
Nocera Inferiore	40 45N	14 37 E
Noda	47 30N	142 5 E
Nogales, Mexico	31 36N	94 29W
Nogales, U.S.A.	31 33N	110 59W
Nõgata	33 48N	130 54 E
Noggerup	33 32S	116 5 E
Noginsk	55 50N	38 25 E
Noire, Mts.	48 11N	3 40W
Noirmoutier, Î. de	46 58N	2 10W
Nok Kundi	28 50N	62 45 E
Nokhuysk	60 0N	117 45 E
Nome	64 30N	165 30W
Nonda	20 40S	142 28 E
Nong Khai	17 50N	102 46 E
Noonamah	12 38S	131 4 E
Noondoo	28 35S	148 30 E
Noord Beveland, I.	51 45N	3 50 E
Noord Brabant □	51 40N	5 0 E
Noord Holland □	52 30N	4 45 E
Noordoost-Polder	52 45N	5 45 E
Noordwijk	52 14N	4 26 E
Nootka I.	49 40N	126 50W
Noranda	48 20N	79 0 E
Nord □	50 15N	3 30 E
Nord-Ostsee Kanal	54 5N	9 15 E
Nordegg	52 29N	116 5W
Nordkapp	71 11N	25 48 E
Nordland □	65 40N	13 0 E
Nordrhein Westfalen □	51 45N	7 30 E
Nordvik	73 40N	110 57 E
Nore, R.	52 25N	6 58W
Norfolk, Nebr.	42 3N	97 25W
Norfolk, Va.	36 52N	76 15W
Norfolk □	52 39N	1 0 E
Norfolk I.	28 58S	168 3 E
Norilsk	69 20N	88 0 E
Normal	40 30N	89 0W
Norman	35 12N	97 30W
Norman Wells	65 40N	126 45W
Normandie, Reg.	48 45N	0 10 E
Normandin	48 49N	72 31W
Normandy, Reg.= Normandie, Reg.	48 45N	0 10 E
Normanton	17 40S	141 10 E
Nornalup	35 0S	116 49 E
Norquinco	41 51S	70 55W
Norrbotten □	66 45N	23 0 E
Nørresundby	57 5N	9 52 E
Norristown	40 9N	75 15W
Norrköping	58 37N	16 11 E
Norrland, Reg.	64 25N	18 0 E
Norrtälje	59 46N	18 42 E
Norseman	32 8S	121 43 E
Norsk	52 30N	130 0 E
Norte, C. do	1 40N	49 55W
North, C.	34 23S	173 4 E
North I.	38 0S	176 0 E
North Adams	42 42N	73 6W
North America	45 0N	100 0W
North Battleford	52 50N	108 10W
North Bay	46 20N	79 30W
North Belcher Is.	56 30N	79 0W
North Bend, Canada	49 50N	121 35W
North Bend, Oreg.	43 28N	124 7W
North Berwick	56 4N	2 44W
North Borneo□=		

Sabah □	6 0N	117 0 E
North Carolina □	35 30N	80 0w
North Channel	55 0N	5 30w
North Chicago	42 19N	87 50w
North Dakota □	47 30N	100 0w
North Dandalup	32 31s	115 58 E
North Down □	54 40N	5 45w
North Downs	51 17N	0 30w
North East Frontier Agency= Arunachal Pradesh	28 0N	95 0 E
North Esk, R.	56 54N	2 38w
North European Plain	55 0N	25 0 E
North Foreland, Pt.	51 22N	1 28 E
North Horr	3 20N	37 8 E
North Kamloops	50 40N	120 25w
North Korea ■	40 0N	127 0 E
North Lakhimpur	27 15N	94 10 E
North Magnetic Pole	76 5N	101 3w
North Minch	58 5N	5 55w
North Platte	41 10N	100 50w
North Ronaldsay, I.	59 20N	2 30w
North Saskatchewan, R.	53 15N	105 6w
North Sea	55 0N	5 0 E
North Sydney	46 12N	60 21w
North Tonawanda	43 5N	78 50w
N.-Trøndelag □	64 30N	12 30 E
North Truchas Pk.	36 0N	105 30w
North Tyne, R.	54 59N	2 8w
North Uist, I.	57 40N	7 15w
North Vancouver	49 25N	123 20w
North Village	32 15N	64 45w
North Walsham	52 49N	1 22 E
North West, C.	21 45s	114 9 E
North West Highlands, Mts.	57 35N	5 2w
North West Territories □	65 0N	100 0w
North York Moors	54 25N	0 50w
North Yorkshire □	54 10N	1 25w
Northallerton	54 20N	1 26w
Northam	31 35s	116 42 E
Northampton, Australia	28 21s	114 33 E
Northampton, U.K.	52 14N	0 54w
Northampton, Mass.	42 22N	72 39w
Northampton □	52 16N	0 55w
Northampton Downs	24 35s	145 48 E
Northcliffe	34 36s	116 7 E
Northern □	9 0N	1 30w
Northern Circars, Reg.	17 30N	82 30 E
Northern Ireland □	54 45N	7 0w
Northern Mid-Atlantic Ridge	30 0N	40 0w
Northern Rhodesia■= Zambia ■	15 0s	28 0 E
Northern Territory □	16 0s	133 0 E
Northfield	44 37N	93 10w
Northumberland □	55 12N	2 0w
Northumberland, Is.	21 45s	150 20 E
Northumberland Str.	46 20N	64 0w
Northwich	53 16N	2 30w
Norton	17 52s	30 40 E
Norton Sd.	64 0N	165 0w
Norwalk, Conn.	41 7N	73 27w
Norwalk, Ohio	41 15N	82 37w
Norway ■	67 0N	11 0 E
Norway House	53 55N	98 50w
Norwegian Dependency	75 0s	15 0 E
Norwegian Sea	66 0N	1 0 E
Norwich, U.K.	52 38N	1 17 E
Norwich, N.Y.	42 32N	75 30w
Nosok	70 10N	82 20 E
Nosratabad	29 55N	60 0 E
Noss Hd.	58 29N	3 4w
Nossob, R.	26 55s	20 37 E
Nosy Bé, I.	13 20s	48 15 E
Nosy-Varika	20 35s	48 32 E
Noteć R.	52 44N	15 26 E
Notikewin	57 15N	117 5w
Noto	36 52N	15 4 E
Notre Dame B.	49 45N	55 30w
Notre Dame de Koartac=Koartac	60 55N	69 40w
Notre Dame d'Ivugivik= Ivugivik	62 20N	78 0w
Nottawasaga B.	44 40N	80 30w
Nottingham	52 57N	1 10w
Nottinghamshire □	53 10N	1 0w
Nouadhibou	21 0N	17 0w
Nouakchott	18 20N	15 50w
Nouméa	22 17s	166 30 E
Noupoort	31 10s	24 57 E
Nouveau Comptoir	53 2N	78 55w
Nova Cruz	6 28s	35 25w
Nova Friburgo	22 10s	42 30w
Nova Granada	20 29s	49 19w
Nova Lima	20 5s	44 0w
Nova Lisboa= Huambo	12 42s	15 54 E
Nova Scotia □	45 10N	63 0w
Nova Sofala	20 7s	34 48 E
Nova Venecia	18 45s	40 24 E
Novara	45 27N	8 36 E
Novaya Ladoga	60 7N	32 16 E
Novaya Lyalya	58 50N	60 35 E
Novaya Sibir, Os.	75 10N	150 0 E
Novaya Zemlya, I.	75 0N	56 0 E
Nové Zámky	47 59N	18 11 E
Novgorod	58 30N	31 25 E
Novi-Sad	45 18N	19 52 E
* Novo Redondo	11 10s	13 48 E
Novocherkassk	47 27N	40 5 E
Novokazalinsk	45 40N	61 40 E
Novokiybyshevsk	53 7N	49 58 E
Novo-kuznetsk	54 0N	87 10 E
Novomoskovsk	54 5N	38 15 E
Novorossiyk	44 43N	37 52 E
Novoshakhtinsk	47 39N	39 58 E
Novosibirsk	55 0N	83 5 E
Novosibirskiye Os.	75 0N	140 0 E
Novotroitsk	51 10N	58 15 E
Novouzensk	50 32N	48 17 E
Novska	45 19N	17 0 E
Now Shahr	36 40N	51 40 E
Nowa Nowa	37 44s	148 3 E
Nowgong	26 20N	92 50 E
Nowra	34 53s	150 35 E
Nowy Sącz	49 40N	20 41 E
Nowy Tomyśl	52 19N	16 10 E
Noyon	49 34N	3 0 E
Nsanje	16 55s	35 12 E
Nsawam	5 50N	0 24w
Nsukka	7 0N	7 50 E
‡ Nuanetsi	21 22s	30 45 E
‡ Nuanetsi, R.	22 40s	31 50 E
† Nuatja	7 0N	1 10 E
Nubian Des.	21 30N	33 30 E
Nûbîya, Es Sahrâ en	21 30N	33 30 E
Nueva Rosita	28 0N	101 20w
Nueve de Julio	35 30s	60 50w
Nuevitas	21 30N	77 20w
Nuevo, G.	43 0s	64 30w
Nuevo Laredo	27 30N	99 40w
Nuevo León □	25 0N	100 0w
Nuhaka	39 3s	177 45 E
Nukheila	19 1N	26 21 E
Nukus	42 20N	59 40 E
Nulato	64 43N	158 6w
Nullagine	21 53s	120 6 E
Nullarbor	31 26s	130 55 E
Nullarbor Plain	31 20s	128 0 E
Numan	9 29N	12 3 E
Numata	36 38N	139 3 E
Numazu	35 7N	138 51 E
Numurkah	36 0s	145 26 E
Nuneaton	52 32N	1 29w
Nunivak I.	60 0N	166 0w
Nunkiang	49 11N	125 12 E
Nunspeet	52 21N	5 45 E
Núoro	40 20N	9 20 E
Nuremburg= Nürnberg	49 26N	11 5 E
Nürnberg	49 26N	11 5 E
Nusa Tenggara Barat	8 50s	117 30 E
Nusa Tenggara Timur □	9 30s	122 0 E
Nushki	29 35N	65 59 E
Nutak	57 30N	61 59w
Nuweveldberge	32 10s	21 45 E
Nyabing	33 30s	118 7 E
Nyahanga	2 20s	33 37 E
Nyahua	5 25s	33 23 E
Nyahururu	0 2N	36 27 E
Nyakanazi	3 2s	31 10 E
Nyakanyazi	1 10s	31 13 E
Nyakrom	5 40N	0 50w
Nyálâ	12 2N	24 58 E
Nyalikungu	2 35s	33 17 E
Nyanguge	2 30s	33 12 E
Nyanza	2 20s	29 42 E
Nyasa, L.	12 0s	34 30 E
Nybro	56 44N	15 55 E
Nyda	66 40N	73 10 E
Nyenchen, Ra.	30 30N	95 0 E
Nyeri	0 23s	36 56 E
Nyika Plat.	10 30s	36 0 E
Nyíregyháza	48 0N	21 47 E
Nykarleby	63 32N	22 31 E
Nykøbing	54 56N	11 52 E
Nykøping	58 45N	17 0 E
Nylstroom	24 42s	28 22 E
Nynäshamn	58 54N	17 57 E
Nyngan	31 30s	147 8 E
Nyong, R.	3 17N	9 54 E
Nyora	38 20s	145 41 E
Nysa	50 40N	17 22 E
Nysa, R.	52 4N	14 46 E
Nyurba	63 17N	118 20 E
Nzega	4 10s	33 12 E
Nzérékoré	7 49N	8 48w

O

Oahe Dam	44 28N	100 25w
Oahe Res.	45 30N	100 15w
Oahu, I.	21 30N	158 0w
Oak Creek	40 15N	106 59w
Oak Park	41 55N	87 45w
Oak Ridge	36 1N	84 5w
Oakdale	30 50N	92 28w
Oakengates	52 42N	2 29w
Oakesdale	47 11N	117 9w
Oakey	27 25s	151 43 E
Oakham	52 40N	0 43w
Oakland	37 50N	122 18w
Oakleigh	37 54s	145 6 E
Oakover, R.	20 43s	120 33 E
Oakridge	43 47N	122 31w
Oakville, Man.	49 56N	97 58w
Oamaru	45 6s	170 58 E
Oaxaca □	17 0N	97 0w
Ob, R.	62 40N	66 0 E
Oba	49 4N	84 7w
Oban	56 25N	5 30w
Obed	53 30N	117 10w
Ober-Österreich □	48 10N	14 0 E
Oberhausen	51 28N	6 50 E
Obiaruku	5 51N	6 9 E
Obihiro	42 55N	143 10 E
Obluchye	49 10N	130 50 E
Obskaya Guba	70 0N	73 0 E
Obuasi	6 17N	1 40w
Obudu	6 40N	9 10 E

* *Renamed Sumbe*
‡ *Renamed Mwenezi*
† *Notsé*

Ocala 29 11N 82 5w
Ocaña, Col. 8 15N 73 20w
Ocaña, Sp. 39 55N 3 30w
Occidental, Cord. . 5 0N 76 0w
Ocean City 39 18N 74 34w
Ocean Falls 52 25N 127 40w
Oceanlake 45 0N 124 0w
Oceanside 33 13N 117 26w
Ochil Hills 56 14N 3 40w
Oconto 44 52N 87 53w
Ocatlán 20 21N 102 42w
Ocumare del Tuy .. 10 7N 66 46w
Ocussi .... 9 20s 124 30 E
Ôda 5 50N 1 5w
Odádahraun 65 5N 17 0w
Odawara .... 35 20N 139 6 E
Odda .... 60 3N 6 35 E
Oddur .... 4 0N 43 35 E
Ödemiş .... 38 15N 28 0 E
Odendaalsrus ..... 27 48s 26 43 E
Odense .... 55 22N 10 23 E
Oder=Odra R. ... 53 33N 14 38 E
Oder Haff .... 53 46N 14 14 E
Odessa .... 46 30N 30 45 E
Odessa 31 51N 102 23w
Odienné 9 30N 7 34w
Odra, R. .... 53 33N 14 38 E
Odzi .... 18 58s 32 23 E
Oeiras 7 0s 42 8w
Oelwein 42 39N 91 55w
Oenpelli .... 12 20s 133 4 E
Offa □ .... 8 13N 4 42 E
Offaly □ 53 20N 7 30w
Offenbach ...... 50 6N 8 46 E
Ofir 41 30N 8 52w
Ogahalla 50 6N 85 51w
Ôgaki .... 35 25N 136 35 E
Ogallala 50 6N 85 51w
Ogbomosho ...... 8 1N 3 29 E
Ogden 41 13N 112 1w
Ogdensburg 44 40N 75 27w
Oglio, R. .... 45 15N 10 15 E
Ogmore .... 22 37s 149 35 E
Ogoja .... 6 38N 8 39 E
Ogoki 51 35N 86 0w
Ogooué, R. ..... 1 0s 10 0 E
Ogun □ .... 6 55N 3 38 E
Oguta .... 5 44N 6 44 E
Ogwashi-Uku .... 6 15N 6 30 E
O'Higgins, L. ... 49 0s 72 40w

Ohakune .... 39 24s 175 24 E
Ohio, R. 38 0N 86 0w
Ohio □ 40 20N 83 0w
Ohre, R. .... 50 10N 12 30 E
Ohrid .... 41 8N 20 52 E
Ohrid, L.=
  Ohridsko, J. ... 41 8N 20 52 E
Ohridsko, J. .... 41 8N 20 52 E
Ohrigstad .... 24 41s 30 36 E
Oiapoque 3 50N 51 50w
Oil City 41 26N 79 40w
Oise □ .... 49 28N 2 30 E
Ôita .... 33 15N 131 36 E
Ojos del Salado,
  Cerro, Mt. 27 0s 68 40w
Okahandja ...... 22 0s 16 59 E
Okanagan 48 24N 119 24w
Okarito .... 43 15s 170 9 E
Okavango, R. ... 17 40s 19 30 E
Okavango Swamps 19 30s 23 0 E
Okaya .... 36 0N 138 10 E
Okayama .... 34 40N 133 54 E
Okayama □ ..... 35 0N 133 50 E
Okazaki .... 34 36N 137 0 E
Oke-Iho .... 8 1N 3 18 E
Okeechobee, L. .. 21 0N 80 50w
Okefenokee Swamp. 30 50N 82 15w
Okehampton 50 44N 4 1w
Okene .... 7 32N 6 11 E
Okha .... 53 40N 143 0 E
Okhotsk .... 59 20N 143 10 E
Okhotsk, Sea of .. 55 0N 145 0 E
Okhotskiy
  Perevoz ...... 61 52N 135 35 E
Oknotsko
  kolymskoy ..... 63 0N 157 0 E
Oki-Shotō ...... 36 15N 133 15 E
Okiep .... 29 39s 17 53 E
Okigwi .... 5 52N 7 20 E
Okija .... 5 54N 6 55 E
Okinawa, I. ..... 26 40N 128 0 E
Okinawa-guntō, Is. 26 0N 127 30 E
Okitipupa ...... 6 31N 4 50 E
Oklahoma □ 35 20N 97 30w
Oklahoma City ... 35 25N 97 30w
Okmulgee 35 38N 96 0w
Okrika .... 4 47N 7 4 E
Oktyabriskoy
  Revolyutsii Os... 79 30N 97 0 E
Oktyabrski ...... 53 11N 48 40 E

Okura .... 43 55s 168 55 E
Okushiri-To, I. ... 42 15N 139 30 E
Okuta .... 9 14N 3 12 E
Öland, I. .... 56 45N 16 50 E
Olary .... 32 17s 140 19 E
Olathe 38 50N 94 50w
Olavarría 36 55s 60 20w
Ólbia .... 40 55N 9 30 E
Old Castille=
  Castilla la Vieja . 39 45N 3 20w
Old Crow 67 35N 139 50w
Old Factory 52 36N 78 43w
Old Town 45 0N 68 50w
Oldcastle 53 46N 7 10w
Oldeani .... 3 25s 35 35 E
Oldenburg ...... 53 10N 8 10 E
Oldenzaal ...... 52 19N 6 53 E
Olds 51 50N 114 10w
Olean 42 8N 78 25w
Olekminsk ...... 60 40N 120 30 E
Olenegorsk ..... 68 9N 33 15 E
Olenek .... 68 20N 112 30 E
Oléron, Î. d' 45 55N 1 15w
Oleśnica .... 51 13N 17 22 E
Olga .... 43 50N 135 0 E
Olga, Mt. ...... 25 20s 130 40 E
Olifants, R. 24 10s 32 40s
Olimbos, Oros ... 40 6N 22 23 E
Oliver 49 20N 119 30w
Ollague 21 15s 68 10w
Olney 38 40N 88 0w
Olomouc .... 49 38N 17 12 E
Olovyannaya .... 50 50N 115 10 E
Olsztyn .... 53 48N 20 29 E
Olt, R. .... 43 50N 24 40 E
Oltenita .... 44 7N 26 42 E
Olympia 47 0N 122 58w
Olympic Mts. 48 0N 124 0w
Olympic Nat. Park 47 35N 123 30w
Olympus Mt. 47 52N 123 40w
Omagh 54 36N 7 20w
Omagh □ 54 35N 7 20w
Omaha 41 15N 96 0w
Omak 48 25N 119 24w
Oman ■ .... 23 0N 58 0 E
Oman, G. of .... 24 30N 58 30 E
Omaruru .... 21 26s 16 0 E
Omate 16 45s 71 0w
Ombai, Selat, Str . 8 30s 124 50 E
Omdurmân ...... 15 40N 32 28 E

Omez .... 32 22N 35 0 E
Ōmiya .... 35 54N 139 38 E
Omo, R. .... 8 48N 37 14 E
Omsk .... 55 0N 73 38 E
Ōmura .... 33 8N 130 0 E
Ōmuta .... 33 0N 130 26 E
Onda 39 55N 0 17w
Ondangua ...... 17 57s 16 4 E
Ondo .... 7 4N 4 47 E
Ondo □ .... 7 0N 5 5 E
Ondörhaan ...... 47 22N 110 31 E
Onega .... 64 0N 38 10 E
Onega, R. ...... 63 0N 39 0 E
Onehunga ...... 36 55N 174 30 E
Oneida 43 5N 75 40w
Onezhskaya Guba . 64 30N 37 0 E
Onezhskoye, Oz... 62 0N 35 30 E
Ongarue .... 38 42s 175 19 E
Ongerup .... 33 58s 118 29 E
Ongole .... 15 33N 80 2 E
Onilahy, R. ..... 23 34s 43 45 E
Onitsha .... 6 6N 6 42 E
Onoda .... 34 2N 131 10 E
Onslow .... 21 40s 115 0 E
Onstwedde ..... 52 2N 7 4 E
Ontake-San, Mt. . 35 50N 137 15 E
Ontario 34 2N 117 40w
Ontario, L. 43 40N 78 0w
Ontario □ 52 0N 88 10w
Oodnadatta ..... 27 33s 135 30 E
Ooldea .... 30 27s 131 50 E
Oorindi .... 20 40s 141 1 E
Oostende ...... 51 15N 2 50 E
Oosterhout ..... 51 38N 4 51 E
Oosterschelde, R. . 51 30N 4 0 E
Ootacamund .... 11 30N 76 44 E
Opala, U.S.S.R. .. 52 15N 156 15 E
Opala, Zaïre ..... 0 37s 24 0 E
Opari .... 2 56N 32 0 E
Opava .... 49 57N 17 58 E
Opelousas 30 35N 92 0w
Ophir 63 10N 156 31w
Opi .... 6 36N 7 28 E
Opobo .... 4 35N 7 34 E
Opole .... 50 42N 17 58 E
Oporto=Pôrto ... 41 8N 8 40w
Opotiki .... 38 1s 177 19 E
Opp 31 19N 86 13w

Oppland □ ...... 61 15N 9 30 E
Optic Lake 54 46N 101 13w
Opua .... 35 19s 174 9 E
Opunake .... 39 26s 173 52 E
Or Yehuda ...... 32 2N 34 50 E
Oradea .... 47 2N 21 58 E
Öraefajökull, Mt... 64 2N 16 15w
Orai .... 25 58N 79 30 E
Orán 23 10s 64 20w
Oran 35 37N 0 39w
Orange, Australia . 33 15s 149 7 E
Orange, Fr. ..... 44 8N 4 47 E
Orange, U.S.A. ... 30 0N 93 40w
Orange=Oranje, R. 33 38s 18 0 E
Orange, C. 4 20N 51 30w
Orange Free
  State .... 28 30s 27 0 E
Orange Walk 17 15N 88 47w
Orangeburg 33 27N 80 53w
Orangeville 43 55N 80 5w
Oranienburg .... 52 45N 13 15 E
Oranje, R. ...... 28 41s 16 28 E
Oranje-Vrystaat □ 28 30s 27 0 E
Oranjemund .... 28 32s 16 29 E
Orapa .... 24 13s 25 25 E
Orbetello .... 42 26N 11 11 E
Orbost .... 37 40s 148 29 E
Orchy, Bridge of . 56 30N 4 46w
Ord, Mt. .... 17 20s 125 34 E
Ord, R. .... 15 30s 128 21 E
Ord of Caithness . 58 35N 3 37w
Ord River ...... 17 23s 128 51 E
Ordu .... 40 55N 37 53 E
Ordzhonkidze .... 43 0N 44 35 E
Ore Mts.=
  Erzgebirge .... 50 25N 13 0 E
Örebro .... 59 20N 15 18 E
Örebro □ .... 59 27N 15 0 E
Oregon □ 44 0N 120 0w
Oregon City 45 21N 122 35w
Orekhovo-Zuyevo . 55 50N 38 55 E
Orel .... 52 59N 36 5 E
Orem 40 27N 111 45w
Orenburg .... 51 45N 55 6 E
Orense 42 19N 7 55w
Orepuki .... 46 19s 167 46 E
Orford Ness, C. .. 52 6N 1 31 E
Orient Bay 49 20N 88 10w
Oriental, Cord. ... 5 0N 74 0w
Orihuela 38 7N 0 55w

Orillia 44 40N 79 24w
Orinoco, R. 8 37N 62 15w
Orion 49 28N 110 49w
Orissa □ .... 21 0N 85 0 E
Oristano .... 39 54N   8 35 E
Oristano, G. di .. 39 50N   8 22 E
Orizaba 18 50N 97 10w
Orkanger .... 63 18N   9 52 E
Orkla, R. .... 63 18N   9 50 E
Orkney .... 26 42s 26 40 E
Orkney □ 59 0N   3 0w
Orland 39 46N 120 10w
Orlando 28 30N 81 25w
Orléanais, Reg. .. 48 0N   2 0 E
Orléans, Fr. ..... 47 54N   1 52 E
Orleans, I. d' 46 54N 70 58w
Orléansville = El
  Asnam .... 36 10N   1 20 E
Orlik .... 52 30N 99 55 E
Ormara .... 25 16N 64 33 E
Ormoc .... 11 0N 124 37 E
Ormond .... 38 33s 177 56 E
Ormskirk 53 35N   2 54w
Orne □ .... 48 40N   0 0 E
Örnsköldsvik ..... 63 17N 18 40 E
Orocué 4 48N 71 20w
Orodo .... 5 34N   7 4 E
Oromocto 45 54N 66 37w
Oron, Israel ..... 30 55N 35 1 E
Oron, Nigeria .... 4 48N   8 14 E
Orós 6 15s 38 55w
Oroville 39 40N 121 30w
Ororoo .... 32 44s 138 37 E
Orsha .... 54 30N 30 25 E
Orsk .... 51 20N 58 34 E
Orşova .... 44 41N 22 25 E
Ortegal, C. 43 43N   7 52w
Orthez 43 29N   0 48w
Ortigueira 43 40N   7 50w
Ortles, Mt. ...... 46 31N 10 33 E
Ortona .... 42 21N 14 24 E
Oruro 18 0s 67 19w
Orvieto .... 42 43N 12 8 E
Orwell, R. .... 51 57N   1 17 E
Osa, Pen. de 8 0N 84 0w
Osage, R. 38 35N 91 57w
Ōsaka .... 34 40N 135 30 E
Ōsaka □ .... 34 40N 135 30 E
Osborne 39 30N 98 45w
Osceola 35 40N 90 0w

Oshawa 43 50N 78 45w
Oshikango .... 17 9s 16 10 E
Oshkosh 44 3N 88 35w
Oshogbo .... 7 48N   4 37 E
Osijek .... 45 34N 18 41 E
Osipenko=
  Berdyansk ..... 46 45N 36 49 E
Oskaloosa 41 18N 92 40w
Oskarshamn ...... 57 15N 16 27 E
Oslo .... 59 55N 10 45 E
Oslofjorden ...... 58 30N 10 0 E
Osmaniye .... 37 5N 36 10 E
Osnabrück .... 52 16N   8 2 E
Osorio 29 53s 50 17w
Osorno 40 25s 73 0w
Oss .... 51 46N   5 32 E
Ossa, Mt., Austral. 41 54s 146 0 E
Ossa, Mt., Greece . 39 47N 22 42 E
Ossining 41 9N 73 50w
Ostend=Oostende . 51 15N   2 50 E
Österdalälven, R.. 60 33N 15 8 E
Östergötlands □ .. 58 24N 15 34 E
Östersund .... 63 10N 14 38 E
Østfold □ .... 59 25N 11 25 E
Ostfriesische Is. .. 53 45N   7 15 E
Ostia .... 41 43N 12 17 E
Ostrava .... 49 51N 18 18 E
Ostróda .... 53 42N 19 58 E
Ostrołeka .... 53 4N 21 38 E
Ostrów
  Wielkopolski .. 51 39N 17 49 E
Ostrowiec-
  Swietokrzyski .. 50 57N 21 23 E
Ōsumi-Kaikyo,
  Str. .... 30 55N 131 0 E
Ōsumi-Shotō, Is. . 30 30N 130 45 E
Osuna 37 14N   5 8w
Oswego 43 29N 76 30w
Oswestry 52 52N   3 3w
Otago □ .... 44 45s 169 10 E
Ōtake .... 34 27N 132 25 E
Otaki .... 40 45s 175 10 E
Otaru .... 43 13N 141 0 E
Otavalo 0 20N 78 20w
Othello 46 53N 119 8w
Otira Gorge ...... 42 53s 171 33 E
Otjiwarongo ...... 20 30s 16 33 E
Otorohanga .... 38 11s 175 12 E
Otranto .... 40 9N 18 28 E
Otranto, C. d' .... 40 7N 18 30 E

Otranto, Str. of ... 40 15N 18 40 E
Ōtsu .... 42 35N 143 40 E
Ottawa, Canada .. 45 27N 75 42w
Ottawa, Ill. 41 20N 88 55w
Ottawa, Kans 38 40N 95 10w
Ottawa Is. 59 50N 80 0w
Ottawa, R. 45 20N 73 58w
Otter Rapids 55 42N 104 46w
Ottumwa 41 0N 92 25w
Otu .... 8 14N   3 22 E
Otukpa .... 7 9N   7 41 E
Oturkpo .... 7 10N   8 15 E
Otway, B. 53 30s 74 0w
Otway, C. .... 38 52s 143 31 E
Otway, Seno de .. 53 5s 71 30w
Otwock .... 52 5N 21 20 E
Ouagadougou 12 25N   1 30w
Ouahigouya 13 40N   2 25w
Ouallene .... 24 41N   1 11 E
Ouargla .... 31 59N   5 25 E
Ouarzazate 30 55N   6 55w
Oubangi, R. ...... 0 30s 17 42 E
Oudenaarde ...... 50 50N   3 37 E
Oudtshoorn ...... 33 35s 22 14 E
Oueme, R. .... 6 29N   2 32 E
Ouessant, I. d' ... 48 28N   5 6w
Ouesso .... 1 37N 16 5 E
Ouezzane 34 51N   5 42w
Ouidah .... 6 25N   2 0 E
Oujda 34 41N   1 45w
Ouled Djellal .... 34 28N   5 2 E
Oulu .... 65 1N 25 29 E
Oulu □ .... 64 36N 27 20 E
Oulujärvi, L. ..... 64 25N 27 0 E
Our, R. .... 49 53N   6 18 E
Ouricuri 7 53s 40 5w
Ouro Prêto 20 20s 43 30w
Ouse .... 42 25s 146 42 E
Ouse, R.,
  E. Sussex ..... 50 47N   0 3 E
Ouse, R.,
  N. Yorks 53 42N   0 41w
Outjo .... 20 5s 16 7 E
Outlook 51 30N 107 0w
Ouyen .... 35 1s 142 22 E
Ovalau, I. .... 17 40s 178 48 E
Ovalle 30 33s 71 18w
Ovamboland, Reg. 17 20s 16 30 E
Ovar .... 40 51N   8 40 E
Over Flakkee, I. .. 51 45N   4 5 E

Overijssel □ ...... 52 25N   6 35 E
Overpelt .... 51 12N   5 20 E
Oviedo 43 25N   5 50w
Owaka .... 46 27s 169 40 E
Owase .... 34 7N 136 5 E
Owatonna 44 3N 93 17w
Owen Falls .... 0 30N 33 5 E
Owen Sound 44 35N 80 55w
Owendo .... 0 17N   9 30 E
Owensboro 37 40N 87 5w
Owerri .... 5 29N   7 0 E
Owo .... 7 18N   5 30 E
Owosso 43 0N 84 10w
Oxelösund .... 58 43N 17 15 E
Oxford, U.K. 51 45N   1 15w
Oxford, N.C. 36 19N 78 36w
Oxford □ 51 45N   1 15w
Oxford House 54 46N 95 16w
Oxnard 34 10N 119 14w
Oyama .... 36 18N 139 48 E
Oyem .... 1 37N 11 35 E
Oymyakon .... 63 25N 143 10 E
Oyo .... 7 46N   3 56 E
Oyo □ .... 8 0N   3 30 E
Ozamiz .... 8 15N 123 50 E
Ozark 31 29N 85 39w
Ozark Plat. 37 20N 91 40w
Ozarks, L. of the .. 38 10N 93 0w

P

Pa Sak, R. .... 15 30N 101 0 E
Paan .... 30 0N 99 3 E
Pa-an .... 16 45N 97 40 E
Paarl .... 33 45s 18 46 E
Pabna .... 24 1N 89 18 E
Pacaraima, Sa. ... 5 0N 63 0w
Pacasmayo 7 20s 79 35w
Pachpadra ...... 25 57N 72 10 E †
Pachuca 20 10N 98 40w
Pacific Groves ... 37 36N 121 58w
Pacific Ocean 10 0N 140 0w
Padalarang ...... 7 50s 107 30 E
Padang .... 1 0s 100 20 E
Paddockwood 53 30N 105 30w
Paderborn ...... 51 42N' 8 44 E
Padlei 62 10N 97 5w

Padloping Island .. 67 0N 63 0w
Pádova .... 45 24N 11 52 E
Padstow 50 33N   4 57w
Padua=Pádova ... 45 24N 11 52 E
Paducah, Ky. 37 0N 88 40w
Paducah, Tes. 34 3N 100 16w
Paeroa .... 37 23s 175 41 E
Pag, I. .... 44 50N 15 0 E
Pagadian .... 7 55N 123 30 E
Pagalu, I. .... 1 35s   3 35 E *
Page 47 11N 97 37w
Paghman .... 34 36N 68 57 E
Pago Pago 14 16s 170 43w
Pagosa Springs .. 37 16N 107 1w
Pagwa River 50 2N 85 14w
Pahala 20 25s 156 0w
Pahiatua .... 40 27s 175 50 E
Paicheng .... 45 40N 122 52 E
Paignton 50 26N   3 33w
Painesville 41 42N 81 18w
Paint Hills=
  Nouveau
  Comptoir 53 2N 78 55w
Painted Des. 36 40N 112 0w
Paisley 55 51N   4 27w
Paita 5 5s 81 0w
Paiyin .... 36 45N 104 4 E
Pak Phanang .... 8 21N 100 12 E
Pakanbaru ...... 0 30N 101 15 E
Pakhoi .... 21 30N 109 10 E
Pakistan ■ ...... 30 0N 70 0 E
Pakokku .... 21 30N 95 0 E
Pakongchow ..... 23 50N 113 0 E
Pakse .... 15 5N 105 52 E
Paktya □ .... 33 0N 69 15 E
Palamós .... 41 50N   3 10 E
Palana .... 59 10N 160 10 E
Palangkaraya .... 2 16s 113 56 E
Palanpur .... 24 10N 72 25 E
Palapye .... 22 30s 27 7 E
Palatka 29 40N 81 40w
Palau Is. .... 7 30N 134 30 E
Palauk .... 13 10N 98 40 E
Palawan, I. ...... 10 0N 119 0 E
Palawan Is. ..... 10 0N 115 0 E
Palayancottai .... 8 45N 77 45 E
Paleleh .... 1 10N 121 50 E
Palembang ...... 3 0s 104 50 E
Palencia 42 1N   4 34w
Palenque .... 38 8N 13 20 E

Palestine 31 42N 95 35W
Paletwa .... 21 30N 92 50 E
Palghat .... 10 46N 76 42 E
Pali .... 25 50N 73 20 E
* Palimé .... 6 57N   0 37 E
Palisade 40 35N 101 10W
Palitana .... 21 32N 71 49 E
Palk B. .... 9 30N 79 30 E
Palk Str. .... 10 0N 80 0 E
Palm, Is. .... 18 40 S 146 35 E
Palm Beach 26 46N 80 0W
Palm Springs ... 33 51N 116 35W
Palma, Moz. ..... 10 46 S 40 29 E
Palma, Spain .... 39 33N   2 39 E
Palma Soriano ... 20 15N 76 0W
Palmares .... 8 41 S 35 36W
Palmas, C. 4 27N   7 46W
Palmas, G. di ... 39 0N   8 30 E
Palmeira dos
  Indios .... 9 25 S 36 30W
Palmer 61 35N 149 10W
Palmer Ld. ...... 73 0 S 60 0W
Palmerston ...... 45 29 S 170 43 E
Palmerston North . 40 21 S 175 39 E
Palmi .... 38 21N 15 51 E
Palmira, Col. 3 32N 76 16W
Palmyra Is. 5 52N 162 5W
Palo Alto 37 25N 122 8W
Palopo .... 3 0 S 120 16 E
Palos, C. de 37 38N   0 40W
Palu .... 38 45N 40 0 E
Pama .... 11 19N   0 44 E
Pamekason .... 7 10 S 113 29 E
Pamiencheng ..... 43 16N 124 4 E
Pamirs, Mts. ..... 38 0N 73 30 E
Pamlico Sd. 35 20N 76 0W
Pampa 35 35N 100 58W
Pampanua .... 4 22 S 120 14 E
Pampas, Reg. .... 34 0 S 64 0W
Pamplona, Col. ... 7 23N 72 39W
Pamplona, Spain . 42 48N   1 38W
Panaji .... 15 25N 73 50 E
Panama 9 0N 79 25W
Panamá ■ 8 48N 79 55W
Panamá, B. de ... 8 50N 79 20W
Panamá, G. de ... 8 4N 79 20W
Panama Canal 9 10N 79 56W
Panama City 30 10N 105 41W
Panarukan .... 7 40 S 113 52 E
Panay, I. .... 11 10N 122 30 E

Panay G. .... 11 0N 122 30 E
Pančevo .... 44 52N 20 41 E
Pandharpur ...... 17 41N 75 20 E
Panfilov .... 44 30N 80 0 E
Pang-Long .... 23 11N 98 45 E
Pangani .... 5 25 S 38 58 E
Panjinad Barr. ... 29 22N 71 15 E
Pangfou=Pengpu .. 33 0N 117 25 E
Pangkalanberandan 4 1N 98 20 E
Pangkalansusu ... 4 2N 98 42 E
Pangnirtung 66 8N 65 44W
Panguitch 37 52N 112 30W
Pangyang .... 22 10N 98 45 E
Panitya .... 35 15 S 141 0 E
Panjao .... 34 21N 67 0 E
Panjgur .... 27 0N 64 5 E
Panjim=Panaji .. 15 25N 73 50 E
Pankalpinang .... 2 0 S 106 0 E
Pankshin .... 9 25N   9 25 E
Panorama .... 21 21 S 51 51W
Panshih .... 42 55N 126 3 E
Pantellaria, I. .... 36 52N 12 0 E
Pánuco 22 10N 98 25W
Panyam .... 9 27N   9 8 E
Paochang .... 41 46N 115 30 E
Paoki .... 34 25N 107 15 E
Paoshan .... 25 7N 99 9 E
Paoting .... 38 50N 115 30 E
Paotow .... 40 35N 110 3 E
Paoying .... 33 10N 119 20 E
Papá .... 47 22N 17 30 E
Papagayo, G. del . 10 4N 85 50W
Papakura .... 37 4 S 174 59 E
Papantla 20 45N 97 41W
Papar .... 5 45N 116 0 E
Papua
  New Guinea ■ .. 8 0 S 145 0 E
Pará=Belém ...... 1 20 S 48 30W
Pará □ .... 3 20 S 52 0W
Paracatú .... 7 23 S 46 50W
Parachilna ...... 31 10 S 138 21 E
Paradise 47 27N 114 54W
Paragould 36 5N 90 30W
Paraguaipoa 11 21N 71 57W
Paraguaná, Penide . 12 0N 70 0W
Paraguari .... 25 36 S 57 0W
Paraguay ■ ...... 23 0 S 57 0W
Paraguay, R. .... 27 18 S 58 38W
Paraiba=
  João Pessoa ... 7 10 S 34 52W

Paraiba □ .... 7 0 S 36 0W
Parainen .... 60 18N 22 18 E
Parakou .... 9 25N   2 40 E
Paramaribo 5 50N 55 10W
Paraná, Arg. .... 32 0 S 60 30W
Paraná, Brazil ... 12 30 S 47 40W
Paraná, R. ...... 33 43 S 59 15W
Paraná □ .... 24 30 S 51 0W
Paranaguá .... 25 30 S 48 30W
Paranapanema, R. . 22 40 S 53 9W
Paranapiacaba,
  Sa. do .... 24 31 S 48 35W
Paratinga .... 12 40 S 43 10W
Paratoo .... 32 42 S 139 22 E
Parbhani .... 19 8N 76 52 E
Pardes Hanna ... 32 28N 34 57 E
Pardubice .... 50 3N 15 45 E
Pare .... 7 43 S 112 12 E
Pare Mts. .... 4 0 S 37 45 E
Paren .... 62 45N 163 0 E
Parent 47 55N 74 35W
Parepare .... 4 0 S 119 40 E
Parfuri .... 22 28 S 31 17 E
Parguba .... 62 58N 34 25 E
Paria, G. de 10 20N 62 0W
Pariaguan 8 51N 64 43W
Pariaman .... 0 47 S 100 11 E
Parigi .... 0 50 S 120 5 E
Parika 6 50N 58 20W
Paringul-Mare, Mt. 45 20 S 23 37 E
Parintins .... 2 40 S 56 50W
Paris, Canada ... 43 20N 80 25W
Paris, Fr. .... 48 50N   2 20 E
Paris, Tenn. 36 20N 88 20W
Paris, Tex. 33 40N 95 30W
Paris □ .... 48 0N   2 20 E
Park City 40 42N 111 35W
Park Ra. 40 0N 106 30W
Park Rynie ...... 30 25 S 30 35 E
Parkano .... 62 5 S 23 0 E
Parker, Ariz. 34 8N 114 16W
Parker, S.D. 43 25N 97 7W
Parkersburg 39 18N 81 31W
Parkerview 51 28N 103 18W
Parkes .... 33 9 S 148 11 E
Parksville 49 20N 124 21W
Parma, Italy .... 44 50N 10 2 E
Parma, U.S.A. ... 43 49N 116 59W
Parnaguá .... 10 10 S 44 10W
Parnaíba, Piauí ... 3 0 S 41 40W

Parnaiba, São
  Paulo .... 19 34 S 51 14W
Parnaiba, R. .... 3 0 S 41 50W
Parnassós, Mt. ... 38 17N 21 18 E
Pärnu .... 58 12N 24 33 E
Páros, I. .... 37 5 S 25 12 E
Parowan 37 54N 112 56W
Parral .... 36 10 S 72 0W
Parramatta ...... 33 48 S 151 1 E
Parras 25 30N 102 20W
Parrett, R. 51 13N   3 1W
Parrsboro 45 30N 64 10W
Parry Is. 77 0N 110 0W
Parry Sd. 42 20N 80 0W
Parsons 37 20N 95 10W
Parvatipuram .... 18 50N 83 25 E
Parwan □ .... 35 0N 69 0 E
Parys .... 26 52 S 27 29 E
Pasadena, Calif. . 34 5 S 118 0W
Pasadena, Tex. ... 29 45N 95 14W
Pasaje .... 3 10 S 79 40W
Pascagoula 30 30N 88 30W
Pasco 46 10N 119 0W
Pas-de-Calais □ .. 50 30N   2 30 E
Pasir Mas .... 6 2N 102 8 E
Pasirian .... 8 13 S 113 8 E
Pasley, C. ...... 33 52 S 123 35 E
Paso de Indios ... 43 55 S 69 0W
Paso Robles 35 40N 120 45W
Paspébiac 48 3N 65 17W
Passage West 51 52N   8 20W
Passau .... 48 34N 13 27 E
Passero, C. ..... 36 42N 15 8 E
Passo Fundo .... 28 10 S 52 30W
Passos .... 20 45 S 46 29W
Pasto 1 13N 77 17W
Pasuruan .... 7 40 S 112 53 E
Patagonia, Reg. .. 45 0 S 69 0W
Patchogue 40 46N 73 1W
Patea .... 39 45 S 174 30 E
Pategi .... 8 50N   5 45 E
Patensie .... 33 46 S 24 49 E
Paterno .... 37 34N 14 53 E
Paterson 40 55N 74 10W
Pathankot ...... 32 18N 75 45 E
Pathfinder Res. .. 42 0N 107 0W
Patan .... 23 52N 72 4 E
Patani .... 0 20N 128 50 E
Pataokiang ..... 41 58N 126 30 E
Patiala .... 30 23N 76 26 E

Patkai Bum, Mts... 27 0N 95 30 E
Patmos, I. ...... 37 21N 26 36 E
Patna .... 25 35N 85 18 E
Patos, L. dos ... 31 20 S 51 0W
Patos de Minas ... 18 35 S 46 32W
Pátrai .... 38 14N 21 47 E
Pátraikos Kól. ... 38 17N 21 30 E
Patrocínio ...... 18 57 S 47 0W
Pattani .... 6 48N 101 15 E
Patti .... 31 17N 74 54 E
Patuca, R. 15 50N 84 18W
Pátzcuaro 19 30N 101 40W
Pau 43 19N   0 25W
Pauillac 45 11N   0 46W
Pauk .... 21 55N 94 30 E
Paulistana ..... 8 9 S 41 9W
Paulo Afonso ... 9 21 S 38 15W
Paulpietersburg .. 27 23 S 30 50 E
Paul's Valley ... 34 40N 97 17W
Pavia .... 45 10N   9 10 E
Pavlodar .... 52 33N 77 0 E
Pavlograd ...... 48 30N 35 52 E
Pavlovo, Gorkiy .. 55 58N 43 5 E
Pavlovo, Yakut
  A.S.S.R. ...... 63 5N 115 25 E
Pavlovsk .... 50 26N 40 5 E
Pawtucket 41 51N 71 22W
Payakumbuh .... 0 20 S 100 35 E
Payette 44 0N 117 0W
Payne Bay=Bellin . 60 0N 70 0W
Payne L. 59 30N 74 30W
Paynes Find .... 29 15 S 117 42 E
Paysandú ...... 32 19 S 58 8W
Payson 40 8N 111 41W
Pazardzhik ..... 42 12N 24 20 E
Pe Ell 46 30N 123 29W
Peace, R. 59 30N 111 30W
Peace River 56 15N 117 18W
Peace River, Res. . 55 40N 123 40W
Peak, The., Mt. .. 22 17 S 148 11 E
Peak Downs Mine . 22 17 S 148 11 E
Peak Hill ...... 32 39 S 148 11 E
Peake .... 35 25 S 140 0 E
Pearl City 21 21N 158 0W
Pearl Harbor ... 21 20N 158 0W
Pearston .... 32 33 S 25 7 E
Pebane .... 17 10 S 38 8 E
Pebas .... 3 10 S 71 55W
Peč .... 42 40N 20 17 E
Pechenga .... 69 30N 31 25 E

Pechora . . . . 65 15N 57 0 E
Pechora, R. . . . . 68 13N 54 10 E
Pechorskaya Guba . 68 40N 54 0 E
Pecos 31 25N 103 35w
Pecos, R. 29 42N 101 22w
Pécs . . . . 46 5N 18 15 E
Pedra Asul 16 1s 41 16w
Pedregal 8 22N 82 27w
Pedro Afonso 9 0s 48 10w
Pedro Juan
  Caballero 22 30s 55 40w
Peebles 55 40N 3 12w
Peekskill 41 18N 73 57w
Peel 54 14N 4 40w
Peel, R. 67 0N 135 0w
Pegasus, B. . . . . 43 20s 173 10 E
Pegu . . . . 17 20N 96 29 E
Pegu Yoma, Mts. . . 19 0N 96 0 E
Peh Kiang, R. . . . . . 23 10N 113 10 E
Pehan . . . . . . 48 17N 120 31 E
Pehpei . . . . . . 29 44N 106 29 E
Pehuajó 36 0s 62 0w
Peiping . . . . . 39 45N 116 25 E
Peixe 12 0s 48 40w
Pekalongan . . . . . . 6 53s 109 40 E
Pekin 40 35N 89 40w
Peking=Peiping . 39 45N 116 25 E
Pelabuhan Ratu,
  Teluk, G. . . . . 7 0s 106 32 E
Pelabuhanratu . . . 7 5s 106 30 E
Peleaga, Mt. . 45 22N 22 55 E
Peleng, I. . . . . . 1 20s 123 30 E
Pelican Narrows . . 55 12N 102 55 E
Pelican Portage . . . 55 51N 113 0w
Pelican Rapids . . . 52 38N 100 42 E
Pelly, R. 62 47N 137 19w
Pelly Bay 68 53N 89 51w
Peloponnese□=
  Pelopónnisos . 37 40N 22 15 E
Pelopónnisos □ . . . 37 40N 22 15 E
Peloro, C. . . . . 38 15N 15 40 E
Pelorus, Sd. . . . . . 40 59s 173 59 E
Pelotas 31 42s 52 23w
Pelvoux, Massif du. 44 52N 6 20 E
Pemalang . . . . . . 6 53s 109 23 E
Pematang . . . . 0 12s 102 4 E
Pematangsiantar . . 2 57N 99 5 E
Pemba, I. . . . . . 16 31s 27 22 E
Pemba I. . . . . . 5 0s 39 45 E
Pemberton,

Australia . . . . 34 30s 116 0 E
Pemberton, Canada 50 25N 122 50w
Pembroke, Canada 45 50N 77 15w
Pembroke, N.Z.=
  Wanaka . . . . 44 33s 169 9 E
Pembroke, U.K. . . . 51 41N 4 57w
Penang□=
  Pinang □ . . . . . . 5 25N 100 15 E
Penápolis 21 24s 50 4w
Peñas, C. de 43 42N 5 52w
Penas, G. de 47 0s 75 0w
Pendembu 8 6N 10 45w
Pendleton 45 35N 118 50w
Penedo 10 15s 36 36w
Penetanguishene . 44 50N 79 55w
Penganga, R. . . . . . 19 53N 79 9 E
Penghu, I. . . . . . . 23 30N 119 30 E
Penglai . . . . . . 37 49N 120 47 E
Pengpu . . . . . . 33 0N 117 25 E
Penguin . . . . . . 41 8s 146 6 E
Penhalonga . . . . . . 18 54s 32 40 E
Peniche 39 19N 9 22w
Penicuik 55 50N 3 14w
Penki . . . . . . 41 20N 132 50 E
Penn Yan 42 40N 77 3w
Pennine Ra. 54 50N 2 20w
Pennsylvania □ . . . 40 50N 78 0w
Penny 53 58N 121 1w
Penobscot, R. 44 30N 68 50w
Penola . . . . . . 37 25s 140 47 E
Penonomé 8 37N 80 25w
Penrhyn Is. 9 0s 150 30w
Penrith, Australia . 33 43s 150 38 E
Penrith, U.K. 54 40N 2 45w
Pensacola 30 30N 87 10w
Penticton 49 30N 119 30w
Pentland . . . . . . 20 32s 145 25 E
Pentland Firth 58 43N 3 10w
Pentland Hills 55 48N 3 25w
Pen-y-Ghent, Mt. . . 54 10N 2 15w
Penza . . . . . . 53 15N 45 5 E
Penzance 50 7N 5 32w
Peoria 40 40N 89 40w
Perabumilih . . . . . . 3 27s 104 15 E
Perche, Reg. . . . . . . 48 30N 1 0 E
Percival Lakes . . . . 21 25s 125 0 E
Percy, Is. . . . . . 21 39s 150 16 E
Perdu, Mt. . . . . . . 42 40N 0 1 E
Pereira 4 49N 75 43w
Perekop . . . . 46 0N 33 0 E

Perenjori . . . . 29 26s 116 16 E
Pereyaslav
  khmelnitskiy . . . 50 3N 31 28 E
Pérez, I. 22 40N 89 30w
Peribonca, R. 48 45N 72 5w
Perico 24 25s 65 10w
Perigord, Reg. . . . 45 0N 0 40 E
Périgueux . . . . . . 45 10N 0 42 E
Perim, I. . . . . . . 12 39N 43 25 E
Perm . . . . . . 58 0N 57 10 E
Pernambuco=
  Recife 8 0s 35 0w
Pernambuco □ 8 0s 37 0w
Pernik . . . . . . 42 36N 23 2 E
Peron, C. . . . . . . 25 30s 113 30 E
Perpignan . . . . . . 42 42N 2 53 E
Perry, Iowa 41 48N 94 5w
Perry, Okla. 36 20N 97 20w
Persia=Iran ■ . . . . 35 0N 50 0 E
* Persian G. . . . . . . 27 0N 50 0 E
Perth, Australia . 31 57s 115 52 E
Perth, Canada . . . 44 55N 76 20w
Perth, U.K. 56 24N 3 27w
Perth Amboy 40 31N 74 16w
Peru 8 0s 75 0w
Peru, Ill. 41 18N 89 12w
Peru, Ind. 40 42N 86 0w
Perúgia . . . . . . 43 6N 12 24 E
Pervomaysk . . . . . 48 5N 30 55 E
Pervouralsk . . . . . 56 55N 60 0 E
Pésaro . . . . . . 43 55N 12 53 E
Pescara . . . . . . 42 28N 14 13 E
* Peshawar □ . . . . . 35 0N 72 50 E
Pesqueira 8 20s 36 42w
Petah Tiqwa . . . . . 32 6N 34 53 E
Petauke . . . . . . 14 14s 31 12 E
Petawawa 45 54N 77 17w
Petén Itzá, L. . . . 16 58N 89 50w
Peterbell 48 36N 83 21w
Peterborough,
  Australia . . . . . . 32 58s 138 51 E
Peterborough, Can. 44 20N 78 20w
Peterborough, U.K. 52 35N 1 14w
Peterhead 57 30N 1 49w
Peterlee 54 45N 1 18w
Petersburg, Alas. . 56 50N 133 0w

Petersburg, Va. . . . 37 17N 77 26w
Petit Cap 48 58N 63 58w
Petit Goâve 18 27N 72 51w
Petit St. Bernard,
  Col du . . . . . . 45 41N 6 53 E
Petitcodiac 45 57N 65 11w
Petite Saguenay . . 47 59N 70 1w
Petlad . . . . . . 22 30N 72 45 E
Petone . . . . . . 41 13s 174 53 E
Petoskey 45 21N 84 55w
Petrich . . . . . . 41 24N 23 13 E
Petrolandia 9 5s 38 20w
Petrolia 52 54N 82 9w
Petrolina 9 24s 40 30w
Petropavlovsk . . . . 55 0N 69 0 E
Petropavlovsk-
  kamchatskiy . . . 53 16N 159 0 E
Petrópolis 22 33s 43 9w
Petrovaradin . . . . 45 16N 19 55 E
Petrovsk . . . . . . 52 22N 45 19 E
Petrovsk-
  Zdbaykalskiy . . . 51 17N 108 50 E
Petrozavodsk . . . . 61 41N 34 20 E
Petrusburg . . . . . . 29 8s 25 27 E
Peureulak . . . . . . 4 48N 97 45 E
Pevek . . . . . . 69 15N 171 0 E
Pforzheim . . . . . . 48 53N 8 43 E
Phagwara . . . . . . 31 13N 75 47 E
Phala . . . . . . 23 45s 26 50 E
Phalodi . . . . . . 27 12N 72 24 E
Phan Rang . . . . . . 11 34N 108 59 E
Phan Thiet . . . . . . 11 1N 108 9 E
Phangan, Ko . . . . 9 45N 100 4 E
Phangna . . . . . . 8 28N 98 30 E
Phanh Bho
  Ho Chi Minh . . . 10 58N 106 40 E
Pharo Dzong . . . . 27 45N 89 14 E
Phatthalung . . . . . 7 39N 100 6 E
Phenix City 32 30N 85 0w
Phetchabun . . . . . 16 24N 101 12 E
Phetchaburi . . . . . 16 25N 101 8 E
Philadelphia 40 0N 75 10w
Philippi . . . . . . 41 0N 24 19 E
Philippines ■ . . . . 12 0N 123 0 E
Philippolis . . . . . . 30 19s 25 13 E
Philipstown . . . . . 30 26s 24 29 E
Phillip, I. . . . . . . 38 30s 145 12 E
Phillott . . . . . . 27 53s 145 50 E
Philomath 44 28N 123 21w
Phitsanulok . . . . . 16 50N 100 12 E

Phnom Dangrek
  Ra. . . . . 14 15N 105 0 E
Phnom Penh . . . 11 33N 104 55 E
Phoenix 33 30N 112 10w
Phoenix Is. 3 30s 172 0w
Phong Saly . . . . . 21 41N 102 6 E
Phra Nakhon Si
  Ayutthaya . . . 14 25N 100 30 E
Phu Quoc, I. . . . . 10 15N 104 0 E
Phuket . . . . . . 8 0N 98 28 E
Phuoc Le . . . . . . 10 30N 107 10 E
Piacenza . . . . . . 45 2N 9 42 E
Pialba . . . . . . 25 20s 152 45 E
Pian Creek . . . . . . 30 2s 148 12 E
Piatra Neamt . . . . 46 56N 26 22 E
Piani □ 7 0s 43 0w
Picardie, Reg. . . . . 50 0N 2 15 E
Picardy, Reg.=
  Picardie, Reg. . 50 0N 2 15 E
Picayune 30 40N 89 40w
Pichilemú . . . . . . 34 23s 72 2 E
Pickering 54 15N 0 46w
Pickle Crow 51 30N 90 0w
Pico Truncado . . . 46 40s 68 10w
Picton, Australia . 34 12s 150 34 E
Picton, Canada . . 44 1N 77 9w
Picton, N.Z. . . . . . 41 18s 174 3 E
Pictou 45 41N 62 42w
Picture Butte 49 55N 112 45w
Picún Leufú 39 30s 69 5w
Pidurutalagala, Mt. 7 10N 80 50 E
Piedras Blancas Pt. 35 45N 121 18w
Piedras Negras . . 28 35N 100 35w
Piermonte □ . . . . 45 0N 7 30 E
Pierre 44 23N 100 20w
Piet Retief . . . . . . 27 1s 30 50 E
Pietermaritzburg . 29 35s 30 25 E
Pietersburg . . . . . 23 54s 29 25 E
Pietrosu, Mt. . . . . 47 8N 25 11 E
Pietrosul, Mt. . . . 47 36N 24 38 E
Pigeon River 48 1N 89 42w
Pigüé 37 36s 62 25w
Piketberg . . . . . . 32 55s 18 40 E
Pikeville 37 30N 82 30w
Piła . . . . . . 53 10N 16 48 E
Pilar 26 50s 58 10w
Pilar 14 30s 49 45w
Pilcomayo, R. 25 21s 57 42w
Pilibhit . . . . . . 28 40N 79 50 E
Pilica, R. . . . . . . 51 52N 21 17 E

* Renamed The Gulf
* Now part of
North West Frontier

Pilos .... 36 55N 21 42 E
Pilsen=Plzeň ..... 49 45N 13 22 E
Pilzen=Plzeň ..... 49 45N 13 22 E
Pima 32 54N 109 50W
Pimba .... 31 18 S 136 46 E
Pinang, I. .... 5 25N 100 15 E
Pinar del Rio 22 26N 83 40W
Pinawa 50 15N 95 50W
Pincher Creek 49 30N 113 35W
Pinczów .... 50 32N 20 35 E
Pindar .... 28 30 S 115 47 E
Pindiga .... 9 58N 10 53 E
Pindos Óros ...... 40 0N 21 0 E
Pindus Mts.=
    Pindos Óros ... 40 0N 21 0 E
Pine, C. 46 37N 53 30W
Pine Bluff 34 10N 92 0W
Pine Creek .... 13 49 S 131 49 E
Pine Falls 50 51N 96 11W
Pine Point 60 50N 114 40W
Pinega, R. .... 64 8N 41 54 E
Pinehill .... 23 38 S 146 57 E
Pinerolo .... 44 47N 7 21 E
Pinetown .... 29 48 S 30 54 E
Pineville 31 22N 92 30W
Ping, R. .... 15 42N 100 9 E
Pingaring .... 32 40 S 118 32 E
Pingelly .... 32 29 S 116 59 E
Pingkiang .... 28 45N 113 30 E
Pingliang .... 35 32N 106 50 E
Pingsiang .... 22 2N 106 55 E
Pingtingshan ..... 33 43N 113 28 E
Pingtung .... 22 38N 120 30 E
Pingyao .... 37 12N 112 10 E
Pinhel 40 18N 7 0W
Pinhsien .... 35 10N 108 10 E
Pinios, R. .... 39 54N 22 45 E
Pinjarra .... 32 37 S 115 52 E
Pinkiang=
    Harbin .... 45 46N 126 51 E
Pinnaroo .... 35 13 S 140 56 E
Pinos, I. de 21 40N 82 40W
Pinos, Pt. 36 50N 121 57W
Pinrang .... 3 46 S 119 34 E
Pinsk .... 52 10N 26 8 E
Pinto Butte, Mt. .. 49 22N 107 25W
Pintumba .... 31 50 S 132 18 E
Pinyang .... 23 12N 108 35 E
Pinyug .... 60 5N 48 0 E
Pioche 38 0N 114 35N

Piombino .... 42 54N 10 30 E
Piotrków
    Trybunalski .... 51 23N 19 43 E
Pipestone 44 0N 96 20W
Pipinas .... 35 30N 57 19 E
Pipmuacan Res. ... 49 40N 70 25W
Pippingarra ...... 20 27 S 118 42 E
Piqua 40 10N 84 10W
Piracicaba .... 22 45 S 47 30W
Piracuruca .... 3 50 S 41 50W
Piraeus=
    Piraiévs ...... 37 57N 23 42 E
Piraiévs .... 37 57N 23 42 E
Pirané .... 25 44 S 59 7W
Pírgos .... 37 40N 21 25 E
Piripiri .... 4 15 S 41 46W
Piru .... 3 3 S 128 12 E
Pisa .... 43 43N 10 23 E
Pisagua .... 19 40 S 70 15W
Pisciotta .... 40 7N 15 12 E
Pisco .... 13 50 S 76 5W
Pisek .... 49 19N 14 10 E
Pistóia .... 43 57N 10 53 E
Pitcairn I. .... 25 5 S 130 5W
Pitea .... 65 20N 21 25 E
Piteşti .... 44 52N 24 54 E
Pithapuram .... 17 10N 82 15 E
Pithara .... 30 20 E 116 35 E
Pitlochry 56 43N 3 43W
Pittsburg, Calif. .. 38 1N 121 50W
Pittsburg, Kans. .. 37 21N 94 43W
Pittsburgh, Pa. ... 40 25N 79 55W
Pittsburgh, Tex. .. 32 59N 94 58W
Pittsfield 42 28N 73 17W
Pittston 41 19N 75 50W
Pittsworth .... 27 41 S 151 37 E
Piura .... 5 5 S 80 45W
Pizzo .... 38 44N 16 10 E
Placentia 47 20N 54 0W
Placerville 38 47N 120 51W
Placetas 22 15N 79 44W
Plainfield 40 37N 74 28W
Plainview 34 10N 101 40W
Plaquemine 30 20N 91 15W
Plasencia 40 3N 6 8W
Plaster Rock 46 53N 67 22W
Plata, R. de la ... 34 45 S 57 30W
Plate, R.=
    Plata, R. de la .. 34 35 S 57 30W
Plateau ☐ .... 8 30N 8 45 E

Plato 9 47N 74 47W
Platte, R. 41 4N 95 53W
Platteville 40 18N 104 47W
Plattsburgh 44 41N 73 30W
Plattsmouth 41 0N 96 0W
Plauen .... 50 29N 12 9 E
Pleasantville 39 25N 74 30W
Plenty, B. of ..... 37 45 S 177 0 E
Plesetsk .... 62 40N 40 10 E
Plessisville 46 14N 71 46W
Pleven .... 43 26N 24 37 E
Płock .... 52 32N 19 40 E
Ploieşti .... 44 57N 26 5 E
Plovdiv .... 42 8N 24 44 E
Plumtree .... 20 27 S 27 55 E
Plymouth,
    Montserrat 16 42N 62 13W
Plymouth, U.K. ... 50 23N 4 9W
Plymouth, Ind. ... 41 20N 86 19W
Plzeň .... 49 45N 13 22 E
Pô 11 10N 1 9W
Po, R. .... 44 57N 12 4 E
Po Hai, G. .... 38 40N 119 0 E
Pobé .... 6 58N 2 41 E
Pobedino .... 49 51N 142 49 E
Pocatello 42 50N 112 25W
Poços de
    Caldas .... 21 50 S 46 45W
Podkamenndya
    Tunguska ..... 61 50N 90 26 E
Podolsk .... 55 30N 37 30 E
Podporozny ...... 60 55N 34 2 E
Pofadder .... 29 10 S 19 22 E
Pohang .... 36 8N 129 23 E
Point Edward 43 10N 82 30W
Pointe-Noire ..... 4 48 S 12 0 E
Pointe-à-Pitre 16 10N 61 30W
Poitiers .... 46 35N 0 20 E
Poitou, Reg. 46 25N 0 15W
Pokaran .... 26 55N 71 55 E
Pokataroo .... 29 30 S 148 34 E
Poko .... 3 7N 26 52 E
Pokotu .... 48 46N 121 54 E
Pokrovsk .... 61 29N 129 0 E
Polacca 35 52N 110 25W
Poland ■ .... 52 0N 20 0 E
Polcura .... 37 17 S 71 43W
Polden Hills 51 7N 2 50W
Poli .... 8 34N 12 54 E
Polillo Is. .... 14 56N 122 0 E

Poljanovgrad ..... 42 35N 26 58 E
Pollachi .... 10 35N 77 0 E
Polnovat .... 63 50N 66 5 E
Polotsk .... 55 30N 28 50 E
Polson 47 45N 114 12W
Poltava .... 49 35N 34 35 E
Polyarny .... 69 8N 33 20 E
Pombal, Brazil .... 6 45 S 37 50W
Pombal, Port. 39 55N 8 40W
Pomona 34 2N 117 49W
Pompano 26 12N 80 6W
Ponca City 36 40N 97 5W
Ponce 18 1N 66 37W
Pond Inlet 72 30N 75 0W
Pondicherry ...... 11 59N 79 50 E
Pondoland .... 31 10 S 29 30 E
Ponferrada 42 32N 6 35W
Ponnyadaung, Mts. 22 0N 94 10 E
Ponoi .... 67 0N 41 0 E
Ponoka 52 35N 113 40W
Ponorogo .... 7 52 S 111 29 E
Pont Lafrance 47 40N 64 58W
Ponta Grossa ..... 25 0 S 50 10W
Pontarlier .... 46 54N 6 20 E
Pontchartrain, L. .. 30 12N 90 0W
Ponte Nova ...... 20 25 S 42 54W
Pontedera .... 43 40N 10 37 E
Pontefract 53 42N 1 19W
Ponteix 49 46N 107 29W
Pontevedra 42 26N 8 40W
Pontiac, Ill. 40 50N 88 40W
Pontiac, Mich. 42 40N 83 20W
Pontianak .... 0 3 S 109 15 E
Pontine Mts.=
    Karadeniz
    Daĝlari, Mts. .. 41 30N 35 0 E
Pontypool 51 42N 3 1W
Ponytpridd ...... 51 36N 3 21 S
Ponziane, Ís. .... 40 55N 13 0 E
Poochera .... 32 43 S 134 51 E
Poole 50 42N 2 2W
Poona=Pune ...... 18 29N 73 57 E
Poopó, L. .... 18 30 S 67 35W
Popanyinning ..... 32 40 S 117 2 E
Popayán 2 27N 76 36W
Poperinge .... 50 51N 2 42 E
Popigay .... 71 55N 110 47 E
Poplar Bluff 36 45N 90 22W
Popocatepetl, Mt. . 19 10N 98 40W
Porbandar .... 21 44N 69 43 E

Porcupine, R. 66 35N 145 15W
Pori .... 61 29N 21 48 E
Porjus .... 66 57N 19 50 E
Porkkala .... 59 59N 24 26 E
Porlamar 10 57N 63 51W
Poronaysk .... 49 20N 143 0 E
Port Adelaide ..... 34 46 S 138 30 E
Port Alberni 49 15N 124 50W
Port Albert
    Victor .... 21 0N 71 30 E
Port Alfred, Canada 48 18N 70 53W
Port Alfred, S. Afr. 33 6 s 26 55 E
Port Alice 50 25N 127 25W
Port Allegany 41 49N 78 17W
Port Angeles 48 0N 123 30W
Port Arthur,
    Canada=
    Thunder Bay ... 48 25N 89 10W
Port Arthur, China=
    Lushun .... 38 48N 121 16 E
Port Arthur,
    U.S.A. 30 0N 94 0W
Port Arthur=
    Thunder Bay ... 48 25N 89 10W
Port Augusta ..... 32 30 S 137 50 E
Port aux Basques .. 47 32N 59 8W
Port-Bergé Vaovao 15 33 s 47 40 E
Port Bou .... 42 25N 3 9 E
Port Broughton ... 33 37 S 137 56 E
Port Canning ..... 22 18N 88 40 E
Port Cartier 50 10N 66 50W
Port Chalmers .... 45 49 S 170 30 E
Port Chester 41 0N 73 41W
Port Colborne 42 50N 79 10W
Port Coquitlam ... 49 20N 122 45W
Port Darwin ...... 12 18 S 130 55 E
Port de Paix 19 50N 72 50W
Port Dickson ..... 2 30N 101 49 E
Port Douglas ..... 16 30 S 145 30 E
Port Edward 54 14N 130 18W
Port Elgin 44 25N 81 25W
Port Elizabeth .... 33 58 S 25 40 E
Port Ellen 55 39N 6 12W
Port Erin 54 5N 4 45W
Port Étienne=
    Nouadhibou ... 21 0N 17 0W
Port Fairy .... 38 22 S 142 12 E
Port-Gentil ...... 0 47 S 8 40 E
Port Glasgow 55 57N 4 40W
Port Harcourt .... 4 43N 7 5 E

Port Hardy	50 41N	127 30W
Port Harrison=		
Inoucdouac	58 25N	78 15W
Port Hedland	20 25S	118 35 E
Port Henry	44 0N	73 30W
Port Hood	46 0N	61 32W
Port Hope	44 0N	78 20W
Port Jefferson	40 57N	73 4W
Port Kelang	3 0N	101 24 E
Port Kembla	34 29S	150 56 E
Port Laoise	53 2N	7 20W
Port Lavaca	28 38N	96 38W
Port Lincoln	34 42S	135 52 E
Port-Lyautey=		
Kenitra	34 15N	6 40W
Port Macquarie	31 25S	152 54 E
Port Maitland	44 0N	66 2W
Port Mellon	49 32N	123 31W
Port Menier	49 51N	64 15W
Port Moller	00 00 0N	00 00 0W
Port Moresby	9 24S	147 8 E
Port Nelson	57 5N	92 56W
Port Nolloth	29 17S	16 52 E
Port Nouveau-		
Quebec	58 30N	65 50W
Port of Spain	10 40N	61 20W
Port Orchard	47 31N	122 47W
Port Perry	44 6N	78 56W
Port Pirie	33 10S	137 58 E
*Port Radium	66 10N	117 40W
Port Said=		
Bûr Saïd	31 16N	32 18 E
Port St. Johns=		
Umzimvubu	31 38S	29 33 E
Port St. Servain	51 21N	58 0W
Port Shepstone	30 44S	30 28 E
Port Simpson	54 30N	130 20W
Port Stanley	42 40N	81 10W
Port Sudan=		
Bûr Sûdân	19 32N	37 9 E
Port Talbot	51 35N	3 48W
Port Townsend	48 0N	122 50W
Port-Vendres	42 32N	3 8 E
Port Vladimir	69 25N	33 6 E
Port Wakefield	34 12S	138 10 E
Port Weld	4 50N	100 38 E
Portadown	54 27N	6 26W
Portage	43 31N	89 25W
Portage la Prairie	49 58N	98 18W
Portalegre	39 19N	7 25W
Portales	34 12N	103 25W
Portarlington	53 10N	7 10W
Port-au-Prince	18 40N	72 20W
Porterville, S. Afr.	33 0S	19 0 E
Porterville, U.S.A.	36 5N	119 0W
Porthcawl	51 28N	3 42W
Portimão	37 8N	8 32W
Portland,		
Australia	33 13S	149 59 E
Portland, Me.	43 40N	70 15W
Portland, Oreg.	45 35N	122 30W
Portland Bill	50 31N	2 27W
Portland I.	50 32N	2 25W
Portland		
Promontory	59 0N	78 0W
Portmadoc	52 51N	4 8W
Portneuf	46 43N	71 55W
Porto, Port.	41 8N	8 40W
Pôrto Alegre	30 5S	51 3W
Porto Amélia=		
Pemba	12 58S	40 30 E
Pôrto de Móz	1 41S	52 22W
Porto Empédocle	37 18N	13 30 E
Porto Franco	9 45S	47 0W
Porto Grande	0 42N	51 24W
Pôrto Mendes	24 30S	54 15W
Pôrto Murtinho	21 45S	57 55W
Porto Nacional	10 40S	48 30W
Porto-Novo	6 23N	2 42 E
Porto Seguro	16 20S	39 0W
Porto Torres	40 50N	8 23 E
Porto União	26 10S	51 0W
Porto-Vecchio	41 35N	9 16 E
Porto Velho	8 46S	63 54W
Portoferráio	42 50N	10 20 E
Portola	39 49N	120 28W
Portoscuso	39 12N	8 22 E
Portoviejo	1 0S	80 20W
Portpatrick	54 50N	5 7W
Portree	57 25N	6 11W
Portrush	55 13N	6 40W
Portsmouth, U.K.	50 48N	1 6W
Portsmouth, N.H.	43 5N	70 45W
Portsmouth, Ohio	38 45N	83 0W
Portsmouth, Va.	36 50N	76 50W
Portsoy	57 41N	2 41W
Porttipahta, I.	68 5N	26 40 E
Portugal ■	40 0N	7 0W
Portuguese		
Guinea■=		
Guinea Bissau ■	12 0N	15 0W
Portumna	53 5N	8 12W
Porvenir	53 10S	70 30W
Provoo	60 27N	25 50 E
Posadas	27 30S	56 0W
Poseh	23 50N	106 0 E
Poshan=Tzepo	36 28N	117 58 E
Poso	1 20S	120 55 E
Posse	14 4S	46 18W
Poste de la Baleine	55 20N	77 40W
Poste Maurice		
Cortier	22 14N	1 2 E
Postmasburg	28 18S	23 5 E
Postojna	45 46N	14 12 E
Potchefstroom	26 41S	27 7 E
Potenza	40 40N	15 50 E
Potgietersrus	24 10S	29 3 E
Poti	42 10N	41 38 E
Potiskum	11 39N	11 2 E
Potomac, R.	38 0N	76 20W
Potosí	19 38S	65 50W
Potatan	10 56N	122 38 E
Potow	38 8N	116 31 E
Potrerillos	26 26S	69 29W
Potsdam,		
E. Germany	52 23N	13 4 E
Potsdam, U.S.A.	44 40N	74 59W
Pottstown	40 15N	75 38W
Pottsville	40 39N	76 12W
Pouce Coupe	55 40N	120 10W
Poughkeepsie	41 40N	73 57W
Poverty B.	38 43S	178 0 E
Póvoa de Varzim	41 25N	8 46W
Povenets	62 48N	35 0 E
Powassan	46 5N	79 25W
Powder, R.	46 44N	105 26W
Powder River	43 5N	107 0W
Powell	44 45N	108 45W
Powell, L.	37 25N	110 45W
Powell River	49 48N	125 20W
Powys □	52 20N	3 30W
Poyang	28 59N	116 40 E
Poyang Hu, L.	29 10N	116 10 E
Poyarkovo	49 38N	128 45 E
Požarevac	44 35N	21 18 E
Poznań	52 25N	17 0 E
Pozo Almonte	20 10S	69 50W
Pra, R.	5 1N	1 37W
Prachuap Khiri		
Khan	11 48N	99 47 E
Prado	17 20S	39 20W
Prague=Praha	50 5N	14 22 E
Praha	50 5N	14 22 E
Prainha	1 45S	53 30W
Prairie	20 50S	144 35 E
Prairie City	45 27N	118 44W
Prairie du Chien	43 1N	91 9W
Prairies,Coteau des.	44 0N	97 0W
Praja	8 39S	116 37 E
Prata	19 25S	49 0W
Prato	43 5N	11 5 E
Pratt	37 40N	98 45W
Pravia	43 30N	6 12W
Preeceville	52 0N	102 50W
Premier	56 4N	130 1W
Prenzlau	53 19N	13 51 E
Prepansko, J.	40 45N	21 0 E
Prerov	49 28N	17 27 E
Prescott, Canada	44 45N	75 30W
Prescott, U.S.A.	34 35N	112 30W
Presidencia Roque		
Saenz Peña	26 50S	60 30W
Presidente Epitácio	21 46S	52 6W
Presidente Prudente	15 45S	54 0W
Prešov	49 0N	21 15 E
Presque Isle	46 40N	68 0W
Pressburg=		
Bratislava	48 10N	17 7 E
Prestea	5 22N	2 7W
Presteign	52 17N	3 0W
Preston	53 46N	2 42W
Prestonpans	55 58N	3 0W
Prestwich	53 30N	2 18W
Prestwick	55 30N	4 38W
Pretoria	25 44S	28 12 E
Préveza	38 57N	20 47 E
Pribilov Is.	56 0N	170 0W
Příbram	49 41N	14 2 E
Price	39 40N	110 48W
Prieska	29 40S	22 42 E
Prikaspiyskaya		
Nizmennost	47 30N	50 0 E
*Prikumsk	44 30N	44 10 E
Prilep	41 21N	21 37 E
Priluki	50 30N	32 15 E
Prince Albert	53 15N	105 50W
Prince Albert		
Nat. Park	54 0N	106 25W
Prince Albert Pen.	72 30N	116 0W
Prince Albert Sd.	70 25N	115 0W
Prince Charles I.	68 0N	76 0W
Prince Edward Is.	45 15S	39 0 E
Prince Edward I. □	44 2N	77 20W
Prince George	53 50N	122 50W
Prince of Wales, C.	53 50N	131 30W
Prince of Wales, I.,		
Australia	10 35S	142 0 E
Prince of Wales I.,		
Canada	73 0N	99 0W
Prince of Wales I.,		
U.S.A.	53 30N	131 30W
Prince Rupert	54 20N	130 20W
Princess Charlotte,		
B.	14 15S	144 0 E
Princeton, Canada	49 27N	120 30W
Princeton, Ind.	38 20N	87 35W
Princeton, Ky.	37 6N	87 55W
Princeton, W.Va.	37 21N	81 8W
Príncipe, I.	1 37N	7 25 E
Prins Albert	33 12S	22 2 E
Priozersk	61 2N	30 4 E
Pripet, R.=		
Pripyat, R.	51 20N	30 20 E
Pripyat, R.	51 20N	30 20 E
Priština	42 40N	21 13 E
Pritchard	30 47N	88 5W
Probolinggo	7 46S	113 13 E
Proddatur	14 45N	78 30 E
Progreso	21 20N	89 40W
Prokopyevsk	54 0N	87 3 E
Prome	18 45N	95 30 E
Propriá	10 13S	36 51W
Proserpine	20 21S	148 36 E
Prosser	46 11N	119 52W
Prostĕjov	49 30N	17 9 E
Provence, Reg.	43 40N	5 46 E
Providence	41 41N	71 15W
Providence Bay	45 41N	82 15W
Providencia I. de	13 25N	81 26W
Provideniya	64 23N	173 18W
Provincial Cannery	51 33N	127 36W
Provins	48 33N	3 15 E
Provo	40 16N	111 37W
Provost	52 25N	110 20W
Prudhoe, I.	21 23S	149 45 E
Prudhoe Bay	70 10N	148 0W
Prudhomme	52 22N	105 47W
Pruszków	52 9N	20 49 E
Prut, R.	45 28N	28 12 E
Przemyśl	49 50N	22 45 E
Przeworsk	50 6N	22 32 E

* Renamed Echo Bay

* Renamed Budennovsk

Przhevalsk . . . . 42 30N 78 20 E
Pskov . . . . 57 50N 28 25 E
Puán 37 30s 63 0w
Pucallpa 8 25s 74 30w
Puchi . . . . 29 42N 113 54 E
Pudukkottai . . . . . 10 28N 78 47 E
Puebla 19 0N 98 10w
Puebla □ 18 30N 98 0w
Pueblo 38 20N 104 40w
Pueblo Hundido . . 26 20s 69 30w
Pueblonuevo 38 20N 5 15w
Puelches 38 5s 66 0w
Puente Alto 33 32s 70 35w
Puente Genil 37 22N 4 47w
Puerh . . . . 23 11N 100 56 E
Puerto Armuelles . . 8 20N 83 10w
Puerto Asís 0 30N 76 30w
Puerto Ayacucho . . 5 40N 67 35w
Puerto Barrios . . 15 40N 88 40w
Puerto Berrío 6 30N 74 30w
Puerto Bolívar . . 3 10s 79 55w
Puerto Cabello . . . 10 28N 68 1w
Puerto Cabezas . . 14 0N 83 30w
Puerto Carreño . . 6 12N 67 22w
Puerto Casado . . 22 19s 57 56w
Puerto Cortes . . 15 51N 88 0w
Puerto Cortés . . . 8 20N 82 20w
Puerto Coyle . . . 50 54s 69 15w
Puerto Cumarebo . 11 29N 69 21w
Puerto de Santa
    María 36 35N 6 15w
Puerto del Rosario . 28 30N 13 52w
Puerto Deseado . . 47 45s 66 0w
Puerto Páez 6 13N 67 28w
Puerto Leguizamo . 0 12s 74 46w
Puerto Lobos . . . 42 0s 65 3w
Puerto Madryn . . 42 48s 65 4w
Puerto Montt . . 41 28s 72 57w
Puerto Natales . . 51 45s 72 25w
Puerto Padre . . . 21 13N 76 35w
Puerto Pirámides . 42 35s 64 20w
Puerto Piritu . . . 10 5N 65 0w
Puerto Plata . . . 19 40N 70 45w
Puerto Princesa . 9 55N 118 50 E
Puerto Quellón . 43 7s 73 37w
Puerto Rico, I. . . 18 15N 66 45w
Puerto Saavedra . 38 47s 73 24w
Puerto Suárez . . 18 58s 57 52w
Puerto Varas . . 41 19s 72 59w
Puertollano 38 43N 4 7w

Pueyrredón, L. 47 20s 72 0w
Pugachev . . . . 52 0N 48 55 E
Puget Sd. 47 15N 123 30w
Puglia □ . . . . 41 0N 16 30 E
Pukaki, L. . . . . . . 44 4s 170 1 E
Pukatawagan . . . 55 45N 101 20w
Pukekohe . . . . . 37 12s 174 55 E
Pula . . . . 39 0N 9 0 E
Pulacayo 20 25s 66 41w
Pulantien . . . . . 39 25N 122 0 E
Pulaski, N.Y. . . 43 32N 76 9w
Pulaski, Tenn. . . 35 10N 87 0w
Pulaski, Va. . . . 37 4N 80 49w
Puławy . . . . . . 51 23N 21 59 E
Pulicat L. . . . . . 13 40N 80 15 E
Pullman 46 49N 117 10w
Puloraja . . . . . . 4 55N 95 24 E
Pułtusk . . . . . . 52 43N 21 6 E
Puluntohai . . . . 47 2N 87 29 E
Punch . . . . 33 48N 74 4 E
Pune . . . . 18 29N 73 57 E
Punjab □ . . . . . 31 0N 76 0 E
Puno 15 55s 70 3w
Punta Alta . . . 38 53s 62 4w
Punta Arenas . . . 53 0s 71 0w
Punta de Díaz . . . 28 0s 70 45w
Punta Delgada . . 42 43s 63 38w
Punta Gorda . . 16 10N 88 45w
Punta Rieles . . . 22 20s 59 40w
Puntabie . . . . . 32 12s 134 5 E
Puntarenas . . . 10 0N 84 50w
Punto Fijo 11 42N 70 13w
Purace, Mt. . . . 2 21N 76 23w
Purbeck, I. of . . 50 40N 2 5w
Puri . . . . 19 50N 85 58 E
Purnea . . . . . . 25 45N 87 31 E
Pursat . . . . . . 12 34N 103 50 E
Purulia . . . . . 23 17N 86 33 E
Purus, R. 3 42s 61 28w
Purwakarta . . . 6 35s 107 29 E
Purwodadi, Jawa . 7 7s 110 55 E
Purwodadi, Jawa . 7 51s 110 0 E
Purwokerto . . . 7 25s 109 14 E
Purworedjo . . . 7 43s 110 2 E
Pusan . . . . . . 35 5N 129 0 E
Pushchino . . . 54 20N 158 10 E
Pushkino . . . . 51 16N 47 9 E
Putao . . . . . . 27 28N 97 30 E
Putaruru . . . . 38 3s 175 47 E
Putehachi . . . . 48 4N 122 45 E

Putien . . . . 22 28N 119 0 E
Puttalam . . . . . . 8 4N 79 50 E
Puttgarden . . . . 54 28N 11 15 E
Putumayo, R. . . . 3 7s 67 58 E
Puy de Dôme, Mt. . 45 46N 2 57 E
Puyallup 47 10N 122 22w
Puy-de-Dôme □ . . 45 47N 3 0 E
Pweto . . . . 8 25s 28 51 E
Pyatigorsk . . . . 44 2N 43 0 E
Pyinmana . . . . 19 45N 96 20 E
Pyŏngyang . . . 39 0N 125 30 E
Pyrenees, Mts. . . 42 45N 0 20 E
Pyrénées-
    Atlantiques □ . . 43 15N 0 45w
Pyrénées-
    Orientales □ . . . 42 35N 2 25 E
Pyu . . . . 18 30N 96 35 E

Q

Qabatiya . . . . 32 25N 35 16 E
Qadam . . . . 32 55N 66 45 E
Qadhima . . . . . 22 20N 39 13 E
Qal'at al Mu'azzam . 27 43N 37 27 E
Qal'at Sālih . . . 31 31N 47 16 E
Qal'at Sura . . . . 26 10N 38 40 E
Qala-i-Kirta . . . 32 15N 63 0 E
Qala Nau . . . . . 35 0N 63 5 E
Qalqīlya . . . . . 32 12N 34 58 E
Qâra . . . . 29 38N 26 30 E
Qasr-e Qand . . . 26 15N 60 45 E
Qasr Farâfra . . . 27 0N 28 1 E
Qasr Hamam . . 21 5N 46 5 E
Qatar ■ . . . . . . 25 30N 51 15 E
Qattara
    Depression=
    Qattara,
    Munkhafed el . . . 29 30N 27 30 E
Qattara,
    Munkhafed el . . . 29 30N 27 30 E
Qazvin . . . . . . 36 15N 50 0 E
Qena . . . . 26 10N 32 43 E
Qesari . . . . 32 30N 34 53 E
Qeshm . . . . . . 26 55N 56 10 E
Qeshm, I. . . . . 26 50N 56 0 E
Qeys, Jazireh-ye . 26 32N 53 56 E
Qezi'ot . . . . . . 30 52N 34 28 E

Qila Safed . . . . . . 29 0N 61 30 E
Qila Saifullah . . . . 30 45N 68 17 E
Qiryat Bialik . . . . 32 50N 35 5 E
Qiryat Gat . . . . 31 36N 35 47 E
Qiryat 'Eqron . . . 31 52N 34 49 E
Qiryat Hayyim . . 32 49N 35 4 E
Qiryat Mal'akhi . . 31 44N 34 45 E
Qiryat Shemona . . 33 13N 35 35 E
Qiryat Tiv'om . . 32 43N 35 8 E
Qiryat Yam . . . 32 51N 35 4 E
Qīzān . . . . 16 57N 42 3 E
Qom . . . . 34 40N 51 4 E
Quairading . . . . 32 0s 117 21 E
Qualeup . . . . . . 33 48s 116 48 E
Quan Long . . . . 9 7N 105 8 E
Quang Ngai . . . . 15 13N 108 58 E
Quang Tri . . . . 16 45N 107 13 E
Quantock Hills . . 51 8N 3 10w
Quaraí 30 15s 56 20w
Qūchān . . . . . 37 10N 58 27 E
* Que Que . . . . . . 18 58s 29 48 E
Queanbeyan . . . 35 17s 149 14 E
Québec 46 52N 71 13w
Québec □ 50 0N 70 0w
Queen Charlotte
    Is. 53 10N 132 0w
Queen Charlotte
    Str. 51 0N 128 0w
Queen Elizabeth Is. 75 0N 95 0w
Queen Maud G. . . 68 15N 102 0w
Queensland □ . . . 15 0s 142 0 E
Queenstown,
    Australia . . . . . 42 4s 145 35 E
Queenstown, N.Z. . 45 1s 168 40 E
Queenstown,
    S.Africa . . . . . 31 52s 26 52 E
Queimadas 11 0s 39 38w
Quela . . . . 9 10s 16 56 E
Quelimane . . . . 17 53s 36 58 E
Quemoy, I. =
    Kinmen, I. . . . . 24 25N 118 25 E
Quequén 38 30s 58 30w
Querétaro 20 40N 100 23w
Querétaro □ . . . 20 30N 100 30w
Quesnel 53 5N 122 30w
Quetico 48 45N 90 55w
Quetico Prov. Park 48 15N 91 45w
Quetta . . . . . . 30 15N 66 55 E
† Quetta □ . . . . . 30 15N 68 30 E

Quezaltenango 14 40N 91 30w
Quezon City . . . . 14 38N 121 0 E
Qui Nhon . . . . . 13 40N 109 13 E
Quibdo 5 42N 76 40w
Quiberon 47 29N 3 9w
Quilân, C. 43 15s 74 30w
Quilengues . . . . 14 12s 15 12 E
Quillota 32 54s 71 16w
Quilon . . . . . . 8 50N 76 38 E
Quilpie . . . . . . 26 35s 144 11 E
Quimilí 27 40s 62 30w
Quimper 48 0N 4 9w
Quimperlé 47 53s 3 33w
Quincy, Mass. . . 42 14N 71 0w
Quincy.Fla. . . . 30 34N 84 34w
Quincy, Ill. . . . 39 55N 91 20w
Quines 32 14s 65 48w
Quintana Roo □ . 19 0 E 88 0w
Quintanar de la
    Orden 39 36N 3 5w
Quintero 32 45s 71 30w
Quito 0 15s 78 35w
Quixadá 4 55s 39 0w
Qumran 31 43N 35 27N
Quoin, I. . . . . 14 54s 129 32 E
Quorn . . . . . . 32 25s 138 0 E
Qurug-Tagh, Mts. . 41 30N 90 0 E
Qûs . . . . 25 55N 32 50 E
Quseir . . . . . . 26 7N 34 16 E

R

Ra'anana . . . . 32 12N 34 52 E
Raane . . . . 64 40N 24 28 E
Raasay, I. 57 25N 6 4w
Raba . . . . 8 36s 118 55 E
Rabai . . . . 3 50s 39 31 E
Rabat 34 2N 6 48w
Rabaul . . . . . 4 24s 152 18 E
Rabigh . . . . . . 22 50N 39 5 E
Race, C. 46 40N 53 18w
Racibórz . . . . 50 7N 18 18 E
Racine 42 41N 87 51w
Radford 37 8N 80 32w
Radom . . . . . 51 23N 21 12 E
Radomir . . . . 42 37N 23 4 E
Radomsko . . . 51 5N 19 28 E

* Renamed Kwekwe
† Now part of Baluchistan

Radstock 51 17N   2 25W
Radville 49 30N 104 15W
Rae 62 45N 115 50W
Rae Bareli .... 26 18N 81 20 E
Rae Isthmus 66 40N 87 30W
Raetihi .... 39 25s 175 17 E
Rafaela 31 10s 61 30W
Rafhä .... 29 35N 43 35 E
Rafsanjän .... 30 30N 56 5 E
Rãgã .... 8 28N 25 41 E
Ragama .... 7 0N 79 54 E
Raglan, Australia .. 23 42s 150 49 E
Raglan, N.Z. ..... 37 55s 174 55 E
Ragusa .... 36 56N 14 42 E
Rahad el Bardi .... 11 20N 23 40 E
Raichur .... 16 10N 77 20 E
Raigarh .... 21 56N 83 25 E
Railton .... 41 25s 146 28 E
Rainier, Mt. 46 50N 121 50W
Rainy River 48 50N 94 30W
Raipur .... 21 17N 81 45 E
Raith 48 50N 90 0W
Raj Nandgaon .... 21 5N 81 5 E
Rajahmundry .... 17 1N 81 48 E
Rajapalaiyam ..... 9 25N 77 35 E
Rajasthan □ ...... 26 45N 73 30 E
Rajgarh .... 24 2N 76 45 E
Rajkot .... 22 15N 70 56 E
Rajshahi .... 24 22N 88 39 E
Rajshahi □ .... 25 0N 89 0 E
Rakaia .... 43 45s 172 1 E
Rakaia, R. .... 43 54s 172 12 E
Rakatau, P. ...... 6 10s 105 20 E
Raleigh, Australia . 30 27s 153 2 E
Raleigh, Canada .. 49 30N 92 5W
Rám Alläh .... 31 55N 35 10 E
Ram Head .... 37 47s 149 30 E
Rama .... 32 56N 35 21 E
Ramanathapuram .. 9 25N 78 55 E
Ramat Gan .... 32 4N 34 50 E
Ramat Ha Sharon . 32 7N 34 50 E
Ramat Ha Shofet . 32 36N 35 5 E
Rambre Kyun, I. .. 19 0N 94 0 E
Ramelau, Mt. ..... 8 55s 126 22 E
Ramgarh .... 23 39N 85 31 E
Rãmhormoz ...... 31 15N 49 35 E
Ramisi .... 4 35s 39 15 E
Ramla .... 31 55N 34 52 E
Ramnad .... 9 25N 78 55 E
Ramona 33 1N 116 56W

Ramoutsa .... 24 50s 25 52 E
Rampart 65 30N 150 10W
Rampur .... 23 25N 73 53 E
Rampur Hat ...... 24 10N 87 50 E
Ramsey, Canada .. 47 25N 82 20W
Ramsey, U.K. 54 20N   4 21W
Ramsgate .... 51 20N   1 25 E
Ranaghat .... 23 15N 88 35 E
Rancagua 34 10s 70 50W
Ranchester 44 57N 107 12W
Ranchi .... 23 19N 85 27 E
Ranco, L. 40 15s 72 25W
Randers .... 56 29N 10 1 E
Randfontein ..... 26 8s 27 45 E
Randolph 43 55N 72 39W
Rãneã .... 65 53s 22 18 E
Rangaunu, B. ..... 34 51s 173 15 E
Rangia .... 26 15N 91 20 E
Rangitaiki, R. .... 37 54s 176 53 E
Rangitata, R. ..... 44 11s 171 30 E
Rangkasbitung ... 6 22s 106 16 E
Rangon=
  Rangoon .... 16 45N 96 20 E
Rangoon .... 16 45N 96 20 E
Rangpur .... 25 42N 89 22 E
Raniganj .... 23 40N 87 15 E
Rankin Inlet 62 30N 93 0W
Rankins Springs .. 33 49s 146 14 E
Rannoch 56 41N   4 20W
Rannoch, L. 56 41N   4 20W
Ranohira .... 22 29s 45 24 E
Ranong .... 9 56N 98 40 E
Rantauprapat .... 2 15N 99 50 E
Rantemario, Mt. .. 3 15s 119 57 E
Rantis .... 32 4N 35 3 E
Rantoul 40 18N 88 10W
Rapa Iti, Is. 27 35s 144 20W
Rapang .... 3 45s 119 55 E
Rapid City 44 0N 103 0W
Rarotonga, I. 21 30s 160 0W
Rasa, Pte. 40 55s 63 20N
Ras al Khaima .... 25 50N 56 5 E
Ra's Al-Unuf .... 30 25N 18 15 E
Ra's al Tannurah .. 26 40N 50 10 E
Rashad .... 11 55N 31 0 E
Rashīd .... 31 21N 30 22 E
Rasht .... 37 20N 49 40 E
Rat Is. .... 51 50N 178 15 E
Ratangarh .... 28 5N 74 35 E

Rath Luirc 52 21N   8 40W
Rathdrum, Eire .. 52 57N   6 13W
Rathdrum, U.S.A . 47 50N 116 58W
Rathenow .... 52 38N 12 23 E
Rathkeale 52 32N   8 57W
Rathlin, I. 55 18N   6 14W
Ratisbon=
  Regensburg .... 49 1N 12 7 E
Ratlam .... 23 20N 75 0 E
Ratnagiri .... 16 57N 73 18 E
Raton 37 0N 104 30W
Rattray Hd. 57 38N   1 50W
Raukumara, Ra. .. 38 5s 177 55 E
Rauma .... 61 10N 21 30 E
Ravar .... 31 20N 56 51 E
Ravenna .... 44 28N 12 15 E
Ravensburg ...... 47 48N   9 38 E
Ravenshoe ...... 17 37s 145 29 E
Ravensthorpe .... 33 35s 120 2 E
Ravi, R. .... 30 35N 71 38 E
Ravine .... 0 15s 36 15 E
Rawalpindi ...... 33 38N 73 8 E
Rawalpindi □ .... 33 38N 73 8 E
Rawdon 46 3N 73 40W
Rawene .... 35 25s 173 32 E
Rawlinna .... 30 58s 125 28 E
Rawlins 41 50N 107 20W
Rawson 43 15s 65 0W
Ray, C. 47 33N 59 15W
Rayagada .... 19 15N 83 20 E
Raychikhinsk .... 49 46N 129 25 E
Raymond, Canada . 49 30N 112 35W
Raymond, U.S.A. . 46 45N 123 48W
Raymondville 26 30N 97 50W
Raymore 50 25N 104 31W
Rayne 30 16N 92 16W
Raz, Pte. du 48 2N   4 47W
Ré, I. de 46 12N   1 30W
Reading, U.K. 51 27N   0 57W
Reading, U.S.A. .. 40 20N 75 53W
Realicó 35 0s 64 15W
Rebi .... 5 30s 134 7 E
Recife 8 0s 35 0W
Reconquista 29 10s 59 45W
Recreo 29 25s 65 10W
Red, R. 48 10N 97 0W
Red Bluff 40 11N 122 11W
Red Deer 52 20N 113 50W
Red Lake 51 1N 94 1W
Red Oak 41 0N 95 10W

Red Sea .... 20 0N 39 0 E
Red Wing 44 32N 92 35W
Redbridge ...... 51 35N   0 7 E
Redcar 54 37N   1 4W
Redcliff 50 10N 110 50W
Redcliffe .... 27 12s 153 0 E
Redcliffs .... 34 16s 142 10 E
Redding 40 30N 122 25W
Redditch 52 18N   1 57W
Redlands 34 0N 117 0w
Redmond,
  Australia ..... 34 55s 117 40 E
Redmond, U.S.A. . 44 19N 121 11w
Redonda, I. 16 58N 62 19w
Redondela 42 15N   8 38w
Redondo 38 39N   7 37w
Redondo Beach .. 33 52N 118 26w
Redruth 50 14N   5 14w
Redstone 52 8N 123 42w
Redvers 49 35N 101 40w
Redwater 53 55N 113 0w
Redwood City ... 37 30N 122 15w
Ree, L. 53 35N   8 0w
Reedley 34 40N 119 27w
Reedsport 43 45N 124 4w
Reefton .... 42 6s 171 51 E
Regavim .... 32 32N 35 2 E
Regensburg ..... 49 1N 12 7 E
Reggio nell'Emilia . 44 42N 10 38 E
Réggio di Calábria . 38 7N 15 38 E
Regina 50 30N 104 35w
Registan, Reg. ... 30 15N 65 0 E
Rehoboth .... 17 55s 15 5 E
Rehovot .... 31 54N 34 48 E
Reichenbach .... 50 36N 12 19 E
Reid .... 35 17s 149 8 E
Reid River ..... 19 40s 146 48 E
Reidsville 36 21N 79 40w
Reigate 51 14N   0 11w
Reims .... 49 15N   4 0 E
Reina .... 32 43N 35 18 E
Reina
  Adelaida, Arch. . 52 20s 74 0w
Reindeer L. 57 20N 102 20w
Reinga, C. ...... 34 25s 172 43 E
Reinosa 43 2N   4 15w
Reisengebirge ... 50 40N 15 5 E
Reitz .... 27 48s 28 29 E
Rekinniki .... 60 38N 163 50 E
Remanso 9 41s 42 4w

Rembang .... 6 42s 111 21 E
Remeshk .... 26 55N 58 50 E
Remscheid ...... 51 11N   7 12 E
Rendsburg ...... 54 18N   9 41 E
Rene 66 2N 179 25w
Renfrew, Canada .. 45 30N 76 40w
Renfrew, U.K. ... 55 52N   4 24w
Rengat .... 0 30s 102 45 E
Renkum .... 51 58N   5 43 E
Renmark .... 34 11s 140 43 E
Rennes 48 7N   1 41w
Reno 39 30N 119 0w
Renton 47 30N 122 9w
Republican, R. ... 39 3N 96 48w
Repulse Bay 66 30N 86 30w
Reserve 33 50N 108 54w
Resistencia 27 30s 59 0w
Reşiţa .... 45 18N 21 53 E
Resolution I.,
  Canada 61 30N 65 0w
Resolution, I., N.Z. 45 40s 166 40 E
Ressano Garcia .. 25 25s 32 0 E
Retalhulen 14 33N 91 46w
Réthímnon ..... 35 15N 24 40 E
Réunion, Í. ..... 22 0s 56 0 E
Reus .... 41 10N   1 5 E
Reutlingen ..... 48 28N   9 13 E
Revelstoke 51 0N 118 0w
Revilla Gigedo Is. . 18 40N 112 0w
Rewa .... 24 33N 81 25 E
Rewari .... 28 15N 76 40 E
Rexburg 43 45N 111 50w
Rey Malabo ..... 3 45N   8 50 E
Reykanes, Pen. .. 63 48N 22 40w
Reykjavik ...... 64 10N 21 57 E
Reynosa 26 5N 98 18w
Reza'iyeh .... 37 40N 45 0 E
Rhayader 52 19N   3 30w
Rheden .... 52 0N   6 3 E
Rhein, R. .... 51 42N   6 20 E
Rhein-Donau-Kanal 49 45N 11 0 E
Rheine .... 52 17N   7 25 E
Rheinland-Pfalz □ . 50 50N   7 0 E
Rhine, R. =
  Rhein, R. ..... 51 42N   6 20 E
Rhinelander 45 38N 89 29w
Rhir, C. 30 38N   9 54w
Rhode Island □ .. 41 38N 71 37w
Rhodes, I. =

Ródhos, I. . . . . . . 36 15N 28 10 E
Rhodesia ■ . . . . . . 20 0 s 28 30 E
Rhodope, Mts. =
Rhodopi Planina 41 40N 24 20 E
Rhodopi Planina . . 41 40N 24 20 E
Rhön, Mts. . . . . . . 50 25N 10 0 E
Rhondda 51 39N   3 30w
Rhône □ . . . . 45 54N   4 35 E
Rhône, R. . . . . . . 43 28N   4 42 E
Rhum, I. 57 0N   6 20w
Rhyl 53 19N   3 29w
Riachão . . . . 7 20 s 46 37w
Riau □ . . . . 1 0N 102 35 E
Riau, Kep. . . . . . . 0 30N 104 20 E
Ribadeo 43 35N   7 5w
Ribas do Rio Pardo 20 27 s 53 46w
Ribatejo, Reg. 39 15N   8 30w
Ribble, R. 54 13N   2 20w
Ribe . . . . 55 19N   8 44 E
Ribeirão Prêto . . 21 10 s 47 50w
Riccarton . . . . . . 43 32 s 172 37 E
Rice Lake 44 10N 78 10w
Richards B. . . . . . 28 48 s 32 6 E
Richibucto 46 42N 64 54w
Richland 44 49N 117 9w
Richmond,
Australia . . . . . 20 43 s 143 8 E
Richmond, N.Z. . . 41 4 s 173 12 E
Richmond, C. Prov 31 23 s 23 56 E
Richmond, Natal
S. Africa . . . . . 29 54 s 30 8 E
Richmond, Surrey . 51 28N   0 18w
Richmond, Yorks. . 54 24N   1 43w
Richmond, Calif. . . 38 0N 122 30w
Richmond, Ind. . . 39 50N 84 50w
Richmond, Ky. . . 37 40N 84 20w
Richmond, Utah . 41 55N 111 48w
Richmond, Va. . . 37 33N 77 27w
Richmond Gulf, L. 56 20N 75 50w
Richwood 38 17N 80 32w
Ridgedale 53 0N 104 10w
Ridgetown 42 26N 81 52w
Ridgway 41 25N 78 43w
Riding Mountain
Nat. Park 50 55N 100 25w
Ried . . . . 48 14N 13 30 E
Riet, R. . . . . 29 0 s 23 54 E
Rieti . . . . 42 23N 12 50 E
Rifle 39 40N 107 50w
Riga . . . . 56 53N 24 8 E

Rigolet 54 10N 58 23w
Rijau . . . . 11 7N   5 14 E
Rijeka . . . . 45 20N 14 21 E
Rijssen . . . . 52 19N   6 30 E
Rijswijk . . . . 52 4N   4 22 E
Riley 39 18N 96 50w
Rima, R. . . . . 13 10N   5 15 E
Rimi . . . . 12 58N   7 43 E
Rímini . . . . 44 3N 12 33 E
Rîmnicu Sărat . . 45 26N 27 3 E
Rîmnicu Vîlcea . . 45 9N 24 21 E
Rimouski 48 27N 68 30w
Rineanna 52 42N 85 7w
Ringim . . . . 12 8N   9 10 E
Ringkøbing . . . . . 56 5N   8 15 E
Rio Amazonas,
Estuario do 1 0N 49 0w
Rio Branco, Brazil 9 58 s 67 49w
Rio Branco,
Uruguay . . . . . . 32 34 s 53 25w
Rio Claro 10 20N 61 25w
Rio Cuarto . . . . . 33 10 s 64 25w
Rio de Janeiro . . 23 0 s 43 12w
Rio de Janeiro □ . . 22 50 s 43 0w
Rio do Sul . . . . . 27 95 s 49 37w
Rio Gallegos . . . . 51 35 s 69 15w
Rio Grande, Brazil 32 0 s 52 20w
Rio Grande, R. . . 37 47N 106 15w
Rio Grande do
Norte . . . . 5 45 s 36 0w
Rio Grande do
Sul . . . . 30 0 s 54 0w
Rio Largo . . . . . . 9 28 s 35 50w
Rio Mulatos . . . . 19 40 s 66 50w
Rio Muni □ . . . . . 1 30N 10 0 E
Rio Negro, Brazil 26 0 s 50 0w
Rio Verde, Brazil 17 43 s 50 56w
Río Verde,
Mexico 21 56N 99 59w
Rio Vista 38 11N 121 44w
Riobamba . . . . . . 1 50 s 78 45w
Ríohacha 11 33N 72 55w
Ríosucio 5 30N 75 40w
Rioscio 7 27N 77 7w
Ripon, U.K. 54 8N   1 31w
Ripon, U.S.A. . . . 43 51N 88 50w
Rishon Le Zion . . 31 58N 34 48 E
Rishpon . . . . 32 12N 34 49 E
Risør . . . . 58 43N   9 13 E
Riti . . . . 7 57N   9 41 E

Ritzville 47 10N 118 21w
Riva . . . . 45 53N 10 50 E
Rivadavia, Arg. . . 24 5 s 63 0w
Rivadavia, Chile . 29 50 s 70 35w
Rivas 11 30N 85 50w
Rivera . . . . 31 0 s 55 50w
Riverhead 40 53N 72 40w
Riverhurst 50 55N 106 50w
Rivers □ . . . . 5 0N   6 30 E
Riversdale . . . . . . 34 7 s 21 15 E
Riverside, Calif. . . 34 0N 117 15w
Riverside, Wyo. . . 41 12N 106 57w
Riverton, Australia 34 10 s 138 46 E
Riverton, Canada . 51 5N 97 0w
Riverton, N.Z. . . 46 21 s 168 0 E
Riverton, U.S.A. . 43 1N 108 27w
Riviera di Levante . 44 23N   9 15 E
Riviera di Ponente . 44 0N   7 58 E
Rivière Bleue 47 26N 69 2w
Rivière du Loup . . 47 50N 69 30w
Rivière Pentecôte . 49 57N 67 1w
Riyadh = Ar Riyád 24 41N 46 42 E
Rize . . . . 41 0N 40 30 E
Rjukan . . . . 59 54N   8 33 E
Roanne . . . . 46 3N   4 4 E
Roanoke, Ala. . . . 33 9N 85 23w
Roanoke, Va 37 19N 79 55w
Roanoke Rapids . 36 36N 77 42w
Roatán, I. de 16 23N 86 26w
Robertson . . . . . . 33 46 s 19 50 E
Roberval 48 32N 72 15w
Roblin 51 21N 101 25w
Robson, Mt. 53 10N 119 10w
Robstown 27 47N 97 40w
Roca, C. da 38 40N   9 31w
Rocadas . . . . 16 45 s 15 0 E
Rocas, Is. . . . . . . 4 0 s 34 1w
Rocha . . . . 34 30 s 54 25w
Rochdale 53 36N   2 10w
Rochefort 45 56N   0 57w
Rochelle 41 55N 89 5w
Rocher River . . . 61 12N 114 0w
Rochester,
Australia . . . . . 36 22 s 144 41 E
Rochester, U.K. . 51 22N   0 30 E
Rochester, Minn. . 44 1N 92 28w
Rochester, N.H. . . 43 19N 70 57w
Rochester, N.Y. . . 43 10N 77 40w
Rock Hill 34 55N 81 2w
Rock Island 41 30N 90 35w

Rock Sound 24 54N 76 12w
Rock Springs 46 55N 106 11w
Rockall, I. 57 37N 13 42w
Rockford, Ill. 42 20N 89 0w
Rockford, Mich. . . 43 7N 85 33w
Rockhampton . . . 23 22 s 150 32 E
Rockingham . . . . 32 15 s 115 38 E
Rockland, Mass. . 44 6N 69 8w
Rockville, Md. . . . 39 7N 77 10w
Rocky Gully . . . . 34 30 s 117 0 E
Rocky Mount . . . 35 55N 77 48w
Rocky Mountain
House 52 22N 114 55w
Rocky Mts. 48 0N 113 0w
Rockyford 51 13N 113 8w
Rødbyhavn . . . . . 54 39N 11 22 E
Roddickton 50 51N 56 8w
Rodez . . . . 44 21N   2 33 E
Ródhos . . . . 36 15N 28 10 E
Ródhos, I. . . . . . 36 15N 28 10 E
Rodney, C. . . . . . 36 17 s 174 50 E
Rodriguez, I. . . . . 20 0 s 65 0 E
Roebourne . . . . . 20 44 s 117 9 E
Roebuck, B. . . . . 18 5 s 122 20 E
Roebuck Plains
P.O. . . . . 17 56 s 122 28 E
Roermond . . . . . 51 12N   6 0 E
Roes Welcome Sd. 65 0N 87 0w
Roeselare . . . . . . 50 57N   3 7 E
Rogaland □ . . . . . 59 12N   6 20 E
Rogers 36 20N 94 0w
Roggan River . . . 54 24N 78 5w
Roggeveldberge . . 32 10 s 20 10 E
Rohri . . . . 27 45N 68 51 E
Rohtak . . . . 28 55N 76 43 E
Rolândia . . . . . . 23 5 s 52 0w
Rolla 38 0N 91 42w
Rollingstone . . . . 19 2 s 146 24 E
Rolleston . . . . . . 43 35 s 172 24 E
Rolleville 23 41N 76 0w
Roma, Australia . 26 32 s 148 49 E
Roma, Italy . . . . 41 54N 12 30 E
Roma, Sweden . . 57 32N 18 28 E
Roman . . . . 43 8N 23 54 E
Romania ■ =
Rumania ■ . . . . 46 0N 25 0 E
Romanzof, C. . . . 61 49N 165 56w
Rome, Italy =
Roma . . . . 41 54N 12 30 E
Rome, Ga. 34 20N 85 0w

Rome, N.Y. 43 14N 75 29w
Romney Marsh . . . 51 0N   1 0 E
Romorantin-
Lanthenay . . . . . 47 21N   1 45 E
Romsdalen, R. . . . 62 25N   7 50 E
Ronaldsay,
North I. 59 23N   2 26w
Ronaldsay,
South I. 58 47N   2 56w
Roncador, S. do . . 12 30 s 52 30w
Roncevoux 43 0N   1 23w
Ronda 36 46N   5 12w
Rondônia □ . . . . . 11 0 s 63 0w
Rondonópolis . . . 16 28 s 54 38w
Rongai . . . . 0 10 s 35 51 E
Rønne . . . . 55 6N 14 44 E
Ronsard, C. . . . . 24 46 s 113 10 E
Ronse . . . . 50 45N   3 35 E
Roodepoort-
Maraisburg . . . . 26 11 s 27 54 E
Roorkee . . . . 29 52N 77 59 E
Roosendaal . . . . . 51 32N   4 29 E
Roosevelt Res. . . 33 46N 111 0w
Roper, R. . . . . . . 14 43 s 135 27 E
Roraima □ 2 0N 61 30w
Roraima, Mt. 5 10N 60 40w
Rosa, Mte. . . . . . 45 57N   7 53 E
Rosario, Arg. . . . 33 0 s 60 50w
Rosário, Brazil . . . 3 0 s 44 15w
Rosario, Mexico . 23 0 s 105 52w
Rosario de la
Frontera . . . . . . 25 50 s 65 0w
Rosário do Sul . . 30 15 s 54 55w
Rosas . . . . 42 19N   3 10 E
Rosas, G. de . . . . 42 10N   3 15 E
Roscommon 53 38N   8 11w
Roscommon □ . . . 53 40N   8 15w
Roscrea 52 57N   7 47w
Rose Blanche . . . 47 38N 58 45w
Rose Harbour . . . 52 15N 131 10w
Rose Valley 52 19N 103 49w
Roseau 48 56N 96 0w
Rosenberg 29 30N 95 48w
Rosebud 31 5N 97 0w
Roseburg 43 10N 123 10w
Rosedale . . . . . . 38 11 s 146 48 E
Rosetown . . . . . . 57 33N 108 0 E
Rosetta = Rashîd . 31 21N 30 22 E
Roseville 38 46N 121 41w
Rosewood . . . . . 35 38 s 147 52 E

Rosh Ha'Ayin .... 32 5N 34 47 E
Rosh Pinna ...... 32 58N 35 32 E
Rosignol 6 15N 57 30w
Roskilde .... 55 38N 12 3 E
Roslavl.......... 53 57N 32 55 E
Ross, N.Z. ...... 42 53s 170 49 E
Ross, U.K. 51 55N 2 34w
Ross □.......... 70 0s 170 5w
Ross
  Dependency □ .. 70 0s 170 0w
Ross Sea .... 74 0s 178 0 E
Rossland 49 6N 117 50w
Rosslare 52 17N 6 23w
Rosso 16 30N 15 49w
Rossosh .... 50 15N 39 20 E
Rosthern 52 40N 106 20w
Rostock .... 54 4N 12 9 E
Rostov .... 47 15N 39 45 E
Roswell 33 26N 104 32w
Rosyth 56 2N 3 26w
Rother, R. 50 59N 0 40w
Rotherham 53 26N 1 21w
Rothes 57 31N 3 12w
Rothesay 55 50N 5 3w
Roti, I. .... 10 50s 123 0 E
Roto .... 33 0s 145 30 E
Rotorua .... 38 9s 176 16 E
Rotorua, L. ...... 38 5s 176 18 E
Rotterdam .... 51 55N 4 30 E
Rottnest, I. ...... 32 0s 115 27 E
Rottweil .... 48 9N 8 38 E
Rotuma, I. ...... 12 25s 177 5 E
Roubaix .... 50 40N 3 10 E
Rouen .... 49 27N 1 4 E
Rouergue, Reg. .. 44 20N 2 20 E
Roumania■=
  Rumania ■ .... 46 0N 25 0 E
Round, Mt. ...... 30 26s 152 16 E
Roundup 46 25N 108 35w
Rousay, I. 59 10N 3, 2w
Roussillon, Reg. .. 45 24N 4 49 E
Rouxville .... 30 11s 26 50 E
Rouyn 48 20N 79 0w
Rovaniemi .... 66 29N 25 41 E
Rovereto .... 45 53N 11 3 E
Rovigo .... 45 4N 11 48 E
Rovinj .... 45 18N 13 40 E
Rovno .... 50 40N 26 10 E
Roxas .... 11 36N 122 49 E
Roxburgh .... 45 33s 169 19 E

Roy Hill .... 22 37s 119 58 E
Royal Oak 42 30N 83 5w
Royale, I. 48 0N 89 0w
Royan 45 37N 1 2w
Rtishchevo ...... 52 35N 43 50 E
Ruapehu, Mt. ... 39 18s 175 35 E
Rubeho Mts. .... 6 50s 36 25 E
Rubio 7 43N 72 22w
Rubtsovsk ...... 51 30N 80 50 E
Ruby .... 38 27s 145 55 E
Rudall .... 33 43s 136 17 E
Rudnichny ...... 59 38N 52 26 E
Rudnogorsk .... 57 15N 103 42 E
Rudnyy .... 52 57N 63 7 E
Rudolf, L. =
  Turkana, L. .... 4 10N 36 10 F
Rufa'a .... 14 44N 33 32 E
Rufiji, R. .... 8 0s 39 20 E
Rufino 34 20s 62 50w
Rufisque 14 43N 17 17w
Rugby, U.K. 52 23N 1 16w
Rugby, U.S.A. .. 48 21N 100 0w
Rügen, I. .... 54 22N 13 25 E
Ruhâma .... 31 31N 34 43 E
Ruhengeri ...... 1 30s 29 36 E
Ruhr, R. .... 51 27N 6 44 E
Ruki, R. .... 0 5N 18 17 E
Rukungiri .... 0 53s 29 58 E
Rukwa, L. ...... 7 50s 32 10 E
Rum Jungle .... 13 0s 130 59 E
Rumania ■ ..... 46 0N 25 0 E
Rumbalara ..... 25 20s 134 29 E
Rumford 44 30N 70 30w
Rumoi 43 56N 141 39w
Rumuruti ...... 0 17N 36 32 E
Runanga .... 42 25s 171 15 E
Runcorn 53 20N 2 44w
Rungwa .... 6 55s 33 32 E
Rungwe, Mt. ... 9 11s 33 32 E
Runka .... 12 28N 7 20 E
Rupat, I. .... 1 45N 101 40 E
Rupert House =
  Fort Rupert 51 30N 78 40w
Rusape .... 18 35s 32 8 E
Ruse .... 43 48N 25 59 E
Rushden 52 17N 0 37w
Rushville 39 38N 85 22w
Rushworth ..... 36 32s 145 1 E
Russas 4 56s 37 58w
Russell, Canada .. 50 50N 101 20w

Russell, U.S.A. .. 38 56N 98 55w
Russellville, Ala. .. 34 30N 87 44w
Russellville, Ark. .. 35 15N 93 0w
* Russian Soviet
    Federal Socialist
    Rep. .... 60 0N 80 0 E
Russkaya Polyana . 53 47N 73 53 E
Rustenburg ...... 25 41s 27 14 E
Ruston 32 30N 92 40w
Ruteng .... 8 26s 120 30 E
Ruth 39 15N 115 1w
Rutherglen,
  Australia ...... 36 5s 146 29 E
Rutherglen, U.K. .. 55 50N 4 11w
Rutland 43 38N 73 0w
Rutshuru .... 1 13s 29 25 E
Ruvu .... 6 49s 38 43 E
Ruvuma, R. ..... 10 29s 40 28 E
Ruwenzori, Mts. .. 0 30N 29 55 E
Ruzomberok .... 49 3N 19 17 E
Rwanda ■ ...... 2 0s 30 0 E
Ryan, L. 55 0N 5 2w
Ryazan .... 54 38N 39 44 E
Ryazhsk .... 53 40N 40 7 E
Rybache .... 46 40N 81 20 E
Rybachiy Pol. .... 69 43N 32 0 E
† Rybinsk .... 58 3N 38 52 E
Rybinskoye, Vdkhr. . 58 30N 38 25 E
Ryde 50 44N 1 9w
Rye .... 50 57N 0 46 E
Rye, R. 54 12N 0 53w
Rypin .... 53 3N 19 32 E
Ryūkyū, Is. ..... 26 0N 128 0 E
Rzeszów .... 50 5N 21 58 E
Rzhev .... 56 15N 34 18 E

S

Sa'ad .... 31 28N 34 33 E
Sa'ádatábád ..... 30 10N 53 5 E
Saale, R. .... 51 57N 11 55 E
Saar, R. .... 49 20N 6 45 E
Saarbrücken .... 49 15N 6 58 E
Saaremaa, I. .... 58 30N 22 30 E
Saarland □ ...... 49 20N 0 75 E
Saba, I. 17 30N 63 10w
Sabadell .... 41 28N 2 7 E

Sabah □ .... 6 0N 117 0 E
Sabalan, Kuhha-ye 38 15N 47 49 E
Sabanalargo 10 38N 74 55w
Sabang .... 5 50N 95 15 E
Sabará 19 55s 43 55w
Sabastiya .... 32 17N 35 12 E
Sabáudia .... 41 17N 13 2 E
Sabhah .... 27 9N 14 29 E
Sabie .... 25 4s 30 48 E
Sabinas 27 50N 101 10w
Sabinas Hidalgo . 26 40N 100 10w
Sabine, R. 30 0N 93 45w
Sable, C., Canada . 43 29N 65 38w
Sable, C., U.S.A. . 25 5N 81 0w
Sable I. 44 0N 60 0w
Sabou 12 1N 2 28w
Sabzevár .... 36 15N 57 40 E
Sabzvāran ...... 28 45N 57 50 E
Saco 43 29N 70 28w
Sacramento .... 38 39N 121 30 E
Sacramento, R. .. 38 3N 121 56w
Sacramento Mts. . 32 30N 105 30w
Sádaba 42 1N 1 12w
Sadd el Aali .... 24 5N 32 54 E
Sade .... 11 22N 10 45 E
Sado, I. .... 38 15N 138 30 E
Safaniya .... 28 5N 48 42 E
Safed Koh ...... 34 15N 64 0 E
Safford 32 54N 109 52w
Saffron Walden .. 52 5N 0 15 E
Safi 32 20N 9 17w
Saga, Indonesia .. 2 40s 132 55 E
Saga, Japan .... 33 15N 130 18 E
Saga □ .... 33 15N 130 20 E
Sagaing .... 22 0N 96 0 E
Sagar .... 23 50N 78 50 E
Sagil .... 50 15N 91 15 E
Saginaw 43 26N 83 55w
Saginaw B. 43 50N 83 40w
Saglouc 62 30N 74 15w
Sagres 37 0N 8 58w
Sagua la Grande . 22 50N 80 10w
Saguache 38 10N 106 4w
Saguenay, R. 48 10N 69 45w
Sagunto 39 42N 0 18w
Sahagun 42 18N 5 2w
Sahara .... 23 0N 5 0 E
Saharanpur ..... 29 58N 77 33 E
Sahiwal .... 30 45N 73 8 E
Sa'idābād ...... 29 30N 55 45 E

Saidapet .... 13 0N 80 15 E
Saidu .... 34 50N 72 15 E
Saighan .... 35 10N 67 55 E
Saigon=Phanh
    Bho Ho Chi Minh 10 58N 106 40 E
Saihut .... 15 12N 51 10 E
Saijo .... 34 0N 133 5 E
Saiki .... 32 35N 131 50 E
St. Abbs Hd. 55 55N 2 10w
St. Albans, U.K. .. 51 46N 0 21w
St. Albans, U.S.A. . 44 49N 73 5w
St. Albans Hd. ... 50 34N 2 3w
St. André, C. .... 16 0s 44 27 E
St. Andrews 56 20N 2 48w
St. Arnaud ..... 36 32s 143 16 E
St. Asaph 53 15N 3 27w
† St. Augustin ... 51 19N 58 48w
St. Augustine ... 29 52N 81 20w
St. Austell 50 20N 4 48w
St. Barthélémy, I. . 17 50N 62 50w
St. Bees Hd. .... 54 30N 3 38 E
St. Boniface 49 50N 97 10w
St. Bride's B. ... 51 48N 5 15w
St. Brieuc 48 30N 2 46w
St. Catherine's Pt. . 50 34N 1 18w
St. Charles 38 46N 90 30w
St. Christopher, I. . 17 20N 62 40w
St. Clair, L. 42 30N 82 45w
St. Claude 49 40N 98 22w
St. Cloud 45 30N 94 11w
St. Cœur de Marie . 48 39N 71 43w
St. Cricq, C. .... 25 17s 113 6 E
St. Croix, I. 17 30N 64 40w
St. Davids 51 54N 5 16w
St. David's Hd. .. 51 54N 5 16w
St. David's I. ... 32 22N 64 39w
St. Denis .... 48 56N 2 22 E
St. Elias, Mt. 60 20N 141 59w
St. Étienne ..... 45 27N 4 22 E
St. Félicien 48 40N 72 25w
St. Fintan's 48 10N 58 50w
St. Flour .... 45 2N 3 6 E
St. Francis, C. .. 34 14s 24 49 E
St. Gabriel
    de Brandon ... 46 17N 73 24w
St. Gallen ...... 47 25N 9 23 E
St. George,
    Australia ..... 28 1s 148 41 E
St. George,
    Bermuda 32 24N 64 42w

* Renamed Russian Soviet
  Federative Socialist Republic
† Renamed Andropov

† Renamed Anatsogno

St. George, Canada 45 11N 66 57w
St. George, U.S.A. 37 10N 113 35w
St. George, C. 29 36N 85 2w
St. George Hd.... 35 11s 150 45 E
St. George West . 50 33N 96 7w
St. Georges,
    Belgium ...... 50 37N   4 20 E
St. Georges,
    Canada 46 42N 72 35w
St. George's, Fr.
    Guiana 4 0N 52 0w
St. Georges,
    Grenada 12 5N 61 43w
St. George's B.... 48 20N 59 0w
St. George's Chan. 52 0N   6 0w
St. George's I. ... 32 22N 64 40w
St. Helena, I. 15 55s   5 44w
St. Helenabaai .... 32 40s 18 10 E
St. Helens,
    Australia .... 41 20s 148 15 E
St. Helens, U.K. . 53 28N   2 44w
St. Helens, U.S.A. 45 55N 122 50w
St. Hyacinthe ... 45 40N 72 58w
St. Ives, Cambridge 52 20N   0 5w
St. Ives, Cornwall . 50 13N   5 29w
St. Jean 45 20N 73 50w
St. Jean Baptiste . 49 15N 97 20w
St. Jérôme 45 55N 74 0w
St. John 45 20N 66 8w
St. John, L. 48 40N 72 0w
St. John's, Antigua 17 6N 61 51w
St. John's, Canada . 47 45N 52 40w
St. Johnsbury 44 25N 72 1w
St. Joseph, Mich. . 42 6N 86 29w
St. Joseph, Mo. ... 39 46N 94 51w
St. Jovite 46 8N 74 38w
St. Kilda .... 45 53s 170 31 E
St. Kilda, I. 57 50N   8 40w
St. Kitts, I.=
    St. Christopher, I. 17 20N 62 40w
St. Laurent 50 25N 97 58w
St. Lawrence 54 25N 55 23w
St. Lawrence, G. of 48 25N 62 0w
St. Lawrence, I. ... 63 0N 170 0w
St. Lawrence, R. .. 49 15N 67 0w
St. Leonard 47 12N 67 58w
St. Lin 45 44N 73 46w
St. Lô 49 7N   1 5w
St. Louis, France .. 47 35N   7 34 E
St. Louis, Senegal . 16 8N 16 27w

St. Louis, U.S.A. .. 38 40N 90 20w
St. Lucia, C. ...... 28 32s 32 29 E
St. Lucia, I. 14 0N 60 50w
St. Lucia, L. ...... 28 5s 32 30 E
St. Lucia Chan. ... 14 15N 61 0w
St. Maarten, I. 18 0N 63 5w
St. Malo 48 39N   2 1w
St. Marc 19 10N 72 5w
St. Maries 47 17N 116 34w
St. Martin, I. 18 0N 63 0w
St. Martins 45 22N 65 38w
St. Marys, Australia 41 32s 148 11 E
St. Marys, U.S.A. . 41 30N 78 33w
St. Marys, I. 49 55N   6 17w
St. Matthew I. 60 30N 172 45w
St. Michael's Mt. .. 50 7N   5 30w
St. Moritz .... 46 30N   9 50 E
St. Nazaire 47 17N   2 12w
St. Neots 52 14N   0 16w
St. Niklaas ...... 51 10N   4 8 E
St. Omer .... 50 45N   2 15 E
St. Pacôme 47 24N 69 58w
St. Pamphile 46 58N 69 48w
St. Pascal 47 32N 69 48w
St. Paul, Canada .. 51 34N 57 47w
St. Paul, U.S.A. .. 44 54N 93 5w
St. Paul, I.,
    Atlantic Oc. 0 50N 31 40w
St. Paul, I.,
    Indian Oc. ... 30 40s 77 34 E
St. Peter 44 15N 93 57w
St. Peter Port 49 27N   2 31w
St. Petersburg ... 27 45N 82 40w
St. Pierre 46 40N 56 0w
St. Pierre, L. 46 10N 72 50w
St. Pierre et
    Miquelon □ ... 46 49N 56 15w
St. Quentin ...... 49 50N   3 16 E
St. Siméon 47 51N 69 54w
St. Stephen 45 16N 67 17w
St. Thomas, Canada 42 47N 81 12w
St. Thomas,
    Virgin Is. 18 21N 64 56w
St. Tite 46 45N 72 40w
St. Tropez .... 43 17N   6 38 E
St. Troud .... 50 48N   5 10 E
St. Valéry .... 50 10N   1 38 E
St. Vincent, I. 13 10N 61 10w
St. Vincent Pass. .. 13 30N 61 0w
St. Walburg 53 39N 109 12w

Ste. Anne de
    Beaupré 47 2N 70 58w
Ste. Cecile 47 56N 64 34w
Ste. Marie 14 48N 61 1w
* Ste. Marie, C. ..... 25 36s 45 8 E
Ste. Marie de la
    Madeleine 46 26N 71 0w
Ste. Rose 16 20N 61 45w
Ste. Rose du lac .. 51 10N 99 30w
Saintes 45 45N   0 37w
Saintonge, Reg. .. 45 40N   0 50w
Sairang .... 23 50N 92 45 E
Saitama □ .... 36 25N 137 0 E
Sajama, Mt. 18 6s 68 54w
Saka .... 0 11s 39 30 E
Sakai .... 34 30N 135 30 E
Sakaide .... 34 32N 133 50 E
* Sakaiminato ..... 35 33N 133 15 E
Sakata .... 38 55N 139 56 E
Sakété .... 6 40N   2 32 E
Sakhalin .... 51 0N 143 0 E
Sakhnin .... 32 52N 35 12 E
Sakishima-
    gunto, Is. .... 24 30N 124 0 E
Sakrivier .... 30 54s 20 28 E
Sala .... 59 58N 16 35 E
Sala-y-Gomez, I. .. 26 28s 105 28w
Saladillo 35 40s 59 55w
Salado, R.,
    Buenos Aires ... 36 0s 57 30w
Salado, R., Sta. Fe. 31 40s 60 41w
Salaga 8 31N   0 31w
Salamanca, Chile . 32 0s 71 25w
Salamanca, Sp. ... 40 58N   5 39w
Salamanca, U.S.A. 37 56N 78 42w
Salamis .... 37 56N 23 30 E
Salatiga .... 7 19s 110 30 E
Salavat .... 53 21N 55 55 E
Salaverry 8 15s 79 0w
Salawati, I. ...... 1 7s 130 54 E
† Salazar .... 9 18s 14 54 E
Saldanha .... 33 0s 17 58 E
Sale, Australia ... 38 7s 147 0 E
Sale, U.K. 53 26N   2 19w
Salé 34 3N   6 48w
Salekhard .... 66 30N 66 25 E
Salem, India ..... 11 40N 78 11 E
Salem, Mass. 42 29N 70 53w
Salem, Ohio 40 52N 80 50w
Salem, Oreg. 45 0N 123 0w

Salem, Va. 37 19N 80 8w
Sälen .... 64 41N 11 27 E
Salerno .... 40 40N 14 44 E
Salford 53 30N   2 17w
Salihli .... 38 29N 28 9 E
Salima .... 13 47s 34 26 E
Salina 38 50N 97 40w
Salina I. .... 38 35N 14 50 E
Salina Cruz 16 10N 95 10w
Salinas, Brazil ... 16 20s 42 10w
Salinas, U.S.A. ... 36 40N 121 38w
Salinas, B. de 11 4N 85 45w
Salinas Grandes .. 29 30s 65 0w
Salinópolis 0 40s 47 20w
Salisbury,
    Australia ...... 34 46s 138 38 E
* Salisbury,
    Rhodesia ..... 17 50s 31 2 E
Salisbury, U.K. ... 51 4N   1 48w
Salisbury, Md. ... 38 20N 75 38w
Salisbury, N.C. ... 35 42N 80 29w
Salisbury Plain ... 51 13N   2 0w
Salmon 45 12N 113 56w
Salmon, R. 45 51N 116 46w
Salmon Arm 50 40N 119 15w
Salmon Gums ... 32 59s 121 38 E
Salmon River Mts. 45 0N 114 30w
Salo .... 60 22N 23 3 E
Salonica=
    Thessaloniki .... 40 38N 23 0 E
Salonta .... 46 49N 21 42 E
Salop □ 52 36N   2 45w
Salsk .... 46 28N 41 30 E
Salt Lake City ... 40 45N 111 58w
Salta 24 47s 65 25w
Saltcoats 55 38N   4 47w
Saltillo 25 30N 100 57w
Salto 31 20s 58 10w
Salton Sea 33 20N 116 0w
Saltpond 5 15N   1 3w
Saltspring 48 54N 123 37w
Salûm .... 31 31N 25 7 E
Salur .... 18 27N 83 18 E
Saluzzo .... 44 39N   7 29 E
Salvador, Brazil .. 13 0s 38 30w
Salvador, Canada . 52 20N 109 25w
Salvador ■ 13 50N 89 0w
Salween, R. ..... 16 31N 97 37 E
Salzburg .... 47 48N 13 2 E
Salzgitter □ ..... 47 25N 13 15 E

Salzgitter .... 52 2N 10 22 E
Sam Rayburn Res. 31 15N 94 20w
Sama .... 60 10N 60 15 E
Samagaltai....... 50 36N 95 3 E
Samangan □ ..... 36 15N 67 40 E
Samar, I. .... 12 0N 125 0 E
Samaria, Reg.=
    Shomron, Reg. .. 32 15N 35 13 E
Samarinda .... 0 30s 117 9 E
Samarkand ...... 39 40N 67 0 E
Sambalpur ...... 21 28N 83 58 E
Sambhal .... 28 35N 78 37 E
Sambhar .... 26 52N 75 5 E
Sambiase .... 38 57N 16 17 E
Sambre, R. ...... 50 28N   4 52 E
Samchŏk .... 37 27N 129 10 E
Same .... 4 2s 37 38 E
Samoa Is. 14 0s 171 0w
Sámos, I. .... 37 45N 26 50 E
Samothráki, I. ... 40 28N 25 38 E
Sampacho 33 20s 64 50w
Sampang .... 7 11s 113 13 E
Sampit .... 2 20s 113 0 E
Samshui .... 23 7N 112 58 E
Samsun .... 41 15N 36 15 E
Samui, Ko ...... 9 30N 100 0 E
Samut Prakan ... 13 32N 100 40 E
Samut Songkhram 13 24N 100 1 E
San 13 15N   4 45w
San, R., Cambodia 13 32N 105 57 E
San, R., Poland .. 50 45N 21 51 E
San Ambrosio, I. . 26 21s 79 52w
San Andrés, I. de . 12 42N 81 46w
San Andrés Tuxtla 18 30N 95 20w
San Angelo 31 30N 100 30w
San Antonio, Chile 33 40s 71 40w
San Antonio, Sp. .. 38 58N   1 27 E
San Antonio, U.S.A. 29 30N 98 30w
San Antonio,
    C., Arg. 36 15s 56 40w
San Antonio,
    C., Cuba 21 50N 84 57w
San Antonio de
    los Banos 22 54N 82 31w
San Antonio
    Oeste 40 40s 65 0w
San Benedetto ... 45 2N 10 57 E
San Benito 26 5N 97 32w
San Bernardino .. 34 7N 117 18w
San Bernardino Str. 12 37N 124 12 E

French nameform
St-Jean, L.

* Renamed Vohimena, T. 'i
† Renamed Ndalatando

* Renamed Harare

San Bernardo 33 40s 70 50w
San Bernardo, I. de 9 45N 75 50w
San Blas, Cord. de   9 15N 78 30w
San Carlos, Arg. .. 33 50s 69 0w
San Carlos,
  Philippines ..... 10 29N 123 25 E
San Carlos,
  Uruguay 34 46s 54 58w
San Carlos, Ven. .. 1 55N 67 4w
San Carlos, Ven. .. 9 40N 68 36w
San Carlos de
  Bariloche 41 10s 71 25w
San Carlos del
  Zulia 9 1N 71 55w
San Carlos L. 33 13N 110 24w
San Clemente,
  U.S.A. 33 29N 117 45w
San Clemente I. .. 33 0N 118 30w
San Cristóbal,
  Dom. Rep. 18 25N 70 6w
San Cristóbal, Arg. 30 20s 61 10w
San Cristóbal, Ven. 7 46N 72 14w
San Cristóbal de
  las Casas 16 50N 92 33w
San Diego, C. 32 50N 117 10w
San Diego, C. 54 40s 65 10w
San Felipe, Chile . 32 43s 70 50w
San Felipe, Ven. .. 10 20N 68 44w
San Felíu de
  Guíxals .... 41 45N   3 1 E
San Felix, I. 26 30s 80 0w
San Fernando,
  Philippines ..... 15 5N 120 37 E
San Fernando,
  Philippines ..... 16 40N 120 23 E
San Fernando, Sp. . 36 22N   6 17w
San Fernando,
  Trinidad 10 20N 61 30w
San Fernando,
  U.S.A. 34 15N 118 29w
San Fernando de
  Apure 7 54N 67 28w
San Fernando de
  Atabapo 4 3N 67 42w
San Francisco, Arg. 31 30s 62 5w
San Francisco,
  U.S.A. 37 35N 122 30w
San Francisco, R. . 32 59N 109 22w
San Francisco de
  Macoris 19 19N 70 15w

San Francisco de
  Monte del Oro . . 32 36s 66 8w
San Francisco del
  Oro 26 52N 105 50w
San Gil 6 33N 73 8w
San Gottardo,
  P. del .... 46 33N   8 33 E
San Ignacio 26 52s 57 3w
San Joaquin, R. ... 36 43N 121 50w
San Jorge, G. de,
  Arg. 46 0s 66 0w
San José,
  Costa Rica 10 0N 83 57w
San José,
  Guatemala 14 0N 90 50w
San Jose,
  Philippines ..... 15 45N 120 55 E
San Jose,
  Philippines ..... 10 50N 122 5 E
San Jose, U.S.A. .. 37 20N 122 0w
San José, G. 42 20s 64 20w
San José de Jáchal . 30 5s 69 0w
San José de Mayo . 34 27s 56 27w
San José de Ocune   4 15N 70 20w
San José del
  Boquerón 26 5s 63 38w
San José del Cabo . 23 0N 109 50w
San José del
  Guaviare 2 35N 72 38w
San José do
  Rio Prêto 21 0s 49 30w
San Juan, Arg. ... 31 30s 68 30w
San Juan, Dom.
  Rep. 18 49N 71 12w
San Juan, Mexico . 21 20N 102 50w
San Juan,
  Puerto Rico 18 40N 66 11w
San Juan, R. 37 18N 110 28w
San Juan
  Capistrano 33 29N 117 46w
San Juan de
  los Morros 9 55N 67 21w
San Juan del
  Norte, B. de ... 11 30N 83 40w
San Juan Mts. ... 38 30N 108 30w
San Julián 49 15s 68 0w
San Justo 30 55s 60 30w
San Leandro 37 40N 122 6w
San Lorenzo,
  Ecuador 1 15N 78 50w

San Lorenzo, Mt... 47 40s 72 20w
San Lucas, C. de .. 22 50N 110 0w
San Luis 33 20s 66 20w
San Luis de la Paz . 21 18N 100 31w
San Luis Obispo . 35 17N 120 40w
San Luis Potosí .. 9N 100 59w
San Luis Potosí □ . 22 30N 100 30w
San Marcos,
  Guatemala 14 59N 91 52w
San Marcos, U.S.A. 29 53N 98 0w
San Marino ...... 43 56N 12 25 E
San Marino ■ .... 43 56N 12 25 E
San Mateo 37 32N 122 25w
San Matías, G. ... 41 30s 64 0w
San Miguel,
  Salvador 13 30N 88 12w
San Miguel de
  Tucumán 26 50s 65 20w
San Nicolás de
  los Arroyos 33 17s 60 10w
San Pedro, Arg. ... 24 10s 57 15w
San Pedro,
  Dom. Rep. 18 30N 69 18w
San Pedro de las
  Colonias 25 50N 102 59w
San Pedro del
  Paraná 26 43s 56 13w
San Pedro Sula .. 15 30N 88 0w
San Quintin .... 16 1N 120 56 E
San Rafael 34 40s 68 30w
San Remo ...... 43 48N   7 47 E
San Roque 28 15s 58 45w
San Rosendo 37 10s 72 50w
San Salvador ... 13 40N 89 20w
San Salvador, I. .. 24 0N 74 40w
San Salvador de
  Jujuy 23 30s 65 40w
San Sebastián, Arg. 53 10s 68 30w
San Sabastián,
  Spain 43 17N   1 58w
San Severo ..... 41 41N 15 23 E
San Simon 32 14N 109 16w
San Valentín, Mt. . 46 30s 73 30w
San Vicente de la
  Barquera 43 30N   4 29w
Sana .... 15 27N 44 12 E
Sana, R. .... 45 3N 16 23 E
Sanaga, R. ..... 3 35N   9 38 E
Sanana .... 2 5s 125 50 E
Sanandaj ...... 35 25N 47 7 E

Sancti Spíritus ... 21 52N 79 33w
Sand Lake 47 46N 84 31w
Sand Springs 36 12N 96 5w
Sandakan .... 5 53N 118 10 E
Sanday, I. 59 14N   2 30w
Sanders 35 12N 109 25w
Sandgate ...... 27 20s 153 5 E
Sandikli .... 38 30N 30 20 E
Sandnes .... 58 50N   5 45 E
Sandomierz .... 50 40N 21 43 E
Sandoway ..... 18 20N 94 30 E
Sandpoint 48 20N 116 40w
Sandringham ... 52 50N   0 30 E
Sandstone ..... 28 0s 119 15 E
Sandusky 41 25N 82 40w
Sandveld ...... 32 0s 18 15 E
Sandviken ..... 60 38N 16 46 E
Sandwip Chan... 22 35N 91 35 E
Sandy, C. ..... 24 41s 153 8 E
Sanford, Fla. ... 28 45N 81 20w
Sanford, N.C. .. 35 30N 79 10w
Sanford, Mt. ... 62 30N 143 0w
Sanger 36 47N 119 35w
Sanggau .... 0 5N 110 30 E
Sanghe, Pulau . 3 45N 125 30 E
Sangli .... 16 55N 74 33 E
Sangmelima .... 2 57N 12 1 E
Sangonera, R. .. 37 59N   1 4w
Sangre de
  Cristo Mts. ... 37 30N 105 0w
Sangsang ...... 29 30N 86 0 E
Sangwa .... 5 30s 26 0 E
Sanlucar de
  Barrameda ... 36 47N   6 21w
Sanlúcar-la-
  Mayor 37 26N   6 18w
Sanmenhsia ... 34 46N 111 30 E
Sanok .... 49 35N 22 10 E
Sanquhar 55 21N   3 56w
* Sansanné-Mango . 10 20N   0 30 E
Santa Ana,
  Ecuador 1 10s 80 20w
Santa Ana,
  Mexico 30 31N 111 8w
Santa Ana,
  Salvador 14 0N 89 40w
Santa Ana,
  U.S.A. 33 48N 117 55w
Santa Barbara,
  Mexico 26 48N 105 50w

Santa Bárbara,
  U.S.A. 34 25N 119 40w
Santa Catalina,
  G. of 33 0N 118 0w
Santa Catalina I. .. 33 20N 118 30w
Santa Catarina □ . 27 25s 48 30w
Santa Clara,
  Cuba 22 20N 80 0w
Santa Clara,
  U.S.A. 37 21N 122 0w
Santa Cruz,
  Arg. 50 0s 68 50w
Santa Cruz,
  Canary Is. 28 29N 16 26w
Santa Cruz,
  Costa Rica 10 15N 85 41w
Santa Cruz,
  Philippines .... 14 20N 121 30 E
Santa Cruz,
  Calif. 36 55N 122 10w
Santa Cruz,
  N. Mex. 35 59N 106 1w
Santa Cruz, I. ... 0 38s 90 23w
Santa Cruz, R. .. 50 10s 68 20w
Santa Cruz
  do Sul 29 42s 52 25w
Santa Fe, Arg. ... 31 35s 60 41w
Sante Fe, U.S.A. . 35 40N 106 0w
Santa Filomena . 9 0s 45 50w
Santa Inés, I. ... 54 0s 73 0w
Santa Isabel ... 36 10s 67 0w
Santa Lucia Ra. . 36 0N 121 30w
Santa Margarita, I. 24 30N 112 0w
Santa Mariá,
  Brazil 29 40s 53 40w
Santa Maria,
  U.S.A. 34 58N 120 29w
Santa Maria de
  Vitória 13 24s 44 12w
Santa Maria di
  Leuca, C. .... 39 48N 18 20 E
Santa Marta ... 11 15N 74 13w
Santa Monica .. 34 0N 118 30w
Santa Paula ... 34 20N 119 2w
Santa Rosa, Arg. . 36 40s 64 30w
Santa Rosa,
  Brazil 27 52s 54 29w
Santa Rosa,
  Honduras 14 40N 89 0w
Santa Rosa,

* Renamed Mango

Calif. 38 20N 122 50W
Santa Rosa,
  N. Mex. 34 58N 104 40W
Santa Rosa I. 34 0N 120 15W
Santa Rosalía 27 20N 112 30W
Santa Vitória do
  Palmar 33 32S 53 25W
Santai . . . . 31 10N 105 2 E
Santana do
  Livramento 30 55S 55 30W
Santander 43 27N 3 51W
Santaquin 40 0N 111 51W
Santarem, Brazil . . 2 25S 54 42W
Santarém, Port. . . . 39 12N 8 42W
Santiago, Brazil . . . 29 11S 54 52W
Santiago, Chile . . . 33 24S 70 50W
Santiago, Dom.
  Rep. 19 30N 70 40W
Santiago, Panama . 8 0N 81 0W
Santiago de
  Compostela 42 52N 8 37W
Santiago de
  Cuba 20 0N 75 49W
Santiago del
  Estero 27 50S 64 15W
Santiago
  Ixcuintla 21 50N 105 11W
Santo Amaro 12 30S 38 50W
Santo Ângelo 28 15S 54 15W
Santo Domingo . . . 18 30N 70 0W
Santo Tomé 28 40S 56 5W
Santoña 43 29N 3 20W
Santos 24 0S 46 20W
Santu . . . . 25 59N 113 3 E
Santuaho . . . . 26 36N 119 42 E
Sanur . . . . 32 22N 35 15 E
Sanyuan . . . . 34 35N 108 54 E
São Borja 28 45S 56 0W
São Carlos 22 0S 47 50W
São Cristóvão 11 15S 37 15W
São Domingos 13 25S 46 10W
São Francisco 6 0S 44 50W
São Francisco, R. . . 10 30S 36 24W
São Francisco
  do Sul 26 15S 48 36W
São Gabriel 30 10S 54 30W
São João del Rei . . 21 8S 44 15W
São João do
  Araguaia 5 23S 48 46W
São João do

Piauí 8 10S 42 15W
São Leopoldo 29 50S 51 10W
São Lourenço 16 30S 55 5W
São Luís 2 39S 44 15W
São Marcos, B. de . 2 0S 44 0W
São Mateus 18 44S 39 50W
São Paulo 23 40S 56 50W
São Paulo □ 22 0S 49 0W
São Roque, C. de . 5 30S 35 10W
† São Salvador
  do Congo . . . . . . 6 18S 14 16 E
São Sebastião,
  I. de 23 50S 45 18W
São Tomé, I. . . . . . 0 10N 7 0 E
São Vicente,
  C. de 37 0N 9 0W
Saône, R. . . . . 45 44N 4 50 E
Saône-et-
  Loire □ . . . . 46 25N 4 50 E
Sapele . . . . 5 50N 5 40 E
Saposoa 6 55S 76 30W
Sapporo . . . . 43 0N 141 15 E
Sapulpa 36 0N 96 40W
Saqqez . . . . 36 15N 46 20 E
Saragossa=
  Zaragoza 41 39N 0 53W
Sarajevo . . . . 43 52N 18 26 E
Saranac Lake 44 20N 74 10W
Saranda . . . . 5 45S 34 59 E
Sarandí del Yí 33 21S 55 58W
Sarangani B. . . . . . 6 0N 125 13 E
Saransk . . . . 54 10N 45 10 E
Sarapul . . . . 56 28N 53 48 E
Sarasota 27 10N 82 30W
Saratoga Springs . . 43 5N 73 47W
Saratov . . . . 51 30N 46 2 E
Saravane . . . . 15 42N 106 3 E
Sarawak □ . . . . . . 2 0S 113 0 E
Sarbāz . . . . 26 38N 61 19 E
Sarbisheh . . . . 32 30N 59 40 E
Sarda, R. . . . . 27 22N 81 23 E
Sardarshahr . . . . . 28 30N 74 29 E
Sardegna, I. . . . . . 39 57N 9 0 E
Sardinia, I.=
  Sardegna, I. . . . . 39 57N 9 0 E
Sargodha . . . . 32 10N 72 40 E
* Sargodha □ . . . . . 31 45N 72 0 E
Sarh . . . . 9 5N 18 23 E
Sarī . . . . 36 30N 53 11 E
Sarikamiş . . . . 40 22N 42 35 E

Sarikei . . . . 2 8N 111 30 E
Sarina . . . . 21 22S 149 13 E
Sariwon . . . . 38 31N 125 44 E
Sark, I. 49 25N 2 20W
Sarlat-la-
  Canéda . . . . 44 54N 1 13 E
Sarmiento 45 35S 69 5W
Sarnia 42 58N 82 29W
Sarny . . . . 51 17N 26 40 E
Saronikós Kól. . . . . 37 45N 23 45 E
Sarpsborg . . . . 59 16N 11 12 E
Sarthe □ . . . . 47 58N 0 10 E
Sarthe, R. 47 30N 0 32W
Sartynya . . . . 63 30N 62 50 E
Sarur . . . . 23 17N 58 4 E
Sary Tash . . . . 39 45N 73 40 E
Saryshagan . . . . . . 46 12N 73 48 E
Sasabeneh . . . . 7 59N 44 43 E
Sasaram . . . . 24 57N 84 5 E
Sasebo . . . . 33 15N 129 50 E
Saskatchewan □ . . . 53 40N 103 30W
Saskatchewan, R. . . 53 12N 99 16W
Saskatoon 52 10N 106 45W
Sasklylakh . . . . 71 55N 114 1 E
Sasolburg . . . . 26 46S 27 49 E
Sasovo . . . . 54 25N 41 55 E
Sassandra 5 0N 6 8W
Sassandra, R. 4 58N 6 5W
Sássari . . . . 40 44N 8 33 E
Sassnitz . . . . 54 29N 13 39 E
Satara . . . . 17 44N 73 58 E
Satka . . . . 55 3N 59 1 E
Satmala Hills . . . . . 20 15N 74 40 E
Satna . . . . 24 35N 80 50 E
Sátoraljaújhely . . . 48 25N 21 41 E
Satpura Ra. . . . . . . 21 40N 75 0 E
Satu Mare . . . . 47 48N 22 53 E
Satun . . . . 6 43N 100 2 E
Sauda . . . . 59 38N 6 21 E
Saudarkrókur 65 45N 19 40W
Saudi Arabia ■ . . . 26 0N 44 0 E
Sault Ste. Marie,
  Canada 46 30N 84 20W
Saulte Ste. Marie,
  U.S.A. 46 27N 84 22W
Saumur 47 15N 0 5W
Saurbaer 64 24N 21 35W
Sauri . . . . 11 30N 6 35 E
Sava, R. . . . . 44 50N 20 26 E
Savaii, I. 13 35S 172 25W

Savalou . . . . 7 57N 2 4 E
Savanna 42 5N 90 10W
Savannah 32 4N 81 4W
Savannah, R. 32 2N 80 53W
Savannakhet . . . . . 16 30N 104 49 E
Savant Lake 50 20N 90 40W
Savé . . . . 8 2N 2 17 E
Save, R. . . . . 43 47N 1 17 E
Sáveh . . . . 35 2N 50 20 E
Savelugu 9 38N 0 54W
Savoie □ . . . . 45 26N 6 35 E
Savoie, Reg. . . . . . 45 30N 5 20 E
Savona . . . . 44 19N 8 29 E
Sawai . . . . 3 0S 129 5 E
Sawankhalok . . . . . 17 19N 99 54 E
Sawatch Mts. 38 30N 106 30W
Sawknah . . . . 29 4N 15 47 E
Sawmills . . . . 19 30S 28 2 E
Sawu Sea . . . . 9 30S 121 50 E
Saya . . . . 9 30N 3 18 E
Sayabec 38 35N 67 41W
Sayda . . . . 33 35N 35 25 E
Saynshand . . . . . . 44 55N 110 11 E
Sayre 42 0N 76 30W
Sazin . . . . 35 35N 73 30 E
Sca Fell, Mt 54 27N 3 14W
Scandinavia, Reg. . 65 0N 15 0 E
Scapa Flow 58 52N 3 0W
Scarborough 54 17N 0 24W
Schaffhausen . . . . 47 42N 8 36 E
Schefferville 54 50N 66 40W
Schelde, R. . . . . . . 51 22N 4 1 E
Schenectady 42 50N 73 58W
Scheveningen . . . . 52 6N 4 18 E
Schiedam . . . . 51 55N 4 25 E
Schio . . . . 45 42N 11 21 E
Schleswig-
  Holstein □ . . . . . 54 10N 9 40 E
Schouten, Kep. . . . 1 0S 136 0 E
Schreiber 48 45N 87 20W
Schumacher 48 30N 81 6W
Schurz 38 59N 118 57W
Schwäbische Alb,
  Mts. . . . . 48 30N 9 30 E
Schwangcheng . . . 45 27N 126 27 E
Schwangyashan . . . 46 35N 131 15 E
Schwarzrand, Mts. . 26 0S 17 0 E
Schwarzwald . . . . . 48 0N 8 0 E
Schweinfurt . . . . . . 50 3N 10 12 E
Schweizer-Reneke . 27 11S 25 18 E

Schwerin . . . . 53 37N 11 22 E
Schwyz . . . . 47 2N 8 39 E
Sciacca . . . . 37 30N 13 3 E
Scilla . . . . 38 15N 15 44 E
Scillave . . . . 6 22N 44 32 E
Scilly Is. 49 55N 6 15W
Scobey 48 47N 105 30W
Scone, Australia . . 32 0S 150 52 E
Scone, U.K. 56 25N 3 26W
Scotia Sea 56 5S 56 0W
Scotland ■ 57 0N 4 0W
Scott City 38 30N 100 52W
Scottsbluff 41 55N 103 35W
Scottsburgh . . . . . 30 15S 30 47 E
Scottsdale . . . . . . 41 9N 147 31 E
Scranton 41 22N 75 41W
Scunthorpe 53 35N 0 38W
Sea Lake . . . . 35 28S 142 55 E
Seaforth 43 35N 81 25W
Seal, R. 59 4N 94 48W
Searchlight 35 31N 111 57W
Searcy 35 15N 91 45W
Seattle 47 41N 122 15W
Sebastián
  Vizcaíno, B. 28 0N 114 0W
Sebastopol 38 16N 122 56W
Sebring 27 36N 81 47W
Secretary, I. . . . . . 45 15S 166 56 E
Secunderabad . . . . 17 28N 78 30 E
Sedalia 38 40N 93 18W
Sedan . . . . 49 43N 4 57 E
Seddon . . . . 41 40S 174 7 E
Seddonville . . . . . . 4133S 172 1 E
Sede Ya'aqov . . . . 32 43N 35 7 E
Sedgewick 52 48N 111 41W
Sedom . . . . 31 5N 35 20 E
Sedro Woolley . . . 48 30N 122 15W
Seeheim . . . . 26 32S 17 52 E
Segamat . . . . 2 30N 102 50 E
Ségou 13 30N 6 10W
Segovia 40 57N 4 10W
Segre, R. . . . . 41 40N 0 43 E
Séguéla 7 57N 6 40W
Seguin 29 34N 97 58W
Segura, R. 38 6N 0 54W
Sehkonj, Kuh-e . . . 30 0N 57 30 E
Sehore . . . . 23 10N 77 5 E
Seille, R. . . . . 49 7N 6 11 E
Seinäjoki . . . . 62 47N 22 50 E
Seine, R. . . . . 49 30N 0 20 E

† Renamed Mbanza Congo
* Now part of Punjab

Seine-et-Marne □ . 48 45N 3 0 E
Seine-Maritime □ . 49 40N 1 0 E
Seine-St.-Denis □ . 48 55N 2 28 E
Seke .... 3 20s 33 31 E
Sekenke .... 4 18s 34 11 E
Sekondi-Takoradi . 5 2N 1 48w
Selatan □,
  Kalimantan ..... 3 0s 115 0 E
Selatan □,
  Sulawesi .... 3 0s 120 0 E
Selatan □,
  Sumatera ...... 3 0s 105 0 E
Selby 53 47N 1 5w
Seldovia 59 27N 151 43w
Selebi-Pikwe ..... 22 0s 27 45 E
Selenge .... 49 25N 103 59 E
Sélibaby 15 20N 12 15w
Selkirk, Canada .. 50 10N 97 20w
Selkirk, U.K. 55 33N 2 50w
Selkirk Mts. 51 0N 117 10w
Selma, Ala. 32 30N 87 0w
Selma, Calif. 36 39N 119 30w
Selsey Bill 50 43N 0 48w
† Selukwe .... 19 40s 30 0 E
Selva 29 50s 62 0w
Semarang .... 7 0s 110 26 E
Semeru, Mt. ..... 8 4s 113 3 E
Seminoe Res. 42 0N 107 0w
Seminole, Okla. .. 35 15N 96 45w
Seminole, Tex. ... 32 41N 102 38w
Semiozernoye .... 52 35N 64 0 E
Semipalatinsk .... 50 30N 80 10 E
Semnān .... 35 55N 53 25 E
Semnān □ .... 36 0N 54 0 E
Semporna .... 4 30N 118 33 E
Sena Madureira ... 9 5s 68 45w
Senador Pompeu .. 5 40s 39 20w
Senanga .... 16 2s 23 14 E
Sendai, Kagoshima 31 50N 130 20 E
Sendai, Miyagi .. 38 15N 141 0 E
Seneca 44 10N 119 2w
Seneca Falls 42 55N 76 50w
Senegal ■ 14 30N 14 30w
Senegal, R. 16 30N 15 30w
Senegambia, Reg. . 14 0N 14 0w
Senekal .... 28 18s 27 36 E
Senhor-do Bonfim . 10 30s 40 10w
Senj .... 45 0N 14 58 E
Senlis .... 49 13N 2 35 E
Sennâr .... 13 30N 33 35 E

Senneterre 48 25N 77 15w
Sens .... 48 11N 3 15 E
Sentolo .... 7 55s 110 13 E
Senya Beraku 5 28N 0 31w
Seo de Urgel ..... 42 22N 1 23 E
Seoul=Soul ...... 37 20N 126 15 E
Separation Pt..... 53 40N 57 16w
Sept Iles 50 13N 66 22w
Sequim 48 3N 123 9w
Sequoia Nat. Park . 36 20N 118 30w
Seraing .... 50 35N 5 32 E
Seram, I. .... 3 10s 129 0 E
Seram Sea .... 3 0s 130 0 E
Serampore .... 22 44N 88 30 E
Serang .... 6 8s 106 10 E
Serbia □ .... 43 30N 21 0 E
Šerdobsk .... 52 28N 44 10 E
Seremban .... 2 43N 101 53 E
Serengeti Nat. Park 2 40s 35 0 E
Serenje .... 13 11s 30 52 E
Sergipe □ 10 30s 37 30w
Seria .... 4 37N 114 30 E
Serian .... 1 10N 110 40 E
Sérifos .... 37 8N 24 34 E
Serov .... 59 40N 60 20 E
Serowe .... 22 25s 26 43 E
* Serpa Pinto ..... 14 48s 17 52 E
Serpentine .... 32 22s 115 59 E
Serpukhov .... 54 55N 37 28 E
Sérrai .... 41 5N 23 32 E
Serrezuela 30 40s 65 20w
Serrinha 11 39s 39 0w
Sertania 8 5s 37 20w
Serule .... 21 57s 27 11 E
Sese Is. .... 0 30s 32 30 E
Sesheke .... 17 29s 24 13 E
Sestao 43 18N 3 0w
Sète .... 43 25N 3 42 E
Sete Lagôas 19 27s 44 16w
Sétif .... 36 9N 5 26 E
Seto .... 35 14N 137 6 E
Setonaikai .... 34 10N 133 10 E
Settat 33 0N 7 40w
Setté Cama ...... 2 32s 9 57 E
Settle 54 5N 2 18w
Setúbal 38 30N 8 58w
Setúbal, B. de ... 38 40N 8 56w
Seulimeum .... 5 27N 95 15 E
Sevan L. .... 40 30N 45 0 E
Sevastopol ...... 44 35N 33 30 E

Severn, R., Canada 56 2N 87 36w
Severn, R., U.K. .. 51 25N 3 0w
Severnaya
  Zemlya, I. ...... 79 0N 100 0 E
Severnyye
  Uvaly, Reg. ..... 58 0N 48 0 E
Severodvinsk ..... 64 27N 39 58 E
Sevilla 37 23N 6 0w
Seville=Sevilla ... 37 23N 6 0w
Seward 60 0N 149 40w
Seward Pen. 65 0N 164 0w
Seychelles, Is. .... 5 0s 56 0 E
Seyðisfjörður 65 16N 14 0w
Seymour, Australia 36 58s 145 10 E
Seymour, U.S.A. .. 39 0N 85 50w
Sfax .... 34 49N 10 48 E
Sfîntu-Gheorghe .. 45 52s 25 48 E
's-Gravenhage .... 52 7N 4 17 E
Shaba, Reg. ..... 8 30s 25 0 E
† Shabani .... 20 17s 30 2 E
Shabunda .... 2 40s 27 16 E
Shadrinsk .... 56 5N 63 38 E
Shaffa .... 10 30N 12 6 E
Shaftesbury 51 0N 2 12w
Shagamu .... 6 51N 3 39 E
‡ Shāhābād ...... 37 40N 56 50 E
● Shāhbād .... 34 10N 46 30 E
Shahcheng ...... 40 18N 115 27 E
Shahdād .... 30 30N 57 40 E
Shahdadkot ..... 27 50N 67 55 E
Shahhat .... 32 40N 21 35 E
Shāhī .... 36 30N 52 55 E
†† Shāhpūr ...... 38 12N 44 45 E
‡‡ Shahrezā ...... 32 0N 51 55 E
Shahrig .... 30 15N 67 40 E
* Shāhrūd .... 36 30N 55 0 E
●● Shahsavar ..... 36 45N 51 12 E
Shaikhabad ...... 34 0N 68 45 E
Shajapur .... 23 20N 76 15 E
Shakhty .... 47 40N 40 10 E
Shakhunya ...... 57 40N 47 0 E
Shaki .... 8 41N 3 21 E
Shalu .... 24 24N 120 26 E
Sham, Jabal ash .. 23 10N 57 5 E
Shama 5 1N 1 42w
Shamil .... 29 32N 77 18 E
Shamo, L. ...... 5 45N 37 30 E
Shamokin 40 47N 76 33w
Shamva .... 17 18s 31 34 E
Shan □ .... 21 30N 98 30 E

Schanchengtze .... 42 2N 123 47 E
Shanga .... 9 1N 5 2 E
Shangani, R. ..... 18 41s 27 10 E
Shangchih .... 45 10N 127 59 E
Schangchwan
  Shan, I. .... 21 35N 112 45 E
Shanghai .... 31 10N 121 25 E
Shangjao .... 28 25N 117 25 E
Shangkiu .... 34 28N 115 42 E
Shangshui .... 33 42N 115 4 E
Shanh .... 47 5N 103 5 E
Shani .... 10 14N 12 2 E
Shannon .... 40 33s 17 25 E
Shannon, R. 52 30N 9 53w
Shansi □ .... 37 0N 113 0 E
Shantou=
  Shantow .... 23 25N 116 40 E
Shantow .... 23 25N 116 40 E
Shantung □ ...... 37 0N 118 0 E
Shanyang .... 33 39N 110 2 E
Shaohing .... 30 0N 120 32 E
Shaowu .... 27 25N 117 30 E
Shaoyang .... 27 10N 111 30 E
Shapinsay, I. 59 2N 2 50w
Shaqra .... 25 15N 45 16 E
Sharin Gol ...... 49 12N 106 27 E
Sharjah .... 25 23N 55 26 E
Shark, B. .... 25 15s 133 20 E
Sharon 41 14N 80 31w
Sharya .... 58 12N 45 40 E
Shashi .... 21 40s 28 40 E
Shashi, R. ...... 22 14s 29 20 E
Shasi .... 30 16N 112 20 E
Shasta, Mt. 41 45N 122 0w
Shasta Res. 40 50N 122 15w
Shaunavon 49 35N 108 40w
Shawano 44 45N 88 38w
Shawinigan 46 35N 72 50w
Shawnee 35 15N 97 0w
Shebele, Wabi ... 2 0N 44 0 E
Sheboygan 43 46N 87 45w
Shebshi Mts. .... 8 30N 12 0 E
Shediac 46 14N 64 32w
Sheerness ...... 51 26N 0 47 E
Shefar'am ...... 32 48N 35 10 E
Sheffield 53 23N 1 28w
Shekhupura .... 31 42N 73 58 E
Shekki .... 22 30N 113 15 E
Sheklung ...... 23 5N 113 55 E
Shelburne,

  Nova Scotia 43 47N 65 20w
Shelburne, Ont. ... 44 4N 80 15w
Shelby, Mont. 48 30N 111 59w
Shelby, N.C. 35 18N 81 34w
Shelbyville, Ind. .. 39 30N 85 42w
Shelbyville, Tenn. . 35 30N 86 25w
Sheldrake 50 20N 64 51w
Shelikhova Zaliv .. 59 30N 157 0 E
Shell Lake 53 19N 107 6w
Shellbrook 53 13N 106 24w
Shelter Bay 50 30N 67 20w
Shelton, Alaska .. 55 20N 105 0w
Shelton, Wash. ... 47 15N 123 6w
Shemakha .... 40 50N 48 28 E
Shenandoah, Iowa . 40 50N 95 22w
Shenandoah, Pa. . 40 49N 76 13w
Shenandoah, R. .. 39 19N 77 44w
Shendam .... 9 10N 9 30 E
Shendi .... 16 46N 33 33 E
Shensi □ .... 35 0fi109 0 E
Shenyang .... 41 35N 123 30 E
Shepparton ..... 36 18s 145 25 E
Sherborne 50 56N 2 31w
Sherbro I. 7 30N 12 40w
Sherbrooke 45 24N 71 57w
Sheridan 44 50N 107 0w
Sherman 33 40N 96 35w
Sherridon 55 10N 101 5w
s'Hertogenbosch . 51 41N 5 19 E
Sherwood Forest . 53 5N 1 5w
Shesheke .... 17 50s 24 0 E
Shetland □ 60 30N 1 30w
Shevchenko .... 44 25N 51 20 E
Shevut'Am ..... 32 19N 34 55 E
Shibam .... 16 0N 48 36 E
Shibarghan ..... 36 40N 65 48 E
Shibushi .... 31 25N 131 0 E
* Shickshock Mts. . 48 40N 66 30w
Shiel, L. 56 48N 5 32w
Shiga □ .... 35 20N 136 0 E
Shigatse .... 29 10N 89 0 E
Shihchiachuangi=
  Shihkiachwang . 38 0N 114 32 E
Shihkiachwang .. 38 0N 114 32 E
Shihpu .... 29 12N 121 58 E
Shihwei .... 51 28N 119 59 E
Shikarpur ..... 27 57N 68 39 E
Shikoku, I. ..... 33 45N 133 30 E
Shikoku □ ..... 33 30N 133 30 E
Shillelagh 52 46N 6 32w

† Renamed Shurugwi
* Renamed Menongue
† Renamed Zvishavane
‡ Renamed Ashkhāneh
● Renamed Eslāmābād-e Gharb
** Renamed Qā'emshahr
†† Renamed Salmās
‡‡ Renamed Qomsheh
* Renamed Emāmrud
●● Renamed Tonekābon
* French nameform Chic-Chocs, Mts.

Shilka .... 52 0N 115 55 E
Shillong .... 25 30N 92 0 E
Shimada .... 34 49N 138 19 E
Shimane □ .... 35 0N 132 30 E
Shimanovsk ...... 52 15N 127 30 E
Shimizu .... 35 0N 138 30 E
Shimodate .... 36 20N 139 55 E
Shimoga .... 13 57N 75 32 E
Shimonoseki ..... 33 58N 131 0 E
Shimpek .... 44 50N 74 10 E
Shin, L. 58 7N   4 30w
Shin Dand .... 33 12N 62 8 E
Shingú .... 33 40N 135 33 E
Shinyanga .... 3 45s 33 27 E
Shippegan 47 45N 64 45w
Shirane-San, Mt. .. 35 40N 138 15 E
Shiráz .... 29 42N 52 30 E
Shire, R. .... 17 42s 35 19 E
Shiukwan .... 24 58N 113 3 E
Shivpuri .... 25 18N 77 42 E
Shizuoka .... 35 0N 138 30 E
Shizuoka □ .... 35 15N 138 40 E
Shkodra .... 42 6N 19 20 E
Shoal Lake 50 30N 100 35w
Shoeburyness ..... 51 13N   0 49 E
Shohsien .... 39 30N 112 25 E
Sholapur .... 17 43N 75 56 E
Shologontsy ...... 66 13N 114 14 E
Shomera .... 33 4N 35 17 E
Shómrón, Reg. ... 32 15N 35 13 E
Shoshone 43 0N 114 27w
Shoshong .... 22 0s 26 30 E
Show Low 34 16N 110 0w
Shreveport 32 30N 93 50w
Shrewsbury 52 42N   2 45w
Shucheng .... 31 25N 117 2 E
Shuikiahu .... 32 14N 117 4 E
Shumagin Is. 55 0N 159 0w
Shumikha .... 55 15N 63 30 E
Shunat Nimran .. 31 54N 35 37 E
Shunchang .... 26 52N 117 48 E
Shungnak 66 53N 157 2w
Shuqra .... 13 22N 45 34 E
Shúsf .... 31 50N 60 5 E
Shushtar .... 32 0N 48 50 E
Shuweika .... 32 20N 35 1 E
Shwangliano ..... 43 39N 123 40 E
Shwebo .... 22 30N 95 45 E
Shwegu .... 24 15N 96 50 E
Shyok .... 34 15N 78 5 E

Shyok, R. .... 35 13N 75 53 E
Si Racha .... 13 20N 101 10 E
Siahan Ra. .... 27 30N 64 40 E
Siakwan .... 25 45N 100 10 E
Sialkot .... 32 32N 74 30 E
Siam=Thailand ■ . 15 0N 100 0 E
* Siam, G. of ..... 11 30N 101 0 E
Sian .... 34 2N 109 0 E
Sian Kiang, R. .... 22 30N 110 10 E
Siangfan .... 32 15N 112 2 E
Siangtan .... 28 0N 112 55 E
Siangyang .... 32 18N 111 0 E
Siao Hingan
   Ling, Mts. ..... 49 0N 127 0 E
Siargao, I. .... 9 52N 126 3 E
Siauhai .... 55 56N 23 15 E
Sibbald 51 24N 110 10w
Sibenik .... 43 48N 15 54 E
Siberia, Reg. ..... 66 0N 120 0 E
Siberut, I. .... 1 30s 99 0 E
Sibi .... 29 30N 67 48 E
Sibiti .... 3 38s 13 19 E
Sibolga .... 1 50N 98 45 E
Sibsagar .... 27 0N 94 36 E
Sibu .... 2 18N 111 51 E
Sibutu Pass. ...... 4 50N 120 0 E
Sibuyan, I. .... 12 25N 122 40 E
Sibuyan Sea ...... 12 50N 122 20 E
Sichang .... 28 0N 102 10 E
Sicilia .... 37 30N 14 30 E
Sicilia, I. .... 37 30N 14 30 E
Sicuani 14 10s 71 10w
Sìdi Barrâni ...... 31 32N 25 58 E
Sidi bel Abbès 35 13N   0 10w
Sidi Ifni 29 29N 10 3w
Sidlaw Hills 56 32N   3 10w
Sidmouth 50 40N   3 13w
Sidney, Canada ... 48 39N 123 24w
Sidney, U.S.A. ... 40 18N 84 6w
Sidoardjo .... 7 30s 112 46 E
Siedlce .... 52 10N 22 0 E
Siegen .... 50 52N   8 2 E
Siem Reap .... 13 20N 103 52 E
Siena .... 43 20N 11 20 E
Sieyang .... 34 20N 108 48 E
Sierra Gorda 23 0s 69 15w
* Sierra Leone ■ .. 9 0N 12 0w
Sierra Nevada, Mts. 40 0N 121 0w
Sifnos, I. .... 37 0N 24 45 E

Sighet .... 47 57N 23 32 E
Sighisoara .... 46 12N 24 50 E
Sigli .... 5 25N 96 0 E
Siglufjördur 66 12N 18 55w
Sigsig 3 0s 78 50w
Sigtuna .... 59 36N 17 44 E
Sigüenza 41 3N   2 40w
Siguiri 11 31N   9 10w
Sigurd 38 57N 112 0w
Sihanoukville =
   Kompong Som . 10 40N 103 30 E
Sihsien .... 29 55N 118 23 E
Siirt .... 37 57N 41 55 E
Si Kiang, R. ...... 22 0N 114 0 E
Sikandarabad ..... 28 30N 77 39 E
Sikar .... 27 39N 75 10 E
Sikasso 11 7N   5 35w
Sikeston 36 52N 89 35w
Sikhote
   Alin Khrebet ... 46 0N 136 0 E
Sikkim □ .... 27 50N 88 50 E
Sil, R. 42 27N   7 43w
Silamulun, R. .... 43 20N 121 0 E
Silat adh Dhahr .. 32 19N 35 11 E
Silesia, Reg.=
   Slask, Reg. ..... 51 0N 16 45 E
Silghat .... 26 35N 93 0 E
Siliguri .... 26 45N 88 25 E
Silistra .... 44 6N 27 19 E
Siljan, L. .... 60 55N 14 45 E
Silkeborg .... 56 10N   9 32 E
* Silva Porto=Bié . 12 22s 16 55 E
Silver City,
   Panama Canal
   Zone 9 21N 79 53w
Silver City, U.S.A. 32 50N 108 18w
Silver Creek 42 33N 79 9w
Silwan .... 31 59N 35 15 E
Simanggang ...... 1 15N 111 25 E
Simba .... 2 11s 37 35 E
Simcoe, Canada ... 42 50N 80 20w
Simcoe, L. 44 20N 79 20w
Simenga .... 62 50N 107 55 E
Simeria .... 45 51N 23 1 E
Simeulue, I. ...... 2 45N 95 45 E
Simferopol .... 44 55N 34 3 E
Simla 31 2N 77 15
Simmie 49 56N 108 6w
Simplonpass ..... 46 15N   8 0 E
Simpson, Des. .... 25 0s 137 0 E

Sinâ', Gebel el
   Tih Es .... 29 '0N 33 30 E
Sinai = Es Sinâ' .. 29 0N 34 0 E
Sinaloa □ 25 50N 108 20w
Sincelejo 9 18N 75 24w
Sincheng 34 25N 113 56w
Sincorá, Sa. do .. 13 30s 41 0w
Sind Sagar Doab .. 32 0N 71 30 E
Sindangbarang ... 7 27s 107 9 E
Sines .... 37 56N   8 51 E
Sinfeng .... 26 59N 106 55 E
Singa .... 13 10N 33 57 E
Singaparna .... 7 23s 108 4 E
Singapore ■ ...... 1 17N 103 51 E
Singida .... 4 49s 34 48 E
Singitikós Kól. .... 40 6N 24 0 E
Singkling Hkamti . 26 0N 95 45 E
Singkawang ...... 1 0N 109 5 E
Singkep .... 0 30s 140 20 E
Singora=Songkhla . 7 13N 100 37 E
Singtai .... 37 2N 114 0 E
Singtze .... 29 30N 116 4 E
Sinhailien .... 34 31N 119 0 E
Sinhsien .... 38 25N 112 45 E
Sinhwa .... 27 36N 111 6 E
Sining .... 36 35N 101 50 E
Sinjär .... 36 19N 41 52 E
Sinjil .... 32 3N 35 15 E
Sinkat .... 18 55N 36 49 E
Sinkiang .... 35 35N 111 25 E
Sinkiang-Uigur □ .. 42 0N 86 0 E
Sinkin .... 39 30N 122 29 E
Sinnamary .... 5 23N 52 57 E
Sinnûris .... 29 26N 30 31 E
† Sinoia .... 17 20s 30 8 E
Sinop .... 42 1N 35 11 E
Sinsiang .... 35 15N 113 55 E
Sintang .... 0 5N 111 35 E
Sintra 38 47N   9 25w
Sinuiju .... 40 5N 124 24 E
Sinyang .... 32 6N 114 2 E
Sion .... 46 14N   7 20 E
Sioux City 42 32N 96 25w
Sioux Falls 43 35N 96 40w
Sioux Lookout ... 50 10N 91 50w
Siparia 10 15N 61 30w
Siping .... 33 25N 114 10 E
Siquia, R. 12 30N 84 30w
Sir Bani Yas, I. .. 24 20N 54 0 E
Sir Edward Pellew

Group, Is. .... 15 40s 137 10 E
Sir James
   McBrien, Mt. ... 62 7N 127 41w
Siracusa .... 37 4N 15 17 E
Sirajganj .... 24 25N 89 47 E
Siret, R. .... 47 55N 26 5 E
Siros .... 37 28N 24 56 E
Sirsa .... 29 33N 75 4 E
Sisak .... 45 30N 16 21 E
Sisaket .... 15 8N 104 23 E
Sisophon .... 13 31N 102 59 E
Sistan
   Baluchistan □ . 27 0N 62 0 E
Sitapur .... 27 38N 80 45 E
Sitges .... 41 17N   1 47 E
Sitka 57 4N 135 14w
Sittang Myit, R. .. 18 20N 96 45 E
Sittard .... 51 0N   5 52 E
Situbondo .... 7 45s 114 0 E
Sivand .... 30 5N 52 55 E
Sivas .... 39 43N 36 58 E
Siverek .... 37 50N 39 25 E
Siwa .... 29 11N 25 31 E
Siwalik Ra. ...... 28 0N 83 0 E
Sizewell .... 52 13N   1 38 E
Sjaelland, I. ...... 55 30N 11 30 E
Skadarsko,
   Jezero, L. ..... 42 10N 19 15 E
Skagen .... 57 43N 10 35 E
Skagerrak, Str. ... 57 30N   9 0 E
Skagway 59 30N 135 20w
Skara .... 58 25N 13 30 E
Skaraborg □ ..... 58 20N 13 30 E
Skardu .... 35 20N 73 35 E
Skeena, R. 54 15N 130 5w
Skenna Mts. 56 40N 128 0w
Skegnwss .... 53 9N   0 20 E
Skeldon 6 0N 57 20w
Skellefteå .... 64 45N 20 59 E
Skelleftehamn ... 64 41N 21 14 E
Skibbereen 51 33N   9 16w
Skiddaw, Mt. 54 39N   3 9w
Skien .... 59 12N   9 35 E
Skierniewice ..... 51 58N 20 19 E
Skikda .... 36 50N   6 58 E
Skipton 53 57N   2 1w
Skíros, I. .... 38 55N 24 34 E
Skive .... 56 33N   9 2 E
Skoghall .... 59 20N 13 30 E
Skopje .... 42 1N 21 32 E

* Thailand, G. of   * Renamed Kuito   † Renamed Chinhoyi

Skoplje=Skopje ... 42 1N 21 32 E
Skövde .... 58 24N 13 50 E
Skovorodino ..... 53 59N 123 55 E
Skowhegan 44 49N 69 40W
Skudeneshavn .... 59 10N 5 10 E
Skull 51 32N 9 40W
Skwierzyna ...... 52 46N 15 30 E
Skye, I. 57 15N 6 10W
Slaney, R. 52 52N 6 45W
Slask, Reg. ..... 51 0N 16 45 E
Slatina .... 44 28N 24 22 E
Slaton 33 27N 101 38W
Slave Coast ...... 6 0N 2 30 E
Slave Lake 55 25N 114 50W
Slavgorod .... 53 10N 78 50 E
Slavyansk .... 45 15N 38 11 E
Sleaford 53 0N 0 22W
Sleat, Sd. of 57 5N 5 47W
Sliedrecht ...... 51 50N 4 45 E
Sliema .... 35 55N 14 29 E
Sligo ◊ 54 17N 8 28W
Sligo □ 54 10N 8 40W
Slite .... 57 42N 18 45 E
Slobodskoy ...... 58 40N 50 6 E
Slough 51 30N 0 35W
Slovenia◊ =
 Slovenija ...... 45 58N 14 30 E
Slovenija □ ..... 45 58N 14 30 E
Slovenské
 Rudohorie, Mts.. 50 25N 13 0 E
Słupsk .... 54 28N 17 1 E
Slyudyanka ...... 51 40N 103 30 E
Smeaton 53 30N 105 49W
Smederevo ...... 44 40N 20 57 E
Smith 55 10N 114 0W
Smith Arm, B. ... 66 30N 123 0 E
Smithers 54 45N 127 10W
Smithfield, S. Afr . 30 13 s 26 32 E
Smithfield, U.S.A. . 35 31N 78 16W
Smiths Falls 44 55N 76 0W
Smithton .... 40 53N 145 6 E
Smoky Falls 50 10N 82 10W
Smoky Hill, R. ... 39 3N 96 48W
Smolensk .... 54 45N 32 0 E
Smolikas, Mt. .... 40 9N 20 58 E
Smooth Rock Falls 49 17N 81 37W
Snaefell, Mt. 54 18N 4 26W
Snaefellsjökull.Mt.. 64 49N 23 49W
Snake, R. 46 12N 119 2W
Snake River Plain . 43 13N 113 0W

Sneek .... 53 2N 5 40 E
Sneeuberg ...... 31 46 s 24 20 E
Sněžka, Mt. ..... 50 41N 14 55 E
Snøhetta, Mt. .... 62 19N 9 16 E
Snow Lake 54 53N 101 2W
Snowdon, Mt. 53 4N 4 8W
Snowflake 34 30N 110 4W
Snowshoe Pk. 48 13N 115 41W
Snowy, Mts. ..... 36 15s 148 20 E
Snyder 32 45N 100 57W
Soalala .... 16 6s 45 20 E
Soap Lake 47 29N 119 31W
Sobral 3 50s 40 30W
Soche .... 38 24N 77 20 E
Sochi .... 43 35N 39 40 E
Society Is. 17 0s 151 0W
Socorro, Col. 6 29N 73 16W
Socorro, U.S.A. ... 34 3N 106 58W
Socotra, I. ...... 12 30N 54 0 E
Soda Creek 52 25N 122 10W
Soda Springs 42 4N 111 40W
Söderhamn ...... 61 18N 17 10 E
Söderköping ..... 58 31N 16 35 E
Södermanlands □ . 59 10N 16 30 E
Södertälje ...... 59 12N 17 50 E
Sodo .... 7 0N 37 57 E
Soekmekaar ..... 23 30s 29 55 E
Soest, Neth. ..... 52 9N 5 19 E
Sofala = Beira ... 19 50s 34 52 E
Sofia = Sofiya ... 42 45N 23 20 E
Sofiya .... 42 45N 23 20 E
Sogamoso 5 43N 72 56W
Sogn og Fjordane □ 61 40N 6 0 E
Sohâg .... 26 27N 31 43 E
Soignes .... 50 35N 4 5 E
Soissons .... 49 25N 3 19 E
Soke .... 37 48N 27 28 E
Sokodé .... 9 0N 1 11 E
Sokol .... 59 30N 40 5 E
Sokółka .... 53 25N 23 30 E
Sokoto .... 13 2N 5 16 E
Sokoto, R. ...... 11 20N 4 10 E
Sokoto □ .... 11 40N 5 15 E
Solai .... 0 2N 36 12 E
Solano .... 16 25N 121 15 E
Soledad, Col. 10 55N 74 46W
Soledad, U.S.A. .. 36 27N 121 16W
Soledad, Ven. 8 10N 63 34W
Solent 50 45N 1 25W
Soligalich .... 59 5N 42 10 E

Solikamsk .... 59 38N 56 50 E
Sollefteå .... 63 10N 17 20 E
Sóller .... 39 43N 2 45 E
Sologne, Reg. .... 47 40N 2 0 E
Solok .... 0 55s 100 40 E
Sololá .... 14 49N 91 10 E
Solomon Is. ..... 8 0s 159 0 E
Solothurn ...... 47 13N 7 32 E
Soltânabâd ..... 36 29N 58 5 E
* Soltâniyeh ..... 36 20N 48 55 E
Sölvesborg ..... 56 5N 14 35 E
Solvychegodsk ... 61 21N 46 52 E
Solwezi .... 12 20s 26 26 E
Solway Firth 54 45N 3 38W
† Somabula ..... 19 40s 29 38 E
Somali Rep. ■ ... 7 0N 47 0 E
Somerset, Bermuda 32 20N 64 55W
Somerset, Ky. 37 5N 84 40W
Somerset □ 51 9N 3 0W
Somerset East ... 32 42s 25 35 E
Somerset West ... 34 8s 18 50 E
Somerset I.,
 Bermuda 32 20N 64 55W
Somerset I., Canada 73 30N 93 0W
Someş, R. ...... 47 9N 23 55 E
Somme □ ...... 40 0N 2 15 E
Somme, R. ..... 50 11N 1 39 E
Somovit .... 43 45N 24 48 E
Somport, Pto. de . 42 48N 0 31W
Sondags, R. ..... 33 44s 25 51 E
Sonderborg ..... 54 55N 9 49 E
Søndre Strømfjord 66 30N 50 52W
Sonepat .... 29 0N 77 5 E
Sonepur .... 20 55N 83 50 E
Songea .... 10 40s 35 40 E
Songefjorden ... 61 10N 5 30 E
Songkhla ...... 7 13N 100 37 E
Sonmiani ...... 25 25N 66 40 E
Sonora 30 33N 100 37W
Sonora □ 37 59N 120 27W
Sonsonate 13 45N 89 45W
Soochow ...... 31 18N 120 41 E
Sopot .... 54 27N 18 31 E
Sopron .... 47 41N 16 37 E
Sop's Arm 49 46s 56 56W
Sør Trøndelag □ . 63 0N 11 0 E
Sorata 15 50s 68 50W
Sorel 46 0N 73 10W
Sorgono .... 40 1N 9 7 E
Soria 41 43N 2 32W

Sorkh, Kuh-e ..... 35 40N 58 30 E
Sorocaba 23 31s 47 35W
Sorong .... 0 55s 131 15 E
Soroti .... 1 43N 33 35 E
Sørøya, I. ...... 70 35N 22 45 E
Sorrento .... 40 38N 14 23 E
Sorsele .... 65 31N 17 30 E
Sortavala .... 61 42N 30 41 E
Sosnogorsk ..... 63 37N 53 51 E
Sosnovka ...... 54 9N 109 35 E
Sosnowiec ..... 50 20N 19 10 E
Souanke .... 2 10N 14 10 E
Soûdas, Kol. .... 35 28N 24 10 E
Soul .... 37 33N 126 58 E
Sources, Mt. aux . 28 45s 28 50 E
Soure 0 35s 48 30W
Souris 49 40N 100 20W
Souris, R. 49 39N 99 34W
Sousa 7 0s 38 10W
Sousel 2 38s 52 29W
Sousse .... 35 50N 10 33 E
South Africa ■ ... 30 0s 25 0 E
South America ... 10 0s 60 0W
South Australia □ . 32 0s 139 0 E
South Bend, Ind.
 U.S.A. 41 38N 86 20W
South Bend,
 Wash. 46 44N 123 52W
South Boston 36 42N 78 58W
South Carolina □ . 33 45N 81 0W
South Charleston . 38 20N 81 40W
South China Sea . 10 0N 111 0 E
South Dakota □ .. 45 0N 100 0W
South Esk, R. 56 40N 2 40W
South Georgia, I. . 54 30s 37 0W
South Glamorgan □ 51 28N 3 26W
South Grafton ... 42 11s 71 42W
South Haven ... 42 22N 86 20W
South Horr ..... 2 12N 36 56 E
South Invercargill . 46 26s 168 23 E
South Island ... 43 50s 171 0 E
South Korea ■ ... 36 0N 128 0 E
South Magnetic
 Pole .... 66 30s 139 30 E
South Milwaukee . 42 50N 87 52W
South Orkney Is. . 63 0s 45 0W
South Platte, R. .. 41 7N 100 42W
South Porcupine . 48 30N 81 12W
South River 45 52N 79 21W
South Sandwich Is. 57 0s 27 0W

South
 Saskatchewan, R. 53 15N 105 5W
South Shetland Is. . 62 0s 59 0W
South Shields 54 59N 1 26W
South Sioux City . 42 30N 96 30W
South Tyne, R. ... 54 59N 2 8W
South Uist, I. 57 10N 7 10W
* South West Africa ■ 22 0s 18 0 E
South Yemen ■ ... 15 0N 48 0 E
South Yorkshire □ . 52 45N 1 25W
Southampton,
 Canada 44 30N 81 25W
Southampton,
 U.K. 50 54N 1 23W
Southampton,
 U.S.A. 40 54N 72 22W
Southampton I. ... 64 30N 84 0W
Southend ...... 51 32N 0 43 E
Southern Alps, Mts. 43 41s 170 11 E
Southern Cross ... 31 12s 119 15 E
Southern Mid-
 Atlantic Ridge .. 30 0s 15 0W
Southern Ocean .. 62 0s 160 0W
Southern
 Uplands, Mts. ... 55 30N 4 0W
Southport,
 Australia ...... 28 0s 153 25 E
Southport, U.K. .. 53 38N 3 1W
Southwold ..... 52 19N 1 41 E
Soutpansberge .. 22 55s 29 30 E
Sovetsk .... 57 38N 48 53 E
Sovetskaya Gavan . 48 50N 140 0 E
Spain ■ 40 0N 5 0W
Spalding 52 47N 0 9W
Spandau ...... 52 32N 13 13 E
Spaniard's Bay .. 47 38N 53 20W
Spanish Fork 40 10N 111 37W
Spanish Pt. 32 12N 64 45W
Spanish Town ... 18 0N 77 20W
Sparks 39 30N 119 45W
Sparta 43 55N 91 10W
Spartanburg ... 35 0N 82 0W
Spárti .... 37 5N 22 25 E
Spartivento,
 C., Italy ...... 37 56N 16 4 E
Spartivento,
 C., Sardinia ... 38 52N 8 50 E
Spassk-Dal'niy ... 44 40N 132 40 E
Spátha, Ákra ... 35 42N 23 43 E
Spearfish 44 32N 103 52W

* Renamed Sa'īdiyah
† Renamed Somabhula

* Renamed Namibia

Speed .... 35 21 s 142 27 E
Speightstown 13 18N 59 30W
Speke G. .... 2 20 s 32 50 E
Spenard 61 0N 149 50W
Spence Bay 69 32N 93 31W
Spencer 43 5N 95 3W
Spencer, G. .... 34 30 s 137 0 E
Spenser, Mts. .... 42 15 s 172 45 E
Sperrin Mts. 54 50N 7 0W
Spey, R. 57 40N 3 6W
Speyer .... 49 19N 8 26 E
Spezia=La Spezia . 44 8N 9 50 E
Spinazzola .... 40 58N 16 5 E
Spirit River 55 45N 119 0W
Spithead 50 46N 1 12W
Split .... 43 31N 16 26 E
Spokane 47 45N 117 25W
Spoleto .... 42 44N 12 44 E
Sporades, Is.=
 Voríai .... 39 15N 23 30 E
Sporádhes, Voríai . 39 15N 23 30 E
Spree, R. .... 52 32N 13 13 E
Springbok .... 29 42 s 17 54 E
Springburn .... 43 40 s 171 32 E
Springdale, Canada 49 30N 56 6W
Springdale, U.S.A. 36 10N 94 5W
Springerville 34 10N 109 16W
Springfield, N.Z. .. 43 19 s 171 56 E
Springfield, Ill. .. 39 58N 89 40W
Springfield, Mass. . 42 8N 72 37W
Springfield, Mo. .. 37 15N 93 20W
Springfield, Ohio . 39 50N 83 48W
Springfield, Ore. .. 44 2N 123 0W
Springfield, Tenn. . 36 35N 86 55W
Springfontein .... 30 15 s 25 40 E
Springhill 45 40N 64 4W
Springs .... 26 13 s 28 25 E
Springsure .... 24 8 s 148 6 E
Springvale,
 Queens. .... 23 33 s 140 42 E
Springvale,
 W.Australia .... 17 48 s 127 41 E
Springville, N.Y. .. 42 31N 78 41W
Springville, Utah . 40 14N 111 35W
Spurn Hd. .... 53 34N 0 8 E
Squamish 49 45N 123 10W
Squillace .... 38 45N 16 28 E
Sragen .... 7 28 s 110 59 E
Sredinnyy Khrebet 57 0N 160 0 E

Sredne
 Tamborskoye ... 50 55N 137 45 E
Srednekolymsk .... 67 20N 154 40 E
Srednevilyuysk ... 63 50N 123 5 E
Sremska Mitrovica . 44 58N 19 37 E
Srépok, R. .... 13 33N 106 16 E
Sretensk .... 52 10N 117 40 E
Sri Lanka ■ ..... 7 30N 80 50 E
Srikakulam .... 18 14N 84 4 E
Srinagar .... 34 12N 74 50 E
Srnetica .... 44 25N 16 33 E
Staffa, I. 56 26N 6 21W
Stafford 52 49N 2 9W
Stafford □ 52 53N 2 10W
Staines 51 26N 0 30W
Stalingrad =
 Volgograd ..... 48 40N 44 25 E
Stalybridge 53 29N 2 2W
Stamford, Australia 21 15 s 143 46 E
Stamford, U.K. ... 52 39N 0 29W
Stamford, Conn. .. 41 5N 73 30W
Stamford, Tex. ... 32 58N 99 50W
Standerton .... 26 55 s 29 13 E
Stanger .... 29 18 s 31 21 E
Stanke Dimitrov .. 42 27N 23 9 E
Stanley, Australia . 40 46 s 145 19 E
Stanley, Falkland Is. 51 40 s 58 0W
Stanley, U.S.A. ... 44 10N 114 59W
Stanley Falls =
 Chutes Boyoma . 0 12N 25 25 E
Stanleyville =
 Kisangani ..... 0 41N 52 11 E
* Stann Creek 17 0N 88 20W
Stanovoy Khrebet . 55 0N 130 0 E
Stanthorpe .... 28 36 s 151 59 E
Stanton 69 45N 128 52W
Stara Planina .... 43 15N 23 0 E
Stara Zagora ..... 42 26N 25 39 E
Staraya Russa .... 57 58N 31 10 E
Starbuck I. .... 5 37 s 155 55W
Stargard Szczecinski 53 20N 15 0 E
Starkville 37 10N 104 31W
Start Pt. 50 13N 3 38W
Staryy Keydzhan .. 60 0N 144 50 E
State College 40 47N 77 49W
Statesboro 32 26N 81 46W
Statesville 35 48N 80 51W
Staunton 38 7N 79 4W
Stavanger .... 58 57N 5 40 E
Stavrapol .... 45 2N 41 59 E

Stawell .... 36 58 s 142 47 E
Steamboat Springs . 40 30N 106 58W
Steelton 40 17N 76 50W
Steen River 59 40N 117 12W
Steep, Pt. .... 26 8 s 113 8 E
Stefanie, L. =
 Chew Bahir .... 4 40N 30 50 E
Steiermark □ ..... 47 26N 15 0 E
Steilrandberg .... 17 30 s 13 0 E
Steinbach 49 32N 96 40W
Steinkjer .... 63 59N 11 31 E
Stellaland .... 26 45 s 24 50 E
Stellarton 45 34N 62 40W
Stellenbosch ..... 33 58 s 18 50 E
Stelvio, P. de .... 46 32N 10 27 E
Stendal .... 52 36N 11 50 E
Stepanakert ...... 40 0N 46 25 E
Stephen 48 30N 96 53W
Stephens Creek ... 31 50 s 141 30 E
Stephenville,
 Canada 48 31N 58 30W
Stephenville,
 U.S.A. 32 12N 98 12W
Stepnoi =
 Elista .... 46 25N 44 17 E
Stereá Ellás □ .... 38 55N 22 0 E
Sterkstroom ...... 31 32 s 26 32 E
Sterling, Colo. ... 40 40N 103 15W
Sterling, Ill. 41 45N 89 45W
Sterlitamak ...... 53 40N 56 0 E
Stettin = Szczecin . 53 27N 14 27 E
Stettler 52 25N 112 40W
Steubenville 40 21N 80 39W
Stevens Point 44 32N 89 34W
Stewart, I., Chile . 54 50 s 71 30W
Stewart, I., N.Z. .. 46 58 s 167 54 E
Stewart River 63 25N 139 30W
Steynsburg .... 31 15 s 25 49 E
Steyr .... 48 3N 14 25 E
Steytlerville ...... 33 17 s 24 19 E
Stikine, R. 56 40N 132 30W
Stilfontein .... 26 50 s 26 50 E
Stillwater, Minn. .. 45 3N 92 47W
Stillwater, Okla. .. 36 5N 97 3W
Stillwater Mts. 39 45N 118 6W
Štip .... 41 42N 22 10 E
Stirling 56 17N 3 57W
Stockerau .... 48 24N 16 12 E
Stockholm .... 59 17N 18 3 E
Stockholms □ ..... 59 40N 18 45 E

Stockport 53 25N 2 11W
Stockton, Australia 32 56 s 151 47 E
Stockton, U.K. ... 54 34N 1 20W
Stockton, U.S.A. . 38 0N 121 20W
Stoke-on-Trent ... 53 1N 2 11W
Stokes Bay 45 0N 81 22W
Stolbovaya .... 64 50N 153 50 E
Stonehenge,
 Australia ...... 24 22 s 143 17 E
Stonehenge, U.K. . 51 9N 1 45W
Stonehaven 56 58N 2 11W
Stonewall 50 10N 96 50W
Storavan, L. ..... 65 45N 18 10 E
Store Baelt ...... 55 28N 11 0 E
Støren .... 63 3N 10 18 E
Storm Lake 42 35N 95 5W
Stormberg .... 31 16 s 26 17 E
Stornoway 58 12N 6 23W
Storsjön, L. ...... 60 35N 16 45 E
Stoughton 49 40N 103 0W
Stour, R., Dorset .. 50 43N 1 46W
Stour, R., Hereford
 and Worcester .. 52 20N 2 15W
Stour, R., Kent ... 51 18N 1 22 E
Stour, R., Suffolk . 51 52N 1 16 E
Stourbridge 52 28N 2 8W
Stowmarket ...... 52 11N 1 0 E
Strabane 54 50N 7 28W
Strabane □ 54 50N 7 28W
Strahan .... 42 8 s 145 24 E
Stralsund .... 54 17N 13 5 E
Strand .... 34 9 s 18 48 E
Strangford, L. 54 30N 5 37W
Stranraer 54 54N 5 0W
Strasbourg, Canada 51 10N 104 55W
Strasbourg, Fr. ... 48 35N 7 42 E
Stratford, Australia 37 59 s 147 5 E
Stratford, Canada . 43 23N 81 0W
Stratford, N.Z. ... 39 20 s 174 19 E
Stratford-on-Avon . 52 12N 1 42W
Strath Spey 57 15N 3 40W
Strathalbyn ...... 35 13 s 138 53 E
Strathclyde □ 55 30N 5 0W
Strathmore 51 5N 113 25W
Strathmore, Reg. . 58 23N 4 40W
Strathroy 42 58N 81 38W
Strathy, Pt. 58 35N 4 0W
Streaky Bay ...... 32 51 s 134 18 E
Streator 41 9N 88 52W
Strelka .... 58 5N 93 10 E

Strezhevoy .... 60 42N 77 34 E
Strómboli, I. ..... 38 48N 15 12 E
Stromeferry 57 20N 5 33W
Strömstad .... 58 55N 11 15 E
Stronsay, I. 59 8N 2 38W
Stroud 51 44N 2 12W
Struer .... 56 30N 8 35 E
Struma, R. .... 40 47N 23 51 E
Struthers 41 6N 80 38W
Stung Treng ...... 13 26N 106 0 E
Sturgeon Bay 44 52N 87 20W
Sturgeon Falls ... 46 25N 79 57W
Sturt Cr. .... 20 8 s 127 24 E
Stutterheim ...... 32 33 s 27 28 E
Stuttgart, U.S.A. .. 34 30N 91 33W
Stuttgart,
 W.Germany .... 48 46N 9 10 E
Styr, R. .... 52 7N 26 35 E
Suakin .... 19 0N 37 20 E
Suancheng .... 30 58N 118 57 E
Suanhwa .... 40 35N 115 0 E
Suao .... 24 32 s 121 42 E
Subang .... 7 30 s 107 45 E
Subotica .... 46 6N 19 29 E
Suchitato 13 56N 89 0W
Suchou=Soochow . 31 18N 120 41 E
Suchow .... 34 10N 117 20 E
Suck, R. 53 16N 8 3W
Sucre .... 19 0 s 65 15W
Sudan ■ .... 15 0N 30 0 E
Sudbury 46 30N 81 0W
Sûdd .... 8 20N 29 30 E
Sudetes, Mts.=
 Sudety, Mts. ... 50 20N 16 45 E
Sudety, Mts. ..... 50 20N 16 45 E
Sudirman,
 Pengunungan,
 Ra. .... 4 30 s 137 0 E
Sueca 39 12N 0 21W
Suez = El Suweis . 28 40N 33 0 E
Suffolk 36 47N 76 33W
Suffolk □ .... 52 16N 1 0 E
Sufu .... 39 44N 75 53 E
Sugluk = Saglouc . 62 10N 75 40W
Suhar .... 24 20N 56 40 E
Suhbaatar ...... 50 17N 106 10 E
Suhsien .... 33 28N 117 54 E
Suichwan .... 26 26N 114 32 E
Suihwa .... 46 40N 126 57 E

* Renamed Dangriga

Suikhai .... 21 17N 110 19 E
Suiping .... 33 15N 114 6 E
Suir, R. 52 15N 7 0W
Sukabumi .... 6 56s 106 57 E
Sukadana .... 1 10s 110 0 E
Sukhumi .... 43 0N 41 0 E
Sukkur .... 27 50N 68 46 E
Sulaiman Ra. .... 30 30N 69 50 E
Sulam Tsor ...... 33 4N 35 6 E
Sulawesi, I. .... 2 0s 120 0 E
Sulina .... 45 10N 29 40 E
Sulitälma .... 67 17N 17 28 E
Sulitjelma ...... 61 7N 16 8 E
Sullana 5 0s 80 45W
Sullivan 39 5N 87 26W
Sulphur 30 20N 93 22W
Sulphur Springs .. 33 5N 95 30W
Sultanpur .... 26 18N 82 10 E
Sulu Arch........ 6 0N 121 0 E
Sulu Sea .... 8 0N 120 0 E
Suluq .... 31 44N 20 14 E
Sumalata .... 1 0N 122 37 E
Sumatera □ ..... 0 40N 100 20 E
Sumatera, I. .... 0 40N 100 20 E
Sumatra 46 45N 107 37W
Sumatra, I. =
  Sumatera, I. ... 0 40N 100 20 E
Sumba, Selat, Str. . 9 0s 118 40 E
Sumba, I. ...... 9 45s 119 35 E
Sumbawa, I. ..... 8 34s 117 17 E
Sumbawa Besar ... 8 30s 117 26 E
Sumbawanga ..... 7 57s 31 35 E
Sümber .... 46 40N 108 50 E
Sumbing, Mt. .... 7 19s 110 3 E
Sumedang .... 6 49s 107 56 E
Sumenep .... 7 3s 113 51 E
Summerside 46 29N 63 41W
Summit 47 50N 72 20W
Summit Lake 54 20N 122 40W
Summit Pk. 37 20N 106 48W
Sumoto .... 34 21N 134 54 E
Sumperk .... 49 59N 17 0 E
Sumter 33 55N 80 10W
Sumy .... 50 57N 34 50 E
Sunart, L. 56 42N 5 35W
Sunbury 40 50N 76 46W
Sunchon .... 34 52N 127 31 E
Sunda, Selat .... 6 0s 105 45 E
Sundarbans, Reg. . 22 0N 89 0 E
Sunderland 54 54N 1 22W

Sundridge 45 45N 79 25W
Sundsvall .... 62 23N 17 17 E
Sungaigerung .... 4 58s 105 7 E
Sungaipakning ... 1 19N 102 0 E
Sungaipenuh .... 2 1s 101 20 E
Sungaitiram ..... 0 45s 117 8 E
Sungari, R. ..... 47 30N 132 30 E
Sungguminasa .... 5 17s 119 30 E
Sungkiang ...... 31 0N 121 20 E
Sungpan .... 32 50N 103 20 E
Sungtzu Hu, L. .. 30 10N 111 45 E
Sunnyside 46 24N 120 2W
Sunshine .... 37 48s 144 52 E
Sunyani 7 21N 2 22W
Supaul .... 26 10N 86 40 E
Superior, Ariz. .. 33 19N 111 9W
Superior, Wis. ... 46 45N 92 0W
Superior, L. 47 40N 87 0W
Supu .... 27 57N 110 15 E
Sür, Lebanon ... 33 19N 35 16 E
Sür, Oman ..... 22 34N 59 32 E
Sura, R. .... 56 6N 46 0 E
Surabaya .... 7 17s 112 45 E
Surakarta ...... 7 35s 110 48 E
Surat .... 21 12N 72 55 E
Surat Thani .... 9 3N 99 28 E
Suratgarh ...... 29 18N 73 55 E
Surgut .... 61 20N 73 28 E
Suri .... 23 50N 87 34 E
Surif .... 31 40N 35 4 E
Surinam ■ 4 0N 56 15W
Surrey □ 51 16N 0 30W
Surt .... 31 11N 16 46 E
Surt, Khalij .....
Surtsey, I. 63 27N 20 15W
Suruga-Wan, G. .. 34 45s 138 30 E
Susa .... 45 8N 7 3 E
Susaki .... 33 22N 133 17 E
Susanino .... 52 50N 140 14 E
Susanville 40 28N 120 40W
Susquehanna, R. .. 39 33N 76 5W
Susques 23 35s 66 25W
Sussex 45 45N 65 37W
Susuman .... 62 47N 148 10 E
Sutherland, Canada 52 15N 106 40W
Sutherland,
  S. Africa, ... 32 33s 20 40 E
Sutlej, R. ...... 29 23N 71 2 E
Sutton-
  in-Ashfield 52 8N 1 16W

Suva .... 17 40s 178 8 E
Suwałki .... 54 8N 22 59 E
Suwannee, R. ... 29 18N 83 9W
Suwanose-Jima, I. . 29 26N 129 30 E
Suwarrow Is. 13 15s 163 5W
Suweilih .... 32 2N 35 50 E
Suweis, Kañg es .. 28 40N 33 0 E
Suwen .... 20 27N 110 2 E
Suwôn .... 37 17N 127 1 E
Suzdal .... 56 29N 40 26 E
Suzu .... 37 25N 137 17 E
Suzuka .... 34 55N 136 36 E
Svalbard, Is. .... 78 0N 17 0 E
Svappavaara .... 67 40N 21 3 E
Svartisen, Mt. ... 66 40N 14 16 E
Svealand, Reg. ... 60 0N 15 0 E
Sveg .... 62 2N 14 21 E
Svendborg ...... 55 4N 10 35 E
Sverdlovks ..... 56 50N 60 30 E
Sverdrup Is. 79 0N 97 0W
Svishtov .... 43 36N 25 23 E
Svobodnyy ..... 51 20N 128 0 E
Svolvaer .... 68 15N 14 34 E
Swabian Mts.=
  Scwäbische
  Alb., Mts. ..... 48 30N 9 30 E
Swakop, R. ..... 22 38s 14 36 E
Swakopmund .... 22 37s 14 30 E
Swale, R. 54 6N 1 20W
Swan Hill ...... 35 15s 143 31 E
Swan Hills 54 42N 115 49W
Swan Is. 17 22N 83 57W
Swan River 52 10N 101 25W
Swanage 50 36N 1 59W
Swansea, Australia 33 3s 151 35 E
Swansea, U.K. ... 51 37N 3 57W
Swartberge ..... 30 15s 29 23 E
Swartruggens ... 25 39s 26 42 E
Swatow = Shantow 23 25N 116 40 E
Swaziland ■ .... 26 30s 31 30 E
Sweden ■ ...... 67 0N 15 0 E
Swedru 5 32N 0 41W
Sweetwater 32 30N 100 28W
Swellendam .... 34 1s 20 26 E
Świdnica .... 50 50N 16 30 E
Świebodzin ..... 52 15N 15 37 E
Swift Current ... 50 20N 107 45W
Swindon 51 33N 1 47W
Świnoujście .... 53 54N 14 16 E
Switzerland ■ ... 46 30N 8 0 E

Swords 53 27N 6 15W
Sydney, Australia . 33 53s 151 10 E
Sydney, Canada .. 46 7N 60 7W
Sydney Mines ... 46 18N 60 15W
Syktyvkar ...... 61 45N 50 40 E
Sylacauga 33 10N 86 15W
Sylhet .... 24 43N 91 55 E
Sylvan Lake 52 20N 114 10W
Sym .... 60 20N 87 50 E
Syr Darya, R. ... 46 3N 61 0 E
Syracuse 38 0N 101 40W
Syria ■ .... 35 0N 38 0 E
Syul'dzhyukyor .. 63 25N 113 40 E
Syzran .... 53 12N 48 30 E
Szczecin .... 53 27N 14 27 E
Szechwan □ .... 30 15N 103 15 E
Szeged .... 46 16N 20 10 E
Székesfehérvár .. 47 15N 18 25 E
Szekszárd ...... 46 22N 18 42 E
Szemao .... 22 50N 101 0 E
Szengen .... 24 50N 108 0 E
Szentes .... 46 39N 20 21 E
Szeping .... 43 10N 124 18 E
Szolnok .... 47 10N 20 15 E
Szombathely .... 47 14N 16 38 E

T

Ta Hingan Ling,
  Mts. .... 48 0N 120 0 E
Ta Liang Shan, Mts. 28 0N 103 0 E
Tabacal 23 15s 64 15W
Tabagné 7 53N 3 7W
Tabasco □ 17 45N 93 30W
Taber 49 48N 111 5W
Tablas, I. ...... 12 20N 122 10 E
Table Mt. ...... 34 0s 18 22 E
Tableland ...... 17 16s 126 51 E
Tabletop, Mt. ... 23 30s 147 0 E
Tábor .... 49 25N 14 39 E
Tabora .... 5 2s 32 57 E
Tabou 4 30N 7 20W
Tabriz .... 38 7N 46 20 E
Tabuk .... 28 30N 36 25 E
Tachira 8 7N 72 21W
Tacloban ...... 11 1N 125 0 E
Tacna 18 0s 70 20W

Tacoma 47 15N 122 30W
Tacuarembó 31 45s 56 0W
Tademait, Plateau
  du .... 28 30N 2 30 E
Tadjoura ...... 11 50N 44 55 E
Tadmor, N.Z. ... 41 27s 172 45 E
Tadmor, Syria .. 34 30N 37 55 E
Tadoussac 48 11N 69 42W
Tadzhik S.S.R. □ . 35 30N 70 0 E
Taegu .... 35 50N 128 25 E
Taejon .... 35 30N 127 22 E
Tafalla 42 30N 1 41W
Tafelbaai ...... 33 35s 18 25 E
Taff, R. 51 27N 3 9W
Taftan, Küh-e, Mt. 28 36N 61 6 E
Taganrog ...... 47 12N 38 50 E
Tagbilaran ..... 9 42N 124 3 E
Tagliamento, R. .. 45 38N 13 6 E
Taguatinga 12 26s 45 40W
Tahakopa ...... 46 30s 169 23 E
Tahan, Gunong .. 4 38N 102 14 E
Tahcheng ...... 46 50N 83 1 E
Tahiti, I. 17 45s 149 30W
Tahoe, L. 39 6N 120 0W
Tahoua .... 14 57N 5 16 E
Tahsien .... 31 12N 108 13 E
Tahta .... 26 44N 31 32 E
Tai Hu .... 31 10N 120 0 E
Taichow .... 32 30N 119 50 E
Taichung ...... 24 10N 120 35 E
Taihan Shan, Mts. . 36 0N 114 0 E
Taihape .... 39 41s 175 48 E
Taiho .... 26 50N 114 54 E
Taiku .... 37 46N 112 28 E
Tailai .... 46 28N 123 18 E
Tailem Bend ... 35 12s 139 29 E
Taima .... 27 35N 38 45 E
Tain 57 49N 4 4W
Tainan .... 23 0N 120 15 E
Taínaron, Åkra .. 36 22N 22 27 E
Taipei .... 25 2N 121 30 E
Taiping .... 4 50N 100 43 E
Taitao, Pen. de .. 46 30s 75 0W
Taitung .... 22 43N 121 4 E
Taiwan ■ ...... 23 30N 121 0 E
Taiyiba, Israel .. 32 36N 35 27 E
Taiyiba, Jordan . 31 55N 35 17 E
Taiyuan .... 38 0N 112 30 E
Ta'izz .... 13 38N 44 4 E
Tajo, R. 38 40N 9 24W

Tājūra .... 32 51N 13 27 E
Tak .... 17 0N 99 10 E
Takachiho .... 32 42N 131 18 E
Takada .... 37 7N 138 15 E
Takaka .... 40 51s 172 50 E
Takamatsu ...... 34 20N 134 5 E
Takaoka .... 36 40N 137 0 E
Takapuna .... 36 47s 174 47 E
Takasaki .... 36 20N 139 0 E
Takatsuki .... 34 40N 135 37 E
Takaungu .... 3 38s 39 52 E
Takayama .... 36 10N 137 5 E
Takefu .... 35 50N 136 10 E
Takhar □ .... 36 30N 69 30 E
Takla Makan, Reg. 39 40N 85 0 E
Takoradi 4 58N 1 55w
Takum .... 7 18N 10 0 E
Talara 4 30s 81 10w
Talata Mafara ..... 12 35N 6 2 E
Talaud, Kep. ..... 4 30N 127 10 E
Talavera de la Reina 39 55N 4 46 E
Talca 35 20s 71 46w
Talcahuano 36 40s 73 10w
Taldy Kurgan .... 45 10N 78 45 E
Talfit .... 32 5N 35 17 E
Talguppa .... 14 11N 74 51 E
Tali, Shensi ...... 34 48N 109 48 E
Tali, Yunnan .... 25 50N 100 0 E
Taliabu, I. ...... 1 45s 125 0 E
Talien .... 38 53N 121 35 E
Taliwang .... 8 50s 116 55 E
Talkeetna 62 20N 149 50w
Talladega 33 28N 86 2w
Tallahassee 30 25N 84 15w
Tallangatta ...... 36 10s 147 14 E
Tallinn .... 59 29N 24 58 E
Tallulah 32 25N 91 12w
Talluza .... 32 17N 35 18 E
Taltal 25 23s 70 40w
Talwood .... 28 27s 149 20 E
Tamale 9 22N 0 50w
Tamano .... 34 35N 133 59 E
Tamanrasset ..... 22 56N 5 30 E
Tamar, R. 50 22N 4 10w
Tamashima ...... 34 27N 133 18 E
Tamaské .... 14 55N 5 40 E
* Tamatave .... 18 10s 49 25 E
* Tamatave □ ..... 18 0s 49 0 E
Tamaulipas □ 24 0N 99 0w
Tambacounda 13 55N 13 45w

Tambellup .... 34 4s 117 37 E
Tambo .... 24 54s 146 14 E
Tambora, I. ...... 8 14s 117 55 E
Tambov .... 52 45N 41 20 E
Tamchaket 17 25N 10 40w
Tamiahua, Laguna
de 21 30N 97 30w
Tamil Nadu □ .... 11 0N 77 0 E
Taming .... 36 20N 115 10 E
Tammun .... 32 18N 35 23 E
Tampa 27 57N 82 30w
Tampere .... 61 30N 23 50 E
Tampico 22 20N 97 50w
Tamra .... 32 51N 35 12 E
Tamsagbulag ..... 47 15N 117 5 E
Tamworth,
Australia ...... 31 0s 150 58 E
Tamworth, U.K. .. 52 38N 1 2w
Tana .... 70 23N 28 13 E
Tana, L. .... 12 0N 37 20 E
Tana, R. .... 2 32s 40 31 E
Tanabe .... 33 44N 135 22 E
Tanacross 63 40N 143 30w
Tanahgrogot ..... 1 55s 116 15 E
Tanahmerah ...... 6 0s 140 7 E
Tanami, Des. ..... 23 15s 132 20 E
Tanana 65 10N 152 15w
Tanana, R. 64 25N 145 30w
Tananarive =
Antananarivo ... 18 55s 47 31 E
Tananarive □ .... 19 0s 47 0 E
Tánaro, R. ...... 44 9N 7 50 E
Tanda 7 48N 3 10w
Tandil 37 15s 59 6w
Tando Adam ..... 25 45N 48 40 E
Taneatua .... 38 4s 177 1 E
Tane-ga-Shima, I. . 30 30N 131 0 E
Tanen Tong
Dan, Mts. ...... 19 40N 99 0 E
Tanezrouft ...... 23 9N 0 11 E
Tanga .... 5 5s 39 2 E
Tanganyika■ =
Tanzania ...... 6 40s 34 0 E
Tanganyika, L. .... 6 40s 30 0 E
Tanger 35 50N 5 49w
Tangerang ...... 6 12s 106 39 E
Tanghla Shan, Mts. 33 10N 90 0 E
Tangier=Tanger .. 35 50N 5 49w
Tangshan, Anhwei. 34 23N 116 34 E
Tangshan, Hopei .. 39 40N 118 10 E

Tangtu .... 31 37N 118 39 E
Tanguiéta .... 10 37N 1 16 E
Tangyang .... 30 50N 111 45 E
Tanimbar, Kep. ... 7 30s 131 30 E
Tanjung .... 2 10s 115 25 E
Tanjungbalai ..... 2 55N 99 44 E
Tanjungkarang ... 5 25s 105 16 E
Tanjungpandan ... 2 45s 107 39 E
Tanjungredeb .... 2 12N 117 35 E
Tanjungselor ..... 2 55N 117 25 E
Tannin .... 49 40N 91 0 E
Tanout .... 14 58N 8 53 E
Tanta .... 30 45N 30 57 E
Tanunda .... 34 30s 139 0 E
Tanzania ■ ...... 6 40s 34 0 E
Taonan .... 45 30N 122 20 E
Taoyuan .... 25 0N 121 4 E
Tapa Shan, Mts. .. 31 45N 109 30 E
Tapachula 14 54N 92 17w
Tapah .... 4 10N 101 17 E
Tapaktuan ...... 3 30N 97 10 E
Tapanui .... 45 56N 169 18 E
Tapti, R. .... 21 5N 72 40 E
Tapuaenuka, Mt. .. 41 55s 173 50 E
Tara .... 56 55N 74 30 E
Tara, R. .... 56 42N 74 36 E
Tarabagatay,
Khrebet, Mts. ... 47 30N 84 0 E
Tarābulus, Lebanon 34 31N 35 52 E
Tarābulus, Libya .. 32 49N 13 7 E
Tarago .... 35 6s 149 39 E
Tarakan .... 3 20N 117 35 E
Taranaki □ ...... 39 5s 174 51 E
Taranga Hill ..... 24 0N 72 40 E
Táranto .... 40 30N 17 11 E
Táranto, G. di .... 40 0N 17 15 E
Tarapaca 2 56s 69 46w
Tarapoto 6 30s 76 20w
Tarawera .... 39 2s 176 36 E
Tarawera, L. ..... 38 13s 176 27 E
Tarbat Ness 57 52N 3 48w
Tarbela Dam ..... 34 0N 72 52 E
Tarbert 57 54N 6 49w
Tarbes .... 43 15N 0 3 E
Taree .... 31 50s 152 30 E
Tarifa 36 1N 5 36w
Tarija 21 30s 64 40w
Tarim, R. .... 41 5N 86 40 E
Tarkastad ...... 32 0s 26 16 E
Tarkhankut, Mys. . 45 25N 32 30 E

Tarko Sale .... 64 55N 77 50 E
Tarkwa 5 20N 2 0w
Tarlac.......... 15 30N 120 25 E
Tarlton Downs ... 22 40s 136 45 E
Tarn, R. .... 44 5N 1 6 E
Tarn □ .... 43 50N 2 8 E
Tarn-et-Garonne □ 44 8N 1 20 E
Tarnobrzeg ...... 50 35N 21 41 E
Tarnów .... 50 3N 21 0 E
Tarnowskie Góry .. 50 27N 18 54 E
Tarom .... 28 11N 55 42 E
Tarragona ...... 41 5N 1 17 E
Tarrasa .... 41 26N 2 1 E
Tarso Emissi ..... 21 27N 18 36 E
Tarsus .... 36 58N 34 55 E
Tartagal 22 30s 63 50w
Tartu .... 58 25N 26 58 E
Tartūs .... 34 55N 35 55 E
Tarutung .... 2 0N 99 0 E
Tasāwah .... 26 0N 13 37 E
Tashereau 48 40N 78 40w
Tashauz .... 42 0N 59 20 E
Tashigong ...... 33 0N 79 30 E
Tashkent .... 41 20N 69 10 E
Tashkurgan ..... 37 51N 74 57 E
Tashkurghan .... 36 45N 67 40 E
Tashtagol .... 52 47N 87 53 E
Tasikmalaya ..... 7 18s 108 12 E
Taskan .... 63 5N 150 5 E
Tasman, B. ...... 40 59s 173 25 E
Tasman Glacier ... 43 45s 170 20 E
Tasman Sea ..... 42 30s 168 0 E
Tasmania, I. □ ... 49 0s 146 30 E
Tatabánya ...... 47 32N 18 25 E
Tatar A.S.S.R. □ .. 55 50N 51 30 E
Tatarsk .... 55 50N 75 20 E
Tateyama .... 35 0N 139 50 E
Tatien .... 25 40N 118 0 E
Tatra Mts.=
Tatry, Mts. ..... 49 20N 20 0 E
Tatry, Mts. ..... 49 20N 20 0 E
Tatsaitan .... 37 55N 95 0 E
Tatui 23 25s 48 0w
Tatung .... 40 10N 113 10 E
Tatungkow ...... 39 55N 124 10 E
Taubaté 23 5s 45 30w
Taumarunui ..... 38 53s 175 15 E
Taumaturgo 9 0s 73 50w
Taung .... 27 33s 24 47 E
Taungdwingyi .... 20 1N 95 40 E

Taunggyi .... 20 50N 97 0 E
Taungup Taunggya 18 20N 93 40 E
Taunton, U.K. 51 1N 3 7w
Taunton, U.S.A. .. 41 54N 71 6w
Taunus, Mts....... 50 15N 8 20 E
Taupo .... 38 41s 176 7 E
Taupo, L. .... 38 46s 175 55 E
Tauranga .... 37 35s 176 11 E
Taurus Mts. =
Toros Daglari .. 37 0N 35 0 E
Tava Wan, G. .... 22 40N 114 40 E
Tavani 62 10N 93 30w
Tavda 58 7N 65 8w
Tavda, R. .... 57 47N 67 16 E
Taveta .... 3 31N 37 37 E
Taveuni, I. 16 51s 179 58w
Tavira 37 8N 7 40w
Tavistock 50 33N 4 9w
Tavoy .... 14 7N 98 18 E
Taw, R. 51 4N 4 11w
Tawitawi, I....... 5 2N 120 0 E
Tay, Firth of 56 25N 3 8w
Tay, L. 56 30N 4 10w
Tay, R. 56 37N 3 58w
Tayabamba ...... 8 15s 77 10 E
Taylor 30 30N 97 30w
Taylor, Mt. 35 16N 107 50w
Taylorville 39 32N 29 20w
Taymyr Pol. ..... 75 0N 100 0 E
Tayport 56 27N 2 52w
Tayshet .... 55 58N 97 25 E
Tayside □ 56 30N 3 35w
Taytay .... 10 45N 119 30 E
Tayu .... 25 38N 114 9 E
Tayulehsze ...... 29 15N 98 1 E
Taza 34 10N 4 0w
Tazovskiy ...... 67 28N 78 42 E
Tbilisi .... 41 50N 44 50 E
Tchad ■ .... 12 30N 17 15 E
Tchad, L. ...... 13 30N 14 30 E
Tchibanga ...... 2 45s 11 12 E
Te Anau, L. ..... 45 15s 167 45 E
Te Aroha .... 37 32s 175 44 E
Te Awamutu ..... 38 1s 175 20 E
Te Horo .... 40 48s 175 6 E
Te Kuiti .... 38 20s 175 11 E
Te Puke .... 37 46s 176 22 E
Tébessa .... 35 28N 8 9 E
Tebingtinggi .... 3 38s 102 1 E
Tecuala 22 24N 105 30w

Name	Lat	Long
Tecuci	45 51N	27 27 E
Tedzhen	37 23N	60 31 E
Tees, R.	54 34N	1 16w
Teesside	54 37N	1 13w
Tefé	3 25s	64 50w
Tegal	6 52s	109 8 E
Tegelen	51 20N	6 9 E
Tegina	10 5N	6 14 E
Tegucigalpa	14 10N	87 0w
Tehchow	37 28N	116 18 E
Tehrān	35 44N	51 30 E
Tehrān □	35 30N	51 0 E
Tehtsin	28 45N	98·58 E
Tehuacán	18 20N	97 30w
Tehuantepec	16 10N	95 19w
Tehuantepec, Istmo de	17 0N	94 30w
Teifi, R.	52 7N	4 42w
Teign, R.	50 33N	3 29w
Teignmouth	50 33N	3 30w
* Teixeira da Silva	12 12s	15 52 E
† Teixeira de Sousa	10 42s	22 12 E
Tejo, R.	38 40N	9 24w
Tekapo, L.	43 48s	170 32 E
Tekax	20 20N	89 30w
Tekeli	44 50N	79 0 E
Tekirdag	40 58N	27 30 E
Tekkali	18 43N	84 24 E
Tel Aviv-Yafo	32 4N	34 48 E
Tel Mond	32 15N	34 56 E
Tela	15 40N	87 28w
Telanaipura = Jambi	1 38s	103 30 E
Telavi	42 0N	45 30 E
Telegraph Creek	58 0N	131 10w
Telemark □	59 30N	8 30 E
Telford	52 42N	2 29w
Telisze	39 50N	112 0 E
Telkwa	54 41s	126 56w
Tell City	38 0N	86 44w
Tellicherry	11 45N	75 30 E
Telok Anson	4 0N	101 10 E
Telsen	42 30s	66 50w
Telukbetung	5 29s	105 17 E
Telukbutun	4 5N	108 7 E
Telukdalem	0 45N	97 50 E
Tema	5 41N	0 .0 E
Temanggung	7 18s	110 10 E
Tembuland	31 30s	28 20 E
Teme, R.	52 9N	2 18w
Temerloh	3 27N	102 25 E
Temir	49 8N	57 6 E
Temirtou	53 10N	87 20 E
Temiskaming	46 44N	79 5w
Temora	34 30s	147 30 E
Tempe	33 26N	111 59w
Tempino	1 55s	103 23 E
Temple	31 5N	97 28w
Templemore	52 48N	7 50w
Temuco	38 50s	72 50w
Temuka	44 14s	171 17 E
Tenado	12 6N	2 38 E
Tenali	16 15N	80 35 E
Tenancingo	18 98N	99 33w
Tenango	19 0N	99 40w
Tenasserim	12 6N	99 3 E
Tenby	51 40N	4 42w
Tenda, Col di	44 9N	7 34 E
Tende	44 5N	7 34 E
Tenerife, I.	28 20N	16 40w
Tengah□, Java	7 0s	110 0 E
Tengah□, Kalimantan	2 20s	113 0 E
Tengchung	24 58N	98 30 E
Tenghsien	·35 10N	117 10 E
Tengiz, Oz.	50 30N	69 0 E
Tenkasi	8 55N	77 20 E
Tenkodogo	11 55N	0 20w
Tennant Creek	19 30s	134 0 E
Tennessee, R.	37 0N	88 20w
Tennessee □	36 0N	86 30w
Tenryū-Gawa, R.	34 39N	137 47 E
Tenterfield	29 0s	152 0 E
Teófilo Otoni	17 15s	41 30w
Teotihuacan	19 44N	98 50w
Tepic	21 30N	104 54w
Teplice	50 39N	13 48 E
Ter, R.	42 1N	3 12 E
Téra	14 1N	0 50 E
Terang	38 3s	142 59 E
Terek, R.	43 44N	46 33 E
Teresina	5 2s	42 45w
Termez	37 0N	67 15 E
Términi Imerese	37 59N	13 51 E
Términos, L. de	18 35N	91 30w
Térmoli	42 0N	15 0 E
Ternate	0 45N	127 25 E
Terneuzen	51 20N	3 50 E
Terni	42 34N	12 38 E
Terowie	38 10s	138 50 E
Terrace	54 30N	128 35w
Terracina	41 17N	13 12 E
Terralba	39 43N	8 37 E
Terre Adélie	67 0s	140 0 E
Terre Haute	46 30N	75 13w
Terrell	32 44N	96 19w
Terschelling, I.	53 25s	5 20 E
Teruel	40 22N	1 8w
Tervola	66 6N	24 59 E
Tessalit	20 12N	1 0 E
Tessaoua	13 45N	8 0 E
Test, R.	51 7N	1 30w
Tetas, Pta.	22 28s	70 38w
Tete	16 13s	33 33 E
Tete □	16 20s	32 30 E
Tetouan	35 30N	5 25w
Tetyukhe = Dalnergorsk	44 40N	135 50 E
Teuco, R.	25 35s	60 11w
Teulon	50 30N	97 20w
Teutoburger Wald	52 5N	8 15 E
Tevere, R.	41 44N	12 14 E
Teviot, R.	55 36N	2 26w
Tewantin	26 27s	153 3 E
Tewkesbury	51 59N	2 8w
Texarkana, Ark.	33 25N	94 0w
Texarkana, Tex.	33 25N	94 0w
Texas	28 49s	151 15 E
Texas □	31 30N	98 30w
Texas City	27 20N	95 20w
Texel, I.	53 5N	4 50 E
Teziutlán	19 50N	97 30w
Tezpur	26 40N	92 45 E
Thabana Ntlenyana	29 30s	29 9 E
Thabazimbi	24 40s	26 4 E
Thailand ■	16 0N	101 0 E
Thakhek	17 25	104 45 E
Thal	33 28N	70 33 E
Thal Desert	31 0N	71 30 E
Thallon	28 30s	148 57 E
Thame, R.	51 52N	0 47w
Thames	37 7s	175 34 E
Thames, R., Canada	42 19N	82 28w
Thames, R., U.K.	51 28N	0 43 E
Than Hoa	19 48N	105 46 E
Thana	19 12N	72 59 E
Thanet, I.	51 21N	1 20 E
Thangoo P.O.	18 10s	122 22 E
Thangool	24 29s	150 35 E
Thanjavur	10 48N	79 12 E
Thar Des.= Gt. Indian Des.	28 25N	72 0 E
Thargomindah	27 58s	143 46 E
Tharrawaddy	17 30N	96 0 E
Thásös, I.	40 40N	24 40 E
Thatcher	32 54N	109 46w
Thaton	17 0N	97 39 E
Thaungdut	24 30N	94 30 E
Thayetmyo	19 19N	95 11 E
Thazi	21 0N	96 5 E
The Bight	24 19N	75 24w
The Dalles	45 40N	121 11w
The Flatts	32 19N	64 45w
The Great Wall of China	37 30N	109 0 E
The Grenadines	12 40N	61 15w
The Hague = s'Gravenhage	52 7N	7 14 E
The Johnston Lakes	32 25s	120 30 E
The Pas	53 45N	101 15w
Theebine	26 0s	152 30 E
Theodore	24 55s	150 3 E
Thermaikós Kól.	40 15N	22 45 E
Thermopolis	43 14N	108 10 E
Thermopílai Giona, Mt.	38 48N	22 45 E
Thessalía □	39 30N	22 0 E
Thessalon	46 20N	83 30w
Thessaloníki	40 38N	23 0 E
Thetford	52 25N	0 44 E
Thessaly□= Thessalía □	39 30N	22 0 E
Thetford Mines	46 8N	71 18w
Thevenard	32 9s	133 38 E
Thibodaux	29 48N	90 49w
Thicket Portage	55 25N	97 45w
Thief River Falls	48 15N	96 10w
Thiès	14 50N	16 51w
Thika	1 1s	37 5 E
Thionville	49 20N	6 10 E
Thíra, I.	36 23N	25 27 E
Thirsk	54 15N	1 20w
Thisted	56 57N	8 42 E
Thíval	38 19N	23 19 E
Thomasville, Ala.	31 55N	87 42w
Thomasville, Fla.	30 50N	84 0w
Thomasville, N.C.	35 5N	80 4w
Thompson	55 50N	97 34w
Thonon	46 22N	6 29 E
Thori	27 20N	84 40 E
Thornaby on Tees	54 36N	1 18w
Thráki □	41 9N	25 30 E
Three Forks	45 5N	111 40w
Three Hills	51 43N	113 15w
Three Points C.	4 42N	2 6w
Thule	76 0N	68 0w
Thun	46 45N	7 38 E
Thunder Bay	48 25N	89 10 E
Thunder River	52 13N	119 20w
Thung Song	8 10N	99 40 E
Thüringer Wald	50 35N	11 0 E
Thuringian Forest= Thüringer Wald	50 35N	11 0 E
Thurles	52 40N	7 53w
Thursday I.	10 59s	142 12 E
Thurso, Canada	45 36N	75 15w
Thurso, U.K.	58 34N	3 31w
Thurston I.	72 0s	100 0w
Tianjin=Tientsin	39 10N	117 0 E
Tiaret	35 28N	1 21 E
Tiassalé	5 58N	4 57w
Tibati	6 22N	12 30 E
Tiber, R.= Tevere, R.	41 44N	12 14 E
Tiberias	32 47N	35 32 E
Tibesti	21 0N	17 30 E
Tibet □	32 30N	86 0 E
Tibet, Plateau of	35 0N	90 0 E
Tibooburra	29 26s	142 1 E
Tiburón, I.	29 0N	112 30w
Ticino, R.	45 9N	9 14 E
Ticul	20 20N	89 50w
Tidjikdja	18 4N	11 35w
Tiehling	42 25N	123 51 E
Tiel	51 54N	5 5 E
Tielt	51 0N	3 20 E
Tien Shan, Mts.	42 0N	80 0 E
Tienshui	34 30N	105 34 E
Tienching= Tientsin	39 10N	117 0 E
Tienen	50 48N	4 57 E
Tienshui	34 30N	105 34 E
Tientsin	39 10N	117 0 E
Tientung	23 47N	107 2 E
Tierra de Campos	42 5N	4 45w
Tiétar, R.	39 55N	5 50w
Tierra del Fuego, I.	54 0s	69 0w
Tiffin	41 8N	83 10w
Tifrah	31 19N	34 42 E
Tifton	31 28N	83 32w

* Renamed Bailundo
† Renamed Luau

Tifu .... 3 39s 126 18 E
Tignish 46 58N 63 57w
Tigris, R. =
 Dijlah, Nahr .... 31 0N 47 25 E
Tigu .... 29 48N 91 38 E
Tigyaing .... 23 45N 96 10 E
Tijuana 32 30N 117 10w
Tikal 17 2N 89 35w
Tikhoretsk .... 45 56N 40 5 E
Tiko .... 4 4N 9 20 E
Tiksi .... 71 50N 129 0 E
Tilburg .... 51 31N 5 6 E
Tilbury, Canada ... 42 17N 84 23 E
Tilbury, U.K. ..... 51 27N 0 24 E
Tilichiki .... 61 0N 166 5 E
Tillabéri .... 14 10N 1 30 E
Tillsonburg 42 53N 80 55w
Tílos, I. .... 36 27N 27 27 E
Tilpa .... 30 58s 144 30 E
Timanskiy Kryazh . 65 58N 50 5 E
Timaru .... 44 23s 171 14 E
Timbuktu =
 Tombouctou 16 50N 3 0w
Timişoara .... 45 43 1 21 15 E
Timmins 48 28N 81 25w
Timok, R. .... 44 13N 22 40 E
Timon 5 8s 42 52w
Timor, I. .... 9 0s 125 0 E
Timor, Sea ...... 10 0s 127 0 E
Timris, C. 19 15N 16 30w
Timur□, Java .... 7 20s 112 0 E
Timur□,
 Kalimantan ..... 1 15N 117 0 E
Tindouf 27 50N 8 4w
Tinkurrin .... 33 0s 117 38 E
Tinnoset .... 59 45N 9 3 E
Tinogasta 28 0s 67 40w
Tínos, I. .... 37 33N 25 8 E
Tinpak .... 21 40N 111 15 E
Tintinara .... 35 48s 140 2 E
Tioman, Pulau ... 2 50N 104 10 E
Tipongpani ...... 27 20N 95 55 E
Tipperary 52 28N 8 10w
Tipperary □ 52 37N 7 55w
Tipton 52 32N 2 4w
Tîra .... 32 14N 34 56 E
Tîrân .... 32 45N 51 0 E
Tirana .... 41 18N 19 49 E
Tiraspol .... 46 55N 29 35 E
Tirat Karmel .... 32 46N 34 58 E

Tirat Tsevi .... 32 26N 35 51 E
Tirat Yehuda ..... 32 1N 34 56 E
Tire .... 38 5N 27 50 E
Tirebolu .... 40 58N 38 45 E
Tiree, I. 56 31N 6 49w
Tîrgovişte .... 44 55N 25 27 E
Tîrgu-Jiu .... 45 5N 23 19 E
Tîrgu-Mureş ...... 46 31N 24 38 E
Tirich Mir, Mt. .. 36 15N 71 35 E
Tirol, Reg. ...... 46 50N 11 40 E
Tirol □ .... 47 3N 10 43 E
Tiruchchirappalli .. 10 45N 78 45 E
Tirunelveli ...... 8 45N 77 45 E
Tirupati .... 13 45N 79 30 E
Tisa, R. .... 45 15N 20 17 E
Tisdale 52 50N 104 0w
Tit-Ary .... 71 58N 127 1 E
Titicaca, L. 15 30s 69 30w
Titiwa .... 12 14N 12 53 E
Titlagarh .... 20 15N 83 5 E
Titograd .... 42 30N 19 19 E
Titov Veles ...... 41 46N 21 47 E
Titovo Uzice ..... 43 55N 19 50 E
Titule .... 3 15N 25 31 E
Titusville 41 35N 79 39w
Tiverton 50 54N 3 30w
Tívoli .... 41 58N 12 45 E
Tiwi .... 22 45N 59 12 E
Tizi-Ouzou .... 36 48N 4 2 E
Tizimín 21 0N 88 1w
Tlaxcala □ 19 30N 98 20w
Tlaxiaco 17 10N 97 40w
Tlemcen 34 52N 1 15w
Toay 36 50s 64 30w
Toba Kakar Ra.... 31 30N 69 0 E
Tobago, I. 11 10N 60 30w
Tobelo .... 1 25N 127 56 E
Tobermorey,
 Australia .... 22 12s 138 0 E
Tobermory, Canada 45 12N 81 40w
Tobermory, U.K. ... 56 37N 6 4w
Tobolsk .... 58 0N 68 10 E
Tobruk = Tubruq . 32 7N 23 55 E
Tocantinopolis ... 6 20s 47 25w
Tocantins, R. 1 45s 49 10w
Toccoa 34 35N 83 19w
Tochigi .... 36 25N 139 45 E
Tochigi □ .... 36 45N 139 45 E
Tocopilla 22 5s 70 10w
Tocumwal .... 35 45s 145 31 E

Todos os Santos,
 B. de 12 45s 38 40w
Togliatti .... 53 37N 49 18 E
Togo ■ .... 6 15N 1 35 E
Tohoku □ .... 38 40N 142 0 E
Tokaj .... 48 8N 21 27 E
Tōkamachi .... 37 8N 138 43 E
Tokar .... 18 27N 37 43 E
Tokara Kaikyō, Str. 30 0N 130 0 E
Tokara-Shima, I. .. 29 0N 129 0 E
Tokarahi .... 44 56s 170 39 E
Tokat .... 40 22N 36 35 E
Tokelau Is. 9 0s 172 0w
Tokmak .... 47 16N 35 42 E
Tokombere .... 11 18N 3 30 E
Toku-no-Shima, I. .. 27 50N 129 2 E
Tokushima .... 34 4N 134 45 E
Tokushima □ ..... 35 50N 134 50 E
Tokuyama .... 34 0N 131 50 E
Tōkyō .... 35 45N 139 45 E
Tōkyō □ .... 35 40N 139 30 E
Tolaga .... 38 21s 178 20 E
Tolbukhin .... 43 37N 27 49 E
Toledo, Sp. 39 50N 4 2w
Toledo, U.S.A. ... 41 37N 83 33w
Toledo, Mts. de .. 39 30N 4 30w
Tolima, Mt. 4 40N 75 19w
Tolitoli .... 1 5N 120 50 E
Tolleson 33 29N 112 10w
Tolo, Teluk, G. .. 2 0s 122 10 E
Tolosa 43 8N 2 5w
Toluca 19 20N 99 50w
Tolun .... 42 22N 116 30 E
Tom Price .... 22 50s 117 40 E
Tomar 39 36N 8 25w
Tombigbee, R. ... 32 0N 88 6 E
Tombouctou 16 50N 3 0w
Tombstone 31 40N 110 4w
Tomini, Teluk, G. .. 0 10s 122 0 E
Tomintoul 57 15N 3 22w
Tommot .... 58 50N 126 30 E
Tomsk .... 56 30N 85 12 E
Tonalá 16 8N 93 41w
Tonantins 2 45s 67 45w
Tonawanda 43 0N 78 54w
Tonbridge .... 51 12N 0 18 E
Tonga ■ 20 0s 173 0w
Tongaat .... 29 33s 31 9 E
Tongatapu, I. ... 20 0s 174 0w
Tongeren .... 50 47N 5 28 E

Tonghing .... 21 30N 108 0 E
Tongking, G. of ... 20 0N 108 0 E
Tongoy 30 25s 71 40w
Tongue 58 29N 4 25w
Tonj .... 7 20N 28 44 E
Tonk .... 26 6N 75 54 E
Tonlé Sap, L. ... 13 0N 104 0 E
Tonopah 38 4N 117 12w
Tønsberg .... 59 19N 11 3 E
Tooele 40 30N 112 20w
Toompine .... 27 15s 144 19 E
Toowoomba .... 27 32s 151 56 E
Top, Oz. .... 65 35N 32 0 E
Topeka .... 39 3N 95 40 E
Topki .... 55 25N 85 20 E
Topley 54 32s 126 5w
Toppenish 46 27N 120 16w
Torata 17 3s 70 1w
Torbat-e
 Heydariyeh 35 15N 59 12w
Torbay, Canada ... 47 40N 52 42w
Torbay, U.K. 50 26N 3 31w
Tordesillas 41 30N 5 0w
Torgau .... 51 32N 13 0 E
Torhout .... 51 5N 3 7 E
Torino .... 45 4N 7 40 E
Torne, R. .... 65 48N 24 8 E
Torneträsk, L. ... 68 20N 19 10 E
Tornio .... 65 57N 24 12 E
Tornquist 38 0s 62 15w
Toro, Cerro del .. 29 0s 69 50w
Toronaíos Kól. ... 40 5N 23 30 E
Toronto, Canada ... 43 39N 79 20w
Toronto, U.S.A. ... 40 27N 80 36w
Tororo .... 0 45N 34 12 E
Torquay 50 27N 3 31w
Torre Annunziata . 40 45N 14 26 E
Tôrre de Moncorvo 41 12N 7 8w
Torrelavega 43 20N 4 5w
Torremolinos 36 38N 4 30w
Torrens, L. ..... 31 0s 137 45 E
Torreon 25 33N 103 25w
Torres Str. ..... 10 0s 142 0 E
Torres Veldras ... 39 5N 9 15w
Torrevieja 37 59N 0 42w
Torridge, R. 51 3N 4 11w
Torridon 57 35N 5 50w
Torrington 41 50N 73 9w
Tortola, I. 18 19N 65 0w

Tortosa .... 40 49N 0 31 E
Tortosa, C. ..... 40 41N 0 52 E
Toruń .... 53 3N 18 39 E
Tosa-Wan, G. .... 33 15N 133 30 E
Toscana □ .... 43 30N 11 5 E
Tostado 29 15s 61 50w
Toteng .... 20 22s 22 58 E
Totma .... 60 0N 42 40 E
Totnes 50 26N 3 41w
Totness 5 53N 56 19w
Totonicapán 14 50N 91 20w
Tottori .... 35 30N 134 15 E
Tottori □ .... 35 30N 134 12 E
Toubkal,
 Djebel, Mt. 31 0N 8 0w
Touggourt .... 33 10N 6 0 E
Tougué 11 25N 11 50w
Toul .... 48 40N 5 53 E
Toulon .... 43 10N 5 55 E
Toulouse .... 43 37N 1 28 E
Toummo .... 22 45N 14 8 E
Toungoa .... 19 0N 96 30 E
Touraine, Reg. ... 47 20N 0 30 E
Tourane = Da Nang 16 10N 108 7 E
Tourcoing .... 50 42N 3 10 E
Tournai .... 50 35N 3 25 E
Tournon .... 45 4s 4 50 E
Tours .... 47 22N 0 40 E
Touwsrivier ..... 33 20s 20 0 E
Towang .... 27 33N 91 56 E
Townsend, Mt. ... 36 25s 148 16 E
Townsville ...... 19 15s 146 45 E
Towson 39 26N 76 34w
Towyn 52 37N 4 8w
Toyama .... 36 40N 137 15 E
Toyama □ .... 36 45N 137 30 E
Toyama-Wan, G. .. 37 0N 137 30 E
Toyohashi .... 34 45N 137 25 E
Toyokawa .... 34 48N 137 27 E
Toyonaka .... 34 50N 135 35 E
Toyooka .... 35 35N 135 5 E
Toyota .... 35 5N 137 9 E
Tozeur .... 33 54N 8 4 E
Trabzon .... 41 0N 39 45 E
Tracy 44 12N 95 3w
Tradom .... 30 0N 83 59 E
Trafalgar .... 38 14s 146 12 E
Trafalgar, C. ... 36 10N 6 2w
Traiguón 38 12s 72 40w
Trail 49 5N 117 40w

Tralee 52 16N   9 42w
Tramore 52 10N   7 10w
Tranås .... 58 3N 14 59 E
Trancas 26 11s 65 20w
Trang ....   7 33N 99 38 E
Trangan, I. ......   6 40s 134 20 E
Trani .... 41 17N 16 24 E
Tranoroa .... 24 42s 45 4 E
Transcona 49 50N 97 0w
Transilvania, Reg.=
   Transylvania,
   Reg. .... 46 20N 25 0 E
Transkei □ .... 32 15s 28 15 E
Transvaal □ .... 25 0s 29 0 E
Transylvania, Reg. 46 20N 25 0 E
Transylvanian
   Alps, Mts. ..... 45 30N 25 0 E
Trápani .... 38 1N 12 30 E
Traralgon .... 38 6s 146 31 E
Tras os Montes Alto
   Douro, Reg. 41 30N   7 5w
Trasimeno, L. ..... 43 30N 12 5 E
Traverse City 44 45N 85 39w
Travnik .... 44 17N 17 39 E
Trayning .... 31 8s 117 42 E
Třebíč .... 49 13N 15 53 E
Trebinje .... 42 44N 18 22 E
Třeboň .... 48 59N 14 48 E
Tredegar 51 47N   3 16w
Tregaron 52 14N   3 56w
Treinta y Tres 33 10s 54 50w
Trekveld .... 30 35s 19 45 E
Trelew 43 10s 65 20w
Trelleborg .... 55 20N 13 5 E
Tremonton 41 45N 112 10w
Trenggalek .... 8 5s 111 44 E
Trenque Lauquen ... 36 0s 62 45w
Trent, R. 53 40N   0 40w
Trentino-Alto
   Adige □ .... 46 5N 11 0 E
Trento .... 46 5N 11 8 E
Trenton, Canada ... 44 10N 77 40w
Trenton, U.S.A. ... 40 15N 74 41w
Trepassey 46 43N 53 25w
Tres Arroyos 38 20s 60 20w
Três Corações 21 30s 45 30s
Três Lagoas 20 50s 51 50w
Tres Montes, C. ... 47 0s 75 35w
Tres Puentes 27 50s 70 15w
Tres Puntas, C. ... 47 0s 66 0w

Três Rios 22 20s 43 30w
Treungen .... 58 55N   8 27 E
Treviso .... 45 40N 12 15 E
Triabunna .... 42 28s 148 0 E
Trichinopoly=
   Tiruchchirappalli 10 45N 78 45 E
Trichur .... 10 20N 76 18 E
Trier .... 49 45N   6 37 E
Trieste .... 45 39N 13 45 E
Triglav, Mt. ...... 46 30N 13 45 E
Tríkkala .... 39 34N 21 47 E
Trikora,
   Puncak, Mt. ... 4 11s 138 0 E
Trim 53 34N   6 48w
Trincomalee ...... 8 38N 81 15 E
Trindade, I. 20 20s 29 50w
Trinidad, Bolivia . 14 54s 64 50w
Trinidad, Cuba 21 40N 80 0w
Trinidad, U.S.A. .. 37 15N 104 30w
Trinidad, Uruguay . 33 30s 56 50w
Trinidad I., Arg. . 39 10s 62 0w
Trinidad I.,
   Trinidad &
   Tobago 10 30N 61 20w
Trinidad &
   Tobago ■ 10 30N 61 20w
Trinity, R. 29 47N 94 42w
Trinity Is. 56 33N 154 25w
Tripoli, Lebanon=
   Tarābulus ...... 34 34N 35 52 E
Tripoli, Libya=
   Tarābulus ...... 32 49N 13 7 E
Trípolis .... 37 31N 22 25 E
Tripura □ .... 24 0N 92 0 E
Tristan de Cunha, I. 37 6s 12 20w
Trivandrum .... 8 31N 77 0 E
Trnava .... 48 23N 17 35 E
Trois Pistoles 48 5N 69 10w
Trois Rivières 46 25N 72 40w
Troitsk .... 54 10N 61 35 E
Troitsko Pechorsk . 62 40N 56 10 E
Trollhättan .... 58 17N 12 20 E
Trompsburg .... 30 2s 25 5 E
Troms □ .... 69 19N 19 0 E
Tromsø .... 69 40N 19 0 E
Tronador, Mt. 41 53s 71 0w
Trondheim .... 63 25N 10 25 E
Trondheims, Fd. ... 63 40N 10 45 E
Tróodos, Mt. ...... 34 58N 32 55 E
Troon 55 33N   4 40w

Trossachs, Reg. ... 56 14N   4 24w
Trotternish, Reg. . 57 32N   6 15w
Trouville .... 49 21N   0 54 E
Trowbridge 51 18N   2 12w
Troy, Ala. 31 50N 85 58w
Troy, N.Y. 42 45N 73 39w
Troy, Ohio 40 0N 84 10w
Troyes .... 48 19N   4 3 E
Truckee 39 29N 120 12w
Trujillo, Honduras. 16 0N 86 0w
Trujillo, Peru 8 0s 79 0w
Trujillo, Sp. 39 28N   5 55w
Trujillo, Ven. 9 22N 70 26w
Truk, I. .... 7 25N 151 46 E
Trung-Phan, Reg. . 16 0N 108 0 E
Truro, Canada 45 21N 63 14w
Truro, U.K. 50 17N   5 2w
Truslove .... 33 20s 121 45 E
Truth or
   Consequences .. 33 9N 107 16w
Tsaidam, Reg. ..... 37 0N 95 0 E
Tsanghsien .... 38 24N 116 57 E
Tsangpo, R. .... 29 40N 89 0 E
Tsaochwang .... 35 11N 115 28 E
Tsaratanana .... 16 47s 47 39 E
Tsaratanana, Mt. de 14 0s 49 0 E
Tsaring Nor, L. ... 35 0N 97 0 E
Tsau .... 20 12s 22 22 E
Tsavo .... 3 0s 38 27 E
Tselinograd .... 51 10N 71 30 E
Tsetserleg .... 47 46N 101 32 E
Tsévié .... 6 25N   1 13 E
Tshabong .... 26 2s 22 29 E
Tshane .... 24 5s 21 54 E
Tshwane .... 22 24s 22 1 E
Tsiaotso .... 35 11N 113 37 E
Tsihombé .... 25 18s 45 29 E
Tsimlyanskoye,
   Vdkhr. .... 47 45N 42 0 E
Tsin Ling
   Shan, Mts. ..... 34 0N 107 30 E
Tsinan .... 34 50N 105 40 E
Tsincheng .... 35 30N 113 0 E
Tsinghai .... 38 56N 116 52 E
Tsinghai □ .... 36 0N 98 0 E
Tsingkiang, Kiangsi 27 50N 114 38 E
Tsingkiang, Kiangsu 33 30N 119 2 E
Tsingning .... 35 25N 105 50 E
Tsingshih .... 29 43N 112 13 E
Tsingtao .... 36 0N 120 25 E

Tsining,
   Inner Mongolia . 40 59N 112 59 E
Tsining, Shantung . 35 30N 116 35 E
Tsinyang .... 35 2N 112 59 E
Tsiroanomandidy .. 18 46s 46 2 E
Tsitsihar .... 47 20N 124 0 E
Tsivory .... 24 4s 46 5 E
Tskhinvali .... 42 14N 44 1 E
Tsna, R. .... 54 32N 42 5 E
Tsu .... 34 45N 136 25 E
Tsuchiura .... 36 12N 140 15 E
Tsugaru-Kaikyo,
   Str. .... 41 30N 140 30 E
Tsuiluan .... 47 58N 28 27 E
Tsumeb .... 19 9s 17 44 E
Tsumgfa .... 23 35N 113 35 E
Tsungtso .... 22 20N 107 25 E
Tsunyi .... 27 40N 107 0 E
Tsuruga .... 35 35N 136 0 E
Tsushima-Kaikyō,
   Str. .... 34 20N 130 0 E
Tsuyama .... 35 0N 134 0 E
Tswana □ .... 24 0s 27 50 E
Tual .... 5 30s 132 50 E
Tuam 53 30N   8 50w
Tuamotu Arch. 17 0s 144 0w
Tuapse .... 44 5N 39 10 E
Tuatapere .... 48 7s 167 43 E
Tubac 31 45N 111 2w
Tuban .... 6 57s 112 4 E
Tubarão 28 30s 49 0w
Tubas .... 32 20N 35 22 E
Tubayq, Jabal at .. 29 40N 37 30 E
Tubo, R. .... 10 25N   7 10 E
Tubruq .... 32 7N 23 55 E
Tubuai Is. 23 20s 151 0w
Tucacas 10 48N 68 19w
Tuckanarra .... 27 8s 118 1 E
Tucker's Town 32 19N 64 43w
Tucson 32 14N 110 59w
Tucumcari 35 12N 103 45w
Tucupita 9 4N 62 0w
Tucurui 3 45s 49 48w
Tudela 42 4N   1 39w
Tugela, R. .... 29 14s 31 30 E
Tuguegarao .... 17 35N 121 42 E
Tugur .... 53 50N 136 45 E
Tuhshan .... 25 40N 107 30 E
Tuktoyaktuk 69 15N 133 0w

Tukuyu .... 9 17s 33 35 E
Tula, Nigeria ..... 9 51N 11 27 E
Tula, U.S.S.R. .... 54 13N 37 32 E
Tulan .... 37 24N 98 1 E
Tulare 36 15N 119 26w
Tularosa 33 4N 106 1w
Tulbagh .... 33 16s 19 6 E
Tulcán 0 48N 77 43w
Tulcea .... 45 13N 28 46 E
Tuléar .... 23 21s 43 40 E
Tuléar □ .... 21 0s 45 0 E
Tuli .... 1 24s 122 26 E
Tūlkarm .... 32 19N 35 10 E
Tullahoma 35 23N 86 12w
Tullamore 53 17N   7 30w
Tulle .... 45 16N   1 47 E
Tullow 52 48N   6 45w
Tully .... 17 30s 141 0 E
Tulymaythah .... 32 40N 20 55 E
Tulsa 36 10N 96 0w
Tulua 4 6N 76 11w
Tulun .... 54 40N 100 10 E
Tulungagung .... 8 5s 111 54 E
Tuma, R. 13 6N 84 35w
Tumaco 1 50N 78 45w
Tumatumari 5 20N 58 55w
Tumba, L. .... 0 50s 18 0 E
Tumbes 3 30s 80 20w
Tumby Bay .... 34 21s 136 8 E
Tumen .... 42 46N 129 59 E
Tumeremo 7 18N 61 30w
Tumkur 13 18N 77 12w
Tummel, L. 56 43N   3 55w
Tump .... 26 7N 62 16 E
Tumpat .... 6 11N 102 10 E
Tumucumaque
   South 2 0N 55 0w
Tumut .... 35 16s 148 13 E
Tunbridge Wells .. 51 7N   0 16 E
Tunduma .... 9 20s 32 48 E
Tunduru .... 11 0s 37 25 E
Tundzha, R. .... 41 40N 26 34 E
Tungabhadra, R. .. 15 57N 78 15 E
Tungcheng .... 31 10N 117 3 E
Tungchow .... 39 58N 116 50 E
Tungchuan .... 35 4N 109 2 E
Tungfanghsien ..... 18 50N 108 33 E
Tunghwa .... 41 46N 126 0 E
Tungkiang .... 47 40N 132 30 E
Tungkwanshan ..... 31 0N 117 45 E

* Renamed Toliara

Tungliao .... 43 42N 122 11 E
Tunglu .... 29 50N 119 35 E
Tungping .... 35 50N 116 20 E
Tungshan .... 29 36N 144 28 E
Tungshan, I. .... 23 40N 117 31 E
Tungsten 61 52N 128 1W
Tungtai .... 32 55N 120 15 E
Tungting Hu, L. .. 28 30N 112 30 E
Tungtze .... 27 59N 106 56 E
Tunhwa .... 43 27N 128 16 E
Tunhwang .... 40 5N 94 46 E
Tunis .... 36 50N 10 11 E
Tunisia ■ .... 33 30N   9 0 E
Tunja .... 5 40N 73 25 E
Tuoy-khaya 62 30N 111 0W
Tupelo 34 15N 88 42W
Tupik .... 54 26N 119 57 E
Tupiza 21 30s 65 40W
Tupper Lake 44 18N 74 30W
Tupungato, Mt. .. 33 15s 69 50W
Túquerres 1 5N 77 37W
Tur .... 31 47N 35 14 E
Tura, India ..... 25 30N 90 16 E
Tura, Tanz. ..... 5 15s 33 48 E
Turayf .... 31 45N 38 30 E
Turbaco 10 20N 75 25W
Turbo .... 8 6N 76 43 E
Turda .... 46 35N 23 48 E
Turek .... 52 3N 18 30 E
Turfan .... 43 6N 89 24 E
Turfan Depression . 43 0N 88 0 E
Turgovishte ..... 43 17N 26 38 E
Turgutlu .... 38 30N 27 48 E
Turhal .... 40 24N 36 19 E
Turia, R. 39 27N   0 19W
Turiaçu 1 40s 45 28W
Turin=Torino .... 45 3N   7 40 E
Turkana, L. ..... 4 10N 36 10 E
Turkestan .... 43 10N 68 10 E
Turkey ■ .... 39 0N 36 0 E
Turkey Creek P.O. 17 2s 128 12 E
Turkmen S.S.R. .. 39 0N 59 0 E
Turks Is. 21 20N 71 20W
Turku .... 60 27N 22 14 E
Turlock 37 30N 122 55W
Turneffe Is. 17 20N 87 50W
Turnhout 51 19N   4 57W
Tûrnovo .... 43 5N 25 41 E
Turnu Măgurele .. 43 46N 24 56 E
Turnu-Severin ... 44 39N 22 41 E

Turriff 57 32N   2 58W
Turtle 48 52N 92 40W
Turtleford 53 30N 108 50W
Turūbah .... 28 20N 43 15 E
Turun ja Pori □ .. 61 0N 22 30 E
Tuscaloosa 33 13N 87 31W
Tuskegee 32 26N 85 42W
Tutoja 2 45s 42 20W
Tuttlingen ...... 47 59N   8 50 E
Tutuala .... 8 25s 127 15 E
Tutuila, I. 14 19s 170 50W
Turukhansk ...... 65 55N 88 5 E
Tava, A.S.S.R. .. 52 0N 95 0 E
Tuvalu ■ .... 8 0s 176 0 E
Tuwaiq, Jabal ... 23 0N 46 0 E
Tuxpan 20 50N 97 30W
Tuxtla Gutiérrez . 16 50N 93 10W
Tuy 42 3N   8 39W
Tuyun .... 26 5N 107 20 E
Tuz Gölü .... 38 45N 33 30 E
Tuz Khurmātu .... 34 50N 44 45 E
Tweed, R. 55 46N   2 0W
Tweedsmuir Prov.
  Park .... 52 55N 126 5 E
Tweeling .... 27 38s 28 30 E
Twin Falls 42 30N 114 30W
Two Rivers 44 10N 87 31W
Tyler 32 20N 95 15W
Tyndinskiy ...... 55 10N 124 43 E
Tyne, R. 55 1N   1 26W
Tyne & Wear □ ... 54 55N   1 35W
Tynemouth 55 1N   1 27W
Tyre =Sur .... 33 19N 35 16 E
Tyrendarra ...... 38 12s 141 50 E
Tyrifjorden ..... 60 2N 10 3 E
Tyrol, Reg.=
  Tirol, Reg. ... 46 50N 11 40 E
Tyrrhenian Sea ... 40 0N 12 30 E
Tyumen .... 57 0N 65 18 E
Tywi, R. 51 46N   4 22W
Tzaneen .... 23 47s 30 9 E
Tzeki .... 29 40N 117 5 E
Tzekung .... 29 25N 104 30 E
Tzekwei .... 31 0N 110 46 E
Tzepo .... 36 28N 117 58 E
Tzeyang .... 32 47N 108 58 E

U

Uarsciek .... 2 28N 45 55 E
Uaupés 0 8s 67 5W
Ubá 21 0s 43 0W
Ubaitaba 14 18s 39 20W
Ube .... 34 6N 131 20 E
Ubeda 38 3N   3 23W
Uberaba 19 50s 48 0W
Uberlândia 19 0s 48 20W
Ubiaja .... 6 40N   6 20 E
Ubon Ratchathani . 15 15N 104 50 E
Ubundu .... 0 22s 25 30 E
Ucayali, R. 4 30s 73 30W
Uchi Lake 51 10N 92 40W
Uchiura-Wan, G. .. 42 25N 140 40 E
Ucluelet 48 57N 125 32W
Udaipur .... 24 36N 73 44 E
Uddevalla .... 58 21N 11 55 E
Uddjaur, L. ..... 65 55N 17 50 E
Udi .... 6 23N   7 21 E
Údine .... 46 5N 13 10 E
Udipi .... 13 25N 74 42 E
Udmurt A.S.S.R. □ 57 30N 52 30 E
Udon Thani ...... 17 29N 102 46 E
Udzungwa Ra. .... 8 30s 35 30 E
Ueda .... 36 30N 138 10 E
Uelen 66 10N 170 0W
Uelzen .... 53 0N 10 33 E
Uere, R. .... 3 42N 25 24 E
Ufa .... 54 45N 55 55 E
Ufa, R. .... 54 45N 55 55 E
Uganda ■ .... 2 0N 32 0 E
Ugashik Lakes ... 57 0N 157 0W
Ugep .... 5 50N   8 1 E
Uglegorsk .... 49 10N 142 5 E
Uitenhage .... 33 40s 25 28 E
Ujiji=Kigoma-Ujiji 4 55s 29 40 E
Ujjain .... 23 9N 75 43 E
Ujpest .... 47 33N 19 6 E
Ujung Pandang ... 5 10s 119 0 E
Uka .... 57 50N 162 0 E
Ukerewe I. ...... 2 0s 33 0 E
Ukhrul .... 25 10N 94 25 E
Ukhta .... 63 55N 54 0 E
Ukiah 39 10N 123 9W
Ukrainian S.S.R. □ 48 0N 35 0 E
Ulaanbaatar ..... 48 0N 107 0 E
Ulan Bator

= Ulaanbaatar .. 48 0N 107 0 E
Ulan Ude .... 52 0N 107 30 E
Ulanhot .... 46 5N 122 1 E
Ulhasnagar ...... 19 15N 73 10 E
Ulladulla .... 35 21s 150 29 E
Ullapool 57 54N   5 10W
Ullswater, L. ... 54 35N   2 52W
Ulm .... 48 23N 10 0 E
Ulricehamn ...... 57 46N 13 26 E
Ulrichsville 40 27N 81 30W
Ulster □ 54 45N   6 30W
Uluguru Mts. .... 7 15s 37 30 E
Ulverston 54 13N   3 7W
Ulverstone ...... 41 11s 146 11 E
Ulyanovsk .... 54 25N 48 25 E
Uman .... 48 40N 30 12 E
Umaria .... 23 31N 80 40 E
Umbria □ .... 42 53N 12 30 E
Umeå .... 63 45N 20 20 E
Umfuli, R. ...... 17 50s 29 40 E
Umkomaas .... 30 13s 30 48 E
Umm al Qaiwain .. 25 30N 55 35 E
Umm el Fahm ..... 32 31N 35 9 E
Umm Keddada ..... 13 36N 26 42 E
Umm Lajj .... 25 0N 37 23 E
Umnak I. 53 0N 168 0W
Umniati, R. ..... 17 30s 29 23 E
* Umtali .... 18 58s 32 38 E
Umtata .... 31 36s 28 49 E
Umuahia .... 5 33N   7 29 E
† Umvuma .... 19 16s 30 30 E
Umzimvubu .... 31 38s 29 33 E
Umzinto .... 30 15s 30 45 E
Unac, R. .... 44 30N 16 9 E
Unalakleet 63 53N 160 50W
Unalaska I. 54 0N 164 30W
Uncompahgre Pk. . 38 5N 107 32W
Underbool .... 35 10s 141 51 E
Ungarie .... 33 38s 146 56 E
Ungava B. 59 30N 67 0W
Ungava Pen. 60 0N 75 0W
União 4 50s 37 50W
União da Vitoria . 26 5s 51 0W
Unimak I. 54 30N 164 30W
Union 34 49N 81 39W
Union City, Pa. .. 41 53N 79 50W
Union Gap 46 38N 120 29W
Union of Soviet

Socialist
  Republics ■ .... 60 0N 60 0 E
Uniondale .... 33 39s 23 7 E
Uniontown 39 54N 79 45W
United Arab
  Emirates ■ .... 24 0N 54 30 E
United Kingdom ■ 55 0N   3 0W
United States
  of America ■ .. 37 0N 96 0W
Unity 52 30N 109 5W
Unst, I. 60 50N   0 55W
Ünye .... 41 5N 37 15 E
Uozu .... 36 48N 137 24 E
Upata 8 1N 62 24W
Upington .... 28 25s 21 15 E
Upolu, I. 13 58s 172 0W
Upper □ 10 40N   2 0W
Upper Hutt ...... 41 8s 175 5 E
Upper
  Musquodoboit .. 45 10N 62 58W
Upper Volta ■ ... 12 0N   0 30W
Uppsala .... 59 53N 17 42 E
Uppsala □ .... 60 0N 17 30 E
Ur .... 30 55N 46 25 E
Uracará 2 20s 57 50W
Ural, Mt. .... 33 21s 146 12 E
Ural Mts. =
  Uralskie Gory . 60 0N 59 0 E
Ural, R. .... 47 0N 51 48 E
Uralla .... 30 37s 151 29 E
Uralsk .... 51 20N 51 20 E
Uralskie Gory ... 60 0N 59 0 E
Urandangi .... 21 32s 138 14 E
Uranium City 59 28N 108 40W
Urawa .... 35 50N 139 40 E
Uray .... 60 5N 65 15 E
Urbana, Ill. 40 7N 88 12W
Urbana, Ohio 40 9N 83 44W
Urbino .... 43 43N 12 38 E
Ure, R. 54 1N   1 12W
Urengoy .... 66 0N 78 0 E
Urfa .... 37 12N 38 50 E
Urfahr .... 48 19N 14 17 E
Urgench .... 41 40N 60 30 E
Uribia 11 43N 72 16W
Urim .... 31 18N 34 32 E
Urmia, L. =
  Daryâcheh-ye
  Reza'iyeh ..... 37 30N 45 30 E
Uruaca 14 35s 49 16W

* Renamed Mutare
† Renamed Mvuma

Uruapán	19 30N	102 0w
Uruçui	7 20s	44 28w
Uruguay ■	32 30s	55 30w
Uruguay, R.	34 0s	58 30w
Uruguaiana	29 50s	57 0w
Urumchi= Wulumuchi	43 40N	87 50 E
Urungu, R.	46 30N	88 50 E
Uruzgan □	33 30N	66 0 E
Usa, R.	65 57N	56 55 E
Uşak	38 43N	29 28 E
Usakos	22 0s	15 31 E
Usambara Mts.	4 50s	38 20 E
Usedom, I.	53 50N	13 55 E
Usfan	21 58N	39 27 E
Ush-Tobe	45 16N	78 0 E
Ushant, I.= Ouessant, I. d'	48 28N	5 6w
Ushuaia	54 50s	68 23w
Ushuman	52 47N	126 32 E
Usk, R.	51 36N	2 58w
Üsküdar	41 0N	29 5 E
Usman	52 5N	39 48 E
Usoke	5 8s	32 24 E
Usolye Sibirskoye	52 40N	103 40 E
Usoro	5 34N	6 13 E
Uspallata, P.	32 30s	69 28w
Uspenskiy	48 50N	72 55 E
Ussuriysk	43 40N	131 50 E
Ust-Ilga	55 5N	104 55 E
Ust-Ilimsk	58 3N	102 39 E
Ust Ishim	57 45N	71 10 E
Ust-Kamchatsk	56 10N	162 0 E
Ust Kamenogorsk	50 0N	82 20 E
Ust-Kut	56 50N	105 10 E
Ust Kuyga	70 1N	135 36 E
Ust Maya	60 30N	134 20 E
Ust Olenck	73 0N	120 10 E
Ust Port	70 0N	84 10 E
Ust Tsilma	65 25N	52 0 E
Ust-Tungir	55 25N	120 15 E
Ust Usa	66 0N	56 30 E
Ustchaun	68 47N	170 30 E
Ustí nad Labem	50 41N	14 3 E
Ustica, I.	38 42N	13 10 E
Ustye	55 30N	97 30 E
Usulután	13 25N	88 28w
Utah □	39 30N	111 30w
Utara □, Sulawesi	1 0N	120 3 E
Utara □, Sumatera	2 0N	99 0 E
Utete	7 59s	38 47 E
Uthmaniya	25 5N	49 6 E
Utica	43 5N	75 18w
Utrecht, Neth.	52 3N	5 8 E
Utrecht, Neth. □	52 6N	5 7 E
Utrecht, S. Africa	27 38s	30 20 E
Utrera	37 12N	5 48w
Utsunomiya	36 30N	139 50 E
Uttar Pradesh □	27 0N	80 0 E
Uttaradit	17 36N	100 5 E
Uttoxeter	52 53N	1 50w
Uudenmaa □	60 25N	23 0 E
Uuldza	49 8N	112 10 E
Uusikaupunki	60 47N	21 28 E
Uvalde	29 15N	99 48w
Uvat	59 5N	68 50 E
Uvinza	5 5s	30 24 E
Uvira	3 22s	29 3 E
Uvs Nuur, L.	50 20N	92 30 E
Uwajima	33 10N	132 35 E
Uxmal	20 22N	89 46w
Uyo	5 1N	7 53 E
Uyuni	20 35s	66 55w
Uzbek S.S.R.	40 5N	65 0 E

V

Vaal, R.	29 4s	23 38 E
Vaasa	63 10N	21 35 E
Vaasa □	63 6N	23 0 E
Vác	47 49N	19 10 E
Vadodara	22 20N	73 10 E
Vadsø	70 3N	29 50 E
Váh, R.	47 55N	18 0 E
Vaigach	70 10N	59 0 E
Val d'Or	48 7N	77 47w
Val Marie	49 15N	107 45w
Valahia, Reg.	44 35s	25 0 E
Valchete	40 40s	66 20w
Val-d'Oise □	49 5N	2 0 E
Val-de-Marne □	48 45N	2 28 E
Valdayskaya Vozvyshennost	57 0N	33 40 E
Valdepeñas, Ciudad Real	38 43N	3 25w
Valdés, Pen.	42 30s	63 45w
Valdez	61 14N	146 10w
Valdivia	39 50s	73 14w
Valdosta	30 50N	83 48w
Valença, Brazil	13 20s	39 5w
Valença da Piaui	6 20s	41 45w
Valence	44 57N	4 54 E
Valencia, Sp.	39 27N	0 23w
Valencia, Ven.	10 11N	68 0w
Valencia, G. de	39 30N	0 20 E
Valencia, Reg.	39 25N	0 45w
Valencia de Alcántara	39 25N	7 14w
Valenciennes	50 20N	3 34 E
Valentia, I.	51 54N	10 22w
Valentine	42 50N	100 35w
Valera	9 19N	70 37w
Valkenswaard	51 21N	5 29 E
Valladolid, Mexico	20 30N	88 20w
Valladolid, Sp.	41 38N	4 43w
Valle d'Aosta □	45 45N	7 22 E
Valle de la Pascua	9 13N	66 0w
Valle de Santiago	20 25N	101 15w
Vallecas	40 23N	3 41w
Vallejo	38 12N	122 15w
Vallenar	28 30s	70 50w
Valletta	35 54N	14 30 E
Valley City	46 57N	98 0w
Valleyfield	45 15N	74 8w
Valleyview	55 5N	117 25w
Valls	41 18N	1 15 E
Valognes	49 30N	1 28w
Valparaíso	33 2s	71 40w
Valsbaai	34 15s	18 40 E
Valverde del Camino	37 35N	6 47w
Van Buren, Ark.	35 28N	94 18w
Van Buren, Me.	47 10N	68 1w
Van Diemen, C.	16 30s	139 46 E
Van Diemen, G.	12 0s	132 0 E
Van Gölü	38 30N	43 0 E
Van Wert	40 52N	84 31w
Vancouver, Canada	49 20N	123 10w
Vancouver, U.S.A.	45 44N	122 41w
Vancouver I.	49 50N	126 30w
Vandalia	38 57N	89 4w
Vanderbijlpark	26 42s	27 54 E
Vanderhoof	54 0N	124 0w
Vandyke	24 8s	142 45 E
Vänern, L.	58 47N	13 50 E
Vänersborg	58 26N	12 27 E
Vanga	4 35s	39 12 E
Vangaindrano	23 21s	47 36 E
Vankarem	67 51N	175 50w
Vankleek Hill	45 32N	74 40w
Vännäs	63 58N	19 48 E
Vannes	47 40N	2 47w
Vanrhynsdorp	31 36s	18 44 E
Vansbro	60 32N	14 15 E
Vanua Levu, I.	16 33s	179 10 E
Var □	43 27N	6 18 E
Varanasi	25 22N	83 8 E
Varaždin	46 20N	16 20 E
Varberg	57 17N	12 20 E
Vardar, R.	40 35N	22 50 E
Varese	45 49N	8 50 E
Värmlands □	59 45N	13 0 E
Varna	43 13N	27 56 E
Värnamo	57 10N	14 3 E
Vascongadas, Reg.	42 50N	2 45w
Vaslui	46 38N	27 42 E
Västerbotten □	64 58N	18 0 E
Västerdalälven, R.	60 33N	15 8 E
Västernorrlands □	63 30N	17 40 E
Västervik	57 43N	16 43 E
Västmanlands □	59 45N	16 20 E
Vasto	42 8N	14 40 E
Vatnajökull	64 30N	16 30w
Vatomandry	19 20s	48 59 E
Vatra-Dornei	47 22N	25 22 E
Vättern, L.	58 25N	14 30 E
Vaucluse □	44 3N	5 10 E
Vaughan	34 37N	105 12w
Vauxhall	50 5N	112 9w
Växjö	56 52N	14 50 E
Vaygach, Os.	70 0N	60 0 E
Vechte, R.	52 35N	6 5 E
Vedea, R.	43 53N	25 59 E
Veendam	53 5N	6 25 E
Veenendaal	52 2N	5 34 E
Vefsna, R.	65 50N	13 12 E
Vega fjord	65 37N	12 0 E
Vegreville	53 30N	112 5w
Vejer de la Frontera	36 15N	5 59w
Vejle	55 47N	9 30 E
Velay, Mts. du	45 0N	3 40 E
Velddrif	32 42s	18 11 E
Velebit Planina, Mts.	44 50N	15 20 E
Vélez	6 2N	73 43w
Vélez Málaga	36 48N	4 5w
Vélez Rubio	37 41N	2 5w
Velikiy Ustyug	60 47N	46 20 E
Velikiye Luki	56 25N	30 32 E
Velikonda Ra.	14 45N	79 10 E
Velletri	41 43N	12 43 E
Vellore	12 57N	79 10 E
Velsen	52 27N	4 40 E
Velsk	61 10N	42 5 E
Venado Tuerto	33 50s	62 0w
Vendée □	46 40N	1 20w
Veneto □	45 30N	12 0 E
Venézia	45 27N	12 20 E
Venézia, G. di	45 20N	13 0 E
Venezuela ■	8 0N	65 0w
Venezuela, G. de	11 30N	71 0w
Vengurla	15 53N	73 45 E
Venice=Venézia	45 27N	12 20 E
Venlo	51 22N	6 11 E
Venraij	51 31N	6 0 E
Ventnor	50 35N	1 12w
Ventspils	57 25N	21 32 E
Ventura	34 16N	119 25w
Vera, Arg.	29 30s	60 20w
Vera, Sp.	37 15N	1 45w
Veracruz	19 10N	96 10w
Veracruz □	19 0N	96 15w
Veraval	20 53s	70 27 E
Vercelli	45 19N	8 25 E
Verde, R.	41 56s	65 5w
Verden	52 56N	9 15 E
Verdun	49 12N	5 24 E
Vereeniging	26 38s	27 57 E
Verkhniy Baskunchak	48 5N	46 50 E
Verkhoyansk	67 50N	133 50 E
Verkhoyanskiy Khrebet	66 0N	129 0 E
Vermilion	53 20N	110 50w
Vermilion, R.	53 44N	110 18w
Vermilion Bay	49 50N	93 20w
Vermillion	42 50N	96 56w
Vermont □	43 40N	72 50w
Vernal	40 28N	109 35w
Verner	46 25N	80 8w
Vernon, Canada	50 20N	119 15w
Vernon, U.S.A.	34 0N	99 15w
Verona	45 27N	11 0 E
Versailles	48 48N	2 8 E
Verte, C.	14 45N	17 30w
Verulam	29 38s	31 2 E

Verviers .... 50 37N   5 52 E
Veselovskoye,
    Vdkhr. .... 47 0N   41 0 E
Vesoul .... 60 40N   6 11 E
Vest-Agde □ ..... 58 30N   7 0 E
Vestfold □ ...... 59 15N   10 0 E
Vestmannaejar, Is. 63 27N   20 15w
Vesuvio, Mt. ...... 40 50N   14 22 E
Vesuvius, Mt.=
    Vesuvio, Mt. .. 40 50N   14 22 E
Veszprém .... 47 8N   17 57 E
Vetlanda .... 57 24N   15 3 E
Vexin, Reg. .... 49 20N   1 30 E
Viacha 16 30s   68 5w
Viana 3 0s   44 40w
Viana do Castelo .. 41 42N   8 50w
Vianopolis 16 40s   48 35w
Viborg .... 56 27N   9 23 E
Vicenza .... 45 32N   11 31 E
Vich .... 41 58N   2 19 E
Vichy .... 46 9N   3 26 E
Vicksburg 32 22N   90 56w
Vicosa 9 28s   36 25w
Victor Harbour ... 35 30s 138 37 E
Victoria, Australia . 21 16s 149 3 E
Victoria, Cameroon . 1 4N   9 10 E
Victoria, Canada .. 48 30N 123 25w
Victoria, Chile .. 38 22s   72 29w
Victoria,
    Hong Kong ..... 22 25N 114 15 E
Victoria, Malaysia . 5 20N 115 20 E
Victoria, Malta .. 36 2N   14 14 E
Victoria, U.S.A. ... 28 50N   97 0w
Victoria, L. ...... 1 0s   33 0 E
Victoria, R. ...... 15 12s 129 43 E
Victoria □ .... 20 55s   31 50 E
Victoria Beach .. 50 45N   96 32w
Victoria
    de las Tunas 20 58N   76 59w
Victoria Falls .. 17 58s   25 45 E
Victoria I. 71 0N   11 0w
Victoria Ld. ...... 75 0s 160 0 E
Victoria Nile, R. .. 2 14N   31 26 E
Victoria
    Taungdeik, Mt. .. 21 15N   93 55 E
Victoria West .. 31 25s   23 4 E
Victorica 36 15s   65 30w
Victorville 34 32N 117 18w
Vicuña 30 2s   70 44w

Vidalia 32 13N   82 25w
Vidin .... 43 59N   22 52 E
Viedma 40 50s   63 0w
Viedma, L. 49 30s   72 30w
Vienna = Wien .. 48 12N   16 22 E
Vienne .... 45 31N   4 53 E
Vienne, R. ...... 47 13N   0 5 E
Vienne □ .... 45 53N   0 42 E
Vientiane .... 18 7N 102 35 E
Vierzon .... 47 13N   2 5 E
Vietnam ■ .... 16 0N 108 0 E
Vigan .... 17 35N 120 28 E
Vigia 0 50s   48 5w
Vigo 42 12N   8 41w
Vijayawada ...... 16 31N   80 39 E
Vikulovo .... 56 50N   70 40 E
Vila Cabral
    = Lichinga .... 13 13s   35 11 E
Vila da Maganja .. 17 18s   37 30 E
Vila de Manica .. 18 58s   32 58 E
Vila Franca de Xira 38 57N   8 59w
Vila Machado .... 19 15s   34 14 E
Vila Real 41 17N   7 48w
Vila Real
    de Sto. António . 37 10N   7 28w
Vilaine, R. 47 30N   2 7w
Viliga .... 60 2N 156 56 E
Villa Ángela 27 34s   60 45w
Villa Cisneros
    = Dakhla 23 50N   15 53w
Villa Colón 31 38s   68 20w
Villa Hayes 25 0s   57 20w
Villa Julia Molina . 19 5N   69 45w
Villa María 32 20s   63 10w
Villa Mazán 28 40s   66 10w
Villa Ocampo 28 30s   59 20w
Villach .... 46 37N   13 51 E
Villa de Maria .. 29 55s   63 45w
Villagarcia de
    Arosa 42 34N   8 46w
Villaguay 32 0s   58 45w
Villahermosa,
    Mexico 17 45N   92 50w
Villalba 40 36N   3 59w
Villanueva 35 16N 105 31w
Villanueva de
    la Serena 38 59N   5 50w
Villarreal 39 55N   0 3w
Villarrica 39 15s   72 30w
Villavicencio 4 9N   73 37w

Villaviciosa 43 32N   5 27w
Villazón 22 0s   65 35w
Ville Marie 47 20N   79 30w
Ville Platte 30 45N   92 17w
Villena 38 39N   0 52w
Villiers .... 27 2s   28 36 E
Vilna 54 7N 111 55w
Vilnius .... 54 38N   25 25 E
Vilvoorde .... 50 56N   4 26 E
Vilyuysk .... 63 40N 121 20 E
Viña del Mar 33 0s   71 30w
Vinaroz .... 40 30N   0 27 E
Vincennes 38 42N   87 29w
Vindhya Ra. ..... 22 50N   77 0 E
Vinh .... 18 45N 105 38 E
Vinh Loi .... 17 4N 107 2 E
Vinita 36 40N   95 12w
Vinkovci .... 45 19N   18 48 E
Vinnitsa .... 49 15N   28 30 E
Violet Town ..... 36 19s 145 37 E
Viqueque .... 8 42s 126 30 E
Viramgam .... 23 5N   72 0 E
Virden 49 50N 101 0w
Vírgenes, C. 52 19s   68 21w
Virgin Gorda, I. ... 18 45N   64 26w
Virgin Is., Br. 18 40N   64 30w
Virgin Is., U.S. ... 18 20N   64 50w
Virginia, S. Afr. ... 28 8s   26 55 E
Virginia, U.S.A. ... 47 30N   92 32w
Virginia □ 37 45N   78 0w
Virginia Beach .. 36 54N   75 58w
Virginia City ... 45 25N 111 58w
Virton .... 49 35N   5 32 E
Virudunagar .... 9 30N   78 0 E
Vis, I. .... 43 0N   16 10 E
Visalia 36 25N 119 18w
Visayan Sea .... 11 30N 123 30 E
Visby .... 57 37N   18 18 E
Viscount
    Melville Sd. ... 78 0N 108 0w
Visé .... 50 44N   5 41 E
Viseu, Brazil 1 10s   46 20w
Viseu, Port. 40 40N   7 55w
Vishakhapatnam .. 17 45N   83 20 E
Visrisler .... 31 45s   25 20 E
Vistula, R.=
    Wisła, R. ...... 54 22N   18 55 E
Viso, Mte. .... 44 40N   7 7 E
Vitebsk .... 55 10N   30 15 E
Viterbo .... 42 25N   12 8 E

Viti Levu, I. ...... 17 30s 177 30 E
Vitim .... 59 45N 112 25 E
Vitim, R. .... 59 26N 112 34 E
Vitoria, Brazil ... 20 20s   40 22w
Vitoria, Sp. 42 50N   2 41w
Vitória da
    Conquista 14 51s   40 51w
Vitoria de Santo
    Antão 8 10s   37 20w
Vittória .... 36 58N   14 30 E
Vittório Véneto .. 45 59N   12 18 E
Vivero 43 39N   7 38w
Vizianagaram .... 18 6N   83 10 E
Vlaardingen ..... 51 55N   4 21 E
Vladimir .... 56 0N   40 30 E
Vladivostok ..... 43 10N 131 53 E
Vlissingen ...... 51 26N   3 34 E
Vlóra .... 40 32N   19 28 E
Vogelkop, Mt.=
    Doberai,
    Djazirah ...... 1 25s 133 0 E
Vohémar .... 13 25s   50 0 E
Vohipeno .... 22 22s   47 51 E
Voi .... 3 25s   38 32 E
Volga, R. .... 45 55N   47 52 E
Volga Heights, Mts. 51 0N   46 0 E
Volgograd ...... 48 40N   44 25 E
Volgogradskoye,
    Vdkhr. .... 50 0N   45 20 E
Volksrust .... 27 24s   29 53 E
Vollenhove ...... 52 40N   5 58 E
Volochanka ..... 71 0N   94 28 E
Vologda .... 59 25N   40 0 E
Vólos .... 39 24N   22 59 E
Volsk .... 52 5N   47 28 E
Volta, L. .... 7 30N   0 15 E
Volta, R. .... 5 46N   0 41 E
Volta Noire, R. ... 8 41N   1 33w
Volta Redonda ... 22 31s   44 5w
Volterra .... 43 24N   10 50 E
Volzhskiy .... 48 56N   44 46 E
Vondrozo .... 22 49s   47 20 E
Voorburg .... 52 5N   4 24 E
Vor-Arlberg □ ... 47 15N   9 55 E
Vorkuta .... 67 48N   64 20 E
Voronezh .... 51 40N   39 10 E
Voroshilovgrad .. 48 38N   39 15 E
Vosges, Mts. ..... 48 20N   7 10 E
Vosges □ .... 48 12N   6 20 E
Voss .... 60 38N   6 26 E

Vostochnyy Sayan . 54 0N   96 0 E
Vostok, I. 10 5s 152 23w
Votkinsk .... 57 0N   53 55 E
Votkinskoye,
    Vdkhr. .... 57 30N   55 0 E
Vozhe, Oz. ...... 60 45N   39 0 E
Voznesenka ...... 46 51N   35 26 E
Voznesensk ...... 47 35N   31 15 E
Voznesenye ...... 61 0N   35 45 E
Vrangelya, Os. ... 71 0N 180 0 E
Vranje .... 42 34N   21 54 E
Vratsa .... 43 13N   23 30 E
Vrede .... 27 30s   9 6 E
Vredefort .... 27 5s   27 16 E
Vredenburg ..... 32 51s   18 0 E
Vredendal ...... 31 41s   18 35 E
Vršac .... 45 8N   21 18 E
Vryburg .... 26 55s   24 45 E
Vryheid .... 27 54s   30 47 E
Vught .... 51 38N   5 20 E
Vulcan 50 25N 113 15w
Vulcano, I. ...... 38 27N   14 58 E
Vyatskiye .... 56 5N   51 0 E
Vyazma .... 55 10N   34 15 E
Vyborg .... 60 42N   28 45 E
Východné Beskydy 49 30N   22 0 E
Vyg, Oz. .... 63 30N   34 0 E
Vyrnwy, L. 52 48N   3 30w
Vyshniy Volochek . 57 30N   34 30 E
Vytegra .... 61 15N   36 40 E

W

Wa 10 7N   2 25w
Waal, R. .... 51 55N   4 30 E
Wabana 47 40N   53 0w
Wabash 40 48N   85 46w
Wabash, R. 37 46N   88 2w
Wabowden 54 55N   98 35w
Wabrzeźno ...... 53 16N   18 57 E
Wabush City 52 40N   67 0w
Waco 31 33N   97 5w
Wad Banda .... 13 10N   27 50 E
Wad Hamid .... 16 20N   32 45 E
Wâd Medani .... 14 28N   33 30 E
Wadayama ...... 35 19N 134 52 E
Waddeniladen, Is. . 53 30N   5 30 E

Renamed Limbe
Renamed Masvingo

Waddenzee .... 53 15N   5 15 E
Wadderin Hill 32   0s 118 25 E
Waddington, Mt. .. 51 10N 125 20w
Wadena, Canada .. 52 0N 103 50w
Wadena, U.S.A. ... 46 25N 95 2w
Wadi Halfa .... 21 53N 31 19 E
Wageningen ...... 51 58N   5 40 E
Wager Bay 66 0N 91 0w
Wagga Wagga .... 35 7s 147 24 E
Wagin, Austral. .. 33 17s 117 25 E
Wagin, Nigeria .. 12 45N   7 8 E
Wahai .... 2 48s 129 35 E
Wahpeton 46 20N 96 35w
Waiau .... 42 39s 173 5 E
Waiau, R. .... 42 46s 173 23 E
Waigeo, I. .... 0 20s 130 40 E
Waihi .... 37 23s 175 52 E
Waihou, R. .... 37 10s 175 32 E
Waikaremoana, L. . 38 49s 177 9 E
Waikari .... 42 58s 72 41 E
Waikato, R. ...... 37 23s 174 43 E
Waikokopu .... 39 3s 177 52 E
Waikouaiti .... 45 36s 170 41 E
Waimakariri, R. .. 43 24s 172 42 E
Waimarino .... 40 40s 175 20 E
Waimate .... 44 53s 171 3 E
Wainganga, R. .... 18 50N 79 55 E
Waingapu .... 9 35s 120 11 E
Wainwright 52 50N 110 50w
Waiouru .... 39 29s 175 40 E
Waipara .... 43 3N 172 46 E
Waipawa .... 39 56s 176 38 E
Waipiro .... 38 2s 176 22 E
Waipu .... 35 59s 174 29 E
Waipukurau ...... 40 1s 176 33 E
Wairakei .... 38 37s 176 6 E
Wairau, .R. ...... 41 32s 174 7 E
Wairoa .... 39 3s 177 25 E
Waitaki, R. ...... 44 56s 171 7 E
Waitara .... 38 59s 174 15 E
Waiuku .... 37 15s 174 45 E
Waiyeung .... 23 12N 11432 E
Wajima .... 37 30N 137 0 E
Wajir .... 1 42N 40 20 E
Wakasa .... 35 20N 134 24 E
Wakasa-Wan .... 34 45N 135 30 E
Wakatipu, L. .... 45 6s 168 30 E
Wakaw 52 39N 105 44w
Wakayama .... 34 15N 135 15 E

Wakayama □ ..... 34 50N 135 30 E
Wake, I. .... 19 18N 166 36 E
Wakefield, U.K. .. 53 41N   1 31w
Wakefield, N.Z. .. 41 24s 173 5 E
Wakeham Bay =
  Maricourt 61 36N 71 57w
Wakkanai .... 45 28N 141 35 E
Wakkerstroom ... 27 24s 30 10 E
Wakre .... 0 30s 131 5 E
Walachia, Reg.=
  Valahia, Reg. .. 44 35N 25 0 E
Walbrzych ...... 50 45N 16 18 E
Walbury Hill 51 22N   1 28w
Walcha .... 30 55s 151 31 E
Walcheren, I. .... 51 30N   3 35 E
Walden 40 47N 106 20w
Waldron 50 53N 102 35w
Walebing .... 30 40s 116 15 E
Wales ■ 52 30N   3 30w
Walgett .... 30 0s 148 5 E
Walkaway 28 59s 114 48w
Walkerton 44 10N 81 10w
Walla Walla 46 3N 118 25w
Wallace 47 30N 116 0w
Wallaceburg 42 40N 82 30w
Wallal .... 26 32s 146 7 E
Wallal Downs ... 19 47s 120 40 E
Wallaroo .... 33 56s 137 39 E
Wallasey 3 26s   3 2w
Wallerawang .... 33 25s 150 4 E
Wallhallow ..... 17 50s 135 50 E
Wallowa 45 40N 117 35w
Wallsend 54 59N   1 30w
Wallumbilla ... 26 33s 149 9 E
Walmer .... 33 57s 25 35 E
Walney, I 54 5N   3 15w
Walpeup ...... 35 10s 142 2 E
Walsall 52 36N   1 59w
Walsenburg ... 37 42N 104 45w
Waltham 45 57N 76 57w
Walvisbaai ... 23 0s 14 28 E
Walvis Bay =
  Walvisbaai ... 23 0s 14 28 E
Wamba .... 2 10N 27 57 E
Wanaka, L. ... 44 33s 169 7 E
Wanapiri ..... 4 30s 135 50 E
Wanbi .... 34 46s 140 17 E
Wanderer ..... 19 37s 29 59 E
Wandoan ..... 26 5s 149 55 E
Wanganui .... 39 35s 175 3 E

Wangaratta ...... 36 21s 146 19 E
Wangary .... 34 33s 135 29 E
Wangtu .... 38 42N 115 4 E
Wanhsien .... 30 45N 108 20 E
* Wankie .... 18 18s 26 30 E
Wanless 54 11N 101 21w
Wanning .... 18 45N 110 28 E
Wantsai .... 28 1N 114 5 E
Wanyang
  Shan, Mts. ..... 26 30N 113 30 E
Wanyuan .... 32 3N 108 16 E
Wapato 46 30N 120 25w
Warandab ...... 7 20N 44 2 E
Warangal ...... 17 58N 79 45 E
Ward .... 41 49s 174 11 E
Wardak □ ...... 34 15N 68 0 E
Warden .... 27 56s 29 0 E
Wardha .... 20 45N 78 39 E
Warialda ...... 29 29s 150 33 E
Warkopi .... 1 12s 134 9 E
Warkworth ..... 36 24s 174 41 E
Warley 52 30N   2 0w
Warman 52 25N 106 30w
Warmbad ...... 24 51s 28 19 E
Warmbad, S.W.
  Africa .... 28 25s 18 42 E
Warmbad, S.W.
  Africa .... 19 14s 13 51 E
Warncoort ..... 38 30s 143 45 E
Warnemünde .... 54 9N 12 5 E
Warner Ra. 41 30s 120 20w
Warner Robins .. 32 41N 83 36w
Waroona ...... 32 50s 115 55 E
Warracknabeal . 36 9s 142 26 E
Warragul ..... 38 10s 145 58 E
Warrego, R. ... 30 24s 145 21 E
Warren, Australia . 31 42s 147 51 E
Warren, Ohio ... 41 18N 80 52w
Warren, Pa. 41 52N 79 10w
Warren 33 35N 92 3w
Warrenpoint ... 54 7N   6 15w
Warrensburg ... 38 45N 93 45w
Warrenton, S.
  Africa .... 28 9s 24 47 E
Warrenton, U.S.A. 46 11N 123 59w
Warri .... 5 30N   5 41 E
Warrington, U.K. . 53 25N   2 38w
Warrington, U.S.A. 30 22N 87 16w
Warrnambool .. 38 25s 142 30 E
Warsak Dam ... 34 10N 71 25 E

Warsaw 41 14N 85 50w
Warsaw=Warszawa 52 13N 21 0 E
Warszawa ...... 52 13N 21 0 E
Warta, R. .... 52 35N 14 39 E
Warwick □ 52 20N   1 30w
Warwick, Australia 28 10s 152 1 E
Warwick, U.K. ... 52 17N   1 36w
Warwick, U.S.A. . 41 43N 71 25w
Wasa 49 45s 115 50w
Wasatch Mts. ... 40 30N 111 15w
Wasbank .... 28 15s 30 9 E
Wasco, Calif. ... 35 37N 119 16w
Wasco, Oreg. ... 45 45N 120 46w
Waseca 44 3N 93 31w
Wash, The 52 58N   0 20w
Washington 47 45N 120 30w
Washington, D.C. . 38 52N 77 0w
Washington, Ind. . 38 40N 87 8w
Washington, Iowa . 41 20N 91 45w
Washington, Mo. . 38 33N 91 1w
Washington, N.C. . 35 35N 77 1w
Washington, Ohio . 39 34N 83 26w
Washington, Pa. . 40 10N 80 20w
Washington, Mt. . 44 15N 71 18w
Wassenaar ...... 52 8N   4 24 E
Waswanipi 49 30N 77 0w
Watangpone .... 4 29s 120 25 E
Waterberg ..... 24 14s 28 0 E
Waterbury 41 32N 73 0w
Waterford □ 52 16N   7 8w
Waterford 51 10N   7 40w
Waterloo, Belgium 50 43N   4 25 E
Waterloo, Canada . 43 30N 80 32w
Waterloo, Iowa .. 42 27N 92 20w
Watertown, N.Y. . 43 58N 75 57w
Watertown, S.D. . 44 57N 97 5w
Watertown, Wis. . 43 15N 88 45w
Waterval-Boven .. 25 40s 30 18 E
Waterville 44 35N 69 40w
Watervliet 42 46N 73 43w
Wates .... 7 53s 110 6 E
Watford 51 38N   0 23w
Watheroo 30 15s 116 0w
Watkins Glen .. 42 25N 76 55 E
Watling, I. 24 0N 74 30w
Watrous 51 40N 105 25w
Watsa .... 3 4N 29 30 E
Watson .... 30 19s 131 41 E
Watson Lake .. 60 12N 129 0w
Watsonville ... 37 58N 121 49w

Waubra .... 37 21s 143 39 E
Wauchope ...... 31 28s 152 45 E
Waugh 49 40N 95 20w
Waukegan 42 22N 87 54w
Waukesha 43 0N 88 15w
Waupun 43 38N 88 44w
Wausau 44 57N 89 40w
Wauwatosa 43 6N 87 59w
Wave Hill ..... 17 32N 131 0 E
Waveney, R. ... 52 28N   1 45 E
Waverley ..... 39 46s 174 37 E
Waverly 42 40N 92 30w
Wavre .... 50 43N   4 38 E
Wāw .... 7 45N 28 1 E
Waxahachie ... 32 22N 96 53w
Wayatinah .... 42 19s 146 27 E
Waycross 31 12N 82 25w
Waynesboro, Pa. . 39 46N 77 32w
Waynesboro, Va. . 38 4N 78 57w
Waynesville ... 35 31N 83 0w
Wazirabad,
  Afghanistan . 36 44N 66 47 E
Wazirabad,
  Pak. .... 32 30N 74 8 E
Weald, The .... 51 7N   0 9 E
Wear, R. 54 55s   1 22w
Weatherford ... 32 45N 97 48w
Webster City ... 42 30N 93 50w
Webster Green .. 38 38N 90 20w
Weda .... 0 30N 127 50 E
Weddell I. 51 50s 61 0w
Weddell Sea .. 72 30s 40 0w
Wedderburn ... 36 20s 143 33 E
Wedgeport 43 44N 65 59w
Wee Waa ..... 30 11s 149 26 E
Weed 41 29N 122 22w
Weenen ..... 28 57s 30 3 E
Weert .... 51 15N   5 43 E
Wei Ho, R. ... 35 45N 114 30 E
Weifang ..... 36 47N 119 10 E
Weihai ...... 37 30N 122 10 E
Weimar ..... 51 0N 11 20 E
Weinan ..... 34 30N 109 35 E
Weipa ...... 12 24s 141 50 E
Weir River .. 57 0N 94 10w
Weiser 44 10N 117 0w
Wejherowo .. 54 35N 18 12 E
Wekusko ... 54 45N 99 45w
Welch 37 29N 81 36w
Welkom .... 28 0s 26 50 E

* Renamed Hwange

Welland 43 0N 79 10w
Welland, R. ...... 52 53N 0 2 E
Wellesley, Is. ..... 17 20s 139 30 E
Wellingborough ... 52 18N 0 41w
Wellington,
　Australia .... 32 30s 149 0 E
Wellington, Canada 43 57N 77 20w
Wellington, N.Z. .. 41 19s 174 46 E
Wellington, U.K. .. 52 42N 2 31w
Wellington, U.S.A. 37 15N 97 25w
Wellington □ ...... 40 8s 175 36 E
Wellington, I. 49 30s 75 0w
Wells, Norfolk .... 52 57N 0 51 E
Wells, Somerset .. 51 12N 2 39w
Wells, U.S.A. 41 8N 115 0w
Wells, L. 26 44s 123 15w
Wellsboro 41 45N 77 16w
Wellsville, N.Y. ... 42 9N 77 57w
Wellsville, Ohio .. 40 36N 80 40w
Wels .... 48 9N 14 1 E
Welshpool,
　Australia .... 38 42s 146 26 E
Welshpool,
　U.K. 52 40N 3 9w
Wem 52 52N 2 45w
Wenatchee 47 30N 120 17w
Wenchang .... 19 38N 110 42 E
Wenchi 7 46N 2 8w
Wenchow=
　Wenchow ...... 28 0N 120 35 E
Wenchow .... 28 0N 120 35 E
Wendell 42 50N 114 51w
Wensiang .... 34 35N 110 40 E
Wensleydale 54 20N 2 0w
Wensu .... 41 15N 80 14 E
Wenteng .... 25 15s 23 16 E
Wentworth .... 34 2s 141 54 E
Wepener .... 29 42s 27 3 E
Werda .... 25 15s 23 16 E
Werra, R. .... 51 26N 9 39 E
Werribee .... 37 54s 144 40 E
Werris Creek ..... 31 8s 150 38 E
Weser, R. .... 53 32N 8 34 E
Wesleyville 49 8N 53 36w
Wessel, Is. .... 11 10s 136 45 E
West Bend 43 25N 88 10w
West Bengal □ .... 25 0N 90 0 E
West Bromwich .. 52 32N 2 1w
West Des Moines . 41 30N 93 45w
West Falkland, I. .. 51 30s 60 0w

West Frankfort 37 56N 89 0w
West Germany ■.. 51 0N 9 0 E
West Glamorgan □ 51 40N 3 55w
West Helena 34 30N 90 40w
West Indies 20 0N 65 0w
West Memphis ... 35 5N 90 3w
West Midlands □ .. 52 30N 2 0w
West Monroe 32 32N 92 7w
West Palm Beach . 26 44N 80 3w
West Pt. 18 14N 78 30w
West Point, Miss. .. 33 36N 88 38w
West Point, Va. ... 37 35N 76 47w
West Sussex □ 50 55N 0 30w
West Virginia □ ... 39 0N 18 0w
West Wyalong ... 33 56s 147 10 E
West Yorkshire □ . 53 45N 1 40w
Westbrook 43 41N 70 21w
Westbury .... 41 30s 146 51 E
Western □ 6 0N 2 20w
Western
　Australia □ ..... 25 0s 118 0 E
Western Ghats,
　Mts. .... 15 30N 74 30 E
Western Isles □ ... 57 30N 7 10w
Western Samoa ■. 14 0s 172 0w
Westerschelde, R. . 51 25N 4 0 E
Westerwald, Mts... 50 39N 8 0 E
Westland □ .... 43 33s 169 59 E
Westlock 54 20N 113 55w
Westmeath □ 53 30N 7 30w
Westminster 39 34s 77 1w
Westmorland 33 2N 115 42w
Weston, Malaysia . 5 10N 115 35 E
Weston, U.S.A. ... 39 3N 80 29w
Weston-super-Mare 51 20N 2 59w
Westphalia□=
　Nordrhein-
　Westfalen □ ... 51 45N 7 30 E
Westport, Eire 53 44N 9 31w
Westport, N.Z. ... 41 46s 171 37 E
Westray, I. 59 18N 3 0w
Westview 49 50N 124 31w
Westwood 40 26N 121 0w
Wetar, I. .... 7 30s 126 30 E
Wetaskiwin 52 55N 113 24w
Wetteren .... 51 0N 3 53 E
Wetzlar .... 50 33N 8 30 E
Wewaka 35 10N 96 35w
Wexford 52 20N 6 28w
Wexford □ 52 20N 6 40w

Weyburn 49 40N 103 50w
Weymouth, U.K. .. 50 36N 2 28w
Whakatane .... 37 57s 177 1 E
Whale, R. 57 40N 67 0w
Whale Cove 62 10N 93 0w
Whalsay, I. 60 22N 1 0w
Whangamomona .. 39 8s 174 44 E
Whangarei .... 35 43s 174 21 E
Whangaroa,
　Harbour .... 35 4s 173 46 E
Wharfe, R. 53 51N 1 7w
Wheatland 42 4N 105 58w
Wheeler Pk. 38 57N 114 15w
Wheeling 40 2N 80 41w
Whernside, Mt. ... 54 14N 2 24w
Whitby 54 29N 0 37w
White, R., Ind. 38 25N 87 44w
White, R., Ark. 33 53N 91 3w
White Cliffs ...... 30 50s 143 10 E
White Nile, R. =
　Nîl el Abyad .... 9 30N 31 40 E
White River,
　Canada 48 35N 85 20w
White River, S. Afr. 25 20s 31 0 E
White Sea=
　Beloye More .... 66 30N 38 0 E
White Sulphur
　Springs 46 35N 111 0w
White Volta, R. ... 9 10N 1 15w
Whitecliffs .... 43 26s 171 55 E
Whitefish 48 25N 114 22w
Whitehall, Wis. ... 44 20N 91 19w
Whitehaven 54 33N 3 35w
Whitehorse 60 45N 135 10w
Whiteshell
　Prov. Park 50 0N 95 25w
Whitewood .... 21 28s 143 30 E
Whitewood 50 20N 102 20w
Whithorn 54 55N 4 25w
Whitianga .... 36 47s 175 41 E
Whitney, Mt. 36 35N 118 14w
Whitstable .... 51 21N 1 2 E
Whitsunday, I. .... 20 15s 149 4 E
Whittier 60 46N 148 48w
Whittle, C. 50 11N 60 8w
Whyalla .... 33 2s 137 30 E
Wiarton 44 50N 81 10w
Wiawso 6 12N 2 29w

Wichita .... 37 40N 97·29w
Wichita Falls 33 57N 98 30w
Wick 58 26N 3 5w
Wickenburg 33 58N 112 45w
Wickepin .... 32 50s 117 30 E
Wicklow 53 0N 6 2w
Wicklow □ 52 59N 6 25w
Wicklow Mts. 53 0N 6 30w
Widgiemooltha ... 31 30s 121 34 E
Widnes 53 22N 2 44w
Wieliczka .... 50 0N 20 5 E
Wieluń .... 51 15N 18 40 E
Wien .... 48 12N 16 22 E
Wiener Neustadt .. 47 49N 16 16 E
Wierden .... 52 22N 6 35 E
Wiesbaden .... 50 7N 8 17 E
Wigan 53 33N 2 38w
Wigtown 54 52N 4 27w
Wigtown B. 54 46N 4 15w
Wilcannia .... 31 30s 143 26 E
Wildwood 39 5N 74 46w
Wilhelmshaven ... 53 30N 8 9 E
Wilkes-Barre 41 15N 75 52w
Wilkes Ld. .... 69 0s 120 0 E
Wilkie 52 27N 108 42w
Willcox 32 13N 109 53w
Willemstad 12 5N 69 0w
Willeroo .... 15 14s 131 37 E
William Creek .... 28 58s 136 22 E
Williams, Australia 33 2s 116 52 E
Williams, U.S.A. .. 35 16N 112 11w
Williams Lake 52 20N 122 10w
Williamsburg 37 17N 76 44w
Williamson 37 46N 82 17w
Williamsport 41 18N 77 1w
Williamstown,
　Australia .... 37 46s 144 58 E
Williston, S. Afr. .. 31 20s 20 53 E
Williston, U.S.A. .. 48 10N 103 35w
Willits 39 28N 123 17w
Willmar 45 5N 95 0w
Willow Tree ...... 31 40s 150 45 E
Willowmore ...... 33 15s 23 30 E
Willows, Australia . 23 45s 147 25 E
Willows, U.S.A. .. 39 30N 122 10w
Wilmette 42 6N 87 44w
Wilmington, Del. .. 39 45N 75 32w
Wilmington, N.C. . 34 14N ·77 54w
Wilmington, Ohio . 39 29N 83 46w
Wilson 35 44N 77 54w

Wilson, Mt. 37 55N 105 3w
Wilson's
　Promontory ..... 39 5s 146 28 E
Wilton 51 5N 1 52w
Wiltshire □ 51 20N 2 0w
Wiluna .... 26 40s 120 25 E
Winburg .... 28 30s 27 2 E
Winchester, U.K... 51 4N 1 19w
Winchester, Ind. .. 40 10N 84 56w
Winchester, Ky. .. 38 0N 84 8w
Winchester, Va. ... 39 14N 78 8w
Windber 40 14N 78 50w
Windermere, L. ... 54 20N 2 57w
Windhoek .... 22 35s 17 4 E
Windorah .... 25 24s 142 36 E
Windrush, R. 51 42N 1 25w
Windsor, Australia 33 34s 150 44 E
Windsor,
　Nova Scotia 44 59N 64 5w
Windsor, Ont. 42 25N 83 0w
Windsor, U.K. 51 28N 0 36w
Windsor, U.S.A. .. 43 30N 72 25w
Windward Is. 13 0N 63 0w
Winfield, Canada .. 52 58N 114 26w
Winfield, U.S.A. .. 37 15N 97 0w
Wingen .... 31 50s 150 58 E
Wingham 43 55N 81 25w
Winisk, R. 55 17N 85 5w
Winkler 49 15N 98 0w
Winneba 5 25N 0 36w
Winnemucca 41 0N 117 45w
Winnepegosis, L. .. 52 40N 100 0w
Winnetka 42 8N 87 46w
Winnfield 31 57N 92 38w
Winning .... 23 9s 114 32 E
Winnipeg 49 50N 97 15w
Winnipeg, L. 52 30N 98 0w
Winnipegosis 52 40N 100 0w
Winona 44 2N 91 45w
Winooski 44 31N 73 11w
Winschoten ...... 53 9N 7 3 E
Winslow 35 2N 110 41w
Winston-Salem ... 36 7N 80 15w
Winter Haven 28 0N 81 42w
Winter Park 28 34N 81 19w
Winterhoek, Mt. .. 33 5s 19 35 E
Winterthur .... 47 30N 8 44 E
Winton .... 22 21s 143 0 E
Winton .... 46 8s 168 20 E
Wirrulla .... 32 24s 134 31 E

Wisbech . . . . 52 39N 0 10 E
Wisconsin □ 44 30N 90 0w
Wisconsin Rapids . 44 25N 89 50w
Wishaw 55 46N 3 55w
Wisła, R. . . . . 54 22N 18 55 E
Wismar . . . . 53 53N 11 23 E
Witbank . . . . 25 51s 29 14 E
Witham, R. . . . . . . 52 56N 0 4 E
Withernsea 53 43N 0 2w
Witney 51 47N 1 29w
Witsand . . . . 34 24s 20 50 E
Wittenberg . . . . . . 51 51N 12 39 E
Wittenberge . . . . . . 53 0N 11 44 E
Wittenoom . . . . . . 22 15s 118 20 E
Witu . . . . 2 23s 40 26 E
Wlingi . . . . 8 5s 112 25 E
Włocławek . . . . . . 52 39 19 2 E
Włodawa . . . . 51 34N 23 32 E
Wodonga . . . . 36 5s 146 50 E
Wokam, I. . . . . 5 45s 134 28 E
Wolfe I. . . . . 44 7N 76 27 E
Wolin, I. . . . . 53 55N 14 31 E
Wollaston, Is. 55 40s 67 30w
Wollaston L. 58 20N 103 30w
Wollaston Pen. 69 30N 113 0w
Wollongong . . . . . . 34 25s 150 54 E
Wolmaransstad . . . . 27 12s 26 13 E
Wolseley, Canada . 50 25N 103 15w
Wolseley, S. Afr. . . 33 26s 19 12 E
Wolstenholme, C. . . 62 50N 78 0w
Wolverhampton 52 35N 2 6w
Wonarah P.O. . . . . 19 55s 136 20 E
Wondai 26 20s 151 49E
Wongan Hills . . . . 30 53s 116 42 E
Wŏnju . . . . 37 30N 127 59 E
Wŏnsan . . . . 39 20N 127 25 E
Wonthaggi . . . . . . 39 29s 145 31 E
Wood Buffalo Nat.
Park 59 30N 113 0w
Woodanilling . . . . 33 31s 117 24 E
Woodend . . . . 37 20N 144 33 E
Woodland 38 40N 121 50w
Woodridge 49 20N 96 20w
Woodroffe, Mt. . . . 26 20s 131 45 E
Woods, L. of the . 49 30N 94 30w
Woodstock,
Australia . . . . . 19 22s 142 45 E
Woodstock, Ont. . 43 10N 80 45w
Woodstock, N.B. . 46 11N 67 37w
Woodstock, U.K. . 51 51N 1 20w

Woodstock, Ill. . . . 42 17N 88 30w
Woodville . . . . . . 40 20s 175 53 E
Woodward 36 24N 99 28w
Woolgangie . . . . . 31 12s 120 35 E
Woolgoolga . . . . . 30 7s 153 12 E
Woombye . . . . 26 40s 152 55 E
Woomelang . . . . . . 35 37s 142 40 E
Woomera . . . . 31 9s 136 56 E
Woonona . . . . 34 32s 150 49 E
Woonsocket 42 0N 71 30w
Woonsockett 44 5N 98 15w
Wooramel . . . . 25 45s 114 40 E
Wooramel, R. . . . . 25 47s 114 10 E
Wooroloo . . . . 31 45s 116 25 E
Wooster 40 38N 81 55w
Worcester, S. Africa 33 39s 19 27 E
Worcester, U.K. . 52 12N 2 12w
Worcester, U.S.A. . 42 14N 71 49w
Workington 54 39N 3 34w
Worksop 53 19N 1 9w
Worland 44 0N 107 59w
Worms . . . . 49 37N 8 21 E
Worsley . . . . 33 15s 116 2 E
Worthing 50 49N 0 21w
Worthington 43 35N 95 30w
Wosi . . . . 0 15s 128 0 E
Wrangell 56 30N 132 25w
Wrangell Mts. . . . 61 40N 143 30w
Wrath, C. 58 38N 5 0w
Wrekin, The, Mt. . 52 41N 2 35w
Wrexham 53 5N 3 0w
Wright, Canada . . 51 45N 121 30w
Wright, Philippines 11 42N 125 2 E
Wrigley 63 0N 123 30w
Wrocław . . . . 51 5N 17 5 E
Września . . . . 52 21N 17 36 E
Wubin . . . . 30 8 15N 116 30 E
Wuchang,
Heilungkiang . . 44 51N 127 10 E
Wuchang, Hupei . 30 34N 114 25 E
Wuchow . . . . 23 26N 111 19 E
Wuchung . . . . 38 4N 106 12 E
Wuhan . . . . 30 32N 114 22 E
Wuhsi=Wusih . . 31 30N 120 30 E
Wuhu . . . . 31 21N 118 30 E
Wukari . . . . 7 57N 9 42 E
Wulumuchi . . . . . 43 40N 87 50 E
Wum . . . . 6 23N 10 4 E
Wun . . . . 19 59N 78 52 E
Wuntho . . . . 23 55N 95 45 E

Wuppertal . . . . . . 51 15N 7 8 E
Wurarga . . . . 28 15s 116 12 E
Würzburg . . . . . . 49 46N 9 55 E
Wusih . . . . 31 30N 120 30 E
Wusu . . . . 44 10N 84 55 E
Wutai Shan . . . . . 39 4N 113 35 E
Wutunghliao . . . . 29 25N 104 0 E
Wuwei . . . . 38 0N 102 30 E
Wuyi Shan, Mts. . 26 40N 116 30 E
Wuying . . . . 48 10N 129 20 E
Wuyo . . . . 10 25N 11 50 E
Wuyuan . . . . 41 45N 108 30 E
Wyalkatchem . . . . 31 8s 117 22 E
Wyandotte 42 14N 83 13w
Wyandra . . . . 27 12s 145 56 E
Wycheproot . . . . . 36 0N 143 17 E
Wye, R. 51 37N 2 39w
Wymondham . . . . 52 34N 1 7 E
Wynberg . . . . 34 0s 18 30 E
Wyndham . . . . . . 15 33s 128 3 E
Wynnum . . . . 27 29s 152 58 E
Wynyard,
Australia . . . . . 40 59s 145 45 E
Wynyard, Canada . 51 45N 104 10w
Wyoming □ 42 48N 109 0w
Wyong . . . . 33 14s 151 24 E
Wytheville 37 0N 81 3w

X
Xánthi . . . . 41 10N 24 58 E
Xenia 39 42N 83 57w
Xi'an=Sian . . . . . 34 2N 109 0 E
Xieng Khouang . 19 17N 103 25 E
Xinavane . . . . 25 2s 32 47 E
Xingu, R. 1 30s 51 53w
Xique-Xique 10 40s 42 40w

Y
Yaamba . . . . 23 8s 150 22 E
Yaan . . . . 30 0N 102 59 E
Yabassi . . . . 4 32N 10 2 E
Yablonovy

Khrebet . . . . 53 0N 114 0 E
Ya'Bud . . . . 32 27N 35 10 E
Yacuiba 22 0s 63 25w
Yadgir . . . . 16 45N 77 5 E
Yagur . . . . 32 45N 35 4 E
Yaicheng . . . . 18 14N 109 7 E
Yajua . . . . 11 25N 12 50 E
Yakima 46 42N 120 30w
Yako 13 2N 2 15w
Yakoshih . . . . 49 13N 120 35 E
Yaku-Shima, I. . . . 30 20N 130 30 E
Yakuluku . . . . 4 22N 28 45 E
Yakut A.S.S.R. □ . 66 0N 125 0 E
Yakutat 59 50N 139 44w
Yakutsk . . . . 62 5N 129 40 E
Yala . . . . 6 45N 101 15 E
Yalboroo . . . . 20 50s 148 30 E
Yalgoo . . . . 28 16s 116 39 E
Yalkubul, Pta. . . . 21 32N 88 37w
Yallourn . . . . 38 10s 146 18 E
Yalta . . . . 44 30N 34 10 E
Yalu, R. . . . . 47 30N 123 30 E
Yalung Kiang, R. . 32 0N 100 0 E
Yalutorovsk . . . . . 56 30N 65 40 E
Yamagata . . . . . . 37 55N 140 20 E
Yamagata □ . . . . . 38 30N 140 0 E
Yamaguchi . . . . . . 34 10N 131 32 E
Yamaguchi □ . . . . 34 20N 131 40 E
Yamal Pol. . . . . . 71 0N 70 0 E
Yamanashi □ . . . . 35 40N 138 40 E
Yamba . . . . 29 30s 153 22 E
Yamdena, I. . . . . . 7 45s 131 20 E
Yamethin . . . . . . 20 26N 96 9 E
Yamil . . . . 12 55N 8 5 E
Yampi, Sd. . . . . . 15 15s 123 30 E
Yamhsien . . . . . . 21 45N 108 31 E
Yamrat . . . . 10 10N 9 55 E
Yamun . . . . 32 29N 35 14 E
Yamuna, R. . . . . . 27 0N 78 30 E
Yan . . . . 10 5N 12 15 E
Yanai . . . . 33 58N 132 7 E
Yanaul . . . . 56 25N 55 0 E
Yanda Bayo . . . . . 11 30N 10 55 E
Yandanooka . . . . . 29 18s 115 29 E
Yandoon . . . . 17 2N 95 39 E
Yangambi . . . . . . 0 47N 24 20 E
Yangchow . . . . . . 32 25N 119 25 E
Yangchuan . . . . . . 38 0N 113 29 E
Yangi-Yer . . . . . . 40 17N 68 48 E

Yangtze Kiang, R. . 31 40N 122 0 E
Yankton 42 55N 97 25w
Yanna . . . . 26 58s 146 0 E
Yanping . . . . 22 25N 112 0 E
Yao Shan, Mts. . . 24 0N 110 0 E
Yaoundé . . . . 3 50N 1 35 E
Yap Is. . . . . 9 30N 138 10 E
Yapen, I. . . . . . . 1 50s 136 0 E
Yapen, Teluk, G. . 1 30s 136 0 E
Yaraka . . . . 24 53s 144 3 E
Yaransk . . . . 57 13N 47 56 E
Yare, R. . . . . 52 40N 1 45 E
Yarensk . . . . 61 10N 49 8 E
Yarkand= Soche . 38 24N 77 20 E
Yarkhun, R. . . . . 36 30N 72 45 E
Yarmouth 43 53N 65 45w
Yaroslavl . . . . 57 35N 39 55 E
Yarra Yarra Lakes 29 12s 115 45 E
Yarraloola . . . . . . 21 34s 115 52 E
Yarraman . . . . . . 26 46s 152 1 E
Yar-Sale . . . . 66 50N 70 50 E
Yartsevo . . . . 60 20N 90 0 E
Yarumal 6 58N 75 24w
Yasawa Is. . . . . . 17 0s 177 23 E
Yashi . . . . 12 25N 7 58 E
Yass . . . . 34 50s 149 0 E
Yas'ur . . . . 32 54N 35 10 E
Yathkyed, L. 63 0N 98 0w
Yatsushiro . . . . . . 32 30N 130 40 E
Yattah . . . . 31 27N 35 6 E
Yavne . . . . 31 52N 34 45 E
Yawatehama . . . . 33 27N 132 24 E
Yazd . . . . 31 55N 54 27 E
Yazdan . . . . 33 30N 60 50 E
Yazoo City 32 48N 90 28w
Ye . . . . 15 15N 97 51 E
Yealering . . . . . . 32 35s 117 30 E
Yebyu . . . . 14 15N 98 13 E
Yegros 26 20s 56 25w
Yehsien . . . . 37 12N 119 58 E
Yelanskoye . . . . . 61 25N 128 0 E
Yelarbon . . . . . . 28 33s 150 49 E
Yelets . . . . 52 40N 38 30 E
Yell, I. 46 42N 2 20w
Yellow, R.=
Hwang Ho, R. . 37 32N 118 19 E
Yellow Sea . . . . . 35 0N 124 0 E
Yellowdine . . . . . 31 18s 119 39 E
Yellowhead P. . . . 53 0N 118 30w
Yellowknife 62 30N 114 10w

Yellowknife, R. 63 30N 113 30w
Yellowstone
  Nat. Park...... 44 35N 110 0w
Yellowtail Res... 45 6N 108 8w
Yelvertoft ...... 20 13s 138 53 E
Yelwa............ 10 50N 4 50 E
Yemen ■ ...... 15 0N 44 0 E
Yenangyaung ... 20 30N 95 0 E
Yencheng .... 36 44N 110 2 E
Yendi........... 9 17N 0 22 E
Yeniseysk .... 58 39N 92 4 E
Yenisey, R. ...... 68 0N 86 30 E
Yeniseyskiy Zaliv . 72 20N 81 0 E
Yenki .... 43 12N 129 30 E
Yentai .... 37 30N 121 22 E
Yenyuka .... 58 20N 121 30 E
Yeo, R. 51 1N 2 46w
Yeola .... 20 0N 74 30 E
Yeotmal .... 20 20N 78 15 E
Yeovil 50 57N 2 38w
Yeppoon .... 23 5s 150 47 E
Yerevan .... 40 10N 44 20 E
Yermakovo .... 52 35N 126 20 E
Yerofey Pavlovich . 54 0N 122 0 E
Yeroham .... 30 59N 34 55 E
Yershov .... 51 15N 48 27 E
Yerushalayim=
  Jerusalem ...... 31 47N 35 10 E
Yes Tor .... 50 41N 3 59 E
Yeu, Î.d' 46 42N 2 20w
Yeungchun .... 22 15N 111 40 E
Yeungkong .... 21 55N 112 0 E
Yeysk Stavo ..... 46 40N 38 12 E
Yiannitsa .... 40 46N 22 24 E
Yibal .... 22 10N 56 8 E
Yilan .... 24 47N 121 44 E
Yin Shan, Mts. ... 41 0N 111 0 E
Yinchwan .... 38 30N 106 20 E
Yingcheng .... 31 0N 113 44 E
Yingkow .... 40 38N 122 30 E
Yingtan .... 28 12N 117 0 E
Yirga Alem ...... 6 34N 38 29 E
Ýíthion .... 36 46N 22 34 E
Yitu .... 36 40N 118 24 E
Yiyang .... 28 45N 112 16 E
Yizre'el .... 32 34N 35 19 E
Ylivieska .... 64 4N 24 28 E
Yoakum 29 20N 97 10w
Yobe, R. .... 13 0N 13 45 E
Yogyakarta ...... 7 49s 110 22 E

Yokkaichi .... 35 0N 136 30 E
Yokohama .... 35 30N 139 32 E
Yokosuka .... 35 20N 139 40 E
Yola .... 9 10N 12 25 E
Yom, R. .... 16 40N 100 14 E
Yonago .... 35 25N 133 19 E
Yongchon .... 35 55N 138 55 E
Yonkers 40 57N 73 51w
Yonne □ .... 47 50N 3 40 E
Yonne, R. .... 48 23N 2 58 E
Yoqne'am .... 32 39N 35 7 E
York, Australia .. 31 52s 116 47 E
York, U.K. 53 58N 1 7w
York, Nebr. 40 55N 97 35w
York, Pa. 39 57N 76 43w
York, C. 75 55N 66 25w
York, Sd. .... 14 30s 125 0 E
York Factory 57 0N 92 30w
York Wolds 54 0N 0 30w
Yorke, Pen. ..... 34 40s 137 35 E
Yorkton 51 11N 102 28w
Yornup .... 34 2s 116 10 E
Yosemite Nat. Park 31 50N 119 30w
Yoshkar Ola ..... 56 49N 47 10 E
Yosu .... 34 47N 127 45 E
Yotvata .... 29 53N 35 2 E
Youghal 51 58N 7 51w
Young .... 34 19s 148 18 E
Younghusband,
  Pen. .... 34 45s 139 15 E
Youngstown 43 16N 79 2w
Yoweragabbie .... 28 10s 117 30 E
Yoyang .... 29 27N 113 10 E
Ypsilanti 42 18N 83 40w
Yreka 41 44N 122 40w
Ystad .... 55 26N 13 50 E
Ythan, R. 57 26N 1 12w
Ytyk-kel .... 62 20N 133 28 E
Yu Shan, Mt. .... 23 30N 121 0 E
Yuan Kiang, R. .. 28 40N 110 30 E
Yuanling .... 28 30N 110 5 E
Yuanyang .... 23 10N 102 58 E
Yuba City 39 12N 121 45w
Yucatán □ 21 30N 86 30w
Yucatán, Canal de . 22 0N 86 30w
Yucca 34 56N 114 6w
Yudino .... 55 10N 67 55 E
Yuendumu .... 22 16s 131 49 E
Yugoslavia ■ .... 44 0N 20 0 E
Yukikow .... 31 29N 118 17 E

Yukon Territory □ 63 0N 135 0w
Yukon, R. 65 0N 150 0w
Yukti .... 63 20N 105 0 E
Yülin, Hainan ... 18 10N 109 31 E
Yülin
  Kwangsi-Chuang 22 30N 110 50 E
Yuma, Ariz. 32 45N 114 45w
Yuma, Colo. 40 10N 102 43w
Yumen .... 41 13N 96 55 E
Yuna .... 28 20s 115 0 E
Yunndaga .... 29 45s 121 0 E
Yungan .... 25 50N 117 25 E
Yungchun .... 25 20N 118 15 E
Yungfu .... 24 59N 109 59 E
Yungshun .... 29 3N 109 50 E
Yungtsi .... 34 50N 110 25 E
Yunlin .... 23 45N 120 30 E
Yunnan □ .... 25 0N 102 30 E
Yunsiao .... 24 0N 117 20 E
Yunta .... 32 35s 139 33 E
Yurga .... 55 42N 84 51 E
Yuribei .... 71 20N 76 30 E
Yurimaguas 5 55s 76 0w
Yütu .... 5 0N 115 24 E
Yutze .... 37 45N 112 45 E
Yuyang .... 28 44N 108 46 E
Yuyao .... 30 0N 121 20 E
Yuzhno-Sakhalinsk 47 5N 142 5 E
Yvelines □ ...... 48 40N 1 45 E
Yvetot .... 49 37N 0 44 E

Z

Zaandam .... 52 26N 4 49 E
Zabaykalskiy .... 49 40N 117 10 E
Zabid .... 14 10N 43 17 E
Zabol .... 31 0N 61 25 E
Zäboli .... 27 10N 61 35 E
Zabrźe .... 50 24N 18 50 E
Zabul □ .... 32 0N 67 15 E
Zacapa 14 59N 89 31w
Zacatecas 22 49N 102 34w
Zacatecas □ 23 30N 103 0w
Zacatecoluca 13 29N 88 51w
Zadar .... 44 8N 15 8 E
Zadawa .... 11 30N 10 22 E
Zadetkyi Kyun, I. . 10 0N 98 25 E

Zafra 38 26N 6 30w
Zagań .... 51 39N 15 22 E
Zagazig .... 30 40N 31 12 E
Zagnanado .... 7 15N 2 15 E
Zagreb .... 45 50N 16 0 E
Zagros, Kudhā-ye . 33 45N 47 0 E
Zahala .... 32 8N 34 49 E
Zähedān .... 29 30N 60 50 E
Zahlah .... 33 52N 35 50 E
Zaïre ■ .... 3 0s 23 0 E
Zaïre, R. .... 6 4s 12 24 E
Zakamensk .... 50 23N 103 17 E
Zakavkazye ...... 42 0N 44 0 E
Zakhū .... 37 10N 42 50 E
Zákinthos .... 37 47N 20 54 E
Zákinthos, I. ... 37 45N 27 45 E
Zalingei .... 13 5N 23 10 E
Zambeze, R. ..... 18 46s 36 16 E
Zambézia □ ...... 16 15s 37 30 E
Zambia ■ 15 0s 28 0w
Zamboanga .... 6 59N 122 3 E
Zamora, Mexico .. 20 0N 102 21w
Zamora, Sp. 41 30N 5 45w
Zamość .... 50 50N 23 22 E
Zandvoort .... 52 22N 4 32 E
Zanesville 39 56N 82 2w
Zanjan .... 36 40N 48 35 E
Zante, I.=
  Zákinthos, I. .. 37 47N 20 54 E
Zanthus .... 30 55s 123 29 E
Zanzibar .... 6 12s 39 12 E
Zanzibar, I. .... 6 12s 39 12 E
Zaouiet Reggane . 26 32N 0 3 E
Západné
  Beskydy, Mts. . 49 30N 19 0 E
Zapadnyy Sayan .. 53 0N 94 0 E
Zapala 39 0s 70 5w
Zapolyarnyy ..... 69 26N 30 48 E
Zaporozhye ...... 47 50N 35 10 E
Zaragoza 41 39N 0 53w
Zarand .... 30 46N 56 34 E
Zaraza 9 21N 65 19w
Zari .... 13 5N 12 44 E
Zaria 11 0N 7 40w
Zaruma 3 40s 79 30w
Żary .... 51 37N 15 10 E
Zarzis .... 33 31N 11 2 E
Zashiversk ...... 67 25N 142 40 E
Zaskar Mts. ..... 33 15N 77 30 E
Zastron .... 30 18s 27 7 E

Zavareh .... 33 35N 52 28 E
Zavitinsk .... 50 10N 129 20 E
Zawiercie .... 50 30N 19 13 E
Zayarsk .... 56 20N 102 55 E
Zaysan, Oz. ..... 48 0N 83 0 E
Zduńska Wola .... 51 37N 18 59 E
Zealand=
  Sjaelland ..... 55 30N 11 30 E
Zeballos 49 49N 126 50w
Zeebrugge .... 51 19N 3 12 E
Zeehan .... 41 52s 145 25 E
Zeeland □ .... 51 30N 3 50 E
Zeerust .... 25 33s 26 6 E
Zefat .... 32 58N 35 29 E
Zeila .... 11 15N 43 30 E
Zeist .... 52 5N 5 15 E
Zeita .... 32 23N 35 2 E
Zemun .... 44 51N 20 23 E
Zerbst .... 51 59N 12 8 E
Zeya .... 54 2N 127 20 E
Zêzere, R. 40 0N 7 55w
Zhanatas .... 43 11N 81 18 E
Zhdanov .... 47 5N 37 31 E
Zheleznogorsk-
  Ilimskiy ...... 56 34N 104 8 E
Zhigansk .... 66 35N 124 10 E
Zhitomir .... 50 20N 28 40 E
Zhlobin .... 52 55N 30 0 E
Zhupanovo .... 51 59N 15 9 E
Zielona Góra .... 51 57N 15 31 E
Ziguinchor 12 25N 16 20w
Zikhron Ya'aqov . 32 34N 34 56 E
Zile .... 40 15N 36 0 E
Žilina .... 49 12N 18 42 E
Zillah .... 28 40N 17 41 E
Zilling Tso, L. . 31 40N 89 0 E
Zima .... 54 0N 102 5 E
Zimbabwe■=
  Rhodesia ...... 20 0s 28 30 E
Zimnicea .... 43 39N 25 21 E
Zinder .... 13 48N 9 0 E
Ziniaré 12 35N 1 18w
Zinjibar .... 13 5N 46 0 E
Zion Nat. Park ... 37 25N 112 50w
Zipaquira 5 0N 74 0w
Zippori .... 32 64N 35 16 E
Zirko, I. .... 25 0N 53 30 E
Zitácuaro 19 20N 100 30w
Zlatoust .... 55 10N 59 30 E
Zlitan .... 32 25N 14 35 E

Znojmo .... 48 50N 16 2 E
Zoar .... 33 30s 21 58 E
Zohar .... 31 36N 34 42 E
Zomba .... 15 30s 35 19 E
Zonguldak .... 41 28N 31 50 E
Zorgo 12 15N   0 36w

Zorritos .... 3 50 s 80 40w
Zouérabe 22 35N 12 30w
Zrenjanin .... 45 22N 20 23 E
Zuba .... 9 5N   7 10 E
Zuetina .... 30 58N 20 7 E
Zufar, Reg. .... 17 40N 54 0 E

Zug .... 47 10N   8 31 E
Zuid Holland □ ... 52 0N   4 35 E
Zuider Zee=
  Ijsselmeer, L. ... 52 45N   5 20 E
Zula .... 15 17N 39 40 E
Zululand .... 28 15s 31 45 E

Zumbo .... 15 35s 30 26 E
Zürich .... 47 22N   8 32 E
Zuru .... 11 25N   5 12 E
Zutphen .... 52 9N   6 12 E
Zuwarah .... 32 58N 12 1 E
Zverinogolovskoye 55 0N 62 30 E

Zwettl .... 48 35N 15 9 E
Zwickau .... 50 43N 12 30 E
Zwolle .... 52 31N   6 6 E
Zyryanka .... 65 45N 150 51 E
Zyryanovsk ...... 49 43N 84 20 E
Żyrardów .... 52 3N 20 35 E

BIOGRAPHY OF DISCOVERERS

Roald Amundsen was born in Norway in 1877. In 1894 he broke off his medical studies to be trained as a polar explorer. His first journey was to the Antarctic, and it was also here that he made his greatest achievements. From 1897 to 1899 he went as the first officer on the *Belgica* on an expedition to the Antarctic. The ship was icebound for 13 months; so Amundsen took part, involuntarily, in the first wintering in the Antarctic. In 1903–6 he and the Dane Godfred Hansen were the first to sail through the Northwest Passage from Greenland to Alaska. En route they did some extensive magnetic measuring. In 1918–22 he sailed through the Northeast Passage from Norway past the northern coast of the U.S.S.R. The ships were icebound on both voyages for long periods. Amundsen tried in vain to reach the North Pole by drifting with the ice, but he succeeded in crossing the North Pole in 1926 in the airship *Norge.* Perhaps Amundsen's greatest achievement was during the 1910–13 expedition, when he was the first to reach the South Pole, on December 14, 1911.

The expedition traveled 1,400 km (870 miles) in 99 days in order to reach this objective. The Englishman Scott and his men died in an attempt to do the same thing, having crossed the South Pole one month after Amundsen.

Christopher Columbus was born in Genoa in northern Italy in 1451, the son of a wool spinner. After an unsettled boyhood, during which on his many travels he learned to read and write, he married the daughter of a Portuguese courtier in 1479, thereby gaining access to the leading circles of society. However, his plan to find a passage to India by sailing west did not meet with favor in Portugal, and Columbus did not succeed in persuading the Spanish king and queen to equip an expedition until 1492. On August 3, 1492, three ships (the *Santa Maria,* the *Pinta,* and the *Nina*) with a crew of 100 men, under the command of Columbus, sailed across the Atlantic. The following year he returned home with two of the ships, having been to the Canary Islands, the Bahamas, Cuba, and Haiti.

Columbus received a wonderful welcome and left again the same year (second voyage, 1493–96), this time with 17 ships and 1,500 men. On his voyage he visited the Lesser Antilles, Puerto Rico, and Jamaica, but when he returned home without any wealth, the enthusiasm was restrained. However, Columbus went on two more voyages (1498–1500 and 1502–4), on which he discovered the mouth of the river Orinoco and visited Central America (Honduras). His last voyages were eclipsed by the achievements of other seafarers, and Columbus – who believed throughout his life that he had discovered India – died in 1506, a disappointed man.

James Cook, born in Yorkshire in England, the son of a farmer, worked his way up through the ranks in his young days, first as the captain on colliers in English coastal waters and then in the Canadian navy, for which he did some very exact surveys of the coast of Newfoundland. Thus he was a very experienced navigator when he was given the task by the English government in 1768

BIOGRAPHY OF DISCOVERERS

of exploring the Pacific Ocean, which was still thought to be covered by large areas of land between the equator and 50° southern latitude. Cook made his first voyage from August 1768 to June 1771. From England he sailed south of South America and via the Society Islands to areas where it was thought there was land, but where Cook found only water. And from there to New Zealand, where he discovered the passage between the two main islands (Cook Strait). During the following exploration of the east coast of Australia, the ship ran aground on a coral reef but came free and sailed to Batavia, where the damage was repaired. The crew, who had received exemplary treatment from Cook by the standards of those days, were afflicted by illness here, so many died before their return to England.

On the next voyage (1772–74) Cook had two ships – again of a rather broad, flat-bottomed type – which could sail close to the shore. This time he succeeded in making the first circumnavigation of the world from west to east, and by going far south in the Pacific Ocean finally killed the myth of the "southern continent." He also explored a large number of the islands in the ocean.

On his third voyage (1776–79), Cook tried in vain to find a passage from the Pacific Ocean to Hudson Bay (the Northwest Passage). On the way home he reached Hawaii, where he was killed by the natives in a minor battle.

Leif Ericsson was born in Iceland in about 970, the son of the chieftain Eric the Red. His father was banished, for committing murder, for three years from about 985 and traveled west and explored the coasts of western Greenland during the following years. His son Leif, who went along on these expeditions as a boy, went off on long voyages himself in the years around 1000. In 999 he was in Norway, where he was baptized, and in the following years he went on his famous voyages to the east coast of North America. It is difficult to locate the places Leif Ericsson and his people visited from the sagas, but a settlement from about 1000, found on the northern point of Newfoundland, is considered to be from his expedition, and it is likely that he was in Labrador and maybe even as far south as Cape Cod (near what is now Boston).

During their stay in Vinland (= grassland) the Norsemen met the natives, with whom they had minor clashes. During the next decades the Norsemen from Greenland often sailed across to North America for timber, but they do not appear to have settled anywhere.

Vasco da Gama was born in 1469, the son of a high-ranking Portuguese court official.

In the latter half of the 14th century the Portuguese were very intent on finding the passage south of Africa to India. Already in 1448 Bartolomeu Diaz rounded the southern point of Africa, but only in July 1497, when King Manoel sent Vasco da Gama off with four small ships and about 150 men, was there any great progress in the explo-

BIOGRAPHY OF DISCOVERERS

ration of the Indian Ocean: the ships sailed via the Cape Verde Islands south of Africa and explored parts of the east coast of Africa, where they met Arab traders, from whom they tried to get information about a passage farther across the Indian Ocean. On May 20, 1498, the expedition landed at Calicut on the Malabar Coast. After what was often a dramatic journey along the coast (to Goa, among other places), the expedition returned home in October and reached Lisbon in July 1499, with vast supplies of spices. Vasco da Gama received a peerage, was appointed admiral, and sent back to India in 1502–3, this time with a larger fleet. First, they sailed to Brazil, down the coast of South America and from there via the Cape of Good Hope to India, where the Portuguese put down Indian and Arab resistance, often with great cruelty. Within a short time their fleet had military control of the Indian Ocean and its coasts, and their trade ships were able to return home with very handsome profits.

During the following years Vasco da Gama worked at home in Portugal planning voyages. When trouble broke out in India in 1524, he was sent out with the title of viceroy but died shortly after.

Alexander von Humboldt was born in Berlin in 1769 into a German noble family. After a successful career in the city administration, from 1797 he turned to research and became one of the greatest geographers and naturalists of his day. In the years 1799–1804 he traveled to Venezuela, where he made detailed studies and collected scientific material, especially from the Orinoco area. He also traveled to Colombia, Ecuador, Peru, Mexico, and Cuba. These expeditions have been called the "second discovery of South America."

In 1829 he explored farther west – and south Siberia. His aim was to write a book in which all aspects of nature – everything known both on earth and in the universe – were dealt with. The result: the work *Cosmos* in five volumes was of a fantastic quality for the times, and von Humboldt is considered a pioneer particularly within the fields of plant geography and climatology.

Ferdinand Magellan was born in about 1480 in Portugal. In his youth he went on voyages all the way to Malacca, but after several disappointing refusals from the Portuguese king, he entered the services of the king of Spain. Thus his dream of looking for a passage to the Moluccas, south of America, came within his reach. On September 20, 1519, five ships with a crew of 270 men sailed from San Lucar in Spain under the command of Magellan. On December 13 they reached the bay at Rio de Janeiro, but only on December 1, the following year, did the three remaining ships manage to sail through what later became known as the Strait of Magellan. After much hunger, thirst, and illness, Magellan reached the Mariana Islands on March 6, 1521, and thus Europeans had crossed the Pacific Ocean for the first time. The voyage continued to the Philippines, where they made friends with the king of Cebu, who granted Spain a trade monopoly with the island.

BIOGRAPHY OF DISCOVERERS

Magellan was killed when he tried to help the king quell a local uprising. The two remaining ships with 115 men sailed on to the Moluccas, among other places, but only one – the *Victoria* – arrived back in Spain, on September 6, 1522, with 18 of the original 270 men. The first circumnavigation of the world was at an end. The Moluccas remained Portuguese, but Spain secured control of the Philippines.

The Nautilus *expedition.* During the years 1952–54 the U.S.A. built the first nuclear-powered submarine in the world and named it *Nautilus,* after the submarine in Jules Verne's *Twenty Thousand Leagues Under the Sea,* published in 1870. *Nautilus* could sail fast (up to 20 knots) and, unlike other submarines, could stay underwater for long periods. This attribute was made use of in 1958, when the submarine was the first to cross the Arctic Ocean under the ice. The voyage had a military purpose and was also part of the intensive exploration of the seabed that took place during the International Geophysical Year

1957/58. The *Nautilus* sailed, under the command of Comdr. W. R. Anderson, from Pearl Harbor on July 23, 1958, dived under the ice at Point Barrow, Alaska, on August 1, and reached the North Pole after 1,830 miles on August 3 at 11:15 P.M. (EDT). The voyage under the ice continued for an additional 1,200 miles until the *Nautilus* reached open water between Svalbard and Greenland. The journey beneath the ice had taken 96 hours, and in that time the crew had, by means of an echo sounder, gained further knowledge of the ranges of mountains and chasms that lie beneath the ice, the first of which (the Lomonosov Range) had been found by the U.S.S.R. in 1948. Later surveys, both from stations on ice islands and from nuclear-powered submarines, have increased this knowledge so that the Arctic Ocean has by and large been charted.

Robert E. Peary, born in 1856 in the U.S.A., started his career as a marine engineer and ended up as a rear admiral. Inspired by the Swede Nordenskiöld's

book about Greenland, he traveled there in 1886 and was so fascinated by the country that he spent almost all his life exploring the polar region. His main objective was to reach the North Pole itself, which he succeeded in doing on April 6, 1909; he was the first to do so.

There was a lot of lengthy preparation, but this in itself led to several discoveries: during the 1891–95 expedition Peary proved that Greenland is an island by exploring the northern coast right up to Independence Bay. From 1898 to 1902 he surveyed the northern coast even more thoroughly, and the northernmost part of Greenland has since been called Peary Land.

Around the turn of the century there was a veritable race to get to the North Pole. During the 1890's it was established that the area around the North Pole is sea and not land. Therefore, meticulous preparation was necessary in order to be able to cross the ice to the North Pole. Peary had depots set up and sent reconnaissance teams in advance, so that it was easier for the actual expedition, and as the ice situation in

BIOGRAPHY OF DISCOVERERS

1909 was favorable, he and Matthew Henson succeeded in reaching their goal. They tried to sound the depth of the sea at the North Pole but were only able to ascertain that their 2,300-meter (7,546-foot) sounding line was too short (the depth was later measured to be 4,290 meters, or 14,075 feet). Peary and Henson were only at the North Pole for a short time and traveled the 776 km (428 miles) back in 16 days.

Abel Janszoon Tasman, born in about 1603 in Groningen, is considered the greatest Dutch seafarer and discoverer. From the beginning of the 1630's he sailed for the Dutch East India Company to Thailand, Cambodia, and Japan, among other countries.

In 1642 he was assigned the task of exploring the Antarctic Ocean and looking for the "southern continent," which was thought to exist as a southern extension of Australia. For this voyage he was given two extremely well-equipped ships. After sailing for 10 months, only 10 men out of the crew of 110 had died of illness, a very small number in those days.

On October 8, 1642, they sailed from Mauritius southeast to latitude 44° and then east until on November 23 they reached the island that was named Tasmania after the leader of the expedition. On December 13, the ships reached New Zealand and from there sailed to New Guinea via Tonga and Fiji. In June 1643 Tasman reached Batavia and had thus – without knowing it – sailed around Australia. The "southern continent," after this discovery, could not go farther south than Tasmania, but it was not known how far east it extended. In 1644 Tasman was sent to explore the area between New Guinea and Australia. He did not find the Torres Strait, and when he observed barren coast along the Gulf of Carpentaria and along the east coast of Australia, the company was not interested in further voyages of discovery.

Tasman worked for the company until 1653 and died in 1659.

Charles Wilkes, born in New York in 1798, started his career in the U.S. Navy at the age of 20. In 1838 he was given the task of leading the first expedition sent to the Antarctic continent by the American Congress. The expedition included people from many fields of science. They sailed from the U.S.A. to Sydney and from there to the Antarctic, where they explored the ice barrier from 150° to 97° east. Since then the area has been called Wilkes Land. On the outward journey the expedition visited Samoa and New South Wales, and on the way north Fiji and Hawaii (1840), among other places. During 1841 Wilkes explored the west coast of the U.S.A., and from there he sailed across the Pacific Ocean to the islands south of Asia and onward south of Africa to New York, where he arrived in June 1842.

From 1844 to 1861 Wilkes worked on publishing 19 large volumes – 7 of which he wrote himself – on the results of the expedition.

Voyages of Discovery

Roald Amundsen	1897–1899
	1903–1906
Christopher Columbus	1492–1493
	1493–1496
	1498–1500
	1502–1504
James Cook	1768–1771
	1772–1774
	1776–1779
Leif Ericsson	about 1000
Vasco da Gama	1497–1499
	1502–1503
Alexander von Humboldt	1799–1804
	1829
Ferdinand Magellan	1519–1522
Nautilus Expedition	1958
Robert E. Peary	1891–1895
	1898–1902
	1909
Abel Janszoon Tasman	1642–1643
	1644
Charles Wilkes	1838–1840
	1841–1842

Space Travel

Vostok 1	U.S.S.R.	Gagarin	4/12/61	The first man in space
Freedom 2	U.S.A.	Shepard	5/5/61	The first American in space
Apollo 11	U.S.A.	Armstrong	7/16/69 to	The first man on the moon
		Collins	7/24/69	
		Aldrin		

Summary of the First Six Manned Apollo Experiments

	Apollo 7	Apollo 8	Apollo 9	Apollo 10	Apollo 11	Apollo 12
sent up	10/11/68	12/21/68	3/3/69	5/18/69	7/16/69	11/14/69
taken down	10/22/68	12/27/68	3/13/69	5/26/69	7/24/69	11/24/69
duration	$10^د20^h09^m$	$6^د03^h00^m$	$10^د01^h01^m$	$8^د00^h03^m$	$8^د03^h18^m$	$10^د04^h36^m$
distance (km)	7,200,000	990,000	6,800,000	1,220,000	1,170,000	1,360,000
orbited earth	163 times	2 times	151 times	2 times	2 times	2 times
orbited moon	no	10 times	no	31 times	30 times	45 times
carried sections	CM + SM	CM + SM	CM + SM + LM	CM + SM + LM	CM + SM + LM	CM + SM + LM
landing site on the earth	27°N, 64°W in western Atlantic	8°N, 165°W in central Pacific	23°N, 66°W in western Atlantic	15°S, 164°W in central Pacific	13°N, 169°W in central Pacific	15°S, 165°W in central Pacific
landing site on the moon	none	none	none	none	0.8°N, 23.5°E Sea of Tranquility	3.0°S, 23.4°W Ocean of Storms
commanding pilot in LM	Walter M. Schirra	Frank Borman	James A. McDivitt	Thomas P. Stafford	Neil A. Armstrong	Charles Conrad, Jr.
CM pilot	Donn E. Eisele	James A. Lowell	David R. Scott	John W. Young	Michael Collins	Richard F. Gordon, Jr.
LM pilot	R. Walter Cunningham	William A. Anders	Russell L. Schweickart	Eugene A. Cernan	Edwin E. Aldrin, Jr.	Alan L. Bean

NB: CM means command module, SM service module, LM lunar module.

Ever since antiquity, people of inquiring minds have wanted a picture of the earth we live on. You are now the owner of a globe, the only accurate reproduction of the earth. With this globe you can see the correct size of lands and oceans, measure distances and areas, find differences in time, locate historic places, and follow daily events mentioned in newspapers and on radio and television. You can put your finger on the political and strategic focal points and better understand the influence of geographical conditions. Schoolwork becomes more enjoyable and understandable, and students are more interested and well informed.

Besides being a source of knowledge, this globe is decorative. Your family and friends will admire its elegant design and the beautiful lithographed maps printed in 10 colors.

History of the Globe

Today everyone knows the earth is round, but when Pythagoras, a Greek mathematician and philosopher who lived about 2,500 years ago, postulated this, his views were considered very farfetched. Somewhat later – about 200 B.C. – the Greek astronomer Eratosthenes was able to compute the size of the earth fairly accurately by observing the height of the sun above the horizon in two places on the same longitude and measuring the distance between the two spots. However, notions of the earth were mainly guesswork, since large parts of it had not yet been discovered.

The first known model of the earth in the shape of a globe – made by a Greek, Crates, in 150 B.C. – showed four continents separated by oceans because people thought that four continents were necessary for the sake of balance.

For hundreds of years the Greek theories about the earth's shape were ignored in Europe, but when the great voyages of discovery were about to begin, these ideas were revived and extended, and one of the greatest revolutions in the intellectual life of Europe

Fig. 1. Gerardus Mercator and Jodocus Hondius, famous Dutch mapmakers of the 16th century, in an engraving from a Mercator-Hondius atlas of about 1612.

took place. By completing the first voyage around the world, Magellan's expedition (1519–22) supplied incontrovertible proof that the world was round. At the same time astronomers Copernicus (1473–1543) and Kepler (1571–1630) discovered that the earth was a planet like all the other planets that move around the sun. However, the old notions of the earth as the flat and stationary center of the universe died very slowly. Thus, because he had taught otherwise, the Italian astronomer Galileo (1564–1642) was sentenced by the church to a weekly recital of seven penitential psalms and was compelled to swear that the earth did not turn on its own axis. In 1600 the Italian philosopher Giordano Bruno died at the stake for contending, among other things, that the earth was round.

Naturally, the voyages of discovery gave renewed impetus to the manufacturing of globes, which were greatly prized by scientists as well as statesmen. They were exceedingly difficult to make and very expensive to buy. Thus, in the 17th century a Venetian, Coronelli, could demand a life annuity for making only two globes (which are now among the oldest in existence).

Nowadays globes are mass-produced and are available to everyone. At the same time, there is a greater need for globes because of the necessity of keep-

Fig. 2. Nicolaus Copernicus (1473-1543) demonstrated that the sun was the center of the solar system, not the earth, as earlier astronomers had believed.

Fig. 3. The Abbé Picard's quadrant of 1669 (modeled on an instrument made by the Danish astronomer Tycho Brahe) replaced the usual pinhole sights with a telescope.

Fig. 4. Vasco da Gama, Portuguese explorer, rounded Africa to reach India in 1498.

ing up with rapid changes in social, economic, cultural, religious, and political affairs and seeing how they are influenced by geographical conditions.

The most important voyages of discovery after the 15th century
1. Christopher Columbus (1492–93)
2. Amerigo Vespucci (1497–99)
3. Vasco da Gama (1497–98)
4. Ferdinand Magellan (1519–22)
5. Sir Francis Drake (1577–80)
6. Abel Janszoon Tasman (1642–44)
7. James Cook (1768–71)
8. Charles Wilkes (1840)
9. Roald Amundsen (1911)
10. The *Nautilus* cruise (1955–58)

Fig. 5. Ferdinand Magellan, Portuguese explorer, sailed west toward the Moluccas in 1519 and claimed them for Spain.

Why a globe?

What makes a globe a necessary supplement to good maps? For one thing, the surface of the earth can be depicted completely correctly only on a globe. The earth's spherical shape, as can be mathematically proved, cannot be represented with true fidelity on a flat surface. This means that all available maps contain errors – area errors, angular errors, and distance errors – and the larger an area the maps cover, the more pronounced the errors become; these are especially noticeable in maps of the whole world.

For example, maritime maps or charts, which are often drawn on the Mercator projection, may depict the whole earth except for the polar regions. It is important that the maps not have angular errors, so that one can chart a course directly on the map. However, as a closer look will reveal, there is so much distortion in area sizes that South America covers almost the same area as Greenland, even though South America is actually more than six times the size of Greenland.

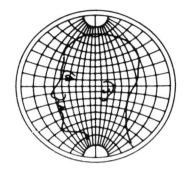 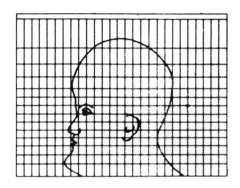

Fig. 6. Different projections (as the mapmaker's methods of presenting the shape of the earth's surface are called) will give very different versions of the same thing. The two illustrations show the same face, drawn in the same grid used for map drawing. A globe presents the earth's face without distortions.

A globe has a uniform scale, thus enabling you to make direct comparisons of different areas, to recognize their location relative to one another, and to determine the distance between them. The globe has a meridian attached to the two poles divided into degrees, nautical miles, and kilometers, so it is easy to measure the shortest distance between any two points on the earth.

Another advantage of a globe is that it gives a true idea of some of the important astronomical conditions of the earth. This will be explained in the sections on the earth and the solar system, the rotation of the earth, the earth's revolution around the sun, and the astronomical year.

How to Use Your Globe

Determination of location on the earth
When determining the location of a place on the earth, you use a number of imaginary lines: the lines of longitude, or meridians, which are great circles – circles with the same diameter as the equator – connecting the poles (Fig. 7A), and the lines of latitude, which are parallel to the equator, itself a line of latitude (Fig. 7B). Lines of latitude and lines of longitude intersect at right angles (Fig. 7C).

The meridian running through the original site of the Royal Observatory at Greenwich, near London, is the prime meridian (0°), and from it longitude is measured 180 degrees east and 180 degrees west, giving a total of 360 degrees. The reason for choosing Greenwich was probably London's vital importance in international trade. Among the lines previously suggested for prime meridian are the line running through the observatory at Paris and the line running through the westernmost point of Europe, Cape Finisterre ("the end of the earth") in Spain. Latitude is measured 90 degrees north and 90 degrees south

Fig. 7.

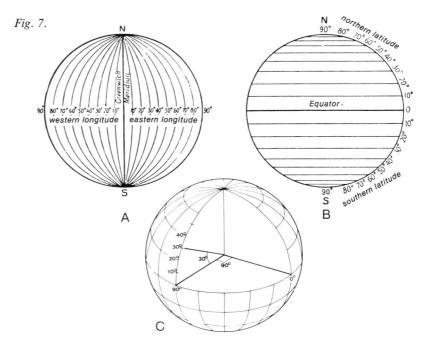

of the equator, which is designated 0°, giving a total of 180 degrees. To describe the location of a place, state the number of the nearest line of longitude and whether it is east or west of the Greenwich meridian (east longitude or west longitude, abbreviated E and W). Then give the number of the nearest line of latitude and its location north or south of the equator (north latitude or south latitude, abbreviated N and S). Your globe shows every 15 meridians and every 10 parallels.

Example: You want to describe the location of Paris. Rotate the globe so that one edge of the metal meridian (the one with the figures) goes through Paris. You can now read that Paris is located a little south of 50° N. Then checking where the edge of the metal meridian cuts the equator, you can see it is a little east of 2° E. For a more precise determination of location, you can use the finer division into minutes and seconds. Each degree, that is, the distance between two lines of longitude or latitude, is divided into 60 minutes and each minute into 60 seconds. The exact

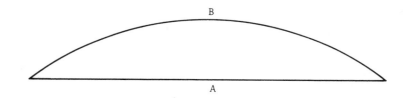

Fig. 8. On the earth's curved surface, line B is shorter than line A.

location of Paris (the observatory) is then 48°50′0″ N and 2°20′14″ E.

Shortest distance between any two points on the earth

The shortest distance between any two points on the earth is the arc of the great circle passing through them. Determine the length of the arc by laying a strip of material – marked for miles or degrees (1° = 68.9 miles = 111 km) – between the two points on the globe. Prepare the strip by placing it along the equator, marking out the distances between the degrees of longitude. With globes having a detachable meridian divided into degrees, you can directly measure distances.

Time

From time immemorial the position of the sun in the sky has determined the measurement of time. When the sun is highest, it is true noon according to solar time. All points located on the same longitude have noon at the same time. Because of the rotation of the earth from west to east, a place located 15 degrees to the west of another will have noon an hour later (360° ÷ 24 hours = 15°), or in other words, a difference in longitude of 15 degrees corresponds to a difference in time of one hour, and a difference in longitude of one degree corresponds to a difference in time of four minutes (Fig. 9).

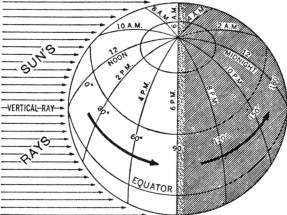

Fig. 9. Solar time when it is noon on the Greenwich meridian. The arrows to the left indicate the direction of the sun's rays. The arrows on the earth indicate the direction of rotation.

Time dial

Around the North Pole of your globe there is a time dial, a metal dial divided into 24 equal parts corresponding to the meridians of the globe. With this dial you can quickly see the difference in true solar time between any two points on the earth.

True solar time is not practical for train schedules and the like, so the earth has been divided into time zones. Each zone is 15 degrees and extends 7½ degrees on either side of 0°, 15°, 30°, 45°, and so forth. However, in many places the boundaries of the zones follow the political boundaries nearby (see Fig. 10). Although the time dial indicates solar time, you can see from Figure 10 whether zone time deviates from solar time.

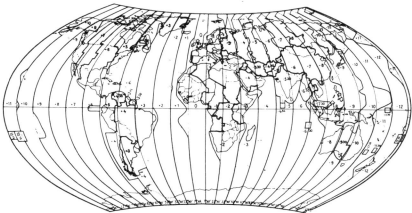

Fig. 10. Standard time zones. Certain countries, such as India, use the zone time throughout the nation. Other countries use only local solar time.

The international date line

Often called the Sunday-Monday line, the international date line runs largely along the 180th meridian (Fig. 10). If you travel from the west to the east, you will have to set your watch one hour ahead for every 15 degrees you travel, which means that by traveling that way around the world, you will gain 24 hours, so simply count the same date twice when you pass the date line. It is just the opposite if you travel from the east to the west: you will have to set your watch back one hour for every 15 degrees and will thus lose 24 hours during a trip around the world, so when passing the date line, tear an extra page out of your calendar.

We can illustrate this by using the time dial. When it is midnight in Paris, the night between Sunday and Monday, it is 11 : 30 A.M. Monday just west of the date line and 11 : 30 A.M. Sunday just east of the date line.

Shape and size of the earth

Precise measurements have shown that the earth is not completely spherical but a little flattened at the poles because of the earth's rotation on its axis, an imaginary line through its poles and its center. However, the flattening is so slight that it would hardly be visible on an ordinary globe.

The earth's polar radius is 3,947 miles (6,356.9 km).

The earth's equatorial radius is 3,961 miles (6,378.4 km).

The earth's polar circumference is 24,842 miles (40,003.4 km).

The earth's equatorial circumference is 24,884 miles (40,070.4 km).

The earth's surface is 193,781,271 square miles (509,950,714.0 km^2).

The earth's volume is 259,318,800,000 cubic miles (1,082,841,300,000.0 km^3).

Rotation (equator): 23 hours and 56 minutes

Speed: 1,037 miles (1,670 km) per hour

Inclination of the equator to the plane of the earth's orbit: 23.5°

Average speed of rotation of the earth around the sun: 67,068 miles (108,000 km) per hour

Distance to the moon

Nearest at perigee: 221,076 miles (356,000 km)

Farthest away at apogee: 252,747 miles (407,000 km)

Average: 238,464 miles (384,000 km)

On globes with a diameter of 30 cm the equatorial circumference is 0.96 m and the scale thus 1 : about 42,000,000. For globes with a diameter of 25 cm the figures are 0.80 m and 1 : about 50,000,000. For globes with a diameter of 15 cm the figures are 0.48 m and 1 : about 84,000,000.

The earth and the solar system

The globe is a good picture of the earth, but this picture has been further improved and supplemented by observations and photographs of the earth from satellites (Fig. 11). These photographs have given us proof that the earth is spherical and that it moves. Space research has also provided information about the other planets and their moons and about the sun. Nothing has dispelled the idea that among the countless

stars there may be other solar systems with planets, including some similar to our earth. They could be in our Milky Way galaxy or in one of the many others thousands of light-years away.

The earth is the third planet from the sun, one of nine planets moving – together with their moons – in elliptical orbits around the sun (Fig. 12). Planets and moons are dark, or nonluminous, celestial bodies (moonshine as well as earthshine on the moon is reflected sunshine), whereas the sun is one of the innumerable luminous stars in our galaxy.

The rotation of the earth

Let us look more closely at the two motions of the earth in the solar system: as already mentioned, it rotates on its own axis and at the same time it revolves around the sun. These two motions do not occur in the same plane, and that is why the axis runs obliquely through a globe.

If we imagine that the earth revolves around the sun in a plane parallel to the base of the globe, then the plane of the

Fig. 11. Clouds over the equator. Clouds over the Amazon delta photographed from Apollo 9. The cloud cover is not continuous; there is no general layer, and the clouds are chiefly of the cumulus type.

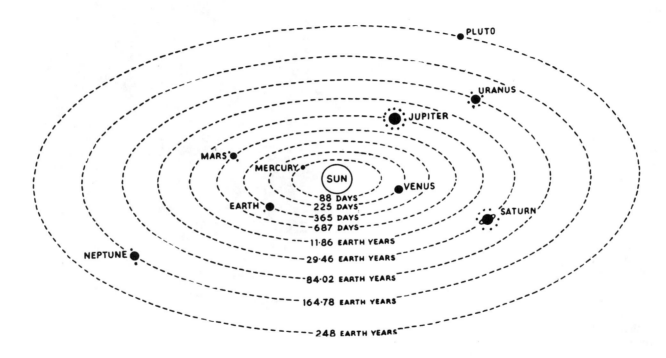

Fig. 12. The solar system showing the planets and their moons and their orbits around the sun. The figures indicate the time it takes the planets to complete one revolution around the sun.

equator, which is at a right angle to the axis of rotation, forms an angle of 23 ½ ° with the former plane, as shown in Figure 14. Today the exact angle between the two planes is 23°27′8″, but it varies in the course of an unknown period that is at least 20,000 years.

The earth moves from west to east (counterclockwise) on its axis, shown on the globe by a metal rod on which the globe rotates. It takes the earth about 24 hours (23 hours, 56 minutes, 4.09 seconds) to complete such a rotation; this means that a point at the equator is moving at a speed of about 1,037 miles (1,670 km) per hour. Naturally, this speed decreases with the distance from the equator and is 0 at the poles. The earth's rotation causes day and night: it is day on the side facing the sun and night on the side away from the sun.

Compass needle

Fig. 13. Demonstration of the revolution of the earth around the sun. The earth's North Pole must always point in the same direction as the north pole of the compass needle.

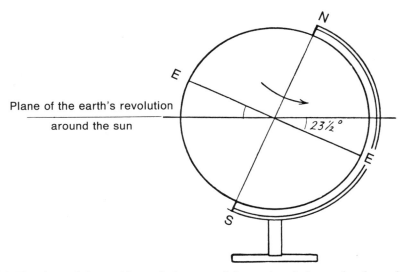

Fig. 14. The plane of the earth's revolution around the sun in relation to the plane of the equator. N = North Pole. S = South Pole. E–E = Equator.

The earth's revolution around the sun

The earth revolves counterclockwise around the sun, taking a year to complete the distance of about 577 million miles (930 million km). The earth's orbit is not a circle, as was formerly assumed, but an ellipse. Since the sun is at one focus of the ellipse (Fig. 15), the distance between the earth and the sun is not the same throughout the year, and the speed of the earth's revolution varies accordingly, being highest when the distance between the two bodies is shortest (December 31). The average speed is 18.6 miles (30 km) per second, or 67,068 miles (108,000 km) per hour.

When the earth revolves around the sun, its axis points toward the north pole of the heavens (approximately the location of the North Star). Using a compass, you can place the globe correctly and demonstrate the earth's revolution around the sun.

The astronomical year

While the calendar year commences on January 1, the astronomical year starts on March 21, when the sun is said to

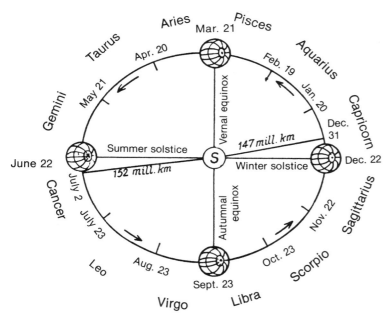

be at the vernal equinox (see Fig. 15). The astronomical year – the time it takes the sun to return to the vernal equinox – is exactly 365 days, 6 hours, 9 minutes, 11 seconds. This is the reason for intercalary days, days that are inserted in the calendar once in a while.

Fig. 15. The earth's revolution around the sun. Note that the earth's greatest distance from the sun falls on July 2 and the shortest distance on December 31. Around the earth's orbit are the names of the constellations that make up the zodiac. The figure shows how the sun, as seen from the earth, passes through the constellations of the zodiac. Note, for instance, that on December 22 the sun enters the sign of Capricorn and on June 22 the sign of Cancer. On March 21 the sun enters the sign of Aries and is then at the vernal equinox.

The seasons; astronomical zones

If the earth's axis were perpendicular to the plane of the earth's orbit, the temperature at any one place on the earth would be the same all year, and large parts of the earth would be uninhabitable because of the cold. However, due to the tilting of the earth's axis, more heat alternately hits the Northern and Southern hemispheres (see Fig. 16 – note that vertical rays heat more than oblique rays).

Let us look first at June 22 (summer solstice): a–a are the sun's rays, which are tangent to the earth; b–b are the polar circles, 66½° N and S (90° − 23½°); c–c is the Tropic of Cancer, which is at 23½° N, where the sun is overhead. Thus, the Northern Hemisphere has summer because here the sun's rays form wider angles than on the Southern Hemisphere, and the sun's rays strike all of the earth north of the Arctic Circle, while everything south of the Antarctic Circle is in darkness.

In the figure to the right (December 22, winter solstice) the sun is overhead at the Tropic of Capricorn (d–d), and

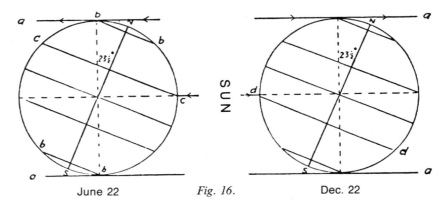

June 22   *Fig. 16.*   Dec. 22

then the Southern Hemisphere has summer. On March 21 and September 23 the sun is overhead at the equator, and both poles receive the same amount of sunshine.

From the above it appears that the earth has five astronomical zones (Fig. 17). In the middle zone, the torrid zone, once or twice a year the sun is directly overhead (at zenith) at all places between the zone's boundaries, the Tropic of Cancer and the Tropic of Capricorn.

The two belts surrounding the poles are called the frigid zones; they have one or several days of midnight sun in the summer and one or several days of midwinter dark. At the poles the length of the day is six months, and so is the length of the night. Between the torrid zone and the frigid zones are the two Temperate Zones, or the middle latitude zones, where the sun is never at zenith and where there is never any midnight sun.

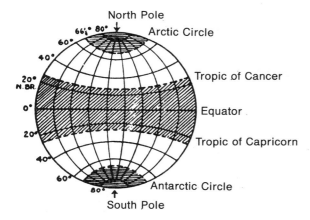

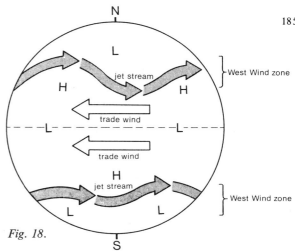

Fig. 17. The astronomical zones. Horizontally shaded: Places with midnight sun. Cross-shaded: Places where the sun can be at zenith, that is, perpendicular to the earth. In the zones in between, neither phenomenon occurs.

Fig. 18.

The climatic zones of the earth are divided in approximately the same way, but due to the distribution of land and oceans, which are not heated equally, nor cooled equally, the climatic zones show rather great deviations from the astronomical zones.

Jet streams

The heating of the earth and its atmosphere by the sun varies widely from place to place, and the heated air masses expand and move upward. This and the earth's rotation on its axis cause currents (winds) to arise in the atmosphere. At an altitude of three to six miles (5 to 10 km) they will form a pattern similar to the one in Figure 18. The jet streams are largely westerlies; in these, whirls form in different ways and move in the direction of the main current, that is, mostly eastward.

Satellite photographs of the earth are invaluable aids to meteorology, particularly for weather forecasting, because they show these whirls very clearly. The whirls can provide exact information about the air pressure and the corresponding cloud formations and precipitation. Since meteorologists receive satellite photographs at short intervals, they can see how the whirls move and can measure their speed and direction.

Oceans

One of the first things you notice on a globe is that most of the earth is covered with water. On earlier globes the ocean was plain blue, and on some globes arrows of different colors indicated ocean currents, blue for cold currents, red for warm ones. (A warm or cold current is one that is warmer or colder than the average temperature of the ocean at the given latitude.)

There is a connection between the steadier winds or wind systems at the surface of the earth and the big ocean currents. In turn the ocean currents influence the climate. It is generally known that the warm Gulf Stream affects the temperature in western Europe. It may be less well known that the cold Canaries Current is largely responsible for the dry climate in North Africa. The air gets dry when passing from the cold ocean to the warm land, and there is little precipitation.

More recent globes show the relief of the ocean floor, which is just as varied as the dry surfaces of the earth. There are enormous mountain ranges, steep slopes, deep canyons, and large plains. This varied terrain results from the movement of large plates that make up the earth's crust. These plates move both horizontally and vertically because of currents in the interior of the earth (Fig. 19). There is evidence of this in the Atlantic where a submerged mountain range, the Mid-Atlantic Ridge, extends throughout the middle and length of the ocean. Here the American plate moves west while the Eurasian and African plates move east, producing a fracture where the fluid interior of the earth pushes surfaceward as lava, forming volcanoes. Iceland is situated on part of the Mid-Atlantic Ridge that has become land. The volcanic fracture practically traverses the island. On the globe you can see that the Mid-Atlantic Ridge describes a curve south of Africa into the Indian Ocean, where it divides and continues through the Red Sea and on land into the big African trough fault (Great Rift valley), where there are also a number of volcanoes.

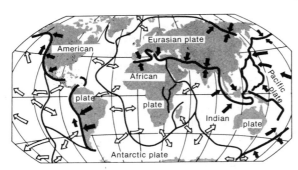

Fig. 19. Areas with upward-flowing convection currents (white arrows) and areas where the crustal plates are sinking (black arrows) (Wilson, 1963).

In other places the land is sinking, for instance, near the West Coast of the United States; at the same time the westerly plate gets displaced northward relative to the easterly plate. Between the two plates is the San Andreas Fault, which extends through California. The displacement along the fault does not take place smoothly but jerkily, thus causing earthquakes. Figure 19 gives you an idea of the areas where earthquakes are prevalent.

The globe also shows the shallow parts of the oceans where the floor is actually part of the continent. Many such places, for instance, in the North Sea, the Gulf of Mexico, and the Persian Gulf, have become oil fields.

Vegetation

Technical developments have made it possible to show several things on the same globe. The old globes showed either the earth's political divisions or its elevations. Now that the relief, mountain ranges, and plains of the earth can be shown on a political globe, important types of vegetation appear instead of elevations. On the globe you get a clear picture of the surprisingly small area of the earth that is cultivated and the large stretches of tundra and forests.

Weather and Weather Instruments

Weather plays a vital role in our daily lives. Its severity may threaten our emotional and physical health, and it can determine the prosperity of an entire area. Weather has even decided the outcome of battles and wars, thereby affecting the destiny of nations. Every day, even every hour, weather influences human decisions. It is understandable, therefore, that we should want to know something about meteorology.

During the past few decades meteorology has developed into an accurate science. The results of this research, visible to the public, are the daily weather forecasts. These cover an extended region and, therefore, can only indicate the general atmospheric conditions. One's own observations and a good barometer can supplement these forecasts to predict local weather.

The barometer

The mercury barometer (invented in 1643 by Torricelli) consists of an 80-centimeter glass pipe that is void of air and closed on the top. The lower end opens into a container filled with mercury. Because of the vacuum the mercury rises about 76 cm in the pipe. The rise or fall of the column of mercury indicates the changes in the weight of the air, or atmospheric pressure. These changes are read on a scale divided into millimeters.

The metal, or aneroid, barometer is a flat metal box, nearly void of air, with a pointer on the top. Changes in atmospheric pressure bend the top of the box in or out and move the pointer. Increasing atmospheric pressure (high) moves the pointer to the right, the barometer rises; falling atmospheric pressure (low) moves the arrow to the left, the barometer falls.

Atmospheric pressure

The atmosphere surrounds the earth, and the atmospheric pressure constantly changes, depending on temperature and water content. Cold, dry air is heavier than warm, humid air. A barometer can determine the temperature and the water content from the weight of the air. A thermometer indicates only the present temperature, a hygrometer indicates only the present water content, but a barometer registers the current climatic state and monitors the development of atmospheric conditions.

The movement of warm and cold air masses creates air currents (wind). Air masses warmed by the sun expand, press against colder air masses, and move on top. This movement causes temperature changes that may result in precipitation (rain, snow, hail, etc.). This constant collision of air masses causes air waves/air mountains (a high) and air valleys/funnel-shaped vortices (a low). The weight of the air for a high is greater than for a low.

With the help of the recorded curve of the register barometer, one can observe how air mountains and air valleys are moving over a given location. During high pressure the weather is generally lovely. During low pressure the weather is usually rainy and stormy. In the overlapping areas the weather is subject to change.

Weather rules
1. Stable atmospheric pressure: continuance of the present atmospheric condition.
2. Slowly rising atmospheric pressure: good, stable weather.
3. Slowly falling atmospheric pressure: bad, continuous weather.
4. Rapidly rising atmospheric pressure: fast, temporary change to good weather.
5. Rapidly falling atmospheric pressure: fast change to bad weather.
6. Strong fall of atmospheric pressure: storm.

How to set a barometer
The aneroid barometer is set for low altitudes and registers correctly in locations no higher than approximately 100 feet (30 m) above sea level. At higher elevations, because of the diminishing air pressure, the pointer moves to the left and must be brought back to the right. You can do this by turning the adjusting screw on the back of the case *slowly and carefully* to the left.

The table at right shows how far the

Table

Feet above sea level (approx.)	Meters above sea level (approx.)	Inches (approx.)	Millimeters (approx.)	Millibars (approx.)
160	60	0.2	4	5
270	90	0.3	7	9
360	120	0.4	10	13
450	150	0.5	13	17
540	180	0.6	15	20
630	210	0.7	16	21
720	240	0.8	21	28
810	270	0.9	24	32
900	300	1.0	26	35
990	330	1.1	28	37
1,080	360	1.2	30	40
1,170	390	1.3	32	43
1,260	420	1.4	35	47
1,350	450	1.5	37	49
1,440	480	1.6	40	53
1,530	510	1.7	43	57
1,620	540	1.8	46	61
1,710	570	1.9	48	64
1,800	600	2.0	51	68
1,900	630	2.1	53	70
2,000	655	2.2	56	75
		etc.		

pointer must be moved to the right (clockwise) at a given elevation. Check with your local town hall, city engineer, or library to determine your community's elevation, or check with a radio or weather station for the current barometric reading. Suppose you live at an elevation of 700 feet (210 m) and that the pointer of the barometer is at 29.2 inches (742 mm). It must be moved 0.8 inch (20 mm) to the right, that is, to 30.0 inches (762 mm). The barometer will then show a reading corrected to sea level.

For elevations over 3,000 feet (1,000 m) a barometer requires special adjustment, and you should have this done at a weather bureau.

Atmospheric humidity; the hygrometer

Your health and well-being at home and at work are dependent on the right humidity. Humid air is a combination of steam and dry air and can be measured in several ways. The generally known concepts are the relative and the absolute (unconditional) humidity. The relative humidity is the ratio between

Barometrical rules

Corrected sea-level readings

Winter	Above 30 inches (760 mm)	Summer
increasing frost, mist	rising rapidly	windy, rapidly clearing
clear and frost	rising slowly	steady, very dry
continuous frost	unchanged after rising	clear, dry, warm
at times clear, frost	unchanged after falling	cloudy to clear
cloudy, snow, thaw	falling slowly	warm followed by rain
windy, snow, glazed frost	falling rapidly	sultry, thunderstorm

Between 29 inches and 30 inches (740 mm and 760 mm)

gusty, showers, cooler	rising rapidly	gusty, showers, cool
clearing up, cooler	rising slowly	slowly clearing up
falling wind, misty	unchanged after rising	cloudy, at times clear
light wind, damp	unchanged after falling	light wind, dull, cool
light wind, snow, thaw	falling slowly	continuous rain
windy, showers, warmer	falling rapidly	windy, showers, cool

Below 29 inches (740 mm)

gusty, showers, damp	rising rapidly	gusty, showers, cloudy
falling wind, cooler	rising slowly	falling wind, clearing
falling wind, cloudy	unchanged after rising	falling wind, light rain
continuous showers	unchanged after falling	continuous showers
windy, much rain	falling slowly	windy, much rain
storm, rain or snow	falling rapidly	storm, rain, hail

(Falling/rising wind refers to change in velocity.)

present and maximum steam saturation, measured in percent, at the same temperature. The absolute humidity is the maximum steam quantity, measured in grams, that can absorb one cubic meter of air at a given temperature. Warm air can hold more steam than cold air.

The relative humidity is measured with a humidity gage, the hygrometer. The comfort zone lies within the temperature range of 64° to 71°F (18° to 22°C) and a relative humidity of 40 percent to 60 percent. During the winter with the heating of rooms, the relative humidity often reaches only 15 percent to 30 percent. This is the cause of many respiratory ailments, such as colds and inflammation and irritation of the respiratory tract. Thus it is useful to monitor the humidity with a hygrometer.

To check the saturation, wrap the instrument in a damp (not dripping wet) towel and place it in a vertical position for half an hour. The indicator should then read 94 percent to 96 percent.

The thermometer
The thermometer is indispensable for every household, indicating the comfort zone and preventing energy from being wasted for heating or cooling.